WORD
BIBLICAL
COMMENTARY

General Editors
David A. Hubbard
Glenn W. Barker †

Old Testament Editor
John D. W. Watts

New Testament Editor
Ralph P. Martin

WORD

BIBLICAL

COMMENTARY

VOLUME 12

1 Kings

SIMON J. DeVRIES

WORD BOOKS, PUBLISHER • WACO, TEXAS

Word Biblical Commentary
1 Kings
Copyright © 1985 by Word, Incorporated

Library of Congress Cataloging in Publication Data
Main entry under title:

Word biblical commentary.

Includes bibliographies.
1. Bible—Commentaries—Collected works.
BS491.2.W67   220.7'7   81–71768
ISBN 0–8499–0211–8 (vol. 12)   AACR2

Printed in the United States of America

Scripture quotations in the body of the commentary marked RSV are from the Revised Standard Version of the Bible, copyright 1946 (renewed 1973), 1956, and © 1971 by the Division of Christian Education of the National Council of the Churches of Christ in the USA and are used by permission. Those marked NIV are from the New International Version of the Bible, copyright © 1973 by New York Bible Society International. The author's own translation of the text appears in italic type under the heading "Translation."

67899   AGF   98

In memory of my mother

Contents

Author's Preface

In every generation, Christian scholars need to search and listen, striving to learn from Scripture itself how better to interpret it, and accordingly how better to subject themselves to it. In my opinion, this need is perhaps more urgent with regard to biblical historiography than to any other scriptural material, and that for two reasons: (1) the OT (Gen, Exod, Josh–2 Chr) and the NT (Gospels, Acts) historiographic literature is more extensively covered in church-school curriculums; and (2) the traditional Christian hermeneutic respecting this particular literature has been weak. In effect, the sacred events along with the good and evil personages tend to be handled as role-models. We are invited to moralize about them, and to follow their good (or avoid their bad) examples. But the Christian religion is more—far more—than a right *ethic.* At its heart is a right *belief,* not so much a doctrinal confession as a personal knowing, trusting, and commitment to the one true God in his Son Jesus Christ. It is not enough to emulate Christ: one must embody Christ. So, by analogy, the other biblical personages, Abraham and Moses and David, Jehoshaphat and Hezekiah and Zerubbabel. None of these is alive in the sense that Christ is alive; but what they confessed in word and action must become alive. And that is what the Christian church must proclaim from the pulpit and teach to the young and the old. If this long lineage of personages from the historiographic literature belong among "the great cloud of witnesses" that surrounds us (Heb 12:1), we are charged to do more than just admire and imitate them. In hearing the books that tell of them as theological testimony—and that is what the historiographic writings are in essence— we are called to share their testimony and become part of their company.

Deep as the writer's respect remains for church tradition, he has taken up the call to this generation of Scripture scholars to listen to the Bible again. To him, obedience to God's Word entails letting it reveal how it must be interpreted, for only then can its testimony be fully and truly heard. As the Word of God, the Bible is verily the word of man. The reader will discover, then, that the most advanced methods have been usefully employed in preparing this commentary on I Kings. These are methods shaped not only by science, but learned from Scripture itself. The writer's fond hope is that those who use this book will learn the new methods, such as form criticism, tradition criticism, and redaction criticism, along with the factual content of the biblical material. Better, more biblical, methods need to be learned and appreciated by all who give serious study to the Bible and endeavor to shape their lives by it.

SIMON J. DE VRIES

Delaware, Ohio
March 1985

Editorial Preface

The launching of the *Word Biblical Commentary* brings to fulfillment an enterprise of several years' planning. The publishers and the members of the editorial board met in 1977 to explore the possibility of a new commentary on the books of the Bible that would incorporate several distinctive features. Prospective readers of these volumes are entitled to know what such features were intended to be; whether the aims of the commentary have been fully achieved time alone will tell.

First, we have tried to cast a wide net to include as contributors a number of scholars from around the world who not only share our aims, but are in the main engaged in the ministry of teaching in university, college and seminary. They represent a rich diversity of denominational allegiance. The broad stance of our contributors can rightly be called evangelical, and this term is to be understood in its positive, historic sense of a commitment to scripture as divine revelation, and to the truth and power of the Christian gospel.

Then, the commentaries in our series are all commissioned and written for the purpose of inclusion in the *Word Biblical Commentary*. Unlike several of our distinguished counterparts in the field of commentary writing, there are no translated works, originally written in a non-English language. Also, our commentators were asked to prepare their own rendering of the original biblical text and to use those languages as the basis of their own comments and exegesis. What may be claimed as distinctive with this series is that it is based on the biblical languages, yet it seeks to make the technical and scholarly approach to a theological understanding of scripture understandable by—and useful to—the fledgling student, the working minister as well as to colleagues in the guild of professional scholars and teachers.

Finally, a word must be said about the format of the series. The layout in clearly defined sections has been consciously devised to assist readers at different levels. Those wishing to learn about the textual witnesses on which the translation is offered are invited to consult the section headed "Notes." If the readers' concern is with the state of modern scholarship on any given portion of scripture, then they should turn to the sections on "Bibliography" and "Form/Structure/Setting." For a clear exposition of the passage's meaning and its relevance to the ongoing biblical revelation, the "Comment" and concluding "Explanation" are designed expressly to meet that need. There is therefore something for everyone who may pick up and use these volumes.

If these aims come anywhere near realization, the intention of the editors will have been met, and the labor of our team of contributors rewarded.

General Editors: *David A. Hubbard*
Glenn W. Barker†
Old Testament: *John D. W. Watts*
New Testament: *Ralph P. Martin*

Abbreviations

ConB	Coniectanea biblica
CTA	A. Herdner, *Corpus des tablettes en cunéiformes alphabétiques*
DTT	*Dansk teologisk tidsskrift*
EchB	Echter-Bibel
EHAT	Exegetisches Handbuch zum Alten Testament
EI	*Eretz Israel*
ErbAuf	*Erbe und Auftrag*
EstBib	*Estudios bíblicos*
EstEcl	*Estudios Eclesiásticos*
EvT	*Evangelische Theologie*
ExpB	Expositor's Bible
FOTL	The Forms of the Old Testament Literature
FRLANT	Forschungen zur Religion und Literatur des Alten und Neuen Testaments
Hen	*Henoch*
HKAT	Handkommentar zum Alten Testament
HTR	*Harvard Theological Review*
HUCA	*Hebrew Union College Annual*
IB	*Interpreter's Bible*
ICC	International Critical Commentary
IDB	*Interpreter's Dictionary of the Bible*, ed. G. A. Buttrick
IDBSup	*Supplementary volume to IDB*
IEJ	*Israel Exploration Journal*
Int	*Interpretation*
JAAR	*Journal of the American Academy of Religion*
JAOS	*Journal of the American Oriental Society*
JBR	*Journal of Bible and Religion*
JETS	*Journal of the Evangelical Theological Society*
JHI	*Journal of the History of Ideas*
JNES	*Journal of Near Eastern Studies*
JPOS	*Journal of the Palestine Oriental Society*
JQR	*Jewish Quarterly Review*
JSOTS	*Journal for the Study of the Old Testament*, Biblical Studies
JSS	*Journal of Semitic Studies*
JTS	*Journal of Theological Studies*
KAT	Kommentar zum Alten Testament, ed. E. Sellin
KB	L. Kohler and W. Baumgartner, *Lexikon in Veteris Testamenti libros*
KHCAT	Kurzer Hand-Commentar zum Alten Testament
KKAT	Kurzgefasster Kommentar zu den Heiligen Schriften Alten und Neuen Testaments
KV	Korte Verklaring
LASBF	*Liber Annuus Studii Biblici Franciscani*
Leš	*Lešonénu*
LingBib	*Linguistica Biblica*
OBO	Orbis Biblicus et Orientalis
OTL	Old Testament Library
OTS	*Oudtestamentische Studien*

PCB	*Peake's Commentary on the Bible*, ed. M. Black and H. H. Rowley
PEFQS	*Palestine Exploration Fund, Quarterly Statement*
PEQ	*Palestine Exploration Quarterly*
Ra	A. Rahlfs, ed., *Septuaginta* (Württembergische Bibelanstalt Stuttgart 1935)
RB	*Revue biblique*
RBiblt	*Rivista biblica italiana*
RHR	*Revue de l'histoire des religions*
RSO	*Rivista degli studii orientali*
SAB	*Sitzungsberichte der Deutschen Akademie der Wissenschaft zu Berlin*
SANT	Studien zum Alten und Neuen Testament
SBLSCS	Society of Biblical Literature Septuagint and Cognate Studies
SBT	Studies in Biblical Theology
SEÅ	*Svensk exegetisk årsbok*
Sem	*Semitica*
SOTSMS	Society for Old Testament Study Monograph Series
ST	*Studia theologica*
StSemNed	Studie Semitica Nederlandica
TBT	*The Bible Today*
THAT	*Theologisches Handwörterbuch zum Alten Testament*, ed. E. Jenni and C. Westermann
ThEx	*Theologische Existenz Heute*
TLZ	*Theologische Literaturzeitung*
TRu	*Theologische Rundschau*
TS	*Theological Studies*
TTZ	*Trierer theologische Zeitschrift*
TZ	*Theologische Zeitschrift*
UF	*Ugaritische Forschungen*
VD	*Verbum domini*
VT	*Vetus Testamentum*
VTSup	*VT* Supplements
WMANT	Wissenschaftliche Monographien zum Alten und Neuen Testament
WO	*Die Welt des Orients*
WuD	*Wort und Dienst*
ZAW	*Zeitschrift für die alttestamentliche Wissenschaft*
ZDMG	*Zeitschrift der deutschen morgenländischen Gesellschaft*
ZDPV	*Zeitschrift des deutschen Palästina-Vereins*
ZKT	*Zeitschrift für katholische Theologie*
ZTK	*Zeitschrift für Theologie und Kirche*

THE HEBREW TEXT AND ANCIENT TRANSLATIONS

A	Arabic version	C		Coptic version
Arm	Armenian version	E		Ethiopic version

G	Greek Septuagint (= LXX)	Or	The Oriental MS family
G^A	Codex Alexandrinus	Q	Qere
G^B	Codex Vaticanus (and its recension)	Seb	Sebir (C. Ginsburg)
G^L	The (proto-)Lucianic recension	OG	"Old Greek" = Alexandrian LXX
G^O	The Origenic (Hexaplaric) recension	OL	Old Latin (Vetus Latinus)
G^s	Codex Sinaiticus	P	Priestly Source
Jos	Fl. Josephus	Par	Paralipomenon (Greek Chronicles)
Kaige	Kaige recension of LXX	Syr	Syriac
		Syr^h	Syro-Hexaplar
LXX	see G	Tg	Targum
MT	Masoretic Text (BHS)	"The Three":	
		A	Aquila
Chr	Chronicles	θ	Theodotion
K	Kethibh	Σ	Symmachus
		Vg	Vulgate

The LXX text is cited from A. E. Brooke, N. McLean, and H. St. J. Thackeray, *The Old Testament in Greek*, II, ii (Cambridge 1930).

MODERN AUTHORITIES

Burney   C. F. Burney, *The Book of Judges (etc.) and Notes on the Hebrew Text of the Book of Kings*. New York: KTAV, 1970 (reprint of 1918 ed.).

Gray   J. Gray, *I & II Kings, A Commentary*. OTL. 2nd rev. ed. Philadelphia: Westminster, 1970.

HOTTP   D. Barthelemy *et al.*, eds., *Preliminary and Interim Report on the Hebrew Old Testament Text Project*. Vol. 2. Stuttgart: United Bible Societies, 1976.

Noth   M. Noth, *Könige*. BKAT IX/1. Neukirchen-Vluyn: Neukirchener Verlag, 1968.

YTT   S. J. De Vries, *Yesterday, Today and Tomorrow: Time and History in the Old Testament*. Grand Rapids: Eerdmans; London: SPCK, 1975.

BIBLICAL AND APOCRYPHAL BOOKS

Old Testament

Gen	Genesis	Josh	Joshua
Exod	Exodus	Judg	Judges
Lev	Leviticus	Ruth	Ruth
Num	Numbers	1 Sam	1 Samuel
Deut	Deuteronomy	2 Sam	2 Samuel

1 Kgs	1 Kings	Ezek	Ezekiel
2 Kgs	2 Kings	Dan	Daniel
1 Chr	1 Chronicles	Hos	Hosea
2 Chr	2 Chronicles	Joel	Joel
Ezra	Ezra	Amos	Amos
Neh	Nehemiah	Obad	Obadiah
Esth	Esther	Jonah	Jonah
Job	Job	Mic	Micah
Ps	Psalms	Nah	Nahum
Prov	Proverbs	Hab	Habakkuk
Eccl	Ecclesiastes	Zeph	Zephaniah
Cant	Song of Solomon	Hag	Haggai
Isa	Isaiah	Zech	Zechariah
Jer	Jeremiah	Mal	Malachi
Lam	Lamentations		

New Testament

Matt	Matthew	1 Tim	1 Timothy
Mark	Mark	2 Tim	2 Timothy
Luke	Luke	Titus	Titus
John	John	Phlm	Philemon
Acts	Acts	Heb	Hebrews
Rom	Romans	Jas	James
1 Cor	1 Corinthians	1 Pet	1 Peter
2 Cor	2 Corinthians	2 Pet	2 Peter
Gal	Galatians	1 John	1 John
Eph	Ephesians	2 John	2 John
Phil	Philippians	3 John	3 John
Col	Colossians	Jude	Jude
1 Thess	1 Thessalonians	Rev	Revelation
2 Thess	2 Thessalonians		

Apocrypha

1 Kgdms	1 Kingdoms	Ep Jer	Epistle of Jeremy
2 Kgdms	2 Kingdoms	1 Macc	1 Maccabees
3 Kgdms	3 Kingdoms	2 Macc	2 Maccabees
4 Kgdms	4 Kingdoms	3 Macc	3 Maccabees
Add Esth	Additions to Esther	4 Macc	4 Maccabees
Bar	Baruch	Pr Azar	Prayer of Azariah
Bel	Bel and the Dragon	Pr Man	Prayer of Manasseh
1 Esdr	1 Esdras	Sir	Sirach
2 Esdr	2 Esdras	Sus	Susanna
4 Ezra	4 Ezra	Tob	Tobit
Jdt	Judith	Wis	Wisdom of Solomon

OTHERS

act	active	MS(S)	manuscript(s) (When
art	the article		appearing as first
	(grammatical)		entry, the
chap(s).	chapter(s)		reference is to
cj	conjecture		manuscripts of
consec	consecutive		MT)
corr	corruption, is corrupt	niph	niphal
Dtr	Deuteronomistic	opt	optative
	history/redaction/	pass	passive
	redactor	pers	person (grammatical)
Eng.	English verses	pl	plural
ET	English translation	*praem*	*praemittit*(*unt*), sets
fem	feminine		forward
Fs	Festschrift	ptcp	participle
gl	gloss	qal	the basic stem of
Gr.	Greek		Heb. verbs
hab	*habet*(*nt*) has/have	*rell*	*reliqui,* the remaining
Heb.	Hebrew		witnesses
hiph	hiphil	sing	singular
hithp	hithpael	tr	transpose(s)
h.l.	*hapax legomenon*	v, vv	verse, verses
hoph	hophal	Vrs	(all) the ancient
impf	imperfect		versions
impv	imperative	+	add(s), addition
ind	indicative	+	additional material at
inf	infinitive		the verse cited
init	*initium,* at the		(=ᵃ⁻ᶻ)
	beginning	x	with preceding
juss	jussive		numeral: times,
lit.	literally		occurrences
masc	masculine	*	the original hand in
mg	margin		a MS cited
min	(some or all)		
	minuscules		

Main Bibliography

COMMENTARIES

Barnes, W. E. *Kings*. The Cambridge Bible. Cambridge: Cambridge University Press, 1908. **Benzinger, I.** *Die Bücher der Könige erklärt*. KHCAT 9. Freiburg i. B., Leipzig & Tübingen: J. C. B. Mohr (Paul Siebeck), 1899. **van den Born, A.** *Koningen uit de grondtekst vertaald en uitgelegd*. BOT IV/2. Roermond-Maaseik: J. J. Romen, 1958. **Burney, C. F.** *Notes on the Hebrew Text of the Book of Kings, with an Introduction and Appendix*. Oxford: Clarendon Press, 1903. **Farrar, F. W.** *The First Book of Kings*. ExB. New York: Funk & Wagnalls, 1893. **Fichtner, J.** *Das Erste Buch der Könige*. BotAT 12/1. Stuttgart: Calwer Verlag, 1964. **van Gelderen, C.** *De Boeken van Koningen*, 3 vols. KV. Kampen: J. H. Kok, 1936–37. **Gray, J.** *I and II Kings, a Commentary*. OTL. Philadelphia-London: Westminster, 1964; 2nd ed. 1970. **Gressmann, H.** *Die älteste Geschichtsschreibung und Prophetie Israels (von Samuel bis Amos und Hosea) übersetzt, erklärt und von Einleitungen versehen*. Göttingen: Vandenhoeck & Ruprecht, 1921. ———. *Die Schriften des Alten Testament in Auswahl*, II, 2. Göttingen: Vandenhoeck & Ruprecht, 1910–15; 2nd ed., 1911–25. **Kittel, R.** *Die Bücher der Könige*. HKAT. Göttingen: Vandenhoeck und Ruprecht, 1900. **Klostermann, A.** *Die Bücher Samuelis und der Könige*. KKAT. Nördlingen: Beck, 1887. **Long, B. O.** *1 Kings, with an Introduction to Historical Literature*. FOTL IX. Grand Rapids: Eerdmans, 1984. **Mauchline, J.** "I and II Kings," *PCB*. London: T. Nelson, 1962. **Montgomery, J. A.**, and **Gehman, H. S.** *A Critical and Exegetical Commentary on the Books of Kings*. ICC. Edinburgh: T. & T. Clark, 1951. **Noth, M.** *Könige* (1. Teilband). BKAT IX/1. Neukirchen-Vluyn: Neukirchener Verlag, 1968. **Rehm, M.** *Die Bücher der Könige*. EchB, AT. Würzburg: Echter Verlag, 1954. **Robinson, J.** "The First Book of Kings," *The Cambridge Bible Commentary*. Cambridge: Cambridge University Press, 1972. **Sanda, A.** *Die Bücher der Könige*. EHAT. 2 vols. Münster i. W.: Aschendorff, 1911–12. **Schlögl, P. N.** *Die Bücher der Könige (etc.) übersetzt und erklärt*. KAT I, 3, 2. Vienna: Mayer, 1911. **Skinner, J.** *I and II Kings*. CenB. London & Edinburgh: T. C. & E. C. Jack, 1893; rev. ed., 1904. **Snaith, N. H.** "The First and Second Books of Kings, Introduction and Exegesis," *IB* III. New York–Nashville: Abingdon, 1954. **Thenius, O.** *Die Bücher der Könige erklärt*. KHCAT. Leipzig: S. Hirzl, 1873. **Trinquet, J.** (with E. Osty). "Premier et deuxième Livre des Rois," *La Bible*. Paris: Editions Rencontre, 1970. **Ubach, B.** *I i II dels Reis*. La Biblia (Montserrat), VI. Viena: Monestir de Montserrat, 1957. **de Vaux, O. P., R.** *Les Livres des Rois*. La Bible de Jérusalem. Paris: Editions de Cerf, 1949; 2nd ed., 1958. **Würthwein, E.** *Das Erste Buch der Könige übersetzt und erklärt*. ATD 11/1. Göttingen: Vandenhoeck & Ruprecht, 1977.

SPECIAL STUDIES

Barrick, W. B. "On the 'Removal of the "High-places,"'" in 1–2 Kings." *Bib* 55 (1974) 257–59. **Döller, J.** *Geographische und ethnographische Studien zum III. und IV. Buche der Könige*. Theologische Studien der Leo-Gesellschaft, 9. Vienna: Mayer, 1904. **Ehrlich, A. B.** *Randglossen zur hebräischen Bibel, textkritisches, sprachliches und sachliches*. Vol. 7, *Könige*. Leipzig: J. C. Hinrichs, 1914. **Jenni, E.** "Zwei Jahrzehnte Forschung an den Büchern Josua bis Könige." *TRu* n.F. 27 (1961) 1–34, 97–146.

Introduction

THE WORLD OF 1 KINGS

The break between 2 Sam and 1 Kgs is arbitrary, and the break between 1 Kgs and 2 Kgs is arbitrary. 1 Kgs 1–2 is definitely the original conclusion to the document broken off at 2 Sam 20, widely known as the Succession or Throne-succession History. These first two chapters of 1 Kgs were evidently severed from the foregoing material by some ancient editor, dividing up the Scriptures into lectionary-rolls of convenient length, and consigning these chapters to Kgs because they tell of Solomon (though they tell us also of David), the dominant subject of the ensuing chapters. There is far less rationale for the break that has been made between 1 Kgs 22 and 2 Kgs 1, for the latter chapter continues to tell of Elijah, the great hero of 1 Kgs 17–19 and 21. How strange it seems, indeed, to read of the death of Jehoshaphat in 1 Kgs 22:50, and then encounter him on the march to battle in 2 Kgs 3! The reader feels that the story told in 1 Kgs has been left an incomplete torso; but fortunately he is able to continue it in the "book" that follows. Broken off merely for lectionary purposes, 2 Kgs remains attached to 1 Kgs in all copies of Scripture since ancient times.

THE GEOGRAPHICAL AND CULTURAL SITUATION

Bibliography

Aharoni, Y. *The Land of the Bible; a Historical Geography.* Philadelphia: Westminster, 1967. —— **and Avi-Yonah, M.** *The Macmillan Bible Atlas.* New York–London, 1968. **Baly, D.** *The Geography of the Bible,* rev. ed. New York: Harper, 1974. —— **and Tushingham, A. D.** *Atlas of the Biblical World.* New York: World, 1971. **Kenyon, K. M.** *Archaeology of the Holy Land.* New York: Praeger, 1960. **Noth, M.** *Die Welt des Alten Testaments,* 4th ed. Berlin: Töpelmann, 1962. **Smith, G. A.** *The Historical Geography of the Holy Land.* 4th ed. New York–London, 1894. **Wright, G. E.** *Biblical Archaeology,* rev. ed. Philadelphia: Westminster, 1962.

Biblical commentaries often assume that the reader is well acquainted with the geographical and historical background against which the Bible's story is told, and accordingly launch directly into matters of composition and text. Veteran students of the Old Testament may in fact be trusted to know just where and when the events of 1 Kgs took place, but beginners and laymen read the Bible too, and it is for them that some guidelines are in order so that this particular portion of Scripture may come alive in its proper time and place.

The present commentary will begin by providing some essential information concerning "the world of 1 Kgs." That world was, first of all, geographically delineated and culturally defined. As readers of 1 Kgs move from chapter to chapter, they need to recall all they know about where the events in question took place and what cultural conditions played a role in shaping these events. To begin with, it is important to know that most of the narration is told from a Judahite perspective and concerns occurrences of special consequence to the land and kingdom of Judah. Jerusalem, captured but a few decades before by David, is here the sole great capital of Israel; or so it is from chap. 1 to chap. 11, and on into chap. 12. The great schism, or division, of the land recounted in chap. 12 brings a drastic shift in scene, for from here on Jerusalem is scarcely mentioned, and that in the sparse notices of the deuteronomistic redactor (Dtr) concerning the southern kings, Rehoboam, Abijam, Asa, and Jehoshaphat; meanwhile, various cities of the north—first Tirzah, then Samaria—rival it for importance.

A former Jebusite enclave, Jerusalem lay at the precise tribal boundary between Benjamin (Saul's tribe) and Judah. Five miles to the south lay Bethlehem, the birthplace of David. Jerusalem also lay athwart the main north-south ridge reaching from the barren Negeb in the distant south northward to the Carmel range and the Jezreel valley, many dozens of miles away. Throughout the period of the Hebrew kings, walled Jerusalem occupied the southeast Ophel hill, directly adjacent to the Kidron Valley—with an extension for the temple northward. 2 Sam reports that the city was indeed heavily fortified, yet Solomon had occasion to improve its walls and construct a palace complex for conducting the administration of his increasingly complex realm.

Jerusalem is where most of the events in 1 Kgs 1–11 take place, yet the surrounding countryside is in the background too. Shimei runs off to Gath, just outside the boundaries of Judah (2:40). Solomon journeys to Gibeon, a few miles north of Jerusalem, to worship and receive revelation (3:4–9). The Judahite-Benjaminite hill-country occupies terrain that is rugged and rocky, with sparse vegetation. Chap. 4 tells how Solomon's realm outside Judah was divided up among twelve prefects. This description presents a broad panorama of terrain, climate, and cultural peculiarities, for as one journeys northward toward Galilee, westward toward the Shephelah and the coastal plain, or eastward toward the Jordan depression and the Transjordanian plateau, rich variety prevails. And this variety is found not only in nature. In Solomon's administration, it appeared in the mixture of nationalities and ethnic groups. David's conquests, consolidated now by Solomon, had incorporated the native Canaanite population, the residents of erstwhile city-states, into the corporate body of his kingdom. Though their social status remained lower than that of the freeborn Israelites, and though their allegiance to Yahweh may have been nominal at best, they were indeed citizens (or at least subjects) of the United Kingdom of Israel.

But 1 Kgs also draws attention to countries outside Palestine: to Tyre of Phoenicia (modern-day Lebanon), whence came Hiram's cedars and a wife for Ahab; to southern Arabia or the Horn of Africa, whither Solomon sent for gold and similar precious objects; to Edom and Ammon, the first dependencies to rebel against Solomon's rule; and most of all to Egypt, of which Solomon was a probable dependent and from which he took a wife. The route to many of these nations was sometimes through the desert, but increasingly the sea became important. The sea on the south led to Arabia and Africa; the sea to the west led to Egypt, Phoenicia, and far-off Tarshish. More than anything else, the sea offered to open up this landlocked, hill-isolated kingdom to the culture of great and famous civilizations. It is small wonder that archeological remains from the beginning of Iron Age II (the period of 1–2 Kgs) show the sale and importation of strange and precious wares, manufactured outside the borders of Israel.

The narratives in chaps. 12–22 are mainly played out at the shrines and capitals of the Northern Kingdom, now split off from Jerusalem. Many events take place at the chief ancestral sites of the once-dominant Rachel tribes (Benjamin, Ephraim, Manasseh), and most particularly at the new residence of a prominent new dynasty, Samaria. Jerusalem had been a Jebusite town before becoming David's capital, but Samaria was brand new (16:24). Built on a high, isolated hill, Samaria dominated the rich countryside while itself remaining half hidden from marauding bands and marching kings on the major highways through the land.

There were some who knew where Samaria lay and how to hold it captive— Syria in particular. (This is the familiar Greco-Roman name; the Semitic name for Syria was "Aram.") The ancient Aramean empire had held its center along the upper Euphrates (Mari) or in the valley of the Orontes (Hamath; cf. Ebla), but by biblical times the Damascus region had become independent. It lay between the mountains of the Antilebanon and the eastern desert; it was in a strategic location for dominating Israel's Jezreel valley and the central mountains of Samaria to the west, as well as the towns of Gilead to the south. It is with Syria's serious threat against Northern Israel—evil harbinger of things to come—that 1 Kgs comes to an end.

THE POLITICAL SITUATION

Bibliography

History

Bright, J. *A History of Israel.* Philadelphia: Westminster, 1959. **Hayes, J. H.,** and **Miller, J. M.,** eds. *Israelite and Judaean History.* Philadelphia: Westminster, 1977. **Herrmann, S.** *Geschichte Israels in alttestamentlicher Zeit.* Munich: Kaiser, 1973. ET, *A History of Israel in Old Testament Times.* Philadelphia: Fortress, 1975. **Malamat, A.** "The Aramaeans." In *Peoples of Old Testament Times,* J. Wiseman, ed., pp. 134–55. Oxford: Clarendon, 1973. **Noth, M.** *Geschichte Israels,* 2nd ed. Göttingen: Vandenhoeck & Ruprecht, 1956. ET, *The History of Israel,* 2nd ed. New York: Harper, 1960. ———. *Ueberlieferungsgeschichte des Pentateuch.* Stuttgart: Kohlhammer, 1948. ET by B. W. Anderson, *A History of Pentateuchal Traditions.* Englewood Cliffs, N.J.: Prentice-Hall, 1972. **Unger, M. F.** *Israel and the Aramaeans of Damascus.* London: J. Clarke, 1957.

Chronology

Albright, W. F. "The Chronology of the Divided Monarchy of Israel." *BASOR* 100 (1945) 16–22. **Anderson, K. T.** "Die Chronologie der Könige von Israel und Juda."

ST 23 (1969) 64–114. **Begrich, J.** *Die Chronologie der Könige von Israel und Juda.* Tübingen: Mohr, 1929. **De Vries, S. J.** "Chronology of the OT." *IDB* I (1962) 580–99. ⸺. "Chronology, OT." *IDB*Sup (1976) 161–66. **Freedman, D. N., and Cross, F. M.** "Old Testament Chronology." *The Bible and the Ancient Near East* (Albright Fs). Garden City, N.Y.: 1961. **Goldschmied, L.** "Zur Chronologie der Königsbücher." *ZDMG* 54 (1900) 17–36. **Kamphausen, A.** *Die Chronologie der hebräischen Könige, Eine geschichtliche Untersuchung.* Bonn: Max Cohen & Sohn (Fr. Cohen), 1883. **Kleber, A. M.** "The Chronology of 3 and 4 Kings and 2 Paralipomenon." *Bib* 2 (1921) 3–29, 170–205. **Lewy, J.** *Die Chronologie der Könige von Israel und Juda.* Giessen: Alfred Töpelmann, 1927. **Morawe, G.** "Studien zum Aufbau der Neubabylonischen Chroniken in ihrer Beziehung zu den Chronologischen Notizen der Königsbücher." *EvT* 26 (1966) 308–20. **Mowinckel, S.** "Die Chronologie der israelitischen und jüdischen Könige." *AcOr* 9 (1931) 161–277. **Schedl, C.** "Textkritische Bemerkungen zu den synchronismen der Könige von Israel und Juda." *VT* 12 (1962) 88–119. ⸺. "Worte und Jahre. Zehnerverschreibungen und Mitregentschaften." *Bib* 46 (1965) 454–59. **Thiele, E. R.** "A Comparison of the Chronological Data of Israel and Judah." *VT* 4 (1954) 185–95. ⸺. "Coregencies and Overlapping Reigns among the Hebrew Kings." *JBL* 93 (1974) 174–200. ⸺. *The Mysterious Numbers of the Hebrew Kings*, rev. ed. Grand Rapids: Eerdmans, 1965. ⸺. "The Synchronisms of the Hebrew Kings—A Reevaluation." *AUSS* 1 (1963) 121–38; 2 (1964) 120–36. **Thilo, M.** *Die Chronologie des Alten Testaments.* Barmen: Hugo Klein, 1917. **Wifall, Jr., W. R.** "The Chronology of the Divided Monarchy of Israel." *ZAW* 80 (1960) 319–37.

In addition to the foregoing facts concerning peoples and places, there is need also to outline the main political forces that were at work during the period of 1 Kgs. No one can understand Israel or its history who does not reckon with an important detail of ancient Near-Eastern history. That is, the period from Solomon to Ahab (969–852 B.C.) comes toward the end of a long era of international peace. Up until the eighteenth and nineteenth dynasties (fifteenth to thirteenth centuries), Egypt had held domination over much of Palestine and Syria, being kept in check only by the powerful Hittites to the north. The Euro-Asiatic Hyksos (dominating Egypt during the eighteenth-sixteenth centuries) were the last serious menace to traverse Palestine from the east. The end of the Late Bronze Age (*ca.* 1200 B.C.) brought a definite hiatus in the foreign domination of Palestine. The tribal league of the Hebrews, like the adolescent kingdoms eastward of the Jordan (Edom, Moab, Ammon, Syria), was able to follow its own natural course of development. The Hebrews still had to contend with the native city-states, left stranded through the withdrawal of Egyptian support—and, as had been said, the last of these did not succumb until the time of David. There was also the growing problem of the Philistines, newcomers from the Aegean and recent residents of the southern seacoast; but they too were at last subdued by David, and in any case do not appear as any sort of menace in the books of Kgs. One serious Egyptian incursion by Pharaoh Shishak took place during the time of Rehoboam (1 Kgs 14:25–26); although this had painful effects for the cities on Shishak's route of march, Shishak was in no way able to consolidate his success or organize an Asiatic empire.

So until the Syrians became a threat, the Hebrew kingdoms were allowed full freedom to develop their own political and national institutions—which is not to imply that foreign bonds were altogether ignored, as we see especially in the policies of Solomon. David's great achievement had been, first, to throw off the external threats that had brought to ruin the kingdom of Saul (1 Sam 31); second, to unite all the Hebrew tribes in a centralized, permanent realm; and third, to set up a rudimentary bureaucracy for administering this kingdom (2 Sam 8:15–18). In the absence of any imperial claim upon it, Davidic Israel expended its pent-up aggressiveness in campaigns against Philistia, Moab, Zobah, Damascus, Hamath, Edom (2 Sam 8:1–14) and Ammon (chap. 10), creating a far-flung empire for Solomon to inherit. From the point of view of public administration, David's most serious error was his failure to decide the issue of regal succession, a problem that was belatedly dealt with when Adonijah forced David's hand in attempting to seize the crown for himself (1 Kgs 1). Whether or not the throne-succession narrative is historically accurate in every detail, it is certain that Solomon did have influential supporters in Jerusalem able to turn events their way.

In many respects, Solomon's kingship violated the principles of Israel's social heritage. There is no hint that Solomon made any effort to pay even lip service, as Saul and David had done, to tribal autonomy or the popular election of a charismatic individual. Solomon seized the kingdom by force, as his brother Adonijah had tried to do—the only difference being that he enjoyed his father's belated backing. Little wonder that he went on to rearrange the territory of Palestine into administrative districts in a way that completely disregarded the traditional tribal boundaries. He also entered into alliances with foreign powers which his forefathers would have loathed and resisted. He allowed Egyptian cultural influence to become dominant in secular and religious affairs, with significant concessions also to cultural models from Phoenicia and the kingdoms of southern Arabia, without raising the question of incompatibility with the ancestral ideals of primitive Yahwism. The biblical historians recorded Solomon's piety in building Yahweh a great temple. These same historians also recorded the destruction of that temple (2 Kgs 25) as God judged Judah for trusting the shrine rather than its living Lord. Also, Solomon was honored as a model "wise" man, in spite of the fact that he led a life of profligate ease (5:2–8, Eng. 4:22–28b) and notorious self-indulgence (11:1–8).

It is idle speculation to ask whether the United Kingdom might have continued a rise to lasting dominance throughout the eastern Mediterranean, had it only continued to exist as a single united entity under a single dynasty of kings. In spite of the Scripture's paucity of details, chaps. 11 and 12 provide us with sufficient information to allow us to understand the essential elements that were responsible for the schism that created the separate kingdoms of Israel and Judah in the year 931–930 B.C. This rupture was, from the modern historian's point of view, all but inevitable. There was, first of all, a deep social-economic disaffection, a bitter resentment on the part of the non-Judahite Hebrews, because their traditions of tribal freedom and equality were being trampled on through forced labor (the corvée) and heavy taxation— all ostensibly for the purpose of indulging Solomon's lust for luxury and glory. Even more important was a longstanding sense of outrage at the way David, and now Solomon, had relegated the once-dominant tribes in the north—especially the premier tribes of the central highlands, Manasseh,

Ephraim, and Benjamin—to an ancillary status. Where in Israel's great national epic, the Pentateuchal narrative, had Judah been given so dominant a role? As some scholars think, Abraham and Isaac may have once been powerful southern sheikhs, but by all counts it is the patriarch Jacob, with his son Joseph (the eponym of Manasseh and Ephraim), who is remembered for fleshing out the patriarchal promise in terms of a multitribal structure. Northern sensitivity was probably strongest with regard to the way in which the descendants of Benjamin's hero, King Saul, had been dealt with by David (cf. 2 Sam 6, 9, 19), and especially the way in which Solomon liquidated Shimei, ardent advocate of northern recognition (1 Kgs 2:36–46). This left a dull ache of despair that was destined to flame up in revolution, once a monarch less resolute than Solomon came to the throne.

The break did come; and when it did, tempers flared and skirmishes were fought, but in the end both sides settled for separation as a permanent arrangement. The bad element in this was that Israel, now divided rather than united, would never again be able to aspire to world power; alliances might be possible, but never an effective union. In religious terms, this meant also that the model union of twelve tribes was shattered. A process of sloughing off incongenial elements from an "ideal" Israel—continued century by century until the separation of Christianity and Judaism—had now begun. This breakup did give one part of erstwhile Israel (Judah) a chance to survive when the other part (the Northern Kingdom) succumbed to foreign aggression (723–22 B.C.).

In the *Commentary* the individual kings will be identified, and as much will be said about each of them as can be said. For the moment it will suffice to characterize briefly each separate realm, throwing out some hints regarding its historical destiny.

The Northern Kingdom comprised the tribes that had once been dominant and in which Israel's most cherished traditions continued to be preserved. There appears to have remained no tangible link with the Saulide monarchy, perhaps because Saul's ignominious death had marked him as one rejected by Yahweh. A nobody, Jeroboam, became king—to all appearances for no other reason than that he was the only northerner previously known to have been a rebel against King Solomon (11:26–27). He lived long, but his son Nadab was killed soon after he acceded to the throne. The same pattern of long and short reigns repeated itself with Baasha and Elah; also with Ahab and his two sons, Ahaziah and Joram. There were recurrent insurrections, those of Zimri, Omri, and Tibni; in the next century (narrated in 2 Kgs) by those also of several others. To be sure, Israel had strong kings, specifically, Baasha, Omri, and Ahab. One could speculate whether the ancient principle of charismatic designation still played any significant role in the risings and fallings of these kings; the likelihood is that it was honored with the lips only. The northern kings tended to become as despotic as their Judahite counterparts, while lacking the latter's dynastic stability.

It can be plainly discerned, therefore, that the Northern Kingdom was going nowhere; it showed no awareness of a national destiny. Indeed, the eventual intrusion of Baalism suggests that Israel had very little sense of self-identity or covenantal calling. Apart from the external religious accouterments that lay on every side, this people's public life had become essentially secular.

The Southern Kingdom, meanwhile, did show some sense of national destiny, epitomized in an idealized image of David. Every Judahite king was a direct descendant of this king and aimed to perpetuate his image. Supposing that the common citizens of Judah shared this same ideal, we can understand why they attempted no insurrections against the Davidic dynasty as such. As 2 Kgs tells it, Athaliah, baalist and daughter of Ahab, did attempt to wipe it out (chap. 11), but without complete success. When certain Judahite kings were assassinated, it was in order to substitute more worthy persons from within the Davidic line (2 Kgs 12:20–21; 14:19–21; 21:23–24). In the judgment of the deuteronomist (Dtr, the compiler and editor of the books of Kgs and probably of the books of Joshua, Judges, and Samuel, which work is explained below in more detail), only two Judahite kings, Hezekiah and Josiah, fully lived up to the image of their forefather David (18:3, 22:2). What counted in the end is that this same single dynasty had managed to survive from David (*ca.* 1000 B.C.) down to Zedekiah (*ca.* 586), a span of more than four hundred years. No wonder that the psalms and the prophecies allude to this as "the eternal dynasty"!

The reader of Kings needs to know, furthermore, that Israel was more exposed to foreign penetration than was Judah. Our previous sketch of geography is relevant here. Israel was surrounded by Phoenicia on the north and by Syria and Ammon on the east, while Judah had Moab, Edom, and Arabia on its eastern flank, with Egypt to the southwest across the barren reaches of the Sinai. Except at the time of Shishak's invasion (926–925 B.C.), Egypt behaved more as an ally than a menace to Judah. There is no record of trouble with Arabia, and Judah had no more than border skirmishes with Edom (2 Kgs 14:7). The other eastern principalities struggled for some measure of independence but otherwise offered no aggression. As for Phoenicia, the bond of friendship that Hiram had forged with David and Solomon became a firm alliance with Ahab through his marriage to the king's daughter, Jezebel (1 Kgs 16:31). It was with Syria that serious trouble began, first in the time of Baasha (15:16–22) and later in the time of Ahab and his successors. All the stories of 1 Kgs 20, 22, 2 Kgs 1–10, 13, are played out against this background. Hazael, the assassin of Ben-Hadad II (2 Kgs 8:15), was able to rampage pretty much at will over the Northern Kingdom (cf. 2 Kgs 13:3), and he even threatened Jerusalem (12:17–18). This was because Assyria, the great power to the east of the Euphrates, remained comparatively weak and unaggressive throughout this period. But a day was ordained when Assyria would become strong, Syria weak, and the two Hebrew kingdoms relatively strong once again. This is a story that lies beyond the reaches of 1 Kgs. 1 Kgs begins with Syria still a restive dependency of Solomon in the heyday of his empire and it concludes with Ahab and his sons beginning to stand up to the relatively mild bullying of Ben-Hadad, just prior to Jehu's blow against the house of Ahab and Hazael's assassination of Ben-Hadad.

The intricate problem of the overlapping reigns of the Hebrew kings will be taken up by the *Commentary* at its treatment of 1 Kgs 14:21 in a special section titled "The Chronology of the Hebrew Kings."

THE RELIGIOUS SITUATION

Bibliography

Albright, W. F. *From the Stone Age to Christianity.* Baltimore: Johns Hopkins Press, 1946. ———. *Archaeology and the Religion of Israel.* Baltimore: Johns Hopkins Press, 1956. **Cross, F. M.** *Canaanite Myth and Hebrew Epic.* Cambridge: Harvard University Press, 1973. **Fohrer, G.** *Geschichte der israelitischen Religion.* Berlin: de Gruyter, 1969. ET by D. E. Green, *History and Israelite Religion.* Nashville: Abingdon, 1972. **Harrelson, W.** *From Fertility Cult to Worship.* Garden City, N.Y.: Doubleday, 1969. **Jepsen, A.** *Nabi; sozialogische Studien zur alttestamentliche Literatur und Religionsgeschichte.* Munich: Beck, 1934. **Kraus, H. J.** *Gottesdienst in Israel,* 2nd ed. Munich: Kaiser, 1962. ET by G. Buswell, *Worship in Israel; a Cultic History of the Old Testament.* Oxford: Blackwell, 1966. **Lindblom, J.** *Prophecy in Ancient Israel.* Philadelphia-London: Muhlenberg Press, 1962. **von Rad, G.** *Die Botschaft der Propheten.* Munich-Hamburg: 1967. ET by D. Stalker, *The Message of the Prophets.* New York: Harper, 1962. ———. *Die Theologie des Alten Testaments,* II. Munich: Kaiser, 1960. ET by D. Stalker, *Old Testament Theology,* II. New York: Harper, 1965. **Vriezen, T. C.** *De godsdienst van Israel.* Zeist-Arnhem: W. de Haan, 1963. ET by H. Hoskins, *The Religion of Ancient Israel.* Philadelphia: Westminster, 1963.

1 Kgs is not a book of history so much as a book of religion. The story it tells would be of little interest to us were it not that, through the historic events that it relates, the religion of the Hebrew people was being shaped into the great universal faith that gave birth to Judaism and Christianity.

In this book a dominant place is occupied by those chapters that tell of preparations for the Jerusalem temple, its construction and embellishment, and its dedication (chaps. 5–8). As will be argued, Solomon very likely followed a Phoenician pattern and incorporated structures from a pre-existent Jebusite shrine, but this in no way changes the fact that Solomon's temple was intended as a sanctuary of high honor to the true official God of Israel, Yahweh. A most fateful step was here being taken. Heretofore, Yahweh had allowed himself to be worshiped wherever he appeared. He was the God of loosely knit and rambling tribes. As the Pentateuch, Joshua, Judges, and Samuel inform us, he met them in the desert, spoke to them on the mountain, moved about with them to their new encampments. Not even David had dared build Yahweh's permanent dwelling-place in Zion (2 Sam 7). There existed, to be sure, some cherished tokens of his presence, in particular the ark, which David installed in a tent. That he went no further than this shows David's respect for the tribal traditions. That he did go so far, however, foretokened the step that Solomon was destined to take.

Once the kingdom had been consolidated, the empire secured, and the city of Jerusalem turned into an increasingly pompous showplace for regal glory and power, Solomon took the logical, yet ultimately dangerous, step of building the temple. Clearly, the temple was meant to be recognized by the entire population of Israel, with its political dependencies, as the grand residence of Yahweh the champion God. Just as Solomon had adopted the Near Eastern ideology of the supreme resident God, with himself as king representing and serving the Deity, so did he adopt the Near Eastern concept of the temple as the divine residence.

This temple was to stand until destroyed by Nebuchadrezzar in 586 B.C.

Living in the era of Nebuchadrezzar was the great redactor (Dtr) who put much of 1 Kgs together, and who in any event gave it its final polish. In his day Solomon's temple was still standing (or, as some scholars think, was at least still vividly remembered), and the deuteronomist most definitely approved of it. He tells proudly of what Solomon had accomplished. He also speaks disapprovingly of rival shrines to Yahweh's, praising or upbraiding the respective kings for either fostering or suppressing them. Our problem is that most, if not all, of these shrines had already seen long service in the days of Solomon. Solomon and his successors evidently tolerated a great deal of shrine worship in and away from Jerusalem, and the question is whether at least some of this was not legitimate worship of Yahweh.

There are three particular problems concerning shrines other than Solomon's temple: (1) the status of clearly heathen shrines in the vicinity of Jerusalem (cf. 11:7–8); (2) the status of the במות (RSV "high places"), referred to in such passages as 3:3–4, 12:32, etc.; and (3) the legitimacy of cult objects such as the Dan and Bethel calves, installed in honored Yahweh-shrines of great antiquity, yet of questionable influence in themselves (12:28–30).

The deuteronomist condemns each of these—yet the reader is surprised to read how comparatively mild he actually is in 11:5–6, 9–13, when the most serious of Solomon's improprieties, that of tolerating foreign cults outside Jerusalem, has just been described. A complete discussion of this phenomenon must be deferred for the *Commentary*, yet it is clear that Solomon here receives the benefit of the doubt from the deuteronomist, who chastises with less intensity the idolatries of Judahite kings (cf. also 14:22–24) than he employs for the northern kings, whom he often judges without citing any specific details to support his complaint, for "walking in the sin of Jeroboam the son of Nebat."

In chap. 11 we actually read the names of Ashtoreth and Milcom, representative of numerous other unnamed gods to whom shrines were erected for the convenience of Solomon's various foreign wives (v 8). Since these foreign wives were of royal, or at least noble, rank, and since the practical purpose of attracting them to Solomon's harem probably was to secure favorable political treatment from the peoples they represented, it may be conjectured that the building of these foreign altars was meant as much to be an honor to the foreign peoples they represented as a convenience for the wives personally. Although in the case of Pharaoh's daughter (3:1, 9:24, 11:1) the relationship of countries was that of strict equality—or perhaps even of marked subservience on the part of Solomon—it is probable that in most other cases the foreign wives came from minor principalities or fiefdoms inside and outside Palestine. In the latter instance, Solomon may have intended to station these images of foreign gods in close proximity to Yahweh's temple in order to create a literal symbol of the nations waiting in humble attendance upon the God of Israel. Although this explanation hardly coincides with that of the deuteronomist, it is probably close to historical reality. It presupposes that, in Solomon's understanding, Yahweh had risen to a status scarcely higher than that of a national god, now for the while ruling supreme over the gods of subject peoples. This was no outright idolatry. Yet it was a clear violation of the commandment to prohibit "any other gods before me" (Exod 20:3).

The *Commentary* will argue that the במות were simply local shrines, whether dedicated to Yahweh or to other deities. The term is neutral. As has been said, it is the deuteronomist who is their chief critic. It may very well be that he condemns them purely from the point of view of his own period, and it may be that by that time some בּמוֹת that once had been Yahweh-shrines had now become tainted with idolatry and eclecticism. Besides this, no doubt the deuteronomist objected to them from the ideological viewpoint of the entire Deuteronomic movement of which he was a part, insisting on the sole and exclusive legitimacy of the Jerusalem temple over against every sort of local temple (Deut 12:10–14; cf. 2 Kgs 23). One can be sure, in any event, that the champions of Judahite legitimacy did everything in their power, long before Deuteronomy, to encourage worship at the Jerusalem temple and discredit worship at the shrines in the countryside—particularly those across the border, i.e., at Bethel and further north, in the ancestral territory of the central Israelite tribes.

Finally, a few words about Jeroboam's golden calves (12:28–29). With regard to the question of the material object itself, some scholars assert that these were ornaments, or emblems, or some special kind of special cultic implement. Others say that they were intended as actual images of Yahweh himself—thus a direct violation of the commandment prohibiting the making of idols (Exod 20:4). In the absence of any other references to Yahweh-images, it seems most plausible to choose the first interpretation, thereby making due allowance for the perspective of the deuteronomist. But even if the "calves" (more probably, bulls) were mere accouterments, they did introduce the ideology of fertility worship in a most perilous and objectionable manner. There is nothing that a bull can symbolize beside lusty fecundity. This is the vital force that was positively deified throughout the ancient Near East, and it came to special expression in the myths, rituals, and images of Baal, Asherah, and Astarte, the leading fertility deities of Canaan and Phoenicia. Later, Hosea's polemic against Baalism was to show how prevalent fertility ideology was destined to become (mid-eighth century). So also the earlier stories of Elijah.

That Yahweh, the purely spiritual God of Sinai, should tolerate the image of a golden bull in his temple at Bethel is a surprising demonstration of how widespread eclecticism had become even in this early period. It is to Solomon's credit that he tolerated nothing similar to it in his temple. But Israelite religious ideology was still in chaos, north and south. The deeds of the various kings were destined to influence it and be influenced by it.

Prophecy was a burgeoning new religious impulse of the period of 1 Kgs. Two special points must be made: (1) prophecy was a familiar phenomenon, as is now known, in the entire region west of the Euphrates, and especially at Mari, where numerous references to it have been found; and (2) having played but a supporting role in the conquest and settlement period, Hebrew prophecy came into prominence only in the period of the Divided Kingdom, and especially at times of great crisis. Mari was a once-prominent city on the upper Euphrates, where excavations have unearthed a quantity of texts from the second millennium B.C. Biblical scholars have studied the proper names, which are morphologically similar to those of the Bible, but have been specially interested in the various classes of individuals who acted as recipients of revelation and waited on the king to guide him in important political decisions. Apart from being a strong supporter of the ritual cult, Mari prophetism shared with biblical prophetism every individual characteristic, including the ecstatic trance, except monotheism. It is this that makes the vital difference. Some biblical prophets were ecstatic and others were not; some biblical prophets were political and others were not; some were attached to the shrine and others were not; but in all things they all claimed to be devout adherents of the one and only God, Yahweh.

As for the occasion of their emergence: Elijah appeared to oppose Baal; Elisha appeared to oppose the Jehuites and the marauding Syrians. The first of the "writing" prophets, Amos and Hosea, began their prophetic ministries at the appearance of an overpowering menace from the Assyrians. This may be interpreted to mean that stirring and troubling events stimulated spiritual men to interpret them in terms of Yahweh's will for his people. One should not be at all surprised to read, then, of prophets and "men of God" who come upon the scene at a propitious hour in order to show the intent of God's Spirit amid all the comings and goings of kings. Hebrew nationalism as a secular phenomenon was doomed to perish, but biblical prophecy carried the promise of the future. One prophet (Nathan) already directs the first scene of the book. Another prophet (Micaiah) directs its last. 1 Kgs is, then, a strikingly prophetic book. In telling the story of Israel's kings, it speaks most clearly of the God who ruled in them and directed them to his purpose, whether of judgment or of salvation.

SACRED HISTORY AS THEOLOGICAL TESTIMONY

THE BIBLICAL UNDERSTANDING OF HISTORY

Bibliography

Baly, D. *God and History in the Old Testament.* New York: Harper, 1976. **De Vries, S. J.** "History as Responsible Dialogue with God," *The Achievements of Biblical Religion,* pp. 289–372. Washington: University Press of America, 1983. ———. *Yesterday, Today and Tomorrow: Time and History in the Old Testament.* Grand Rapids: Eerdmans, and London: SPCK, 1975. **Galling, K.** *Die Erwählungstraditionen Israels.* Giessen: Töpelmann, 1928. **von Rad, G.** "A History of Yahwism and of the Sacral Institutions of Israel in Outline," *Old Testament Theology,* I, pp. 3–102. New York: Harper, 1962. **Rowley, H. H.** *The Biblical Doctrine of Election.* London: Lutterworth, 1950. **Vriezen, T. C.** *Die Erwählung Israels nach dem Alten Testament.* ATANT 24. Zürich: Zwingli Verlag, 1953.

Only human beings can have history because only they can trace cause and effect, and only they can direct their efforts toward the fulfillment of a conscious goal and purpose. But not every culture has been able to interpret history or record its meaning. For some, its record has been little more than the potsherds left behind in ancient tells; for others it has been imposing monuments and towering pyramids. With the discovery of writing, and the preservation of this writing on durable materials, a sense of continuity began to develop. Even so, many ancient cities have been altogether lost to human memory, no longer existing even in the songs of balladeers. In any event, it was long after the invention of writing (ca. 3000 B.C.) that the first written interpretations of history began. Classical civilization had it, as we know—but many will be surprised to learn that the first written histories were those of the Hebrews.

Evidence will presently be offered to support this assertion. But to prepare the user of this commentary to savor its significance, it is necessary first to offer a brief explanation of the biblical understanding of history. Once this is seen, one can comprehend why the Hebrews were the first to come up with genuine historiography.

First, take note of the irrelevancy of history in the surrounding, nonbiblical cultures: Egypt, Mesopotamia, Asia Minor, Greece, and the rest. We must make a sharp distinction between mythical and nonmythical cultures. The former existed as far back as the human mind can remember; the latter arose, chiefly in Greece, when popular faith in mythology began to die. Now, the mythical mind creates a great variety of fantastic stories as an explanation for the bewildering array of experiential phenomena that confronts puny man in his pilgrimage through life. Myth, usually connected with ritual, is essentially a holy tale about the gods, who are each the embodiment of an irrational force demanding to be respected and placated. Many myths have to do with the birth of the different deities; some also are about the origin of man and human culture. In hearing the recital of a myth, the awed listener participates in it sympathetically, sharing in its very essence. Thus, listening to the account of how Osiris dies and then rises from the dead, the Egyptian worshiper identifies himself with Osiris with the hope and expectation of sharing his power over death. Experiencing the phenomenon that we call history, a mythologic believer seeks not for purpose nor to comprehend the forces of change. The future—and the present too, for that matter—can be endured only as it is related to and rooted in the primeval past from which it sprang. Everything that is and ever shall be is a pale embodiment of the ideal perfection that once was.

In the Golden Age of Greece (fourth century B.C.), many intellectuals had ceased believing in that country's ancient myths. This had several causes. In the social and political upheavals of the time, the priesthood had lost the respect of the people because of their venality. A succession of great philosophers from Thales onward were teaching the rule of reason, and therewith the ridiculousness of myth. Undoubtedly the most important single cause was the prolonged and bitter struggle with the Persians, who had come perilously close to conquering the Greeks. A series of thrilling victories, including those of Alexander the Great in his long march to inner Asia, now called for rehearsal in tale and song, and it was these that eventually inspired the great "histories" of Thucydides, Herodotus, and Xenophon. In comparison with the biblical histories, these must be criticized for a comparative lack of critical discernment in separating the factual from the nonfactual, but, on the whole, they represent a remarkable cultural achievement. The point, however, is that they contain no sense of movement or purpose. This is pure secular history, utterly disregarding the gods, but it consists only of a more or less ordered recording of events. Many modern historians have essentially the same model of history. Things just happen—they have no teleological significance. The warring and politicking of the nations are essentially no different than the pecking of chickens in the henyard, or the jostling of monkeys on a branch. Secularistic nonmythical culture reduces history as effectively as does the superstition of mythical culture. The former turns everything over to man as the latter turns everything over to the gods.

In the culture sphere of the ancient Near East, Israel's concept of the Deity was different in two decisive aspects, and these, taken together, explain why Israel took history seriously while her neighbors did not. First, the Israelites believed in a transcendent monotheism; and second, they believed in the authentic personhood of their God.

A few words, first, need to be said about the element of monotheism. Without denying that Israel weaned itself only gradually from the notion of a tribal and national god, and while acknowledging that official Yahwism had to struggle long and hard against apostasy and eclecticism, we gratefully record the remarkable fact that this nation alone believed in only one God. This does not mean that he was just the supreme god in a heavenly pantheon, comparable to what we find in the mythologies of Egypt, Ugarit, and Mesopotamia. Echoes of this concept appear in the Bible only where they have been fully sanitized of mythological ideology (Gen 1:26, 3:22, 11:7, Ps 82:1); that is, it was safe to use as an analogy or figure of speech because orthodox Israelites could no longer be tempted to take mythic polytheism seriously. Polytheism goes with myth because it is a system by which every separate dynamic force and irrational power is deified. It is also immanentistic because these forces and powers exist on earth in nature and in the life of mankind as well as in heaven. Monotheism, on the other hand, concentrates every transcendental power in the one Deity, whose being can neither be divided nor poured out into the cosmos as the essential substance of all that exists.

Next, some remarks about the element of personalism are in order. The various ancient mythologies also personified their deities. This occurred through analogy from human life, as a device for communicating with the supernatural. Each separate god or goddess is nothing more than the caricature of some single aspect of human behavior. This is to say that there were separate gods/goddesses of the sun, of the wind, of death, of war, of pestilence, of fertility, and so forth. The "personality" of the deity, as recited in myth, was a caricature of something human that resembled the domain of the particular deity. Now, a caricature is the drastic reduction of authentic personhood. Moderns are especially aware of the richness and complexity of human personality, and, if we are well schooled, we are also aware of the constant temptation to reduce the personhood of individual human beings. This is precisely what the ancient mythologists were doing with their gods. Israel's amazing achievement was a transcendental theology by which it approached God as a single, whole, complete, and sovereign Person. Though Lord over all things, his personhood was not caught up in any of them. He refused to be caricatured, distorted, diluted. He refused to be used or manipulated, like a thing. He refused to allow any aspect of his being to be taken as its whole.

This is the meaning of Yahweh's self-designation, "I am a jealous God," אֵל קַנָּא (Exod 20:5). In some OT passages, the word may better be translated "zealous." But, either way, it implies passionate concern and absolute commitment, qualities that this God demands also of his people Israel. Yahweh is a God who is totally committed and involved, but he refuses to be used by his people in bits and pieces. It is all or nothing. Thus Israel has to do with only one God, also with the totality of this only one God.

All of this implies and makes inevitable the concepts of election and covenant. Yahweh chooses, and invites his chosen to choose in return. He covenants with them to be their God, on condition that they agree to be his people. The laws they agree to keep are designed not only as a vehicle for observing this covenant, but for realizing the richer potential of human life.

We come now to ask what this has to do with history and the writing of historiography. In asking this, we uncover the one truly unique thing about Israel as compared with other nations of its cultural area. Israel was not different from them in believing that Deity intrudes into human history; some scholars have claimed this, but we know that the Babylonians and Hittites explicitly mention the determinative presence of their gods in their wars and other historical events. No, Israel's uniqueness lay simply in the fact that they, and they alone, defined themselves in historical rather than mythological language. In Mesopotamian mythology, the Sumerians and the Babylonians directly derived their peoplehood from primordial man, who was made, according to their Creation Myth, for the sole purpose of cultivating the gods' fields and tending the gods' temples. In the Egyptian myths man was simply part of the total world which the gods created, that world being essentially the land of Egypt and no more. Thus these peoples saw themselves as belonging to their respective lands from creation, which defined who and what they were. Not so Israel. They remembered that they had once been no people, had possessed no land. Abraham, their wandering forefather, had been no Adam. He left his land, kin, and family, walking toward the land of promise. His offspring did not become a nation until one great day in history when Yahweh led them out of Egyptian bondage. Prior to the Exodus and Reed-Sea crossing, the Hebrews had been no true nation, in spite of Deut 25:6, which is a somewhat simplistic statement that they were already a nation when in slavery. As one reads Exodus, the downtrodden Hebrews had all but given up on history and nationhood, having no true historic self-awareness whatsoever. It was Yahweh's mighty act, occurring in historical time, that constituted them to be a people and a nation.

Conscious of the demands of divine election, and committed to the fulfillment of the covenant, this people moved from the patriarchal promise toward its fulfillment, striving to become Yahweh's people living in his land. But the Bible's historiographic writings show that the Israelites could never fully enjoy the promise because they never fully carried out their obligation. Because of persistent backsliding, the promise of complete possession of the land and abundant peoplehood remained unfulfilled, held ever before them as an eschatological ideal. There were apparently many in Israel who took the cheap way and seized upon this nation's election and Yahweh's self-commitment to a covenant as absolute givens, irrespective of Israel's performance.

This of course was a violation of Yahweh's jealous personhood. Punishment therefore had to come with blessing; yet true spokesmen of Yahweh's purpose rose up to urge them on toward the ultimate realization of the promise. It is this that gave Israel a sense of history. It had been constituted as a nation in memorable historical event. It was related to the God of history in dynamic interpersonalism. Through frequent failure, it learned the significance of the struggle for perfection. It learned too that the jealous God was a faithful, loving, and forgiving God (Exod 20:6), a God willing to give his erring people a second, a third, a fourth chance. Here is primitive eschatology; here is theological history. Only where striving has purpose, that is, has the prospect of reward as well as the possibility of failure, does authentic history occur.

THE THEOLOGICAL WITNESS OF BIBLICAL HISTORIOGRAPHY

Bibliography

Alonso Diaz, J. "La retribución divina en el libro de las Reyes o una teología de la Historia," *XXVI Semana Biblica Española* (Madrid 1965) I. **Hölscher, G.** *Die Anfänge der hebräischen Geschichtsschreibung.* Sitzungsberichte der Akademie, Heidelberg, Philos.-hist. Klasse 1941/42. Heidelberg: C. Winter, 1942. **von Rad, G.** "Die deuteronomistische Geschichtstheologie in den Königsbüchern." *Deuteronomium-Studien,* Teil B. FRLANT, n.F. 40 (Göttingen: Vandenhoeck & Ruprecht, 2nd ed., 1948), 52–64 = *Gesammelte Studien zum AT* (Theologische Bücherei, 8; Munich: C. Kaiser, 1958), 189–204. ET, *Studies in Deuteronomy,* tr. by D. Stalker. SBT 9. London: S.C.M. Press, 1953. **Rendtorff, R.** "Beobachtungen zur altisraelitischen Geschichtsschreibung anhand der Geschichte vom Aufstieg Davids." *Probleme biblischer Theologie. Gerhard von Rad zum 70. Geburtstag.* Munich: Chr. Kaiser Verlag, 1971. **Wolff, H. W.** "Das Kerygma des deuteronomistischen Geschichtswerks." *ZAW* 73 (1961) 171–86.

We have stated that the OT, and not the histories of the Greeks, constitutes the earliest genuine historiography, and this can be substantiated by measuring it against the commonly recognized criteria of authentic historiography. This is not the academic "history" offered in modern textbooks, but popular historiography. Such historiography may incorporate random materials that do not measure up to the document's normal standards of historicity. These may have been included for edification, for illustration, or even for amusement. But a document that presents itself as historiographical must in general conform to the following four criteria: (1) it must derive its information from authenticated sources, treating this information with due respect and discretion; (2) it must trace an organic line of development from beginning to end; (3) it must show the interaction of cause and effect in a realistic way; and (4) it must offer a believable and essentially reliable portrait of the persons involved.

1 Kgs is part of one such historiographic document, the deuteronomistic history, and it contains the concluding section of another—the throne-succession narrative—that has been included within the former. In *Überlieferungsgeschichtliche Studien* (1943) and *Die Überlieferungsgeschichte des Pentateuchs* (1948), Martin Noth has outlined the now widely accepted theory that Dtr, the so-

called deuteronomistic historian, a member of the group of ancient divines who were responsible for Deuteronomy, published an authentic historiographic document reaching at least as far back as Joshua (perhaps also including Deuteronomy, provided with its own introductory and concluding framework) and forward to the end of 2 Kgs. In many places, such as Solomon's prayer in 1 Kgs 8 and especially in his own great paraenesis of 2 Kgs 17, this writer directly shows us his style and theology, but for the large part he works simply as an editor, arranging ancient sources in a generally chronological order with the ostensible purpose of teaching Yahweh's way through history.

Further treatment of the deuteronomistic history will come in the next section. The discussion in the present section is concerned with two facts: (1) that Dtr meets all the criteria of authentic historiography and (2) that according to every viable theory, it predates by far the Greek histories. As for the date: there may have been previous editions, but the final redaction is set by 2 Kgs 25:27; it comes from late in the exile, ca. 550 B.C. As for the operative criteria: Dtr does use source material with discrimination; he writes to show Israel's tragic progress through repeated apostasy, wearing out, in the end, the patience of Yahweh; he arranges his materials precisely with the purpose of showing cause and effect; and he introduces us to many of the real people who lived out the events he records.

Now surely, such historians as disallow a role for God in history would quibble, pointing to explicit intrusions of theological opinion as well as a tendency to exaggerate and schematize, particularly in the source-material. Our contention would be that although Dtr may indeed contain inaccuracies, he is effectively writing authentic history. Our own investigations can, it is to be hoped, help us deal with the inaccuracies and exaggerations; but we are blind if we cannot see that it is meaningful *historical event* that Dtr is recording and interpreting. What he writes is given credence and respectability particularly by the fact that it does not, in the end, glorify the people of Israel, but rather condemns them. Only Yahweh comes out clean in this story. Thus it is theology of the highest kind; and yet it is history because it tells the meaningful story of a history-rooted and history-determined people.

Embedded in the deuteronomistic history are shorter historiographic documents, of which we may mention three as revealing a specially high level of historiographic methodology. First there is the accession history of David, 1 Sam 16 to 2 Sam 5; next there is the throne-succession narrative of 2 Sam 9 through 1 Kgs 1–2; then also there is the Jehu accession history (2 Kgs 9–10), which I have analyzed in my book, *Prophet against Prophet* (102–103, 122). The throne-succession document has often been praised for the skill and realism with which it has been written. Although the writer gives no account of the sources that lie behind what he writes (he reports, perhaps, as an eyewitness), he shows organic interconnection from beginning to end; he interweaves episodes to accentuate cause and effect; above all, he paints his characters with candor and unmistakable realism. True, this document has a propagandistic aim (to authenticate Solomon's right to kingship instead of David's elder sons). Furthermore, a very subtle theological viewpoint is interjected in such asides as at 2 Sam 11:27, "But the thing that David had done displeased Yahweh." These ulterior elements detract nothing from its historicality while adding the dimension of transcendence, so that we have at the same time history, political propaganda, and theology. What then is its date? As virtually all agree, it is during Solomon's reign, 970–931 B.C. This makes it several centuries earlier than Dtr. This is a document of Israel's youthful maturity, then, not a document of despair and crisis like Dtr. In it, as in Dtr, human beings act in purposeful historical striving, while God acts as judge and savior, superintending all the human designs.

These considerations aim to persuade the reader that a book like 1 Kgs requires of him more than an idle love for narrative or a sober search for historical detail. We all need to learn to read the Bible with the same interest that guided those who wrote it. 1 Kgs—and the other sections of the historiographic collection—was written by men who wished to bear testimony to Yahweh's self-revelation in historical event. It is not the actors on the stage that claim their attention, but the master-director who manipulates the stage props and prompts the actors from the wings. True, in Hebraic understanding, the actors are no puppets; but they can create effective drama only as they respond to the supreme Producer and Director and carry out his design. If the play is poor instead of good, it is because they have wandered off on their own way instead of responding to his teaching and his direction.

One more remark should be made about history and 1 Kgs: although Christians have commonly referred to the writings from Josh to 2 Kgs as "historical" books, Jews rightly retain the name "Former Prophets." Christians should keep this designation in mind when reading 1 Kgs. The reason for speaking of 1 Kgs as a "prophetic" book is not that we ascribe it to prophetic authorship, but that it comes out of a prophetic spirituality and expresses the most essential concern of classical prophetism, namely, God's way with Israel through history. Those who are familiar with the great prophetic collection (Isa, Jer, Ezek, and "The Twelve") know that Israel's prophets were neither mystics nor philosophers, but very practical, pastorally concerned proclaimers of Yahweh's demand in times of peril. They too knew that history is a great stage, and that Yahweh's covenant people, called to play their part, were on the brink of ruining everything by forsaking the way of Yahweh. True, 1 Kgs records the events of a period long before the time of the great prophets (its events date from *ca.* 971 to *ca.* 852 B.C., as compared with the prophetic period, *ca.* 750 to 300 B.C.), but here as there a great dialogue was taking place, the dialogue between God and Israel concerning life and death, with the prophets as chief spokesmen and interpreters.

THE HISTORICALITY OF BIBLICAL NARRATIVE

Bibliography

De Vries, S. J. "The Anthropomorphism of God." In *The Achievements of Biblical Religion,* 78–104. Washington: University Press of America, 1983. ———. "Miracle and Wonder in the Old Testament," *idem,* 326–34. ———. *Prophet against Prophet,* 100–12. Grand Rapids: Eerdmans, 1978. **Gunkel, H.** *What Remains of the Old Testament and Other Essays.* New York: Macmillan, 1928. **Hayes, J. H.,** ed. *Old Testament Form Criticism.* San Antonio:

Trinity University Press, 1979. **Rogerson, J.** *The Supernatural in the Old Testament.* Guild-ford-London: Lutterworth, 1976. **Terrien, S.** *The Elusive Presence: Toward a New Biblical Theology.* New York: Harper, 1978.

Sufficient emphasis has been placed on the origin and purpose of biblical historiography to make superfluous any extended discussion of its historicality. (We distinguish carefully between the terms "historicity" and "historicality"; the former has to do with factual occurrence and accurate reporting, while the latter has to do with self-awareness in historical existence.) As has been said, documents like the throne-succession history and the deuteronomistic history are suffused with historicality; they are concerned with real historical event, interpreted from a transcendental perspective. So documents like these intend to be received as witnesses to God's way with Israel in history. They do not require the language of supernaturalism in order to express this theological truth. But a great redactional collection like that of Dtr does contain embedded materials, some of which have a great antiquity, expressing theological truth in a highly imaginative and directly supernaturalistic way. One must beware of two errors, opposite to each other: (1) to reject them because they clash with the naturalism of the modern mind, or (2) to interpret them only literally while insisting that the biblical God always works in this way.

One must learn to let the Bible say what it intends to say, without first laying down rules about what it has to mean. If the truth of God can come to us as realistic, factually grounded historiography—let us marvel at the achievement. If that truth should come as an imaginative and didactic narrative, full of the metaphors of supernatural power, let us marvel while querying humbly for the lesson which the narrative aims to teach us. There are such stories in 1 Kgs, and we read them correctly only when we acknowledge that they are different from a purely historiographic account, that the purpose of their narration is exemplary.

One discipline that has significantly advanced OT exegesis in the twentieth century is form-criticism. It is important because it has enabled scholars to deal with each separate pericope as an individual unit, even when incorporated into a larger redactional whole; also because it has paid attention to the structure of each pericope, with the aim of determining its genre (literary form), life-setting, and function. It is especially crucial that the reader pay close attention to these matters when coming to 1 Kgs 17–22, then reading on into 2 Kgs. With conscious purpose Dtr placed these chapters here: they illustrate his sparse previous report concerning Ahab's wickedness. 1 Kgs 16:29–34 has been drawn entirely from official records available to Dtr; it invites no particular skepticism regarding the historical factuality of what is written down in it. The prophet narratives in chaps. 17–22, however, have been derived from the schools of the prophets and intend to convey a spiritual message, to illustrate what a model prophet can do. It is my contention that they do not at all *intend* to be taken as literal historical records, and therefore are assessed wrongly when judged by standards of historical accuracy. But most certainly, they are far richer than the aforementioned annalistic records (e.g., 1 Kgs 16:29–34) in terms of theological reflectivity and spiritual suggestiveness. Their purpose is to teach the people how to discern between true and false revelation, between righteous and wicked politics, between pious and hypocritical religion. Because they show us the marvelous deeds of spirit-endowed "men of God," we ought to find a proper genre name for them. In my book *Prophet against Prophet* (52–92), I have argued for the name "prophet legend." But because "legend" can be popularly misconstrued as meaning fanciful or unreal, "prophet story" is the genre name that will be used in this commentary.

One may imagine that everything narrated in the Bible has to be taken literally, as possessing a divinely revealed and absolute historicity. This would apply to the prophet stories as well as any other type of narrative. But a moment of reflection indicates the wrongness of this supposition. The parables of Jesus, for instance, are certainly fictional; there was no actual good Samaritan, no actual prodigal son, no actual repentant publican. Jesus' stories are clearly didactic and exemplary. Anyone might be a good Samaritan or a prodigal son. But as for what we call the historicality of the parables, we would not hesitate at all to claim that each parable tells the ultimate meaning of history. Just so the stories of the prophets. Any type of story or legend (especially those of the Christian martyrs) draws an example of pious behavior for all to follow, just like a parable. Its function is to teach and inspire, rather than to record bare objective occurrence.

One will note that in the prophet stories (but in some more than in others) stress is placed upon the wondrous and the supernatural. This is different from the emphasis in Jesus' parables because the prophets in question were described as filled with the spirit of God. Now, to show that one has the spirit of God, either God acts in response to the prophet's request (as in 1 Kgs 18:38) or the prophet himself performs a wonder (as in 2 Kgs 6:1–7). The important point to remember is that the aim of these stories is less to record what God *has done* (historically, at one particular time and place), than to declare what God *can do* (throughout history, in every time and place). The prophet stories must be studied, then, for what they teach, not simply for what they tell. The telling is an imaginative technique but the truth taught is profoundly theological.

The function of supernaturalistic narrative in general ought to be studied in close connection with the numerous titles and descriptions of the Deity as found scattered throughout Scripture. Yahweh is holy, and righteous, and mighty, and attentive to his people, and jealous of his covenant. So says one text or another. These adjectival appellatives gradually lose some of their awe-eliciting force as they are recited in praise and in ritual. A narrative that actually tells the story of Yahweh coming in theophanous glory, however, may seize the congregation's imagination more powerfully than a dozen repetitions of "holy, holy, holy!" A narrative about his coming in judgment on Israel's enemies may prove to the listener the righteousness of God more than the ritual cry "righteous is he!" It is not necessary to continue with examples: the point is that narrative is an especially effective linguistic form, capable of doing more to communicate the majesty of God than mere words of ritual praise. One may cherish the more, therefore, the stories of the prophets found in 1 Kgs and elsewhere. If one would see God, one may look first here. For here the God of history, the God of the covenant, comes to view, showing not just one single event in which he was present but a model scene that occurs repeatedly, whenever his people come under judgment or reach out to him for deliverance. Let the exegete be prepared, then, to listen for what God has to say in special forms, to recognize the special genres of Scripture for what they intend to be. Those who have a special love for history will find plenty of it in 1 Kgs, but not all that is here is simple historiography. If Israel had wanted to record a bare and literal history of the prophet movement, it would have been able to do so. It had all the tools for writing it; it knew what history was and how to write historiography. It could have given us a thumbnail sketch of Elijah "as he truly was"—and Elisha, and the others (a kind of "biography of the prophets"). But the men who were prophets knew that they as human individuals did not matter; only God matters—he and his needy people Israel. So the prophet stories, so-called, are actually stories about God. More than challenging our intellectual curiosity, they demand of us the response of repentance and of faith.

Whether appearing as historiography or as pious story, the contents of 1 Kgs offer themselves as testimonies to the ways of God with men. The scene is history; the players are kings and prophets; behind the curtain is the Lord of history, challenging his players to make history the scene of salvific revelation. This theological truth must remain uppermost in the exegete's mind as he makes his way through this ancient book, for he will not understand it truly if he interprets it outside the context of a faith in the God who calls his people to a more perfect peoplehood and a more complete possession of his promised land.

1 KINGS AS A LITERARY COMPOSITION

A HISTORY OF THE INTERPRETATION OF 1 KINGS

Bibliography

Benzinger, I. *Jahvist und Elohist in den Königsbüchern.* BZAW II, 2. Berlin-Stuttgart-Leipzig: Töpelmann, 1921. **Bin-Nun, S. R.** "Formulas from Royal Records of Israel and Judah." *VT* 18 (1968) 414–32. **Day, E.** "The Deuteronomic Judgments of the Kings of Judah." *JTS* 11 (1910) 74–83. **Dietrich, W.** *Prophetie und Geschichte. Eine redaktionsgeschichtliche Untersuchung zum deuteronomistischen Geschichtswerk.* FRLANT 108. Göttingen: Vandenhoeck & Ruprecht, 1972. **Garbini, G.** "Le fonti citate nel 'Libro dei Re' (etc.)." *Hen* 3 (1981) 26–46. **Haran, M.** "Problems in the Composition of the Former Prophets" (Heb). *Tarbiz* 37 (1967–68) 1–14. **Hölscher, G.** "Das Buch der Könige, seine Quellen und seine Redaktion." *Eucharisterion Hermann Gunkel zum 60. Geburtstag.* FRLANT 36. Göttingen: Vandenhoeck & Ruprecht, 1927. **Jepsen, A.** *Die Quellen der Königsbuches.* Halle (Saale): M. Niemeyer, 1953. **Langlamet, F.** "Pour ou contre Salomon? La rédaction prosalomonienne de 1 Rois, I–II." *RB* 83 (1976) 321–79, 481–529. **Liver, J.** "The Book of the Acts of Solomon." *Bib* 48 (1967) 75–101. **Maly, E. H.** "1 and 2 Kings." *TBT* 18 (1980) 295–302. **Montgomery, J. A.** "Archival Data in the Book of Kings." *JBL* 53 (1934) 46–52. **Nelson, R. D.** *The Double Redaction of the Deuteronomistic History.* SOTSMS 18. Sheffield: Department of Biblical Studies,

University of Sheffield, 1981. **Noth, M.** *Überlieferungsgeschichtliche Studien: Die sammelnden und bearbeitenden Geschichtswerke im Alten Testament,* 2nd ed. Tübingen: Mohr, 1957. ET of pp. 1–110, *The Deuteronomistic History.* SOTSMS 15. Sheffield: Department of Biblical Studies, University of Sheffield, 1981. **Porten, B.** "The Structure and Theme of the Solomon Narrative (I Kings 3–11)." *HUCA* 38 (1967) 93–128. **Radday, Y. T.** "Chiasm in Kings." *LingBib* 31 (1974) 52–67. **Smend, R.** "JE in den geschichtlichen Büchern des Alten Testament, herausgegeben von H. Holzinger." *ZAW* 39 (1921) 204–15. **Veijola, T.** *Die ewige Dynastie. David und die Entstehung seiner Dynastie nach der deuteronomistischen Darstellung.* Annal. Acad. Sc. Fennicae, Ser. B, 193. Helsinki: Suomalainen Tiedeakatemia, 1975. **Vernès, M.** "De la place faite aux légendes locales par les livres historiques de la Bible (Juges, Samuel, Rois)." *Annuaire, École pratique des Hautes-Études—Sciences religieuses.* Paris 1897–98. **Walker, J. C.** "The Axiology of the Books of Kings." *JBR* 27 (1959) 218–22. **Weippert, H.** "Die 'deuteronomistischen' Beurteilungen der Könige von Israel und Juda und das Problem der Redaktion der Königsbücher." *Bib* 53 (1972) 301–39. **Wellhausen, J.** *Die Composition des Hexateuchs und der historischen Bücher des Alten Testaments.* Berlin: Georg Reimer, 1889; 4th ed., 1963.

Although 1 and 2 Kgs, which belong together, bear no author's name, they are attributed in *Baba Bathra 15 a* to the prophet Jeremiah, mainly because Jer 52 is identical to 2 Kgs 24:18—25:30. Without committing itself to this identification, traditional Christian scholarship was quite willing to accept a single exilic author, acknowledging that he made generous use of those written sources that are mentioned in the biblical text, viz., a "Book of the Acts of Solomon," a "Book of the Chronicles of the Judahite Kings," and a "Book of the Chronicles of the Israelite Kings" (cf. 1 Kgs 11:41, 14:29, 15:31).

Such habitual reference to source documents strengthens the impression of Kings' historical trustworthiness. It is not surprising, therefore, to find conservative scholars staunchly defending the complete historicity of these books. A more critical view began to gain widespread respectability during the closing decades of the nineteenth century and the early decades of the present century. This came about mainly through the impressive achievements of Julius Wellhausen and others who followed his methods in biblical criticism. Wellhausen published a widely influential study, *Die Composition des Hexateuchs und der historischen Bücher des Alten Testaments,* in 1889. The first part of this work was the section most attentively studied because of its controversial argumentation in favor of documentary sources within the Pentateuch, demanding a complete restructuring of Israel's religious history; but many scholars studied the second part as well, and were strongly influenced by it. This section treated the books of Kings. Under Wellhausen's influence, a whole array of commentators on Kings found themselves open to—and sometimes eager for—evidences of unhistoricity; they were ready to rationalize tales of the supernatural; they were inclined to search for signs, real or unreal, of compositional discontinuity.

Scholars have disagreed as to whether 1-2 Kgs was pretty well fleshed out when the deuteronomistic redactor got it. The earlier decades of this century saw the effort of several writers to show that the predeuteronomistic material was itself a redactional combination—and not just of unknown documents but specifically of J and E, the primitive literary sources that had purportedly been intertwined to form the Pentateuch or Hexateuch. In 1921 came two studies: I. Benzinger wrote *Jahvist und Elohist in den Königsbüchern* and R. Smend wrote his article, "JE in den geschichtlichen Büchern des Alten Testament" (*ZAW* 39 [1921] 204–15). These were in basic agreement, even though the latter identified J¹ and J² where the former found J and E. In 1923 G. Hölscher defended a JE source analysis in his article for the Gunkel *Festschrift* ("Das Buch der Könige, seine Quellen und seine Redaktion," *Eucharisterion*, I, 158–213). The influential scholar Otto Eissfeldt, in his *Einleitung in das Alten Testament* (Tübingen: Mohr, 1934) agreed on the existence of underlying documents while cautioning against the attempt to make a sharp separation into J and E sources. Eissfeldt's *caveat* was needed, for sharp separation cannot be made. The reason is that the Pentateuchal sources are not to be found here. The text of Kings lacks evidence both of affinity with J and E and of documentary continuity from the Pentateuch.

Far more fruitful has been the work of Martin Noth in his *Ueberlieferungsgeschichtliche Studien*, published in 1943. In this study Noth treated both the work of the deuteronomist and the work of the chronicler, but it was in the first that most readers were interested. Noth startled the scholarly world with the penetrating simplicity of his hypothesis. He attributed a wider range to the deuteronomistic material than anyone before, and he ascribed a far greater activity to his redactorship. In fact, "author" and "redactor" were close to synonymous in Noth's definition, for the deuteronomist was one who wrote and composed as well as a man who compiled, edited, and rearranged. His work actually commences with the introductory chapters of Deuteronomy, forming its framework. It subsequently arranges all the material belonging to Josh, Judg, and 1–2 Sam, carrying on to the end of 2 Kgs. Numerous source documents are utilized, such as the Throne-Succession Document in 2 Sam 9–20, 1 Kgs 1–2, but this redactor inserts numerous comments along the way and even composes long sections of his own, such as Solomon's prayer in 1 Kgs 8 and the peroration of 2 Kgs 17. It is especially these programmatic passages that show an affinity with the language and ideology of the Deuteronomistic reform.

Scholars have found much to praise in Noth's treatment, but some have also felt that he claimed far too many individual passages for the deuteronomist. Others are not satisfied with his claim that there was only one redactor, living *ca.* 550 B.C., writing this book as Israel's final epitaph. Almost all competent scholars who have written on the subject complain about Noth's excessively gloomy appraisal of the deuteronomist's intent, and most have argued that there were two distinct redactors associated with the deuteronomistic school. These are usually dated around Josiah's time (*ca.* 610) and in the period of the exile (cf. B. S. Childs, *Introduction to the Old Testament as Scripture* [Philadelphia: Fortress, 1979], 281–301). To the eye of the careful scholar there is indeed evidence that the work of this school may have begun considerably earlier. Helga Weippert claims, in her impressive study, "Die 'deuteronomistischen' Beurteilungen der Könige" (*Bib* 53 [1972] 301–39), that some of this work was already in place at the time of King Hezekiah, *ca.* 700 B.C. See now also the work of R. D. Nelson, *The Double Redaction of the Deuteronomistic History* (Sheffield, 1981).

Noth's work was first published while World War II was raging, but after the war it was widely read. Not so fortunate was the work of another German scholar, A. Jepsen's *Die Quellen der Königsbuches*. By the time it appeared (1953), the city of its publication, Halle, was firmly behind the iron curtain, and communication with the west was difficult. It has become the habit for scholars to describe Jepsen's treatment of Kings as virtually identical with Noth's; thus, e.g., B. S. Childs in his *Introduction*, p. 285: "The basic monograph of Noth has been at the centre of the debate. . . . The appearance of Jepsen's book . . . offered an additional confirmation of this new scholarly direction." In matter of fact, Jepsen and Noth took opposite directions on some important issues. On the source materials Jepsen and Noth would basically agree, except that Jepsen posits a separate Prophet source, consisting of 1 Kgs 1–2 and some other materials in addition to the prophet narratives themselves. Jepsen argued for three redactors: an early Priestly redactor, the deuteronomist, and an exilic redaction.

The present writer's work on the prophet narratives (*Prophet against Prophet*) has supported the existence of a separate prophet document. He has also found reason to agree that within the deuteronomistic school there was more than a single stage of redaction. Some recent studies of this question have been going much too far. Thus, specifically, W. Dietrich in his *Prophetie und Geschichte* (1972) and T. Veijola in his book, *Die ewige Dynastie* (1975). Add to this R. Smend in his article, "Das Wort Jahwes an Elia," *VT* 25 (1975) 523–43. The users of biblical commentaries are perhaps destined to see more argumentation in this direction when Smend eventually publishes the second part of Kings in *BKAT*. Dietrich and Veijola were Smend's pupils at Göttingen, and both share his method. Deeper and deeper layers of redaction are added (in the manner of Jepsen), while what scholars have generally taken to be source material is often assigned to one of these redactional levels. This method has been applied by Richter and Veijola to Samuel as well as to Kings, and the whole tendency is to transfer more and more material from the realm of early tribal tradition into that of the sheer literary activity associated with court and temple. The present writer's criticism is that this approach follows an erroneous method in starting from the end-product rather than from elemental oral and written units. This removes us further away from a direct approach to a unit's original structure, setting, and intention, where we must look for the real possibility of perceiving—and receiving—an authentic word of God within the words of man.

Almost a century after Wellhausen, it is possible to set aside both the naïve supernaturalism and the vaunting hypercriticism of the pioneer era here described. One may maintain scientific integrity while holding fast to the revelational truth that Kings offers. Inspired by Wellhausen's literary method, documentary study in the twentieth century has produced valuable insights for the understanding of the books of Kings. The present generation has begun to reap the rich harvest of previous controversy. This has occurred through the uncovering of individual primitive units within 1–2 Kgs; through the identification of these units' genre, structure, setting, and intention; and through the ability to suggest just how and to what purpose these individual units present a transcendental word of God for humankind.

Odil H. Steck has been prominently successful in applying elements of this method in his book, *Überlieferung und Zeitgeschichte in den Elia-Erzählungen* (WMANT, 26, Neukirchen-Vluyn: Neukirchener Verlag, 1968). The present writer has carried it further in his analysis in *Prophet against Prophet* of the Micaiah traditions, and this method will be applied to the interpretation of individual passages within this commentary. It is gratifying also to see the publication of B. O. Long's treatment of 1 Kgs in a new publishing endeavor devoting itself entirely to a thoroughgoing form- and tradition-critical methodology (*1 Kings, with an Introduction to Historical Literature*, FOTL IX, 1984).

It will be observed by careful readers that this new method does not set aside the positive results of the documentary analysis that has held sway so long. Although neither the work of conservative scholars nor that of liberal scholars on Kings has resolved the impasse or shown the relevance of pure literary dissection for unlocking the work of revelation in these ancient writings, we will always need to have a clear understanding of just what the sources were, or how, why, and when they were written, and of how, why, and when they were all brought together in a grand redactional whole. All sides agree that other collections of material must have been available to the final redactor besides the three sources that are specifically named in the biblical text—but there has been little agreement as to just what these additional sources may have been. Likewise all agree that an editor-redactor— someone living in the exile period, later than the last event recorded—brought all this material together into a single book. The Dutch Calvinist, G. C. Aalders, accepts such a redactor even while denying him the name "deuteronomist" (*Oud-Testamentische Kanoniek* [Kampen: J. H. Kok, 1952], 191–99). Actually, it is not the strict evidence of the text that keeps Aalders from admitting a close affinity between the redaction of Kings and the book of Deuteronomy, but rather his rejection of Wellhausen's view that Deuteronomy was compiled in the reign of Josiah, *ca.* 622 B.C. Nonetheless there is clear and positive affinity in language, style, and ideology between that Pentateuchal book and the redaction of 1–2 Kgs. Without this acknowledgement, it is impossible to make sound progress in the literary analysis of these books.

HOW THE DEUTERONOMIST WROTE HIS BOOK

We shall now proceed to outline the way in which the deuteronomist told his story. When we say "deuteronomist" or use the symbol Dtr, we are actually thinking of the school that produced the deuteronomistic redaction, whether that be evidenced in two distinct hands or more. In a way, the use of the symbol Dtr deliberately sets aside the question of multiple redaction since it generally has no relevance for the exegesis of individual passages. In any event, all the members of the Dtr school were sufficiently of one mind and committed to the same distinctive style and vocabulary to make the problem irrelevant in most passages. Dtr is the deuteronomist who happens to be at work in a given text.

It goes without question that 1 Kgs contains nothing that is older than the events recorded. That is, a report or an interpretation can be from shortly after the event down to hundreds of years later, but it cannot be prior to it. Since the work as a whole is a part of the deuteronomistic history, composed most probably by a contemporary of King Josiah and revised by a member of the same school living during the Babylonian exile, *ca.* 550 B.C., we are dealing with a period of perhaps four hundred years for all the materials in I Kgs to have been selected, reshaped, and made to assume final literary form—final, that is, apart from isolated glosses or comments that are even later than the work of the (second) deuteronomist (see now R. Nelson, *The Double Redaction of the Deuteronomistic History*).

It stands as a general rule that if one wishes to know what a story is about, one should look at how it ends. This is certainly true of the deuteronomistic history, and of the history of the kings specifically. This is to say that one should not study 1 Kgs without already knowing the story of 2 Kgs, scrutinizing especially the way in which that book ends. It ends, as we know, with the story of failure and ruin. First the Northern Kingdom comes to disaster (2 Kgs 17), and at the last the Southern Kingdom also (2 Kgs 24–25). We may be certain, therefore, that Dtr is telling the story (rather, letting his sources tell the story) from Solomon to Ahab with this final judgment in mind. The Assyrians were just appearing on the horizon in Ahab's day, yet that king's wickedness is seen as so severe that it guarantees the ultimate downfall of the North, which in turn forecasts the downfall of the South. Dtr's account usually highlights the good deeds and at times downplays the evil deeds of the Judahite kings, in the end pinning all the blame for Judah's ruin on the one king Manasseh (2 Kgs 23:26–27; 24:3–4). About the kings of Israel it can find precious little good to say. They all committed gross evil, from Jeroboam onward; hence Israel's downfall was their fault collectively. Ahab and his "house" were by far the most wicked, to be sure, even though Jehu's bloody purge (2 Kgs 9–10) was to recompense them directly for their evil.

As one notes Dtr's perspective, one is better able to appreciate the pattern in which the account's material has been arranged in 1 Kgs, and at the same time we see the purpose of its repeatedly interpolated comments. The following passages are mainly editorial: first, literary transitions at 1 Kgs 3:8, 16; 14:1, 16:34 and 21:1; second, extracts and comments from various annalistic documents, appearing at 2:24; 6:1; 7:1; 11:41–43; 14:19–20, 21–22, 29–31; 15:1–5, 7, 8, 9–14, 23–24, 25–31; 15:33—16:6; 16:8–14, 15, 19–20, 23, 25–28, 29–33; 22:39–40, 41–46, 50, 51–53.

Let us look closely, then, at the way in which Dtr's book is written. It begins with the finale of the throne-succession history, chaps. 1–2, in order to tell how Solomon became king instead of Adonijah. Chap. 2 already contains a number of Dtr's moralizing interpretations. And now Dtr is able to carry out a plan to use extracts from "the book of the acts of Solomon" (11:41). The first item chosen from it is about Solomon's betrothal to Pharaoh's daughter (3:1)—no very flattering report in Dtr's estimation. But Dtr has reassuring materials to counteract this report, first a story of divine legitimation in which Yahweh gives Solomon "a wise and understanding heart" for governing the people, with riches and honor added on (3:12–13); Dtr inserts this and expands it with his own ideology, having first reported his estimate of the true state of Solomon's heart ("And Solomon loved Yahweh, walking in the statutes of his father David," v 3a), apologizing meanwhile for Solomon's resort to a suspect shrine outside Jerusalem ("for a temple for Yahweh's name had not been built prior to those days," v 2b).

Dtr next inserts a moving narrative, possibly already in popular circulation

and perhaps not originally about Solomon: the story of the two harlots in
3:16–28. This is used to illustrate the "wisdom" that Yahweh has just bestowed
on him. He inserts it with no interruption, except his own transition, the
temporal word זָא "then," at the very beginning (cf. Burney, *Notes*, 35).

Chap. 4 consists entirely of extracts from the Book of Solomon's Acts,
interrupted by a number of what may be very late (post-deuteronomistic)
interpolations. Dtr makes an extensive expansion in chap. 5, where he tells
how Solomon made preparations for building the temple. Dtr is able to use
a number of extracts from the Book of Solomon's Acts, including the notice
in vv 15, 24–26 (Eng. 1, 10–12) about Hiram's providing of timber for the
temple. In vv 16–23 (Eng. 2–9), Dtr shows his skill as a creative narrator,
recounting at length the negotiations between the two kings. Dtr adds his
own climax in v 26 (Eng. 12): "And Yahweh gave Solomon wisdom, as he
had said to him."

Now Dtr is ready to incorporate the diverse materials taken from the Book
of Solomon's Acts having to do with the temple and the palace complex,
the building of which was Solomon's most noteworthy deed. But first Dtr
adds a date for the beginning of the temple (6:1), with a highly schematic
number (12x4x10 years) symbolically designed to identify the building of
the temple as the perfect fulfillment of the Exodus. In 7:1 Dtr makes a transitional annotation to connect the account of the temple's construction with
the account of the construction of the palace-complex, 7:2–13. Although there
are numerous further interpolations into the text of both chaps. 6 and 7,
the above additions, with the cautionary note of 6:11–13, are all that can
be attributed to Dtr himself.

In chap. 8, where Dtr makes use of an ancient *hieros logos* (legitimation
recital) for the dedication of the temple, his interpolations far outnumber
and outweigh all glosses from later hands. Some of Dtr's additions are well
integrated into their contexts; Solomon's extensive address and prayer in
vv 14–66 is his long expansion. But the temporal word זָא in v 1 and again
in v 12 functions as his introduction to new material, i.e., the account of
the bringing up of the ark and Solomon's hymn of dedication, respectively.
In addition, the original narrative of the conclusion of the ceremony (vv
62, 63b, 66aβb) has again been heavily expanded by Dtr. He cannot finish
with this subject, however, until he surprisingly brings Solomon back to receive
his version of a second warning and promise (now presumably superfluous!)
as at Gibeon (9:1–5, with a note seemingly added by an exilic editor in vv
6–9).

Apart from a few late glosses and some comments of Dtr's own in vv
21a, 22, the rest of chap. 9 consists of unedited random notes from the
Book of Solomon's Acts. At 9:26 Dtr begins to draw upon a new source, a
series of unidentified annotations, incorporating among them the popular
story of the Queen of Sheba. Expanded by a number of late glosses, these
annotations, together with the story, fulfill the purpose of enlarging upon
Solomon's wisdom and wealth. But by the end of chap. 10, Dtr has exhausted
the store of account and putative narrative concerning Solomon's reign, except
for two brief items (11:3a, 7) which militate against everything he has reported
in praise of Solomon. They mention his vast number of wives and concubines

and the shrines he built to Chemosh and Molech. This redactor first explains it as arising from Solomon's advancing senility (v 4), then adds that it was the result of his being seduced by so many foreign wives. But such an explanation is no excuse, so Dtr carefully adds Yahweh's grim threat (vv 9–13) to take away every tribe but one.

It is Dtr's firm belief that sin deserves punishment, if not directly on the culprit himself, then on his posterity. He knows very well, of course, that Solomon did die in peace, full of riches and honor; thus the division of the kingdom at the beginning of his son Rehoboam's reign is understood as that punishment (11:12). The histories of the guerrilla chieftains, Hadad the Edomite (vv 14–22) and Rezon of Damascus (vv 23–25), implying trouble for Solomon of an incidental nature, are intended to be taken as preliminary punishment upon him. At the same time they serve to introduce his history of Jeroboam (vv 26–43), which incorporates a prophet story in which Ahijah of Shiloh symbolically offers the kingdom to Jeroboam. Dtr's annotations in this passage emphasize the theme that one tribe out of twelve is to be retained for Solomon's son, but simply because of the promise to David (vv 32–33, 36). In 12:15 Dtr breaks into the story of Rehoboam's rejection with a comment that this was indeed the fulfillment of Ahijah's word, thus making his lesson unambiguously clear.

From various sources Dtr records Jeroboam's accession and the introduction of that king's religious innovations (12:25–32). It is the incorporation of another prophet story, however (13:1–32), that underscores his denunciation of what that king had done. The story is from a group of prophets associated with the shrine at Bethel. As I have argued in *Prophet against Prophet* 59–61, this narrative is ancient and was introduced into the text by Dtr because it seemed an accurate prediction of what King Josiah was later to do to the Bethel shrine (cf. 2 Kgs 23:15–19). In 12:33 Dtr brings Jeroboam to the Bethel altar so that he is present for what is about to transpire (cf. 13:1b); then in 13:2–3 he has a Judahite man of God, who in the original prophet story is not quoted at all, cry out in bitter words against the altar, mentioning Josiah by name. Dtr has the man of God in fact predict that the altar would be split open, adding in v 5 that this occurred directly, even though it has no thematic connection with the story as a whole. Dtr then allows the story to proceed to its conclusion without further interruption, contenting himself to denounce at the end Jeroboam's patronage of the country shrines (vv 32b–34).

The next literary block is the story about the death of Jeroboam's child, the crown prince. The underlying material is another prophet story about Ahijah the Shilonite, in which he predicted to Jeroboam's wife, who came to him by stealth, that the child was to die. His death would be the symbolic token of the end of the dynasty (14:13; cf. 15:29). For Dtr, this is an irresistible invitation; he does not allow this tale to stand as it was. In v 1 he draws a close temporal connection to the preceding condemnation of Jeroboam, using the introductory phrase "at that time." Allowing the story to proceed to the point where Jeroboam's wife asks for help, he creates at v 7 a Yahweh speech denouncing Jeroboam for not acting like David and making idols for himself. Perhaps Dtr borrows from fellow Judahites the language of vv 10–

11, but surely it represents also his own sentiment. Vv 15–16 are especially important to our understanding because these verses express precisely what Dtr means when he constantly condemns the various northern kings for "the sin of Jeroboam the son of Nebat." Although Ahijah has long since finished speaking in the original prophet story, Dtr attributes these additional words to him:

> And Yahweh will smite Israel just as a reed is battered in the water; and he will uproot Israel from this good ground which he gave to their father, and will scatter them beyond the Euphrates because they made their Asherim, infuriating Yahweh. So he will give up on Israel on account of Jeroboam's errors, by which he sinned and by which he made Israel to sin (vv 15–16).

It is now the intent of Dtr to tell the story of the two separate kingdoms, but how shall he proceed? He decides upon a very simple device, carried out consistently to the end of the Northern Kingdom as recorded in 2 Kgs 17. Employing synchronisms for the beginning of each successive reign in terms of the years of reign in the opposite kingdom, Dtr keeps the parallel kings comparatively contemporaneous by writing all he wants to tell about the one king, then switching over to do the same with his opposite number. Since many kingships were quite short, especially in the north, several stories of the same kingdom might be told successively before there is a return to the other kingdom. Dtr continues to make germane comments—though not so many as previously—and pauses to incorporate items, large or small, wherever these have special importance for his theme. The largest noticeable break comes at 1 Kgs 17—2 Kgs 10, 13, where Dtr inserts an ancient book of the prophets, illustrating the special depravity of the houses of Ahab and Jehu, respectively. After telling of this inspirational material, Dtr continues on his way as before, balancing off the reigns of Judah and Israel until the latter finds its end.

Once he is finished telling about Jeroboam, Dtr takes up a succession of Judahite kings and stays with them for three generations. His report about them is in every case rather brief: Rehoboam, 14:21–24, 29–31; Abijam, 15:1–8; Asa, 15:9–24. 1 Kgs will tell at the end about one more Judahite king, Jehoshaphat (22:41–51). In between these first three and the single king at the end, we have Dtr's account of six successive Israelite kings; they are Nadab, 15:25–32; Baasha, 15:33–16:6; Elah, 16:8, 14; Zimri, 16:15a, 20; Omri, 16:23–27; Ahab, 16:29–31, 22:39–40.

In chaps. 14–16 Dtr had little original source material to rely upon; i.e., apart from the aforementioned Ahijah story in 14:1–18. He makes constant reference, however, to "the Book of the Chronicles of the Judahite Kings" (e.g., 14:29) and "the Book of the Chronicles of the Israelite Kings" (e.g., 14:19), to which he refers his readers for further information, but to every appearance he has made little use of this material himself. We may probably identify three notices from the Judahite book at 14:25–26; 15:6, 7b; and 15:16. But there is nothing from the Israelite book, so far as we can tell. In 14:27–28 and 15:15 we also have probable items from the temple archives. In 16:21–22, 24, and 34 we find notices of unknown origin. What did Dtr rely on, then? Apparently on a synchronistic book of annals (cf. A. Jepsen, *Die Quellen des Königbuches,* 1953) compiled from the official court records of the separate kingdoms. The compilation would very likely have been done by Judahite scribes in the time of King Hezekiah (*ca.* 700 B.C.), salvaging materials rescued from now-demolished Samaria. The rough similarity of the notices for the Israelite and Judahite kingdoms, respectively, argues for at least a minimal degree of editorial reworking prior to their use by Dtr.

These synchronistic annals, then, offer the framework for his story up to the time of Ahab and beyond. Although the Northern and Southern notices differ in some significant details, the general structure is as follows:

A. Introductory formula
   1. Date when reign commenced and length of reign
   2. Place of reign
   3. Theological assessment
B. Concluding formula
   1. Mention of most notable deeds
   2. Reference to further sources
   3. Notice of death and burial.

One special feature of the Judahite notices is that they record the name of the king's mother—important because this made her the גבירה, the official queen-mother, with important powers (e.g., Bathsheba, Jezebel). Another feature is that in the theological assessment, the northern kings get unalleviated condemnation while the southern kings generally receive some approval. When Judahite kings are condemned, it is because they have somehow tolerated or abetted idolatry, but this is seldom the charge against the kings of the North (exception: Ahab; cf. 16:30–33). They are uniformly berated for participating in "the sin of Jeroboam the son of Nebat," which may mean no more than that they did not suppress the Yahweh-shrines at Bethel, Dan, and elsewhere.

From this review it has become clear to us that Dtr was not simply recounting events but communicating ideals. The facts may speak for themselves; but he is not going to let them speak for themselves, lest someone misunderstand. Therefore we are reading Israel's history as seen through the "spectacles" of Dtr.

Listed here are the main passages in 1 Kgs in which Dtr makes explicit mention of his theological ideals:

1. Jerusalem as the place that Yahweh chose: 11:13, 32, 36.
2. Denunciation of idolatry and of worship at the country shrines: 11:1–6, 9–13; 12:33; 13:2–5; 14:9; 15:12–15; 16:31–33; 21:26; 22:43, 46.
3. Retribution on wrongdoers: 8:33, 35, 46; 14:10–11; 15:30; 16:2–4, 7, 13, 19; 21:21–24.
4. Yahweh's election and covenant with Israel: 6:13; 8:51–53.
5. The temple as a place of revelation: 8:6, 10–11, 18–19, 43, 54–61, 65–66.
6. Deeds done in fulfillment of prophecy: 2:27; 12:15; 15:25–31; 16:8–14, 34b.
7. Continuity of the Davidic dynasty: 2:2–4, 24; 3:5–8, 13–14; 5:2–5, 22 (Eng. 4:22–25; 5:7); 8:15–21, 24; 9:4–5; 11:12–13, 32–36, 38–39; 14:7–8; 15:4–5, 11.

8. Keeping of the commandments: 3:14; 6:12; 8:57–61; 9:4; 11:10–11, 38; 14:8; 15:3, 5, 11; 22:43.
9. Solomon's wisdom: 3:10–12, 5:11–12 (Eng. 4:31); 5:26 (Eng. 5:12); 11:41.

One who peruses this list carefully will be impressed by how fragile a basis Dtr offers for the long-popular notion (beginning already with Proverbs and Ecclesiastes, which present themselves as writings of Solomon, the premier wise man) that his main character, Solomon, is to be remembered chiefly for his great wisdom. True enough, certain of Dtr's source documents do make this their major theme. Passages that emphasize Solomon's wisdom, however, are often deemed to be late as well as somewhat hyperbolic (e.g., 5:9–14 [Eng. 4:29–34]). Dtr himself repeats it from his annalistic record about Solomon at 11:41. He states it also as his own assessment in 5:26 (Eng. 5:12), but largely on the basis of the legitimation story in 3:10–12.

Actually, Solomon could have been called a great fool also for the idolatrous practices into which he allowed his numerous wives to lead him (11:1–13). There are three likely reasons why he is not: (1) Solomon was the son of David himself; (2) he had been declared wise by Yahweh; and (3) he built the temple. If Dtr could find it in his heart to forgive the follies of an Abijam (15:1–8), an Asa (15:9–15), and a Jehoshaphat (22:41–43), noting that even David himself had not been without sin (15:5), certainly he could now allow Solomon to "sleep with his fathers" without consigning him to the outer darkness of condemnation. All the same, we note that it is not Solomon who receives the praise of Dtr, but his father David.

So central and persistent is Dtr's mention of the continuity of the Davidic dynasty that no careful reader can doubt that this is his major theme. Repeatedly it is mentioned as the basis of Yahweh's favor toward a new king, and constantly it is cited as requiring obedience to Yahweh's law. Especially impressive are the three occasions when Yahweh refers to it in separate revelations to Solomon: the Gibeon legitimation story (3:5–14), Dtr's second Gibeon-like revelation (9:4–5), and Yahweh's bitter censure of Solomon's idolatry at the very end (11:11–13). But all along, Dtr's most effective incorporation of this theme into his account had been in the opening material from the throne-succession narrative, chaps. 1–2. Just at the break between chap. 1 and chap. 2, as the underlying narrative depicts David on his death-bed, Dtr adds thematic words of his own. The throne-succession narrative may have intended to have the dying David call Solomon to his side to urge him to deal severely with Joab and Shimei. "You are a wise man," hints David (2:9)—meaning shrewd, clever, politically perceptive. But Dtr expands the text, giving "wise" his own peculiarly religious meaning (vv 3–4):

Keep the charge of your God, walking in his paths, keeping his statutes, his commandments, his ordinances, and his testimonies, as written in the law of Moses, so that you may prosper in all that you do and in all to which you turn your attention; so that Yahweh may establish his word which he spoke concerning me, saying, "If your sons guard their way, walking before me in fidelity with all their heart and with all their soul, no one of yours shall be cut off from upon the throne of Israel."

Writing towards the very end of Judah's independent nationhood, with the ultimate survival of the Davidic dynasty in peril, Dtr has every reason to fear that this remarkable kingly line will soon be cut off. The northern kingship has, of course, been an aberration and has deserved the early fate that befell it. But the example it taught has been ill learned. The Davidic house is now at the brink of disaster, and this because it has never wholly committed itself to the keeping of the commandments. After all, the promise has been conditional, so that without the fulfillment of the condition it must surely come to nought.

SOURCE MATERIAL IN 1 KINGS

Bibliography

Garbini, G., "Le fonti citate nel 'Libro dei Re' (etc.)." *Hen* 3 (1981) 26–46. **Liver, J.** "The Book of the Acts of Solomon." *Bib* 48 (1967) 75–101. **Montgomery, J. A.** "Archival Data in the Book of Kings." *JBL* 53 (1934) 46–52. **Porten, B.** "The Structure and Theme of the Solomon Narrative (I Kings 3–11)." *HUCA* 38 (1967) 93–128. **Vernès, M.** "De la place faite aux légendes locales par les livres historiques de la Bible (Juges, Samuel, Rois)," *Annuaire, École Pratique des Hautes-Études—Sciences religieuses.* Paris, 1897–98.

Most of the individual items recorded in 1 Kings have a directly factual basis, and require interpretation more than historical evaluation. Here and there, however, one comes across more imaginative material, some of which may prove to have a higher level of historicality (concern for historical event) than of literal historicity. Dtr may not have been aware of this difference, but it is important to us as modern readers because we want to know its testimony, and not just the mechanics of how it makes that testimony. Keeping firmly in mind all that has been said in section 2 regarding sacred history as theological testimony, we scrutinize the materials that the deuteronomist was able to use, dividing them into the two groups, (a) literal reports and (b) imaginative interpretations.

Literal Reports

Here are placed the throne-succession narrative; the Book of Solomon's Acts, with annotations; the histories of Hadad, Rezon, and Jeroboam; the narrative of Rehoboam's rejection; the books of the Judahite and Israelite kings; a report and complaints concerning Jeroboam's religious innovations; temple archives; the narrative of Asa's alliance; the narrative of Omri's rebellion; notices concerning Tibni versus Omri, Samaria, Jericho, and Jehoshaphat's maritime ventures; and finally, details taken up into the structure of the various annalistic formulae at the beginnings and endings of the respective reigns.

Most of the above material has simply been copied from official records. Once we have carried out a careful text-critical and source-critical analysis to make sure that we are dealing with the original statement, we have no reason to question whether it was reliably recorded from the original observation (or report) of the event in question. This material is, accordingly, of high value to the historian, and would be more so if it were not so broken and sporadic. That is to say, there are not enough interconnections, and not enough interpretations, to allow the use of this material in the extensive reconstruction of history that our contemporary approach to history would like. This leads us to add that it is precisely the redacting done by Dtr that does provide the necessary interconnection and interpretation, turning an otherwise atomistic reporting of events into authentic history.

Some words of explanation are necessary regarding one or two of the documents placed in this list. First, there is the throne-succession narrative (or history, as some scholars would call it). 1 Kgs 1–2 contains only its conclusion, and this makes one inquire about its overall theme from its beginning. Is it not imaginative and interpretive? Is it not propaganda, as many believe? The answer is that high art most certainly has gone into its composition. Nevertheless, we may emphasize once again that this is authentic and trustworthy historiography. The reader will see that the author has mainly told his story through numerous speeches, and these speeches can in no way be accepted as the literal transcripts of what was said. All the same, the underlying events really did happen substantially as reported. More will be said about this in the *Commentary*, but this should suffice to justify our placing it on this list.

A similar question arises with regard to the narrative of Rehoboam's rejection in chap. 12. The structure has been very cunningly devised. The respective speakers use suspiciously stereotyped speech. Did it all happen, just as reported? The answer must come from a careful consideration of the probable authorship and function of this material. As the *Commentary* will argue, this is a factual report to the Jerusalem public concerning King Rehoboam's offensive behavior, made by the "elders" whose counsel he had rejected.

Careful scrutiny would reveal that each of the items listed has some level of special shaping, and the reader must take account of this in leveling his historical assessment. Nonetheless, it often turns out that precisely this special shaping provides that perspective and interpretation that the reader desires.

Imaginative Interpretations

Materials in 1 Kgs belonging in the second category are the following: a story of divine legitimation at Gibeon (chap. 3, imitated by Dtr in chap. 9); the anecdote of the abused harlot; the *hieros logos* for the temple dedication; the story of the Queen of Sheba; the two Ahijah stories in chaps. 11 and 14; a prophecy for Rehoboam's inaction; the Bethelite prophet story; and the collection of prophet stories in chaps. 17–22 featuring Ahab and Elijah.

A full discussion of the genre "prophet story" will be offered as a special introduction to chaps. 17–22. Each individual example appearing on our roster will, of course, receive individual analysis when its place comes up in the *Commentary*. It may surprise some readers to see the Gibeon story and the Queen of Sheba story referred to as "stories" or even "legends," but story is a fairly broad genre, broad enough to apply to any particular "hero" who demonstrates paradigmatic virtues. The Gibeon story is quite old, surely having been created—probably orally at first—as a recital designating King Solomon as one approved by Yahweh and endowed with the special qualities (wisdom, riches, and honor) required by a model king. The Queen of Sheba story has much the same focus and intent: Solomon's proverbial wisdom is his most prominent virtue, but his riches and honor are featured too. To call these two narratives story implies that their prime purpose is to exemplify gifts and virtues, as might be required by the "hero" in question as his peculiar manifestation of Yahweh's spirit. Whether or not they contain historical elements is incidental. In the case of these two stories a historical basis is highly probable; Solomon *did* go to Gibeon to seek a dream-revelation from Yahweh early in his reign, and the Queen of Sheba *did* pay him a visit. But precisely what the Deity and the human persons said has to be the free composition of such a one as first told each story.

The anecdote of the abused harlot is a beloved story. It too could have rested—and almost certainly did rest—on a real historical incident, but the dialogue is the storyteller's free creation. The reader notes that this anecdote does not mention time or place, just the situation. The king is not identified by name, and the story could have happened anywhere (see Gressmann, who derives it from Indian folk wisdom). Dtr believes that Solomon is the king in question. As a story about Solomon, it functions in the same way as the two above-mentioned stories, exemplifying in a peculiarly touching way this king's paradigmatic wisdom.

In the *hieros logos* for the temple dedication (chap. 8) a high level of historicity is to be expected. The reason is that it recounts an event to which numerous living persons were witness; and in any case it details a ceremony that could scarcely have proceeded otherwise. Yet there is an element of special individualistic interpretation in the climactic report that "the glory of Yahweh filled the temple," preventing the priests from standing and causing the king to turn away his face (vv 11, 14). Here the reader confronts sheer unsupported spiritual testimony. It was no external event that could have been corroborated by historical investigation that provoked it, but the need to witness to revelation received.

Finally, a word needs to be said about the prophecy in 12:21–24. It tells us that Rehoboam massed a great force to recover the just-separated Northern tribes, but did not proceed because a certain "man of God" by name of Shemaiah told him that Yahweh did not want him to do so. Here once again historical elements are present, probably including the fact of Shemaiah's oracle (more or less accurately transcribed). What may not be strictly historical in this account is the conclusion: "And they listened to the word of Yahweh and turned back, in order to behave in accordance with the word of Yahweh." The oracle probably only urged Rehoboam to do what he really wanted to do on his own initiative, but dared not do for fear of the charge of cowardice. In other words, this passage is propaganda, reporting the truth only in an incomplete and distorted form.

This last example shows us once again that historicity may be present in varying degrees, but every passage, without exception, has a concern for genuine historicality, Yahweh's purpose in Israel's history. In terms of popular Judahite understanding, and definitely in terms of Dtr's overall perspective,

Rehoboam's not attacking Jeroboam *was* Yahweh's will. In the final analysis, it is this theological testimony to transcendental purpose that matters more than the level of a particular passage's literal historicity.

Post-deuteronomistic Expansions

Once completed by Dtr, 1 Kgs did not lie sacrosanct and untouched, but continued to receive minor additions from a variety of glossators and commentators. We take note of their contribution to the final form of the text not so much because of any intrinsic value in this material but to be reminded that the Scriptures retained the force of dynamic growth for a considerable period after the definitive work had been completed. The glossators and interpreters in question had one obvious aim: to make the book relevant to their own generation. Their method of accomplishing this was either (1) to instruct by adding new information or (2) to shape the readers' opinion by the insertion of ideological argument.

We shall list the passages in question, dividing them into two separate lists. Passages on the first list tend to be relatively early (some are earlier than Dtr), while those on the second list tend to be relatively late.

1. *Instructional:* 2:12b; 3:2, 4aβ; 7:18a, 19, 22a; 8:1aβ, 2b, 6aβ, 11aβ; 9:13b, 16–17a; 12:2–3aα, 17, 29; 13:1b, 18b; 18:3b–4, 10–11, 13–14; 20:14a, 43aβba; 22:4bd.
2. *Ideological:* 4:19bβ–20, 5:4–5 (Eng. 4:24–25), 9–14 (Eng. 4:29–34); 6:7, 18–19, 21aba, 22, 27, 29–30, 32–35; 7:48–50; 8:3b, 4aβb, 6aβb, 7a, 10b, 44–53, 64; 9:6–9; 10:21b, 23–25, 27; 11:33a; 14:1aβb, 15–16, 22b–24; 16:7; 17:20; 18:30b; 21:23; 22:28b.

In addition to these, the MT and the LXX each have a large number of idiosyncratic glosses deserving no consideration as an original part of the text.

TOWARD THE ORIGINAL TEXT OF 1 KINGS

AVAILABLE RESOURCES

Bibliography

Allen, L. C. "Further Thoughts on an Old Recension of Reigns in Paralipomena." With R. W. Klein, "Supplements in the Paralipomena: a Rejoinder." *HTR* 61 (1968) 483–95. **Barthélemy, D.** "Les problèmes textuels de 2 Sam 11.2—1 Rois 2.11 reconsidérés à la lumiere de certaines critiques des 'Devanciers d'Aquila'." SBLSCS 2 (1972). **Gehman, H. S.** "The Old Ethiopic Version of I Kings and its Affinities." *JBL* 50 (1931) 81–114. **Jellicoe, S.** *The Septuagint and Modern Study.* Oxford: Clarendon, 1968. **Klein, R. W.** *Textual Criticism of the Old Testament from the Septuagint to Qumran.* Philadelphia: Fortress, 1974. **Lemke, W. E.** *Synoptic Studies in the Chronicler's History.* Diss., Harvard University, 1964. **Muraoka, T.** "The Greek Texts of Samuel-Kings: Incomplete Translations or Recensional Activity?" SBLSCS 2 (1972). **Pietersma, A., and Cox, C.** *De Septuaginta. Studies in honour of John William Wevers on his sixty-fifth birthday.* Mississauga, Ont.: Benben, 1984. **Rahlfs, A.** *Luciens Rezension der Königsbücher.* Septuaginta-Studien, 3. Göttingen: Vandenhoeck & Ruprecht, 1911. ———. *Studien zu den Königsbüchern. Septuaginta-Studien*, 1. Göttingen: Vandenhoeck & Ruprecht, 1904. **Rudolph, W.** "Zum Text der Königsbücher." *ZAW* 69 (1951) 201–16. **Swete, H. B.** *An Introduction to the Old Testament in Greek.* Rev. by R. R. Ottley. Cambridge: University Press, 1914. **Thackeray, H. St. J.** "The Greek Translators of the Four Books of Kings." *JTS* 8 (1907) 262–78. ———. *The Septuagint and Jewish Worship, A Study in Origins.* London: H. Milford (for the British Academy), 1921. **Ulrich, E. C., Jr.** *The Qumran Text of Samuel and Josephus.* HSM 19. Missoula: Scholars Press, 1978. **Vannutelli, P.** *Libri synoptici Veteris Testamenti seu librorum Regum et Chronicorum loci paralleli,* 2 vols. Rome: Pontifical Biblical Institute, 1931–34. **Walters, P.** *The Text of the Septuagint; its Corruptions and their Emendation,* ed. by D. W. Gooding. Cambridge: University Press, 1973. **Wevers, J. W.** "A Study in the Textual History of Codex Vaticanus in the Book of Kings." *ZAW* 70 (1952) 178–89.

Like other OT volumes in this series, this commentary offers an original translation of the Hebrew text, making use of a set of symbolic keys to relevant information in the section labeled *Notes.* Anyone who reads this commentary carefully is likely to discover that it makes generous use of such *Notes,* and if one takes the trouble to compare the translation with that of one of the standard versions, such as the RSV or NEB, one will find words and phrases that imply more than an optional rendering of the Hebrew. This results from the author's willingness to give perhaps more than the usual amount of consideration to variant readings in ancient languages other than the Hebrew. He rejects any foregone stance of favoritism, whether preference for the MT or for the LXX. Each individual passage is scrutinized for what the most important textual witnesses have to say, and is then interpreted. The resulting translation reflects a Hebrew text restored by means of judicious weighing of the witnesses.

The translation of 1 Kgs has been made particularly difficult by the fact that the most important ancient version, the LXX, offers widely differing readings in various recensions; also because the parallel canonical book, Chr, presents its own account of the events recorded, sometimes copying Kgs word for word but most of the time dropping out certain words and phrases, paraphrasing the Kgs text very freely, or omitting it altogether.

The apparatus in the *Notes* differs from that found in most commentaries in the degree of fullness with which it records important differences. It differs from the critical apparatus to *Biblia Hebraica* in being, on the one hand, far more complete, and, on the other hand, noticeably more selective in its citation of particular versions and recensions. Most of the time, as the reader will see, MT (Masoretic Text) is cited along with G^B and G^L (Codex Vaticanus and the Lucianic recension of the LXX, respectively), but with frequent reference also to Chr in the MT and Par (*Paralipomenon,* the LXX rendering of the same). Occasionally other versions are cited. As will be explained, this relative selectivity is justified by the general dependence of these other versions on either MT or LXX. A pragmatic reason for it is that all who are not specialists need textual notes that they themselves can interpret, understand, and apply. In a commentary like this, it is of no use to present the reader with an enormous, undigested mass of textual information. The author hopes that what is included will prove to be right for most. In any case, the *Notes* serve to justify the translation, allowing the reader to make an intelligent decision regarding its validity.

Let us survey the ancient witnesses to the original text of 1 Kgs. Information offered in Montgomery-Gehmann, *A Critical and Exegetical Commentary on the Book of Kings* (1951), 8–24, J. Gray, *I and II Kings, A Commentary* (1970), 43–55, and especially H. B. Swete, *An Introduction to the Old Testament in Greek* (1914) is summarized here. First of all there is the MT, our standard text of the Hebrew Bible. Earlier printings of this text were made from the recension of Ben Naphtali, but *Biblia Hebraica* since the third edition has followed the recension of Ben Asher, as recorded specifically in the famous Codex Petropolitanus (L), dated A.D. 1008 or 1009. The Hebrew University Bible Project, currently in progress, is reproducing a damaged Aleppo codex from the eighth century A.D. This leaves a gap of eight hundred or a thousand years since the only extant ancient manuscripts, those of the Qumran community at the Dead Sea. Fortunately, this community left us with at least the fragments of hundreds of biblical manuscripts, all dating from the fourth century B.C. to the first century A.D. Only morsels (5QK and 6QK) of Hebrew Kings remain; they preserve a few verses from 1 Kgs 1, 3, 12, and 22, leaving little idea about variant readings, but generally supporting a proto-Masoretic text. Nevertheless, the study of more generously preserved manuscripts, particularly those of Isaiah (1QIsa^a, second century B.C.; 1QIsa^b first century A.D.), has shown scholars the trend of textual preservation in the centuries just prior to the beginning of our era. The older Isaiah manuscript exercises relative freedom, with some tendencies in the direction of the LXX text, while the younger manuscript is a virtual carbon copy of our MT. In other words, the biblical text was somewhat fluid in the centuries before the beginning of our era, but became rigidly fixed after it. One cannot know what historical forces brought about this change (probably the Roman war of A.D. 66–70 had something to do with it), but we do know now not to show undue concern about the time-gap prior to the work of the Masoretes who gave us our great codices. The changes that came into the Hebrew Bible following the first century of our era are relatively minute, and for the large part inconsequential.

The Greek versions are the Septuagint (LXX), Theodotion (Θ), Aquila (A), and Symmachus (Σ). Greek Bibles were cherished and widely distributed, especially among Christians—but not all Greek Bibles. The last three versions mentioned—preserved today only in fragments—were made in the second and third centuries of our era, and by Jews or Jewish proselytes. They are actually of little use to the nonspecialist because they were specifically designed to correct the LXX by a more literal rendering of the Hebrew text that was then in use, i.e., the proto-Masoretic text from which ancient variants had already been removed. It is different with the LXX. This was the early Christian OT, but had been in use among the Jews since about 250 B.C. Following the lead of the apocryphal Letter of Aristeas, one is safe in assuming that all or most of the OT was translated at about this date by Jews living in Ptolemaic Alexandria, as much for the edification of the Jewish community as for supporting conversations with Greek philosophers and literary men. Not all books of the Greek OT produced in Alexandria show the same style or translation technique; therefore we must assume that a group of individuals (not necessarily the fabulous seventy-two of the Aristeas legend!) worked on it, perhaps at various times. Moreover, certain books present a text that is completely at variance with the Old Greek (OG) of Alexandria. There is the Theodotionic text of Daniel, as well as a strikingly composite text in Codex Alexandrinus (A) of Judges. Again, there is the quite different translation technique followed in sections of Reigns (= 1–2 Sam, 1–2 Kgs) in Codex Vaticanus (B); this is a problem to which we shall return.

Inasmuch as the LXX served as the church's OT during the first several centuries of our era, and continued as such in the Eastern church long after the Roman church produced its Vulgate and went its own way ecclesiastically and theologically, it is understandable that copies of all or part of it survive in considerable numbers. The great majority of these are, to be sure, minuscules from A.D. 1000 or later. Only a small number are uncials, dating from the fourth and following centuries. It is uncritical to assume that the minuscules necessarily have an inferior text, or that the uncials naturally have a superior one. In some instances, an obscure minuscule may actually preserve a correct reading that is all but lost from the uncials, and, on the other hand, we know that the uncials incorporate errors and tendentious readings that arise from their specific translation tradition. G^B is of course the oldest, and also the most consistent. Yet it offers countless problems to the translator. G^A and G^S, from the fifth century, are mixed texts, showing no consistent principle of rendering the original. We now understand, perhaps, why it is naïve to correct the MT, as represented by Codex L or other late medieval mss., on the basis of a LXX reading simply because the Greek is older. Again it is a question of textual tradition, not of the date of manufacture. If the MT has in a certain instance preserved the original Hebrew, it makes no difference that we get that reading from a manuscript such as Codex L, which may be five or six centuries later than LXX Codex Vaticanus.

To be sure, some fragments of premajuscule LXX exist, paralleling the Qumran MSS of the Hebrew Bible. Fragments of the Minor Prophets in Greek have been found at Qumran, but the remains can tell us little about the nature of the LXX text used there. We mention also the John Rylands Papyrus 458, dating about 150 B.C., and a number of other early papyri. But this is not enough to go by if we are to gain some sense of inner-Septuagintal development. We must get this, if we can, from a knowledge of the recensions or revisions of OG that we know were actually produced. The one that is by far the best known is the famous Origenic text (G^O). About A.D. 240 Origen produced his text-critical work, the *Hexapla*. This presented the OT in parallel columns, with a transliterated Hebrew and a corrected LXX followed by A, Θ, Σ, and several other Greek versions (Quinta, Sexta, Septima). In this work we can see a powerful influence on the part of an already standardized Hebrew Bible. Origen got to see only this—none of the maverick Hebrew manuscripts that we know were in circulation before the Christian era. The rabbis he consulted could, or would, show him nothing else. He accepted without question their claim that this, and this alone, was the very word of God. Thus his transliterated Hebrew is essentially the MT. His LXX was a problem for him because its content and order so often differed from that of the MT, but he solved it with the use of text-critical marks to show pluses and minuses in the LXX as compared with the MT. Where he had to fill in gaps, it was Θ, a Greek translator slavishly close to the Hebrew, that he followed. The consequence of this method is that G⁰ never allows us to get behind the Hebrew (=MT) that Origen was using. The same is true of A, Θ, and Σ, although occasionally they do offer us what appears to be a pre-MT text.

Next there is the Lucianic text of the LXX. The Deacon Lucian of Antioch (d. A.D. 312) prepared this recension for use in the Byzantine church. As such, it shows the learned vocabulary and refined style demanded by the classical revival. This text has been influenced by Origen's Hexaplaric text, yet Lucian consistently copies a Greek prototype that is close to the OG as known in Codex Vaticanus. This old text appears to be pre-Christian, and is certainly pre-Origenic. Its value for Septuagint-criticism can immediately be seen. When it is cited, scholars prefer to speak of the "proto-Lucianic recension," though a briefer designation is simply "Lucian" (Gᴸ)—adequate if one keeps in mind that the final text of Lucian simply builds upon this recension. We are indebted chiefly to two great Septuagint scholars, Paul de Lagarde (*Librorum Vetus Testamentum canonicorum pars prior*, 1883) and Alfred Rahlfs (*Septuaginta-Studien*, Heft 3, 1911) for identifying Gᴸ and the family of MSS that contain it, with the extrabiblical citations that witness to it. Josephus and perhaps the NT read a LXX text that has close affinities with Gᴸ, and now its Hebrew *Vorlage* has definitely been identified in fragments from Cave 4 at Qumran. This in turn has stimulated studies that have been able to show that the MT of Chr often follows a Kgs text that is close to this *Vorlage*, giving the Kgs scholar all the more reason for keeping a close eye on parallel texts in Chr.

In *The Septuagint and Jewish Worship* (1921) and supporting studies H. St. John Thackeray argued that Gᴮ in I–IV Reigns shows the work of two different translators. Thackeray interpreted this as arising from a first translator's unwillingness to render certain "unedifying" sections, viz., II Reigns (= 2 Sam) 11:2—III Reigns (= 1 Kgs) 2:11, 22:1—IV Reigns (= 2 Kgs) 25:30. It was a second translator, accordingly, who rendered the intervening sections. Each translator had his own peculiar style and vocabulary. A striking phenomenon is that the second translator used far more Hebraisms and was consistently supportive of the MT. It was thirty years or more before further research has been able to reveal the significance of this discovery. Among the documents recovered from the Qumran caves was a text of the Minor Prophets strikingly similar to the MT. In his book, *Les Devanciers d'Aquila* (VTSup 10, Leiden, 1963), D. Barthélemy took this as evidence for the character of the pre-Christian Hebrew text in Palestine, from which the material for Thackeray's second "translator" in Sam-Kgs has been translated into Greek. Here we recognize a fourth LXX revision or recension alongside OG, Gᴸ, and G⁰. Barthélemy was able to give it the name *Kaige* recension, from the fact that it offers the Greek Καίγε wherever the Hebrew idiom וגם appears. Other scholars have been able to extend the list of literalizing renderings by which *Kaige* can be recognized. It still has not been established why just the sections mentioned show the marks of this *Kaige* recension, but at least we know that they do represent a distinct text-type (that exhibited in the Qumran

Former Prophets text) and not just the peculiarities of an individual translator.

None of the other ancient versions of the OT is so old as the OG rendering of the LXX, yet the student of Scripture must know about them because each supports either the MT or one of the recensions of the LXX. Nonsemitic versions are the Old Latin (OL), which derives from a Greek text closely similar to proto-Lucian; the Vulgate (Vg), translated directly from the Hebrew but with influence from the LXX plus the Three (A, Θ, Σ); also the Armenian (A^rm), translated from the LXX. So-called Oriental (i.e., Semitic) versions are the following: the Coptic (K), derived from the LXX; the Arabic (A), derived from G⁰; the Ethiopic (E), derived from the OG Septuagint; the Syriac Peshitta (Syr), derived from the Hebrew with influence from the Greek; the Syro-Hexaplar (Syr^h), translating G⁰, and our best extant witness to the Origenic text; finally, the Targum (Tg), rendering the Hebrew and strongly supportive of the MT. As has been said, it is only on occasion that our notes will cite these secondary versions. Their chief utility lies in those readings where they stand with the versions they are supposed to disagree with, or in opposition to one they are supposed to support. This would be the case, e.g., if E agreed with MT or a later Greek recension over against OG, if OL disagreed with G^L in favor of MT or one of the other Greek recensions, or if Tg disagreed with MT in favor of the Greek.

PROBLEMS AND METHODS

Bibliography

Debus, J. *Die Sünde Jerobeams. Studien zur Darstellung Jerobeams und der Geschichte des Nordreichs in der deuteronomistische Geschichtsschreibung.* FRLANT 93. Göttingen: Vandenhoeck & Ruprecht, 1967. **Gooding, D. W.** "Pedantic Timetabling in the 3rd Book of Reigns." *VT* 15 (1965) 155–66. ———. "Problems of Text and Midrash in the Third Book of Reigns." *Textus* 7 (1969) 1–29. ———. *Relics of Ancient Exegesis. A Study of the Miscellanies in 3 Reigns 2.* SOTSMS 4. Cambridge: University Press, 1976. ———. "The Septuagint's Rival Versions of Jeroboam's Rise to Power." *VT* 17 (1967) 173–89. ———. "The Shimei Duplicate and its Satellite Miscellanies in 3 Reigns II." *JSS* 13 (1968) 76–92. ———. "Temple Specifications: A Dispute in Logical Arrangement Between the MT and the LXX." *VT* 17 (1967) 143–72. **Gordon, R. P.** "The Second Septuagint Account of Jeroboam: History or Midrash?" *VT* 25 (1975) 368–93. **Hänel, J.** "Die Zusätze der Septuaginta in Reg. 2.35a-o und 46a-l," *ZAW* 47 (1929) 76–79. **Montgomery, J. A.** "A Study in Comparison of the Texts of Kings and Chronicles," *JBL* 50 (1931) 115–16. ———. "The Supplement at the End of 3 Kingdoms 2 (I Reg 2)." *ZAW* 50 (1932) 124–29. **Rehm, M.** *Textkritische Untersuchungen zu den Parallelstellen der Samuel-Königsbücher und der Chronik.* ATAbh XIII, 3. Münster i. W.: Aschendorff, 1937. **Shenkel, J. D.** *Chronology and Recensional Development in the Greek Text of Kings.* HSM, 1. Cambridge: Harvard University Press, 1968. **Sheppard, H. W.** "Variants in the Consonantal Text of G. 1 in the Books of Samuel and Kings." *JTS* 22 (1921) 36–37. **Stade, B.** "Der Text des Berichtes über Salomos Bauten von 1 Kö. 5–7." *ZAW* 3 (1883) 129–77. **Wevers, J. W.** "Double Readings in the Books of Kings." *JBL* 65 (1946) 307–10. ———. "A Study in Hebrew Variants in the Book of Kings." *ZAW* 61 (1945/48) 43–76.

One assumes that, since 1 Kgs and the rest of the OT were written in Hebrew, it is altogether natural and proper to follow the MT as the basis for an English translation. But since we are aware that the MT represents a normalized text—one that suppresses rival variants—we must regularly consult the LXX and other ancient versions for a possible original. In Kgs we have a remarkably smooth Hebrew. Its chief problems appear in those passages where the Masoretes seem to have forgotten the original meaning of certain highly technical terms and for which they substituted something familiar but perhaps incorrect. Outside the temple section, such occurrences are rare. The narrative flows on unhindered by notorious occurrences of textual disturbance, by so-called *cruces interpretum*. Yet an uneasiness remains in the mind of the careful translator, for he reads in many a passage a different Greek or Latin text—or whatever—than can be called upon to support the Hebrew. In other words, the smoothness of the MT may be an argument against the antiquity of the MT rather than an argument for it. It often appears as if the Masoretes have ironed out the difficulties that once were there. Thus it inevitably comes to a balancing out of the MT with the LXX, with constant attention to readings from the other versions. When the LXX is found to be in close agreement with the MT, we can no longer take this as proof that the text is secure. It may be just the opposite, since the OG LXX is often free and paraphrastic while the later LXX recensions support the Hebrew. In other words, the passage of time brought closer conformity. Where the OG makes sense, therefore, it must be seriously considered as possibly superior to the MT.

If one is to follow the LXX, it stands to reason that one should not adopt, except with compelling reason, a reading from G^O since it offers a Greek text that has been thoroughly normalized to what eventually became the MT (the same is true of the Three—the Jewish Greek versions). Likewise *Kaige*—if one can recognize it—tends to follow a refined Hebrew text, and therefore offers little independent witness. G^L, however, definitely presents a pre-Christian Greek in its proto-Lucianic readings, though it too has been influenced by a modified Hebrew. G^L should be relied upon when it makes good sense, when OG is missing, and when the MT is under serious suspicion. In translating 1 Kgs one is often in precisely this position. We follow G^B, Codex Vaticanus with its supporting minuscules, as the oldest complete text of 1 Kgs. Thackeray's scheme allows one to designate 2:12 to the end of chap. 21 as OG, and the rest (1:1—2:11, chap. 22) as *Kaige*. Where we have *Kaige* in Codex B, the best counsel is to switch over to G^L, preserved chiefly in the MSS boc_2e_2, for G^L stands a far better chance of offering the original Greek, and therefore the original Hebrew, than G^B's *Kaige*.

It goes without saying that, even where OG is clearly preserved or can be conjectured, it does not automatically offer a reading superior to that of the MT. Codex B shows a variety of inner-Greek corruptions, as well as numerous readings where (1) its Hebrew *Vorlage* may have been inferior to that of the MT, or (2) its translator(s) did an inferior job of rendering the Hebrew, as compared with the MT. G^B and G^L make palpable mistakes, most often in the temple section, where technical terms were simply not understood.

All the while, the translator of 1 Kgs must keep in mind that the OT contains the parallel Hebrew text, viz., that of Chr. As students of Chr realize, this later historiographic document often goes its own way, offering a tendentious order and a tendentious text. Nevertheless, Chr has been shown to follow an ancient Palestinian Hebrew text that is often close to that which underlies the early Greek translation of Kgs. The LXX text of Chr (*Par*) is sometimes even closer, for it has not been normalized to the MT of Kgs, as Chr itself has been.

The serious reader of 1 Kgs (and 2 Kgs) will need to be aware (1) that the LXX has a number of remarkable additions that have no equivalent in the MT and (2) that its order frequently differs from that of the MT. Although some Septuagintal scholars have argued that the LXX differences are to be preferred, the one scholar, D. W. Gooding, who has made a career of analyzing these differences has conclusively proven their inferiority (see especially his book, *Relics of Ancient Exegesis*). In 1 Kgs there are four long Septuagintal additions. 2:35[a-o] is a haphazard gleaning of statements about Solomon, chosen from various contexts; so likewise 2:46[a-l]. These are best explained as a late editor's attempt to include random and often tendentious scriptural notices from deviant textual traditions. In 12:24[a-z], moreover, there is a tendentious rival account made up of materials concerning Jeroboam and Rehoboam. In 16:28[a-h] there are the Jehoshaphat materials that the MT and many LXX MSS (including G[B]) present in 22:41–51. Gooding has shown that this last long addition results from the LXX's misguided endeavor to revise the entire chronological system of the MT.

Scholars speak of these additions as "miscellanies." They have not been translated for our commentary because they have no claim to represent the original Hebrew text. Similarly, most of the Septuagintal variations in order can be rejected because they are palpably tendentious and secondary. The Greek translators wanted to put such things as the daughter of Pharaoh's residence in Jerusalem in a better light. They wanted to remove the offensiveness of Solomon's numerous marriages. They desired to make the description of the temple more understandable by presenting it in a more logical order. Here the rule of *lectio difficilior* must often prevail, for a difficult Hebrew text has every reason to be preferred over one that tries to smooth it out. Often the opposite relationship is true, of course, and here we must carefully consider the claims of the Greek. We must also weigh carefully whether the shorter Greek text that appears in many places does not deserve priority over what appears to be an expansive Hebrew text.

The following table will help the reader locate parallels among the various translations. G is as cited in the Brooke-McLean Cambridge edition while the symbol Ra represents Rahlfs's smaller edition published in Stuttgart (see *Abbreviations*).

Parallel Texts in 1 Kings = 3 Reigns

Eng.*	MT	G	Ra**	Misc.
	1:1–2:8	1:1–2:8		
	2:9–10	2:9–10		2:35l-o
	11–29a	11–29a		
	om	29bα		
	29b–35	29bβ–35		
	om	35a-o		
	36–42a	36–42		
	42b	om		
	43–46	43–46		
	om	46a-l		
	3:1	4:31	5:14a	2:35cα
	2–8bα	3:2–8b		
	8bβ	om		
	9–22aα	9–22a		
	22aβ	om		
	22b–28	22b–28		
	4:1	4:1		2:46l
	2–6a	2–6aα		2:46h
	om	6aβbα		2:46h
	6b	6bβ		2:46h
	7–13	7–13a		
	13baא	om		
	13baٮβ–16	13b–16		
	17	19		
	18	17		
	19	18		
	20	om		2:46a,g
4:21	5:1	10:30		2:46b,f,k
4:22–23	5:2–3	4:22–23	5:2–3	2:46e
24	4	24	4	2:46f,gα
25	5	om		2:46gβ
26	6	10:29a	10:26a	
27–28	7–8	4:20–21	5:1	
29–30	9–10	25–26	9–10	2:35a-b
31–34	11–14	27–30	11–14	
5:1–14	15–28	5:1–14	15–28	
15	29	15	29	2:35d
16	30	16	30	2:35h
17–18a	31–32a	6:2–3	6:1ab	
18b	32b	5:17	5:32	
	6:1	6:1		
	2–3	6–7	6:2–3a	
	4–10	9–15	4–10	
	11–13	om		
	14	8	3b	

* Where different from MT.
** Where different from G.

Eng.	MT	G	Ra	Misc.
	15–17	16–18a	15–17	
	18	om		
	19	18b	19	
	20a	19	20a	
	20b	20a	20b	
	21a	om		
	21b	20b	21	
	22a	21	22	
	22b	om		
	23–31a	22–30a	23–31	
	31b–33a	om	32–33a	
	33b–36	31–34a	33b–36	
	om	34b	36^a	
	37–38a	4–5	1^{cd}	
	38b	om		2:35$^{c\beta}$
	7:1a	7:38		
	1b	50		
	2–7a	39–44		
	7b	om		
	8–12a	45–49		
	12b	om		
	13–14	1–2		
	15	3		2:35$^{c\gamma}$
	16–18a	4–6a		
	18bα	om		
	18bβ	6b		
	19	8		
	20a	9a		
	20bα	om		
	20bβ	9b		
	21	7		
	22	om		
	23abα	10		2:35$^{e\alpha}$
	23bβ	om		
	24a	11		2:35$^{e\beta}$
	24b	om		
	25	13		
	26	12		
	27–30a	14–17a		
	30bα	17b		2:35$^{e\gamma}$
	30bβ–32aα	om		
	32aβ–35	18–21		
	36–45bα	22–31a		
	om	31bα		
	45bβ	31bβ		
	46	33		
	47	32		
	48–51	34–37		
	om	8:1aα		
	8:1aα	1aβ		
	1aβ	om		
	1b	1b		

Eng.	MT	G	Ra	Misc.
	2aα,b	om		
	2aβ	2		
	3a	om		
	3b	3		
	4aα,bβ	om		
	4aβba	4		
	5–8a	5–8		
	8b	om		
	9–11	9–11		
	12–13	53[a]		
	14–41a	14–41		
	41b–42a	om		
	42b–49a	42–49		
	49b	om		
	50–66	50–53, 54–66		
	9:1–9	9:1–9bα		
	10–14	10–14		
				15–25 G[A]
	15	10:23a	22[aα]	2:35[iαk]
	16–17aα	4:32–33	5:14[b]	
	17aβb	10:23bα	10:22[aβ]	2:35[iβ]
	18aα	om		2:35[iγ]
	18aβb	om		2:46[d]
	19aα	om		
	19aβ–22	10:23bβ–25	22[aγ-c]	
	23	om		2:35[h]
	24	9:9bβ	9[b]	2:35[f]
	25	om		2:35[g]
	26–28	26–28		
	10:1–22	10:1–22		
	23–25	26–28	23–25	
	26	29	26	2:46[i]
	27–29	31–33	27–29	
	11:1aα	11:1aαא		
	1aβb–2	1aβb–2		
	3a	1aαב		
	3b	om		
	4aα	3a	4aα	
	4aβ	4	4b	
	4b	3b, 10b	4aβ	
	5a	6		
	5b	om		
	6	8		
	7a, bβ	5a, bβ		
	7bα	om		
	8	7		
	9–10	9–10a		
	11–14a	11–14a		
	14b	14bβב		
	15–22b	15–22bα		
	om	22bβ		
	23–25aα	14baβא		

Eng.	MT	G	Ra	Misc.
	25aβb	25aβb		
	26aα	26		12:24[b]
	26aβb	om		
	27	27		2:35[f]
	28	28		
	29–31	29–31		12:24[o]
	32–38	32–38		
	39	om		
	40	40		12:24[c]
	41–42	41–42		
	43	43a, bβℶ		12:24[aα]
	12:1	12:1		12:24[nβ]
	2	11:43baβא		
	3a	om		
	3b–20	12:3–20		12:24[p-u]
	21–24	21–24		12:24[x-z]
	om	24[a-z]		
	25–33	25–33		
	13:1–26a	13:1–26		
	26b–27	om		
	28–34	28–34		
	14:1–2	om		12:24[g]
	3–7a	om		12:24[h-lα]
	7b–9	om		
	10–11	om		12:24[mα]
	12	om		12:24[lβ]
	13	om		12:24[mβ]
	14–16	om		
	17	om		12:24[mγ]
	18–20	om		
	21–22a	14:21–22a		12:24[aβ]
	22b–31	22b–31		
	15:1–5bα	15:1–5		
	5bβ–6	om		
	7–31	7–31		
	32	om		
	33–34	33–34		
	16:1–6	16:1–6bα		
	om	6bβ		
	7	7		
	8aα	om		
	8aβb–10aα	8–10a		
	10aβ	om		
	10b–11aα	10b–11		
	11aβb–12a	om		
	12b–14	12–14		
	15aα	om		
	15aβ–21	15–21		
	22aα	om		
	22aβ–28	22–28		
	om	28[a-h]		
	29–34	29–34		

Eng.	MT	G	Ra	Misc.
	17:1–21	17:1–21		
	22	om		
	23–24	23–24		
	18:1–29a	18:1–29		
	29b	om		
	30a	30		
	30b	om		
18:31–33a	31–33	31–33		
33b	34a	34a		
34	34b	34b		
	35–43	35–43bα		
	om	43bβ–44aα		
	44–46	44aβ–46		
	19:1–21	19:1–21		
	20:1aα	21:1aαא		
	om	1aαב		
	1aβ–20aα	1aβ–20aαא		
	om	20aαב		
	20aβ–43	20aβ–43		
	21:1aα	om		
	1aβ–2	20:1–2bβא		
	om	2bβב		
	3–4aα	3–4a		
	4aβ	om		
	4b–10aα	4b–10		
	10aβ–13aαא	om		
	13aαב–15aαא	13–15a		
	15aαב	om		
	15aβ–16a	15b–16a		
	om	16bα		
	16b–19	16bβ–19bβא		
	om	19bβב		
	20	20abα		
	om	20bβ		
	21–27	21–27bα		
	om	27bβ		
	28–29a	28–29a		
	29bα	om		
	29bβ	29b		
	22:1–28a	22:1–28		
	28b	om		
	29–35a	29–35a		
	om	35bα		
	35b–41	35bβ–41		
	42	42		16:28[a]
22:43–45	43–46	43–46		16:28[b-c]
46–49	47–50	om		16:28[d-g]
50	51	51		16:28[h]
51–53	52–54	52–54bα		
	om	54bβא		
	2 Kgs 1:1	54bβב		

Conclusion to the
Throne-Succession Narrative
Chapters 1–2

Solomon Becomes King (1:1–53)

Bibliography

Ackroyd, P. R. "The Succession Narrative (so-called)." *Int* 35 (1981) 383–96. **Ball, E.** "The Co-regency of David and Solomon (1 Kings I)." *VT* 27 (1977) 268–79. **Bar-Ephrat, S.** "Literary Modes and Methods in the Biblical Narrative." *Immanuel* 8 (1978) 19–31. **Brueggemann, W.** "David and his Theologian." *CBQ* 30 (1968) 156–81. ————. "On Trust and Freedom. A Study of Faith in the Succession Narrative." *Int* 36 (1972) 3–19. ————. "Life and Death in Tenth Century Israel." *JAAR* 40 (1972) 96–109. **Delekat, L.** "Tendenz und Theologie der David-Salomo-Erzählung." *Das ferne und nahe Wort* (L. Rost Fs). BZAW 105. Berlin: Töpelmann, 1967. **Flanagan, J. W.** "Court History or Succession Document? A Study of 2 Samuel 9–20 and 1 Kings 1–2." *JBL* 91 (1972) 172–81. **Fokkelman, J. P.** *Narrative Art and Poetry in the Books of Samuel. A Full Interpretation Based on Stylistic and Structural Analyses.* Vol. I, *King David (II Sam. 9–20 and I Kings 1–2).* StSemNed. Assen: van Gorcum, 1981 (on 1 Kgs 1–2, 345–410). **Gunn, D. L.** "David and the Gift of the Kingdom (2 Sam. 2–4, 9–10, 1 Kgs. 1–2)." *Sem* 3 (1975) 14–45. **Long, B. O.** "A Darkness Between Brothers." *JSOT* 19 (1981) 79–94. **McCarter, Jr., P. K.** "'Plots, True or False': The Succession Narrative as Court Apologetic." *Int* 35 (1981) 355–67. **Mettinger, T. N. D.** *King and Messiah. The Civil and Sacral Legitimation of the Israelite Kings.* Lund: C. W. K. Gleerup, 1976 (on 1 Kgs 1:5–31, 119–24). **von Rad, G.** "Das judäische Königsritual." *TLZ* 72 (1947) 211–16. **Rost, L.** *Die Überlieferung von der Thronnachfolge Davids.* BWANT, III 6. Stuttgart: W. Kohlhammer, 1926. **Smith, M.** "The So-called 'Biography of David' in the Books of Samuel and Kings." *HTR* 44 (1951) 167–69. **Veijola, T.** *Die ewige Dynastie. David und die Entstehung seiner Dynastie nach der deuteronomistischen Darstellung.* Helsinki 1975 (on 1 Kgs 1–2, 16–26). **Waterman, L.** "Some Historical and Literary Consequences of Probable Displacement in I Kings 1–2." *JAOS* 60 (1940) 383–90. **Wharton, J. A.** "A Plausible Tale: Story and Theology in II Samuel 9–20, I Kings 1–2." *Int* 35 (1981) 341–54. **Whybray, R. N.** *The Succession Narrative. A Study of II Samuel 9–20; I Kings 1 and 2.* SBT II, 9. Naperville–London: A. R. Allenson, 1968. **Würthwein, E.** *Die Erzählung von der Thronfolge Davids-theologische oder politische Geschichtsschreibung?* ThS 115. Zurich: Theologischer Verlag, 1977. **Zalewski, S.** "The Struggle Between Adonijah and Solomon over the Kingdom" (Heb.). *BMik* 63 (1975) 490–510.

Translation

[1] Now King David had become [a] old, well advanced in years, so that even when they covered him with blankets he could not get warm. [2] So his servants said,[a] "Let

us seek out [b] *for* [c]*the king* [c] *a pure young woman to attend the king,* [d] *lie* [e]*in his bosom,* [e] *and warm* [f] *the king.'' * [3] *Then they looked for a beautiful young woman throughout* [a]*all Israel* [a] *and found Abishag, a Shunemite, and brought her to the king.* [4] *Now the young woman was extremely beautiful* [a] *and became his bedfellow, waiting on his desires, but the king had no intercourse with her.*

[5] *Now Adonijah* [a] *son of Haggith* [b] *took airs, saying, "I want to be king''; so he prepared for himself chariots and horsemen, with fifty men to run before him.* [6] *But his father had never chided* [a] *him, saying; "Why did you do this?''* [b] *What is more, he was exceedingly good-looking; she had borne him after Absalom was born.* [7] *His confidants were Joab son of Zeruiah and Abiathar the priest, and they* [a]*supported Adonijah.* [a] [8] *But Zadok the priest and Benaiah son of Jehoiada and Nathan the prophet and Shimei and Rei, and the warriors who were associated with David, were not with* [a] *Adonijah.* [9] *So Adonijah sacrificed* [a]*oxen and sheep* [a] *at the sliding stone* [b] *which is near Rogel spring,* [c] *having invited all* [d] *his brothers* [e] *the king's sons* [e] *and* [f] *the Judahites who were* [g]*royal officials;* [g] [10] *but Nathan the prophet and Benaiah and the warriors and Solomon* [a] *he did not invite.*

[11] *Then Nathan said* [a] *to Bathsheba Solomon's mother, "Haven't you heard that Adonijah Haggith's son reigns, while our lord David is unaware of it?* [12] *So now come,* [a] *let me offer you counsel to save your life and the life of your son.* [b] [13] *Go enter in to King David and say to him, 'Did you not, my lord king, swear* [a] *to your maidservant as follows: "Surely* [b]*Solomon your son* [b] *shall reign after me, and he shall sit on my throne?'' So why does Adonijah reign?'* [14] *While* [a] *you are still there speaking with the king, I will follow* [b] *and confirm your words.''*

[15] *So Bathsheba entered in to the king in the bedchamber. Now the king was very old, and Abishag the Shunemite was ministering to the king.* [16] *And Bathsheba bowed to show homage to the king. And the king said,* [a] *"What is it?''* [17] *And she* [a] *said,* [b] *"My lord,* [c] *you swore by* [d] *your god to your maidservant, 'Surely* [e]*Solomon your son* [e] *shall* [f] *reign after me, and he shall sit on my throne.'* [18] *But now, behold, Adonijah reigns, and you,* [a] *my lord the king, do not know about it!* [19] *And he has sacrificed* [a]*sheep and oxen* [a] *and has invited all the king's sons and Abiathar the priest and Joab, general of the army,* [b]*but Solomon your servant* [c] *he has not invited.* [b] [20] [a] *As for you, my lord king,* [a] *the eyes of all Israel* [b] *are on you to tell them who shall sit on the throne of my lord the king after him;* [21] *and it may be that when my lord the king sleeps with his fathers I will be—with* [a]*my son Solomon* [a]*—reckoned as guilty.''*

[22] *And behold, while she was still speaking with the king, Nathan the prophet entered.* [23] *And they told the king, "Here is Nathan the prophet.'' And he entered into* [a]*the king's* [a] *presence and prostrated himself on his face to the king, all the way to the ground.* [24] *And Nathan* [a] *said, "My lord king, you must have said, 'Adonijah shall reign after me, and he shall sit on my throne,'* [25] *for he has gone down today and sacrificed* [a]*oxen and sheep* [a] *in great number, and has invited all the king's sons and* [b]*the commanders of the army* [b] *and Abiathar the priest, and behold, these are eating and drinking before him, and they say, 'Long live King Adonijah!'* [26] *But me—even me, your servant—and Zadok the priest and Benaiah son of Jehoiada and Solomon your son* [a] *he has not invited.* [27] *Has this business actually proceeded from my lord the king, while you have not told your servants* [a] *who is to sit on the throne of my lord the king after him?''*

[28] *Then David* [a] *responded by saying, "Call me Bathsheba,''* [b]*and she came into*

the king's presence and stood before him.[b] [29] And the king took an oath and said, "By the life of Yahweh, who has redeemed my life from every adversity, [30] even as I swore to you by Yahweh the God of Israel, saying, 'Surely Solomon your son shall reign after me, and he shall sit on my throne in my place,' thus shall I do this day!" [31] And Bathsheba bowed face to the ground, doing homage to the king and saying, "May [a]my lord King David[a] live forever!"

[32] And the king[a] said, "Call me Zadok the priest, Nathan the prophet, and Benaiah son of Jehoiada"; and they came into the king's presence. [33] And the king said to them, "Take with you the servants of your lords[a] and mount [b]my son Solomon[b] on the mule that belongs to me and bring him down to Gihon; [34] and let Zadok the priest, with Nathan the prophet, anoint[a] him there as king over Israel;[b] then you shall blow on the ram's horn and say, 'Long live King Solomon!' [35][a] So shall he sit on my throne and[b] reign in my place; and him[c] do I appoint as leader [d]over Israel." [d] [36] And Benaiah son of Jehoiada responded to the king and said, "Amen. May the god[a] of my lord the king [b]confirm it![b] [37] As Yahweh has been with my lord,[a] so [b]may he be[b] with Solomon and make his throne even greater than the throne of my lord King David!"

[38] So Zadok the priest went down, with Nathan the prophet, Benaiah son of Jehoiada, and the Cherethites and Pelethites, and they mounted Solomon on King David's mule, and [a]brought him[a] to Gihon. [39] And Zadok the priest took a horn of oil from the Tent and anointed Solomon; then they blew the ram's horn and all the people said, "Long live King Solomon!" [40] And all the people came up after him; [a]and [b]the people[b] were [c]playing on pipes[c] and rejoicing with loud merriment,[a] so that the land resounded[d] with their noise.

[41] Now Adonijah heard it, [a]and all his guests,[a] just as they finished eating; and when Joab heard the sound of the ram's horn[b] he said, [c]"Why this noise of the city in tumult?"[c] [42] While he was yet speaking, behold, Jonathan son of Abiathar the priest![a] And Adonijah said, "Enter, for a worthy man are you, the bringer of good news!" [43] And Jonathan gave response and said,[a] "No, our lord King David has made Solomon king [44] and has sent[a] with him Zadok the priest, Nathan the prophet, Benaiah son of Jehoiada, and the Cherethites and Pelethites, and they have mounted him on the king's mule. [45] And Zadok the priest and Nathan the prophet have anointed[a] him;[b] and they [c]have come up[c] from there rejoicing, [d]so that the city is in tumult.[d] This is the noise[e] you have heard. [46] So Solomon sits on the royal throne. [47] And when the king's servants came in to bless our lord King David,[a] saying, 'May [b]your God[b] do even better for Solomon's fame than for your own, and may he exalt his throne over your throne,' then the king did homage in bed.[c] [48] What is more, the king responded to this by saying, 'Blessed be Yahweh the God of Israel for providing today[a]—while my own eyes behold it—one who may sit on my throne!'" [49] Then, trembling, all the guests who were with Adonijah [a]rose up[a] and departed, each going his own way.

[50] Now Adonijah, being fearful of[a] Solomon, rose and went[b] to grasp the horns of the altar.[c] [51] And it was reported to Solomon as follows: "Behold, Adonijah is afraid of King Solomon; and behold,[a] he has laid hold on the horns of the altar, saying, 'Let[b] Solomon first swear to me not to kill his servant with the sword!'" [52] And Solomon said, "If he behaves as a gentleman, not one of [a]his hairs[a] will fall to the ground, but if evil is found in him he shall die." [53] Then Solomon[a] sent and brought him down from the altar; and he entered and did homage to Solomon.[b] And Solomon said to him, "Go to your house."

Notes

1.a. G^L adds σφόδρα "very."

2.a. G^B. MT and G^L address the words to the king.

2.b. Probably MT יבקשו supported by G^B ζητησάτωσαν (cf. G^L λαβέτωσαν "let them bring") has been corrupted by v 3 from original נבבקש "let us seek out."

2.c-c. With G^B, omitting "my lord" of MT, which keeps the speech in the mouth of one servant, addressed to the others. G^L adds "lord" without the possessive pronoun.

2.d. Influenced by v 4, MT and G^B (here a hebraizing *Kaige*) add "and be his bedfellow."

2.e-e. G^L ἐν τῷ κόλπῳ is a literalizing idiom, "in the bosom." The lack of a possessive pronoun, as in MT "in your bosom," or in G^B "with him," endeavors to mitigate the apparent lustiness of the scene.

2.f. See note c-c. Here again G^L is to be followed in omitting "my lord" before "the king."

3.a-a. G^L ἐν πάντι Ἰσραήλ "in all Israel" is more probable than the stereotyped locution, "in the whole Israelite domain," read in MT and G^B (*Kaige*).

4.a. MT and G^B "in appearance" is explicative.

5.a. G^L "Ornia," here and wherever the name occurs (ד *dáleth* is read as a ר *rēsh*). G^B (*Kaige*) reproduces MT.

5.b. G^L "David," identifying according to the familiar patronymic formula, scarcely deserves preference to the matronymic identification, relevant in a text emphasizing rivalry between David's wives.

6.a. MT עצב "chide" is well reproduced in G^L ἐπιτιμάω. G^B ἀπεκώλυσεν "persecute," "treat harshly" reads Heb. עצר. This may a very early error since it is in the pre-exilic Canaanite script that ב and ר appear the most alike.

6.b. G^B lacks both a direct object and a comparative phrase (compare G^L, which translates the MT closely). But "this" is implied in the Greek διὰ τί σὺ ἐποίησας "why have you behaved?"

7.a-a. G^L ἀντιλαμβάνοντο "share with" may be an idiomatic rendering of MT, which is literally rendered by G^B (*Kaige*).

8.a. G^L μετὰ "with" literally renders MT עם, but G^B may be OG. Its ὀπίσω "behind" may be a scribal error from the end of v 7.

9.a-a. G^L, with two animals (βόας καὶ πρόβατα "oxen and sheep"), has been expanded in MT and G^B (*Kaige*) to include three (MT צאן ובקר ומריא, G^B πρόβατα καὶ μόσχους καὶ ἄρνας "sheep and cattle and fatlings"). Whenever this formula occurs, the various witnesses are likely to list the animals differently.

9.b. G^B corrupts Heb. אבן "stone" (so G^L) to אש "fire." See Burney, *Notes* xx.

9.c. G^B omits.

9.d. MT and G^L. G^B's omission is a corruption according to Burney, *Notes* xx.

9.e-e. MT and G^L. G^B omits.

9.f. G^{BL}. MT's "all" is late and idealizing.

9.g-g. MT and G^B. G^L is explicative in adding the proper name "David," overlooking the fact that the Heb. עבד־המלך is a technical title, complete in itself.

10.a. G^L has only the proper name. MT and G^B (*Kaige*) add an explicative "his brother," as if to emphasize the insult intended in not including Solomon among "all his brothers," v 9.

11.a. MT and G^B. G^L introduces the sentence with the verb "and came," an effective stylistic device for producing more action, but of doubtful originality.

12.a. Heb. לכי, an imperative arousing to action (cf. Gen. 12:1) is read both by G^B's literalizing δεῦρο "come on" (*Kaige*) and G^L's idiomatic δή "please."

12.b. That "Solomon" is explicative appears from its alternating position before and after "your son" in G^L and MT with G^B, respectively.

13.a. MT and G^B deserve preference because G^L's "by Yahweh God" is explicative.

13.b-b. So MT, G^{BL} reversing the order. The case is not as in note 12.b. because the promise form requires the naming of Solomon emphatically at the beginning.

14.a. G^L omits the "(and) behold" read in MT and G^B, which expand the original in classical Heb. style.

14.b. G^B is to be preferred to MT and G^L, adding the explicative "you."

16.a. MT and G^B are preferred to G^L, which adds the explicative "to her."

17.a. MT and G^B have the simple pronoun, explicated in G^L's "Bathsheba."

17.b. G^{BL} are preferred to MT's explicative "to him."

17.c. MT and G^B. G^L adds "O king."

17.d. G^B's "your god" is regular styling in this document in polite address to the king (1:47) hence MT and G^L's addition, "Yahweh," is pleonastic.

17.e-e. The MT styling, repeated from v 12, deserves preference over G^{BL}'s reversal of the order.

17.f. MT and G^B. G^L reads "he," normal before this stereotyped second line of a familiar royal formula. G^B's omission is Hellenistic stylization.

18.a. G^{BL} καὶ σύ "and you" calls attention to David as the new subject. MT ועתה "and now" is an error from the preceding ועתה. Cf. *HOTTP*, 290.

19.a-a. G^L has the two sacrificial animals. MT and G^B expand this to three each. See note on v 9.

19.b-b. G^L omits, but MT and G^B "but Solomon your servant has not invited" is required for good sense.

19.c. Cf. v 26.

20.a-a. G^L substitutes the equivalent of v 28, "and whether this matter has occurred through my lord the king, because."

20.b. MT and G^B. G^L "the people."

21.a-a. MT "my son Solomon" is here to be preferred to G^{BL} "Solomon my son" because of the more natural connection of mother and son in the anticipated blood-purge.

23.a-a. MT and G^B. G^L's additional "David" is explicative.

24.a. MT and G^B. G^L σύ = אתה may be a corruption of the name נתן. It is normal good style that Nathan should here be introduced by name as the new speaker.

25.a-a. G^L's dual number of sacrificial animals is again to be preferred to the three's of MT and G^B.

25.b-b. MT and G^B "the commanders of the army" constitutes a more difficult reading than G^L's "General Joab" since the latter had been the only high military officer on Adonijah's side previously mentioned. Cf. *HOTTP*, 291.

26.a. G^L. MT and G^B (*Kaige*) normalize to "your servant" from v 19, but cf. "son" in vv 13, 17.

27.a. MT, referring to the entire privy council. G^{BL}, with sing, assume that Nathan is speaking only of himself.

28.a. G^{BL}. MT "King David" is pleonastic in this context.

28.b-b. G^B has the most natural style because "the king's presence" pervades the entire chamber; hence our translation, over against MT, which repeats "in the king's presence" twice, and G^L "and she entered and stood in the king's presence."

31.a-a. MT and G^B. G^L has an awkward "the king my lord David" (corr?).

32.a. G^L. MT and G^B add an explicative "David."

33.a. MT's pl is difficult and requires explanation, hence G^{BL} sing.

33.b-b. Since no emphasis on Solomon's identity seems intended, it is preferable to read our text, with G^B, rather than MT and G^L's "Solomon my son."

34.a. MT and G^B's sing is exegetically correct because only a priest performs the rite of anointing. G^{BL} pl shows this translator's unfamiliarity with Heb. law as he assumes that the two chief sacral officials shared this function also.

34.b. MT and G^B. "Israel" is suitable because this is the name of the sacral union and of the united kingdom. G^L's addition, "and Judah," is a postexilic gloss.

35.a. G^B. MT and G^L add the pleonastic "and you shall ascend."

35.b. G^B, which is to be preferred to MT and G^L, which for no good reason begin with the emphatic subject pronoun, "and he."

35.c. MT and G^L rightly place the pronoun object foremost for emphasis. G^B is probably corrupt, reading ואני in the place of ואתו.

35.d-d. Editorial conjecture from v 34 and from the fact that the main witnesses add "and Judah" inconsistently (MT and G^B have it follow, G^L has it precede).

36.a. G^B does not name David's god in direct address to him; cf. v 17. MT supplies "Yahweh," while G^L has a paraphrastic conflation.

36.b-b. G^{BL}. MT "say it"; Mss and Syr "do it."

37.a. G^{BL}. MT's addition of "the king" is pleonastic.

37.b-b. Reading K יְהִי "may he be" (so G^B εἴη, opt) rather than Q יִהְיֶה "he will be" (so G^L ἔσται, ind). The pious wish of the juss/opt is natural in Benaiah's mouth, but the Sopherim who recommended the indicative with their Q pointing were offended at the thought that Yahweh might not be with Solomon.

38.a-a. MT's hiph, ויֹלכו "and they brought him," supported by G^B ἀπήγαγον, suits the sense of actually conducting Solomon to the scene of anointing, contrary to G^L, (ἐπορεύοντο "they went"), which reads the Heb. as a qal with a corruption of אתו "him" to אחריו "after him."

40.a-a. G^L conflates the reading of MT and that of G^B, showing that they existed together in his oral tradition.

40.b-b. MT, which is probably correct since the first clause, with "all the people," concludes the preceding narrative sequence. G^L and OL repeat "all the people" while G^B omits the new subject for the sake of style.

40.c-c. MT מְחַלְלִים בַּחֲלִלִים "playing on pipes" offers a less startling picture than G^B's "whirling in dances," reading the Heb. as מְחֹלְלִים בַּמְחֹלוֹת; thus Syr, Tg.

40.d. Reading G^L (ἤχησεν, from ἤχω, "resound"), whose Heb. is the more believable תֵּהֹם. MT, followed by G^B, has the astounding וַתִּבָּקַע, from the root meaning "split"—as though an earthquake had occurred.

41.a-a. G^B, with the simplest text. MT has "and the guests who were with him"; G^L, with the simplest text. MT has "and the guests who were with him"; G^L paraphrases with "and all those eating and drinking with him."

41.b. MT and G^B. G^L's "noise" may be influenced by the verb ἤχεω in the preceding verse; cf. v 45.

41.c-c. MT and G^B. G^L's "Why the outcry of the sound of the loud noise?" is a conflation.

42.a. G^L follows a Heb. text without the verb, a style of great dramatic force. MT and G^B (Kaige) pedantically supply the verb "entered."

43.a. G^B. MT and G^L add an explicative "to Adonijah."

44.a. G^L. MT and G^B add the subject explicatively: "the king."

45.a. MT and G^B follow an original text in employing the pl (G^L has the sing consistently with v 39) because such a minor inaccuracy would be entirely natural in the excited report of this young priest, a point not neglected in our writer's skillful narration.

45.b. G^{BL}. MT's "as king" is explicative.

45.c-c. MT and G^B. In adding "him" as pronoun object, G^L reads the final wāw of וַיַּעְלוּ as a pronominal suffix; or, more likely, had a surplus wāw in its Vorlage. The verb is, of course, read as a hiphil rather than as a qal.

45.d-d. MT and G^B, with a fresh expression, are more original than G^L, which keeps "land" from v 40, subject in a nominal clause with the noun κραυγή "outcry," which is not to be derived from the verb הום "be in tumult."

45.e. MT and G^B. G^L tries to make sense in his confused text with "sound of the noise."

47.a. MT and G^B. G^L's addition, "and they came individually and said," is explicative.

47.b-b. MT, deserving preference in this address to the king; see above G^B "God," without the possessive pronoun. G^L κύριος = Yahweh.

47.c. MT and G^B have the idiomatic "the bed." G^L adds an explicative pronoun suffix.

48.a. MT, signalizing the day as a day of resolution and revelation. G^{BL} rather spoil the speaker's point with their explicative "from my posterity."

49.a-a. MT and G^L. Good Heb. style often inserts the verb קום "arise" before verbs of motion. G^B omits.

50.a. MT and G^B. G^L "King Solomon." One should note that vv 50–53 consistently have the proper name alone, showing the narrator's sensitivity to the fact that here it is the rivalry of brothers that still holds center stage. Contrast 2:17–25, where "King Solomon" is regularly used as Solomon acts in his judicial capacity.

50.b. MT and G^B. From 2:29 G^L draws his explicative addition, "to the tent of Yahweh."

50.c. G^L adds words from v 51 (conflation).

51.a. MT and G^L follow a good text in reading a double "behold" (the second is omitted by G^B) because the second clause points out a climactic phenomenon demonstrative of the first.

51.b. G^{BL}. MT's "King Solomon" is unmotivated in this passage (see above).

52.a-a. MT and G^B. G^L's "the hairs of his head" is explicative.

53.a. G^L. MT and G^B "King Solomon"; see above.

53.b. G^{BL}. MT adds "king."

Form/Structure/Setting

Throne-succession narrative, Episode 13: Solomon's party makes a successful
countercoup
  I. The perilous situation: David's advancing debilitude
      A. Exposition: His physical degeneration, 1:1
      B. A putative remedy: Abishag
          1. The proposal, v 2
          2. The search, v 3
          3. The service rendered and its negative result, v 4
 II. Adonijah's coup frustrated
      A. The provocation: Adonijah's move to have himself crowned
          1. Exposition: The conspiracy
              a. Adonijah's disposition, vv 5–6
              b. The rival parties, vv 7–8
          2. Adonijah's feast of investiture, vv 9–10
      B. Nathan's preventive countermeasure
          1. Scene 1: A contrived corroboration
              a. Advice to Bathsheba, vv 11–14
              b. Bathsheba's appeal to David
                  (1) Approach to the king, vv 15–16
                  (2) Bathsheba's speech
                      (a) An oath recalled, v 17
                      (b) Apprisal of Adonijah's coup, vv 18–19
                      (c) Reminder of the king's responsibility, vv 20–21
              c. Nathan's appeal to David
                  (1) Approach to the king, vv 22–23
                  (2) Nathan's speech
                      (a) Report of Adonijah's coup, vv 24–26
                      (b) Query of the king's intent, v 27
          2. Scene 2: David orders Solomon's investiture
              a. The oath confirmed
                  (1) David summons Bathsheba, v 28
                  (2) David swears to crown Solomon immediately, vv 29–30
                  (3) Bathsheba's response, v 31
              b. David instructs his officials
                  (1) The summons, v 32
                  (2) Order for anointing and investiture, vv 33–35
                  (3) Benaiah's laudatory confirmation, vv 36–37
              c. Fulfillment: anointing and acclamation of Solomon, vv 38–40
          3. Scene 3: Nullification of Adonijah's investiture
              a. The festal party seeks intelligence, vv 41–42
              b. Report of Solomon's investiture, vv 43–46
              c. Report of David's confirmation
                  (1) The court blesses Solomon through David, v 47
                  (2) David blesses Yahweh through Solomon, v 48
      C. The dispersal of Adonijah's party, v 49

III. Adonijah accepts conciliation
  A. His flight to sanctuary, v 50
  B. Scene 4: Solomon offers clemency
    1. Report and instructions, vv 51-52
    2. Adonijah summoned and dismissed, v 53

A close study of this outline will show the reader that structure may have communicative function alongside material content. *How* a story is told may be as important as *what* is told. Our outline is designedly functional, thus no mere logical arrangement of subtopics. It aims to reproduce the plan that was in the narrator's mind as he chose precisely certain elements, arranged in a cunningly effective way, to convey the powerful effect that he intended.

1 Kgs 1-2 is a severed trunk, to be sure, and can never be adequately appreciated except as the continuation of 2 Sam 9-20. It is the conclusion and climax of the throne-succession narrative. (See *Introduction* for details.) At one time Sam and Kgs must have belonged together as one continuous document, but a late editor inserted a variety of mainly late materials in 2 Sam 21-24 in order to wrap up the history of King David, cutting 1-2 Kgs adrift as a separate book and allowing 1 Kgs 1-2 to function as an introduction to the history of Solomon. The modern reader must resist the effect of this misalignment and read 1 Kgs 1-2 for what it originally was, i.e., the grand finale of the David-Solomon story.

This commentary's general procedure is to treat the text pericope by pericope, but when dealing with a longer document like the throne-succession narrative it is better to handle it by episodes, for each episode has its own distinct theme and structure. The fourteen episodes within the throne-succession document are as follows:

  (1) David's kindness to Mephibosheth, 2 Sam 9
  (2) The Ammonite–Syrian war (I), 2 Sam 10
  (3) David's sin with Bathsheba and its consequences, 2 Sam 11:1—12:25
  (4) The Ammonite–Syrian war (II), 2 Sam 12:26-31
  (5) Amnon's sin and Absalom's vengeance, 2 Sam 13
  (6) Absalom's restoration and its consequences, 2 Sam 14:1—15:6
  (7) Absalom's revolt and David's flight, 2 Sam 15:7—16:14
  (8) Hushai's counsel saves David from pursuit, 2 Sam 16:15—17:23
  (9) The battle of the Ephraim forest, 2 Sam 17:24—18:7
  (10) Absalom's death and its consequences, 2 Sam 18:8—19:9ab (Eng. 8ab)
  (11) David's return and Sheba's rebellion, 2 Sam 19:9b (Eng. 8b)—20:3
  (12) The suppression of Sheba's rebellion, 2 Sam 20:4-22
  (13) Solomon's party makes a successful countercoup, 1 Kgs 1:1-53
  (14) Solomon establishes his rule, 1 Kgs 2:1-46a
       Summarizing conclusion, 1 Kgs 2:46b

It is the distinguished German scholar Leonhard Rost who once for all disposed of the claim of certain late Wellhausenians that the material in Sam-Kgs should be divided up among the two early sources of the Pentateuch, J and E (*Die Überlieferung von der Thronnachfolge Davids*, 1926). Rost persuasively argued that 2 Sam 9-20, 1 Kgs 1-2 was a propaganda piece legitimizing

Solomon's selection over David's other sons to be his father's successor. The vast majority of scholars have been won over to this position, some of whom (e.g., R. N. Whybray, *The Succession Narrative*, 1968) have offered important studies in confirmation of it. From time to time differing assessments appear, but generally with little lasting effect. We may mention an imposing study by Timo Veijola, *Die Ewige Dynastie* (1975), which rather shatters Rost's synthesis and, in particular, assigns to Dtr a substantial amount of material in 1 Kgs 1–2, as follows: 1:35–37, 46–48 (with expansion in v 30), 2:1–2, 4aαb, 5–9, 24, 26b–27, 31b–33, 37b, 44–45 (with expansion in vv 42a and 43a). Veijola follows much the same methodology as W. Dietrich (*Prophetie und Geschichte*), whom I have sharply criticized in my book *Prophet against Prophet*, 129–30. Veijola allows his redaction-critical presuppositions to dominate the criticism of the earliest literary levels in the David story from 1 Sam 16 to 1 Kgs 2. He neglects the structure of the elemental units, hence has no eye for their function and aim, whether in isolation or in early combinations. He little perceives the skill of the throne-succession document in introducing narrative elements, creating tension and dramatic effect. He loses much of the element of subtle irony in this document's way of resolving the rivalry between various contenders for the throne. All that seems to disturb a simplistic image of David's reign is assigned to Dtr, which is of course much too late to be taken as the original, creative author of this particular material. We may say immediately of 1 Kgs 1 that it definitely needs vv 35–37 and 46–48. This chapter is an absolute unity, with no evidence of the deuteronomistic redaction whatever.

In order to appreciate 1 Kgs 1 for what it truly is, one needs to take full account of the author's rare skill and effectiveness. As in earlier sections of the throne-succession narrative, he employs an alternation of description and dialogue. Interestingly, he uses description mainly in the positions of opening exposition (vv 1, 5–8) and concluding denouement (vv 9–10, 38–40, 49); these are elements that either prepare for or resolve the main action, which is actually carried forward in the sections of dialogue. This is to say that the narrator sees action as occurring essentially in dialogue, a verbal interaction between and among contending parties. Our author is noteworthy for creating a succession of effective scenes (vv 11–27, 28–37, 41–48, 51–53) where such action takes place. Such scenes are, perhaps, comparable to those of Shakespeare's plays. An actor may appear on the stage, speak his part, and depart in favor of someone else. Thus in scene 1, Nathan first speaks to Bathsheba, then she enters into David's bedroom to speak to him, and finally Nathan enters the bedroom to corroborate Bathsheba's appeal. Scene 2 is simpler. Scene 3 is simpler still. And scene 4 is the simplest of all.

Another notable technique on the part of this author is his balancing of reminiscence and prolepsis (glimpse of the future). We recognize an element of reminiscence in v 15, where we are told that the king was very old and was being ministered to by Abishag. This has been put in neither to remind the reader who may have forgotten vv 1–4 nor to suggest that Bathsheba was somehow unaware of it, but to recall the theme of David's dangerous impotence, narrated in vv 1–4. Another instance of reminiscence is Nathan's question in v 27, "Has this business actually proceeded from my lord the king?" In historical fact Nathan may have wondered about the answer to this question; David may theoretically have surreptitiously designated Adonijah. But Nathan actually speaks for the reader, who asks the same question even though he has not read of it in the preceding account.

An even more important instance of reminiscence is found in Bathsheba's (and Nathan's) reminder to David about his oath to appoint Solomon as his successor (vv 13, 17; cf. v 30). Nathan presents this merely as a query, but Bathsheba, presumably in a position to know for sure, states it as a fact. This reference to an unfulfilled oath is clearly thematic for this entire chapter, for it is the sole effective element able to move David from his lassitude (vv 1–4) to appropriate action (vv 28–40). One who is already familiar with the throne-succession narrative realizes that this issue has been central to the entire document, which early on presents the story of David's sin with Bathsheba and the birth of Solomon, then continues to show a succession of calamities as the outworking of Yahweh's punishment for David's deed. Scholars have taken note of the fact that this document nowhere specifically narrates the event of David making this oath, and this has led some (like Veijola) to remove references to the oath in chap. 1 as secondary intrusions. The only effective answer to those who are of such a mind is that the chapter is limp and pointless without them. Perhaps the author overlooked the fact that he had neglected to narrate the taking of the oath. After all, he was only human, with all his skill, was he not? The likelihood is, however, that he expected the reader to assume the oath. Why must everything be directly stated? In this case, if Nathan and Bathsheba and David were all so clear that David had indeed made such an oath, it should go without saying that it had actually occurred.

The main example of prolepsis that we recognize in this chapter is the brief narration about Solomon and Adonijah in vv 50–53. This is an effective foreshadowing of 2:13–25. It does just what is sufficient to set the main theme of what is to come. It shows Adonijah in despair, his coup frustrated, fleeing to the altar for refuge. The author intends this as Adonijah's confession of guilt; Solomon will not need further cause against him in the event of another confrontation. But Solomon shows himself as king by (1) summoning Adonijah from the altar and (2) extending him conciliation upon condition. Thus chap. 1 ends on the note: Adonijah is a culprit, Solomon is king.

Various commentators have called attention to the especially clever way in which our author records the climactic event of this episode, the investiture of Solomon. This is stated in markedly enthusiastic language in vv 38–40 ("the land resounded" [RSV, "the earth was split"] "with their noise," v 40), but the significance of what had been done is communicated in the message of Jonathan to Adonijah's guests. The unmistakable meaning of what had been done comes to expression in this herald's reports of how the court had blessed Solomon through David (v 47), and of how David had then blessed Yahweh through Solomon (v 48). In all this, the reader can scarcely miss the pathos of Adonijah in hearing this told just at the moment when he and his guests are at the climax of their feast (v 41).

Finally, the writer has subtly but effectively done his preaching by putting his sentiment in the mouth of key persons in the story. We should view as designedly interpretive Bathsheba's response in v 31, Benaiah's response in vv 36–37, and the two previously mentioned reports placed in the mouth of Jonathan, vv 42–48. It is precisely these materials that hypercriticism like that of Veijola has first excised. But they would have far less purpose as late glosses than they have as original elements in the throne-succession narrative. When David finally gets around to recognizing his oath and promising that he will fulfill it "this day" (vv 29–30), Bathsheba replies, "May my lord King David live forever!" It is not that she actually wants him to go on living, but that his word may be given enduring validity, so that Solomon may actually become king. This response pattern is carried on into the following verses, where Benaiah first expresses the wish that Yahweh might confirm David's word (v 36) and then states the somewhat paradoxical sentiment that Yahweh may make Solomon's throne even greater than David's (v 37). Evidently this is no moment for regal vanity, for the entire court—as reported by Jonathan—expresses the identical quizzical sentiment in v 47, just prior to David's own prayer of thanksgiving (v 48) for being able to live long enough to see his successor installed. There have been all sorts of pro and con arguments whether the throne-succession narrator actually wrote his history to legitimize Solomon in the place of his older brother, or wrote it disparagingly, to show how ruthless Solomon and his party had been in seizing what properly belonged to another. If the just-mentioned verses are original—and there is no valid reason for denying it—then we know perfectly well which of the two the writer intended. Bathsheba and Benaiah, the court personnel, and even David all speak for the writer himself.

The main element of tension within chap. 1 is whether David can summon sufficient power of will in an hour of crisis to assure the accession of Solomon. There are three main subsections, two very short and one remarkably long. The four verses at the beginning tell us all we need to know about the perilous situation: David has become too feeble to respond even to the intimate presence of a lively beauty. The four verses at the end are, as we have seen, proleptic, laying the groundwork for chap. 2. In the long middle section the author needs no more than six verses to tell us all we need to know about Adonijah and those who supported and opposed him. One verse at the end of this middle section (v 49) states the dispersal of Adonijah's party. The long central section contains the three gripping scenes that we have identified, in which (1) David is aroused to action, vv 11–27; (2) David's order for Solomon's investiture is carried out, vv 28–40; and (3) Adonijah's feast is spoiled by news of what has occurred, vv 41–48.

Comment

1–4 Some commentators, viewing v 15a as a repetition of these verses, have suggested that they are a later expansion, but this fails to recognize the deliberate element of reminiscence (see above). The function of these verses is to know why imminent peril might actually fall on the favorite and his mother, why Adonijah and his supporters could move so boldly to seize the throne. Students of the throne-succession narrative see a consistent and certainly historical portrayal of David's character, for he had been as vacillating and indecisive in dealing with Amnon (2 Sam 13) and Absalom (2 Sam 14–15) as he was now in deciding between Adonijah and Solomon. Our verses suggest that the debilitude of old age was exaggerating this character fault, but one should keep in mind also an ideological factor, i.e., the novelty of kingship in Israel, with no precedent regarding the validity of primogeniture as the basis of succession.

"Now King David had become old": with subject foremost, as in v 5, this noun-clause properly stands at the beginning, serving as "exposition"—i.e., a statement of essential facts—for the following sequence of verbal clauses. Though G and M repeatedly supply "king" where only "David" or "Solomon" is original (or vice versa), it is here required because it is David's very ability to function as king that is in question. Since "old" can be relative, the narrator clarifies the condition by explaining that he was well advanced in years, and by the illustrative detail that no amount of blankets (not "cloaks," "robes," more common equivalents for בגדים, because of the verb, "cover," כסה) could make him warm. This detail does not favor the suggestion that חמם pi. might refer to the arousal of sexual passion as evidence of the king's virility (based on a widespread primitive belief that a king could no longer function if lacking in sexual potency, and that sleeping next to a lusty young virgin could restore this potency; cf. J. Gray, *Kings*, 77). It is sufficiently explained as evidence for advanced arteriosclerosis.

"His servants": עבד, widely used in the OT and common as a cognate in the other Semitic languages, ranges in meaning from "slave" to "chief official," and here it unmistakenly refers to men empowered to act *in loco regi*. "Said,": G^B consistently, and correctly, represents the officials as speaking of David in the third person (i.e., acting for him, perhaps without his consent); MT and G^L alter the text to make it seem that they are addressing him. "A pure young woman," נערה בתולה; cf. "beautiful young woman" in v 3. Although OT scholars have long recognized that בתולה means basically any unmarried woman, and that the meaning "virgin" cannot be demonstrated for the crucial text Isa 7:14, the latter meaning does occur (Gen 24:16; cf. Deut 22:14–20) and is made probable here by its occurrence with a virtual synonym, נערה. Obviously the king could receive to a position of high intimacy no woman heretofore claimed by, or defiled by, another man.

"Then they looked for": perhaps there was a contest somewhat like that of Esth 2:1–18, but it appears that the officials made the choice. "Throughout all Israel": reading G^L in place of MT and G^B's more wordy text (here G^B is *Kaige* and dutifully follows a proto-MT). "Israel" probably includes Judah, though later the two are distinguished (David's own tribe, Judah, would certainly not be excluded in this important matter). "Abishag": here as elsewhere, etymologies have no symbolic significance for the development of the story; the name is typically Hebraic and is quite appropriate to the religious situation (with the theophoric element, אב, "Father") of the period. "A Shunemite": from a town in the eastern Jezreel valley (cf. Josh 19:18, 2 Sam 28:4, 2 Kgs 4:8); oral tradition, embellishing her description, likewise modifies the name to "Shulammite" in Cant 6:13. "His bedfellow": סכנת is the fem. act. participle of סכן, meaning, to judge by Job 15:3, "to be helpful," but our translation accords to it a special nuance in light of v 2 and the end of v 4, "He had no intercourse with her." We would judge that Abishag became a sort of female valet along with her duty to sleep with David (cf. M. J. Mulder, *VT*, 22 [1972], 43–54). In a culture that accepted polygamy and the institution of concubinage, this arrangement had nothing in it that was shocking. "But the king had no intercourse with her": literally, "did not sleep with her," a common biblical euphemism for coitus. That the king could not be enticed (whether or not this were in fact the purpose of bringing Abishag) is conclusive proof of his debilitude.

5–10 "Adonijah": spelled inconsistently in chaps. 1–2; he was David's fourth (2 Sam 3:4), and apparently eldest surviving son (we know of Amnon's and Absalom's deaths from 2 Sam 13:28 and 18:15, respectively; Chileab's death is not mentioned). "Son of Haggith": so v 11, where Nathan, speaking to Bathsheba, would not be expected to speak otherwise; its occurrence in v 5 is no correction from v 11, but MT and G^B's authentic original (G^L "son of David" is a normalization), as the third-personal singular verb in v 6 ("she had borne him") requires. "I want to be king": the context requires a cohortative force in spite of the fact that the MT has not preserved the full cohortative form in אֶמְלֹךְ; in any event, the simple future indicative, "I will be king" (RSV), is inappropriate because Adonijah cannot be sure of becoming king, but knows that he must take determined action if he would be king. The independent personal pronoun (אֲנִי) strengthens this interpretation.

"Chariots and horsemen": רֶכֶב is the collective, "chariotry," and פָּרָשִׁים can be either the chariot-drivers or "cavalrymen," "horsemen." Chariots had already been introduced in the ancient Near East by the Hyksos in the Middle Bronze Age, yet the hill-dwelling Israelites had made little use of them. Dtr's statement in 2 Sam 8:4 that David neglected them may not be entirely reliable, but Adonijah may in fact have somehow learned how potent they could be and now relied on them to undergird his coup. "Fifty men to run": essentially a guard of honor; the number is proportionate to his total force. "Had never chided": G^B's "grieved" is based on the misreading of Hebrew as עָצַר (very similar in Canaanite script, or possibly it may be the text underlying MT and G^L that committed the misreading); the difference is exegetically important because MT and G^L suggest that David had neglected parental discipline while G^B suggests that he had never disciplined him *wrongly*. "What is more," וְגַם: characteristic of our narrator for use at an emphatic climax (see vv 47, 48). "Exceedingly good-looking": the resemblance to Absalom's description in 2 Sam 14:25 makes the reader think also of that rebellious son's willfulness; the Israelites praised physical beauty not so much out of a fleshly orientation as for the fact that it was taken as a token of Yahweh's spirit, driving its possessor to uncommon deeds, whether of good or of evil. "She had borne . . . after Absalom": this cannot refer to Absalom's mother Maacah because she was not Adonijah's mother; the remote antecedent has to be Haggith.

"Joab son of Zeruiah": a cousin of David, along with Abishai and his deceased brother Asahel, he had often advanced David's interests through deeds of ruthless violence (2 Sam 3:27, 18:15, 20:10), but was skilled also in the use of stealth when needed (2 Sam 14:1–24, 20:8–10); indeed, to have Joab at the head of his conspirators gave Adonijah access to Israel's entire army

(2 Sam 20:23; cf. 1 Kgs 1:19), far more powerful than the palace guard that Benaiah commanded. "Abiathar the priest": son of Ahimelech, priest of Nob, he had served David from the beginning of his struggles (cf. 1 Sam 22:20–23), but perhaps a longstanding rivalry with Zadok (cf. 2 Sam 20:25), who had become David's favorite, led him now to join forces with Adonijah and Joab. "Zadok the priest": the want of narrative material makes probable the thesis that this man had all along been priest of the Jebusite shrine in Jerusalem (cf. H. H. Rowley, *JBL* 58 [1939], 113–41; G. Ch. Macholz, *DBAT* 10 [1975], 18–20); to him and his descendants belonged the future highpriesthood in Israel. "Benaiah son of Jehoiada"; see 2 Sam 20:23, 23:20–23. "Nathan the prophet": so in 2 Sam 7:2; cf. 12:1; wherever Nathan is mentioned, his role seems more political-institutional than charismatic-prophetic, yet he does act to superintend politics in the name of a transcendental purpose. "Shimei and Rei": the lack of patronym and title leads some scholars to suspect the text as perhaps corrupted from "Shimei the friend (רֵעַ) of David (or "the king"), but this remains unsupported conjecture (the Benjaminite Shimei of 2:36–46 is not intended); for mention of the office of king's friend see 4:5. "The warriors . . . with David": cf. 2 Sam 23:8–39.

"Sacrificed oxen and sheep": reading the briefer text of G^L; in further references in this chapter, MT and the versions continue in disagreement— a common phenomenon in the transmission of familiar formulae like this. "The sliding stone," אֶבֶן הַזֹּחֶלֶת, sometimes explained to mean "Serpent Stone," by way of etymology from זָחַל, "serpent," "worm," more probably refers to a place where stones have slidden into the wadi (so Gray, *Kings;* M. Noth, *Könige,* 18, citing Arabic *Az-zahweileh,* name of a landslide near the Rogel spring). "Rogel spring": a sacred spot mentioned in Josh 15:7, 18:16, 2 Sam 17:17, the present-day *Bir Ayyub* in the Kidron valley. "All his brothers": G^B removes "all" because Solomon is not included. "His brothers the king's sons": the highest level in the royal entourage, higher than the "royal officials," עַבְדֵי הַמֶּלֶךְ, from Judah. "Solomon": following G^L in preference over MT and G^B because the last is explicative.

11–14 "Bathsheba Solomon's mother": in 2 Sam 11:3 identified with reference to her father and her husband, is here important because of her relationship to Solomon. With him she will be exalted or demoted (cf. v 21). "Adonijah . . . reigns": the noun-subject foremost with the verb in the perfect, following כִּי "that," emphasizes Adonijah's identity while expressing the state of affairs (contra Gray, 88). "So now come": G^L substitutes "please" to avoid the unusual notion that Bathsheba might be requested to move physically toward Nathan, but the throne-succession narrator's art leads him to choose this idiom in order to suggest the positive action that is immediately demanded. "Your son": the different position of "Solomon" in M, G^{BL}, indicates that the proper name is an explicative (but quite unnecessary) addition. "Maidservant," אָמָה, literally a female slave, but used, like עֶבֶד, "male slave," "manservant," as a term of self-effacement in speech to royalty (cf. A. Jepsen, *VT* 8 [1958] 293–97). "Surely," כִּי, though often serving to introduce direct discourse, here follows another indicator of direct discourse, לֵאמֹר "to say," hence is preferably read as an asseverative. This is entirely natural here because Bathsheba intends to recall the emphatic nature of David's previous oath.

"Shall reign . . . shall sit": these are constantly repeated as a traditional phrase-pair, indeed almost as a set formula, throughout these two chapters. Gray, 88 suggests that Nathan wants Bathsheba to practice auto-suggestion on a senile King David, getting him to think he has given such an oath even though he never did; such subtle psychologizing has to be beyond the naïve art of the narrator, however much of it may possibly have motivated the historical Nathan and Bathsheba. "While": G^L's simple form has been normalized to a fuller style in MT and G^B. "Confirm your words": ומלאתי את־דבריך has been identified as a technical juridical term in the Yabneh-Yam lawsuit (V. Sasson, *BASOR* 232 [1978], 56–65).

15–21 "In the bedchamber," החדרה: noting the distinguishing *Kaige* equivalent, Ταμεῖον, in G^B, one sees also that the *Kaige* translator is further removed temporally from the original text than G^L because his word, meaning "storeroom," yields an unsatisfactory sense; G^L κοιτῶνα, "bedroom," is of course demanded even though Heb. can mean any sort of inner room lying outside the central court. "And she said": MT adds the unnecessary explicative "to him." "Your god": so G^B; disturbed by the notion that David's God might not be Bathsheba's god, MT and G^L add "Yahweh." "Surely . . . shall reign . . . shall sit": cf. v 13; in typical fashion, our writer repeats the wording of previous speech, with only subtle changes. "Solomon your servant he has not invited": now for the first time the fact narrated in v 10 makes its impact on Bathsheba's consciousness; in Nathan's repetition of these words in v 26, the wording "Solomon your son" (G^L) is to be preferred because Nathan would avoid Bathsheba's self-effacing terminology and because MT and G^B have apparently harmonized it with v 19.

"The eyes of all Israel are on you": typically Hebraic in its graphic realism, this phrase urges David to action while chiding him for his indecisiveness; David is accorded a level of autocratic authority not previously seen in Israel, in which political appointment traditionally depended on divine designation and the popular acclamation (so at David's own accession reported in 2 Sam 5:1–3). "To tell them," להגיד להם: see on v 35. "Sleeps with his fathers": to judge from Hadad's speech in 1 Kgs 11:21, where David rates this formula while Joab is only said to be dead (מת), it applied only to royalty, and, as I have shown in my book *Prophet against Prophet* 97–99, solely to such as passed away in peace and honor. "I will be—with my son Solomon—": although a singular verb may often precede a compound subject (*GKC* § *145ᵏ*), this styling expresses closely Bathsheba's evident concern first of all for her own safety, which naturally depends on that of Solomon. "Reckoned as guilty," חטאים: the root חטא, whose basic meaning is "to miss the mark" (cf. S. J. De Vries, "Sin, Sinners," *IDB* IV, 361–76), here has a relational and political meaning, "to be on the wrong side," which Bathsheba correctly sees as leading to inevitable false accusations and condemnation.

22–27 Nathan's speech to David, completing scene 1, is climactic. "Prostrated himself . . . to the ground": an idiomatic rendering of an unusual Hebrew phrasing, lit., "And he bowed to the king upon his nose, earthward." "You must have said," אתה אמרת: this could be read as a question (RSV), but is better handled as an ironic exaggeration; the fact that Nathan feels the need to inform the king in detail shows that he does not actually believe that David ordered Adonijah's coronation, an attitude which his question of v 27 underscores. "Long live King Adonijah!": Nathan adds this detail, not previously reported, to move David to action (for its implicit ideology cf. P. A. H. de Boer, "'Vive le roi'," *VT* 5 [1955] 225–31); our narrator has David counter Adonijah's acclamation with identical words for Solomon, v 34. "Has this actually proceeded . . .": introductory Hebrew אם, "if," "or," makes the following question elliptical, entertaining hypothetically a notion which Nathan hints in the preceding to be beyond belief. "Your servants": so MT, rightly including the entire privy council, but the LXX wrongly corrects this to singular, imagining that Nathan speaks only of himself.

28–31 "David": preferred by the LXX, the proper name without the title may show the narrator's sensitivity to the fact that the king acts first in scene 2 as the husband of Bathsheba, but shifts immediately and in the second part of this scene to the title "the king" in order to present him as the supreme political authority that he is. "She . . . stood": since Bathsheba is no longer the supplicant, she does not now bow to him as in v 16, but stands to await his pleasure. "The king took an oath": what David swears to Bathsheba involves complex syntax (cf. *GKC* § 149). First comes an appeal to Yahweh as witness (29b), followed by a comparative clause quoting David's previous oath (30a), and finally the content of David's present oath (30b). The last is the actual protasis of a conditional sentence in which the apodosis ("may he do so and so to me!") is elliptically omitted. The previous oath is not strictly styled after this pattern since David only cites its substance in summary form.

"By the life of Yahweh": lit., "As Yahweh lives." The use of this appeal, normative to the OT, shows David as a committed monotheist since polytheists would appeal to all the gods that exist. "Who has redeemed my life from every adversity": the familiar Deuteronomic word, פדה, refers to the ransoming of captives and the manumission of slaves; David refers to it in identical words in 2 Sam 4:9; cf. 1 Sam 14:45, 2 Sam 7:23 (Dtr) (see J. J. Stamm in *THAT* II, 390–406). "Surely": see on v 13. "Thus shall I do this day": the time identification is emphatic; cf. *YTT* 223. "And Bathsheba bowed": cf. v 23. "May my lord King David live forever": she does not indulge in wishful thinking for an endless life, but rather expresses a desire that David's life-power should continue in his posterity.

32–37 "The servants of your lords": MT is to be retained over simplifying LXX "lord" precisely because of its unusualness; David is referring to the retainers of all the high officials, i.e., the total party loyal to him. "Mount": in vv 33, 38, 44 the hiph. of רכב means "cause to mount" rather than the usual translation, "cause to ride"; cf. R. de Langhe, "Betekenis van het Hebreeuwse werkwoord רכב," *Handelingen van het XVIIIe Vlaamse Filologencongres* (1949) 89–96. "The mule that belongs to me": an animal of special honor and distinction (cf. 2 Sam 13:29), probably because the Hebraic law against crossbreeding (Lev 19:19) would allow only rare, expensive, imported animals to be used; Solomon's riding on David's private mule (a female) was intended as dramatic and visual evidence that David was actually turning all his authority over to Solomon. "Gihon": the present *Ain Umm ad-Daraj*, known to Europeans as "The Spring of the Virgin" and lying in the Kidron valley close to the temple site (later Hezekiah built the Siloam tunnel from it, 2 Kings 20:20), thus much closer to the city than Adonijah's Rogel; again a spring is identified as a sacred site.

"And let Zadok the priest, with Nathan the prophet, anoint him": although an initial singular verb may govern a compound subject (see above on v 21), our translation is responsive to the plain statement of v 39, and brings out the important distinction that, although Nathan is the real power behind the throne, it is a priest who does the anointing; Jonathan's plural verb according to the superior text of v 45 is quite understandable as a somewhat garbled account of what occurred (see below). In his book, *King and Messiah, The Civil and Sacral Legitimation of the Israelite Kings* (Lund: Gleerup [1976], 185–232), Tryggve N. D. Mettinger tendentiously argues that anointing is a contractual ritual symbolizing the promise of the performer to the person receiving the oil. This interpretation is unduly restrictive, for why cannot various conceptions of a ritual enjoy concurrent status? Failing to allow for possible confusion and eclecticism in the various sources referring to anointing, Mettinger hypothesizes that Solomon was first anointed by the people, then by Zadok as priest, and finally by God. He has no explanation for the striking fact that anointing is mentioned only for Solomon, not for Adonijah.

"Blow on the ram's horn": this common Hebrew custom is mentioned for Solomon (cf. v 39), but was evidently not employed for Adonijah in order to preserve stealth. "I appoint as leader": Heb. נָגִיד represents an office previously received by Saul (1 Sam 10:1) and David (2 Sam 7:8), deliberately avoiding the title מֶלֶךְ, "king." Its derivation is uncertain even though it is etymologically related to נָגַד, "tell," "recount." Mettinger, in the above-mentioned work (158–62), argues that the verb הִגִּיד "tell" in v 20 is a reference to Solomon's technical designation as נָגִיד "leader," but he is forced to identify all references to a נָגִיד "leader" in 1–2 Sam as post-Solomonic theologizations, an erroneous concept dependent on Veijola's *Die ewige Dynastie.* "Over Israel": although M and G (so RSV) add "and Judah," the fact that G^L reverses the order makes it probable that the reference to Judah is an addition, which in any event would make little sense in a United Kingdom context.

"May the god of my lord the king": Benaiah, like Bathsheba in v 17, refrains from naming the deity, even though it is obviously Yahweh who is meant; this was apparently a peculiar usage for address to the king (cf. v 47). "Confirm it": although LXX πιστώσαι may be interpretive of MT, there is some probability that יֹאמַר has intruded as a scribal mistake from the foregoing יֹאמַר. Benaiah's desire that the Deity confirm the king's appointment will be—in his intent—fulfilled in Solomon's becoming a greater king than David (v 37).

38–40 The narrative denouement of scene 2. "The Cherethites and Pelethites": because of the mention of Benaiah, their commander (see 2 Sam 20:23), David's mercenary bodyguard are not specifically identified as Solomon's personal escort, required as protection against the forces that are with Adonijah; the names are collective singulars and probably refer to Philistines and Cretans in David's service (cf. 2 Sam 18:2, Ittai the Gittite = Gathite). "A horn of oil": our translation does not express the definiteness indicated by the Heb.; the horn in question is one specially reserved for this purpose, though the usage that would make it such was still future, not past or present.

The oil used was the purest oil from the olive tree, and was employed also in the investiture of Saul (1 Sam 10:1) and (proleptically) of David (1 Sam 16:1, 13). "The Tent": this can scarcely be any other than the sacred tent pitched by David for the ark, 2 Sam 6:17. According to 1 Kgs 2:28–30 it was definitely a shrine to Yahweh.

"All the people," vv 39, 40: a technical designation for the common people; obviously it does not mean "the total population" because at least the Adonijah party is absent. Mettinger (*King and Messiah*, 119–24) interprets this as a reference to a popular assembly entrusted with official powers of confirmation, but our narrator's description suggests a spontaneous gathering. "Playing on pipes": although the Hebrew reading differs from the Greek *Vorlage* only in its vocalization, and although the Greek concept is quite appropriate, it is better to follow the Hebrew because of the text's pointed reference to lôud noisemaking (vv 40, 41, 45). "The land resounded": the root בקע, "split," attested by G^B (*Kaige*) as well as by MT, would make an astounding metaphor if original (so RSV); hence it is better to read the G^L *Vorlage*, from the root תקע, "resound."

41–49 Here Jonathan son of Abiathar adds details, especially in vv 47–48, not provided in the foregoing section. "Just as they finished eating": translating a Hebrew circumstantial clause with foremost independent pronoun. "And when Joab heard": with the foregoing intended as exposition, this clause commences the narration proper (cf. E. Sutcliffe, S. J., "Simultaneity in Hebrew," *JSS* 3 [1958] 80–81). "While he was yet speaking, behold Jonathan . . . !": an effective expression of simultaneity; Joab represents massive military force behind Adonijah's coup, but Jonathan's report effectively negates his power. "Jonathan son of Abiathar the priest": fulfilling the role of messenger, as in 2 Sam 15–17; since he is sufficiently highly placed to have otherwise been a guest at the coronation feast, he had probably been deliberately left behind in some strategic post to spy on Solomon's entourage. "A worthy man," איש חיל: one of high social standing, cf. KB in loco. "Bringer of good news," תבשר טוב, lit., "so it is good which you announce"; cf. 2 Sam 18:19. "Have anointed him": in v 45 the foremost וימשחו unmistakably indicates a plural subject, otherwise than in v 39 and in spite of G^L's sing.; Jonathan's report is summarizing and is perhaps based on other eyewitnesses (contra B. Stade, *ZAW* 3 [1883] 186–87, arguing that the plurals in both verses are impossible). "This is the noise you have heard": an explanatory summary. "So Solomon sits on the royal throne": an epitome of the entire section.

"And when the king's servants came in": though suspected by some (Veijola) as a redactional afterthought, this is our narrator's device placed in Jonathan's mouth for providing an irrefutable corroboration. It is not reasonable to doubt that Jonathan could have known what is reported in vv 47–48 because a tumult surrounded the king and Jonathan was of sufficiently high status to have joined it unnoticed. On וגם "and also" introducing emphatic climaxes, see on v 6. "To bless our lord King David": like the curse, the blessing had a potency independent of the verbal pronouncement (cf. J. Pedersen, *Israel, Its Life and Culture*, I [1926] 182–212), and this particular blessing is clearly designed to benefit another than the addressee, in this case Solomon, who is to be greater in his reign than David. "The king did homage in bed": Hebrew המשכבו, with the determinative, designating David's particular bed, is best translated in our idiomatic English. G^L "his bed," which may well represent OG in the place of G^B's hebraizing *Kaige*, is nonetheless a normalization to Greek idiom rather than literal translation of a hypothetically more original Hebrew. David cannot get out of bed, so feeble is he; yet in his weakness and decline he confirms the people's "blessing," underscoring that Solomon really is king.

"The king responded": David has the last word, and uses it to draw in an otherwise missing note of transcendence; he too blesses, but his "blessing" is actually a thanksgiving to the God who has provided what he himself had no more strength to do. "Providing today": an effective epitome of the entire narrative, this clause with the time-designative states what the event has been all about (cf. *YTT*, 224). "While my own eyes behold it": David is still alive to witness what Yahweh intended to arrange with respect to his succession. "One who may sit on my throne": as David sees it, the issue has not been strictly that Solomon should win out over Adonijah (Bathsheba's concern), but that his personal hold on the throne should be secured in one of his own sons, rather than passing over to an interloper. Our narrative is clear in stating that Solomon took regal authority while David was still alive. David did not simply abdicate but shared the power, though feebly and behind the scenes, with Solomon. Cf. E. Ball, *VT* 27 (1977) 268–79, where it is argued that this arrangement was based on Egyptian models, soon to become prominent in Solomon's court (in Ball's opinion, this gives support to E. Thiele's arguments [see below on Chronology] and undermines Veijola's thesis that Solomon did not begin to reign so long as David lived).

50–53 The party of Adonijah is dispersed (v 49) and he is left alone. But he quickly departs the scene of banqueting and makes off for a place of sanctuary. "To grasp the horns of the altar": dismissing the G^L plus as an explicative addition borrowed from 2:28, we are obliged to rely on the last-mentioned passage for an indication of what the first readers already knew, viz., that the altar pertained to the aforementioned "tent" (v 39). According to 2:30, it must have been inside the tent. To seek refuge in a sanctuary, protected from summary execution, was widely practiced in the ancient world, so much so that the Romans had to abolish it (Tacitus, *Annals* III, lx–lxiii). In Israel's sanctuary the altar had raised projections or "horns" on the four corners. Smeared with the blood of the sacrifice (Exod 27:2, Ezek 43:20), they offered the refugee a convenient point where he might come into direct physical contact with the sacral, and hence claim the Deity's immediate attention. But this practice was really intended for an innocent (or relatively innocent) man; hence for it to be seized by an Adonijah or a Joab was to abuse the intent of an otherwise useful, or even necessary, custom. We are not to wonder, then, that Solomon felt no compunction, here or with Joab, to respect the sanctuary.

"King Solomon": the full title, appropriate in an address of Solomon's servants, has intruded itself in vv 51b and 53a, where it is doubtful in light of its inconsistent representation in the LXX. In chap. 2, where either "Solomon" or "the king" generally suffices, the more official "King Solomon" appropriately appears at vv 19 and 45. "Let Solomon first swear to me": Adonijah still imagines that he has power to bargain; this is designedly proleptic of 2:13–18. "His servant": Adonijah acknowledges his subordination. "Behaves as a gentleman": Heb. חַיִל בֶּן is a characterization often applied to warriors (e.g., Deut 3:18, 1 Sam 18:17) rather than to men of high social station, for which see the idiom חַיִל אִישׁ "worthy man" in v 42. Since prowess in battle can hardly be the condition that Solomon would here impose, our translation stresses the sense of honor and loyalty that soldiers characteristically display. "If evil is found in him": most likely Solomon is speaking of treason and disloyalty, for which death must be the unremitting penalty. "Go to your house": since Solomon imposes no restrictions on Adonijah's movement similar to those of 2:36–38, this command must be interpreted not as a house arrest but as a release.

Explanation

At this point the reader desires to know what this chapter of Scripture really says. Like a human body, which is more than the total of all its parts, a text of Scripture is more than all the words and verses that it contains. It will not do, therefore, to seize upon a few words or a few verses, but we must ask for *the word* among all the words.

The exegete, and specifically the Christian exegete, needs to recognize that even for the initial author, not everything narrated need be endowed with spiritual authority, but may have been included only as a setting or communicative framework for what the author intended to say. How much more is this true for the latter-day Christian scholar, who must judge according to Christian standards both what the author reports and what the author intends to say.

If only this distinction were more generally observed, there would be far less suspect proof-texting and far less idiosyncratic preaching. First of all, non-normative elements—elements not intended for our spiritual celebration or emulation—would be identified and eliminated from candidacy for normative application. Let us review what are the most notable non-normative elements in 1 Kgs 1. There are elements derived not from revelation but from the culture, such as the notion that kings possess a direct claim on their special God (vv 17, 36, 47), that latent sacrality resides in springs and in the residue of sacrifices on the altar, and that the power to renew vitality resides in active sexuality. There are social and ethical practices which the throne-succession narrator may not have fully accepted but which he does not in any event condemn; these would be the practice of polygamy and concubinage, the possible deceit that David may have practiced on Bathsheba in not fulfilling his oath, as well as the possible deceit that she and Nathan may in turn have practiced on David. Finally, we point to non-normative political practices exhibited in this account, specifically the cynical seizure and ruthless employment of autocratic power. As the historians and biblical theologians have often pointed out, Adonijah's coup and Solomon's counter-coup represent a drastic departure from Israel's traditional ideals. In the tribal period there was no kingship (Judg 8:23), and political power was held either by a modified democracy or a limited autocracy. Individual leaders were charismatic persons, empowered by the divine spirit for a short while to perform a special act of deliverance. Saul and next David had taken moderate steps that historians judge to have been necessary, but in Solomon's accession we observe a cynical jockeying for power. It was inevitable that, once installed in power, Solomon should have developed into an absolute ruler. Not only is his image non-normative for Christians (and Jews); it violates the Bible's own standards of social interaction.

Apart from the inevitability of this moderately negative value-judgment on the event itself, we need to pay careful attention to the biblical text in order to observe how it identifies what it considers decisive. Here the art of the narrator follows the course of history. Not each and every historical occurrence is of equal significance and value, but each has to be ranked in its order of importance (Americans would probably put the signing of the Declaration of Independence at the top of their list). In the struggle that actually took place between the historical Adonijah and the historical Solomon, some things happened that prepared for what was to come; other things happened as its effect. These were all part of the picture, but not the picture's central subject. In the specific case that we are referring to, it was not Adonijah's coup that occupied the central position, but Solomon's countercoup. Adonijah's coup had no lasting result except that it precipitated the accession of Solomon. The throne-succession historian understands this and skillfully draws his outline to express it. If we desire to speak in theological language, we can say that Solomon's accession involved a revelation of God (i.e., of divine purpose), but the verbal testimony of the throne-succession historian is required in order to preserve that revelatory event for generations to come.

If we do not keep this firmly in mind, we will be apt to succumb to moralizing and vapid sentimentality. What may we appropriate from vv 1–4 except some subjective moral judgment of David? What may we take from vv 5–10 except some observations about male vanity or a condemnation of pride, greed, and party rivalry? In vv 11–31 we receive an effective illustration of scheming cleverness, possibly also of male power to manipulate a woman, and of a woman's compensating power to influence a man. All these verses are, however, the narrator's preparation for the central event, the investiture of Solomon. This is recounted three times, first in David's instructions (vv 32–35), next in the straight narrative of vv 38–40, and finally in Jonathan's report to Adonijah and his guests (vv 41–48). The story goes on for a few more verses to dispose (temporarily) of Adonijah (vv 49–53), but we now know precisely what our narrator is trying to say. He says, Solomon was made king.

But we might know little more than the external political event—raw secular history—were it not for the narrator's aforementioned technique of placing interpretive speeches in the mouths of key personages in the story. If the sacred text is to become revelation for modern man, this must be at the point where the light of transcendental truth emerges. In v 31 Bathsheba says, having heard David's promise to fulfill his oath to Solomon *this day,* "May my lord King David live forever!" In v 36 Benaiah replies to David's order with his "Amen! May the god of my lord the king confirm it!" Then in v 37 he adds the ironic wish, "As Yahweh has been with my lord, so may he be with Solomon and make his throne even greater than the throne of my lord King David." In v 47 the people say, "May your god do even greater for Solomon's fame than for your own, and may he exalt his throne over your throne." Then in v 48 the king himself replies, "Blessed be Yahweh the God of Israel for providing today—while my own eyes behold it—one who may sit on my throne!" Bathsheba envisages perpetual life for the Davidic dynasty. Benaiah declares that (1) Yahweh must confirm what David says or it will have no effect, and (2) Yahweh will increase Solomon over David. The people second this sentiment in their paradoxical "blessing," and David praises Yahweh for providing a successor, giving continuity to David's rule.

The central truth for the throne-succession historian is that Yahweh was at work to frustrate Adonijah and to establish Solomon. Phrased in the words of the characters in his story and culminating in the speech of David, this truth is transcendentalized so that it reaches beyond the immediacy of the present in order to bring testimony for future generations. This writer did not himself see how far his light was destined to shine. He was thinking only of one generation; the link from David to Solomon was firm. Dtr knew that the link had become a chain, that there had been numerous "Davids," down to the end of the kingdom. But Christian readers know that the chain was destined to become longer still, hanging loose for centuries as messianic ideologies threatened to smolder out, and at last finding another to sit on David's throne, one who would be more righteous than David and wiser than Solomon.

Solomon Disposes of His Rivals (2:1-46)

Bibliography

Gooding, D. W. "The Shimei Duplicate and Its Satellite Miscellanies in 3 Reigns II." *JSS* 13 (1968) 76–92. Rehm, M. "Die Beamtenliste der Septuaginta in 1 Kon 2, 46h." FzB 1. *Festschrift für J. Ziegler.* Würzburg: Echter Verlag, 1972. Trebolle, J. "Testamento y muerte de David." *RB* 87 (1980) 87–103. Yaron, R. "A Ramessid Parallel to 1 K ii 33, 44–45." *VT* 8 (1958) 423–33. Zalewski, S. "The Character of Adonijah" (Heb.). *BMik* 57 (1974) 229–55.

Translation

¹ *When David's days to die drew near he charged*[a] *Solomon his son*[b] *as follows:* ² *"I am going the way of all the earth; so be strong and act as becomes a man*[a] ³ *and keep the charge of*[a] [b]*your god,*[b] *walking* [c]*in his paths,*[c] [d]*keeping his statutes, his commandments, his ordinances, and his testimonies,*[d] [e]*as written*[e] *in the law of Moses, so that you may prosper in all*[f] *that you do and in all to which* [g]*you turn your attention;*[g] ⁴ *so that Yahweh may establish his word*[a] *which he spoke* [b]*concerning me,*[b] *saying, 'If your sons guard their way,*[c] *walking before me in fidelity with all their heart* [d]*and with all their soul,*[d] *no one of your sons shall be cut off from upon the throne of Israel.*

⁵ [a]*So now,*[a] *you know what Joab son of Zeruiah did to me; that is, what he did to the two commanders of Israel's armies, Abner son of Ner and Amasa son of Yether:*[b] *he murdered them, avenging*[c] *the blood of war in peacetime* [d]*and putting innocent blood*[d] *on the girdle of my*[e] *loins and on my*[e] *sandals which are on my*[e] *feet.* ⁶*So act according to your wisdom and do not*[a] *let his gray hairs go down in peace to Sheol.* ⁷ *And with the sons of Barzillai the Gileadite practice loyalty, letting them be among those who eat at your table, for thus did they welcome me when I was fleeing from* [a]*your brother Absalom.*[a] ⁸ *And* [a]*behold, with you*[a] *is Shimei son of Gera, Benjaminite from Bahurim; now he cursed me with a potent curse on the day when I was marching to Mahanaim, but he did come down to meet me at the Jordan, so that I swore to him by Yahweh, saying, 'I won't kill you with the sword,'* ⁹[a]*But as for you,*[a] *do not leave him guiltless, for a wise man are you; and you know what you should do to him, bringing his gray hairs with blood down to Sheol."*

¹⁰ *So David slept with his fathers. And he was buried in the city of David.* ¹¹ *Now the years when David reigned over Israel were forty years; in Hebron he reigned seven years and in Jerusalem* [a]*he reigned*[a] *thirty-three years.* ¹² *Thus Solomon sat on his father David's throne and his dominion was firmly established.*

¹³ *But Adonijah* [a]*son of Haggith*[a] *came to Bathsheba, Solomon's mother.*[b] *And she said,*[c] *"Do you come in peace?" He said, "In peace."* ¹⁴ [a]*Then he said,*[a] *"I have a matter that concerns you," and she*[b] *said,*[c] *"Speak."* ¹⁵ *So he said,*[a] *"You know that the kingship was mine, and it was to me that all Israel turned their faces to make me king. But the kingship has turned away and become my brother's, for through Yahweh it has become his.* ¹⁶ *But now, a single*[a] *request I ask of you:*

don't turn away my [b] *face." And she* [c] *said, "Speak." * [17] *So he* [a] *said,* [b] *"Please speak to Solomon the king, for he will not turn away your* [c] *face,* [d] *that he give me Abishag the Shunemite as wife."* [18] *And Bathsheba said, "Good, I will speak on your behalf to the king."*

[19] *So Bathsheba went to King Solomon to speak to him on Adonijah's behalf. And the king* [a] *arose to meet her and did homage to her.* [b] *Then he returned to his throne and had a chair placed for the king's mother, so that she might sit at his right side.* [20] *Then she said,* [a] *"A single request I am asking of you: don't turn away my* [b] *face." And the king said to her, "Ask, my mother, for I will not turn away* [c]*your face."* [c] [21] *And she said, "Let Abishag the Shunemite be given to Adonijah your brother as wife."* [22] *And the king* [a] *answered and said to his mother, "And why are you asking just Abishag* [b] *for Adonijah?* [c] *Just as well ask the kingship for him—because he is my elder brother—both for him and for Abiathar the priest and Joab son of Zeruiah!"* [d] [23] *And King Solomon swore by Yahweh, saying, "May God do so to me and more, if at the risk of his life Adonijah has not broached this matter!* [24] *So now, by Yahweh's life—who established me and set me on the throne of David my father and made me a house," as he* [a] *said,* [b] *"today shall Adonijah be put to death!"* [25] *So the king* [a] *sent an order with Benaiah son of Jehoiada, and he fell on him* [b] *and he died.* [cd]

[26] *And to Abiathar the priest the king* [a] *said, "To Anathoth! Go to your fields,* [b] *for you are marked for death!* [c] *And* [d]*on this day* [d] *I will not kill you, only because you bore the ark of Yahweh* [e] *before* [f] *my father, and because you suffered through all that my father suffered."* [27] *Thus did Solomon exile Abiathar from acting as Yahweh's priest, fulfilling Yahweh's word which he spoke against the house of Eli in Shiloh.*

[28] *Now the news came to Joab* [a]*—for Joab had been affiliated with Adonijah and had not been affiliated with Solomon* [b]*—and Joab fled to Yahweh's tent and grasped the horns of the altar.* [29] *And it was reported to Solomon* [a] *that he* [b] *had fled to Yahweh's tent, "and behold, he is* [c]*beside the altar."* [c] [d]*So Solomon sent to Joab saying, "What is the matter with you, that you have fled to the altar?" And Joab said, "It was because I feared you that I have fled to Yahweh."* [d] *Then Solomon* [e] *sent Benaiah son of Jehoiada saying, "Go fall* [f] *upon him."* [g] [30] *And Benaiah* [a] *went to Yahweh's tent and said to him, "Thus says the king, 'Come out!'" But he* [b] *said, "No,* [c] *but I will die here." And Benaiah* [d] *returned word to the king saying, "Thus spoke Joab and thus did he answer me."* [31] *So the king said to him,* [a] *"Do as he said: fall upon him and bury him, and remove today* [b] *the innocent blood which Joab* [c] *shed from me and my father's house;* [32] *and may Yahweh return his bloodguilt* [a] *on his own head, since he fell upon two men more righteous and excellent than himself, murdering them with the sword, while my father David was unaware of it* [b]*—even Abner son of Ner, general of Israel's army, and Amasa son of Yether, general of Judah's army.* [33] *So their blood will return on Joab's head and on the head of his posterity forever, but for David and his posterity, and his house and his throne,* [a]*there will be* [a] *peace forever from Yahweh."* [34] *Then Benaiah* [a] *fell upon* [b] *him* [c] [d]*and killed him,* [d] *and he was buried* [e] *in his house* [f] *in the country.* [35] *And the king* [a] *appointed Benaiah son of Jehoiada in his* [b] *place in charge of the army;* [c] *and Zadok the priest the king* [d] *appointed* [e] *in place of Abiathar.*

[36] *Then the king* [a] *sent and summoned Shimei* [b] *and said to him, "Build for yourself a house in Jerusalem and dwell there, and do not go out from there hither or thither.*

[37] *And it will be on the day when you do go out, if you so much as cross the wadi Kidron, know assuredly that you will certainly die; your blood will be on your own head.''* [a] [38] *And Shimei said to the king, "Your terms are good; as* [a] *my lord the king has said, so shall his servant do." So Shimei dwelt in Jerusalem for* [b]*many days.* [b]

[39] *But it happened after three years that two of Shimei's slaves fled to Achish son of Maacah,* [a] *king of Gath. And they told Shimei as follows: "Behold, your slaves are in Gath."* [40] *Then Shimei arose, saddled his ass, and went* [a]*toward Gath, to Achish,* [a] *looking for his slaves; Shimei went* [b] *and brought back his slaves from Gath.* [41] *And* [a]*it was reported* [a] *to Solomon that Shimei had traveled from Jerusalem to Gath and* [b]*had returned.* [b] [42] *So the king sent and summoned Shimei and said to him, "Did I not adjure you by Yahweh and admonish you as follows: 'On the day when you go out* [a] *and travel hither and thither, know assuredly that you will certainly die';* [b]*and did you not say to me, 'Your terms are good; I obey'?* [b] [43] *So why* [a] *do you disobey Yahweh's oath, and my command with which I charged you?"* [44] *Then the king said to Shimei, "You know all the* [a] *evil—at least your heart acknowledges it—that you did to David my father, so Yahweh has returned your evil on your head.* [45] *But King Solomon is blessed, and the throne of David will be established before Yahweh forever!"* [46] *And the king* [a] *ordered Benaiah son of Jehoiada, and he went out and fell upon him,* [b]*and he* [c] *died.* [b]

[d]*Thus was the kingdom made secure in Solomon's hand.* [d]

Notes

1.a. MT and G[L]. This makes better sense than G[B]'s corruption, "answered" (reading עָנָה for עָנָה).

1.b. MT and G[B]. G[L] as the explicative addition, "before his death" (so also some Heb. mss.).

2.a. MT and G[B]. G[L] adds a strengthening explicative, "mighty man," which reproduces a colorful Heb. idiom but fails to discern the subtlety of the original Heb.

3.a. MT adds "Yahweh."

3.b-b. G[B] "your god" deserves preference over MT and G[L] "the god of Israel," whose divergence supports the originality of G[B].

3.c-c. MT and G[B]. G[L]'s substitution, "before him," is a common idiom that accords little with the Dtr terminology of this notable passage.

3.d-d. MT—but with little to commend it over G[BL], with their varying orders in which these synonyms appear.

3.e-e. MT and G[L]. G[B] "that which is written" is explicative.

3.f. MT and G[L]. G[B]'s omission is paraphrastic.

3.g-g. MT and G[L]. G[B] finds this text too vague, so substitutes "I command you."

4.a. MT and G[B]. G[L] pl has in mind various revelations ("words") to David.

4.b-b. MT and G[L]. G[B] may be tendential in omitting, in view of the reference to others than David in the sequel.

4.c. MT and G[B]. G[L]'s pl is motivated by the plurality of the sons.

4.d-d. MT and G[L]. Through simple haplography, G[B] omits these words. MT and G[B] add "saying," as if to introduce the following clause as a citation.

5.a-a. G[L]'s reading is to be preferred to MT, G[B] "and indeed you," because here commences the consequence section in the original throne-succession narrative, whose original structure has been disrupted by the intrusion of Dtr material in vv 3–4.

5.b. MT and G[B], whose identification of Amasa as one of two Israelite generals takes the translator of G[L] as so strange that he adds here "general of Judah" as a corrective.

5.c. G[L], ἐξεδίκησεν, "avenge," reads the original Heb. וַיִּקֹּם "he avenged." MT and G[B] wish to hear of Joab requiring vengeance on himself, rather than of his own seeking of vengeance; hence Heb. וַיָּשֶׂם, Gr. ἔταξεν, meaning "place," "attribute."

5.d-d. G^L supported by *OL* and Gothic, keeps to the point with "innocent blood," altered in MT to "the blood of war" by influence from the preceding clause. Though G^B omits this phrase, probably through haplography, it is read by most Gr. witnesses.

5.e,e,e. G^L "my" is correct over against MT and G^B, "his," because David is complaining not that Joab has covered himself with blood, but that he has committed bloody deeds in his name and with his authority so as to bring blood-guilt on him, which Joab's death alone could expiate. Cf. *HOTTP*, 292.

6.a. MT and G^L. Gr. οὐ "not" has been read by G^B as σύ "you." Cf. Burney, xxi.

7.a-a. G^L. MT and G^B "Absalom your brother." In an address to Solomon, an identification of brotherly relationship would likely precede the proper name.

8.a-a. G^L "and Shimei son of Gera" is drastically abrupt as introduction to a new section. However G^L may have become corrupt, the text needs MT, G^B, "and behold, with you. . . ."

9.a-a. MT וְעַתָּה "so now" is the normal transition from situation to consequence, but it is an auditory mistake for the *Vorlage* of G^L, אַתָּה = σύ "you." As in v 6, G^B commits the visual error of reading οὐ "not" (Burney, xxi).

11.a-a. In the interest of Gr. style, G^B omits.

13.a-a. From this point onward into chap. 22, G^B largely drops *Kaige* and reproduces OG. More prominent than previously will be its preference for approved Gr. styling. It drops the matronym, perhaps because Adonijah has previously been introduced with it (1:5), but MT, G^L are original because the writer's style is deliberately contrasting the two princely mothers.

13.b. MT. G^BL add "and did homage to her," attributing to the brazen Adonijah a more humble demeanor than the passage justifies. Cf. *HOTTP*, 292.

13.c. MT and G^B. G^L adds explicative "to him."

14.a-a. For stylistic reasons, G^B omits, but MT, G^L suggest a pause by repetition of "and he said."

14.b. MT and G^B. G^L has the explicative "Bathsheba."

14.c. MT. G^BL have explicative "to him."

15.a. MT. G^BL have explicative "to her."

16.a. MT and G^B. G^L adds the interpretive "small"; cf. v 20.

16.b. MT. G^BL "your." The translators did not recognize the Heb. idiom; see *Comment*.

16.c. MT. G^BL add explicative "Bathsheba."

17.a. MT and G^B. G^L adds the explicative "Adonijah."

17.b. MT. G^BL add explicative "to her."

17.c. MT and G^L. G^B "his"; see on v 16.

17.d. MT and G^L. G^B adds a consistent but interpretive "from you."

19.a. MT and G^B. G^L adds "Solomon," influenced by the previous reference.

19.b. MT וַיִּשְׁתַּחוּ לָהּ is perfectly understandable as consistent with Solomon's lifelong habit, but G^BL change the verb to "kissed," perhaps out of awe for the royal position.

20.a. MT. G^BL add explicative "to him."

20.b. MT. G^BL "your"; cf. on v 16.

20.c-c. MT. G^BL "you."

22.a. MT "King Solomon"; G^BL "Solomon the king." The transposition of elements makes it likely that the proper name is not original.

22.b. G^BL. MT adds explicative "the Shunemite."

22.c. MT and G^B. G^L adds explicative "as a wife."

22.d. MT. G^BL have a double explicative, ὁ ἀρχιστράτηγος = הַצָּבָא שַׂר "commander-in-chief" and ἕταιρος = רֵעַ "fellow." Cf. Burney, xxx; *HOTTP*, 293.

24.a. MT. G^BL adds "Yahweh," either explicative, or through the influence of the two foregoing occurrences in vv 23–24.

24.b. MT and G^B. G^L has explicative "to me."

25.a. MT "King Solomon"; G^BL "Solomon the king." See v 22.

25.b. MT, G^B. G^L adds explicative "Adonijah."

25.c. MT. G^BL "Adonijah died" is explicative.

25.d. MT. G^BL add explicative "on that day."

26.a. MT, G^B. G^L adds "Solomon."

26.b. MT, G^B. G^L adds "and to your house," overlooking the point that Solomon is restricting Abiathar's access to the sacrificial offerings and must henceforward live from his own fields.

26.c. Lit. "you are a dead man."

26.d-d. MT. Omitting the "and," G^{BL} attach "on this day" to the preceding threat.

26.e. G^L. MT has an expansion of the Sopherim, "Adonai Yahweh," while G^B preserves the unlikely deuteronomistic "the covenant of Yahweh."

26.f. G^B. MT and G^L add explicative "David."

28.a. MT. G^{BL} add explicative "son of Zeruiah."

28.b. G^L, Syr, Syr^h, Vg. MT and G^B "Absolom"; see *Comment*.

29.a. G^{GL}. MT "King Solomon" is expansive.

29.b. G^L. MT and G^B add explicative "Joab."

29.c-c. MT. G^{BL} "he has grasped the horns of the altar" substitutes 1:51 for a rather obscure Heb.

29.d-d. G^{BL}. MT omits by homoioteleuton. Cf. *HOTTP*, 294.

29.e. MT and G^B. G^L "King Solomon."

29.f. MT, which seems too abrupt to G^{BL}, which reads "and fall."

29.g. MT. G^{BL} add "and kill him" (influenced by v 31b). Cf. Burney, xxx.

30.a. MT. G^{BL} have pleonastic "son of Jehoiada."

30.b. MT. G^{BL} add explicative "Joab."

30.c. MT. G^{BL} "No, I will not come," is pleonastic.

30.d. MT, G^L. G^B adds "son of Jehoiada returned word and said to the king as follows" (pleonastic).

31.a. MT. G^{BL} "Go and do. . . ."

31.b. G^{BL}; MT omits. Cf. *YTT*, 224.

31.c. MT and G^L; G^B omits. The proper name seems fitting in this climactic pronouncement.

32.a. MT. G^{BL}'s addition, "of his iniquity," is pleonastic.

32.b. MT, G^L. G^B "their blood" is explicative.

33.a-a. MT, reading a fitting indicative (יִהְיֶה) to express an assurance recognized as unhistorical by G^{BL}, offering an opt to express a juss (יְהִי "may there be") in their *Vorlage*.

34.a. G^{BL}. MT adds a pleonastic "son of Jehoiada."

34.b. G^{BL}. MT "then went up" in pleonastic in view of the fact that Joab was at the moment in the sacred tent.

34.c. G^L; cf. MT. G^B has explicative "Joab."

34.d-d. G^{BL}. MT "and fell upon him and killed him."

34.e. MT. G^{BL} "and they buried him."

34.f. MT and G^B (*lectio difficilior*). G^L "grave" circumvents difficulties in the idea of burying a person in his house.

35.a. MT and G^B. G^L adds "Solomon."

35.b. MT and G^B. G^L adds explicative "Joab's."

35.c. MT. G^{BL} add pleonastic "and the kingdom was established in Jerusalem."

35.d. MT and G^B. G^L adds "Solomon."

35.e. MT and G^L. G^B has pleonastic "as chief priest." Cf. Burney, xxx.

36.a. MT and G^B. G^L adds "Solomon."

36.b. MT and G^B. G^L has explicative "son of Gera."

37.a. MT. G^{BL} add a gloss from v 42, "and the king adjured him on that day"; cf. Burney, 25–26.

38.a. MT. G^{BL} "what."

38.b-b. MT. G^{BL} "three years" is explicative in light of v 39. Cf. Burney, xxvi.

39.a. MT and G^L. G^B "Amesa."

40.a-a. MT, G^B. G^L substitutes the less lapidary "to Achish king of Gath."

40.b. MT, G^B. G^L adds explicative "out of Jerusalem."

41.a-a. MT, G^B. G^L, avoiding passives, substitutes "they reported."

41.b-b. MT. G^{BL} substitute explicative "had brought back his slaves."

42.a. MT. G^{BL} adds explicative "from Jerusalem."

42.b-b. MT, G^L*rell*. G^B omits.

43.a. G^B καὶ τί ὅτι = MT וּמַדּוּעַ. G^L καὶ νῦν διάτι follows abnormal Heb. syntax, וְעַתָּה מַדּוּעַ "so now why?"

44.a. MT, G^L. G^B has explicative "your."
46.a. MT. G^BL add "Solomon."
46.b-b. G^B omits. *Hab* MT *rell.*
46.c. MT, G^B. G^L has explicative "Shimei."
46.d-d. MT. G omits.

Form/Structure/Setting

Throne-succession narrative, Episode 14: Solomon establishes his rule
I. David's farewell charge to Solomon
  A. Instructions for resolving old tensions
    Transition: summons to strength, 2:1–2a
[Dtr: Charge to keep Yahweh's law, vv 2b–4]
      1. Joab's bloodguilt
        a. The complaint, v 5
        b. The instruction, v 6
      2. Loyalty to the Barzillaites v 7
      3. Shimei's curse
        a. The complaint, v 8
        b. The instruction, v 9
  B. Report of David's death, v 10a
[Dtr: Concluding formula, vv 10b–11]
II. Solomon eliminates his rivals
  A. Solomon deals with Adonijah and Abiathar
    Transition: Solomon reigns, v 12a
[Expansion, 12b]
      1. Scene 1: Adonijah's unwarranted initiative
        a. His approach to Bathsheba, vv 13–14
        b. His appeal to Bathsheba
          (1) The situation, v 15
          (2) Request for Abishag, vv 16–17
        c. Bathsheba's acquiescence, v 18
      2. Scene 2: Solomon's vigorous reaction
        a. Bathsheba's approach and reception, v 19
        b. The request, vv 20–21
        c. Solomon's assessment of Adonijah's motive, v 22
        d. A double oath of doom
          (1) The verdict, v 23
          (2) The order for execution
            (a) Solomon's authority, v 24aα
[Dtr: Expansion v 24aβ]
            (b) The imposition of immediate death, v 24b
        e. Execution of the sentence, v 25
      3. Solomon dismisses Abiathar
        a. Decree of exile, v 26a
        b. Suspension of the death sentence, v 26b
[Dtr: Interpretive comment, v 27]
  B. Solomon deals with Joab
      1. Joab's flight to sanctuary, v 28

2. Scene 3: Solomon acts on Joab's terms
   a. Solomon orders Joab's execution, v 29
   b. Joab chooses death in the sanctuary, v 30
   c. Solomon renews the order of execution
     (1) The command to act on Joab's terms, v 31a
     (2) The command to remove bloodguilt, v 31b
     (3) Rationale:
       (a) Divine retribution, v 32
       (b) Generational solidarity, v 33
   d. Benaiah carries out the execution, v 34
 3. Solomon appoints Benaiah and Zadok, v 35
C. Solomon deals with Shimei
 1. Scene 4: He sets the terms of Shimei's parole
   a. Command to remain in Jerusalem, v 36
   b. Threat of death, v 37
   c. Shimei accepts the terms, v 38a
 2. He punishes Shimei's transgression
   a. Shimei pursues his runaway slaves
     (1) The occasion, vv 38b–39a
     (2) The journey to Gath, vv 39b–40a
     (3) Resumptive conclusion, v 40b
   b. Scene 5: Solomon brings Shimei to account
     (1) He hears of the transgression, v 41
     (2) He accuses Shimei of violating his parole
       (a) The oath and order recalled, v 42
       (b) Demand for an explanation, v 43
     (3) He rationalizes Shimei's death
       (a) Divine retribution, v 44
       (b) Dynastic well-being, v 45
   c. The execution, v 46a
Concluding summary, v 46b

It is very generally conceded that the throne-succession narrative, and this episode, come to an end with the report of Shimei's execution and the concluding summary, "Thus was the kingdom made secure in Solomon's hand" (v 46). 1 Kgs 1 surely cannot stand by itself, and there is nothing in chap. 3 to serve as chap. 2's continuation. Here then the unified but tightly episodic narrative beginning in 2 Sam 9 comes to a climax and conclusion. We expect that it will resolve all loose ends and tell the story to completion. The fact is, however, that serious misgivings concerning the originality of extensive blocks within this chapter have troubled some interpreters. The section about Shimei (vv 36–46a) has been suspect because most of it takes place three years later than the rest of the story (v 39); but who can say when the throne-succession narrative was actually written? More serious is a suspicion about vv 13–35, the section that deals with Adonijah and goes on to describe what happened to Abiathar and Joab as well. If part of this section must go, all of it must go, for the verses that deal with Abiathar (26–27) flow smoothly from the preceding context (the man's name is foremost, following the copula, as indirect object of a verb in the perfect, followed by the subject), and the verses that have to do with Joab (28–35) are attached to the Abiathar section by a copula, foremost noun-subject, verb in the perfect, and prepositional phrase, so that it too stands syntactically dependent on its foregoing context. Thus there are no obvious literary seams in vv 13–35, and the entire section ought to be taken as a unity. Several objections have been raised, however, to attaching vv 12–46 to vv 1–11. One of them is that neither Adonijah nor Abiathar is mentioned in David's instructions to Solomon, though Joab and Shimei are. Another objection is that Barzillai (v 7) is not mentioned in vv 13–46. Again, v 12b, "And his dominion was firmly established," has been taken as the real concluding summary to the throne-succession document (v 46b is then explained as a late gloss). Finally, it has been noted that many MSS in the family G^L insert a heading, "Reigns III," just at v 12, as though to commence a new book and a new document.

Now, if stylistic characteristics clearly did distinguish vv 1–11 from vv 12–35, and vv 12–35 from vv 36–46, some of these objections might assume importance. But the writing is clearly from one hand. We must attribute incongruities of content to the author's art, looking to see what purpose may have guided him. V 46b should be viewed as more original than v 12b on linguistic grounds: the word "kingdom," מַמְלָכָה, is widely attested in pre-exilic literature, whereas 12b's "dominion," מַלְכוּת, occurs mainly in very late literature (Esth, Chr, Dan, Ezra, Neh, Pss). As for the Lucianic book-heading, it proves nothing one way or the other. We are curious about it, of course, and wonder whether it has anything to do with the shift from a *Kaige* text back to OG at this very spot in G^B.

This denial of secondary expansions of the main account does not mean that the text is an absolute unity. Remarkably, that was true of chap. 1, but it is not true here. There are five places within this chapter where late editors or glossators have made insertions, and generally they are easy to recognize. The user of this commentary can readily see where they are from the square brackets in the structural outline. Dtr is responsible for four of them (at vv 2b–4, 10b–11, 24aβ, and 27), and may be responsible for v 12b as well (although the above-cited linguistic evidence makes a post-exilic date more likely). In the *Introduction* to this commentary we have called special attention to 1 Kgs 2:2–4 as Dtr's most strategic opportunity for expressing his special ideology. This is a perfect place for it: David is on his deathbed and is just giving Solomon his farewell charge (Dtr is skillful at using the farewell address as a vehicle for his own preachments; cf. Joshua, Josh 23; Samuel, 1 Sam 12). Dtr's enjoinments about keeping the law and the commandments of course have little to do with the revenge that David has in mind. In spite of the fact that he had previously provided a chronological summary for David in 2 Sam 5:4–5, 1 Kgs 2:10b–11 offers Dtr a suitable place for a similar summary (the wording of each passage differs somewhat from that of the other, suggesting that they may be by different redactors). As we have argued, v 12b is definitely late; it turns what the throne-succession narrator intends as an introductory exposition into a concluding summary, disregarding additional material in vv 13–46. In v 24aβ Dtr throws in a pointed allusion to 2 Sam 7:13, meaning thereby to underscore that the promise to David had been for an entire dynasty, not merely for a single individual. In v 27 Dtr shows a practice that is to become familiar in succeeding passages, pointing to Solomon's dismissal of Abiathar as the fulfillment of the prophetic prediction found in 1 Sam 3:11–14.

1 Kgs 2 is markedly different from 1 Kgs 1 in the fact that its structure does not flow smoothly from beginning to end, but rather places the opening section, vv 1–10a, in sharp disjunction with vv 13–46. It is, of course, this disjunction that has led many scholars into the error of assigning all or parts of the latter section to secondary authorship. Assuming that both sections are by the same writer, we may ask whether vv 1–10a should be viewed as a distinct and separate episode within the throne-succession narrative. The answer is no; these sections are not separate episodes because they share a common theme: the securing of Solomon's reign through the "wise" handling of troublesome individuals. Besides, vv 1–10a have no internal development, hence cannot stand alone. Furthermore, the report of David's death in v 10a (not part of Dtr's expansion) is a conclusion only to this one section, while the statement of Solomon's reign in v 12a must be seen as the introductory exposition to all of vv 13–46.

Anyone who might be tempted to doubt that chap. 2 is by the same author as chap. 1 would do well to take note of the five separate scenes that we have identified. They function as in chap. 1, carrying the action forward while bare third-person narration serves as introduction or denouement. In the three major subsections of vv 13–46, the Adonijah subsection (13–27) requires two scenes in quick succession in order to show Adonijah with Bathsheba, then Bathsheba with Solomon. The Joab subsection (28–34) has only one complex scene in which messages fly back and forth between Joab and Solomon. The Shimei subsection (35–46), finally, requires a scene at the beginning for depicting Solomon's agreement with Shimei, then a scene at the end (actually a monologue) for depicting Solomon's judgment on him for his transgression.

It is not necessary to stumble over the fact that the Adonijah subsection has no prolepsis in vv 1–9, for this has already been presented in 1:49–53 (critics who overlook our narrator's technique of dovetailing thematic elements like this are likely to go astray in claiming that the Adonijah material has no preparation in vv 1–9, like the Joab and Shimei material, and is therefore a secondary addition). Prolepsis is precisely what these verses do provide for the Joab and Shimei subsections; again, some critics go astray in pointing to incongruities between the prolepsis and the fulfillment sections for each person, overlooking the consideration that freedom of phraseology is precisely a distinguishing mark of the throne-succession historian. Joab and Shimei have each seriously offended David, according to narration in 2 Sam (see *Comment*), but our author is skillful in depicting offensive action in the immediate present as Solomon's justification (or pretext) for executing them.

Vv 1–9 is not in itself a scene since all it contains is David's speech (though Solomon is designated as the addressee, he neither says nor does anything). This speech serves as a prologue to what is to follow. It begins with the transitional phrase, "I am going the way of all the earth" (i.e., on the point of dying), and then launches out into three distinct instructions for Solomon's performance after he is gone. Again displaying a sense of symmetry, our writer attaches to the first instruction (Joab) and to the third (Shimei) a complaint of injury, leaving the second instruction (Barzillai) to stand clear and clean in the middle without it. Not only is the charge concerning Barzillai used for structural contrast; its reference to "loyalty," חסד, is meant as a potent rebuke to the "blood" of Joab and the "curse" of Shimei. Once David's speech is completed, our writer brings that king's history to a swift conclusion in his laconic report, "So David slept with his fathers." (This might be assigned to Dtr's stereotyped notice in vv 10b–11 were it not for the consideration that a long, involved document like the throne-succession narrative would certainly not end without some statement of David's death. Dtr very naturally allows his source's notice to stand and expands upon it in his usual fashion.)

As has been said, v 12a is a transitional exposition for vv 13–46. One should note that it is styled as a new beginning, with the subject foremost, followed by the perfect verb (perhaps intended as an active participle, creating a noun-clause, in the unvocalized original) and a prepositional phrase. The whole functions as a circumstantial clause for v 13 and following.

We have noted that the Adonijah subsection contains two separate scenes in direct sequence, plus Solomon's concluding declaration in vv 23–24 and the report of execution in v 25. The link between the two scenes is Bathsheba's acquiescence reported in v 18. Here the abused wife and mother becomes instrumental to the perilous shift from Adonijah's opportunity to Adonijah's downfall. We take special note of the fact that 'Adonijah's boast to be Israel's rightful ruler (v 15) is effectively counterbalanced by Solomon's declaration that he is ruler in fact and intends to act as such (v 24). Both men acknowledge that Yahweh's hand has directed what has come to pass. Adonijah tries to circumvent it, but Solomon is determined to use it for his full advantage.

As has been noted, the two verses about Abiathar are inseparably attached to the Adonijah subsection. The foremost position of the indirect object, ולאביתר הכהן "and to Abiathar the priest," makes the addressee of Solomon's speech prominently distinguished from Adonijah, yet the copula connects him to him. As with the action in v 35, Solomon's dealings with Abiathar are not necessarily in direct temporal sequence from the preceding; i.e., the event in question may have taken place a considerable period later. In that case, it would be only Abiathar's involvement in Adonijah's aborted coup that now leads our narrator to take up his case. On the other hand, there is nothing to show that the Abiathar episode could not have occurred immediately. It is certain that he was not with Adonijah because Solomon speaks directly to him in v 26. On the other hand, he was in disgrace with Solomon and hence would not have been standing around in Solomon's throne room. Evidently our narrator wants to include all cases where Solomon dealt with potential enemies to the religio-political establishment that included Zadok as chief priest, while keeping his design of congruity in three distinct subsections; hence it is here that the Abiathar material is attached.

Subsection 2, about Joab, is less complex in some respects than the foregoing subsection, and in other respects more complex. It has only one scene (Scene 3), framed at the beginning by a narrative report and at the end by another narrative report. This Joab subsection is introduced by a circumstantial clause, "Now the news came to Joab," containing subject foremost with following perfect or (original) participle and the indirect object. There is no indication where Joab might have been, but direct temporal connection to the Adonijah subsection is implied in the immediacy with which Joab reacted. There are some puzzles here and some striking peculiarities. To us it is a puzzle why Solomon should have commanded Joab's execution just because he would not come away from the altar (v 29).

Our writer again seems to be aiming for a triadal structure, with inconclusive dialogue in v 29a (carried on by messenger), more inconclusive dialogue in v 30a (Benaiah in direct contact with Joab), and lastly Solomon's definitive dialogue in vv 30b–33 (Solomon in direct address to Benaiah). Solomon actually gives two commands, the second of which is the consequence of the first. He repeats his order for Joab's execution, adding now the ironic element of acting according to Joab's own words, putting him to death in remorseless reality when Joab had appealed to the altar for refuge to save him from everything except the unthinkable extreme resort to violation of the sanctuary, which he mentions only as a hypothetical possibility. Solomon's second command is that in death Joab's blood should expunge the "blood" that Joab had brought upon the house of David. The rationale that follows, even though it differs in certain details from David's earlier instruction (vv 5–6), is intended as Solomon's fulfillment of his responsibility to his father, but it indicates also the narrator's interpretation of the justification for Joab's death. Joab had to be punished for his bloodthirstiness, but, most important, the house of David needed to be purged of blood-guilt so that it might reign in "peace" forever. The report of Joab's execution is accordingly followed by notices that Benaiah was appointed in the place of Joab and Zadok in the place of Abiathar. The reference to Abiathar is a reminiscence back to v 26, where a mention of his successor would have expanded a mere appendage out of proportion to the writer's intent.

The final subsection, about Shimei, has more simplicity but also more complexity than subsection two. Here Scene 4 at the beginning and Scene 5 at the end envelop the narrative report of Shimei's transgression (vv 38b–40). Real dialogue occurs, of course, in Scene 4, where Solomon lays terms on Shimei and he accepts them. In Scene 5, the only narration is at the beginning, where Solomon summons Shimei. It would be wrong to call what follows a dialogue because Solomon does all the talking in spite of his demand (v 43) for an explanation. We are to understand, no doubt, that Shimei had no explanation, that he stood speechless in terror of the king when he might at least have offered the excuse that he had not actually crossed the Kidron (v 37). Our narrator is not interested, in any case, in idle verbalizings, but only in Solomon's closing words and their impact on the competition between the Davidide monarchy and potential rivals in the Benjaminite tribe that has produced King Saul. We take note of the fact that v 44 again introduces Solomon as talking, suggesting perhaps a pause as the king hurried on from accusation to a rationalization of Shimei's execution. Here we clearly see that Shimei's transgression of his parole is only the pretext by which Solomon shall carry out his father's order in vv 8–9. Just as Joab was not really killed for taking refuge at the altar, but for the "blood" he had brought on David, so Shimei will be killed for cursing David and not for going after his slaves. As in vv 32–33, however, vv 44–45 identify retribution on wrongdoing as the instrumental cause for something more ultimately important, in this case blessing on Solomon and the permanent establishment of the Davidide throne.

Finally, we take note of a number of expressions in 1 Kgs 2 that are well on the way to becoming fixed formulae, or at least fixed usages. "I am going (walking) in the way of all the earth" means, of course, I am on the point of dying; this deathbed formula is used by Dtr in Josh 23:14, though not in Deut 31 or 1 Sam 12, and was probably an ancient locution picked up by the throne-succession narrator. Vv 2–4 are nothing but a thick skein of deuteronomistic phrases: keep the charge; walk in his paths; keep his statutes, commandments, ordinances, testimonies; prosper in all that you do and to which you turn your attention; guard your way, walk before me in fidelity, with all your heart and soul; no one shall be cut off (see the commentaries on Deuteronomy). "So now" in v 16 and in v 5 G^L occurs frequently to connect (1) a statement of the situation to (2) a statement of appropriate action (cf. *YTT,* 41–42). The full oath formula appears in v 23 (cf. 1:29–30) and the messenger formula (later used liberally in introducing prophetic oracles) in v 30. Our narrator is skillful in restricting the formal title, "King Solomon" (elsewhere he uses "Solomon" or "the king") to those precise points in the story (according to the preferred readings, only vv 19, 23, and 45) where (1) he is approached in full solemnity or (2) he (and the narrator) speaks of himself in the full dignity of his august position. Finally, we note the somewhat varied, but generally brief and stereotyped way in which Benaiah's performance of the death sentence is reported (vv 25, 34, 46a).

Comment

1–4 "David's days to die": the infinitive with ל expresses purpose ("for dying"); in Heb. mentality dying often occurs gradually, and the sickness or weakness that precedes it characterizes the closing days of one's life. How old was David at his death? Having been thirty years old at his accession, and having reigned forty years (possibly a schematic figure), he was seventy (2 Sam 5:4)—no exceptional age for a man of such unusual vigor. "Be strong and act as becomes a man": here at the beginning of his long interpolation Dtr borrows a picturesque old locution (1 Sam 4:9) as an appropriate introduction to the rigorous rule that David lays on his son. "Keep the charge of your god," אלהיך . . . משמרת . . . : this is attested mainly as a late cultic expression, appearing in Num, Neh, 1–2 Chr, and meaning "carry out the ritual." It does not appear elsewhere in Deut or in deuteronomistic literature, but this does not warrant identifying this half verse as a late intrusion; rather, it should be recognized as fixed in very ancient tradition and here picked up by Dtr, like the other foregoing expressions.

"Walking in his paths" = "ways": here our term has a narrowly religious-ethical focus, unlike "way" in v 2. The term is precisely defined in the following set of injunctions. "Keeping": infinitive of purpose. "Statutes . . . commandments . . . ordinances . . . testimonies": all had juridical bearing and laid the Israelites under Yahweh's absolute authority. These terms are used synonymously in Deut and with remarkable frequency; their original meaning is largely lost as they become virtual equivalents of *Torah*, "law." It is an impossible task to get behind the Greek translation to check whether Dtr's formulations have been normalized by later scribes and redactors. "As written in the law of Moses": though modern study of the Hebrew law-codes shows that they cannot be ascribed to the historical Moses, Moses was honored nonetheless as the archetypal lawgiver, and hence by the time of Deut and Dtr the term "law of Moses" had come to validate all the legal material that had been collected; although it is a deuteronomistic term (Josh 8:31, 23:6, 2 Kgs 14:6, 23:25), it occurs also in Mal 3:22 (Eng. 4:4) Dan 9:13, Ezra 3:2, 7:6, Neh 8:1, 2 Chr 23:18, 30:16 in a literal sense and with reference to a completed, sacrosanct code of law. "You may prosper": countering W. G. Ahlström's suggestion that שׂכל exclusively refers to victory over suffering (*Psalm 89, eine Liturgie aus dem Ritual des leidendes Königs* [1959] 21–26) is M. Saebo's article on this word in *THAT* II, 824–28. "You turn your attention": lit. "to which you turn."

"Establish his word": lit. "make his word to remain standing"; the Hebrews thought of a word as having a quasi-independent existence, living on through many generations until attaining fulfillment in the event that Yahweh had prepared for it. The word to David that is referred to here is phrased in deuteronomistic language like that of 1 Kgs 8:25, differing in terminology from the deuteronomistically colored narrative in 2 Sam 7, to which this passage obviously intends to refer. "If your sons guard . . .": with the promise at the end, this conditional saying is styled as in covenant form (cf. Exod 19:5–6). "In fidelity," אמת: from the root אמן, this term involves a right attitude of heart more than intellectual and linguistic veracity. "With all their heart . . . soul": cf. Deut 6:5 (the *Shema*): the heart is the moral and intellectual center of man's being, while the soul (נפשׁ) is man's vital life. "No one of your sons shall be cut off": a classic *vaticinium ex eventu*, viewed from Dtr's position in Judah's late history, when the remarkable survivability of the Davidic dynasty had been established as an historical fact.

5–9 "So now": MT וגם אתה, "and moreover you" (dutifully reproduced by G^B's *Kaige kai ge sù*) is dubious because there is no need for an emphatic foremost pronoun immediately following the preceding address to this same person. The גם is a post-Septuagintal insertion, and אתה may be a mishearing of עתה, read by G^L. Its function is to draw a logical consequence from the preceding, in this case David's formulaic statement in v 2a. David's meaning is that he himself will no longer be able to deal with Joab and Shimei, "so now" Solomon must do it. "Did to me . . . did to the two commanders": in the light of Israel's corporate sensibility, crimes done to persons for whom David was responsible were done to him; that they had high offices kept the question of retribution constantly before the public eye. "Abner son of Ner": cf. 2 Sam 3:1—4:1; Saul's general, he had been at the point of concluding a peace treaty with David when Joab and his brother ambushed him (3:27), bringing David to ostentatious public grieving (3:31–39); cf. S. J. De Vries, *YTT*, 92–93. "Amasa son of Yether": cf. 2 Sam 19:14 (Eng. 13), 20:4–13.

"He murdered them, avenging the blood of war in peacetime": Abner had been in Hebron under David's safe-passage to discuss peace, Amasa had been in David's army with David, although Joab's Johnny-come-lately successor had earlier been neutral in the struggle with Absalom. "Putting innocent blood on the girdle . . . on my sandals": V. Kubāč, *VT* 31 (1981) 25–26, takes Joab's deed as deliberate and symbolic, citing Anat's bloody rite in *CTA* 3.ii as showing that the victor would wipe some of the victim's blood on his sandals and belt, the sandals being symbolic of the power to travel about, and the belt of the life-power residing in one's loins. "My loins . . . my sandals . . . my feet": G^L, with the more difficult reading, undoubtedly preserves the ancient Hebrew reading since David is specifically complaining that Joab's guilty deed made him (David) guilty (late Jewish piety, offended at the notion of the increasingly glorified David bearing guilt, produced the reading preserved in MT and G^B, making Joab alone responsible).

"So act according to your wisdom": cf. v 9, "for a wise man are you." Those commentators err who object that Solomon is not given wisdom until chap. 3; this simplistic reading fails to account for the difference in literary sources, but also fails to recognize that "wisdom," חכמה, and "wise," חכם, here refer to shrewdness, cleverness, the pragmatic adapting of the means to the end. Solomon is supposed to figure out some way to accomplish what David for some reason had been unable to do. "Do not let his gray hairs go down in peace to Sheol": Sheol, largely demythologized by the Hebrews, is the grave; though "peace," שלום, is often given meanings such as "harmony," "well-being," it here refers to the quiet and safety that Joab's life of violence has forfeited. "The sons of Barzillai the Gileadite": cf. 2 Sam 17:27–29, 19:31–40; although this person had generously helped David in his flight from Absalom, his advanced age had led him to refuse David's offer to install him as a permanent guest at his table. David now insists that the חסד, "deed of loyalty," that had been practiced demands reciprocation as irresistibly as Joab's and Shimei's deeds demand retribution; because his name (with Aramaic בר, "son") suggests that he was a non-Israelite living in the unstable border region between Israel and Syria, David's insistence that his sons be permanently at his table (= his court) may in fact have been motivated as much by the desire to keep them under surveillance as to reward them for past favors.

"Shimei son of Gera, Benjaminite from Bahurim": cf. 2 Sam 16:5–14, 19:17–24 (Eng. 16–23); Bahurim is just east of Jerusalem; David's apparent humility at Shimei's cursing and his apparent generosity at Shimei's greeting upon his return, both bitterly resented by Joab's brother Abishai, were actually motivated by (1) the large force of armed men at Shimei's side and (2) the need to enlist the help of Saul's erstwhile supporters if David were to survive as king. "I swore to him by Yahweh": cf. 2 Sam 19:24 (Eng. 23). "I won't kill you with the sword": cf. 1:51; this static formula leaves plenty of room for maneuvering; the killing may be done by some other means, or some other person may do it. "But as for you": this preferred reading (G^L) tells Solomon to do what David has been prevented from doing by his oath. "With blood": cf. "peace," v 6; Shimei's potent curse had the power of death, and must be counteracted by blood.

10–11 "Was buried in the city of David": Dtr's regular formula, cf. 1 Kgs 11:43, etc. The tombs of the Judahite kings have been identified on the south slope of Ophel, and it is more probable that David was buried there than at the traditional site, shown to modern-day tourists, on the then-unoccupied southern extremity of the western hill. "Now the years when David reigned . . .": compare Dtr's mention of forty years, with seven in Hebron (this was not over Israel, only over Judah) and thirty-three in Jerusalem, with 2 Sam 5:4–5, which first gives David's age at his accession, then the length of his reign, and then the statement that he reigned over Judah for seven years and six months, and over all Israel and Judah for thirty-three years (a total of forty years and six months). The formulation in Sam seems to be more precise and deserves credence over Dtr's formulation, though probably both have been drawn from the same annalistic source. Dtr rounds off his figure to produce a neat forty. He omits a date for David's age at his accession because this normally is placed in the opening formulae.

12–18 "Thus Solomon sat": with the subject foremost and the perfect or (an original) participle following, this is not part of the foregoing Dtr notice (on the usual form, cf. 11:43b), but rather the exposition to this new section (see above). "Adonijah . . . came to Bathsheba, Solomon's mother": since the reader is quite aware whose mother Bathsheba is, this explanation is best interpreted as a recollection of the foregoing reference to Solomon and as a signal of how risky Adonijah's undertaking actually was. "A matter," דבר: foremost for emphasis; the matter concerns her not only because she has privileged access to Solomon, who must decide, but because as גבירה "queen mother," she has the say-so over every woman in the royal palace.

"You know": as in v 5, this implies acknowledgment along with awareness. "The kingship was mine": Adonijah remains firmly convinced of the right of primogeniture and has no misgivings about the rightness of his move to seize the throne. "All Israel turned their faces": showed favor; see below on "turn away my face." "But the kingship has turned away . . . for through Yahweh it has become his": Adonijah is an orthodox Yahwist, attributing evil as well as good to Yahweh, yet this does not prevent him from seeking to reverse his bad fortune if he can. He tries to overawe Bathsheba with the notion that he is really Israel's proper king and deserves some petty solace for his loss. "Don't turn away my face": so *passim* in this section; MT maintains a strange Hebraic idiom over against G's uncomprehending alteration. The meaning is, "Don't reply in such a manner that I am forced to avert my face in shame and chagrin." "Solomon the king": i.e., Solomon *as* king, for though he is a brother, it is as king that he will reply. "Give me Abishag . . . as wife": to David she had been neither wife nor concubine, thus not a regular member of his harem, yet her former intimacy with David, together with her very special beauty, gave her a special status; one can guess that Solomon intended to take, and did in fact take her as his own wife. "Good, I will speak on your behalf . . .": another of our narrator's enigmatic touches, hinting that Bathsheba's seeming good-natured compliance may have disguised her design to get rid of Adonijah (if she was jealous of Abishag, she may also have intended to get Abishag in trouble).

19–25 "King Solomon": the full official title hints that Solomon will now act in his official capacity; from the endearing scene in which his words encourage his mother he suddenly leaps up like a tiger aroused from sleep. "Arose to meet her . . . did homage to her . . . had a chair placed": showing the respect and affection bred into him through his former life of close intimacy. "The king's mother": mistress of the harem and acting executive in the king's absence (cf. Jezebel). "Sit at his right side": a common custom throughout the ancient world was to make this the place of honor and of delegated authority (hence to speak of Christ at the right hand of the Father should never be taken literally, for it simply means enjoying the position of chief delegated authority). "And why are you asking . . . ? Just as well ask, . . .": this is actually a conditional sentence in which the protasis, though styled as a question, has the object foremost, followed by the verb in participial form, and in which the apodosis is an imperative from the same verb. "Ask the kingship for him—because he is my elder brother": Solomon too believes sufficiently in the theory of primogeniture to realize that Adonijah has everything on his side; Solomon is so touchy about this that he fears that one signal to the people that he is unsure about his own power, as would be the case in handing Abishag over to Adonijah, would encourage a revolt that he could not handle. "For him and . . . Abiathar . . . and Joab:" though the last two mentioned had no doubt been lying quiet, Abiathar is still chief priest and Joab is still general of the army, and together they can very possibly bring Solomon's fears to reality.

"King Solomon," v 23: again the full official title is found in the precise point where Solomon acts in his full capacity as king. What follows in vv 23–24 constitutes a double oath. The first oath states in effect that Adonijah is in deadly peril; the second seems to go further and commands that person's death. This signals a portentous moment for Solomon, for he sees that he must decree execution not only here but wherever it may be required. The first oath has the full literal form. The second, introduced by "so now," ועתה (see above), makes the usual appeal to Yahweh, specifying the gracious deeds that Yahweh had done (cf. 1:29), and then decrees Adonijah's death as the implicit protasis in the oath. "Made me a house": i.e., "dynasty"— meaningful only from Dtr's perspective. "Today": this emphatic time-identifier indicates that this matter must be brought to an immediate resolution. "So the king sent an order with (lit., "by the hand of") Benaiah": we would say, "Sent Benaiah with an order," but the Heb. sees the order as the instrument of death and Benaiah only as its agent. "Fell on him and he died": this shows that the verb פגע, which sometimes implies also the resulting death, does not simply mean "kill," but to strike and wound in such a fashion as to cause death.

26–27 "To Anathoth!": Solomon's abrupt speech dramatically expresses his rage; the site is three and a half miles northeast of Jerusalem (Kefr Anata) and is the hometown of the prophet Jeremiah (Jer 1:1). "Go to your fields": from his estate and nevermore from the sanctuary is to come his sustenance. "You are marked for death": lit. "a man of death," איש מות; Solomon is doing more than threatening Abiathar; he is officially passing the death sentence, even though he suspends this in the sequel. "And on this day": cf. *YTT*, 149, for evidence that this may be the regular form for an accession amnesty; nevertheless Solomon's concession is a parole, threatening Abiathar with execution if he dares to leave Anathoth and come back to Jerusalem. "Because you bore . . . because you suffered": to make Solomon ignore all that his father and his father's house owed Abiathar, strong pressure from Zadok must have been at work, not merely Solomon's resentment of Abiathar's support for Adonijah. "Thus did Solomon exile Abiathar from acting as Yahweh's priest": Dtr's summary of the effect. It is evident that kings had final authority over priests, not priests over kings. "Yahweh's word which he spoke against the house of Eli in Shiloh": cf. 1 Sam 3:12–14 (the genealogy from Eli to Ahimelech, priest of Nob, Abiathar's father, is not clearly drawn, but Dtr assumes, and perhaps has independent tradition to support it, that this is true).

28–35 Solomon deals with Joab. "Joab had been affiliated with Adonijah and had not been affiliated with Solomon": it may seem venturesome to adopt G^L's "Solomon" in preference to MT and G^B's "Absalom," especially since G^B is no longer *Kaige*, slavishly reproducing a proto-MT; also because the verb נטה normally means "turn away," "desert to." But the verb sometimes means "adhere to," and this meaning would be suitable with "Solomon" although the meaning "desert to" would not. Some commentators have supposed that the Joab episode is a secondary intrusion (see above), and that the interpolator would naturally insert this explanatory sentence. However, we recognize here another of the throne-succession narrator's familiar reminiscences, an internal exposition introducing this subsection; and certainly a reference to Absalom would be very much out of place because, if our narrator had intended to compare Absalom with Adonijah in terms of Joab's allegiance, he would have done so the first time Adonijah and Joab had been mentioned together, 1:7. In light of the fierceness of Joab's attack on Absalom (see especially 2 Sam 18:14–15), there would be no point in comparing him with Adonijah within the present context.

"Fled to Yahweh's tent to grasp the horns of the altar": cf. 1:50; here the reference to the tent is needed because of the theme of Benaiah's standing outside, commanding Joab to come out. "And behold, he is beside the altar": a partial quotation breaking into indirect discourse; MT depicts Joab as near the altar, ready to seize it, not actually grasping it (so G^{BL}, influenced by 1:50). "So Solomon sent": שלח regularly implies a messenger, who speaks as, and not only for, the person who is speaking. "Fled to Yahweh": in Joab's thinking Yahweh is firmly identified with his sanctuary.

"Go fall on him": Joab's very fear of Solomon tells him that Joab is worthy of death, otherwise than with Adonijah in 1:49–53. In this case, if dauntless Joab is afraid, it may be assumed that he has good cause to be afraid. Solomon sends Benaiah with an immediate order for execution, but the latter is unable to carry it out so long as Joab hides in Yahweh's tent. "No, but I will die here": no doubt Joab is counting on Solomon's unwillingness to violate sanctuary, but his words also seem to imply that Solomon will not resort to the extreme of death. "Do as he said: fall on him and bury him": Joab has misread Solomon's determination; Solomon will act on Joab's word, killing him in the sanctuary itself, then burying him in order to hide a formidable and obnoxious enemy from human sight; cf. v 34. "Remove today": a command or appeal with היום, "today," has an epitomizing force, offering a succinct summary of an entire pericope; cf *YTT*, 224 (see also at vv 24, 26, 37, 42). "Innocent blood," v 31; "Bloodguilt," v 32; "blood" v 33: cf. v 5; the Heb. word דם (not the pl. דמים which refers to the actual fluid) is a metonymy for the violence that sheds blood, hence stands for all sorts of social wrong (Ezek 22:2) and refuses to be covered up, i.e. silenced (Gen 4:10). By executing Joab, Solomon will now avert "innocent blood" from David's house, putting it back on Joab and his posterity (v 33).

"On his own head," vv 31–32: a judicial papyrus now in Turin, written for Pharaoh Ramses IV in the mid-twelfth century, uses this as a fixed formula: "Let all that they (conspirators against Ramses III) have done fall upon their own heads, while I am protected and defended forever" (R. Yaron, "A Ramessid Parallel to 1 K ii 33, 44–45." *VT* 8 (1958) 432–33). "Two men more righteous and excellent": less a moral judgment than an assessment of the juridical position of each man, respectively, over against the assassin Joab, who in each case murdered a man on the king's business, without the king's authority, In v 32 Amasa is correctly identified as commander of Judah's army (2 Sam 20:4), whereas in v 5 he had been named co-commander of the "armies of Israel" (cf. 2 Sam 19:13). "There will be peace": MT's prediction (future indicative) is more likely here than G^BL's wish. "Buried in his house in the country"; reference to a house-burial is difficult (cf. G), but a tomb may have been attached to Joab's house; "country" for Heb. מדבר, usually translated "desert," shows that its root meaning is "open country," which in Joab's case must have been fertile enough to grow barley (2 Sam 14:30). "And the king appointed": everything popular and democractic is now expurgated, for Benaiah the mercenary replaces Joab, leader of the national militia, and Zadok, probably priest of Jerusalem's erstwhile Jebusite shrine, replaces Yahweh's priest, a man who had represented the popular struggle from the beginning.

36–46a Here the LXX inserts v 35; this is not original and has no exegetical significance (see *Introduction*). "Summoned Shimei": Solomon still feels bound by David's oath, yet seeks a pretext for eliminating Shimei in order to (1) fulfill his father's charge and at the same time to (2) neutralize a constant menace from the Benjaminites. To prevent Shimei from possibly rousing the Benjaminite countryside (just north of Jerusalem), he orders him to permanent residence within the city. "Do not go out from there hither or thither": שם is essentially a determinative of place, having usually the remote reference, "there," but occasionally having a proximate reference, "here," as in Isa 28:10. אנה ואנה, an indeterminate adverb of place with verbs of motion, precludes every conceivable destination. "On the day when . . . know assuredly that you will certainly die": for this threat form, see Gen 2:17. "If you so much as cross . . .": this clause, with the copula, is meant as a restrictive; even crossing the Kidron would uncover Shimei's intent to violate Solomon's prohibition. "The wadi Kidron": dry except in the rainy season, the Kidron lay just east of Ophel hill, Solomon's Jerusalem; Solomon mentions it specifically because this is the way to Bahurim (on the eastward slope of the Mount of Olives), Shimei's ancestral home, but Shimei later seems to have interpreted it as a substitute for the broader "hither or thither," allowing him to travel westward to Gath (vv 39–41). "Your terms are good": Shimei agrees, but there is no mention of an oath, vv 42–43.

"After three years": to judge from 22:1–2, this may be an approximation, equivalent to "many days," ימים רבים. "Two of Shimei's slaves": the detail of number is concrete and specific; for one slave Shimei might not have moved, but two made it an important matter. In Bible times slaves were generally military captives, though occasionally individuals sold their children, or even themselves, into slavery when economic destitution drove them to it. "Achish son of Maacah king of Gath": this is evidently the same Philistine potentate, David's feudal lord, who is identified in 1 Sam 27:2; although the location of Gath is not certain, it probably lay westward of a line from Azekah to Gubrin, in the Shephelah just below the Judean highlands. "Shimei went and brought back his slaves from Gath": a resumptive conclusion, produced by a deficient narrative development at this point due to the fact that the writer is not at all interested in the slaves, but only in what fetching them did to Shimei.

"Had traveled . . . had returned": pluperfects are suitable here because Solomon does not learn of what Shimei had done until after his return. "Did I not adjure you by Yahweh and admonish you": Solomon now says that he had put Shimei under a double obligation, to God and to himself (cf. v 43). "So why . . . ?": as has been pointed out, Solomon's question (with solemn מדוע, "for what reason") demands an explanation; that he does not allow a reply but rushes on to judgment apparently means that there is no excuse—at least none that he can possibly accept. "You know all the evil": this is the real reason why Shimei must die; there being no other witnesses ready to hand, Solomon calls on Shimei himself to verify the charge. "At least your heart acknowledges (ידע) it": if Shimei tries to deny it with his lips, his heart (= mind) will admit it. "So Yahweh has returned your evil on your head": Solomon can see Yahweh's hand in causing Shimei to violate his restraint. "But King Solomon is blessed": again the rare official title; now that Shimei is ready for judgment, nothing whatever stands in the way of the fulfillment of the blessing expressed in 1:47. "The throne of David will be established before Yahweh forever": since עד־עולם means "indefinitely" rather than "eternally," Solomon celebrates the passage of David's dominion to him, not the four-hundred-year-long dynasty that Dtr knew; yet certainly Dtr knew this passage and would have interpreted it in the latter sense.

46b "Thus was the kingdom made secure in Solomon's hand." "Made secure" is from the same root as "established" (כון) in v 45; "in Solomon's hand" = in Solomon's power; i.e., he henceforward has sufficient power to maintain it. Our clause is an epitomizing conclusion to the entire throne-succession narrative, all of which has been recounted in order to record how it came about that a younger son of David came to the throne in place of his elders. Such a summary is obviously needed here, yet its appropriateness does not entirely guarantee its originality, for G^BL do not have it in their text. To some extent, this problem is made less serious by the fact that the LXX likewise omits 3:1, substituting the diverse array of variants contained in v 46 (see *Introduction*).

Explanation

An exposition that seeks valid parallels in the biblical text for contemporary application must first clear the ground by identifying elements that deserve our censure rather than our emulation. There are many items here that modern Jews and Christians would condemn. We mention, first of all, the evident dynamism that David's deathbed speech implies respecting "blood," "fidelity," and "curse," elements that continue alive long after the event. Joab's blood, Barzillai's generosity, and Shimei's curse reach into the present and must be satisfied, and the fact that Joab originally acted for David's good, that Barzillai long ago renounced an offer to be David's guest, and that Shimei atoned for his curse by being the first to abet David's return, can change nothing. This kind of dynamistic fatalism, so endemic in that and many other cultures, can be very dangerous. Living in the modern world, we ought to be grateful for the possibility for a freer, more personalistic understanding of human interaction.

Certainly we will be dismayed to read that David's last recorded act was one of revenge. David has been much flattered in biblical and extrabiblical portraits of him, but vv 1–9 show him as petty and scheming. He debases the exalted word "wisdom" in the way he lays it on his son, advising him to use deceit and cleverness to achieve his vengeful aims. With David as with Solomon, there are at least as many negative lessons for us to learn as positive—especially the dangers of the abuse of power.

We are appalled at the ugly scene of the continuing struggle between the Solomonic party and the party of Adonijah. Equally lamentable is the portrait of Adonijah's haughtiness, lust, and greed, vv 13–25, as well as the absolute despotism that Solomon exercises, using the flimsiest of pretexts for the summary execution of his opponents. He even knew how to arrange things to his liking in the religious establishment so that it could never be able to offer effective resistance. Thoroughly deserving our censure is, furthermore, this new king's gross ingratitude for former deeds of notable service. Abiathar had certainly suffered all that David had suffered, and now deserved better than a summary dismissal. Even our grim and bloody Joab deserved a monument rather than an ignominious burial, for had he not fought with David in the wilderness, tried to rescue him (sometimes mistakenly) from the intrigues of Saul, led his armies to foreign conquests, intervened to make David take Absalom back and later killed Absalom and then made David stop weeping for him, because David was too weak to do so himself? Even in the Amasa matter, Joab had acted as much for David's kingdom as for his own position. And now this, an inglorious death by Solomon's order, at the hand of the butcher who was the king's chief bodyguard!

We may mention also Solomon's complete arbitrariness toward Shimei, which was motivated by the desire to suppress unrest among the northern tribes but probably had an unforeseen negative effect in firing up the growing resentment that led finally to the schism under Rehoboam. The worst thing in Solomon's attitude seems to have been the conviction that God is on the side of the largest divisions or the cleverest politicians and that might makes right. Everyone wants to have God on his side, and if He isn't, he takes measures to ensure that He is!

One can understand why some interpreters (see especially M. Noth 39–41) argue that the throne-succession narrative (or at least 1 Kgs 1–2) is actually anti-Solomon. To claim that Solomon is no hero but an anti-hero is to judge him from a wider perspective. If one would maintain that the throne-succession narrative is anti-Solomon, one would have to demonstrate that 2:12–46 is all or partly an addition, for chap. 1 is undisguisedly enthusiastic about him. But we have effectively shown that, apart from very late additions, chap. 2 is a literary unity, and we must certainly take the enthusiastic statements of 1:47–48 as celebrations of Solomon's rule. Also, there remains the question of how this, the earliest written literary document in the world's history, could have been written except by someone educated and active in Solomon's court. There is also the serious question how it could have been preserved except as an ostensible document in his praise. The throne-succession narrative is in fact the legitimation document for Solomon's accession. That it does not present what we would call a flattering picture of that person is more than anything else an indictment of the low spiritual ideals of the time in which he lived.

In the *Introduction* we have had various things to say about the skill of this narrator as a historian. One thing that was noted there was that, as genuine historiography, the throne-succession narrative presents a realistic and believable portrait of the human persons involved. The throne-succession narrator is able to perceive, and ready to recount, the flawed deeds of human persons. He did this with David, and he does it now with Solomon. Although this may diminish our own admiration for David and Solomon, it only heightens our esteem for the man who told about them. There are here, perhaps, the roots of a high theology, viz., the belief that Yahweh works his purposes even in the base behavior of men.

The student of the history of ideas will inevitably read this tale as the record of spiritual decline. In embracing the exercise of autocratic power in the succession of the nation's highest personage, Solomon and his party were relinquishing every vestige of democratic tradition, but also a meaningful commitment to the charismatic principle. We see no moral distance between Adonijah, asserting the right of primogeniture, and Solomon, cashing in on a private family agreement. The story has no hint of a motivating divine revelation; Yahweh is named, but only to sanction oaths and receive credit for a *fait accompli.* Thus God's will is quite nonoperative. He is not directing Israel's destiny, but is simply being used to sanction deeds of naked power. The story does have some hint of popular acclamation—the second of the two traditional principles along with divine designation. However, the people's shouting and singing follows Solomon's investiture, and the critical reader shall not be blamed for suspecting that this element has been enlarged and embellished in the interests of strengthening the impression of Solomon's legitimation.

Henceforward the Judean kingship will never waver from applying the principle of primogeniture in the succession of its rulers. Not even lip-service will be paid to the concept of charismatic designation. Solomon knew very well that he had not received this gift, and that is why he had to move so relentlessly in the exercise of brutal power, striking down rivals real or imaginary. He knew he had not received this gift, yet he and his historian found a way to add it to the ideology of his kingship. The notion of a divine promise to David *and his house* allowed them to attenuate the charisma that David had personally possessed, so that in effect David did live forever! (1:31). The Judean kingship was to be founded not on a single charismatic individual, but on an entire "charismatic" house! This is the meaning of Solomon's closing word (2:45): "But King Solomon is blessed, and the throne of David will be established before Yahweh forever!"

Historically, Israel is at a crossroads. From this moment on one sees a drastic shift from semidemocratic tribal rule (maintained to some extent in David's administration) to a typical despotic city-state. Greater the efficiency but less the freedom! The most serious question is, can this despotic state serve as the true bearer of biblical religion? Only the passage of years and centuries can give the answer; though from our perspective we know the answer, and that answer is that Hebrew nationalism was doomed. The Assyrians and Babylonians would destroy it, and it would never reappear until the time of the Hasmoneans, the second and first centuries B.C. The Jews would have to live without such a tyrant as Solomon. But what about the promise to David and his house? With the demise of Hebrew nationalism it withered away. Only when it was truly spiritualized and given flesh in Jesus Christ, did it come to be established before Yahweh forever.

Account of Solomon's Reign
Chapters 3–11

Solomon's Divine Legitimation (3:1–15)

Bibliography

Albright, W. F. "The High Places in Ancient Palestine." VTSup 4 (1957) 243–58. Barrick, W. B. "What Do We Really Know about 'High-places?'" SEÅ 45 (1980) 50–57. Fensham, F. C. "Legal Aspects of the Dream of Solomon." Fourth World Congress of Jewish Studies, I. Jerusalem: World Union of Jewish Studies, 1967. Fernandez, S. I. "Geographica: 'El Gran Bamah' de Gabaón." Miscellanea Biblica B. Ubach. Montserrat, 1953. Herrmann, S. "Die Königsnovelle in Ägypten und Israel." Wissenschaftliche Zeitschrift der Karl Marx-Universität 3 (1953–54) 51–62. Kaufmann, Y. "The Opening of the Stories on the Reign of Solomon." Studies in the Bible, Presented to M. H. Segal (Heb.). Jerusalem: Kiryath Sepher, 1964. Malamat, A. "Aspects of the Foreign Policies of David and Solomon." JNES 22 (1963) 1–17. Reymond, P. "Le rêve de Salomon (1 Rois 3:4–15)." Maqqél shâqédh. Hommage à W. Vischer. Montpelier, 1960. Zalevsky, S. "The Revelation of God to Solomon in Gibeon" (Heb.). Tarbiz 42 (1973) 215–58.

Translation

[1] *And Solomon made a marriage alliance with Pharaoh king of Egypt by taking Pharaoh's daughter; and he brought her to the City of David until he could finish building his palace and* [a] *the temple of Yahweh,* [b] *and Jerusalem's encircling wall.* [c] [2] *However,* [a] *the people were sacrificing at the country shrines, for a temple for Yahweh's name* [b] *had not been built prior to those days.* [c]

[3] *And Solomon loved Yahweh, walking in the statutes of David his father; however, at the country shrines he did sacrifice and burn incense.* [4] *And the king* [a] *went to Gibeon to sacrifice there—for it was* [b] *the leading country shrine;* [b] *a thousand burnt offerings Solomon offered upon* [c] *that altar.* [c] [5] *At Gibeon Yahweh appeared to Solomon in a dream at night, and God* [a] *said, "Ask what I shall give you."* [6] *And Solomon said, "Thou hast performed with* [a] *David my father great fidelity, just as he walked before thee in faithfulness, righteousness, and uprightness of heart toward thee; and thou hast observed on his behalf this great fidelity: to appoint* [b] *for him a son* [b] *to sit on his throne, as at present;* [7] *so now, O my God:* [a] *thou hast made thy servant rule in the place of David my father; but I am just a young lad; I don't know* [b] *how to go out or come in,* [b] [8] *and thy servant is in the midst of thy people, whom thou hast chosen, a people so great that they cannot be numbered;* [a] [9] *so give thy servant a* [a] *receptive heart for judging* [a] *thy people,* [b] *discriminating between good and evil, for who is able to judge this thy difficult people?"*

^{10} And it was good in Yahweh's ^{a} eyes that Solomon requested this thing. ^{11} And God ^{a} said to him, "Because you requested ^{b} this thing and did not request for yourself many days, and did not request for yourself riches, and did not request the life of your enemies, but requested for yourself ^{c} ability to discriminate in perceiving justice, ^{c} ^{12} behold, I will act according to your word; ^{a} behold, I give you a wise and understanding heart, one like you ^{b} will not have been before you, nor after you will any arise like you; ^{13} but even what you did not request I give you, both riches and honor, in which none will equal you ^{a} among kings; ^{b} ^{14} and if you walk in my paths, keeping my statutes and my commandments, as David your father walked, then I will lengthen your days."

^{15} Then Solomon awoke, and behold it was a dream! And he went ^{a} to Jerusalem and stood ^{b} before the ark of the covenant of Yahweh. ^{bc} And he offered burnt offerings and performed peace offerings, and made a feast ^{d} for all his servants.

Notes

1.a. MT and G^L. Out of piety G^B omits reference to "his place," lest its mention precede that of Yahweh's temple.

1.b. Underscoring this point, G (2:35^c) adds "at first."

1.c. G (2:35^c) adds "in seven years he made and completed it"; cf. 6:37.

2.a. MT. Connecting directly to 2:46^1, G^L omits "however"; G^B omits "however the people."

2.b. MT and G^L preserve the expected Dtr terminology, reduced in G^B to "for Yahweh."

2.c. MT, restyled in G^{BL} to "until now."

4.a. MT is preferred on form-critical grounds to G^L "Solomon" and to G^B's omission.

4.b-b. MT, which does not hesitate to use the term בָּמָה for a legitimate Yahweh shrine. G^{BL} avoid this with the substitution, "high and great."

4.c-c. MT. G^{BL} borrow from v 5 *init* for the reading, "the altar in Gibeon."

5.a. MT אלהים, *lectio difficilior*, is antecedently preferable on literary-critical grounds to G^{BL} κύριος = Heb. יהוה "Yahweh."

6.a. Chr omits MT and G^{BL} "thy servant."

6.b-b. MT. G^{BL} "his son," a stylistic improvement on the lapidary Heb.

7.a. MT and G^B "Yahweh my god"; G^L "my god Yahweh." The variance in order, together with literary source-analysis, argues for "my God" as original, as in v 5.

7.b-b. Lit., "going or coming" (gerundive); G^{BL} read conjunctive *wāw*'s as *yôd*'s, i.e., pronominal suffixes.

8.a. So G^B; MT adds the familiar parallel, "or counted for multitude." G^L adds "for multitude, or be counted."

9.a-a. MT. Lit., "a listening heart for judging." G^B structures this to clarify the meaning: "a heart to hear and judge," while G^L refines the clarification even further: "intelligence to listen."

9.b. MT. G^{BL} add explicative "in righteousness."

10.a. MT אדנ׳ "Lord" is an indubitable scribal substitution for "Yahweh," supported in this Dtr addition by G^{BL} κύριος "Lord."

11.a. MT אלהים is original over against G^{BL} κύριος "Lord", normalizing to the dominant redactional יהוה "Yahweh"; see vv 5, 7.

11.b. MT. "From me," added before (G^B) or following (G^L) "this thing," is explicative.

11.c-c. Lit., "to understand hearing (= perceiving) justice"; cf. v 9.

12.a. G, Syr, Tg, sing deserve preference over MT pl. The Vrs. show the classical Heb. style.

12.b. MT אשר "which", omitted in G, requires a comparison to לב "heart," rather than, as intended, to the person addressed (Solomon); it has probably been drawn into the text under the influence of אשר "which" in v 13.

13.a. Omitting איש "man" (G ἀνήρ), appearing in variant order in MT and G.

13.b. G^B (cf. G^L); MT adds "all your days" under the influence of v. 14.

15.a. MT, G. Chr adds "Solomon went to the country shrine that is in Gibeon."

15.b-b. MT. For ideological reasons, G^BL add "facing the altar which stands" prior to "before the ark," etc., since in Jewish piety only a high priest was allowed to approach the ark. The term for facing is a literalism, κατὰ πρόσωπον "according to (the) face."

15.c. MT אדני is a scribal alteration for יהוה; cf. v 10.

15.d. G^BL "great feast for himself and."

Form/Structure/Setting

Extract from the Book of Solomon's Acts (1): his Egyptian marriage, 3:1 [Expansion, 2]
A narrative of regal legitimation
[Dtr: Framework interpretation, 3]
   1. The divine offer
     a. The occasion: regular worship at Gibeon, v 4aαb
[Expansion, v 4aβ]
[Dtr introduction, v 5a]
     b. The divine address, v 5b
   2. Solomon's reply
     a. Recall of divine fidelity to David, v 6aα
[Dtr: David's deservingness, 6aβ; Divine fidelity, v 6b]
     b. Request for a perceptive heart
       (1) Solomon's appointment, v 7a
       (2) His inexperience, v 7b
[Dtr: Responsibility for the numerous elect, v 8]
       (3) The perceptive heart and its purpose, v 9a
       (4) Motive: The onus of governing, v 9b
[Dtr: The divine approval, v 10]
   3. The divine response
     a. Promise of a wise and understanding heart, vv 11aα, 12b
[Dtr: Reasons for granting the request, vv 11aβb, 12aα; Solomon's unparalleled distinction, v 12abβ]
     b. Promise of riches and honor, v 13a
[Dtr: Solomon's unparalleled distinction, 13b; Conditional promise of a long life, v 14]
   4. Solomon's reaction
     a. Apprehension of the dream as revelation, v 15a
[Dtr: His return to the Jerusalem shrine, v 15bα]
     b. Appropriate celebration, v 15bβ

As the responsible redactor for this material, Dtr begins to build upon the foregoing account of Solomon's accession to the kingship. Tradition recalls two very special features about this king: his wisdom and his wealth. Both were to be employed to good effect in Solomon's greatest achievement, the building of the temple, but it is necessary to relate first how he got these gifts and how he governed his realm. The tradition about Solomon's wisdom and wealth was not generated out of sheer fancy, because he truly was astute enough in his administration to organize tribute and taxation beyond anything theretofore seen, vastly enriching the coffers of his realm. Nevertheless, the reader who has just finished with 1 Kgs 1–2 will be surprised by the mild, benevolent, and pious ruler of the following chapters. Can this be the same Solomon who used his so-called "wisdom" (2:6, 9) to wage a petty vendetta against brave warriors and a faithful priest, in order to defeat his brother in a struggle for the throne? Dtr recognizes this question, perhaps, and eagerly seizes upon an ancient legitimation narrative, together with a popular anecdote about a judicial decision concerning two harlots, to show how (1) Solomon got his true wisdom (along with riches and honor) and (2) how he demonstrated it. The first story, imaginative as it was, was indeed originally about Solomon, whereas the second was not about him at all.

We designate the narrative in 1 Kgs 3:4-15 as a legitimation story or legend. In the *Introduction* we have said what a legend is: it is an imaginative story exemplifying certain virtues and offered as an example for others. In general, a legend may or may not contain historical elements. This does not matter, for the legend does not intend to communicate historical fact. If there happen to be historical elements present, these are incidental; they are part of the background. Now, such stories were told to legitimize the prophets and to sanctify shrines; at the proper place in this commentary we will have an opportunity to bring these kinds of story under close scrutiny. The present passage shows us that there were also legitimation stories about the kings. Siegfried Herrmann has enriched our understanding of them through his important study of accession stories in ancient Egypt (*Wissenschaftliche Zeitschrift* 3 [1953–54] 51–62). Historically speaking, it is quite possible, and even probable, that Solomon did go to Gibeon to seek and receive a night-revelation. The story about it aims, however, to show that Solomon's wisdom, riches, and honor came from God and not from man. In a sense, this is the missing story concerning Solomon's charismatic empowerment. Wisdom, riches, and honor may seem rather worldly, but the vast abundance of them that this particular king possessed was seen as self-demonstrating evidence that he was indeed the one empowered of the Lord.

There is no place in 1 Kgs where Dtr has so massively intervened in his source material. This is strictly a religious piece, yet its directness and simplicity tempted Dtr to invent extensive theologizings upon it. The work of Dtr can be recognized mainly from his familiar tone of moralizing harmonization, but in this case also from the fact that the original Gibeon narrative uses the divine title "God" while Dtr sticks to "Yahweh." V 2 is a late archeological gloss, thus v 3 is Dtr's first insertion; the statement that Solomon loved Yahweh is meant as a corrective to the notice about that king's suspect marriage mentioned in v 1. In preparation for the Gibeon story, Dtr next acknowledges that Solomon did actually worship at the country shrines (a practice which usually receives his severe censure; cf. 14:22–24). Another late gloss like that of v 2 appears in v 4a, disrupting the story's introductory exposition to the effect that Solomon was worshiping at Gibeon according to his faithful custom; then, before the narrative can introduce God's speech, Dtr spells out the obvious fact that a theophany is occurring (v 5a). In v 6, Solomon's mention of God's great fidelity to David sets Dtr to expounding on the meaning of David's faithfulness to God and God's fidelity to him in providing him with a successor. Following Solomon's declaration of incompetence (v 7), Dtr inserts a corrective statement about the people (v 8) anticipatory of the narrative's own complaint in v 9 that the people were "difficult." The story continues next with its report of God's reply (vv 11–13), but Dtr intrudes at three further points with a moralizing interpretation of Solomon's reticence (vv 11aβb, 12aα), two remarks about Solomon's unparalleled distinction (vv 12abβ, 13b), and a statement of Yahweh's condition for a long life (v 14). In the story, the finale is strikingly brief (v 15), but this is split in two by Dtr's cautionary note that Solomon immediately went to Jerusalem and stood before the ark (v 15bα), thus nullifying the original narrative's point that Solomon worshiped right there at Gibeon in thanksgiving for this momentous revelation.

The final product of Dtr's extensive interpolations can hardly appeal to our aesthetic instincts. One point in Dtr's favor is the evident reverence that he feels for the received text of his source material. He does not create his new version by effacing or rewriting the original source, but simply by adding his own remarks to it.

The redactional analysis that we have offered allows one to isolate the original regal legitimation story, and its structural analysis in turn confirms the correctness of our redactional analysis. When one sees that there is a meaningful place within the original structure for references to David's fidelity (v 6aα) and to Solomon's ruling in the place of David (v 7), one is able to avoid the mistake of those critics who assign these materials to Dtr simply because they speak of the David-to-Solomon succession. What Dtr does in both instances is add an appropriate-sounding comment of his own (vv 6aβb, 8). The original legitimation story has four subelements, varying the subject in an alternating pattern: God, Solomon, God, Solomon: (1) God appears to a waiting Solomon; (2) Solomon admits inadequacy and requests a wise and understanding heart; (3) God grants this along with riches and honor; (4) Solomon celebrates the revelation in a festival of thanksgiving. One notes the almost lapidary brevity, the tightness of construction, in which not a single word is wasted. Unabashedly, the narrative tells that Solomon had gone to Gibeon to worship (verb in imperfect *wāw*-consecutive, common at the beginning of a new narrative), where he commonly and habitually worshiped (verb in repetitive or durative imperfect). He is named "king" at the beginning (later regularly "Solomon") according to MT, the superior reading, because the entire narrative has to do with his kingship. While he is in an attitude of devout anticipation, he hears God invite him to make a request ("God," אלהים, is attested by superior readings in vv 5, 7, 11). Solomon's reply involves two elements: (1) a complaint about the difficulty of ruling as his father David had, and (2) a request for "a receptive heart for judging" the people.

This legitimation story was destined to be cherished not only during Solomon's reign but by successive generations of his sons. The "wisdom" that Solomon requested in the dream was a pragmatic skill for managing his autocratic administration, but in the course of time it stimulated also the development of the tradition that he was the wise man *par excellence*, encyclopaedic in his knowledge and unparalleled in his perception of the truth (so Dtr in v 12; 5:9–14, 26 [Eng. 4:29–34, 5:12]; 10:1–10, 23; cf. also Prov 1:1, Eccl 1:1). Thus Solomon's wisdom came to be "proverbial"; so too his riches and his honor, the like of which were never to be seen again. The story was eventually employed, with extensive modifications, by Dtr for the purpose of bridging the serious gap between the crude opportunist of chap. 2 and the wise and pious administrator presented in chaps. 4–11. So seriously does Dtr commit himself to a favorable portrait of Solomon's wisdom that he is not able to deny it when, in chap. 11, he is obliged to report this king's apostasy. Dtr's explanation there will be, not that Solomon ceases to be wise, but that his many wives have turned away his heart! Wisdom, in this definition, has nothing to do with the attitudes and affections of the heart! Does one discern in this an incipient externalization of religion? It is not, in any case, inconsistent with Dtr's redactional additions here in chap. 3, where the legitimation story identifies God's gracious revelation as the source of Solomon's wisdom, but Dtr's dressed-up version makes the right form of religion the actual source of that wisdom.

Comment

1–3 "Solomon made a marriage alliance": the root חתן refers to having or making a close relationship with someone through marriage. "With Pharaoh king of Egypt": "Pharaoh" transliterates an Egyptian word meaning "king," but the narrator takes it as a proper name. J. Gray (119) is convinced by, and M. Noth (49) accepts as a probable solution, Montet's and Malamat's identification of this Pharaoh as Siamun, next-to-last ruler of the Egyptian twenty-first dynasty, on the basis of his known incursions into the Palestinian coastal region. "Taking Pharaoh's daughter": only marriage can be meant, for a king's daughter could receive no status lower than princess or queen; that the arrangement was mainly political, securing Egypt as ally and protector, is generally agreed. "Brought her to the City of David": Solomon did not try to disguise her presence but presented her at his capital with full honors and public recognition; the name, "City of David," taken in 2:10 from the official chronicles for Dtr's death-notice concerning David, may have had general currency at the time of the United Monarchy and reflects the historical fact that the city actually was David's property because his own men had captured it (2 Sam 5:6–9). "Until he could finish": the structures listed (palace, temple, wall) had priority over a separate residence for the Egyptian queen, but for reasons unknown to us, a residence outside the city was eventually built for her (9:24); the Greek translators, offended by the notion of a heathen woman actually residing in the holy city, have rearranged the text in an effort to avoid it (cf. D. W. Gooding, *Relics of Ancient Exegesis*, 9–12).

"However," v 2: omitted in G, its very difficulty in MT is probable evidence of its originality; this word has an exceptive force scarcely demanded by the preceding context, but it introduces a late gloss about worship in the country shrines in the place of the temple precipitated by the mention of the temple in v 1. "The country shrines," הבמות: on the ambivalent attitude of various biblical writers toward these installations, see the *Introduction*. From the root meaning, "back," traditional exegesis has developed the translation, "high places," but there is nothing in the passages that refer to them to justify the notion that they were necessarily on hills, were open-air sanctuaries out in the country, or were the scene of frivolity and idolatry. They were, on the contrary, located in towns and cities, but generally a distance removed from Jerusalem and its temple (see now W. B. Barrick, *SEÅ* 45 [1980] 50–57), hence our translation, "country shrines." "A temple for Yahweh's name": this characteristic Deuteronomic locution makes it probable that v 2 is a gloss out of the deuteronomistic school, though later than v 3. "Prior to those days": a giveaway as to the very late date of this gloss; this Heb. expression occurs elsewhere only with reference to "Nehushtan" in 2 Kgs 18:4, where it is supported by *G* (G^B = *Kaige*), but here G^{BL} go their own way, reading a Heb. "until now."

"Solomon loved Yahweh": the root אהב "love" is prominent in Deut (twenty-three occurrences, e.g., 6:5, 10:12, 30:16, 20); with reference to the Deity, it implies moral concern and commitment, rather than mere affection. "The statutes of David his father": what is meant is Yahweh's statutes which David had enjoined upon Solomon in the Dtr interpolation at 2:2–4. "However, at the country shrines he did sacrifice . . .": Dtr has to admit this, however distasteful to his ideology, in order to make use of the Gibeon story; the very fact that the legend does take place at Gibeon proves that it is very early, virtually contemporary with the event itself, because if it were of late origin this element would never have been inserted.

4–15 "The king went to Gibeon to sacrifice there": he journeyed the seven miles northwestward to Gibeon rather than worship at Jerusalem's tent-shrine (2:28, 30; cf 2 Sam 6:17); it is noteworthy that the parallel passage in 2 Chr 1:3–13 paraphrases this in such a way as to bring Gibeon inside the Jerusalem city-precincts (something that now has in fact been accomplished in the outward extension of Jerusalem's city limits). The city of Gibeon has been identified with modern El-Jib, not only through the etymological similarity of names, but also through J. B. Pritchard's discovery, in his excavation of this site, of jar handles stamped with GB'N, "Gibeon" (*BASOR* 160 [1960] 2–6). No shrine was actually found in this excavation, hence the biblical reference is very likely intended for the nearby hilltop shrine at *Nebi-Samwil.* "The leading country shrine": this is certainly true in fact, but the expansion has an apologetic purpose, viz., to show that Solomon's worship was justified by the special prominence of the site. "A thousand burnt-offerings . . . upon that altar": this gross exaggeration serves the same purpose as the emphasis on the identity of the altar; by elaborate and persistent cultivation of this holy site, Solomon had put himself in a position to receive a revelation from the God whose presence had sanctified it.

"At Gibeon": emphatic in foremost position, this superfluous identification serves Dtr's desire to underscore the location. "Yahweh appeared . . . in a dream at night": v 5, identifying the vehicle of revelation, is meant to be climactic, but Dtr pedantically gives this away prematurely, stating also the obvious fact that it came to pass at night. "And God said": see *Notes.* The old Gibeon legend, like parts of the Pentateuch and many contemporary sources, uses אלהים "God" instead of "Yahweh"; here its effect is to make the revelation seem more mysterious, for the covenant God is left unnamed. "Ask what I shall give you": the interrogative introducing a relative clause, which constitutes the predicate in this sentence, functions as pronoun object to the imperative; Solomon's asking determines his receiving, and no request is beyond the capacity of God. This pious sentiment articulates the major premise of the entire story, viz., that Solomon may ask whatever he desires, but because he requests only a modest gift, God gives him what he does not ask.

"Thou hast performed with David my father great fidelity": גדול חסד refers to the numerous instances in which God had rescued David from trouble and supplied all his need. "He walked in faithfulness (אמת), righteousness (צדקה), and uprightness of heart (ישרת לבב) toward thee": this refers to trustworthiness, honorableness, and correct behavior, which Dtr sees as ground for deserving Yahweh's responding חסד; "the great fidelity" which Yahweh had performed, according to Dtr, in the appointment of Solomon, not the divine favors to David intended in the underlying story. "Appoint for him a son to sit . . .": LXX makes this more specific with "his son." "As at present" כיום הזה is widely used by Dtr in place of עתה "now."

"So now" ועתה, as in 2:5 and elsewhere, is a consequential link from a statement of the situation to a declaration of appropriate action. "Thou hast made thy servant rule . . .": this in effect introduces a conditional sentence in which the above is the protasis and v 9 the apodosis. God has made Solomon ruler; now let him provide Solomon with what he needs to rule. "I am just a young lad," נער קטן: this is the retarding element in what corresponds to a call narrative (cf. Jer 1:6). The reference to tender youth is certainly a convention and an exaggeration because, after forty years of rule, Solomon is said to have had a forty-one-year-old son (11:42, 14:21), and hence had to have been a married adult at the time of his accession. "I don't know how to go out or come in": carry on daily business (cf. 1 Sam 18:16).

"Thy servant is in the midst of thy people, whom thou hast chosen": a very clear articulation of the doctrine of election, the cornerstone of Deuteronomic theology; e.g., in Deut 7:6–8, Dtr's "in the midst of" means to subordinate Solomon's personal election to the election of Israel as a people. "A people so great that they cannot be numbered": this would not have been true in David's and Solomon's day (cf. 2 Sam 24:1–9), and probably not in the time of the deuteronomist, either; Dtr means this as a laudatory superlative in explanation of the underlying legend's "difficult people," v 9.

"So give thy servant a receptive heart," לב שמע, lit., "a hearing" or "listening heart." The Hebrews meant by "heart" also what we call the mind, particularly when the intellectual aspect is prominent. One must be attentive, receptive, and discriminating if he is to render true justice. T. N. D. Mettinger (*King and Messiah*, 238–46) argues that the "hearing heart" of Solomon is meant as a form of "charisma." H. Brunner claims that the image is Egyptian (*TLZ* 79 [1954] 697–700) contra S. Herrmann ("Steuerruder, Waage, Herz und Zunge in ägyptischen Bildreden," *Zeitschrift für ägyptische Sprache und Altertumswissenschaft*, 79 [1954] 106–15). "For judging thy people, discriminating between good and evil": it is precisely the ability to distinguish good from evil, truth from falsehood, that is indispensable in the administration of justice. "For who is able to judge this thy difficult people (הכבד הזה את־עמך)": not only was the civil life of Israel filled with strife and contention toward the end of David's reign (cf. 2 Sam 15:1–4), but the political situation likewise continued unstable. This prayer was definitely answered in the sense that Solomon did find the means to suppress all outward show of rebelliousness to the end of his reign.

"It was good in Yahweh's eyes": Dtr spells out the obvious. "Because you . . . did not request for yourself many days . . . riches . . . the life of your enemies": although riches (עשׁר) are mentioned in the underlying stratum at v 13, along with honor, longevity and revenge are not; thus Dtr's list of unwanted items is not entirely congruous with the items listed in the legend ("I will lengthen your days" in v 14 represents a belated effort to make up for this). "But requested for yourself ability to discriminate in perceiving justice": this affirmative clause, following the negatives, actually duplicates the initial affirmative clause; Dtr paraphrases לב שׁמע "a receptive heart" (v 9) with his more complex הבין לשׁמע משׁפט "ability to discriminate in perceiving justice" (v 11). "Behold, I give you a wise and understanding heart" (לב חכם ונבון): the adjective נבון "understanding" responds to the infinitive of purpose להבין "to discriminate" in v 9, but we have not encountered the active חכם "wise." Though this word has a wide semantic range, it here signifies the judicious administration of justice for which Solomon has prayed (cf. the more ignoble, though no less pragmatic meaning in chap. 2). The present use of the term is unmistakably positive, and constitutes the historical point of origin for the tradition about Solomon's great wisdom (see our discussion on chap. 4 regarding Noth's and Scott's analyses of the later development of this tradition). "I give you . . . riches and honor": these are the blessings of free, unsolicited grace; Solomon's God is sovereignly uncontrolled in his generosity. "In which none will equal you": Dtr would perhaps add to Solomon's praise beyond what God himself had given! "If you walk . . . then I will lengthen your days": see above on Dtr's intent; a long life is the promise that the Deuteronomic/deuteronomistic school offered to faithful performers of Yahweh's commandments (Exod 20:12; cf. Deut 5:16).

"Behold, it was a dream!": that is, a revelation; it would certainly have effect and come true. "He went to Jerusalem and stood before the ark of the covenant of Yahweh": this is Dtr's special terminology, his ideology too. The ark was there (cf. 2 Sam 6:17), but the idea of Solomon standing before it must have seemed daring for later generations, for whom this was a priestly prerogative. "Burnt offerings": the offering of an entire animal in fire. "Peace offerings": a communal sacrifice in which the worshipers consumed part of the animal. "A feast for all his servants": a banquet of rejoicing, symbolizing that all who waited on Solomon were destined to share in his blessings.

Explanation

Not everything in 1 Kgs 3:1–15 is exemplary for adherents of the Jewish and Christian faiths. This pericope contains elements from ancient Israel's cultural heritage. Their function in this material is to provide part of the narrative background.

We take note of Solomon's political pragmatism as expressed in v 1. This report from the Book of the Acts of Solomon is virtually contemporary with the event recorded and has every claim to absolute historicity. The Solomon that we see here, eager to marry an Egyptian princess in exchange for political favors, is credibly similar to the Solomon of chap. 2. In any event, what he does is simply recorded as historical information and has no paradigmatic value. The text neither praises it nor blames it, though, as we have noted, Dtr does think it useful to assure the reader that, after all, Solomon did love Yahweh and did remain orthodox in his religion (v 3). The modern reader is inclined to ask whether Solomon's "love" and his walking in the statutes of David were not purely formal, whether Solomon's religiosity was not entirely external, for there is nothing worse than a punctilious piety that does not proceed from a truly loving and truly devout inner self.

A critical note must also be placed alongside the legitimation story's statement that Solomon traveled a considerable distance to offer innumerable sacrifices in order to elicit a revelation from God. Diligence, generosity, and the acceptance of physical inconvenience may sometimes be tokens of true devotion, yet when we see such a display we can hardly suppress the query whether the worshiper is just using God for his own self-glorification. Using God comes naturally to the devotees of shrine religion. It is typical of all heathen worship that the gods be worshiped at shrines, and that sacrifices be carried out in order to move them to favorable action on the worshiper's behalf. In spite of a growing awareness in Israelite piety that Yahweh is purely spiritual and freely personalistic, and that he appears to his people wherever he will, there were an abundance of local shrines in the land, taken over mainly from the dispossessed Canaanite population. Yahweh was worshiped at these shrines, but with the ever-present danger of tying him down and domesticating his worship. This is clearly what had occurred at Gibeon, the residence of a subservient people (Josh 9) whose shrine had been taken over by the Israelites. Being accustomed as he apparently was to shrine religion, it can be no surprise that before long Solomon began a program to build Yahweh a "house" in Jerusalem. Surely the intent would be to honor Yahweh, but the temple was destined also to serve the pride and vanity of Judah's kings.

Non-normative for us is the intimation that Solomon might legitimately have asked for longevity and revenge (v 11). According to chap. 2, Solomon had already taken revenge on some of his enemies, and the throne-succession historian had of course interpreted this as from God, yet Dtr withholds this as something deserving God's answer, even while admitting Solomon's right to ask for it. Solomon had a right, no doubt, to request "many days," and Dtr has God promise this to him in v 14 on the condition of circumspect obedience. The NT has taught Christians not to seek revenge (Rom 12:17–20), yet it is legitimate for them to ask for life and to acknowledge "many days" as God's gift. Only, one is not to take it as a token of God's disfavor if sickness or calamity should shorten one's days instead. Other things deserving notice are Dtr's point that Solomon would succeed in observing Yahweh's laws if he only acted just like his father David (parental example), and also Dtr's point that God is at work in important human events, appointing the great ones of the earth (v 6).

But these are incidental. To find the passage's most central witness, the reader should carefully study the structure of the original legitimation story. This structure is dramatic in its simplicity: God offers, Solomon responds; God replies, Solomon worships. What does God offer, and how does he make his offer? "Ask what I shall give you." God's giving will correspond to Solomon's asking. There are no limits except those that our own faith imposes. Solomon can never ask more than God is willing to give. Yet if God is to give, Solomon must ask, and he will be tested by what he asks for. Our requests reveal what sort of persons we are, and Solomon's request for a "receptive heart" showed that he was ready to receive all that God could offer.

Now, the portrait of Solomon that we are here seeing differs significantly from the vengeful opportunist in chap. 2 and the political pragmatist of 3:1. If this implies that the real historical Solomon was not actually like the Solomon of the legitimation story, then so be it. The story is meant to be exemplary rather than literally factual. It tells us about the ideal Solomon, about Solomon as he ought to have been, not necessarily as he was in historical reality. Perhaps the two were not irreconcilably divorced, for elements of the real and the ideal are present in every person.

It is noteworthy that Solomon's reply anticipates two special things from God: (1) that as God has performed great fidelity with David the father he will now be generous in taking care of Solomon the son; and (2) that since God has appointed Solomon to rule in David's place, God will now give him all that is needed for carrying out this responsibility. Knowing that these gifts will have to come from God, Solomon speaks of himself as only a young lad, unable to "go out or come in." Meanwhile, Solomon declares that God's people are "difficult," so his plea is for that openness of heart and mind that will identify good and evil when he is obliged as king to adjudicate among them. Thus the request is for no miracle, but for that rare gift of relating perceptively to human persons in their strivings, helping them identify the good and evil in every situation and encouraging them always to choose the good.

The King's Wise Act of Justice   (3:16–28)

Bibliography

Nestle, E. "Miscellen.—3. I Könige 3,22." *ZAW* 26 (1906) 163–64. **Rupprecht, K.** "Eine vergessene Konjektur von A. Klostermann zu I Reg 3,27." *ZAW* 88 (1976) 415–18.

Translation

16 Then two harlotrous women approached[a] the king:[b] they stood before him; **17** and the first woman said, "Please, my lord, I and this woman are living in the same house, and I gave birth[a] in the house. **18** And it so happened that on the third day after my delivery this woman also gave birth. Now we were together,[a] without any stranger with us;[b] there were only we two in the house. **19** But this woman's son died one night when she lay upon him, **20** and she got up in the middle of the night, snatched my son from alongside me [a]while your maidservant was sleeping,[a] and laid him in her bosom, while her dead son she put in my bosom. **21** Then I got up in the morning to nurse my son and[a] he was dead; but[b] I took a good look at him in the morning, and behold he was not my son, the one whom I had borne!" **22** And the other woman said, "No, but my son is the living one, and her son is the dead one!"[a] Thus they spoke before the king;

23 and the king said, [a]"This one is[a] saying, 'This is my son, the living one, and your[b] son is the dead one,' while [c]this one is[c] saying, 'No, but [d]your son is the dead one and my son is the living one!'"[d] **24** So the king said, "Fetch me[a] a sword." And they brought a sword before the king. **25** Then the king said, "Sever the live baby into two parts and give a half to one[a] and a half to the other."[bc] **26** And the woman whose son was the living one spoke to the king, for her maternal emotions were stirred on behalf of her son, and she said, "Please, my lord, let them give her the baby,[a] but by no means kill him," while the other was saying, "Let him be neither mine nor yours;[b] sever him!"[c] **27** And the king made response and said, "Give her[a] the baby,[b] and by no means kill him; she is his mother." **28** And all Israel heard about the[a] judgment that the king had rendered; and they revered the king because they perceived that divine wisdom was in him for performing justice.

Notes

16.a. MT, which G[BL] "appeared" (ὤφθησαν) seeks to clarify by removing a verb of motion just prior to a verb of position.

16.b. MT and G[B]. G[L] adds "Solomon," furthering Dtr's redactional device (see *Comment*) for attributing this anonymous tale to Israel's king.

17.a. G[L]. G[B], "we give birth," and MT, "I gave birth with her," are anticipatory normalizations.

18.a. MT. G[BL] add explicative "by ourselves."

18.b. G[BL]. MT adds "in the house" under the influence of the following.

20.a-a. MT presents a text offering an indispensable reason for what had occurred. G[BL] omit.

21.a. G^BL. MT "and behold" ignores the implication that the mother did not look at her baby until full morning light.

21.b. MT. G^BL "and behold" is superfluous before "and behold" later in the verse.

22.a. G^B. MT and G^L fill out the dialogue with "But this one said, 'No, but your son is the dead one and my son is the live one!'"

23.a-a. MT. G^BL "to them, 'You are . . . .'" Gr. styles as second-person address.

23.b. MT. G^BL "this one's."

23.c-c. MT. G^BL "you are."

23.d-d. MT. G^BL restyles by reversing the order: "My son is the living one and your son is the dead one."

24.a. MT and G^L. G^B omits.

25.a. MT. G^BL "this one" endeavors greater dramatic impact by pointing to the person intended.

25.b. MT. G^BL "that one": see 25.a.

25.c. MT, G^B. G^L carries the story further with the addition, "and the dead one likewise sever, and give it to the two of them."

26.a. G^BL. MT "live baby" is explicative.

26.b. MT. G^BL "hers" depicts the wrongdoer as speaking objectively, in the third person, of her adversary, whereas the MT has her address her directly, in the second person.

26.c. MT and G^L. G^B's omission of the pronoun object is a haplography from the initial *wāw* in v 27.

27.a. MT. G^BL omit the pronoun object and add the explicative, "to the one who said, 'Give it to her.'" Cf. Burney, xxx.

27.b. G^BL. MT adds "live"; cf. v 26.

28.a. MT. G^BL add "this" (explicative).

Form/Structure/Setting

An illustrative anecdote: judgment for an abused harlot
1. The dispute
   a. Introduction: approach to the king, v 16
   b. The speech of the first woman
      (1) The situation: birth of the two babies, vv 17–18
      (2) Substitution of one baby for another
         (a) An uncaring death, v 19
         (b) A heartless theft, v 20
      (3) Apprehension of the wrong, v 21
   c. The speech of the second woman, v 22a
2. The resolution
   a. The situation: indecisive testimony, vv 22b–23
   b. A threat to kill the live baby
      (1) The king's command
         (a) To produce a sword, v 24
         (b) To divide the live baby, v 25
      (2) The replies of the two women, v 26
   c. The king's decision, v 27
Conclusion: Israel's favorable reaction, v 28

It is Dtr who introduces this story with the temporal adverb אָז (see *Introduction*). This directly links the narrative of God's gift of wisdom to Solomon with an anecdote illustrating the employment of that gift. The MT, which is clearly superior here to the LXX, does not employ the proper name, leaving the king in question quite anonymous were it not for Dtr's linking adverb at the beginning.

If this anecdote actually were about Solomon, we would receive a charmingly favorable glimpse of his character. We would see him as benign in the exercise of his authority, insightful and sympathetic in his understanding. The conclusion in v 28, composed specifically to give the anonymous anecdote as Israelite identification, summarizes this in its laudatory description, "divine wisdom was in him!" This would agree entirely with Dtr's sentiment as he chose this anecdote to illustrate Solomon's wisdom, and we can only marvel at his restraint in allowing the anecdote to stand as he had received it, without adding special touches to solidify the identification with Solomon.

The exact wording of the anecdote may be Israelite, but the story itself comes out of international culture. Hugo Gressmann has identified no fewer than twenty-two stories of an abused mother and her endangered child in the folklores of various peoples. This appeared in his study, "Das salomonische Urteil," *Deutsche Rundschau* 130 (1907) 212ff. The most striking parallel is perhaps a Jātaka story from India, according to which a she-demon claims a child left on the river bank, and the deity threatens to tear the child apart when the mother demands it, but gives it to the mother when the mother refuses to accept half.

As related in our anecdote, the two harlots could have lived in any age and any country; it is only the ending that makes it Israelite. In spite of this ending, the king could be anyone. The situation is as common as human life itself. Nevertheless, and in spite of its striking generality, the anecdote is so touchingly realistic in its portrayal of human pathos that every reader has to identify with it. The harlots are not here to be ridiculed, but to be pitied and wept over. In her degradation and deprivation, the mother of the living child shows the lofty flight of the human spirit, the spirit of self-giving sacrifice on behalf of one beloved. The other harlot typifies the meanness of which the human spirit is capable. She can do nothing but hate, hate, hate, and comes up empty in the end.

I have called this "Judgment for an abused harlot." It is not really about two harlots, though there are two harlots in the story; it is about the harlot whose child was stolen from her, who ventures to appeal to the king, declaring herself willing to sacrifice her child to save him. If we read the text attentively we will discover how the structural outline illumines this intent. The basic structure is strikingly simple: (1) dispute; (2) resolution. The king does not do anything in part 1; on the other hand, the second harlot does nothing except contradict the first harlot in v 22a. Thus it is the first harlot who has the word from v 17 to v 21, and all that the reader needs to know about the case is stated here. The problem is, does this woman speak the truth, or has she stolen the other woman's baby and made up this story because that woman has snatched it back? This is the puzzle with which the reader (and the king) is left, as well as the central point of tension. In part 2 it is the king who holds center stage. He first announces his inability to find the truth in what the two women are telling him, then prepares to divide the living baby in two. One notes that the king does not tentatively propose this test to the two women, for they might think that he were teasing, or that he were offering a mere abstract possibility. No, they must be confronted with an emergency situation. They must be made to believe that he really will kill the baby in order to satisfy them both. Only in such a dire situation will the true mother plead to save the baby. So the sword is brought and the swordsman moves to do the king's command. It is then that the true mother cries out to give it to the other woman, while the second woman is saying, "Divide it!" Now the king has his answer; the true mother has been revealed.

Comment

16–22 "Two harlotrous women": this descriptive title, noun and adjective in the sing or pl, occurs with some frequency in the OT; so also the adjective alone, taking the place of the full expression. Although prostitution is disdained and condemned, some OT passages are unabashed in reporting a resort to prostitutes. Both secular and cultic prostitution were widespread in the ancient Near East. From a moral and sociological point of view, there was nothing that was worthy of praise in this institution. Ancient prostitutes were generally slaves, daughters who had been sold by their own parents. Otherwise they were poor women who had never had an opportunity to marry, or who had lost their husbands. The normal expectation for a woman was to be married and live in her husband's house, bearing his children. Women who had to support themselves by yielding to the lust of strangers, and whose children were destined to grow up as bastards and paupers, were wretched and altogether to be pitied. In our story, not only the one woman who had been aggrieved approached the king, but she and her adversary together. "They stood before him": they assumed an attitude of expectant waiting, subjecting themselves to his judgment; no mention is made of prostration (cf. 1:16), and we are to make no conclusion as to whether their social status prevented this, because the narrator may be omitting mention of it as an unimportant detail. "Please, my lord," בִּי אֲדֹנִי (cf. v 26): the simplest explanation of this striking idiom, which occurs fourteen times in the OT, is the one adopted by Gray (129) and Montgomery-Gehman (112) from A. M. Honeyman (*JAOS* [1944] 81–82) to the effect that בִּי is an elliptical imperative from the root אָבָה, "be willing." This would, however, be a feminine form, and in the Bible it is always a masculine "lord" or "Lord" (= God) who is addressed. Hence KB³, 117, follows L. Koehler and K. Marti (*ZAW* 36 [1916], 26–27, 246) and I. Lande, *Formelhafte Wendungen der Umgangsprache im AT* (1949) 16, in viewing it as an ellipsis for "Upon me, my lord, (come something too unpleasant to mention)."

"We were together, without any stranger . . . only we two": this is offered as essential substantiation for the speaker's story. It is important that the two women were together in the house, for otherwise no one but the first woman could have killed the baby. It is important that no "stranger," i.e., client, had been there, for then he might have killed the baby. "This woman's son died one night when she lay upon him": no doubt by smothering, though it seems strange that the baby did not cry out; in any event, the first woman is telling this by logical deduction, for she had not been awake to witness

it. "I got up in the morning . . . I took a good look at him in the morning":
the Heb. בקר "morning" is broad enough to refer to both the first crack
of dawn and the somewhat later moment when it became light enought to
look clearly at the dead baby. The story builds to a climax: first her baby
was dead; next the baby was not her baby! "He was not my son, the one
whom I had borne": a mother knows her own; since the second woman fully
understood that the first woman would not be fooled, brazenness is added
to knavery in her expectation that a judge will believe her denials and give
that woman's baby to her. "No, but . . . ," לא כי: because of the disjunctive
accent over the second word, E. Nestle (ZAW 26 [1906] 163–64) proposes
an unneeded emendation of the consonantal text.

23–28 "And the king said": to himself or to his advisors, but not to the
two women, in spite of the LXX, which makes him address the women directly
in v 23. "This one is saying . . . this one is saying": as if turning his head
to look at each one separately. "They brought a sword before the king":
this implies a swordsman to use the sword, for the king did not intend to
wield it himself (cf. v 25). "Sever the live baby . . . and give . . .": address
in the second person pl implies that several men would be involved in actually
cutting the baby in two and handing the parts to the two women. "Her maternal instincts were stirred": the verb כמר, "grow hot," "get excited," occurs
only in the niph. and, except in Lam 5:10, where "skin" is the subject, it
always has the subject רחמים (Gen 43:30, Hos 11:8, and here); the primary
meaning of רחם is "womb" and the pl means "maternal compassion." "While
the other was saying . . .": translating a participle by which the narrator
intends to subordinate the role of the second woman. "Neither mine nor
yours": thus MT depicting the second woman as speaking to the first woman,
but G "nor hers" implies that she is addressing the king. "And the king
made response and said": finding difficulty with ויען המלך ויאמר, E. Rupprecht (ZAW 88 [1976] 415–18) proposes an unnecessary emendation in the
text; the root ענה does not necessarily imply a verbal utterance, such as
would preclude "and said," but has the basic meaning, "respond." The two
verbs are useful together because they tell us (1) that the king reacted and
(2) that he spoke out to effectuate his reaction. "Give her the baby . . . she
is his mother": the king's first utterance is a command; his second is a formal
declaration, identifying which of the two women is actually telling the truth.

"And all Israel heard . . .": for the political well-being of the realm, it is
necessary that the whole populace hear about what its king has done; if he
will do this for two of his most despised subjects, he will surely do it for
"all Israel." "They revered the king": ויראו, misspelled as if from the root
ראה, under the influence of ירא, means to hold in dread, hence to honor,
respect, and revere. "Divine wisdom," חכמת אלהים: lit., "the wisdom of/
from God." This expression does not occur elsewhere in the OT, but the
Bible does have the idea that wisdom proceeds from God (cf. Prov 8:22–
31). In our anecdote the king is said to be like God because he has a godlike
wisdom and fearfulness. "For performing justice": משפט is a judicial decree,
a case to be judged, the act of judging, or a case that has received judicial
attention. This concluding phrase is precisely what our redactor, Dtr, would
be looking for in illustrating the operation of God's gift at Gibeon, "a receptive
heart for judging thy people, discriminating between good and evil" (v 9).

Explanation

The fact that the two mothers were prostitutes is important in this story (1) because it shows how the wise king would act on behalf of the very lowest of his subjects, (2) because a house of prostitution, with no man present to adjudicate a dispute, is a central premise to the narrative, and (3) because the common baseness of a life of prostitution forms the background for contrasting displays of self-sacrificing love and heartless cruelty. Otherwise the story does not moralize about prostitution. Nor does it moralize about the wretched behavior of the woman who stole the other woman's baby, lied about it to the king, and was glad to see the live baby's blood gush out rather than allow its true mother to have it. Nor, once again, does this story moralize about the summary execution of a helpless innocent (we are not to guess whether the king would have gone ahead with the execution if the true mother had not made her offer!). These are all realistic elements from ancient society, and any blame that may be intended remains implicit in the story itself.

The inescapable point of the whole story is its model of true motherhood: "Give her the baby, and by no means kill him; she is his mother!" In her speech to the king, the first woman expresses her grief at two of her profession's special sorrows. She has a child; it has no father, but she will love it dearly. The child is taken from her, she thinks, by death, God's mysterious and awful act. As she weeps in submission to God's will, she discovers a more dreadful terror: this is not her baby! Where is her baby then? The other woman has it, and now claims that it is hers. First the true mother was bereaved (so she thought), but now she had been robbed! She has to hear the taunts of the other woman, chiding her for sloth and carelessness in killing her child, when all the while it is that woman's child that has been killed. It is bad enough to have to give up one's little baby in death, but it is unthinkable that she should have to go on living in the same house with the evil woman who stole her baby, and now holds it fast in her bosom. Better to be bereaved by God than to be robbed by such a companion!

This true mother makes her appeal to the king, and naturally everything she says is contradicted. The king does not seem to be able to decide who is telling the truth. How shocked the mother is when she hears him call for a sword and order the baby—her precious child—hewn in two! Faced with the ultimate horror of actually seeing her own child killed, she blurts out her plea that her wicked partner be given her way. The choice now is between the claim of motherhood and the claim of life itself!

Thus the true mother finds herself willing to suffer even more in order to save her child's life, to lose her child in order to let it live. Here is substance, no doubt, for many a Mother's Day service, but we would impoverish ourselves if we did not recognize that it offers also a model for all kinds of human interrelations. Parents to children, husbands and wives to each other, brothers and sisters to each other, any person in close relationship to another, need to learn the danger of stifling another's life and spiritual growth by holding it too close to oneself. Important as the various human relationships may be, the survival and the integrity of the person being held in these relationships must always come first.

Unmistakably, the anecdote's central concern is about the wise king. After all, it is his cryptic order for execution that drives the true mother to disclose herself, and this is held up in the conclusion (v 28) as evidence for his "godlike" wisdom. This is, however, of little spiritual value for modern readers. We do not, after all, know this king, and we are not his subjects. The king's role is important to us only if we take it as an example for all who are called upon to render judgment on human motivations. These may be ministers, teachers, policemen, judges, psychologists; or they may be just anyone, professional or nonprofessional, on whom this responsibility comes to be placed. There are times when each may be called upon to judge, perhaps in drastic confrontation, who is "the true mother."

The Administration of Solomon's Empire (4:1—5:14 [Eng. 4:1-34])

Bibliography

Aharoni, Y. "The Solomonic Districts." *Tel Aviv* 3 (1976) 5–15. Albright, W. F. "The Administrative Divisions of Israel and Judah." *JPOS* 5 (1925) 17–54. Alt, A. "Israels Gaue unter Salomo." *Alttestamentliche Studien für R. Kittel.* BWANT I, 13, 1913 (= *Kleine Schriften zur Geschichte des Volkes Israel*, II [1953] 76–89). ———. "Die Weisheit Salomos." *TLZ* 76 (1951) 134–44 (= *Kleine Schriften* II 90–99). Dougherty, R. P. "Cuneiform Parallels to Solomon's Provisioning System." *AASOR* 5 (1923–24) 23–65. Malamat, A. "Organs of Statecraft in the Israelite Monarchy." *BA* 28 (1965) 34–65. Mendelsohn, I. "State Slavery in Ancient Palestine." *BASOR* 85 (1942) 14–17. Mettinger, T. N. D. *Solomonic State Officials. A Study of the Civil Government Officials of the Israelite Monarchy.* ConB, OT ser. 8. Lund: Gleerup, 1971. Noth, M. "Die Bewährung von Salomos 'Göttlicher Weisheit.'" *VTSup* 3 (1955) (= M. Noth and D. W. Thomas, eds., *Wisdom in Israel and the Ancient Near East,* H. H. Rowley Fs). Pintore, F. "I dodici intendenti di Salomone." *RSO* 45 (1970) 177–207. Redford, D. B. "Studies in Relations between Palestine and Egypt during the First Millennium B.C. I. The Taxation System of Solomon." *Studies in the Ancient Palestinian World Presented to Prof. F. V. Winnett.* Toronto-Buffalo: University of Toronto Press, 1972. Scott, R. B. Y. "Solomon and the Beginnings of Wisdom in Israel." *VTSup* 3 (1955). de Vaux, O.P., R. "Titres et fontionnaires égyptiens à la cour de David et de Salomon." *RB* 48 (1939) 394–405 (= *Bible et Orient.* Paris: Editions Cerf [1967] 189–201). Wright, G. E. "The Provinces of Solomon (I Kings 4:7–19)." E. L. Sukenik Memorial Volume, *EI* 8 (1967) 56–68.

Translation

[1a] *And king Solomon became king over* [b] *Israel.* [2a] *and these were the high officials who served him:*
Azariah son of Zadok: priest, [b]
[3] *Elihaph* [ab] *and Ahijah, sons of Shisha: secretaries,*
Jehoshaphat [a] *son of Ahilud: herald,* [c]
[4a] *(and Benaiah son of Jehoiada: over the army* [a]
and Zadok and Abiathar: priests),
[5] *(and) Azariah son of Nathan: over the district prefects,*
(and) Zabud son of Nathan, a priest: [a] *the king's friend,*
[6] *(and) Ahishar: over the palace property,*
[a] *Eliab son of Joab: over the army,* [a]
(and) Adoniram son of Abda: over the corvée.
[7] *And serving Solomon were (twelve) district prefects* [a] *in charge of all Israel,*
[b] *and they supplied* [b] *the king and his establishment (a month per year it was incumbent on each one* [c] *to make provisions);* [8] *and these were their names:*
Ben-hur: (in) Mount Ephraim, [a]
[9] *Ben-deqer: (in) Maqaz and Shaalbim and Beth-shemesh and Elon* [a] *Beth-hanan,* [b]
[10] *Ben-hesed:* [a] *(in) Arubboth (his was Socoh and all the land of Hepher),* [a]

[11] *Ben-abinadab:* [a]*all the heights of Dor* [a] (*Taphath, Solomon's daughter, became his wife*),[b]
[12] *Baanah son of Ahilud: Taanach* [a] *and Megiddo, and all of* [b]*Beth-shan which is adjacent to Zarethan* [b] *below Jezreel, from Beth-shan to Abel-meholah, to a point across from Jokmeam,* [c]
[13] *Ben-geber:* (*in*) [a] *Ramoth-gilead* [b](*his were the tent-camps of Jair son of Manasseh which are in Gilead*);[b] (*his was the region of Argob,* [c] *which is in Bashan, sixty large cities with wall and bronze bar*),[d]
[14] *Ahinadab son of Iddo:* [a] *Mahanaim,*
[15] *Ahimaaz:* (*in*) *Naphtali* (*it was he who took Basemath daughter of Solomon*),[a]
[16] *Baanah son of Hushai:* (*in*) *Asher* [a] *and Bealoth,* [b]
[17] *Jehoshaphat son of Paruah:* (*in*) *Issachar,* [a]
[18] *Shimei* [a] *son of Elah:* (*in*) *Benjamin,* [b]
[19] (*Geber* [a] *son of Uri in the land of Gilead,* [b] *the land* [c] *of Sihon king of Heshbon* [d] *and Og king of Bashan*), *plus one district prefect* [e] *who was in the land* [20] *of Judah.* [ab]

Now Judah and Israel were many, numerous as the sand that is alongside the sea, eating, drinking and rejoicing.
[5:1(4:21)]**Now Solomon was reigning over all the kings* [a] *from the River to* [b] *the land of the Philistines, even as far as the border of Egypt, who brought tribute and served Solomon as long as he lived.*
[2(22)] *Now this was Solomon's provision for one day: thirty cors of fine flour and sixty cors of meal;* [3(23)] *ten fattened cattle and twenty range-fed cattle and a hundred sheep, besides harts, gazelles, roebucks* [a] *and fattened fowl.* [b] [4(24)] *For he exercised dominion over all Eber-hanahar,* [a]*from Tipsah to Gaza, over all the kings of Eber-hanahar,* [a] *and he enjoyed peace on all the borders* [b] *surrounding him;* [5(25)] *and Judah and Israel dwelt safely, every man beneath his vine and beneath his fig tree, from Dan to Beersheba, as long as Solomon lived.* [6(26)] *Also Solomon had forty* [a] *thousand stalls of horses for his chariots, with twelve thousand horsemen.* [7(27)] *So those* [a] *district prefects supplied the person of King Solomon and every guest at the table of the king,* [b] *each one for his month, neglecting nothing;* [8(28)] *and as for the barley and straw for the horses and chariot teams, they would each bring them to such a place as one would be at* [a] *according to one's assigned order.*

[9(29)] *And God* [a] *gave Solomon wisdom, even exceedingly great understanding and broadness of mind, like the sand which is alongside the shore of the sea.* [10(30)] *And Solomon's wisdom exceeded the wisdom of all the eastern peoples, even all the wisdom* [a] *of Egypt.* [11(31)] *And he was the wisest of all mankind, above Ethan the Ezrahite* [a] *and Heman and Calcol and Darda, choristers;* [b]*so that his fame spread to all the nations round about.* [b] [12(32)] *And he* [a] *uttered three thousand proverbs,* [b]*and his songs were* [b] [c]*five and a thousand:* [c]
[13(33)] *And he spoke about the trees,*
from the cedar which is in Lebanon
to the hyssop growing from the wall;

---

*Verse numbers in parentheses are those of the standard English versions. Those without parentheses are those of the Hebrew text.

and he spoke about beast and about bird,
and reptiles and about fish.
[14(34)] *And* [a]*they came from all the peoples*[a] *to listen to Solomon's wisdom, some from* [b] *every king on earth who might have heard about his wisdom.*

Notes

Verse numbers vary in Heb., G, and Eng. after v 20. Heb. 5:1–14 = Eng. 4:21–34 = G 10:30 and scattered (cf. "Parallel Texts" in the *Introduction*).

1.a. On v 1, cf. LXX 2:46.[1]
1.b. Missing in LXX.
2.a. On vv 2–6, cf. LXX 2:46[h].
2.b. In Heb. הכהן "the priest" is normal for an official list, cf. המזכיר "herald" in v 3. The omission in G[BL] (cf. 2:46[h]) may be corrective in view of v 4.
3.a, a. "And" before these names extends the syndetic tendency of the Heb. *Vorlage*, as seen in vv 4–6.
3.b. A restoration; see *Comment*. MT "Elihoreph"; G[B] "Eliaph" G[L] "Eliab."
3.c. Cf. Note 2.b. above.
4.a-a. MT, G[L]. G[B] omits in view of v 6.
5.a. MT. G[BL]'s omission is corrective; cf. vv 2, 4.
6.a-a. G[L]. MT's omission is corrective in view of v 4; G[B] corr. Cf. *HOTTP*, 296.
7.a. Heb. נִצָּבִים "overseers" cf. v 5 and 5:7 (Eng. 4:27); but several MSS read נְצָּבִ(י)ם "overseers" cf. v 19.
7.b-b. MT. G[BL] have the stylistic improvement "to supply."
7.c. K עַל אֶחָד "upon one," "according to one"; Q הָאֶחָד "the one."
8.a. MT. G[BL] add "one"—as in a tally (see below).
9.a. MT. G[BL] add "as far as" (ἔως), an interpretation of Elon from Beth-hanan. Cf. *HOTTP*, 296.
9.b. MT. G[BL] add "one."
10.a-a. MT, supported by most Gr. MSS. G[B] and G[L] are corrupt. Cf. Burney, 41.
11.a-a. MT. G[BL] corr.
11.b. MT. G[BL] add "one."
12.a. MT. G[BL] corr.
12.b-b. MT. G[BL] corr.
12.c. MT and G[L]. G[B] add "one."
13.a. G[BL] omit, resisting the syndetic tendency of MT and the Vrs.
13.b-b. MT. G[BL] omit (haplography).
13.c. MT and G[L]. G[B] corr.
13.d. MT and G[L]. G[B] adds "one."
14.a. MT. G[BL] corr.
15.a. G[BL]. MT adds "as wife." G[B] adds "one."
16.a. MT. G[BL] omits.
16.b. MT. G[BL] corr; add "one."
17.a. MT, G[B]. G[L] adds "one, one."
18.a. MT, G[L]. G[B] omits.
18.b. MT, G[B]. G[L] adds "one."
19.a. MT. G[BL] omit.
19.b. MT. G[BL] "Gad."
19.c. MT, G[L]. G[B] omits.
19.d. G[BL]. MT substitutes the more familiar "the Amorites."
19.e. MT, G[B]. G[L] "as a district prefect" eases the syntax and the problematical numbering created by the gloss at the end of this verse.
20.a. MT "Judah," appearing at the end of v 19 in G[BL], was an original element in the gloss, but when the additional gloss, "Now Judah and Israel were many," etc., was added in direct juxtaposition, one of the "Judah"s dropped out.

20.b. MT, G^B. G^L adds "one."

5:1(4:21). = LXX 2:46^{b,f,k}, 10:30. Cf. Gooding, 22.

1.a. Chr and G 10:30 (2:46^f aliter). MT "kingdoms" does not agree with the personal character of the rest of the verse.

1.b. C and G 10:30. MT omits "as far as" (haplography).

2(4:22). = LXX 2:46^a; cf. Gooding 73.

3(4:23)a. MT. G^{BL} omit, probably through unfamiliarity with the Heb.

3.b. MT, G^B. G^L adds "foraging (animals)."

4(4:24). = LXX 2:46^{f,g}; cf. Gooding, 27.

4.a-a. MT. G^{BL} omits (homoioteleuton).

4.b. MT מכל עבריו "from all his borders" is supported by G^{BL}, which draw a *mem* from the following מסביב "surrounding."

6(4:26). = LXX 2:46^i, 10:29a; cf. Gooding, 46; HOTTP, 297.

6.a. G^B 10:29a "four"; rell "forty."

7(4:27).a. Heb. הָאֵלֶּה = G^L οὗτοι; G^B corr.

7.b. G^{BL}, avoiding the aimless repetitiousness of MT "king Solomon."

8(4:28).a. The verb יִהְיֶה "would be" is potentative, with indefinite subject but referring to the prefects. G^{BL} add "the king."

9(4:29). = LXX 2:35^a; cf. Gooding, 34.

9.a. MT. G^{BL} κύριος "Lord"; cf. 4:5, 11.

10(4:30).a. MT. G^{BL} "wise men."

11(4:31).a. MT, G^L. G^B corr.

11.b-b. MT. G^{BL} omit.

12(4:32).a. MT and G^L. G^B "Solomon" is explicative.

12.b-b. It is more probable that the difficult MT reading, וַיְהִי שִׁירוֹ, followed by the pl, preserves a stylistic idiom, than that defective spelling has been perpetuated in the unpointed text.

12.c-c. MT (G^{BL} "five thousand") is likely in the light of the stylistic peculiarity of this passage.

14(4:34).a-a. MT. G^{BL} makes the stylistic change, "all the people came."

14.b. Heb. מֵאֵת "from" explicates the preceding statement; cf. Burney, 52; HOTTP, 297. G^B "and from"; G^L "and they brought presents from" (stylistic alterations).

Form/Structure/Setting

Extract from the Book of Solomon's Acts(2): List of his high officials, 4:1–6
Extract from the Book of Solomon's Acts (3): List of his district prefects, 4:7–19a
[Expansions, vv 19b, 20]
Extract from the Book of Solomon's Acts (4): Solomon's empire, 5:1 (4:21)
Extract from the Book of Solomon's Acts (5): Solomon's commissary arrangements, 5:2–3, 6–8 (4:22–23, 26–28)
[Expansion: Solomon's ideal reign, 5:4–5 (4:24–25)]
[Expansion: Laudatory interpretation, 5:9–14 (4:29–34)]

1 Kgs 4 is taken up with a variety of highly historical items concerning the administration of Solomon's realm, plus a number of late, mostly post-deuteronomistic, expansions extolling his glory and wisdom. Dtr himself adds nothing that we can recognize; he allows his source material to speak for itself. He now begins to make frequent incursions into the Book of Solomon's Acts, a practice that he will continue in chap. 5. In this chapter his extracts concern the names of Solomon's high officials, the territories of Solomon's prefects, the extent of his empire, and the quantity and sources for provisioning his regal establishment. There is nothing specially logical in this arrange-

ment apart from the fact that the one item does suggest the next. That the same secretary recorded 5:2-3 (4:22-23) and 5:6-8 (4:26-28) as recorded vv 7-19 is apparent from the fact that "so these district prefects" in v 5:7 (4:27) (not a displacement as some commentators believe) can have no other antecedent than vv 7-19. The probability is that the various entries were made at separate times, but by the same secretary; or if by a different secretary, then that that secretary would have read the previous item before making his own entry.

Before we examine the four extracts, let us take note of the expansions. The last phrase of v 19 together with "of Judah," borrowed from v 20, is a normalizing gloss (see *Comment*). The rest of v 20 is a late eschatological idealization. 5:4-5 (4:24-25) is a very late, idyllic description of the land. 5:9-14 (4:29-34) is an encomium of Solomon's image as the model wise man; 5:13 (4:33) actually contains a popular ditty celebrating his praise. We can perceive a purpose in the first three expansions, for (1) the list of prefectural districts, completed to the ideal number of twelve in the first gloss, suggests the expansion's ideology of a numerous and happy people inhabiting the land; (2) the mention of vast provisions for Solomon's household suggests the widespread realm needed to support it, untroubled by strife or any level of deprivation. There is no obvious logic for 5:9-14 (4:29-34), for what has Solomon's wisdom to do with the delivery of barley and straw? From an overall redactional perspective one can, however, discern a purpose in it. A post-deuteronomistic editor chose this spot, just prior to the new section on Solomon's preparations for the temple, to close off chaps. 1-4, whose central theme has been Solomon's wisdom, using this unrestrainedly eulogistic encomium to summarize that wisdom (see our discussion under *Explanation*).

The first extract begins, "And King Solomon became king over Israel." Some commentators have found difficulty in this seemingly belated report of Solomon's accession to the kingship. One suggestion is to translate, "and King Solomon was confirmed as king." This rather breaks the rules of Heb. grammar, and in any case overlooks the implications of source-analysis. What would be more natural for the archivist of the Book of Solomon's Acts than to report in this way the fact of Solomon's accession? This sentence is in any event needed prior to v 2, where אֲשֶׁר־לוֹ, "who were his," requires Solomon's name as an antecedent. The whole entry constitutes an official roster of high officials serving Solomon. This appears in much its original form, but has received a few additions while still preserved in the archives, prior to being incorporated in Dtr's redaction. A superfluous *wāw* ("and") crept in, probably under the influence of v 4, before the names "Azariah," "Zabud," "Ahishar," and "Adoniram." V 4 is a correction identifiable from the fact that it duplicates the two offices mentioned in v 2 and v 6; it probably comes from a separate, earlier archival source, perhaps reflecting the time of 2 Sam 20:25 for Zadok and Abiathar, and the time of 1 Kgs 2:35 for Benaiah. Apart from v 4, this roster mentions eight distinct offices, as compared with five in 2 Sam 8:16-18 and six in 2 Sam 20:23-25, showing how comparatively more sophisticated Solomon's administration had become. This difference, plus the contrast with v 4 and the evidence of a later generation of personnel (e.g., Azariah son of Zadok is now priest) show us that this roster, and by inference that of vv 7–18 as well, reflect a situation late in Solomon's reign. All the original names are single except "Elihaph and Ahijah," and these may be taken as successive, not contemporary, occupants of the office mentioned. All names are given with a patronym except Ahishar. Four of the original offices are named with foregoing עַל, "in charge of" or "over" (vv 5–6). In v 5b a man is mentioned with his occupation and then his office. We notice, finally, that in lists like this the proper name comes first, then the office, whereas in normal narrative styling the office precedes, followed by the proper name (e.g., "King Solomon").

The second extract begins with the form of a narrative report identifying the officer in question and defining his responsibility. It then lists the names together with the territories over which the various men were in charge. The officers in question were called נִצָּבִים, lit., "those appointed" (cf. the name of their general supervisor in v 5), hence "prefects." There is a similarity to the preceding list in that the proper name comes first, then the identification of the territory which they supervised. From the fact that some listings allow the geographical description to follow immediately after the proper name, without intervening בְּ "in," it seems rather apparent that this preposition has come casually into the text at certain points (vv 8, 9, 10, 13, 15, 16, 17, and 18) while this roster was in the charge of predeuteronomistic scribes. This is the circle that was likewise responsible for explanatory additions in vv 10, 11, 13, 15, and 19. It will be seen that all but the last are comments about the person involved. V 19abα has the complete styling of the other entries, with name, patronym, and territory; the pairing of "Sihon king of Heshbon and Og king of Bashan" marks it as relatively late, and the reference to Gilead is certainly secondary because Gilead (LXX "Gad") is a territory already covered in vv 13–14. It is probably a corrective addition, filling out the number twelve, which this glossator believed was demanded by the reference to "all Israel" in v 7. He may also be responsible for the number "twelve" in v 7, together with the statement that each prefect had responsibility for one month per year. As has been stated, a much later gloss in 19bβ-20aα reinterprets the "twelve" so as to include Judah, supposing that the twelve-tribe system was involved. Finally, we observe that one proper name (in v 15) has no patronym; the explanation for this is as obscure as with respect to Ahishar in v 6. The opposite situation pertains with respect to five patronyms without proper names in vv 8–11, 13 (LXX also, vv 18–19). A. Alt in "Menschen ohne Namen," *Kleine Schriften* III (1959) 198–213, has argued that the "Ben"-names are attested in the Ugaritic literature and ought therefore to be understood as titles of hereditary offices, with possibly a succession of unnamed incumbents. But anonymity would be rather strange at least in the instance of the "Ben-abinadab" who is said to have married Solomon's daughter (v 11). The only other viable explanation seems to be a grasping for straws: the widely accepted view (cf. Noth, 59–61) that the sheet on which this list was written was torn or broken off, just on the upper righthand corner (but then why did "Baanah" in v 12 survive?).

V 21 is a simple notice taken from the Book of Solomon's Acts, evidently written after his death because of the phrase, "as long as he lived." Although "all the kings" may be a slight exaggeration, this notice is essentially historical.

It is self-contained and has nothing to do with the preceding or the succeeding context.

The extract in 5:2–3 (4:22–23), 5:6–8 (4:26–28) is an expanded commissary tabulation. The secretary in question has, however, explained the source of the provisions involved, and since the district prefects who were responsible for supplying Solomon's table were responsible for supplying fodder for his horses, he tabulates the horses too. As has been remarked, "those district prefects" in 5:7 (4:27) shows that the secretary in question had just written or read vv 7–19. There is no justification for a drastic rearranging of the text, as performed by Gray (129–49).

Comment

1–6 In the roster of שׂרים "the high officials" (not "princes"), the following may be observed concerning the names: Zadok, Benaiah son of Jehoiada, Abiathar, Nathan, and Joab are all very familiar, having been introduced in chaps. 1–2. They are now apparently all dead. We have no outside information on any of the others except Adoniram, whose name is mentioned also in 5:29 (Eng. 5:14) and in shortened form in 12:18. Of the others, Azariah, Ahijah, Jehoshaphat, and Azariah are normal Yahweh-names and are typical of these times. Elihaph (MT Elihoreph), Ahilud, Ahishar, Eliab, and Adoniram are theophoric names in the usual Hebrew/Semitic pattern. As has been noted, Ahishar is the only person without a patronym; some commentators say this was because of his humble origin, that he came from slavery or another low social class, but this is pure conjecture. The continuing influence of Zadok, who has one son in office, of Nathan, who has two sons in office, and (surprisingly) of Joab, whose son is back in command of the army, is to be noted. Foreign influence is probable in the name of Adoniram's father, Abda (עבדא), who apparently bears the Phoenician form of the word עבד "servant."

We have adopted in v 3a the results of a thorough study by Tryggve N. D. Mettinger, *Solomonic State Officials* (ConB 5. Lund 1971), 29–30, who argues that Heb. "Elihoreph" is the bastardization of a Hebraized Egyptian name, in which the element *ḥp* represents the god Apis (cf. the LXX transliterations, which show no evidence of a *resh*). Mettinger conjectures that "Ahijah" must disguise still another Egyptian name (but he makes no effort to restore it) because the two persons are "sons" of still another person with an Egyptian name, Shisha. Now, "Shisha" is a Hebraizing of Egyptian *šš*, "scribe," and it seems unlikely that this would have been some person's given name; therefore the meaning may actually be "sons of a scribe," i.e., members of the scribal guild (cf. A. Cody, *RB* 72 [1965] 381–93). In any event, the Egyptian influence is abundantly apparent, and we have invaluable evidence that Solomon was reaching out to his Egyptian father-in-law for help in administering his realm.

The following may be observed with respect to the offices mentioned in vv 1–6. The priest is the royal chaplain; standing at the head, he is certainly the most influential figure on the entire list. The secretary (ספר) keeps the records and prepares the correspondence (the two persons named may have served in succession). The herald (המזכיר) is the official protocol officer (cf. H. Graf Reventlow, *TZ* 15 [1965] 161–75; H. J. Boecker, *TZ* 17 [1961] 212–16). The one "over the army" is of course the commander in chief, perhaps also a sort of secretary of war. The man "over the district prefects" is in overall charge of the provisioning system. The "king's friend" (רעה המלך) is the king's most intimate advisor and a sort of secretary of state (cf. A. Penna, *RBiblt* 14, 459–66; A. van Selms, *JNES* 16, 118–23). The one who is "over the palace property" (על־הבית) is no chief housekeeper or chamberlain, but, in view of the widest semantic reference for the word בית "house," the caretaker of all the royal property, including lands as well as buildings. The supervisor of the corvée (המס) is of course the head tax official, whose very special task is to direct the forced-labor system, of which more will be said below.

7–20 Inasmuch as this is a roster of officials and not a geographical list (see above), primary attention should be given to the proper names. In addition to what has already been mentioned concerning their form, the following can be said about the names and the persons concerned. "Hur" could be Hebrew (the hollow noun means "linen"); some say it goes back to the Egyptian Horus, but Noth derives it from Akkadian "child." "Deqer" could be Hebrew because the root is found in Akkadian and Ugaritic, but this name is found nowhere else in the OT. "Hesed," identical to the familiar Heb. noun, חסד, is unattested as a personal name elsewhere in the OT, but has been found in Palmyrene. "Abinadab" is a Hebrew name in the classical theophoric style; a son of Saul and a son of David are among those who bore it, and the second-mentioned is a possible candidate to be the parent in question. "Baanah" is well attested in the OT, but its meaning and derivation are uncertain. "Ahilud" is Hebrew and theophoric; this could refer to the father of Jehoshaphat, mentioned in v 3. "Geber" occurs only here and at v 19 in the OT; it is obviously cognate to the word meaning "warrior," although the vocalization is an enigma. "Ahinadab" occurs only here but is theophoric and Hebrew. "Iddo" is somewhat uncertain in meaning but is a name borne by Zechariah's grandfather (Zech 1:7). "Ahimaaz" is Hebrew and theophoric; this person may be the same as the son of Zadok mentioned in 2 Sam 15:27, and perhaps too well known to require a patronym in this list. "Baanah": the same as the name recorded in v 12. "Hushai," of uncertain derivation, is also the name of David's "friend" (the formal office; see above). "Jehoshaphat," Hebrew and theophoric (the first in this list with the Yahweh-element!), occurs in v 3 and as the name of Judah's fourth king. "Paruah" is not found elsewhere in the OT but has Semitic cognates. "Shimei," omitted in LXX, is a favored Benjaminite name; cf. chap. 2. "Elah" is a common Hebrew and generally Semitic name, and appears in the OT as the name of Baasha's son. The two female names, "Taphath" (v 11) and "Basemath" (v 15) retain the older fem th-ending and thereby help us date the entire roster, with most of the interpolations, as relatively early. The upshot of this review is that the proper names are all good Hebrew/Canaanite and fit the period in question. Theophoric names do not predominate; the Abi-, Ahi-type reflects the tribal religion of Israel's recent past, while the single Yahweh-name shows that Yahweh exclusivism is just beginning.

Now let us look at the geographic designations. Since this is a biblical commentary and not a gazetteer, we shall restrict ourself to such remarks as may be immediately beneficial to biblical exegesis. Persons interested in locating the places named may get a quick orientation in Y. Aharoni and M. Avi-yonah, *The Macmillan Bible Atlas* (New York–London: Macmillan, 1968), 73. Better yet, in Aharoni's *The Land of the Bible: A Historical Geography* (tr. A. F. Rainey, 2nd ed., Philadelphia: Westminster Press, 1979), 429–43, one will find a cross-listing of ancient names, modern Arab names, and modern Hebrew names, with precise locations on the Israel-Survey grid. Some of the sites mentioned, such as Taanach, Megiddo, and Beth-shan, have been excavated, and for the significance of such work one should study the archeological reports and summaries. Some of the sites mentioned also have importance in terms of recorded biblical history. One thing should be clear to us: our passage does not mean to imply that the towns named themselves produced all that was required, nor are we to understand that these towns marked off boundaries, like those mentioned in Josh 13–22. There are some uncertainties with respect to them. What, for instance, is meant by "Asher and Bealoth" in v 16? Asher is a tribe, but is Bealoth a town, a region, or an unusual adverbial combination meaning "in (the) heights"? (so G. W. Ahlström, *BASOR* 235, 79–80). MT is often difficult, but G is so bad at transliterating geographic names that it can seldom help in restoring the original. And what about the prefecturates? How are we to understand their role and function?

One can get an introduction to the debate concerning them by consulting the extensive literature in our *Bibliography*, but many things remain unsettled. How many prefecturates were there? Almost everyone says twelve, but we agree with Mettinger, *Solomonic State Officials*, 121–24, that the original roster mentioned only eleven (Gilead, v 19, and Judah, v 20, occur in early and late glosses, respectively). If it cannot be certain that they were twelve in number, the argument is less convincing to the effect that they were created to supplant the old tribal territories. The description of the tribal boundaries preserved in Josh 13–22, though from the time of Josiah, is sufficiently precise to assure us that that system was no invention but a tradition retained in informal, idealized application. Since raising provisions is the only mentioned function of these prefects, we must marvel at the confidence of those scholars who assure us that Solomon made a determined, deliberate effort to slight northern traditions and wipe out every vestige of the cherished past.

Our roster does not give actual boundaries, yet such scholars speak readily of Solomon creating new boundaries that would cut across the old tribal territories. We observe that once the first clockwise progression, from the first to the fifth prefecturate, has been completed, there is little sense of direction in the ordering of those that remain. Certainly the entire territory of Israel, including the old Canaanite enclaves, but not counting Judah, was meant to be covered. If we may guess why the prefecturates were arranged as they were, we would say that the season, and the type of produce available, may have had more to do with it than anything else. Why, for instance, join Megiddo in the mid-Jezreel valley with Jokmeam in the mid-Jordan? And how about Judah? Was it so privileged that nothing was to be exacted from its inhabitants? We do not have the answer, for there is no information to go by. We can only suppose that Solomon was not holding the North in tribute, for if he were, such unrest should have arisen there as would have left some mark in the record available to us. Our guess is that he had a separate system of raising provisions in Judah; we just happen to have received a record that does not mention the Judah-system.

Although G^{BL} has lost v 20 (extant only in the miscellany at 2:46ª), it does preserve v 19bβ in a form that drops out the relative "who was" but adds "of Judah" to "the land." Our identification of this quarter-verse as a gloss is clearly justified because it has no proper name at the beginning. MT lacks "of Judah," which must have dropped out by haplography from v 20, where the unusual order "Judah and Israel" is supported by the same order in 5:5 (Eng. 4:25); the relative particle in MT arose, of course, when v 19bβ no longer had "in Judah" identifying the prefect in question, and the meaning now was that there was one unnamed prefect serving as a supernumerary, covering all "the land" where needed. MT is in error, but what we have in this gloss is a probably well-informed remark by a fairly late scribe that Judah also did have a prefect. This means that Judah definitely participated in the prefectural system, but was not included in "all Israel" in v 7 because this term refers there strictly to the North.

4:20, 5:1 (4:21), 5:4-5 (4:24-25)   The promises to the Genesis patriarchs were focused on (1) possession of the land and (2) a prosperous people. Gathered together for comment here are the verses that depict Solomon's reign as an ideal fulfillment of these very promises. The extract from the Book of Solomon's Acts, 5:1 (4:21) presents a somewhat idealized picture of Solomon's dominion, making two absolute statements, viz., that "all" the kings in the region of Syria, Palestine, and the Sinai (perhaps Transjordania also), i.e., from "the River" (the Euphrates) in the north down to "the border of Egypt" at wadi el-Arish, including the "land of the Philistines," were under his dominion; also that these kings brought tribute and served Solomon, accepting vassal status, "as long as he lived" (cf. 5:5 [4:25]). Certainly this comprised an empire far vaster than "the land" that God had promised Abraham, yet in later biblical tradition it often describes the ideal territory of Yahweh's people. Solomon had himself done nothing to secure this empire, but had inherited it intact from his father David (see 2 Sam 8).

The late expansion in 5:4-5 (4:24-25) starts out by saying something similar, yet different, and then goes on to other idealizations. It is stated that Solomon controlled "all Eber-hanahar" (RSV: "the region west of the Euphrates"); this designation describes Syro-Palestine from a point of view eastward from the Euphrates and was actually the official name of this region in the Persian empire, hence a very late date is certain. Tipsah lay on the upper Euphrates and Gaza is the leading town of the Philistines, situated on the Mediterranean. Within this territory Solomon is said to have enjoyed perfect security; no one on any of his borders ventured to attack him. Thus "Judah and Israel dwelt safely." The fact that here and in 4:20 "Judah" precedes "Israel" is another clue to extreme lateness, for the reverse order is found in early documents where the two entities are mentioned together (in the post-exilic period, "Judah" began more and more to assume precedence because the returnees from exile were almost all Judahites). 4:20 has two superlatives respecting the people's happy condition: (1) they were too numerous to count and (2) they did nothing but eat, drink, and rejoice. 5:5 (4:25) has two superlatives likewise: (1) the entire land was safe ("from Dan to Beersheba") and (2) this lasted as long as Solomon lived. Here the image of eating, drinking, and rejoicing is kept rather modest in the familiar locution, "every man beneath his vine and beneath his fig tree," as if to suggest that privacy, quiet, and the simple needs of life are enough to keep a man happy.

5:2–3, 6–8 (4:22–23, 26–28) This is the commissary list of a single day for Solomon's entire palatial establishment, no doubt including servants as well as the guests mentioned in 5:7 (4:27). As such, its proportions are entirely believable, and there is no reason to doubt that its details are factual. A cor is usually a dry measure and equals a homer. Estimates of its capacity in terms of our system vary, but R. B. Y. Scott reckons it at 6.3 imperial bushels (*PCB* § 34k). No mention is made of fruits and vegetables, but only of food items (fine flour, meal) that may be stored in the pantry and animals (fattened cattle, range-fed cattle, sheep, harts, gazelles, roebucks, fattened fowl) that may either be kept in pens or shot in the open land. Because 5:7 (4:27) refers to the provisioning of King Solomon personally, with his invited guests, and then 5:8 (4:28) refers to fodder for the horses, our inclination is to view 5:6 (4:26) as the original continuation of 5:3 (4:23), providing the information about Solomon's numerous horses before 5:7–8 (4:27–28) conclude this commissary list with their statement regarding the responsibility of the district prefects. We have had earlier occasion to comment on the use of horses in the United Kingdom of Israel (see on 1:5). On this question see D. P. Ap-Thomas, "All the King's Horses. A Study of the Term פרש," *Proclamation and Presence. OT Essays in Honor of G. H. Davies* (London: SCM Press, 1970), 135–51; also S. Yeivin, *Tarbiz* 40 (1970–71) 395–96. G[B] reads "four thousand" over against the other G MSS and M. Forty thousand stalls seems excessive, but not when compared with the number of horsemen given. (Much was made of the stalls discovered at Megiddo, but these are now dated later than the time of Solomon.) These stalls would have been at key cities like Lachish, Gezer, Megiddo, Hazor, and the like.

On "those district prefects," 5:7 (4:27), see above. "Each one for his month, neglecting nothing": this is the basis for the early gloss in 4:7. From vv 7–19 it has been assumed that these officers worked on a twelve-month calendar, each taking a given month each year. Perhaps that was the method, but 5:7 (4:27) merely states that they worked a month at a time in such a fashion as to leave no month uncovered, hence the number of months involved in this arrangement cannot be conjectured from this verse. The point is that the needs of Solomon and his guests were never neglected. It is likely that during the "months off" each prefect was hard at work collecting what he would eventually be called upon to deliver. "Barley and straw": the rather lapidary Heb. has invited a variety of translations, but we have taken it to mean that these items would be collected by the king's logistics team at one place, and then another, as called for by the schedule that had been prepared, and this makes sense in light of the fact that the chariots and horses were dispersed at various strong-points throughout the land.

5:9–14 (4:29–34) The encomium of Solomon's wisdom begins by repeating what 3:12 has already stated, that God gave him this wisdom. Two phrases explicate its meaning, "exceedingly great understanding" תבונה הרבה מאד, and "broadness of mind" רחב לב, indicating that encyclopedic knowledge is what the reader really has in mind. This is precisely what the popular ditty taken up in 5:13 (4:33) intends, as also the statements that Solomon's "fame spread to all the nations round about," 5:11 (4:31), and that guests came "from all the people to listen to Solomon's wisdom," 5:14 (4:34). Compare the metaphor of the sand on the seashore, 5:9 (4:29), with 20. Next Solomon's wisdom is compared with that of other famous wise men, 5:10–11 (4:30–31). "The wisdom of all the eastern peoples": cf. Job with his three comforters, but בני קדם "easterners" could be translated "men of old," with such figures as those in the Ugaritic literature (Danel?) in mind, were it not for the parallelism with Egypt, lying on the opposite border of the writer's world. "The wisdom of Egypt": Egypt was renowned for its cultivation of wisdom; cf. *ANET* 405–24. "He was the wisest of all mankind": the syntax of the superlative is interesting, lit., "And he was wise (verb) from all the human race (האדם)." "Ethan . . . Heman and Calcol and Darda": a traditional group, cf. 1 Chr 2:6. "Choristers," בני מחול: better than an anonymous "sons of Mahol" (RSV) because of Ethan's association with the temple singers, Pss 88:1, 89:1. "All the nations" (הגוים): cf. "all the peoples" (העמים), 5:14 (4:34); the first term is political, the second sociological, but they are used interchangeably in much late literature.

"Three thousand proverbs": here משל has its late technical meaning, "wise saying" or "aphorism": although this claim may not directly reveal acquaintance with our Book of Proverbs, it certainly does reflect the tradition behind it. "His songs": for the reading see *Notes;* Solomon is remembered for songs because of Cant, though this was much more the traditional province of David. "Five and a thousand": an oriental way of speaking (cf. "A thousand and one nights") meaning "more than a thousand" (cf. K. Steuernagel, *ZAW* 30 [1910] 70–71). As our translation shows, the ditty of 5:13 (4:33) is a couplet with a tricolon and a bicolon, the first being about "trees" (a term wider than ours, for it includes the hyssop vine; cf. the vine in Ezek 15) and the second being about animals. "From . . . to . . ." is a common Hebraic speech pattern, in which the extremes imply everything in between. This ditty was in popular use and was certainly older than the prose context. "They came from all the peoples" (cf. G). The meaning is that individuals from every people came. This is explicated in 5:14b (4:34b) to mean "some from every king on earth," thus official delegates (cf. the parallel in 10:23–25).

Explanation

There is a striking contrast between the source materials taken up into this chapter and the late expansion. The former are sparse, practical, and based on historical fact; the latter are high-blown, lyrical, and imaginatively laudatory. The reader is hard put to find any theological testimony in the former collection but may be inclined to identify with the symbols employed in the expansions. In other words, it may not be with the real, historical

Solomon that one would empathize, but with the idealized Solomon of the later additions.

One will observe that, although Solomon's riches and splendor are presupposed in the statements about his vast realm and the idyllic security that every subject enjoyed, it is his proverbial wisdom that is featured. Very clearly, the Solomonic wisdom of 5:9–14 (4:29–34) is essentially intellectual, whereas the Solomonic wisdom of chap. 3 (even in Dtr's addition, v 12) is essentially pragmatic. Another way to state the contrast is to say that in the late additions Solomon is presented as a light to the nations round about, whereas in chap. 3 he is simply the administrator of justice to Israel. How did the term "wisdom" come to bridge this rather extreme difference? Or were the two meanings actually combined in the mental and spiritual prowess of this remarkable king?

Traditional exegesis, unregarding of source analysis, has naturally said yes to this last question. The relativizing tendency of nineteenth-century criticism was to regard all references to any kind of Solomonic wisdom as unhistorical. The discovery of an extensive wisdom literature in early Egypt, Mesopotamia, and Ugarit has, however, encouraged many scholars who consider themselves modern in their methodology to date Israel's wisdom tradition as far back as possible, taking literally the statements that credit Solomon with superintending an early renaissance of learning in Israel. Gerhard von Rad, for example, speaks of a "Solomonic humanism." Yet there are many scholars who believe that at least intellectual wisdom had nothing but meager beginnings in Solomon's day, indeed, throughout the entire pre-exilic period.

Two highly respected writers who take the first view have been Albrecht Alt and Martin Noth. Alt argues (*TLZ* 76 [1951] 134–44) that 1 Kgs 5:9–14 (4:29–34) was already in the Book of Solomon's Acts, along with the unredacted version of 3:4–28. His pupil Noth, in VTSup 3 (1955), argues that this same material is fairly early and has been taken from annals and popular tales, and could actually be the formal introduction to a literary collection of wise sayings, now lost. Noth goes on to argue that very early materials (1 Kgs 2:6, 3:28, etc.) speak only of a pragmatic wisdom. In the year that Noth's essay was written, a brilliant and effective essay taking the opposite position was published by R. B. Y. Scott (VTSup 3 [1955]). Turning his attention directly to 1 Kgs 5:9–14 (4:29–34), 10:1–10, 13, 23–25, Scott sought to counter the growing tendency to acknowledge the historicity of an intellectual wisdom in Solomon. According to Scott, the above three passages are folkloristic and parallel the similar outbursts of superlative praise in 4:20; 5:1, 4–5 (4:21, 24–25). The best comparison is the midrashic exuberance displayed in Esth, Dan 1–4, and Chr. Scott bases this assessment on a detailed linguistic analysis, which reveals such data as the following: תבונה, "understanding," in 5:9 (4:29) is rare in pre-exilic documents, common in Prov; ורחב לב "broadness of mind," occurs in Ps 119:32 (in Prov לב generally means "intelligence"); the verb חכם "wise" in 5:11 (4:31) occurs twenty-seven times, but almost everywhere in postexilic passages; the names "Ethan, Heman, Calcol, and Darda" are found in 1 Chr 2:6, Ps 88:1; the pl for "trees" in 5:13 (4:33) is mostly late and poetic (cf. Burney, 52). This massing of details is a strong prop for the claim that 5:9–14 (4:29–34) is post-exilic, and this impression is strengthened by further linguistic evidence for the extreme lateness of related materials in 4:20—5:4 (4:20–24) and 10:1–10, 13, 23–25. The sections mentioned are, says Scott, clearly post-deuteronomistic, which may explain the different order in which the MT and the LXX, respectively, place them (this would assume that their position in the text remained unstable up to the time of the LXX translation). In any event, Scott uses this conclusion to offer Bible students this idea of how the concept of Solomonic wisdom must have developed through the centuries: (1) wisdom as the ability of the successful ruler, 1 Kgs 2:1–2, 5–9, 5:15–26 (5:1–12); these references are authentic and certainly pre-deuteronomistic; (2) wisdom as the insight to distinguish right from wrong, i.e., render justice, 1 Kgs 3:4–15, 16–28; Dtr additions show that this material too is pre-deuteronomistic; (3) wisdom as intellectual brilliance and encyclopedic knowledge, 1 Kgs 5:9–14 (4:29–34), 10:1–10, 13, 23–25; this is a late, imaginative development of the promise of wisdom, riches and honor in 3:12–13. Dtr expansions in 1 Kgs 2:3–4, 3:6–14, 5:4–5 (4:24–25), 6:12–13, 8:14–30, 46–61, 9:3–9 know nothing of this third concept; in fact, Dtr did not actually consider Solomon to be an exemplary king (see our *Introduction*), as can be seen especially from the fact that he gives the same promise to Jeroboam as to Solomon. Scott notes also that Deut 17:14–20 is quite negative regarding the image of a king like Solomon. Who then was the king who inspired this late model of wisdom? In Scott's opinion it was Hezekiah; the period of Hezekiah and Isaiah was the period of the rise of international, intellectual wisdom (cf. Prov 1:1, 25:1).

This argument remains persuasive in spite of a determined effort to refute it by J. Liver (*Bib* 48 [1967] 84–85). The conclusion is that tradition has been kind to Solomon far beyond what he deserves. There can be no doubt that he truly was an efficient ruler. Perhaps he was also just. His close contacts with Egypt, where the tradition of intellectual wisdom was always vital, may lead us to assume that he may have encouraged a guild of "wise men" at his court, but the early texts do not say so and the late ones are too idealized to give us historical certainty.

Which image, then, shall we choose? The tradition of a great king with his three thousand proverbs, surrounded by admirers from every nation, will inspire those who value a combination of cleverness with worldly splendor. For the mass of simple believers, however, Solomon's historical image of possessing wisdom for the urgent practicalities of life may have greater appeal. After all, what good is wisdom if it does not improve the quality of our daily lives?

The Preparation of Materials for Solomon's Temple (5:15-32 [Eng. 5:1-18])

Bibliography

Offord, J. "Archaeological Notes on Jewish Antiquities.—53. How Cedars Were Transported." *PEFQS* 50 (1918) 181–83.

Translation

[15] *And Hiram king of Tyre sent his servants to* [a] *Solomon* [b] *when he heard that they had anointed him king* [b] *in the place of* [c] *his father, for Hiram had always been friends with David.* [16(2)] *And Solomon sent to Hiram as follows:* [17(3)] *"You know about David my father, that he was unable to build a temple to the name of Yahweh his* [a] *God on account of the warfare which surrounded him* [b] *until they should be put* [b] *under the soles of his feet.* [c] [18(4)] *But now Yahweh my God has brought me quiet on every side, free from adversary and evil circumstance.* [a] [19(5)] *So look, I am proposing to build a temple to the name of Yahweh my God, just as Yahweh* [a] *spoke to David my father: 'Your son whom I shall appoint to take your place on your throne, he shall build the temple to my name.'* [20(6)] *So now, command that they cut me cedars* [a] *from Lebanon, and my servants will be with your servants,* [b] *and the wages of your servants* [b] *I will pay you, anything you say; for you know that none* [c] *among us knows how to cut timber like the Sidonians."*

[21(7)] *When Hiram heard Solomon's words he rejoiced greatly and said, "Blessed be Yahweh* [a] *today,* [b] *who has appointed for David a wise son over this great people!"* [22(8)] *And he* [a] *sent to Solomon as follows: "I have heard what you sent to me. I shall do all that you desire with regard to cedar and juniper timber.* [23(9)] *My servants shall fetch them down* [a] *from Lebanon to the sea and I will make them into towrafts to go* [b] *to the place which you shall indicate* [c] *to me, and I will break them up there, and you shall take delivery. And you on your part shall carry out my desire in providing bread for my household."* [24(10)] *And Hiram became Solomon's supplier of* [a] *cedar and juniper,* [a] [b] *so much as he desired.* [b] [25(11)] *And Solomon supplied Hiram with twenty thousand cors of wheat as food* [a] *for his household* [b] *and twenty thousand baths* [b] *of pure oil. (Solomon would supply this much* [c] *for Hiram year by year.)* [26(12)] *And Yahweh gave Solomon wisdom, as he had said to him. And there was peace between Hiram and Solomon;* [a] *and the two of them* [a] *made a treaty.*

[27(13)] *And the king* [a] *levied a corvée* [b] *from all Israel; the corvée came to thirty thousand men.* [28(14)] *And he sent them to Lebanon in relays of ten thousand per month;* [a] *one month they would be in Lebanon, two months they would be home.* [b] *And Adoniram was in charge of the corvée.* [29(15)] *And Solomon had seventy thousand (carriers)* [a] *burden-bearers, and eighty thousand stonecutters in the hills,* [30(16)] *besides Solomon's supervising officers who were in charge of the labor; three thousand three* [a] *hundred were those who directed* [b] *those performing* [b] *the labor.* [31(17)] [a] *The king gave orders* [a] *and they quarried out large stones, costly stones,* [b] *for laying the foundation*

of the temple with[c] *dressed stones.* [32(18)] *And Solomon's builders*[a] *and Hiram's build-ers*[a] *did the shaping*[b] *and gave them edges.*[b]
So did they prepare the timber and the stones[c] *for building the temple.*

Notes

(MT 5:31–32a [Eng. 17–18a] = G 6:23; MT 32b [Eng. 18b] = G 5:17)

15(1).a. MT, G[BL] add "anoint," paraphrasing their following omission.
15.b-b. G[BL] omit. The Gr. translators imagine it to be a great honor for a foreign king to anoint Solomon.
15.c. MT. G[BL]'s addition, "David," is explicative.
17(3).a. MT, accurately reflecting the polite form of address seen, e.g., in 1 Kgs 1:47. G[BL] "my" corrects what seems to be a manifest blunder.
17.b-b. G[B], devoid of the theologizing tendency seen in MT and G[L] "until Yahweh should put them."
17.c. QG; K "foot."
18(4).a. MT and G[L]. G[B] ἁμάρτημα πονηρόν "evil trespass" misreads Heb. פגע "circumstance" as פשע "rebellion," "sin."
19(5).a. MT. G[B] "Yahweh God"; G[L] "God."
20(6).a. MT. G[BL] "trees," "timber," normalizes to עצים "trees" at the end of this verse.
20.b-b. MT and G[L]. G[B] δουλείας σου = עבודתך "your service"; corr.
20.c. MT and G[L] (literalizing ἀνήρ εἰδώς "one knows"); G[B] ἰδίως "privately" is idiomatic.
21(7).a. MT. G[B] "God"; G[L] "Yahweh the God of Israel."
21.b. MT and G[L]; G[B] omits. Cf. *YTT,* 225.
22(8).a. G[B]. MT, G[L] "Hiram" is explicative.
23(9).a. G[BL] read masc pl ptcp; a haplography in MT omits *mēm* before מן.
23.b. G[BL]. MT adds explicative "by sea."
23.c. Heb. תשלח "you shall send" (= Grk. ἀποστείλῃς) implies the sending of a messenger to provide the necessary information.
24(10).a-a. G[L]. G[B] "cedar" seems paraphrastic; MT "cedar logs and juniper logs" is pleonastic.
24.b-b. G[L] (= כחפצו); MT "all that he desired" (כל חפצו) and G[B] "and all that he desired (= וכל-חפצו) are expansive.
25(11).a. MT has an orthographic peculiarity, מכלת for מאכלת. Corruptions in the Gr. render-ings show that it was not understood.
25.b-b. G[BL], reading a more reasonable tally than MT's "twenty cors"; contra *HOTTP,* 298. MT is a dittography from the preceding "twenty thousand cors of wheat"; the Gr. translators would simply have copied, and not tried to correct, their *Vorlage.* Cf. 2 Chr 2:10.
25.c. G[BL], reading a meaningful ככה "like this" for MT כה "thus."
26(12).a-a. MT. G[BL] read תחתיהם "between them," a corruption.
27(13).a. G[B]. MT and G[L] "King Solomon."
27.b. MT. G[BL] add "also" in view of v 20.
28(14).a. MT. MSS, G[BL] add "and" as a stylistic improvement. Cf. 9:20–22.
28.b. The conjectured most simple form; cf. MT "at his home"; G[B] "at their home," and G[L] "at their houses" are explicative or stylistic improvements.
29(15) = LXX 2:35[d]; cf. 2 Chr 2:1, 17.
29.a. Chr omits. MT נשא "carries," is an interpretive gloss for the following סבל "burden-bearers," whose meaning may have become obscure. Cf. G αἴροντες ἄρσιν "bearers of burdens."
30(16).a. MT. Chr, G[B] "six"; G[L] "seven."
30.b-b. G[B]. MT and G[L], explaining a technical term, offer "the people who performed."
31(17).a-a. MT and G[L]. G[B] omits.
31.b. MT, G[L]. G[B] omits.
31.c. MT, G[L]. G[B] adds explicative "and."
32(18).a-a. MT. G[BL] υἱοί reads Heb. בני "builders of" as בני "sons of."
32.b-b. Cj. ויגבלום (*wayyagbilûm;* Thenius); a technical term many not have been understood by G "and they threw them" or MT "and the Giblites."
32.c. MT. G[BL] add explicative "three years."

Form/Structure/Setting

Extract from the Book of Solomon's Acts (6): Solomon's relationships with Hiram, 5:15, 24–25, 26b (Eng. 5:1, 10–11, 12b)
[Dtr: Solomon's message to Hiram 16–20 (2–6); Hiram's message to Solomon 21–23 (7–9) Yahweh provides wisdom, 26a (12a)]
Extract from the Book of Solomon's Acts (7): Solomon's work force for providing building materials for the temple
   1. The Lebanon corvée, vv 27–28 (13–14)
   2. The local quarriers, vv 29–32a (15–18a)
   Concluding resumé, v 32b (18b)

In 1 Kgs 3:3–15 Dtr repeatedly interfered in the flow of the underlying text. Here his material is greater in actual quantity, but it is also more cohesive, comprising as it does all of vv 16–23 (2–9), with a casual comment thrown in at the beginning of v 26 (12). Commentators generally are aware that Dtr's hand is in this passage but have not always been precise in identifying the extent of the Dtr material. The isolation of this material cannot succeed without careful scrutiny of the biblical text. The following are characteristic Dtr locutions: "the name of Yahweh," vv 17, 19 (3, 5) twice, particularly with reference to the temple; "just as Yahweh spoke to David my father," v 19 (5); "Your son . . . I shall appoint to take your place on your throne," v 19 (5), and "who has appointed for David a wise son," v 21 (7) (contrast "they had anointed him king," v 15 [1]); "this great people," v 21 (7) (cf. 3:8); "Yahweh gave Solomon wisdom," v 26 (12) (cf. "wise son" 7). Thus we can immediately discern that much of vv 16–23 (2–9), 26 (12) belongs to Dtr, and it is apparent that the narrative of Solomon's negotiation with Hiram is a continuous and cohesive structure, yet not all of vv 15–26 (1–12) belongs to Dtr. One can start by observing that Dtr uses the verb שלח "send," in a different way than does v 15 (1). Here that verb has "his servants" as an object, but in Dtr's usage vv 16, 22, 23 (2, 8, 9) it has no object. V 15 (1) means that ambassadors or negotiators were sent to Solomon, just as they had been sent to David. No message is mentioned, but we do learn of the results in vv 24–25 (10–11), telling of the agreement that was reached, and in v 26b (12b), where we read that Solomon and Hiram agreed to live as peaceful neighbors and make a treaty. But in vv 16, 22, 23 (2, 8, 9) the sending of a messenger is not mentioned, only the message. This peculiarity, plus the observation that v 15 (1) gives no lengthy speech to Hiram comparable to those of vv 16–20 (2–6) and vv 21–23 (7–9), goes a long way in assuring us that v 15 (1) is not part of Dtr's work; Dtr does not in any case like to start right out with his own material. V 24 (10) would have to be taken as resumptive, if it were part of Dtr's expansion, because it summarizes what Hiram's foregoing speech plainly indicates. Its use of the participle of נתן is parallel to the use of the ptcp of אהב in v 15 (1), suggesting that these two verses come from the same source. The specific details given in v 25 (11) suggest original source material, and the report of the treaty with a foreign idol-worshiper in v 26b (12b) must have been in Dtr's source material, for this is not the kind of detail that he would have been likely to have invented.

It is not often that Dtr consciously composes a lengthy, elaborate narrative like what is found here. It must have been invented because Dtr lived long after the time of Solomon, and verbatim reports of speeches are not preserved in historical records. The basic structure is simple: a message from Solomon to Hiram followed by a message from Hiram to Solomon. In vv 16–20 (2–6) the main break comes with ועתה "so now," in v 20 (6). It is there that Solomon presents his request. "You know . . ." in v 16 (2) apprises Hiram of the situation with regard to David's plan to build the temple. "But now" in v 18 (4) is ועתה but represents one of the very few temporal, rather than situational, uses of this adverb (it introduces a shift from the "then" of David's warfare to the "now" of Solomon's quiet). "So look, I am proposing . . . ," a formula of imminent action simply introduces Solomon's plan to go ahead with what David had been forced to abandon (v 19 [5]). In v 21 (7) Dtr reports Hiram's rather implausible expression of praise to Yahweh, and then in vv 22–23 (8–9) he reproduces his message to Solomon. Its internal structure is chiastic, emphasizing the role of opposites in the negotiating process. V 22 (8) places Hiram's "I" foremost for emphasis; its chiastic counterpart is the second "and you" in v 23 (9). Hiram will give timber; Solomon will give bread. Within this outer structure there appears an internal contrast in the foremost "my servants" over against the first "and you" of v 23 (9): the servants of the respective kings will do what the agreement of their kings implies, Hiram's servants fetching the logs and Solomon's servants taking delivery. The attentive reader of Hiram's speech can detect Dtr's true interest; it is with the delivery of timber destined for Solomon's temple rather than with the delivery of food grains for Hiram. He has no true interest in a great political event except as it produces direct benefit for Solomon and his temple. This is why he does not invent a concluding speech for Solomon. He has skillfully composed this narrative to make Hiram look like Solomon's servant and vassal.

5:1 is an extract from the Book of Solomon's Acts. It is continued in vv 24–25, 26b (10–11, 12b). In v 24 (10) נתן "give" must be read as a participle because of the preceding ויהי "and it will be"; it seems entirely reasonable to read "And Hiram became Solomon's supplier . . ." because this verse tells the results of the negotiations mentioned in v 15 (1). V 25 (11) has "and Solomon" foremost, followed by what has to be the perfect of נתן "give"; the words in parentheses have the durative imperfect of נתן "give" and constitute an early gloss. Still featuring the root נתן "give," Dtr here adds his rather silly gloss of v 26a (12a), trying to make Yahweh parallel to Hiram and Solomon while completely overlooking the frame of reference.

In vv 27–32 (13–18) Dtr inserts a second extract from the Book of Solomon's Acts that leads directly to the narrative of the temple's construction in chap. 6. Some commentators see vv 27–28 (13–14) and vv 29–32 (15–18) as separate notices, but the reference to "timber and stones" at the end of v 32 (18) marks it as a concluding resumé to both sections. Vv 27–28 (13–14) has to do with the fetching of timber, but reports the Jerusalem administration's direct concern with it. It reports the fact of an all-Israel corvée and its size; it reports the arrangement for rotating the workers; it reports who was in charge of it. Vv 29–32a (15–18a) has to do with stone-cutting: the tally of carriers, stone-cutters, and supervisors; also the procedure according to which the king (or his representatives) would order certain stones and then have the design executed at the quarries, while leaving the finishing to special workers employed by Solomon or dispatched by Hiram.

Comment

15–26 (1–12) "Hiram king of Tyre": the name as given is an abbreviation for "Ahiram," attested for a king of Byblos *ca.* 1200 B.C. The form is theophoric, involving a divine epithet, אחי "my brother," that was popular also among the Israelites (see 4:14–15). The king in question had enjoyed good relations with David according to 2 Sam 5:11. Tyre had a mainland base but occupied also an offshore island, which kept it invulnerable to siege warfare up to the time of Alexander the Great, 333 B.C. Because of its strategic strength, Tyre could become a base for the founding of the faraway Carthage colony in the ninth century; it dominated the Mediterranean littoral as late as the Persian period, and for its influence on Judahite politics it was often condemned by the prophets. The Israelite coast was also in its sphere of influence, although always by means of trade and treaty. "When he heard . . . they had anointed him king": this could be read, "because he heard." The temporal translation need not endanger the validity of the theory that Solomon exercised a brief co-regency with David, as assumed in chap. 1, because Solomon would have been the active power, deserving of recognition by foreign kings. "Had . . . been friends . . .": אהב היה, lit., "friendly was," with emphasis on the foremost participle. The ptcp in effect makes this a technical expression, and apparently the root has a political sense here, as in the controverted expression in 1 Sam 18:1, 3, "Jonathan loved [David]."

"Solomon sent . . . as follows": the vehicle could be either a letter, to be read to Hiram, or an oral communication recited by the messenger from memory; cf. vv 7–8. "You know about David my father": How did Hiram know? Would David actually have told Hiram so many intimate details, or, far more likely, is this simply Dtr's convention? "The warfare (המלחמה) which surrounded him until they should be put": although the subject of this relative clause is sing, it is thought of as collective, or even personified in the two pl verbs that follow. "Free from adversary (שטן) and evil circumstance": this claim does not pertain to the conditions of Solomon's later life; cf. 11:14–25. "Build a temple," בית: the word commonly meaning "house" becomes this book's common name for the Jerusalem temple; it implies that Yahweh, or as Dtr would put it, Yahweh's name, resides there as a monarch resides in his palace. "Just as Yahweh spoke to David my father . . .": the sentiment, if not the exact words, is taken from 2 Sam 7. "My servants will be with your servants . . . , and the wages of your servants I will pay you": Hiram says nothing of this in his reply, but at least the participation of Israelites in the timberwork is supported by v 28 (14). "For you know": how would Hiram know that Israelite workmen were deficient in this skill? This is a polite way of speaking, and of course reflects Dtr's rationale for getting things for Yahweh's temple from a foreign land. "The Sidonians": evidently the most renowned among the Phoenicians in timber work; Sidon lies a third of the way north of Tyre toward Beirut, and may have been in commercial, if not political, dependency on Tyre at this time.

"Blessed be Yahweh today": This has nothing to do with the language of treaty documents, but is Dtr's adaptation of a popular pious expression, with הים "today" added to the blessing formula (cf. 1 Sam 25:32-33, 1 Kgs 1:48), but in such a way as to make it modify the act of blessing rather than Yahweh's act of appointing Solomon king (cf. YTT, 225); Dtr makes the queen of Sheba express a similar sentiment, but without הים, in her speech to Solomon, 10:9. "Over this great people": with reference to Israel, this is unthinkable in the mouth of Hiram. "All that you desire": lit., "all your desire"; cf. vv 23-24 (9-10). "Towrafts," דברות: cf. L. Koehler, TZ 5 (1949) 74-75; Hiram agrees to build them, transport them, and break them up at the designated place. "Bread for my household": this means the ingredients for making bread, together with every sort of food, and was intended for the support of Hiram's entire palatial establishment. "Cedar and juniper": in v 24's (10's) itemized list, the common genus "timber," is omitted, whereas in the expansive speech of v 22 (8) "timber" (two times in Hebrew) was appropriate; cf. Solomon's more modest request for "cedars" in v 20 (6), allowing Hiram to seem more generous in his offer than Solomon's request required.

"Twenty thousand cors of wheat as food for his household": for the cor, see on v 2 (4:22); the amount is not at all excessive for a large establishment. מ(א)כלת, "food," is less metaphorical than Dtr's "bread," appropriately so in this extract from official annals. "Twenty thousand baths of pure oil": the substance is lit. "beaten oil," שמן כתית, i.e., olive oil that is purified through processing; our translation follows G rather than MT's "twenty cors of pure oil," which shows first a corruption of "baths" (ca. five and a half gallons; cf. IDB IV, 834) to "cors" under the influence of v 25 aα, and next a reduction of the number to a figure more reasonable with "cors" as the unit. This sale of domestic produce, of which Israel had an abundance and cliff-girded Phoenicia had little, was as beneficial to the seller as to the buyer. "As he said to him": cf. 3:12; Dtr's remark is totally irrelevant; he simply cannot restrain himself from making a parallel to Hiram's and Solomon's giving, or providing (see above). "Peace" שלם: though absence of hostilities is the primary meaning of this word, especially here, cordiality and mutual well-being are included. "Treaty" ברית: the word that also means "covenant" has here its primary political denotation.

27-32 (13-18) "And the king levied a corvée": the word מס means "burden" but it also designates the labor force that is raised to carry a burden, i.e., perform a particular work-project; as in various societies, Solomon made it the obligation of Israel's freemen to work for given periods on projects for the public good. "From all Israel": all Israelites and no foreigners were involved, other than in the various other kinds of work-projects that were carried out during Solomon's reign according to 9:15-23. "And he sent them to Lebanon": here שלח "sent" is used as in v 1. "Adoniram": cf. 4:6. "Carriers, burden-bearers": the word סבל itself means "burden-bearer," thus נשא

"carrier" is superfluous, and an interpretive gloss. "Supervising officers" שרי הנצבים: their number is directly given as three thousand, three hundred, a not unlikely number.

"Large stones (אבנים גדלות), costly stones (אבנים יקרות) . . . dressed stones (אבני גזית)": the first expression communicates the idea that very large blocks were to be used; these were to be costly because many men had to work on them and they were not simply found in the field. The term אבני גזית (note that the first word is in construct, so is to be taken as a distinct noun and not as an adjective) refers to *ashlar:* hewn, squared-off rock. "For laying the foundation of the temple": these special stones were designated for the lower levels of masonry, possibly leaving the upper levels to be completed with brick or with smaller stones (see chaps. 6–7). "Gave them edges": the most desirable reading, suggesting that special care was taken to keep the edges straight and square. The present-day foundation of the temple-mount has impressive squared-off stones, but these were placed by Herod. The temple itself has been razed, and nothing remains except what may be underground. Apparently it was constructed with skill and care to rival that of Herod, even though its date was many centuries earlier.

Explanation

Solomon was crowned king (chap. 1) and took firm measures to remove potential rivals to his rule (chap. 2). His rule was legitimized through divine revelation and put to practical effect in his judgment on behalf of the abused harlot (chap. 3). His organization of his administration gave posterity a firm basis for its developing concept of his unparalleled wisdom (chap. 4). With all these things accomplished, he was ready to propose the single greatest undertaking of his reign, the building of the great temple in Jerusalem. And as he proposed it, he began to put his plan into action, gathering timber and stone for its construction (chap. 5). This is Dtr's conception for arranging his materials for a history of Solomon's reign. The trend of his presentation is quite clear; everything is to center in Solomon's temple, for this is what Dtr and his generation remembered of Solomon, more than his reputed wisdom.

Of course, Dtr continually appeals to David's behavior as the example rather than to Solomon's. He needs a rationale to explain why the more righteous father was not allowed the privilege of building the temple. Dtr could not offer the simple historical reason, viz., that David did not have the means. Nor could he be satisfied with the explanation offered in 2 Sam 7, even with all his own reworking, for that passage states with embarrassing clarity that Yahweh did not want a temple, at least not in David's time. It is clear, of course, that the historical Solomon did want a temple, and the still-standing temple of Dtr's day was testimony to it. No historical record declares what Solomon's original rationale was, but Dtr invents one in Solomon's speech to Hiram: David did want to build the temple, but constant warfare prevented him from carrying it out; Solomon could do it because he reigned in unbroken peace (5:17–18; Eng. 3–4). We can respect this construction, contrived as it is, because it does not demean David or flatter Solomon, and it may be based partly on the truth. It is certainly more worthy than the superstitious, mechanical caricature that 1 Chr 22:8–9 creates, to the effect that David was unfit for building the temple because he was "a man of blood." If it were actually true that nobody would be allowed to render service for God's house except one who was sinless and utterly undefiled, and that those who are in any way tainted with sin are excluded from God's service, very few indeed would qualify to join in such a noble and necessary work.

The temple was to be dedicated solely to Israel's god, Yahweh. Thus it was to be quite unique, for all the shrines where Yahweh was being worshiped at this time had formerly been dedicated to the various gods of the Canaanites and the Amorites who were dwelling in the land. As our discussion of chaps. 6–7 will show, from the very beginning many worshipers in Jerusalem would imagine that this temple was Yahweh's actual dwelling-place, his palace and his throne. This is a superstition which Yahwistic faith had largely surmounted by the time of Dtr; or at least it was no longer current in deuteronomistic circles, and their conception was destined to prevail in the Yahwism that survived the Babylonian exile. Here in his redactional account of how the temple came to be built, Dtr is careful to use the expression "a temple to the name of Yahweh." This avoids the gross and dangerous anthropomorphism that conceives of Yahweh as dwelling in a house, which is the temple. "The name" is a hypostasis of God, a special form in which he appears. All persons, divine or human, need names so that they may be called, for the name is the vital symbol of the person who bears it. As Dtr understood it, the Jerusalem temple was a place where "the name" of Yahweh dwelt, i.e., a specially holy site where he could be summoned and where he would respond (cf. chap. 8).

We have observed how cleverly Dtr constructed the message of Solomon and the message of Hiram so as to make the latter an eager dependent on the former. This attitude over against foreign peoples and nations was quite characteristic of Israel's self-understanding throughout the pre-exilic and much of the post-exilic period. Israel searches everywhere for precious things to bring for Yahweh's temple, but there is no equality between the giver and the receiver. Jerusalem, with its temple, comes to understand itself as the very center of the earth (Ezek 5:5). There is a kind of universalism in which all nations are allowed to contribute to the temple's glory, but get nothing comparable back. Is this spiritual imperialism? Perhaps so, but adherents of the biblical faith must always be clear that, with all the sharing among cultures and religions that is now popular, Jerusalem definitely does have priority; it has something more precious than any other city. Although all faiths possess truth and beauty, biblical faith remains as the paragon by which all other faiths are to be understood and judged.

The Construction of Solomon's Temple (6:1—7:1)

Bibliography

Busink, T. A. *Der Tempel von Jerusalem von Salomo bis Herodes.* Studia Francisci Scholten memoriae dicta, 3. Leiden: Brill, 1970. **Chapman, W. J.** "Zum Ursprung der chronologischen Angabe I Reg. 6:1." *ZAW* 38 (1935) 185–89. **Clements, R. E.** *God and Temple.* Oxford: Clarendon Press, 1965. **Gooding, D. W.** "Temple Specifications: A dispute in Logical Arrangement between the MT and the LXX." *VT* 17 (1967) 143–72. ———. "An Impossible Shrine." *VT* 15 (1965) 405–20. **Möhlenbrink, K.** *Der Tempel Salomos.* BWANT 4, 7. Stuttgart: Kohlhammer, 1932. **Myres, J. L.** "King Solomon's Temple and Other Buildings and Works of Art." *PEQ* 81 (1948) 14–41. **Ouellette, J.** "The Basic Structure of the Solomonic Temple and Archaeological Research." Ed. J. Gutmann, *The Temple of Solomon: Archaeological Fact and Medieval Tradition in Christian, Islamic and Jewish Art.* Religion and the Arts, 3. Missoula, MT: Scholars Press/ AAR-SBL, 1976. ———. "The Solomonic DᵉBIR according to the Hebrew Text of I Kings 6." *JBL* 89 (1970) 338–43. **Rowton, M. B.** "The Date of the Founding of Solomon's Temple." *BASOR* 119 (1950) 20–22. **Rupprecht, K.** "Nachrichten von Erweiterung und Renovierung des Tempels in 1. Könige 6." *ZDPV* 88 (1972) 38–52. ———. *Der Tempel von Jerusalem, Gründung Salomos oder jebusitisches Erbe?* BZAW 144. Berlin-New York: Walter de Gruyter, 1977. **Schmid, H.** "Jahwe und die Kulttraditionen von Jerusalem." *ZAW* 67 (1955) 168–97. ———. "Der Tempelbau Salomos in religionsgeschichtlicher Sicht." *Archäologie und Altes Testament* (Galling Fs). Tübingen: Mohr, 1970. **Schreiner, J.** *Sion-Jerusalem, Jahwäs Königssitz.* SANT 7 (1963). **Schult, H.** "Der Debir im salomonischen Tempel." *ZDPV* 80 (1964) 46–52. **Stolz, F.** *Strukturen und Figuren im Kult von Jerusalem.* BZAW 118 (1970). **Vincent, H.** "La description du Temple de Salomon. Notes exégétiques sur I Rois VI." *RB* 16 (1907) 515–42. **Waterman, L.** "The Damaged 'Blueprints' of the Temple." *JNES* 2 (1943) 284–94. **Yeivin, S.** "Philological Notes. 10 (3)" (Heb.). *Leš* 2 (1967–68) 6–11.

Translation

6:1 *It was in the four-hundred-eightieth[a] year since the Israelites had departed from[b] Egypt, in the fourth year, [c]second month,[c] of Solomon's reign over Israel, [d]that he built the temple.[d]* 2 *Now the temple that the king[a] built for Yahweh: sixty[b] cubits was its length, twenty[c] its width, and thirty[d] cubits its height;* 3 *and the porch before the nave:[a] twenty cubits was its length [b]extending from the temple's breadth;[b] ten cubits was its width in front of the temple.* 4 *And he designed for the temple close-latticed windows.* 5 *And he constructed[a] alongside the wall a platform[b] encircling the walls of the temple, surrounding both the nave and the adytum (a holy of holies). [c]And he made encircling stories;[c]* 6 *the lowest story[a] was five cubits in breadth, the middle one was six [b]cubits in breadth,[b] and the third one was seven cubits in breadth, for he allowed offsets for the temple, surrounding the exterior,[c] to avoid having them joined to the walls of the temple.*

7 [a] *As for the temple[a] during its construction: it was built of completely pre-prepared quarried stone, so that neither hammers nor [b]the hand-adze[bc] was heard in the temple during its construction.*

⁸*And* ᵃ *the doorway to the lower* ᵇ *story was on* ᶜ *the south side of the temple, and by flights of stairs one would ascend to* ᵈ *the middle, and from the middle to* ᵉ *the third.* ᶠ ⁹*And he constructed the temple and dressed it out by ceiling the temple with* ᵃ*cofferwork and rows of beams in* ᵃ *cedar.* ¹⁰*And he erected the platform* ᵃ *along* ᵇ *the entire temple to a height of five cubits, and supported the temple* ᶜ *with cedar beams.* ¹¹*And the word of Yahweh came to Solomon as follows:* ¹²*"As for this temple which you are building, if you walk in my statutes and perform my ordinances, keeping all my commandments by walking according to them, then I will fulfill my word made with you, the one which I spoke to David your father;* ¹³*and I will dwell amidst the Israelites and will not forsake my people Israel."*

¹⁴*Thus did he* ᵃ *build the temple and dress it out.*

¹⁵*And he constructed* ᵃ*the walls* ᵃ *of the temple with cedar boards; from the floor of the temple* ᵇ*up to the rafters* ᵇ *he covered* ᶜ *the interior with wood. And he covered the floor* ᵈ *of the temple with juniper boards.* ¹⁶*And he constructed the twenty cubits* ᵃ*toward the rear* ᵃ *of the temple* ᵇ*with cedar boards,* ᵇ *from the floor to the rafters;* ᶜ *and he constructed* ᵈ *the interior as an adytum (a holy of holies),* ¹⁷ ᵃ*with forty cubits remaining in front of it.* ᵃ ¹⁸*And the cedar for the temple's interior was carved in the form of gourds and flowerbowls; all was cedar, with no stone to be seen.* ¹⁹ ᵃ*The adytum* ᵃ *within the interior of the temple* ᵇ*he prepared* ᵇ *as a place to put the ark of Yahweh's covenant.* ²⁰ ᵃ*And the face of the adytum,* ᵃ *twenty cubits long, twenty cubits wide, and twenty cubits high,* ᵇ *he covered with fine gold. And he constructed* ᶜ *an altar.* ᵈ ²¹*And Solomon covered the temple's interior with fine gold and drew golden chains* ᵃ *across in front of the adytum, and covered it with gold.* ²²*And the entire temple he covered with gold, until all the temple was completed; and all the altar which belonged to the adytum he covered with gold.*

²³*And he made in the adytum two cherubim.* ᵃ *Ten cubits was its height* ᵇ ²⁴ ᵃ*and five cubits its wing—ten cubits between the tips of its wings.* ᵃ ²⁵ ᵃ*Similar was the second cherub.* ᵃ *The same size and same design pertained to both:* ᵇ ²⁶*the* ᵃ *height of the first cherub was ten* ᵇ *cubits, so also the second cherub.* ²⁷*And he placed* ᵃ *the cherubim inside the interior sanctuary; and they spread out* ᵇ*their wings* ᵇ *so that the wing of the one touched the wall while the wing* ᶜ*of the second cherub* ᶜ *was touching the opposite wall, and their* ᵈ *wings inside the sanctuary were touching wing to wing.* ²⁸*And he covered the cherubim with gold.*

²⁹*All* ᵃ *the walls of the temple round about he carved with sculptured figures of cherubim,* ᵇ *inside* ᶜ *and outside,* ³⁰*and the floor of the temple he covered with gold, inside and outside.*

³¹*And the entrance to the adytum he made as doors of oilwood,* ᵃ*the portal consisting of pentagonal posts.* ᵃ ³² ᵃ*And the two doors were of oilwood; and he carved on them figures of cherubim and palmtrees and flowerbowls; and he covered them with gold, and hammered out the gold into the cherubim and palmtrees.*

³³*And similarly did he make posts of oilwood for the entrance to the nave,* ᵃ ᵇ*a square corridor.* ᵇ ³⁴*And the two doors were of juniper; the two panels of* ᵃ *the first door* ᵇ*were hinged* ᵇ *and the two panels* ᶜ *of the second door were hinged.* ³⁵*He* ᵃ *carved cherubim and palmtrees and flowerbowls, and covered the engraving with goldplate.* ³⁶*And he constructed the inner court, using three courses of hewn stone with one course of cedar beams.* ᵃᵇ

³⁷*In the fourth year Yahweh's temple* ᵃ*was started,* ᵃ *in the month Ziv,* ᵇ ³⁸*and in the eleventh year, in the month Bul* ᵃ *(which is the eighth month), he had completed*

the temple in all its details and according to every specification. ᵇ*So he was seven years in building it.*ᵇ

7:1 *But his own house Solomon was building for thirteen years,* ᵃ*completing his entire house.*ᵃ

Notes

In chap. 6, G omits MT vv 11–13, 18, 21a, 22a, 31b–33a, 38b, and rearranges the text so that English/MT material appears in the sequence: 1, 6–7, 9–15, 8, 16–34, 4–5.

1.a. MT and G^L, retaining Dtr's schematic chronology; cf. S. J. De Vries, "Chronology, OT," *IDBSup*, 162. G^BA "fortieth" follows a revisionistic chronology.

1.b. G^B. MT and G^L add pleonastic "the land of."

1.c-c. G^BL. MT "in the month Ziv, which is the second month," is a gloss from v 37.

1.d-d. MT and G^Lrell. G^B omits and substitutes the beginning of v 2.

2.a. G^B, preserving the styling of the archivist (see *Comment*). MT and G^L "King Solomon" (explicative).

2.b. MT. G^BL have "forty," a correction from v 17.

2.c. MT. G^BL add pleonastic "cubits."

2.d. MT. G^BL "twenty-five"; cf. *HOTTP*, 298.

3.a. G^B. MT's addition "of the temple" and G^L's "of Yahweh" are explicative.

3.b-b. MT; lit., "along the face of the breadth of the temple," an ellipsis implying "joining to (= extending from) the temple's breadth." G^B shows *Kaige* editing in its literalistic rendering of the first and third עַל פְּנֵי "along the face of" (κατὰ πρόσωπον τοῦ), but it shows an original אֶל "toward" (εἰς) where G^L ἔτι reads Heb. עַל "against."

5.a. MT and G^L. G^B καὶ ἔδωκεν misreads Heb. וַיָּבֶן as וַיִּתֵּן "and he placed," "provided."

5.b. Q. K "bed." G^BL omit "encircling the walls of the temple" (homoioteleuton).

5.c-c. MT. G^B omits (haplography). G^L adds "the nave and the adytum" (dittography).

6.a. QK as in v 5; here the Q word acquires a different meaning. G^BL πλευρά (lit. "rib") = Heb. צֵלָע.

6.b-b. MT and G^L. G^B omits (haplography).

6.c. MT and G^L. G^B adds explicative "of the temple."

7.a-a. MT; lit., "and the temple" = G^B. G^L "for (ὅτι γαρ) the temple."

7.b-b. MT וַהֲגָרֶזֶן (*lectio difficilior*). G omits art; G^B pl.

7.c. G^L. MT adds "every/any iron instrument" (gl); MSS of G^B add clarifying and/or.

8.a. G^BL, making connection back to v 6. MT omits, following asyndetic syntax created by secondary material in v 7.

8.b. G^BL; MT "middle." Cf. v 6.

8.c. G^L ἐπὶ = עַל "upon." MT אֶל "toward." G^B ὑπο "under" (from ὑποκάτωθεν = מִתַּחַת).

8.d. G^BL εἰς = אֶל "toward." MT עַל "against" is a visual error from preceding יַעֲלוּ "they ascend."

8.e. MT אֶל "toward." G^BL ἐπὶ = עַל "against or upon."

8.f. MSS of Syr. MT and G "the thirty" (corr).

9.a-a. MT. G^BL omit.

10.a. Q; K "bed" (cf. v 5). G^BL τους ἐνδέσμους "bonding"?; cf. v 5 μέλαθρα "ridge poles"?.

10.b. MT. G^BL = לְ "through" (haplography of ע following הַיָּצוּעַ).

10.c. MT. G^BL "the platform(s)," reading Heb. הַיָּצוּעַ, read as ἐνδέσμους "binding," "joining" here (GL) and at the beginning of the verse.

14.a. G^BL. MT adds "Solomon."

15.a-a. G^BL. MT adds explicative "interior" (מביתה; cf. v 15b, v 16).

15.b-b. G^BL, reading עַד קוֹרוֹת. MT "up to the walls" (עד־קירות), adding הַסִּפֻּן "of the ceiling" as explicative. The doublet in G^BL, καὶ ἕως τῶν τοίχων, "and on to the inner walls," reads MT. Cf. *HOTTP*, 304–5.

15.c. MT. G^BL corr.

15.d. MT. G^BL "the interior."

16.a-a. Q modernizes the K spelling.

16.b-b. MT. G^B corr; G^L omits.

16.c. G^BL. MT "walls"; cf. v 15.

16.d. MT. G^BL "made." With G^B, MT (cf. G^L) לו "it," an explicative gl, should be omitted, making מבית "the interior" the verbal object.

17.a-a. The probably original, וארבעים באמה היה לפניו "and forty cubits was before it," has received successive glosses in MT (הבית "the house" and ההיכל הוא "it is the temple," the latter of which is reflected in G^BL, which read an original הדביר "the adytum" from v 19 (cf. OL^Lᵍ, Vg), omitting v 18.

19.a-a. Cf. Note on G^BL in v 17. MT "and an adytum" corr.

19.b-b. MT. G^BL omit.

20.a-a. MT. G^BL omit (haplography); cf. vv 17–19.

20.b. MT and G^BL add suffix wāw, borrowed from the following copula.

20.c. G^BL. MT "covered" corr from v 21.

20.d. G^BL. MT adds explicative "with/from cedar."

21.a. Q and K are variant orthographic forms.

23.a. G^B. MT and G^L add explicative "of oilwood."

23.b. MT. G^BL corr.

24.a-a. G^B reads the original text except for an explanatory gl, δεύτερον δέ (וְהַשֵּׁנִית "and the second"). G^L follows an expansive MT and G^O.

25.a-a. G^B. G^L adds "and." MT "and ten cubits was the second cherub" is explicative.

25.b. G^BL. MT adds explicative "cherubim."

26.a. MT. G^BL "and the" is explicative.

26.b. MT and G^L. G^B omits.

27.a. MT. G^BL add "both," a corr from הֹשֵּׁנִי, v 26.

27.b-b. G^BL. MT "the wings of the cherubim" is pleonastic.

27.c-c. MT and G^L. G^B omits (haplography).

27.d. MT and G^L. G^B "his/its" misinterprets the antecedent because of the foregoing haplography.

29.a. G^B. MT and G^L have "and all," creating a more syndetic syntax.

29.b. G^BL. MT adds "and palmtrees and flowerbowls" under influence of v 32.

29.c. MT מִלְפָנִים corr; cf. לִפְנִימָה in v 30.

31.a-a. G^B omits (haplography from v 33. G^L partially renders MT, reading חֲמוּשׁוֹת "five-folded" for חֲמִישִׁית "pentagonal." Cf. v 33.

32.a-33.a. G^B omits; hab G^Lrell.

33.b-b. G^L στοαὶ τετραπλῶς (G^B pl) and MT (corr) probably read an original אתיק רבעות; cf. Ezek 42:5.

34.a. MT and G^L. G^B "and" destroys the genitival connection between "panels" and "door."

34.b-b. MT. G^BL καὶ στροφεῖς αὐτῶν "and their folds" = Heb. וגלילותם.

34.c. G^BL. MT "carvings" corr from v 35. Cf. HOTTP, 301.

35.a. G^BL. MT "and he" establishes a syndetic relationship to v 34 because of the verb קלע "carve."

36.a. G^BL κατειργασμένης = חרשת "engraved" (cf. Exod 35:23) for MT כרתת "cut," a possible corr through dictation, and adds "surrounding" = סביב.

36.b. MT. G^BL add words resembling MT 7:12b (corr?). Cf. Burney, 83.

37.a-a. MT. G^BL "he started (founded)."

37.b. MT. G^BL "Nisan" is interpretive.

38.a. MT. G^BL have corrupt reading, βααδ (cf. G^mss βααλ).

38.b-b. MT. G^BL omit; = 2:35^cβ.

7:1.a-a. MT. G (v 50) follows MT v 12.

Form/Structure/Setting

[Dtr: Chronological note on the construction of the temple, 6:1]
Extract from the Book of Solomon's Acts (8): Solomon's temple (with supplements from official records)

1. The external structure: walls, foundation, supporting structures, roof
   a. The temple and the porch, vv 2aα, 3aα
      (1) Dimensions from architectural records, vv 2aβb, 3aβb

b. Construction of the windows, v 4
c. Construction of the platform, v 5a
d. Construction of the stories, v 5b
   (1) Dimensions and technical details from architectural records, vv
     6, 8
[Expansion: Use of pre-prepared material, v 7]
e. Construction of the temple, v 9
   (1) Dimensions and technical details from architectural records, v
     10
[Dtr: Yahweh's conditional presence, vv 11–13]
f. Summarizing conclusion, v 14
2. The internal structure: paneling, partitioning, entrances
  a. Construction of the walls and floor, v 15
  b. Construction of the adytum, vv 16–17, 20aαℵβ
    (1) Dimensions from architectural records, v 20aαℷ
[Expansion: Ornamentation, v 18]
[Expansion: The adytum, v 19]
  e. Construction of the altar, vv 20b, 21bβ
[Expansion: The golden chains, v 21abα]
[Expansion: The use of gold throughout, v 22]
  d. Construction of the cherubim, vv 23–24a, 28
    (1) Dimensions from architectural records, vv 24b–26
[Expansion: The positioning of the cherubim, v 27]
[Expansion: Ornamentation of the temple, vv 29–30]
  e. Construction of the entrance to the adytum, v 31
[Expansion: Ornamentation of its doors, v 32]
  f. Construction of the entrance to the nave, v 33
    (1) Technical details from architectural records, v 34
[Expansion: Ornamentation of its doors, v 35]
3. The inner court, v 36
Extract from the Book of Solomon's Acts (9): The time of building, vv 37–38
[Dtr: Addition on the building of Solomon's palace, 7:1]

What follows here pertains to both chap. 6 and chap. 7. They form a single complex. The literary composition of this material has long been a puzzle to biblical interpreters. The Hebrew text is difficult, while the LXX only adds to the confusion. The Greek translators are at their very worst in rendering the plethora of arcane architectural terms found in these two chapters. The difficulty of the text and the inherent interest of the subject matter have stimulated an extensive literature dealing (1) with literary composition and (2) with the structures themselves. Upon consulting this literature, one will find that there has always been a heavy reliance on typology. That is to say, scholars have looked to Greek, Egyptian, Mesopotamian, and Phoenician models (linguistically as well as architecturally) upon which to base their conceptions. (The rabbinic tradition has its own special explanations; Christian models have often been based on medieval conceptions.) The most painstaking, extensive, and judicious analysis of the temple complex yet to appear is Th. A. Busink, *Der Tempel von Jerusalem* (1970). Although Busink does not offer an independent rendering of the Hebrew text, his handling of typological questions is exhaustive. Our discussion will rely heavily upon it.

With reference to the text of 1 Kgs 6–7, it is obvious that the critic needs to put things in order by first identifying the work of Dtr and other late expansions, assuming then that the remainder must be original. This type of literary analysis must of course take account of both the subject matter and the internal structure. One must be wary of following the order offered in the LXX, for the serious confusion that it often displays with regard to translating the Hebrew has led it, inadvisably, to attempt to create a more logical order, but this idealized reconstruction, based on its own failure to understand, cannot be trusted. The fact is that, once Dtr's chronological notes in 6:1 and 7:1 are removed from consideration, and late expansions in 6:7, 11–13, 18–19, 21–22, 27, 29–30, 32–35; 7:18–19, 22, 48–50 are identified, a meaningful progression does emerge, as follows:

A. The temple
   1. External structure
   2. Internal structure
   3. Inner court
B. Palace complex: five buildings
C. Methods of construction
D. Hiram's handiwork
   1. The pillars
   2. The reservoir and watercarts
   3. Utensils (with note on the casting process).

The order here is of course not temporal or derivatory, but logical and relational.

The above approach shows that the text does have a meaningful structure. Some scholars have felt that much can be done by studying syntactical patterns, with special attention to the variation between a long series of noun-clauses appearing in the descriptive sections and a series of narrative sentences beginning with the *wāw*-consecutive imperfect. In his commentary, Martin Noth argues that the text is derived from oral reports of what was in effect an architectural blueprint for the temple, with similar materials for chap. 7 (see also L. Waterman, *JNES* 2 [1943] 284–94). The style certainly suits such a document, and it is our opinion that some kind of architectural records were indeed employed. One notices that the narrative sentences are interwoven with nominal descriptions, as "warp intermeshed with woof," so that more than a mere blueprint is involved.

The literary analyst wishes that he might find some word or expression, common to the entire OT, running through every suspected layer of material in this section, revealing through special usages the hands of various writers. There is in fact just such a term in the word אמה, "cubit," the common unit of measurement appearing throughout chaps. 6–7, but in distinct forms and combinations. A careful analysis of these forms can lead us to a solid literary reconstruction.

A notable peculiarity in 1 Kgs 6–7 is that sixteen times a dimension is given where the MT offers a number followed by the form באמה; ignoring the prefixed ב, this apparently means—and is so translated—"cubits." There appears to be no distinction in meaning and function from the more customary

אמתים/אמה, du./אמות locution which occurs twenty-five times in this same section, except that while the latter consistently follows a normative variation (cf. C. Brockelmann, *Hebräische Syntax,* Neukirchen: Neukirchener Verlag [1956] §83a, 84a) for numbers 3–10 and above 10, באמה never varies in form. It thus shows complete independence of the normative idiom. The biblical commentaries offer no comment on this phenomenon, nor do the grammars. It appears, however, to be related to an antique Semitic idiom. This is identified for Akkadian by W. von Soden, *Grundriss der akkadischen Grammatik* §139ⁱ, where Old Akkadian is cited: *tišē ina ammitim,* "nine cubits"; and Middle Babylonian: *ina ammati,* "a cubit." E. G. Kraeling, *The Brooklyn Museum Aramaic Papyri* (New Haven: Yale University Press, 1953) 173, reports a similar locution in Imperial Aramaic. The preposition *ina* preceding the unit of measure points to a primitive locution, "(number) in (terms of) a cubit."

The form באמה occurs sporadically, intermixed with the אמות/אמה idiom, in two other (quasi) architectural pericopes regarding the sanctuary; i.e., at Exod 26:2 twice, 8 twice, 9, 18; 36:9 twice, 15; 38:9, 11, 12; Ezek 40:5, 21; 47:3. It occurs two times in Zech 5:2 (the ephah). It occurs in 2 Chr 4:2–3, which renders 1 Kgs 7:23–24 verbatim. It occurs in an apparently primitive reading at 1 Chr 11:23, where the parallel text, 2 Sam 23:21, lacks Chr's חמש באמה "five cubits," a corruption supported by G. Finally, it is instructive to observe the shift in Num 35:4–5 from an original אלף אמה סביב "a thousand cubits all around," assigned as Levitical pasture land, to a four-sided strip measuring אלפים באמה "two thousand cubits," in the secondary reinterpretation.

This literary survey could be refined by a detailed analysis of the interrelationships between the באמה and the אמות/אמה occurrences in Exod 26–28 P, and Ezek 40 and following, respectively. Enough has come to light, however, to show that the באמה idiom was an established tradition among the Hebrews. It is difficult to date it in the literature, though clearly the chronicler avoids it except where citing verbatim from passages where it occurs. Yet even he recognizes it as a variant form of expression that is perfectly understandable and acceptable. Nevertheless, it stands out as an oddity over against the more sophisticated אמות/אמה styling, a drawback which the LXX translators of 1 Kgs 6–7 handled inconsistently, but with the general aim of replacing a literalistic rendering with something more normatively Greek.

When the Gᴮ and Gᴸ readings are compared with their Heb. counterparts in 1 Kgs 6–7, we discover evidence for a more extensive original employment of the באמה idiom than what is attested in the sixteen occurrences in MT. Consistently, G offers πῆχυς (see R. Helbing, *Grammatik der Septuaginta, Laut- und Wortlehre* [2nd ed., Göttingen: Vandenhoeck & Ruprecht, 1979] 44–45) as its equivalent for אמה, though in a number of passages it reads a different, often patently tendentious, numeral. It is striking that wherever the אמה/אמות idiom is being translated, G has the pl. of πῆχυς, and this is true whether the governing word is singular or plural. Wherever MT has our peculiar באמה, however, one or both of the principle LXX recensions translates it with the quite unidiomatic ἐν πήχει. It also occurs that Gᴮ or Gᴸ has ἐν πήχει when MT has אמות/אמה, showing that the Heb. *Vorlage* in such instances had באמה, for the Gr. would not offer this uncouth literalism if it were not in the original text. The constant variation within the Greek tradition indicates a struggle to be free from a difficult Heb. *Vorlage* in favor of a more elegant Gr. style. These observations enable us to add several passages to our list of באמה readings, for the Gr. text is as useful a witness as the MT to what the original reading must have been.

This discussion offers an important clue, then, for the literary criticism of these difficult chapters. The alternation between the אמות/אמה idiom and the באמה idiom must be viewed as a stylistic characteristic of the specific underlying documents from which these chapters have been drawn.

The final inventory of באמה readings (Heb. and Gr.) includes the following: 6:2 (three times), 3 (twice), 6 (three times), 10, 24 (3rd), 26, 7:23 (three times), 24, 27 (three times), 38. In 6:2–6 a narrative framework based on action verbs in *waw*-impf consec ("and he made . . . and he built . . . and he made . . . for he provided . . .") is filled out with a sequence of nominal statements that pertain mainly to dimensions, and it is these sections that have the באמה idiom. Our conjecture is that the narrator is here citing verbatim from a written architectural record containing these data; so too in v 10. Passing over vv 15–17 for the moment, to return to it presently, we may assign the original occurrences of באמה in v 24 (3rd) and v 26 to the same or a similar architectural record, used here by the narrator to fill out his own sparse details concerning the cherubim in v 23 and v 24 (however, the LXX is to be followed in vv 24–25 in omitting repetitious dimensions due to expansiveness and pedantry in the MT scribal tradition). When the באמה idiom next appears, it is in the dimensions offered for the "sea" or reservoir (7:23 three times, 24), for the watercarts (7:27 three times), and for the lavers (7:38), all of which, together with certain other design specifications, may have been drawn from the same or similar architectural records.

As for אמות/אמה, we can list as probably original those in 6:16, 17, 20 (3x), 23, 24 (1st, 2nd), 7:2 (3x), 10 (2x), 15 (2x), 16 (2x), 19. The occurrences in 6:16–17, 20 all have to do with the adytum (דביר) and are integrated into the narrative structure in such a way as to suggest the probability that they too were lifted from a separate architectural record. The same style continues in 6:23–24a, marking the אמות occurrences as part of the primary narrator's writing, especially in light of the fact that v 23, עשר אמות קומתו, "ten cubits its height," duplicates the information in v 26, drawn from the architectural record and reading קומת הכרוב האחד עשר באמה "the height of the one cherub was ten cubits." In chap. 7 the אמות/אמה idiom prevails in the sections that pertain to Solomon's building activities within the palace complex (vv 2–12) and to the pillars in front of the temple (vv 15–22). In these sections the same narrative style that was found in chap. 6 continues, but readily gives way to predominating nominal sentence structures. We may attribute the styling of these sections to the primary writer except in 7:19, where the reference to lilywork as ornamentation, in the place of reticulations, chainwork, and pomegranates, marks this verse as a secondary gloss which actually refers to a different set of pillars standing within the porch of the temple (Busink).

To summarize: our study of the "cubits" idiom enables us to hypothesize the composition history of 1 Kgs 6–7 as follows. Dtr, whose hand is directly seen in 6:1, 11–13, 7:1, employed six different extracts from the record called the Book of Solomon's Acts:

(1) Solomon's temple, 6:2–36 (with late glosses at vv 7, 19, 21abα, 22, 27, 29–30, 32, 35)
(2) The time of building, 6:37–38
(3) Solomon's building projects, 7:2–8
(4) Methods of construction, 7:9–12
(5) Hiram's handiwork, 7:13–51a (with glosses at vv 18a, 19, 22a, 48–50)
(6) The deposit of David's gifts, 7:51b.

The dominant style throughout these extracts is that of אמות/אמה; it is in the verbatim citations from architectural records that the באמה idiom appears. These are, understandably, in section (1), dealing with the temple (6:2–3, 6, 10, 24b–26) and in certain parts of section (5), expanding the narrator's information concerning the holy utensils (7:23–24, 27, 38). Not yet mentioned are the four dimensions found in 7:31, 32, 35; all belong to a design specification cited by the framework narrator. For lengths between one-half cubit (7:35) to one and a half cubits (7:31 [2nd], 32) אמה is used. באמה appears in 7:31 and has been translated "one cubit" (rsv), but without warrant; the באמה form may simply be a scribal carryover from באמה in v 27, so that אמה would have been original.

Thus we have identified architectural records as source material. Information for them has been drawn into a narrative account concerning the several buildings. These have been combined in the Book of Solomon's Acts, which in the course of time Dtr extracted for his own presentation, meanwhile adding dates in 6:1 and 7:1, and inserting a noticeably irrelevant admonition in the midst of the construction narrative, 6:11–13. Probably in the post-deuteronomistic period a rather impressive number of explanatory glosses were added, most having to do with ornamentation and the application of gold, showing that Israel's conception of the temple and its accouterments continued to expand with the passage of time.

Comment

1 There can be no mistaking of the special solemnity with which Dtr records the date when the temple began to be built. In all the chronological notices that are to follow in 1–2 Kgs, many dates and years will be casually announced, but two elements mark this particular date as especially portentous: (1) the measurement is in terms of the Exodus, the departure from Egypt, as if the building of the temple marks the fulfillment of the Exodus; and (2) the highly schematic number, 480, which equals 4 x 12 x 10. Each figure had symbolic value for Dtr. Bible students have long struggled with this text because it seems to demand a fourteenth-century B.C. date for the Exodus, but efforts to apply this literally have been largely abandoned. Of course, there is a continuing interest in what Dtr intended, and the most satisfying solution appears to be the one that Martin Noth offers (*Überlieferungs-geschichtliche Studien*, 2nd ed., 1957, 18–27; cf. S. J. De Vries, "Chronology, OT" *IDBSup* 162–65). As Noth shows, Dtr found a total of 76 years in his source material for the "minor judges"; he contrived a total of 154 more years for when Israel had to do penance for backsliding (including the 40 years of wilderness wandering), and he contrived 249 further years, largely in units of 40, for the time when Israel enjoyed victory and peace. See also W. J. Chapman (*ZAW* 38 [1935] 185–89) and M. B. Rowton (*BASOR* 119 [1950] 20–22). "The fourth year, second month of Solomon's reign over Israel" may have been drawn from original sources.

2–36 The narrator begins in a kind of ledger style: "Now the temple that the king built for Yahweh . . . and the porch before the nave" (vv 1–2), but he immediately abandons this in favor of a narrative framework that is filled in with replete details. The temple was built of stone, with a cedar roof and interior wall paneling, and juniper boards on the floor. It stood all alone in the middle of the large inner court described in v 36. The ground underneath was a barren, fairly level rock, having formerly been used as a threshing floor (2 Sam 24). Some of the details given in this chapter are clear; others are not. We know, for instance, that the temple was long and consisted of three separate chambers (it is based on a Phoenician-Syrian model; cf. Busink). The dimensions were sixty cubits (cubit = 1.5 ft.) long, with a porch twenty cubits long in front of it; it was also twenty cubits wide and thirty cubits high. Thus it was not very large by modern standards. Its roof was probably flat, and there was a strange kind of structure built around the outside, the purpose of which was to help support the external walls of the sanctuary itself. This structure served also as a storeroom. Inside there was no furniture, only an altar standing before a closed-in adytum or holy-of-holies. There were beams and cofferwork on the ceiling, and near the ceiling a number of small recessed windows, intended more for letting out the smoke from the altar than for admitting light. All in all, this was a dark and mysterious structure, conducive to a sense of awe. Within the adytum stood two composite mythical beings, the cherubim, who symbolized the presence of Yahweh.

These verses contain a sizable number of architectural terms that unavoidably remain more or less problematical to us. Generally, we must surmise the meaning from analogies in other ancient temples, but occasionally terms are used that also have a common, everyday meaning, from which we may conjecture the special technical meaning. For the reader's benefit, we offer here a list of the architectural terms used in the original sections of this chapter. The identification is usually Busink's, but the choice of English equivalents is our own:

temple בית: the ordinary word for "house"; porch אולם: a roofed, pillared, structure at the entranceway; nave היכל: the interior of the main part of the temple; windows חלונים: deeply recessed and latticed, high near the roof; platform יציע: a high-standing foundation built out of large blocks; adytum דביר: the inner room (20 x 20 x 20 cubits) where Yahweh dwelt; story צלע, lit., "rib": one of the three levels in the surrounding structure; doorway פתח: an opening for a door, as at the front and side of the temple; side כתף, lit., "shoulder": the outside flank; flight of stairs לולים: probably winding or reversing; cofferwork גבים: recessed panels with reticular beams; rows of beams שדרת: the reticular beams; walls קירות: external or internal; floor קרקע; rafters (G קורות M corr): the roof beams (heavy timbers 30 ft. long); altar מזבח: only one in this temple, of cedar covered with gold; cherubim כרובים: composite mythical creatures with wings; portal איל: a recessed entrance to the adytum; doorposts מזוזות: shaped side-pieces for the portal; doors דלתות: not the doorway (*petaḥ*) but the door closing; corridor (G אתיק; M corr): a passageway from the porch to the nave; panels קלעים: folding sections of the outside door; inner court החצר הפנימית: the open, walled-in space surrounding the temple.

It is in vv 2–10 that the narrator tells about the temple, the porch, the windows, the platform, and the stories, with door and stairway. At vv 2, 3, 6, and 8 he incorporates dimensions drawn from his architectural record. According to the preferred reading, the king is not named, though his identification as Solomon would be understood. In v 9 the Heb. reads ויבן את הבית ויכלהו. We translate this, "And he constructed the temple and dressed it out," understanding this to mean that he first built the walls, stories, etc., and then completed it by constructing the roof. In v 14 the Heb. reads an almost identical ויבן שלמה את הבית ויכלהו. The proper name drops out as nonoriginal and we translate, "Thus did he build the temple and dress it out," understanding this as a resumptive summary to all of vv 2–10. M. Görg (*BN* 13 [1980] 22–25) proposes an Egyptian equivalent meaning "roof" for the word אולם in v 2. J. Ouellette (*RB* 76 [1969] 365–78) sees v 4's חלוני, "windows," as justification for his conjecture that this temple was actually a *bit ḥilāni* (Akkadian for an open, pillared portico); this same scholar derives v 4's אטמים, "latticed" from a Dravidian word meaning "raised platform" (*BIJS* 2, 99–102); Ouellette likewise goes far afield for יציע "platform" in v 5 and צלעות "stories" in vv 5–6 (*JNES* 31 [1972] 187–91); M. Gil in *BMik* 50 (1972) 279–301 reads לולים "flights of stairs" in v 8 as "passageways"; M. Görg in *BN* 10 (1979) 12–15, goes to Egyptian to find a new meaning for גבים ושדרת "coffer work and rows of beams" in v 9; he would translate, "side buildings and halls of columns" (on גבים see also P. de Lagarde in *Mittheilungen,* IV, 235). The validity of such suggestions has to be questioned because many of them are drawn from culture-areas far removed from Palestine and because they disrupt the integrated image of the temple that one must derive from all the biblical data taken together (cf. Busink).

V 7 is not deuteronomistic, as some have believed, but clearly does not belong to the original document. It divides the verses dealing with the stories (6, 8) and differs from the original document in style and conception (on its meaning, see H. Schult, *ZDPV* 88 [1972] 53–54). The deuteronomistic intrusion in vv 11–13 likewise disrupts the context, inserting Yahweh's promise to be present among the Israelites on condition of Solomon's obedience to the commandments.

The narrative style continues in vv 15–34, where the temple's walls and floor, the adytum, and the outer entrance to the nave are described. We observe the specification of four special costly materials: cedar for the wall panels, juniper for the floors and door panels, oilwood for the doorways and cherubim, and gold for the front of the adytum, the altar, and the cherubim. Our author turns to his architectural record(s) for the dimensions of the adytum and the cherubim and for the technical details concerning the outer door. It is especially in vv 23–26, 28 that our foregoing analysis of the באמה "cubit" idiom bears fruit, for now the over-full text, separated into the basic construction narrative on the one hand, and an architectural record with באמה on the other, begins to make sense. But the exegete has other hurdles to negotiate: the eight distinct expansions within this section, almost all of which have to do with carved decorations and with the lavish application of gold. An important linguistic clue to the identity of this expansive material is its repeated use of the perfect with conjunctive *wāw* in place of the narrative *wāw*-consecutive imperfect. Once this material is removed, it will be seen that "Jerusalem the Golden" is a figment of someone's imagination. It was only the passing of time (and perhaps the passing of the temple) that encouraged the Jews to think that Solomon's temple had entirely been of gold.

The narrator's description of the temple's outer door leads him to a very brief description of what lay outside it, viz., the "inner court" (see above). The description is similar to that of the walls surrounding the great court, 7:12. H. C. Thomson (*PEQ* 92 [1960] 57–63) identifies the pattern as Syrian and describes it as an earthquake-resisting device, possibly intended for supporting an overburden of brick or small stones.

37–38, 7:1 The Book of Solomon's Acts is the source for a chronological notice for the beginning and end of the construction work on Solomon's temple. "In the fourth year": the king's reign is not mentioned, but is understood; Dtr in v 1 drew on this same notice. "Ziv" and "Bul" are Canaanite names for the second month (Apr-May) and eighth month (Oct-Nov), respectively. Thus seven years and six months were consumed in this work, and the writer states emphatically that absolutely all details were completed in this period. This is rounded off to an even seven years, the number of perfection. Dtr's notice in 7:1 should not be taken as part of 7:2–8 because those verses include a description of Solomon's house (palace) in v 8a. Dtr was perhaps driven by the desire to make every conceivable relevant comment, for 7:1 is needed neither for chap. 6 nor for chap. 7.

Explanation

In the *Introduction* and in the *Explanation* to chap. 6 we have made pertinent observations with regard to the construction of Solomon's temple. Solomon was deliberately breaking with the ancestral tradition that Yahweh could have no central shrine, no "house" to dwell in. This is a necessary and logical implication of monotheistic personalism when taken in dead earnest. Yet biblical historians agree that this was an inevitable consequence of a centralized monarchy. One nation, one capital, one king demanded one temple for its one God. In building that temple, Solomon undoubtedly did just what 1 Kgs said he did: expended extensive wealth and every available skill upon it. Its resulting glory would reflect Yahweh's glory, but it would certainly bring praise as well to Solomon, to Jerusalem, and to Israel. With the temple, there would grow an elaborate system of sacrifices, together with a burgeoning guild of priests with their auxiliary cultic personnel. To them, not to Judah's kings, would belong the ultimate future of the Hebraic-Jewish tradition.

With respect to the architecture of the temple, two features are especially expressive. The temple was built to last, and it stood in an empty space, outside the walls of Ophel, the Solomonic Jerusalem. That it was built of massive stone walls signified the notion that Yahweh was to dwell there indefinitely, and that his "covenant" with the sons of David was to last permanently. Somehow those walls seemed to guarantee that Yahweh would never wish to depart from Jerusalem. They encouraged those who saw them to rely more on the outward symbols of Yahweh's presence than on the pious performance of his commandments and the heartfelt loyalty to his covenant that his spokesmen continually demanded. No wonder that an exasperated Jeremiah would one day cry out, "Do not trust in these deceptive words: 'This is the temple of Yahweh, the temple of Yahweh, the temple of Yahweh!'" (Jer 7:4).

The temple stood in the large open space that is now called "the dome of the rock." It was not in the midst of the city, like most heathen temples of the time. Its isolation symbolized the uniqueness of the deity to whom it was dedicated. And the fact that this was no rededicated temple, taken over from the dispossessed deity of some captive people, emphasizes that the religion devoted to him was radically new. Such indeed is biblical religion, in spite of repeated efforts from many sides to compromise and confuse it.

In 1977, Konrad Rupprecht published his Heidelberg dissertation, *Der Tempel von Jerusalem, Gründung Salomos oder jebusitisches Erbe?* A word must be said about it before we can leave the present subject. Rupprecht argues that there had been no actual tent-shrine in Jerusalem during David's reign, but rather a Jebusite temple mentioned in 2 Sam 12:20, for which the Araunah legend of 2 Sam 24 served as a legitimation narrative prior to its reshaping. Rupprecht argues further that all references to Solomon's building operations in 1 Kgs are secondary reinterpretations, while את־הבית ושלם "and he completed the temple" in 1 Kgs 9:25 reflects the historical fact that Solomon actually reconstructed, remodeled, or modified an existing temple taken over for Yahweh by David. To uphold this thesis, Rupprecht argues that in 1 Kgs 6, only vv 1–3, 9a, 14, 37–38 refer to original work done on the temple, while v 7 is a clue to a remodeling project in which Solomon himself was the builder. He also argues that only vv 1–2 are original in 2 Sam 6; that 2 Sam 7 is nothing but secondary reinterpretation; that references to the "tent" in 1 Kgs 1:39, 2:28–30 are using that word as a symbolic appellation for an actual temple. 1 Kgs 8:4 is a late priestly gloss; Ps 132:3, 5 refer to a temple, not a tent; and 2 Chr 3:1 resurrects authentic historical tradition in identifying the temple site with Araunah's threshing-floor.

The greatest weakness in Rupprecht's thesis is his slipshod textual and form-critical analysis. He is unduly suspicious of ascriptions of temple-building to Solomon, for the Jebusite shrine that must have existed in Ophel would hardly have stood in a separate, open area, such as the temple mount, outside the city walls. Although a threshing-floor may at times be the scene of special revelatory activity, it is not the site of an organized sacrificial cult. It is probable that David did take over an existing Jebusite temple, erecting alongside it a sacred tent as the provisional locus for the ark. On the temple mount was Araunah's threshing floor, where David took over a free-standing altar originally belonging to Araunah. But the architectural design of Solomon's temple, based on Phoenician rather than Palestinian antecedents, argues that he was indeed the builder, not just the remodeler, of Yahweh's proper shrine in Jerusalem.

The Construction of the Palace Complex (7:2–12)

Bibliography

Görg, M. "Lexicalisches zur Beschreibung des salomonischen Palastbezirks (1 Kön 7, 1–12)." *BN* 11 (1980) 7–13. **Mulder, M. J.** "Einige Bemerkungen zur Beschreibung des Libanonwaldhauses in I Reg 7, 2f." *ZAW* 88 (1976) 99–105. **Ussishkin, D.** "King Salomon's Palaces." *BA* 36 (1973) 78–105. **Vincent, H.** "Une antichambre du palais du Salomon. Note de critique textuelle sur I Rois 7, 6." *RB* 14 (1905) 258–65.

Translation

² *And he constructed the House of the Lebanon Forest, a hundred cubits in length and fifty cubits in width and* ᵃ*thirty cubits in height,*ᵃ *upon three*ᵇ *rows of cedar pillars, with cedar beams*ᶜ *atop the pillars,* ³ *covered*ᵃ *above* ᵇ*with cedar*ᵇ *atop* ᶜ*the chambers which were over the pillars,*ᶜ *forty-five, fifteen*ᵈ *per row,* ⁴ *with windowpanes*ᵃ *in three rows,*ᵇ *aperture over against aperture at three separate locations,* ⁵ *and all the doorways and doorposts*ᵃ *square,* ᵇ*at the opening*ᵇ ᶜ*and at the forefront,*ᶜ *aperture over against*ᵈ *aperture at three separate locations;* ⁶ *also the Hall of Pillars,*ᵃ *fifty*ᵇ *long and thirty*ᶜ ᵈ*in width,*ᵈ *with*ᵉ *a hall along their front and pillars with a balustrade along their front;*ᶠ ⁷ *also the Throne Hall where he would render judgment (the Hall of Judgment),*ᵃ ᵇ*covered with cedar from the floor to the rafters;*ᵇᶜ ⁸ *also his*ᵃ *own house where he resided,* ᵇ*in the other court outside the Hall,*ᵇ *similar to this same pattern in construction;*ᶜ *also the house*ᵈ *belonging to Pharaoh's daughter whom Solomon took in marriage, similar to this Hall.* ⁹ *All these were*ᵃ *costly stones,*ᵇ *sawn with a stonesaw inside* ᶜ*and out,*ᶜ *and used from the foundation up to the framework*ᵈ *as far as the great court.* ¹⁰ *It*ᵃ *was footed with precious stones, great stones,* ᵇ*stones of ten cubits and stones of eight cubits;*ᵇ ¹¹ *also the elevation consisted of precious ones,*ᵃ *made to measure out of dressed stone, with cedar.* ¹² *And*ᵃ *the great court on all sides had three courses of dressed stones with a row of cedar beams;* ᵇ*so also the inner court of Yahweh's temple and the nave of the temple.*ᵇ

Notes

In chap. 7, G equivalents to the MT appear in the following order: 38, 50, 39–49, 1–6, 8–9, 7, 10–11, 13, 12, 14–37. G omits MT vv 7b, 12b, 18bα, 20b, 22, 23bβ, 24b

2.a-a. MT. G^{BL} omit (haplography).

2.b. G^{BL}. MT "four."

2.c. G^{BL} ὡμίαι "shoulders" (= וכתפות, corr from וכרתות "and cedar beams" = MT.

3.a. MT; cf. v 7b *plene*. G^{BL} "and he roofed" reads Heb. pass ptcp of ספן as Heb. pf = aor; cf. 6:15.

3.b-b. MT. G^{BL} "the house."

3.c-c. MT. G^{BL} reads the same Heb. but translates "the ribs (stories) of the pillars."

3.d. MT. G^{BL} omits (haplography).

4.a. MT. G^{BL} μέλαθρα "rooftrees" translates יציע "platform" in 6:5.

4.b. MT. In G^{BL} "three" modifies μέλαθρα "rooftrees" (haplography).

5.a. G^BL χῶραι "space" (= והמחזות; cf. מחזה "aperture" twice in v 5.b. MT has erroneous והמזוזות "and the thresholds." See *HOTTP*, 302f.
5.b-b. MT. G^BL corr.
5.c-c. MT ומול "and in front." G^BL καὶ ἀπὸ "and away from" = ומעל (auditory corr?).
5.d. MT אל "towards." G^BL על "upon or against."
6.a. G^BL. MT adds "he made."
6.b. G^B. MT and G^L add "cubits."
6.c. MT and G^L. G^B "fifty" (dittography).
6.d-d. MT. G^BL corr (doublet).
6.e. G^BL omit (haplography).
6.f. MT. G^BL add the explicative gloss, "the halls."
7.a. G^BL. MT adds "he made."
7.b-b. MT. G^BL omit.
7.c. Syr. MT הקרקע "the floor" is corrupt.
8.a. MT. G^BL "their."
8.b-b. MT. G^BL corr.
8.c. G^BL. MT adds "it was."
8.d. G^BA. MT adds "he made." G^L "and Solomon built a house."
9.a. MT. G^BL add "out of."
9.b. G^BL. MT adds gl כמדת גזית "according to measure out of dressed stones" (cf. v 11).
9.c-c. MT. G^BL omit.
9.d. MT. G^BL γεισῶν "cornices." MT and G^BL add "and outward" (haplography). Cf. *HOTTP*, 303.
10.a. G^BL. MT "and it" endeavors a more syndetic style.
10.b-b. MT. G^BL are paraphrastic.
11.a. G^B. MT and G^L add explicative "stones."
12.a. MT. G^BL "of/from" (corr?).
12.b-b. MT. G^BL omit; cf. 6:36 (Burney, 83). MT is elliptical; lit., "both pertaining to Yahweh's interior temple and to the nave of the temple."

Form/Structure/Setting

Extract from the Book of Solomon's Acts (10): Solomon's building projects
1. The House of the Lebanon Forest
    a. Its dimensions, v 2aα
    b. The pillars and beams, v 2aβb
    c. The roof chambers, v 3
    d. The apertures
        (1) Windows, v 4
        (2) Doorways, v 5
2. The Hall of Pillars
    a. Its dimensions, v 6a
    b. Its construction, v 6b
3. The Throne Hall, v 7
4. The royal residence, v 8a
5. The queen's residence, v 8b
Extract from the Book of Solomon's Acts (11): Methods of construction
1. Preparation of the stones, v 9
2. Application of the stones, vv 10–11
3. Construction of the court walls, v 12

With regard to the source-criticism of this section, see on chap. 6. The style is densely descriptive and loaded with technical architectural terms. Our

English translations (cf. RSV) render several verbs as they appear in MT but we rely on G^B in acknowledging only וַיִּבֶן, "and he constructed," at the beginning of v 2 as original, governing each of the structures mentioned in vv 2–8. This is confirmed by the fact that even MT lacks this verb in v 8a, though it does supply it in v 8b. Vv 9–12 are entirely nominal, lacking any verb whatsoever. In v 6 a dimension is given without either of the idioms for "cubit(s)," a kind of ellipsis like our expression, "two by four," meaning "a board two inches broad and four inches wide."

Comment

2–8 Solomon's five edifices. The only building material mentioned is cedar, no gold as in the temple, though there must have been some in David's palace and the palace of Pharaoh's daughter, which are not described. The last two structures are given no special name, but for the first three we are given the names "House of the Lebanon Forest," "Hall of Pillars," and "Throne Hall" (also known as "the Hall of Judgment"). As in chap. 6, there are a sizable number of arcane architectural terms that gave the ancient translators endless vexation, and that continue to attract novel suggestions from modern scholars (see *Bibliography*). We offer the following equivalents: pillar, עַמּוּד: a heavy post, not the עַמּוּד of carved stone, v 15; chamber, צֵלָע: lit., "rib"; a compartment on the second story of the House of the Lebanon Forest; cf. "story," 6:6; beam, עָמֻד: a cross-joist supporting the chambers; windowpane, שֶׁקֶף: for admitting light, unlike the חַלּוֹנִים in the temple; aperture, מְחֱזָה: hole in the wall for windowpane; doorway, פֶּתַח: hole in the wall for door; doorpost, מְזוּזָה: framework for the door; opening, שֶׁקֶף: the inside of the door opening; forefront, נֹל: the exit to the door opening; hall, אוּלָם: a room with pillars; cf. the temple "porch," 6:3; balustrade, עַב: an entrance-barrier; floor, קַרְקַע; rafters, Syr, Vg קוֹרוֹת MT "floor," v 7; other court, חָצֵר הָאַחֶרֶת: alternatively, the "after court."

9–12 The antecedent for "all these" is vague unless we retranslate, "Costly stones were used on all these," which is undoubtedly what is meant. Evidently the Hebrews or Phoenicians had discovered how to apply a hard abrasive to their saws because a finer surface was desired than could be had with hammer and chisel. One must realize, of course, that native limestone was being used, a stone that is not particularly hard. The intent of these verses is to describe how stone was applied to the various structures. A distinction is being made between its application in the various buildings (vv 9–11) in contrast to its application in the walls of the "great" and "inner" courts. A key word for understanding what was involved is הַטְּפָחוֹת in v 9. M. Görg has recently argued (*BN* 11 [1980] 7–13) that it is related to the Egyptian word for "roof," but we need not hesitate to follow Busink, *Der Tempel*, 229, and R. de Vaux, *Ancient Israel, Her Life and Culture* (1961), 316, in giving it the meaning "framework." By this is meant a row of headers and stretchers (of stone or wood) atop the various levels of the foundation. For the terms "costly stones," "precious stones," "great stones," see on 5:17. Stones ten cubits long and eight cubits high are quite believable in view of the massive stones that Herod used at the temple site. The so-called "precious" stones were used not only for the foundation, but for the "elevation" (from the ground up to the top) as well.

"The great court," casually mentioned in v 9, is directly described in v 12 (עד החצר הגדולה, "as far as the great court," v 9, is an enigma; a too-facile solution is to read with the LXX, "outside in the great court"). As with the inner court described in 6:36, cedar beams (כרתת) were alternated with three courses of dressed stones in this great court. A final note recalls the similarity to the inner court and adds that this method was applied also to the nave of the temple; if the text of this final assertion is in order (see *Notes*), we are left in the dark as to the way in which it was actually carried out.

Explanation

There have been all sorts of attempts to reconstruct Solomon's edifices and to draw up a scheme of their arrangement on the temple mount. We can only try to explain the one that seems to satisfy our own understanding, and that is the one of Busink, *Der Tempel*, 128–61. The "House of the Lebanon Forest" was much larger than the temple and was intended to be used as a great audience- or assembly-hall. It had three rows of forty-five-foot-long cedar pillars, each row with fifteen; hence the name comparing it to a forest. The roof was flat, probably with access via outside stairways, and it bore the "chambers," whose walls would have rested squarely on the rows of pillars (Busink; see also M. J. Mulder, *ZAW* 88 [1976] 99–105). Entrance to this great hall was by one door each on the short sides and two doors each on the long sides. There were windows between the doors on the long sides. No height is given for the "Hall of Pillars," nor are we informed about how many pillars there were. Busink believes that the "Throne Hall" was the same building; the writer has simply recorded two different names for it. It appears to have had a pillared porch in front, with some kind of ramp or balustrade, and within, it was paneled with cedar. We are told nothing about Solomon's "house" or the "house" of his Egyptian queen, except that they were "similar to this same pattern of construction." D. Ussishkin, "King Solomon's Palaces," *BA* 36 (1973) 78–105, agrees with Busink in identifying the two palaces as showing a popular Syrian style, that of the *Bit-Ḥilāni*, i.e., with rooms on three sides surrounding an open hall supported by pillars. This seems to fit very well the requirements of the biblical text; according to v 8 this would also have been the style of the building or buildings described in vv 6–7.

A brief word, finally, about the relative situation of the temple over against these secular edifices: Judging from biblical and historical references and from recent archeological work, it is clear that the latter would have been grouped southward of the temple. Solomon's own palace had to have been by far the largest of all the buildings in order to accommodate the large family that was to become his, with all his retainers, and this palace probably had an entrance directly into the "inner court" surrounding the temple and another entrance into the "other/after court" mentioned in v 8. The palace of Pharaoh's daughter would have been directly attached to that of Solomon.

South of the "inner court" and east of the two palaces would have been the "great court," and it contained the "Throne Hall" and the "House of the Lebanon Forest."

This was the great complex on which King Solomon spent his nation's wealth. He did everything imaginable to show that, as Yahweh was a great God, he was a great king. What is displayed here is far more Solomon's "riches and honor" than his "wisdom." His was undoubtedly the piety of worldly success.

Hiram's Artifacts for the Temple
(7:13–51a)

Bibliography

Albright, W. F. "Two Cressets from Marisa and the Pillars of Jachin and Boaz." *BASOR* 85 (1942) 18–27. **van den Branden, A.** "I brucia-incenso Jaken e Bo'az." *BibOr* 4 (1962) 47–52. **von Hummelauer, P. F.** "Salomons ehernes Meer (3 Kg 7, 23–26=2 Chr 4, 2–5)." *BZ* 4 (1906) 225–31. **Kornfeld, W.** "Der Symbolismus der Tempelsäule." *ZAW* 74 (1962) 50–57. **May, H. G.** "The Two Pillars Before the Temple of Solomon (I K 7:15–22)." *BASOR* 88 (1942) 19–27. **Schwally, F.** "Zur Quellenkritik der historischen Bücher.—II. I Kön. 7, 41–45a." *ZAW* 12 (1892) 157. **Scott, R. B. Y.** "The Pillars Jachin and Boaz." *JBL* 58 (1939) 143–47. **Segré, A.** "Il mare fusile del tempio di Salomone." *RSO* 41 (1966) 155. **Stade, B.** "Die Kesselwagen des salomonischen Tempels 1 Kö. 7, 27–39." *ZAW* 21 (1901) 145–90. **Vincent, L.-H.** "Les bassins roulants du Temple du Salomon (I K 7, 27–39)." *Miscellanea Biblica B. Ubach,* Montserrat 1953. **Wright, G. E.** "Solomon's Temple Resurrected." *BA* 4 (1941) 17–31. **Wylie, C. C.** "On King Solomon's Molten Sea." *BA* 12 (1949) 86–90. **Yeivin, S.** "Jachin and Boaz." *PEQ* 91 (1959) 6–22.

Translation

[13] *And King Solomon sent and fetched Hiram* [a] *from Tyre.* [14] *The son of a widow woman was he, from the tribe of Naphtali, though his father had been a Tyrian citizen, a craftsman in bronze. And he was full of skill, comprehension, and* [a]*know-how in crafting* [a] *all kinds of work in bronze. So he came* [b] *to King Solomon and crafted all his work.* [c]

[15] *And he cast* [a] [b]*the two pillars* [b] [c]*of bronze.* [cd] *Eighteen cubits was the height of* [e]*the pillar;* [e] *and a cord of twelve* [f] *cubits could encircle* [g]*it, and its thickness hollowed out was four fingers. Identical to it was the second.* [g] [16] *And two capitals he made to set on top of the pillars, castwork;* [a] *five cubits was the height of the one capital* [b]*and five cubits was the height of the second capital.* [b] [17] [a]*Reticulations shaped like a net, festoons shaped like a chain, belonged to the capitals which were on top of the pillars,* [a] *seven* [b] *for the one capital and seven* [b] *for the second capital.* [18] [a]*And he made the columns;* [a] *and* [b] *there were* [c]*two rows surrounding each reticulation made to cover the capital which was on top of the pomegranates;* [c] *and the same he made for the second capital.* [19] *And* [a]*the capitals which were* [a] *on top of the columns, styled as lilies, in* [b] *the porch, were four cubits.* [20] *And the capitals* [a] *were atop the two pillars; also upward with respect to the protuberance,* [b] [c]*which was distinct from the reticulation; and two hundred pomegranates were in surrounding rows upon* [c] *the second capital.* [21] *And he erected the pillars at the porch of the nave; he erected the first* [a] *pillar and called its name Yakin; he erected the second* [b] *pillar and called its name Boaz.* [c] [22] *And the top of the columns was shaped like lilies. So the construction of the pillars was completed.*

[23] *And he made the reservoir,* [a] *ten cubits from one rim to the other rim, round on its exterior and five cubits in height; and a line* [b] *of thirty* [c] *cubits could encircle it* [d]*on the circumference.* [d] [24] *And gourds were beneath the rim on the outside, encircling it for ten cubits,* [a]*enclosing* [b] *the reservoir* [a] *on the outside;* [c]*in two rows were the*

gourds, cast when it was cast. [c] [25] [a]*It stood upon twelve oxen,* [a] *three facing north, three facing west, three facing south, and three facing east;* [b]*and it was resting upon them from above, with all their hind parts inward.* [b] [26] [a]*And its thickness was a handbreadth,* [a] *and its rim was similar in style to the rim of a cup, a lily bloom.* [b]*It could contain two thousand baths.* [b]

[27] *And he made the watercarts, ten of them, of bronze. Four* [a] *cubits was the length of each watercart, four cubits was its width, and three* [b] *cubits was its height.* [28] *Now this was the design of a watercart:*

They had framing pieces, and the framing pieces were between the crossrungs; [29] *and upon the framing pieces that were between the crossrungs were lions, oxen,* [a] *and cherubim; and upon the crossrungs, identically above and below the lions and the oxen, were wreaths in hammered work.* [30] *And four in number were the bronze wheels belonging to each watercart, with bronze axletrees; also four in number were its cornerposts. They had shoulderpieces beneath the laver;* [a] *the cast shoulderpieces were each adjacent to a wreath.* [31] *And its opening was inside the crown, extending upward one cubit; and the latter's opening was round, of similar design for a cubit and a half, and also on its opening were carvings, although their framing pieces were square rather than round.* [32] *And there were four wheels underneath their own framing pieces,* [a] *with sockets for the wheels fixed to the watercart; and the height of each wheel was a cubit and a half,* [33] *the construction of the wheels being according to the design of a chariot wheel; their* [a] *sockets and their rims* [b]*and their spokes* [b] *and their hubs were all of cast metal.* [34] *And there were four shoulderpieces leading to the four cornerposts of each watercart, whose individual shoulderpiece extended from the watercart.* [35] *And in the top of the watercart, a half cubit tall, was an encircling band; also* [a] *atop the watercart were its handles, with its framing pieces extending from it.*

[36] *And he engraved upon the* [a] *panels of its handles and on* [b] *its framing pieces cherubim, lions,* [c] *and palmtrees,* [d]*adjusted to the amount of empty space, with wreaths surrounding them.* [d] [37] *Like this he made the watercarts, using the* [a]*same casting,* [a] [b]*same dimensions, and same design* [b] *for them all.* [38] *And he made ten bronze lavers, forty baths capacity to each laver;* [a]*each laver measured four cubits.* [a] *The ten watercarts had each one laver per individual watercart.* [39] *And he positioned the watercarts five* [a]*on the right side of the temple* [a] *and five on the left side of the temple. And the reservoir* [b]*he positioned* [b] *away from the right side of the temple, eastward but toward the south.*

[40] *And Hiram made the pots,* [a] *the shovels, and the sprinkling vessels. So Hiram completed crafting all the handcraft which he had been commissioned to make for King Solomon for use in Yahweh's temple:*

[41] *Pillars: two*
(and) bowls for the capitals [a] *(and) bowls* [b]*which were* [b] *atop the pillars: two*
(and) the reticulations: two (for covering the two [c]*bowls of*
the capitals [c] *which were upon* [d] *the pillars)*
[42] *(and)* [a] *the pomegranates: four hundred for the two reticulations*
(two rows of pomegranates to each reticulation covering the
two [b]*bowls of the capitals* [b] *which were* [c]*upon each of* [c] *the*
pillars)
[43] *(and) the watercarts: ten*
(and) the lavers: ten (upon the watercarts)

44 (and) the reservoir: one [a]
(and) the oxen: twelve (beneath the reservoir).
45 Now the pots and the shovels and the sprinkling vessels, with all the [a] utensils, which Hiram crafted for King Solomon for Yahweh's temple [b] out of polished [c] bronze, 46 he [a] cast in the Jordan trough [b]in clay molds[b] between Succoth and Zarethan. 47 [a]But Solomon let all the utensils lie because of their very great abundance; [a] the weight of the bronze could not be determined.
48 And Solomon [a] made [b] all the utensils which were [c] in Yahweh's [d] temple:
the golden altar;
also the table on which was placed the bread [e] of presence: gold;
49 also the lampstands, [a]five on the left and five on the right,[a] in front of the adytum: pure gold;
also the flower [b] and the lamps and the tongs: gold; [c]
50 also the basins and the snuffers and the bowls and the incense dishes and the firepans: pure gold; [a]
also the doorfronts for the inner sanctuary (the holy of holies) and [b] the doors [c]of the nave: [c] gold.

51 So [a]the craftwork[a] which Solomon [b] made for Yahweh's temple was carried to completion.

Notes

13.a. MT's orthography is consistently confirmed by G MSS: χειραμ, χηραμ to Huram-Abi, etc., over against Chr's חורם (but cf. Par חירם). Chr לְחוּרָם אָבִי is corrupt; cf. Par. Hence J. Gray (i.l.) is on shaky ground in conjecturing that Huram-Abi was indeed this craftsman's proper name, particularly because it would contain two distinct theophoric elemens: אחי ("my brother")-רם, ("great")-אכי, ("my Father").

14.a-a. MT הדעת לעשות, "the knowledge of making"; GBL "and he knew how to craft."

14.b. MT. GBL "was brought," perhaps suggesting that Hiram did not belong in Jerusalem and came only because summoned.

14.c. MT. GBL "the work" implies that Solomon was the designer and Hiram was only the executor.

15.a. GBL χωνεύω "melt," "cast," in place of MT's "shaped." These huge pillars were cast in a mold (cf. v 46) rather than carved. MT ויצר is a corruption of an original ויצק "and he cast."

15.b-b. MT, GL.

15.c-c. MT. GBL omit.

15.d. MT. GBL add "for the porch of the temple."

15.e-e. GBL. MT "the one/first pillar" in explicative.

15.f. MT. GBL "fourteen."

15.g-g. GBL. MT "the second pillar" is explicative.

16.a. GB. MT, GL add explicative "of bronze."

16.b-b. MT and GL. GB omits (haplography).

17.a-a. MT. Not understanding the intricate Heb., GBL offer the paraphrastic approximation, "and he made two nets, trellis-like, the capital(s) of the pillars."

17.b. MT. GBL "(and) a net" is corrupt (δίκτυον = Heb. שבכה; cf. שבעה "seven").

18.a-a. MT. GBL "and festoonwork."

18.b. MT. GBL omit.

18.c-c. MT. GBL translate what they do not understand: "two rows of bronze spaces (?), network, network, row on row."

19.a-a. MT. GBL omit.

19.b. MT. GBL "upon."

20.a. MT. G^{BL} μέλαθρον translates MT שקף "windowpane" in 7:4, יצוע "story" in 6:5.
20.b. MT; lit., "belly" (בטן). G^{BL} πλευρῶν "ribs."
20.c-c. MT. G^{BL} omit.
21.a. G^B. MT and G^L "righthand" is explicative.
21.b. G^B. MT and G^L "lefthand" is explicative.
21.c. MT. G^B has auditory corruption; cf. G^L MSS.
23.a. G^{BL}. MT "of cast metal." Contra Burney, 90. The G omission is likely no oversight, as claimed, for in this section the original translator drops out only such technical terms as he despairs to render even by paraphrase.
23.b. Q and K are orthographic variants.
23.c. MT. Chr and G^{BL} "thirty-three."
23.d-d. MT. G^L omits; G^B paraphrases.
24.a-a. MT and G^L. G^B omits.
24.b. MT and G^B. G^L "supporting."
24.c-c. MT. G^{BL} omit.
25.a-a. MT. G^{BL} "and twelve oxen beneath the reservoir."
25.b-b. MT. G^{BL} reverse the order of clauses.
26.a-a. MT. G^{BL} omit.
26.b-b. MT. G^{BL} "and its thickness was ancient" (corr).
27.a. MT. G^{BL} "five."
27.b. MT. G^{BL} "six." The translators tend to augment numerals.
29.a. MT. G^{BL} "and oxen."
30.a—32.a. MT. G^{BL} omit.
33.a. MT, G^B. G^L "and their."
33.b-b. MT. G^{BL} omit.
35.a. MT. G^{BL} omit.
36.a. MT. G^{BL} add explicative "four."
36.b. MT. G^{BL} omit.
36.c. MT. G^{BL} "and lions."
36.d-d. MT. G^{BL} corr.
37.a-a. MT. G^{BL} omit.
37.b-b. MT. G^{BL} "a single design and measure" (stylistic).
38.a-a. MT. G^{BL} omit.
39.a-a. MT. G^B omits; all others have this reading.
39.b-b. MT and G^L. G^B omits.
40.a. Chr and G; cf. v 45. MT has corrupted הסירות "the pots" to הכירות "the posts" or "the stages" under the influence of v 38.
41.a. MT. G^B "and the festoons of the (G^L carved) pillars"; cf. v 17 MT, Deut 22:12.
41.b-b. MT and G^L. G^B omits.
41.c-c. MT. G^{BL} "festoons of the carvings."
41.d. G^{BL}. MT "on top of" על ראש.
42.a. MT and G^L. G^B omits.
42.b-b. MT. G^{BL} "festoons of the watercarts"; corr from v 43.
42.c-c. G^{BL}. MT "in front of."
44.a. G^{BL}. MT "the one."
45.a. G^{BL}. K "of the tent"; Q "these."
45.b. MT. G^B (cf. G^L) adds: "and the forty-eight pillars of the king's house and Yahweh's temple, all the king's craftwork Hiram made" (explicative gl).
45.c. MT. G^{BL} corr.
46.a. G^{BL}. MT adds explicative "the king."
46.b-b. MT. G^{BL} (cf. Chr), unable to understand the hapax legomenon, במעבה, translate "in the clay of the earth/land." Our translation is based on the sense of the passage.
47.a-a. MT. G^{BL} corr: "there was no weighing of the bronze (G^L whatsoever) from which he made all these artifacts (G^L utensils) from its great abundance" (doublet to v 47.b).
48.a. MT. G^{BL} "King Solomon" (from v 40).
48.b. MT. G^B "took" and G^L "gave/dedicated" avoid the notion that Solomon was a craftsman in the same sense as Hiram.
48.c. MT. G^{BL} "he made" probably refers back to Hiram.

48.d. MT and G^L. G^B omits.
48.e. MT. G^{BL} "loaves."
49.a-a. G^B, more likely to be original because the order "left-right" breaks the stereotype seen in MT, G^L "five on the right and five on the left."
49.b. MT. G^{BL} corr (doublet for ואת־מנרות "the lampstands").
49.c. MT and G^B. G^L adds "all of them."
50.a. MT and G^B. G^L adds "all of them."
50.b. G^{BL}. MT has explicative "for."
50.c-c. G^{BL}. MT has the doublet, "of the temple, for the nave."
51.a-a. G^{BL}. MT has explicative "all the craftwork."
51.b. G^{BL} (cf. v 48). MT "King Solomon."

Form/Structure/Setting

Extract from the Book of Solomon's Acts (12): Hiram's handiwork (supplemented with items from official records)

1. Hiram's credentials, vv 13–14
2. The pillars before the temple
    a. The casting of the pillars, v 15
    b. The crafting of the capitals, v 16
        (1) Their ornamentation (from architectural records), vv 17, 18b, 20
[Expansion: The columns in front of the porch, vv 18a, 19]
    c. The erection and dedication of the pillars, vv 21, 22b
[Expansion: Ornamentation of the columns, v 22a]
3. The reservoir and the watercarts
    a. The reservoir and its oxen pedestal
        (1) Its dimensions and ornamentation (from architectural records), vv 23, 24–26
    b. The watercarts: framework narration, vv 27a, 28aα, 36–37
        (1) Its dimensions (from architectural records), v 27b
        (2) Its construction and ornamentation (conflated from two separate design specifications), vv 28aβb–35
    c. The bronze lavers, v 38aα, bβ
        (1) Their capacity and dimensions (from architectural records), v 38aβbα
    d. Positioning of the watercarts and reservoir, v 39
4. Miscellaneous utensils, v 40a
    a. Inventory of Hiram's craftwork (from a separate list), vv 40b–44
5. The casting process, vv 45–47
[Expansion: Solomon makes gold utensils for the temple, vv 48–50]
6. Concluding summary, v 51a

Three late expansions have intruded into the text of 7:13–22; they refer to a pair of columns or pilasters adorned with lilywork and standing within the temple porch; these are distinct from the free-standing pillars being described in the main text. In vv 48–50 a fairly long expansion offers a separate list of items that Solomon had made for the interior of the temple; it has been attracted here by the reference to Solomon in v 51a, which is in fact the final summary for vv 13–47. Dtr has not interfered in this chapter. Vv 13–51a, without these expansions, was evidently taken as a single, long extract from the Book of Solomon's Acts. Its purpose is to describe all that Hiram the Phoenician craftsman fabricated for the exterior of the temple: two pillars with their capitals, a reservoir with watercarts and lavers, and miscellaneous items to be used in the sacrificial cultus. Much space is devoted to the pillars and the water vessels, but just a few words to the miscellaneous items (v 40a). Everything is set within a narrative framework, commencing with an introduction to Hiram in vv 13–14; this begins with a statement of Solomon's action and ends with a statement of Hiram's action, with a descriptive identification of Hiram between the two. Narrative verbs provide the framework for the section on the pillars, vv 15–22: "And he cast (15) . . . he made to set (16) . . . the same he made (18) . . . and he erected . . . he erected . . . he erected" (21). This leads to a summarizing conclusion in v 22, "So the construction of the pillars was completed." Everything else in between is dense description, as in chap. 6's description of the temple.

In the section about the reservoir (vv 23–26) there is only one narrative verb, and that is at the beginning, "And he made. . . ." "It stood" (v 25) and "it could contain" (v 26) belong to description rather than to narrative. As in the preceding section, this material is constructed of noun-clauses and adjectives, providing details numerous enough to enlighten the ancient reader's understanding. This is even more the case with the section about the watercarts and lavers, vv 27–39. Its main part has only two narrative verbs, "and he made" in v 27 plus "and he engraved" in v 36. V 37 is a summarizing conclusion regarding the watercarts. It is followed in v 38 by the narrative verb "and he made," followed by a very brief description of the lavers, which were actually a functional part of the watercarts. Then in v 39 the writer gives us two more narrative verbs, "and he positioned" and "he positioned" (here the verb follows the object, emphasized by being brought forward in order to distinguish it from the watercarts). V 39, having to do with the disposition of the objects named, is parallel to v 21, which mentions the disposition of the two pillars. In v 40 we have the narrative verb "made," and here for the first time following v 13 Hiram is named as the subject. V 40 continues with a summarizing statement intended as the penultimate conclusion: "So Hiram completed crafting all the handcraft (etc.)." This ought to have been able to have stood by itself, but the narrator extends it by appending an inventory (later expanded by a series of explanatory notes) of the items that Hiram had actually made (vv 41–43), plus a note about how Hiram had got the casting done (vv 45–46) and what Solomon had done with what he had cast (v 47). As has been stated, v 51a is intended as the final summary for the whole section.

Finally we mention source materials. Such as can be identified with some probability are notes from architectural records in vv 17, 18b, 20, 23, 24–26, 27b, 38; also a lengthy design specification, evidently conflated from two separate versions, in vv 28–35; also the inventory of Hiram's craftwork, vv 40–44, which may actually go back to a sort of invoice or bill for services. The secondary list in vv 48–50 may also be based on an actual inventory.

Comment

13–14 Hiram is introduced. The narrator wants to tell us that Hiram had all the skill of the Tyrian copper-workers, one of whom had been his father; but in order to ease troubled consciences, he emphasizes, by bringing it forward, the fact that this man was nonetheless a true Israelite, the son of a widow woman from Naphtali. "Skill, comprehension, and know-how": את־הדעת ואת־התבונה ואת־החכמה; though these words may mean something highly intellectual in other contexts, they here refer to great cunning in conceiving and executing artifacts. It seems to be only a coincidence that this craftsman had the same name as his king (see chap. 5), but the name they both bore may have been fairly common in Phoenicia.

15–22 The two pillars with their capitals. Again, arcane architectural terms are used. Here, few parallels exist; thus we must form our conception from etymology, from the use of the relevant words elsewhere in Scripture, and from the general logic of craftsmanship. It helps a great deal that we are able to disregard the glosses in vv 18a, 19, and 22a. The dimensions make good sense as given, though the Greek translators were not always satisfied with them (see *Notes*). A twenty-seven-foot-high pillar with a diameter of about six feet would have been very impressive. It was very likely made in sections, for a ten-foot-high capital rested upon it. Technical terms appearing in this section are as follows:

pillar, עמוד: (same term for "column," vv 18, 19, 22); capital, כתר; cast-work, מצק; reticulation, net, שבכ: an adornment covering the top part of the capital; festoon, גדל: a floral-shaped decoration; chainwork, מעשה שרשרות: a wreath or garland made of festoons; row, טור a straight circle around the capital; pomegranate, רמן; protuberance, בטן: the ordinary word for "belly," "womb"; porch of the nave, אלם ההיכל (see on chap. 6); lilywork, מעשה שושן.

Hiram erected the pillars at ל, not in כ the porch of the nave. In the unlikely event that the pillars were all of one piece, they would have to have been raised with hoists; but almost certainly they were built up in sections with the use of scaffolding. The name "Yakin" ("he shall uphold") was carved on the one, and the name "Boaz" ("may strength be in him") was carved on the other. (On רמן, see M. Görg's Egyptological speculations in *BN* 13 [1982] 17–21; on Yakin and Boaz, see S. Yeivin, *PEQ* 91 [1959] 6–22.)

23–39 Heavy castings of bronze were required for handling water in the temple court: a "sea" or reservoir fifteen feet across, containing 11,000 gallons (see on "bath" at 5:11), and ten watercarts to transfer lavers containing 220 gallons each. The construction and decoration of each artifact is told in considerable detail. Again, technical terms have meanings that are likely to elude the modern reader. In this section we find the following:

the reservoir, הים: lit., "sea"; rim, שפה: lit., "lip"; gourd, פקע: a decoration; watercart, מכנה: lit., "support" or "stand"; framing piece, מסגרה: lit., "that which encloses"; cross-rung, שלב: internal support; wreath, ליה: a decoration; shoulderpiece, כתף: a support running from the corner to the laver; axletree, סרן: support for the axle; laver, כיר: lit., "vessel"; opening, פיה: lit., "mouth"; crown, כתרת: the protuding part of the laver;

wheel, אוֹפָן; carving, מִקְלַע; socket, יָד: lit., "hand"; also "handle," vv 35–36; rim, גַב; spoke, חִשֻּׁק; hub, חִשֻּׁר; band, עָגֹל; cornerpost, פִּנָּה; empty space, מֵעַר; panel, לוּחַ.

Since B. Stade's intensive investigation of the biblical text in 1901 (*ZAW* 21 [1901] 145–90), scholars have agreed that the watercarts had a cylindrical rim to support the laver, which would have been filled in some unspecified way from the reservoir. According to Th. A. Busink, *Der Tempel von Jerusalem*, 337–52, the watercarts were similar in construction to one found in Larnaka, Cyprus. They were purely utilitarian and their decorations were only for adornment.

40–51a   Implements fabricated by Hiram for cultic use in the temple court (v 40) are the following:

pot, סִיר (MT כִּיר): for handling the sacrificial portions; shovel, יָע: for cleansing the ground of meat and ashes; sprinkling vessel, מִזְרָק: for washing away excess blood.

In the inventory of vv 41–43 items are repeated from vv 15–39, and all is familiar except the word "bowl," גֻלָּה. There was one of these for each pillar and each served as a capital; i.e., they were the capitals, this being an alternative designation for them. Expansions in these verses state that the reticulations or network (made of bronze) covered these "bowls." In the late addition concerning Solomon's own artifacts (vv 48–50), special items for the interior of the temple, all wrought in gold, are listed:

the golden altar, מִזְבַּח הַזָּהָב: the same as in 6:20; table, שֻׁלְחָן: for receiving the "bread of presence"; lampstand, מְנֹרָה: the seven-armed candelabra (ten of them); flower, פֶּרַח: a decoration; lamp, נֵר: an additional source of illumination; tong, מֶלְקָח: an implement for handling coals on the altar; basin, סַף: for the same; snuffer, מְזַמְּרָה: for extinguishing the flame; bowl, מִזְרָק: for distributing or sprinkling sacred materials; incense dish, כַּף: lit., "palm (of hand)"; firepan, מַחְתָּה: for supplying coals; doorfront, פֹּת: an inner panel.

This list disagrees with 6:14–35, particularly in its unglossated form. It shows its late origin by making Solomon as rich as Croesus. The influence of Exod 27, 38 is evident.

Explanation

The section concerning Hiram's handiwork (vv 13–47) has entirely to do with bronze artifacts for the temple court. These were all cast in clay forms carved in the ground near the Jordan river between Succoth and Zarethan, some thirty to forty miles northeast of Jerusalem; Hiram was evidently so eager to produce bronze items that Solomon's servants were unable to keep an accurate tally on their weight (vv 46–47). The two tall pillars with the bowl-like capitals have been variously described and interpreted. Since they stood free and did not support anything (two smaller pillars or pilasters stood within the temple porch, v 21), it is evident that they had symbolic significance. The names engraved upon them underscores this. It is irresponsible to suggest that they had a phallic form and symbolized the fertility impulse, for nothing in later references to the Jerusalem temple even hints at ascribing to Yahweh a fertility trait (contra the golden calves of Bethel and Dan!). It is best to interpret the pillar Yakin and the pillar Boaz as proprietary emblems, claiming the temple for Yahweh. Also, the "bowls" may have resembled a flame, symbolizing Yahweh as a God of fire and light. Because these pillars disappear from Ezekiel's temple and the temple of the restoration, it is likely that they were eventually removed precisely because influential leaders did suspect them of having heathen implications.

Daily, a large number of animal sacrifices were brought to be slaughtered in the temple court. Some of these were given by private individuals, others were given by the king or the priests on behalf of the public. Much of the meat was eaten on the spot or offered to the priests. The fat was burned. An unavoidable residue was always an abundance of ashes and blood. The ashes would be carted away but the blood required water, and it is for this that the great reservoir and the ten watercarts were intended. Since the watercarts had wheels, we can depict in our minds how they would have been used in transporting relatively small quantities of water from the reservoir to ten positions adjacent to the areas where the animal victims were slaughtered. Priests and laity would dip lavishly from these lavers in order to cleanse themselves, their victims, and the surrounding earth from the uncleanness of blood. These instruments were well crafted for their purpose, but of bronze, not gold. As has been said, the notion that Solomon used pure gold in the temple is a figment of later imagination. The use of gold to adorn holy objects may reflect human vainglory more than honor to the deity being worshiped.

One of the epistles of the NT emphasizes the unique efficacy of Jesus Christ, sacrificial victim and at the same time high priest. His blood is unique in that it makes sinners clean rather than unclean, according to the Epistle to the Hebrews. "We have confidence to enter the sanctuary by the blood of Jesus, by the new and living way which he opened for us through the curtain, that is, through his flesh" (Heb 10:19–20).

The Dedication of the Temple   (7:51b–9:9)

Bibliography

van den Born, A. "Zum Tempelweihespruch (I Kg viii 12f)." *OTS* 14 (1965) 235–44. **Braulik, G.** "Spuren einer Neubearbeitung des deuteronomistischen Geschichtswerkes in 1 Kön 8, 52–53, 59–60." *Bib* 52 (1971) 20–33. **Friedman, R. E.** "The Tabernacle in the Temple," *BA* 43 (1980) 241–48. **Gamper, A.** "Die heilsgeschichtliche Bedeutung des salomonischen Tempelweihegebete." *ZKT* 85 (1963) 55–61. **Görg, M.** "Die Gattung des sogenannten Tempelweihespruchs (1 Kg 8, 12f.)." *UF* 6 (1974) 53–63. **von Hummelauer, F.** "Salomons Tempelweihe." *BZ* 1 (1903) 43–46. **Loretz, O.** "Der Torso eines kanaanäisch-israelitischen Tempelweihspruches in 1 Kg 8, 12–13." *UF* 6 (1974) 478–80. **Skweres, D. E.** "Das Motiv der Strafgrunderfragung im biblischen und neuassyrischen Texten." *BZ* n.F. 14 (1970) 181–97.

Translation

[51b] *And Solomon fetched the sacral booty that had belonged to David his father;* [c] *the silver and the gold* [d]*and the artifacts* [d] *he deposited in the treasure-rooms of Yahweh's temple.* [8:1] *Then Solomon* [a] *assembled the* [b] *elders of Israel,* [c] [d]*(with all the chiefs of the tribes, leaders of the fathers belonging to the Israelites, to King Solomon in Jerusalem,)* [d] *in order to bring up the ark of Yahweh's covenant from the city of David; that is, Zion.* [2a]*Now every Israelite man was assembled to King Solomon* [a] *in the month Ethanim* [b] *with celebration; this is the seventh month.* [3] *And all the elders of Israel came,* [a] *and the priests picked up the ark,* [4] *and brought up the ark of Yahweh, and the tent of meeting and* [a] *the holy utensils that were in the tent* [b]*of meeting;* [b] [c]*and the priests and Levites brought them up,* [c] [5] *while the king* [a] *and all* [b]*the people* [b] [c]*who had gathered unto him* [c] *before the ark were sacrificing* [d]*sheep and oxen* [d] [e]*without number.* [e] [6] *Then the priests brought up the ark* [a] *to its place; that is, into the adytum of the temple, to the holy of holies, to a position beneath the wings of the cherubim,* [7] *for the cherubim were spreading their wings over* [a] *the place* [b] *of the ark, so that the cherubim sheltered the ark and* [c]*its staves* [c] *from above,* [8] *while* [a]*the staves* [a] *extended so that the ends of* [a]*the staves* [a] *were seen from the holy place in front of the adytum; but they were not seen outside,* [b]*and they are there to the present day.* [b] [9] *There is nothing in the ark except the two stone tablets* [a] *which Moses deposited in it at Horeb, where Yahweh made a covenant with the Israelites upon their departure from the land of Egypt.* [10] *And when the priests emerged from the holy place, and the cloud was filling the temple,* [a] [11] *the priests were unable to stand (in service) on account of the cloud because the glory of Yahweh filled the temple.* [a]

[12] *Then Solomon said,* [a]

[b]*A sun hath Yahweh established in the heavens,* [b]

[c]*but he hath purposed* [c] *to dwell in thick darkness;*

[13a]*I have surely built* [a] *a noble house for thee,*

a residence [b] *where thou shalt dwell perpetually.*

[c]*Is it not written in the Book of the Upright One?* [c]

[14] *And the king turned away his face.*

Then he [a] *blessed the whole assembly of Israel, while the whole assembly of Israel remained standing,* [15] *and said, "Blessed be Yahweh, God of Israel,* [a] *who spoke by his mouth with* [b] *David my father and fulfilled it with his hand, as follows:* [16] *'Ever since the day when I brought* [a] *my people Israel out of Egypt I never chose a particular city* [b] *from all the tribes* [b] *of Israel in order to build a temple for my name to be there, but I did choose David to be over my people Israel.'* [17] *And it came into* [a] *the mind of David* [b] *my father to build a temple to the name of Yahweh, God of Israel,* [18] *but Yahweh said to David my father, 'Inasmuch as it was in* [a] *your mind to build a temple to my name, you have done well in that it came into* [a] *your mind;* [19] [a] *all the same,* [a] *it is not you who is to build the temple; but your son who issues from your loins, he shall build a* [b] *temple to my name.'* [20] *and Yahweh has established his word that he spoke, so that* [a] *I have arisen* [a] *in place of David my father* [b] *and have come to sit* [b] *upon the throne of Israel, as he* [c] *said, and have built the temple to the name of Yahweh, God of Israel.* [21] *And I have provided there a place for the ark, in which is the covenant of Yahweh which he made with our fathers when he brought them out of the land of Egypt."*

[22] *Then Solomon stood in front of Yahweh's altar in the presence of the entire assembly of Israel, spread out his palms toward heaven,* [23] *and said, "O Yahweh God of Israel, there is no god like thee in heaven above or on the earth beneath, keeping the covenant and due fidelity with thy servants* [a] [b] *who walk before thee* [c] *with all their hearts;* [b] [24] *who hast kept with thy servant David my father* [a] *what thou hast said to him,* [a] *not only speaking it with thy mouth but fulfilling it by thy hand this very day.* [25] *So now, O Yahweh God of Israel, keep with thy servant, David my father, what thou didst speak with him, as follows: 'No one of you shall be cut off from me who is to sit on the throne of Israel, on condition that your sons guard their way so as to walk before me, just as you have walked before me.'* [26] *So now,* [a] *O God of Israel, let thy word to David my father be confirmed.* [b] [27] *But shall God actually dwell* [a] *upon earth? Behold, heaven and the heaven of heavens cannot contain thee! How then this temple which I have built?* [b] [28] *But do regard* [a] *my supplication, O Yahweh* [b] *my God,* [b] *hearing the outcry* [c] *which thy servant is praying before thee today,* [29] *so that thy eyes may be open toward this temple* [a] *night and day,* [a] *even the place of which thou didst say, 'My name shall be there,' listening to the prayer which thy servant may pray toward this place.* [b]

[30] *"So listen to the supplication of thy servant and of thy people Israel which they may pray toward this place while thou art listening in the place where thou dwellest, even heaven, so as to hear and forgive:*

[31] *"In any case in which a man offends his neighbor and puts an oath upon him so that he comes under the oath, and the oath comes before the altar, into this temple,* [32] *then do thou hear in heaven and carry it to effect, thus judging* [a] *thy servants,* [a] *condemning a guilty person by putting his way upon his head, and vindicating an innocent person by dealing with him according to his righteousness.*

[33] *"Whenever thy people Israel are defeated* [a] *before an enemy* [b] *in a situation in which they have offended thee, but return* [c] *and praise thy name, and pray and make supplication* [d] *in this temple,* [34] *then do thou hear in heaven and forgive,* [a] *absolving thy people* [a] *Israel and restoring them to the land which thou gavest to their fathers.*

[35] *"When the skies are closed tight and there is no rain, because they have offended thee, but they pray* [a] *toward this place and praise thy name, having turned away*

from their sin ᵇ *because thou hast afflicted them,* ³⁶ *then do thou* ᵃ *hear in heaven and forgive, absolving* ᵇ *thy servant and thy people Israel, for thou dost point out to them the good way* ᶜ*in which they should walk,* ᶜ *and bestowing rain upon* ᵈ*the land* ᵈ *which thou hast given thy people* ᵉ *to inherit.*

³⁷ *"Famine, if it should come;* ᵃ *pestilence, if it should come; blight* ᵇ*or mildew,* ᵇ *grasshopper or locust, if it should come; if one's enemy should attack him* ᶜ*in one of his cities;* ᶜ *whatever plague or illness,* ³⁸ *whatever prayer, whatever supplication which any man may have,* ᵃ *whenever the heart of any individual shall become aware of a plague and he shall spread his palms toward this house;* ³⁹ *oh, hear thou in heaven, the residence where thou dwellest, and forgive, do as he says, and* ᵃ *give to that individual according to* ᵇ*his ways,* ᵇ *as thou shalt know his heart; for thou alone knowest the heart of* ᶜ *the sons of man,* ⁴⁰ *in order that they may fear thee all the days that they remain alive upon* ᵃ *the ground which thou hast given to their fathers.*

⁴¹ *"And even to the foreigner who is not of thy people,* ᵃ ᵇ*who shall come from a distant land because of thy name,* ⁴² *for they shall hear about thy great name and about thy strong hand and outstretched arm,* ᵃ *if one shall come and pray toward this place,* ᵇ ⁴³ᵃ*then listen* ᵃ *in heaven, the residence where thou dwellest, and act with regard to everything concerning which the foreigner may appeal to thee, so that all the peoples* ᵇ *may know thy name,* ᶜ*for the fear of* ᶜ *thee like that of thy people Israel and* ᵈ*for the knowledge* ᵈ *that thy name has been invoked over this temple which I have built.*

⁴⁴ *("When thy people shall go out to war against its enemy along some road on which thou shalt send them, and they shall pray unto Yahweh* ᵃ *in the direction of the city which* ᵇ*thou hast* ᵇ *chosen and the temple which I built for thy name,* ⁴⁵ᵃ*then hear* ᵃ *in heaven* ᵇ*their supplication and their prayer,* ᵇ *and perform what is right for them.*

⁴⁶ *"When they shall sin against thee, for there is no man who does not sin, and thou shalt be furious with them and shalt deliver them up in the face of* ᵃ*an enemy,* ᵃ *and their captors shall deport them to* ᵇ*some land* ᵇ *far or near,* ⁴⁷ *then if they take it to their heart in the land to which they have been deported, and turn* ᵃ*in the land of their captors and supplicate thee* ᵃ *saying, 'We have sinned, we have done wrong, we have rebelled,'* ⁴⁸ *and if they do return to thee with all their heart and all their soul in the land of their enemies who have deported them, and pray unto thee in the direction of their land which thou hast given their fathers, the city which thou hast chosen, and the temple which I have built to thy name,* ⁴⁹ *then hear in heaven, the residence where thou dwellest,* ᵃ ⁵⁰ *and forgive* ᵃ*their wrongs which they* ᵃ *have sinned against thee and all their rebellions in which they have rebelled* ᵇ*against thee,* ᵇ *and destine them for compassion in the presence of their captors so that they may be kind to them.* ⁵¹ *For they* ᵃ *are thy people and thy inheritance, whom thou hast brought out of* ᵇ *Egypt, the inside of an iron furnace,* ⁵² *so that thy eyes* ᵃ *should be open to thy servant's supplication and the supplication of thy people Israel, listening to them in every matter in which they may appeal to thee;* ⁵³ᵃ *thou didst set them apart* ᵇ *from all the peoples of the earth, as thou didst declare through* ᶜ*Moses thy servant* ᶜ *when thou broughtest our fathers out of* ᵈ *Egypt, O Lord Yahweh!)"*

⁵⁴ *When Solomon finished praying to Yahweh this entire prayer and supplication, he got up from in front of Yahweh's altar where he had been kneeling on his knees with his palms outstretched toward heaven,* ⁵⁵ *and he stood to bless the whole assembly of Israel with a loud voice, saying,* ⁵⁶ *"Blessed be Yahweh* ᵃ *who has given* ᵇ *rest to*

*his people Israel in accordance with all that he has spoken! Not one word has failed
of all* ^c*his good word* ^c *which he declared through* ^d*Moses his servant.* ^{d 57} *May Yahweh
our God be with us, as he was with our fathers—may he not forsake or abandon
us!—* ⁵⁸ *inclining our hearts to himself, to walk in* ^a *his ways and to observe his
commandments and statutes* ^b *which he imposed on our fathers.* ⁵⁹ *And may these my
words with which I have made supplication before Yahweh* ^a *find access to Yahweh
our God day and night, so that he may perform what is right for his* ^b *servant* ^c*and
what is right for his people* ^c *Israel, the concern of each day on its day,* ^{d 60} *with a
view to the knowledge on the part of all the peoples of the earth that* ^a*Yahweh, he
is God,* ^a *with* ^b *none other!* ⁶¹ *And your* ^a *heart shall be in accord with* ^b *Yahweh
our God,* ^c *to walk in his statutes and to observe his commandments, as right now."*

⁶² *While the king,* ^a*and all Israel with him,* ^a *were offering sacrifices before Yahweh,*
⁶³ *for Solomon* ^a *offered a sacrifice of communion-offerings* ^b*(which he offered to Yah-
weh)* ^b *consisting of twenty-two thousand oxen* ^c*and one hundred twenty thousand
sheep,* ^c *the king and all the Israelites dedicated Yahweh's temple.* ⁶⁴ *On that day the
king sanctified the center of the court which is in front of Yahweh's temple, because
he performed there the burnt-offering and the cereal-offering and the fat of the communion-offerings, for the bronze altar which is before Yahweh is too small to serve the
burnt-offering,* ^a*the cereal-offering, and the fat of the communion-offerings.* ^{a 65} *And
Solomon made* ^a*a feast,* ^a *and all Israel with him, a great assembly from the approach
to Hamath to the brook of Egypt, in the presence of Yahweh our God* ^b *in the temple
which he had built, eating and drinking and rejoicing* ^c *in the presence of Yahweh
our God* ^b *for seven days.* ^{d 66} *On* ^a *the eighth day he dismissed the people. Then they
blessed him* ^b *and went off* ^c*to their tents,* ^c *rejoicing and with happy hearts for* ^d*all
the good* ^d *which Yahweh had performed on behalf of David his servant and Israel
his people.*

^{9:1} *And it happened that, when Solomon had completed constructing Yahweh's temple,
the king's house, and whatsoever Solomon took a notion to make,* ² *Yahweh appeared
to Solomon a second time, just as he had appeared* ^a *in Gibeon,* ³ *and said to him,* ^a
"I have heard your prayer and your supplication which you have made before me.
^b*I have done for you according to your prayer;* ^b *I have sanctified this temple which
you have built in order to fix my name there forever, and my eyes* ^c *and my heart
will be there every day.* ⁴ *As far as you personally are concerned: if you walk before
me as David your father walked, in integrity of heart and in uprightness, and behave* ^a
according to all that I commanded you ^b*and observe my statutes* ^b *and ordinances,*
⁵ *then I will confirm the throne of your kingdom over Israel perpetually, just as I
spoke to* ^a *David your father, saying, 'No man belonging to you will be cut off from
* ^b*being leader in Israel.'* ^{b 6} *(If you dare turn back, you and your children, from following
me, and do not observe my commandments and* ^a ^b*my statutes* ^b *which I* ^c *placed before
you, and you depart and worship other gods, and bow down to them,* ⁷ *then I will
cut Israel off from* ^a *the ground which I gave them, and this* ^b *temple which I sanctified
to my name I will dismiss from my presence; then Israel will become a proverb and
a taunt among all the peoples,* ⁸ *and the* ^a *temple will be a ruin.* ^b *Everyone passing
it by will be appalled and whistle; and they will say, 'Why did Yahweh behave like
this with respect to this land and this temple?'* ⁹ *And they will say, 'It is because
they forsook Yahweh their God who brought their fathers out of* ^a *Egypt,* ^b *and they
seized on other gods, bowing down* ^c *to them and worshiping them. This is why he* ^d
brought on them ^e*this affliction.)"* ^e

Notes

51.c. MT. G^BL add "and all the sacral booty of Solomon."
51.d-d. MT and G^L. G^B omits.
8:1.a. MT and G^L. G^B "King Solomon."
1.b. MT and G^L. G^B has pleonastic "all the."
1.c. MT and G^L. G^B adds explicative "in Zion."
1.d-d. MT and G^L have this late gl. G^B omits.
2.a-a. MT and G^A. G^BL omit.
2.b–3.a. MT. G^BL omit.
4.a. G^B. MT and G^L add pleonastic "all."
4.b-b. G^BL. MT omits (haplography).
4.c-c. MT. G^BL omit (haplography).
5.a. G^BL. MT "King Solomon."
5.b-b. G^L, which deserves preference over G^B "Israel" and MT "the congregation of Israel" because the group being designated are in contrast to the king and the priests.
5.c-c. C (Par). MT adds אִתּוֹ "with him" (doublet?). G^BL omit.
5.d-d. MT. G^L reverses the order; G^B omits the copula.
5.e-e. G^BL. MT is expansive with the stereotyped phrase, "which could neither be counted nor measured for multitude."
6.a. G^BL. MT has Dtr terminology, "the ark of Yahweh's covenant."
7.a. G^BL and Chr (Par). MT "unto" expresses the pious conceit that the cherubim showed reverence to the ark.
7.b. MT and G^B. G^L corr: τό πρόσωπον "the face" = Heb. קֹדֶם.
7.c-c. MT. G^BL τὰ ἄγια αὐτῆς "its holy things" (= Heb. קָדְשֵׁיו) paraphrases out of despair of rendering בַּדָּיו "its pieces" = "sticks" = "staves."
8.a-a, a-a. See note 7.c-c.
8.b-b. MT, Chr, G^A. G^BL omit.
9.a. MT. G^BL add "the tablets of the covenant," explicating the ellipsis of v 9b (*HOTTP*, 307).
10.a. G^B. MT, Chr, G^L add explicative "of Yahweh."
11.a. G^B. MT, Chr (Par "of God"), G^L add "of Yahweh."
12.a. MT. G^BL add explicative "concerning the temple when he finished building it."
12.b-b. G^L. G^B ἐγνώρισεν "caused to rise." MT omits out of pious ideology.
12.c-c. G^L. MT and G^B "Yahweh hath purposed."
13.a-a-a. MT. "I have built my house." (οἰκοδόμησον οἶκον μου "I built my house" is corr, reading Heb. בְּבִי בִיתִי for בָּנֹה בָנִיתִי "I have surely built.")
13.b. MT. G^BL omit.
13.c-c. G^BL. MT omits. The Gr. MSS must be original, for they would never introduce this ancient rubric except from a Heb. *Vorlage*.
14.a. MT and G^L. G^B "the king" is pedantically explicative.
15.a. MT. G^BL add "today" (see *YTT*, 188).
15.b. MT. G^BL περὶ "concerning" avoids the idea of revelations to David.
16.a. MT and G^L (root יצא). G^L "brought up" = Heb. עלה hiph.
16.b-b. MT, G^L, Par. G^B, C add the corrective, "and I chose Jerusalem, for my name to dwell there."
17.a. MT עַם, misread as עַל by G^BL "upon."
17.b. MT, G^L. G^B omits (haplography).
18.a,a. G^BL "upon"; cf. v 17.
19.a-a. MT and G^L. G^B omits for stylistic reasons.
19.b. G^L. MT and G^B have explicative "the."
20.a-a. MT and G^B. G^L "he raised me" accentuates the divine role.
20.b-b. MT and G^B. G^L "and caused me to sit."
20.c. G^B. MT, G^L "Yahweh" is explicative.
23.a. MT. G^BL sing, making the text refer to David rather than all Israel; G^L adds "David my father." Cf. vv 24–25 (see Burney, 116).
23.b-b. MT. G^BL sing.
23.c. G^L adds "in truth and."

24.a-a. MT. G^BL omit (G^A *hab*).
26.a. MT. G, Tg^L, Syr, Vg, Chr (Par) add "Yahweh," a gloss from v 25.
26.b. G^BL. MT adds "which thou spakest" (from v 25).
27.a. MT. G^BL and Chr (Par) add "with man/men"; cf. Burney, 116; *HOTTP*, 309.
27.b. MT. G^BL add pleonastic "for thy name."
28.a. G^BL. MT adds "my prayer and" (pleonastic).
28.b-b. MT, C. Par "God." G^BL "God of Israel."
28.c. G^B. MT adds pleonastic "and the prayer"; G^L "the supplication and the prayer."
29.a-a. MT (*lectio difficilior;* cf. v 59). G and Chr (Par) "day and night."
29.b. MT. G^BL add "day and night."
32.a-a. MT. G^BL "thy people Israel" from v 33.
33.a. MT, G^B. G^L adds the theological intrusion, "before thee and fall"; cf. Burney 119.
33.b. MT. G^BL "enemies" communicates the ideology of Israel's prowess.
33.c. G^BL. MT adds interpretive "unto thee"; Chr omits.
33.d. G^BL. MT adds explicative "unto thee"; Chr "before thee."
34.a-a. MT. G^BL "the sins of thy servant."
35.a. MT, G^B. G^L adds explicative "unto thee."
35.b. MT. G^BL pl.
36.a. MT. G^BL omit for stylistic reasons.
36.b. MT. G^BL "the sins of" (ταῖς ἁμαρτίαις) has a corrupt text or misreads an infinitive of purpose (MT לחטאת) as a noun (חטאות).
36.c-c. MT. G^BL "to walk in them" = MT.
36.d-d. G^B. MT and G^L have explicative "thy land."
36.e. MT and G^L. G^B "servant" is an obvious corruption and departs from orthodox ideology.
37.a. G^BL. MT adds explicative "into the land."
37.b-b. MT, G^A. G^BL do not know the word and omit its translation.
37.c-c. G^BL. MT "in the land of his gates" is a possible corruption; cf. *HOTTP*, 309.
38.a. G^BL. MT's addition, "thy people Israel may have" seems to express a late ideology of particularism.
39.a. MT, G^B. G^L has pleonastic "and justify all his ways."
39.b-b. G^B. MT and G^L have pleonastic "all his ways."
39.c. Chr (Par). MT and G add "all."
40.a. G^BL. MT adds "the face of."
41.a. G^B. MT and G^L have explicative addition "Israel."
41.b–42.a. MT. G^BL omit (haplography).
42.b. G^BL. MT "temple" guards against the possibility that the "place" in question might be Jerusalem.
43.a-a. Par. MT "do thou listen" and G, Chr "then do thou listen" are pleonastic.
43.b. G^BL. MT adds pleonastic "of the earth."
43.c-c. MT. G^BL "and may fear" (Gr. culture would not appreciate the abstraction involved in the nominal construction).
43.d-d. MT. G^BL "may know" (see previous remark).
44.a. MT. G^BL "in the name of Yahweh" tends toward abstraction.
44.b-b. MT. G^BL "I have" may have been influenced by the following verb.
45.a-a. MT. G^BL "and thou shalt listen."
45.b-b. G^B (the usual Dtr order). MT and G^L transpose.
46.a-a. MT. G^BL, Par pl. See note 33.b.
46.b-b. G^BL, Chr (Par). MT has explicative "the land of the enemy."
47.a-a. G^BL. MT's transposition, "and supplicate thee in the land of their captors" is not favored because the writer intends to make parallel the taking to heart and the turning, "in the land . . ." modifying both.
49.a. G^BL. MT adds "their prayer and their supplication, and perform what is right" (from v 45). Cf. Burney, 125.
50.a-a. G^BL. MT "thy people who."
50.b-b. MT and G^B. G^L omits (haplography).
51.a. MT (G^L paraphrases). G^B omits.
51.b. MT. G^BL's addition "the land of" is pleonastic.
52.a. MT (*lectio difficilior*). G^BL, Chr (Par) add "and thy ears" in view of v 52.b.

53.a. MT and G^L. G^B "and thou."
53.b. G^L. MT and G^B "as an inheritance" is interpretive and pleonastic.
53.c-c. MT, G^L. G^B "thy servant Moses" (the more common locution); cf. v 56.
53.d. MT. G^BL add "the land of"; cf. n. 51.b.
56.a. MT, G^B. G^L "God"; G^B adds "today," as in v 15.
56.b. MT and G^B. G^L adds "today."
56.c-c. MT, G^L. G^B pl.
56.d-d. MT, G^L. G^B "his servant Moses."
58.a. MT. G^BL adds pleonastic "all."
58.b. G^BL. MT adds pleonastic "and his ordinances."
59.a. MT. G^BL add "our God" to harmonize with the following occurrence.
59.b. MT. G^BL "thy" is erratic in this context.
59.c-c. MT, G^L. G^B omits, failing to understand the writer's identification of Yahweh's servant in this context.
59.d. MT, G^L. G^B adds a corruption, "of a year."
60.a-a. MT. G^B "Yahweh, the God, he is God," and G^L, "Thou art Yahweh the God," show the influence of 18:39.
60.b. MT. G^BL "and with"; throughout this verse, G improves the style.
61.a. MT. G^BL "our."
61.b. MT. G^BL "toward."
61.c. MT. G^BL add "and worthily."
62.a-a. MT. G^BL "and all the Israelites" (καὶ πάντες υἱοὶ Ἰσραηλ) fails to understand the covenant symbolism of the title "Israel."
63.a. MT, Par. G^BL and C "King Solomon."
63.b-b. MT and G^BL. This is a gl which Chr (Par) omits.
63.c-c. MT, G^L, Chr. G^B Par om (haplography).
64.a-a. MT and G^L. G^B "and the offering of the communion-offerings to offer up."
65.a-a. G^L. The other textual witnesses have harmonized and interpreted original חֹג; thus G^B "the feast on that day"; MT "at that time the feast"; Chr (Par) "the feast at that time for seven days."
65.b-b. G^BL. MT omits (haplography).
65.c. G^L adds "and singing."
65.d. G^BL. MT adds interpretive "and seven days, fourteen days"; cf. *HOTTP* 310.
66.a. MT. G^BL "and on."
66.b. G^B. MT "the king." G^L corr.
66.c-c. MT. G^BL substitutes the popular phrase, "each one to his own tent."
66.d-d. MT. G^BL attempts a stylistic improvement with "the good things."
9:2.a. G^B. MT and G^L add "to him" under the influence of v 3.
3.a. Chr. MT "and Yahweh said to him." G "and said to him Yahweh" (pleonastic).
3.b-b. G^B. G^L *praem* "behold." MT omits.
3.c. MT, G^L. G^B adds pleonastic "there forever."
4.a. Par = עשׂות "and behave." Chr, G^BL, and MT have inappropriate infinitive forms.
4.b-b. Chr (Par), G^BL. MT "my statutes . . . observe."
5.a. Mss, G^B. MT and G^L "concerning"; cf. 8:25.
5.b-b. G, Chr (Par). MT "upon the throne of Israel" is influenced by 2:4, 8:25.
6.a. G^B. MT omits; G^L, Chr adapts in other ways.
6.b-b. MT, G^B. G^L omits.
6.c. MT. G^BL "Moses" (exegetical correction).
7.a. G^BL. MT adds pleonastic "the surface of."
7.b. G^BL. MT omits. Cf. v 8.
8.a. G^BL. MT "this."
8.b. Original is restored in light of MT, G "exalted" being designated as a pious scribal emendation (*Tiqqune Sopherim*). Cf. *HOTTP*, 310.
9.a. G^BL. MT adds "the land of"; cf. 8:51, 53.
9.b. MT. G^BL adds the familiar phrase "from the house of bondage."
9.c. Q (וישׁתחוו), Chr, G^B pl. K sing. G^L omits.
9.d. G^BL, Chr (Par). MT "Yahweh" is explicative.
9.e-e. G^B. MT, G^L, Chr have pleonastic "all this misfortune."

Form/Structure/Setting

Extract from the Book of Solomon's Acts (13): The deposit of David's gifts for the temple, 7:51b
[Dtr: The dedication of the temple: Framework introduction, 8:1a*a*b]
[Expansion: v 1a*β*]
Hieros logos for the dedication of the temple
   1. The transfer of the ark
     a. The assembly v 2a
[Gloss, v 2b]
     b. The elders present the ark, vv 3a, 4a*a*, 5
[Expansions, vv 3b, 4a*β*b]
     c. The priests deposit the ark in the adytum, vv 6a*a*b, 7b, 8a
[Expansions, vv 6a*β*, 7a]
[Dtr: Details of the ark, vv 8b–9]
     d. The numinous presence of Yahweh, vv 10a, 11a*a*b, 14a*a*
[Expansions, vv 10b, 11a]
[Dtr: An ancient hymn of dedication 12b–13, with editorial introduction, v 12a, and concluding rubric (LXX)]
[Dtr: Solomon's dedicatory recitation
   Narrative introduction, v 14a*β*b
   1. The protocol of legitimation
     a. Ascription of praise, v 15
     b. The divine directives
       (1) The choice of David, v 16
       (2) The redirection of David's plan, vv 17–19
     c. Fulfillment through Solomon, vv 20–21
   2. The supplicatory prayer
   Transition, v 22
     a. For Solomon's posterity
       (1) Ascription of praise, vv 23–24
       (2) Plea for a perpetual dynasty, vv 25–26
     b. For Solomon's sanctuary
       (1) Plea for divine attentiveness
         (a) God's residence in heaven, v 27
         (b) God's attention to the temple, vv 28–29
       (2) Cases inviting God's attention
       Introductory, v 30
         (a) Judging an oath in case of offenses, vv 31–32
         (b) Restoring repentant Israel from exile, vv 33–34
         (c) Giving rain to repentant Israel, vv 35–36
         (d) Relieving all variety of afflictions, vv 37–40
         (e) Accepting the pious foreigner's prayer, vv 41–43]
[Expansion: Support for Israel in foreign warfare, vv 44–45]
[Expansion: Compassion for Israel in foreign captivity, vv 46–53]
[Dtr: continued
   3. Exhortation to mutual devotion
   Transition, vv 54–55

a. Ascription of praise, v 56
b. Appeal to the covenant God
  (1) For the divine presence, vv 57–58
  (2) For the divine attentiveness, vv 59–60
c. Appeal to the covenant people, v 61]
Hieros logos continued
2. The dedication, vv 62, 63b
[Dtr: Narrative conclusion
  a. The offerings, v 63a]
[Expansion, v 64]
[Dtr: continued
  b. The festival, vv 65–66aα]
Hieros logos continued
3. The dismissal, v 66aβb
[Dtr: A confirmatory appearance to Solomon
  1. The narrative setting, 9:1–3aα
  2. Promise for the temple, v 3aβb
  3. Conditional promise for Solomon, vv 4–5]
[Expansion: A warning to Israel against apostasy, vv 6–9]

Modern criticism is unanimous in attributing the bulk of 1 Kgs 8 to Dtr. Only in the great moralizing chapter, 2 Kgs 17, does one encounter so extensive an exposition of this historian/redactor's theological system. 1 Kgs 8 is especially crucial in Dtr's overall plan because he here takes advantage of an opportunity to make Solomon the mouthpiece of his theology. M. Noth (*Überlieferungsgeschichtliche Studien* 5–10) has pointed out that Dtr has done this at crucial points in the preceding history, i.e., with Moses, Joshua, and Samuel. These, with Solomon, do Dtr's preaching for him. In 1 Kgs 8 it is particularly Dtr's philosophy of history that comes to the fore.

This offers the Bible student all the motivation he needs for making a careful study of the deuteronomistic material in this chapter, but before he will be able to do this successfully, it will be necessary to exercise every technique of text and literary criticism, for the text is in fact in serious disarray at some points, and the ancient witnesses have often made things worse by trying to remedy them.

What one needs to see is that there are at least three distinct layers in this chapter: (1) early source materials, (2) the Dtr adaptation and expansion, and (3) post-Dtr expansions and glosses. It is the introduction and the ending that are particularly confused. The first part of v 1 begins with Solomon as subject, the hiph of קהל "assemble" as verb, and "the elders of Israel" as object; the object is then expanded, with a perplexing prepositional phrase "to King Solomon in Jerusalem," by which the same proper name appears both as subject and as part of a prepositional phrase. In v 2 "every Israelite man" serves as subject, substituting for parallel phrases in v 1, and this is governed by the same verb, but in the niph *wāw*-consec impf (the normal narrative verb form). Following this, v 3 mentions that "the elders of Israel came," but only after "every Israelite man" had been assembled. V 1b had informed us that the elders, chiefs, leaders, etc., assembled to bring up the ark, but v 3 states that the priests actually carried it. This is some of the confusion that reigns at the beginning of chap. 8; gradually literary wholeness asserts itself, but again at the end confusion returns. Thus v 62 says that "the king and all Israel with him" were making sacrifices, but immediately v 63 states that "Solomon" offered a sacrifice. In v 66 we read that Solomon dismissed the people, but then we read that the people "blessed him," meaning a formal recitation, hardly to be expected after they had already been dismissed by the king.

These are threads left behind in the redactional process. We are able to put to good effect what we already know of the diction, style, and ideology of Dtr in order to isolate what actually belongs to him, leaving the early source materials on the one hand and the late expansions on the other. The latter may in places be difficult to distinguish from the deuteronomistic material, but there is never any danger of confusing them with the early source materials. Here too, language and style are clues, but we may rely heavily, in addition, on an observation of the way in which the source materials are assimilated to become a significant part of Dtr's own structure, something that does not happen when random late expansions appear in the text.

One of Dtr's early sources is an ancient hymn of dedication in vv 12–13, quoted verbatim along with its concluding rubric, "Is it not written in the Book of the Upright One?" The other early source at his disposal was a *hieros logos* (Gr. "sacred story") for the dedication of the temple. It had the following structure: 1. The transfer of the ark; 2. The dedication; 3. The dismissal. These elements are presently scattered throughout the chapter, providing the framework on which Dtr has strung his own elaborate composition. It is important to identify these dispersed materials because they represent the first and original narrative of how the temple was actually dedicated. A *hieros logos* is the official account, retold on special occasions, of how the shrine in question received the tokens of divine acceptance and approval. In this case it is the appearance of Yahweh's glory (vv 10–11) that shows Yahweh's acceptance; this is so overpowering that the priests cannot stand to minister and even the king is forced to turn away his face (v 14). According to this *hieros logos*, four distinct persons or groups play a role in the dedication: the laity ("every Israelite man") who come to the temple site to offer sacrifices, vv 2, 5; the elders who come collectively to the place where the ark is (the tent) and bring it to the court of the temple, where the sacrificing is taking place, vv 3–4; the priests who then bring the ark into the adytum of the temple, leaving the staves exposed, vv 6, 8; the king who commands the assembly and shares in the sacrifices, vv 2, 5. The *hieros logos* concludes with blunt statements about the dedication, vv 62–63, and a final description of the joy the people feel as they make their way homeward, v 66.

Some of the late expansions are long; some are very brief. In v 1 the expression "elders of Israel" is explained in terms of Israel's primitive tribal structure; the term "fathers" is an indication of lateness. The gloss in v 2 explains a long-obsolete month-name. The expansions in vv 3–4 reflect the postexilic theocracy, with its exclusive priestly prerogative in religious matters. Those in vv 6–7 give the late name for the adytum and labor an obvious point about the cherubim's wings. Those in vv 10–11 anxiously offer a surrogate ("the cloud" הֶעָנָן) for the original term of theophany, "the glory of Yahweh." Very late expansions to Solomon's prayer appear in vv 44–45 and vv 46–53. In v 64 a contemplative glossator tells that the whole center of the temple court was sanctified so as to make possible the sacrificing of the fantastic number of victims reported in Dtr's narrative in v 63.

Dtr himself, writing probably toward the end of Judah's history, prepares his redaction according to a remarkably orderly fashion. Solomon's speaking is structured in three sections, each of which is provided with a narrative transition (vv 14, 22, 54–55). In the first part of his speech, vv 14–21, his stance is not specified, but it is stated that he is addressing the "whole assembly of Israel." He starts out with an ascription of praise to God but turns this into a protocol of legitimation, i.e., a statement of Solomon's divine designation as the temple builder. In the second part of his speech, vv 23–43, Solomon faces the altar with his palms toward heaven and prays first for a blessing on his posterity (Dtr's number one concern) and second for divine attentiveness toward the temple and those who worship in or "toward" it; this section is especially interesting because of the way in which it lists special cases that might invite Yahweh's attention (vv 30–43). It is just here that the long expansions of vv 44–45 and vv 46–53 have been inserted. Then in the third part of Solomon's speech, vv 54–61, he rises from his knees to bless the people, but this time his blessing turns out to be an appeal to God and also an appeal to the people. Finally comes Dtr's narrative conclusion, vv 63–66. Picking up on the final sections of the *hieros logos*, Dtr tells of the offerings, the feasting, and the dismissal.

Included as part of our pericope for the dedication of the temple is the extract from the Book of Solomon's Acts telling how Solomon deposited David's gifts in the temple's treasure-rooms (7:51b); also Dtr's imaginative narrative in 9:1–5, telling how Solomon received a second revelation like that at Gibeon, and the very late expansion of 9:6–9, foretelling the ruin of the temple and the disgrace of Israel as a people.

Comment

7:51b This extract from the Book of Solomon's Acts mentions two things that appear nowhere else in the materials concerning the temple. One is the "sacral booty," lit., "holy things," consisting of silver, gold, and valuable artifacts, evidently confiscated by David in his various wars and designated as booty dedicated to Yahweh (cf. 15:15). The other is the "treasure-rooms," אֹצָרוֹת, which may be a functional description of what 6:6, 8 call the "stories."

8:1–11 Dtr is known in v 1 as in v 12 by his introductory אָז, "then." Consistently, Dtr uses the name "Solomon" (1, 12, 22, 54, 63, 65; 9:1, 2), in distinction from the underlying *hieros logos*, which commences at vv 2, 5 with the formal "King Solomon" and thereafter uses "the king" (vv 14, 63). "The elders of Israel," זִקְנֵי יִשְׂרָאֵל, used by Dtr in v 1 and by the *hieros logos* in v 3, is an old designation found numerous times in the OT, commencing with Exod 3:16; it reflects the sociological situation of the ancient tribal league, in which leading mature men were elevated to a position of authority. "Chiefs of the tribes" ראשי המטות and "leaders of the fathers" נשיאי האבות are artificial and unhistorical. "The ark of Yahweh's covenant": Dtr's phrase, used already at 1 Sam 4:5 and implying with vv 9 and 21 that the ark had no other function than to symbolize the covenant. For the original story of the ark see 1 Sam 4–6, 2 Sam 6. It was actually a war palladium symbolizing Yahweh's presence in battle, and was so used as late as David's time (cf. 2 Sam 11:11). "From the city of David; that is Zion": cf. 2 Sam 5:7; Dtr is careful to indicate that, although David's city would have included the temple mount in his own day, in the time of Solomon it included only Ophel with its citadel Zion.

"Every Israelite man," כל איש ישראל: the *hieros logos* assumes universal adult male participation in the dedication ceremony; no tribal, regional, or social segregation was allowed (cf. 2 Sam 6:1) since the temple was intended to be a powerful unifying symbol. "The month Ethanim": the month is given but not the day; Israel still used the Canaanite names rather than the gloss's numeral. Since 6:38 states that the temple was finished in the eighth month, Bul, it must have stood empty for at least eleven months. "With celebration," בחג: this alternative translation is less troublesome than the usual "at the feast," which would have to refer to the Feast of Booths or Tabernacles, of whose proper celebration (Num 29) the text gives no indication. "The tent of meeting," אהל מועד: this refers not to David's tent (2 Sam 6:17, 1 Kgs 2:29–30) but to the desert tabernacle, which a priestly glossator means by this notice to identify with Solomon's temple. Nothing is said about what was next done with the "tent of meeting"; there is really nothing to justify R. E. Friedman's speculation that it was set up within the adytum (*BA* 43, [1940] 241–48).

"Then the priests brought up the ark to its place": according to the *hieros logos,* the elders had brought the ark to the temple precincts (cf. 2 Sam 6:2–17), but then the priests carried it to the place prepared for it within the adytum, just beneath the wings of the cherubim (more and more it was assumed that only sacral persons like the Levites were entitled to carry the ark, cf. Josh 3). "The staves extended": in P's blueprint, staves were permanently affixed to the ark (Exod 25:12–15), but this passage makes it clear that these were affixed to the long side of the ark and extended through the curtain in front of the adytum so that their ends could be seen from the "holy place" (= the nave, הקדש) before it. Dtr immediately denies this statement (v 8) but assures his readers that the staves are there irregardless. He adds (v 9) that the ark contains nothing besides Moses' stone tablets, deposited there at Horeb; this is a Deuteronomic tradition (Deut 10:5) in conflict with the later Priestly statements that a pot of manna and Aaron's staff had been placed in it (Exod 16:33; Num 17:25 [Eng. 10]). "A covenant": Dtr epitomizes the entire theology of the Book of Deuteronomy; the temple with its ark and its stone tablets symbolizes the covenant that Yahweh made with Israel when they arrived at Mt. Horeb from Egyptian bondage, a complete reversal of the actual historical situation in which the construction of the temple conflicts with the ancient Exodus and Sinai traditions. "The cloud . . . the glory of Yahweh": the former (found in the expansions) is a priestly surrogate (cf. Exod 40:34–38); the latter is normative as late as Ezekiel (cf.

1:28, 10:18, 11:22–23, 43:2, 4–5), but our passage shows how early the "glory" tradition actually was.

12–14a G^L is the best guide in restoring this mangled hymn (see *Notes*). Our translation presupposes a long-verse couplet, 4:3, 4:3; in the first bicolon a contrast is stated between the shining sun in the sky and Yahweh hiding in the dark, and in the second bicolon the royal patron offers parallel statements announcing that he has made for Yahweh a permanent palace. This ancient dedication hymn was written down in the Book of Jasher (the Upright One), mentioned also in Josh 10:12–13 and 2 Sam 1:17–27, where other poetic materials are preserved (see H. St. John Thackeray, *JTS* 12 [1911] 518–32). There is little solid basis for A. van den Born's claim that this hymn belongs to a lost creation epic (*OTS* 14 [1965] 235–44), M. Görg's view that it is based on Egyptian models (*UF* 6 [1974] 53–63), or O. Loretz's effort to identify it as a fragment from a Canaanite-Israelite dedication hymn (*UF* 6 [1974] 478–80). "And the king turned away his face" belongs to the *hieros logos;* it records his natural response to the *mysterium tremendum* (Otto) of Yahweh's glory, but offers a poor preparation for Dtr's "then he blessed. . . ."

14aβb–21 The protocol of legitimation. The narrative introduction states that Solomon blessed the whole assembly (or "congregation," קהל) of Israel as they stood, yet Dtr composes words of blessing for Yahweh, not for them. Another incongruity follows as the blessing becomes a quotation of what Yahweh purportedly said about choosing David rather than a city (v 16), and this in turn becomes Solomon's exposition to the people of how Yahweh refused David's plan to build a temple, promising him a son to perform this in his place (vv 17–19), a promise that has been fulfilled in Solomon's ascent to the throne, construction of the temple, and provision of a place for the ark (vv 20–21). Already in this speech, the observant reader can discern Dtr's priorities, for the security of the Davidic succession remains ever the prerequisite for the establishment of the temple.

22–29 Now Solomon begins his actual prayer. He first praises Yahweh for his incomparability and for his covenant faithfulness (v 23), but immediately returns to his major concern, Yahweh's fidelity toward the Davidides. Reminding Yahweh that he has not only spoken a promise to David but has fulfilled it as well (v 24), Solomon introduces parallel pleas in v 25 and v 26 with the connective particle, ועתה "so now," asking Yahweh to keep the faithful Davidic posterity, a reference to the kings of his own late period, safe from being "cut off." With this plea expressed, Solomon returns to the subject of the temple that he is in the process of dedicating, first expressing the wondering question whether such a God as Yahweh, who is too great for earth and heaven to contain, will indeed dwell on earth, and in a man-made temple (v 27). For this characteristic deuteronomistic sentiment the closest parallel is the postexilic passage, Isa 66:1. But Solomon prays nonetheless that Yahweh may deign to make this temple the place where his Name dwells, the Name being, in deuteronomistic ideology, a hypostasis or extension of Yahweh's true being, but not the Deity in the fullness of his being (vv 28–29). The purpose is that the temple may serve as a listening-post or sounding board, continually receptive to any prayer that may be directed toward it (v 29b; cf. vv 30, 33, 35, 42, 44, 48).

30–43 Solomon next describes five (original) cases or situations in which this function of the temple is to be carried out. He asks that as he or the people pray toward the temple Yahweh will be listening up in heaven and respond (v 30; so also vv 32, 34, 36, 39, 43, 45). The respective petitions are somewhat differently styled: v 31 as in cultic legislation (cf. Lev 1:2, 2:1, etc.), vv 33 and 35 with ב plus the infinitive, v 37 again in casuistic style, but with the various possibilities expressed by foremost noun subjects, and v 41 with an exceptive clause introduced by וגם "and even," preceding the casuistic "if" in v 42b. Vv 31–32 asks that when two men make contradictory oaths, swearing to Yahweh, Yahweh will cause the truth to come out. Vv 33–34 asks that when Israel sins, is punished by being defeated in battle, and prays for forgiveness, Yahweh will forgive and restore. Vv 35–36 asks for forgiveness when Israel sins, is punished by drought, and repents. Vv 37–40 broadens this to include every conceivable calamity and every conceivable prayer, requesting forgiveness as Yahweh knows a man's heart, to the end that all men ("the sons of man") may revere him. Vv 41–43 represents possibly the most marvelously universalistic passage in the OT; it asks that the prayer of every foreigner may be heard, so that all the peoples may fear and know Yahweh.

44–53 The two late expansions in vv 44–45 and vv 46–53, respectively, are again styled casuistically, but now with the particle כי "when." The first is revealed as an addition by the fact that it closely repeats the substance of vv 33–34, but without any acknowledgement of sin (note "the city" alongside "the temple"; Jerusalem becomes like Mecca!). Vv 46–53 clearly reveals an exilic background, with the covenant people far from their land. There is a series of "ifs": the people sin; in fury Yahweh delivers them up; their captors deport them; they take it to heart and supplicate Yahweh; they truly repent and pray—this time toward the "land" as well as toward the "city" and the "temple." Upon all these conditions, Yahweh is asked to "hear," "forgive," and "destine them for compassion." This plea is concluded by a pointed summation of deuteronomistic theology, requesting Yahweh's attention on the ground of Israel's election (for Israel as Yahweh's inheritance see Deut 4:20, 9:29; for Egypt as an "iron furnace," see Deut 4:20, Jer 11:4; for Israel's separation, see Lev 20:24, 26).

54–61 The prayer finished, Solomon launches into a blessing on the "assembly" that is, once again, praise to Yahweh for giving "rest" מנוחה (cf. G. von Rad, *The Problem of the Hexateuch and Other Essays* [New York: McGraw-Hill, 1966] 94–102) and for keeping his word with Moses (v 56; cf. v 53). He next expresses the pious wishes (1) that Yahweh will continue to be with Israel as in the past and (2) that he will incline Israel to do his commandments (vv 57–58). Next the prayer is for continual access to Yahweh, with an appropriate response to the particular prayer of each day, leading to the universal confession of his sole and universal Godship (vv 59–60); see G. Braulik, *Bib* 52 (1971) 20–33. Solomon's final word is a plea to the assembly that their future behavior may be the same as "right now" (on this phrase see *YTT*, 54n).

62–66 On the narrative conclusion, in which deuteronomistic material is mixed with the *hieros logos*, see above. The number of oxen and sheep is utterly fantastic (v 63), so that one scarcely blames the interpolator of v 64 for inserting his notice about using the entire court and not just the bronze altar (on "the same day" see *YTT*, 110). V 65 and the first clause of v 66 is Dtr's conclusion. Yahweh is twice called "our God." The feasting is expansive in two dimensions: (1) it involves an "all Israel" that covers people from the approach to Hamath in upper Syria to the brook of Egypt in Sinai; (2) it lasts seven full days. According to the *hieros logos* in v 66aβb things are more simple: the worshipers bless the king and then depart, thankful for what Yahweh has done for "David" and for Israel.

9:1–5 Dtr places the second Gibeon revelation in a time when Solomon's building operations—named and unnamed—had come to completion. Without telling how Solomon got to Gibeon, or why he went there, Dtr narrates Yahweh's response to the prayer of chap. 8. Yahweh says he has heard it and done it: the temple is sanctified and accepted. His Name is fixed there so that it cannot depart (v 1); his eyes (symbol of all-seeing) and his heart (symbol of all-caring) will be there every day. But again it is with Solomon and the Davidic line that Dtr is ultimately concerned: Yahweh goes on to promise not to cut off any king from this line so long as each king remains obedient to his commandments (vv 4–5).

6–9 In this late addition "you" becomes plural, indicating that it is now Israel rather than Solomon who is being addressed. The condition under consideration is Israel's nonobedience, involving the worship of other gods (v 6), in which event Yahweh threatens to cut them off from the "ground" (= "land"; cf. 8:40) and to "dismiss" the temple from his presence, so that Israel will become a mockery and the temple a ruin (vv 7–8aα). This drastic statement is paralleled by the famous denunciation of the temple in Mic 3:12; cf. Jer 26:18. The rest of v 8, with v 9, is a kind of catechism in which the cause of such devastation and opprobrium is defined in terms of Israel's apostasy.

Explanation

A close study of the text has revealed that Dtr's prime concern was for the Davidic dynasty, not the temple. He keeps on asking that Yahweh's promise may be fulfilled, that no one may be "cut off" from the throne. This clearly alludes to the situation during the last years of Judah's existence, when kings like Jehoiakim were playing fast and loose with the covenant and the law (cf. Hab 1:1–4, 12–13). Dtr continues to emphasize that the perpetuation of the Davidic dynasty depends on their repentance and obedience. Eventually the Davidides showed themselves to be unworthy, so that their lineage was never allowed to be restored and the aspiration for an "everlasting throne" died away, to be brought back to life once again only in the perfect obedience of David's latter-day son, Jesus of Nazareth. As we see in this chapter, it is Israel's basic convenant made through Moses that remains secure even when Dtr has to give up on the promise to David.

The original material in this chapter gives a central place to the laity and their representative "elders" in the dedication of God's temple. Late, post-exilic glosses try to usurp their prerogative for the priests. Thus we can identify a discernible "evangelical" impulse at the heart of Israelite religion. The common people knew that God welcomed them to full participation in his house, and on this occasion they returned home rejoicing for the good that worshiping him betokened for the king and for the nation (v 66).

Rising to the surface here is a tension that always exists between a realistic and a symbolic representation of God's presence. We see the first especially in the "glory כבוד" that fills the temple in the *hieros logos,* and the second in Dtr's insistence that Yahweh dwells in heaven while only his name (שם) abides in the temple. Dtr sees the danger of trying to objectify and capture God, substituting a spiritualizing universalism and transcendence. The trend is toward mere memorialization, or even a kind of nominalism. Bible students as well as theologians are ever challenged to ponder how the "real presence" of God (and of Christ) is to be understood.

Notable Events of Solomon's Reign
(9:10-25)

Bibliography

Fensham, F. C. "The Treaty between Solomon and Hiram and the Alalakh Tablets." *JBL* 79 (1960) 59–60. Gooding, D. W. "Text-sequence and Translation-Revision in 3 Reigns IX, 10–X, 33." *VT* 19 (1969) 448–63. Haran, M. "The Gibeonites, the Nethinim and the Sons of Solomon's Servants." *VT* 11 (1961) 159–69. Naor, M. "Solomon and Hiram and the Land of Cabul." *Western Galilee and the Coast of Galilee.* Jerusalem: Israel Exploration Society, 1965. Yadin, Y. "Solomon's City Wall and Gate at Gezer." *IEJ* 9 (1958) 80–86.

Translation

[10] (*It so happened at the end of the twenty years during which Solomon was occupied in building the two houses, Yahweh's temple and the king's house—* [11] *Hiram king of Tyre providing[a] Solomon with cedar timber and juniper timber and gold as much as he wished—that then*). . . . *The king[b] [c]would trade[c] to Hiram twenty cities in the land of Galilee.* [12] *So Hiram went out of Tyre[a] to inspect the cities which Solomon had offered him, but they did not measure up in his eyes,* [13] *and he said, "What are these cities which you have offered me, my brother?" So they named them, "Land of Kabul,"[a] to this day.* [14] *So Hiram sent the king[a] a hundred twenty talents of gold.[b]*

[15] *And this is an item about the corvée[a] which King Solomon raised in order to construct Yahweh's temple and [b]his own house[b] [c]and the Millo and the wall of Jerusalem;[c] also Hazor, Megiddo, and Gezer;[d]* [16] *(Pharaoh, king of Egypt, went up and captured Gezer, burning it with fire.[a] And the Canaanite residents [b]of the city he slew[b] so that he[c] might be able to present it as a dowry to his daughter, Solomon's wife.* [17] *So Solomon rebuilt Gezer) also Beth-Horon [a]the Lower[a]* [18] *and Baalat and Tamar[a] in the wilderness (in the land);* [19] *also every store-city belonging to Solomon and the cities of the chariotry and the cities of the horsemen—anything whatsoever[a] that Solomon desired to build, be it in Jerusalem [b]or in Lebanon[b] or anywhere in the territory that he governed:* [20] *All the surviving[a] population from [b]the Amorites, the Hittites, the Perizzites, the Hivites, and the Jebusites[b]—those that did not belong among the Israelites—* [21] *their children who remained after them in the land, whom the Israelites were not able to consign to destruction,[a] them did Solomon recruit for a slave[b] corvée to this very day.* [22] *However, from the Israelites, Solomon did not choose any slave,[a] but these were set aside to become men of war and his officials,[b] [c]his commanders, his captains,[c] his chariot commanders and his cavalrymen.*

[23] *These were the chiefs of the prefects who were over Solomon's work: [a]five hundred fifty[a] directors over the people doing the work.*

[24] *To be sure,[a] the daughter of Pharaoh [b]did go up[b] out of the city of David to [c]her own house[c] which he built for her.[d] [e]Then he built the Millo.[e]*

[25] *And Solomon offered up [a]three times each year[a] burnt-offerings and communion-offerings upon the altar that he had built for [b]Yahweh, and he burnt [c]his fire-offerings[cb] before Yahweh.[d] [e]So did he finish off the temple.[e]*

Notes

MT 9:15 = G 10:23a; MT vv 16–17a = G 4:32–33; MT v 17aβb = G 10:23bα; MT vv 19aβ–22 = G 10:23bβ–25; MT v 24 = G 9:9b.

11.a. Reading the qal act ptcp for MT piel pf (נֹשֵׂא, normally נֹשֵׂא).

11.b. G[B]. MT and G[L] "King Solomon."

11.c-c. The impf is modal in a context where past events are rendered by the impf consec or the pf.

12.a. G adds explicative "and went to Galilee."

13.a. MT. G ὅριον "boundary" = Heb. גְּבוּל (auditory corr).

14.a. MT. G "Solomon" is explicative.

14.b. For MT vv 15–25, G has counterparts at various places in the very corrupt *Vorlage* it is following.

15.a. MT. G "plunder."

15.b-b. MT. G "the king's house" is explicative; cf. v 10.

15.c-c. MT. G[BL] paraphrases: "and the wall of Jerusalem and the citadel in order to provide the defense-work for the city of David."

15.d. MT. G adds words from vv 17–19.

16.a. MT, G[L]. G[B] omits.

16.b-b. Mt. G[BL] corr.

16.c. MT. G[BL] have explicative "Pharaoh."

17.a-a. MT. G "the upper."

18a. K and G[B]. Q, Chr, G[L] Syr, Tg, Vg "Tadmor" (correcting the unfamiliar by the familiar).

19.a. Reading "all" with Chr.

19.b-b. MT (*lectio difficilior*). G omits.

20.a. MT. G[BL] corr.

20.b-b. MT. G[BL] have a different list of nations.

21.a. MT, hiph from root חרם "devote to the ban." Chr has piel of כלה, "consume," "wipe out."

21.b. MT. G omits (haplography).

22.a. MT. G πρᾶγμα "world" = Heb. עבודה, corr from עבד "slave." Chr "as slaves to feed him."

22.b. MT. Chr omits.

22.c-c. MT. G[B] omits; G[L] transposes.

23.a-a. MT. G 2:35[h] "three thousand six hundred"; Chr "two hundred fifty."

24.a. MT אַךְ is to be preferred as *lectio difficilior*. Chr אֵת־ן sign of direct obj. accords best with its passive construction. G 2:35[f] = כָּכָה, כֵּן "thus." G 9:9 reads אָז "then," influenced by v 24.b.

24.b-b. MT. For reasons of pious ideology, Chr and G 9:9 read "Solomon brought up."

24.c-c. MT (= G 2:35[f]). G 9:9 "his house"; Chr "to the house."

24.d. MT. G 9:9 "for himself."

24.e. MT (= G 2:35[f]). G 9:9, Chr omit.

25.a-a. MT (= G 2:35[g]). Chr omits.

25.b-b. MT. Chr omits.

25.c-c. MT אֲשֶׁר אִתּוֹ "with him who" makes no sense; G 2:35[g], which generally follows MT closely, omits. With modern commentators (Gray, Noth), we adopt Klostermann's conjecture, reading אֶת־אִשָּׁיו "his fire-offerings."

25.d. MT. Chr "the porch."

25.e-e. MT. Chr omits.

Form/Structure/Setting

Extract from the Book of Solomon's Acts (14): Barter for Galilean cities
    Editorial introduction, vv 10–11a
    1. The proposition, v 11b
    2. Inspection and deprecation, vv 12–13a
[Punning comment, v 13b]

3. Conclusion of the sale, v 14
Extract from the Book of Solomon's Acts (15): What the corvée did and who were in it
1. Its building accomplishments, vv 15, 17b–19
[Archeological note regarding Gezer, vv 16–17a]
2. Its personnel, vv 20, 21b, 23
[Dtr comments, vv 21a, 22]
Extract from the Book of Solomon's Acts (16): Pharaoh's daughter goes to her new house, v 24a
Extract from the Book of Solomon's Acts (17): The Millo, v 24b
Extract from the Book of Solomon's Acts (18): Solomon's ritual devotion, v 25a
Editorial conclusion, v 25b

The collocation of five extracts from the Book of Solomon's Acts which make up this section can be rationalized through observation of the concluding rubric in v 25b, "So did he finish off (שלם piel) the temple." This refers not to constructing or decorating this building, but to performing everything pertinent to the foregoing description of the temple. The item about the barter for twenty Galilean cities is included because, like 5:15–26 (Eng. 1–12), it speaks of Hiram providing Solomon with cedar and juniper timber. The next item is included because, like 5:27–32 (Eng. 13–18), it speaks about the corvée. Next comes the item about Pharaoh's daughter getting a new house, included because 3:1 and 7:8b have left the impression that she continued to live in her original palace within the temple precincts. There follows a very brief item to the effect that Solomon eventually built the Millo, needed because v 15's reference to this structure, preceding the notice about the palace of Pharaoh's daughter, might give the undesired impression that Solomon had waited until everything else had been built before turning to the matter of this queen's palace, as though a heathen woman's presence in the city were a matter of indifference. Finally, the item about Solomon's schedule for offering sacrifices at the temple is required to show that his devotion continued after the dedication of this sanctuary.

We may believe that each of these items is based on factual data, as is the case with all the extracts taken from this archive. It is doubtful that they were written in the precise order in which we now find them. Dtr is probably responsible for their selection, for his usual אז transition at v 24b, and perhaps for the editorial conclusion in v 25b, although this may have been found here or somewhere else in his source document. In any event, Dtr intends this last as a concluding rubric; he will have absolutely nothing more to say about the temple. Dtr does not miss the opportunity to interject comments from his highly ideological point of view in vv 21a and 22. Other additions, from unknown sources, appear in vv 13b and 16–17a.

Comment

10–14 One is suspicious that some early editor, probably not Dtr, had begun to rewrite or paraphrase this extract because v 10 begins in customary narrative style, with ויהי "it so happened" and a temporal clause, after which one would expect a series of *wāw*-consecutive imperfects, but the piel perfect of נשׂא "provide" (we repoint this as a participle) follows, then in v 11b with the imperfect of נתן "trade." The twenty years for building the "two houses" adds the figures from 6:38 and 7:1, which intended them as contemporary. The reference to Hiram providing gold along with cedar and juniper is entirely fanciful. The imperfect of נתן "trade" in v 11 has a modal force (see *Notes*) and implies an offer to trade, not an unconditional gift. To be sure, the elaborate polite procedure of the time (cf. Gen 23) required the fiction of offering an actual gift, and this is reflected in the perfect of this same verb occurring in v 12: Solomon had given Hiram a "gift," but reciprocation was expected. The land of Galilee is adjacent to the territory controlled by Tyre, but the twenty cities (actually villages) that Solomon "gave" must have been on the border, outside the traditional border of Asher. This may therefore have been more a political than a commercial exchange (note the treaty name, "brother"; cf. 20:32–33). Solomon was willing to give up—for a price—"cities" that may have been in dispute between him and Hiram in order to secure the latter's good will (cf. F. C. Fensham, *JBL* [1960] 79, 59–60). Hiram of course goes through the motions of inspecting the "cities," finds them of little account, but concludes a bargain with Solomon to pay him one hundred twenty talents (talent: from 45 to 130 lb.) of gold, a truly magnificent sum, but perhaps insufficient when seen from the perspective of their potential worth (like the seven million dollars paid for Alaska!). There is a town known as Kabul near Acco (cf. Josh 19:27), and the glossator evidently thought it to be among Hiram's twenty "cities." This is by no means certain, for כבול, "like nothing," is a pun strongly suggested by Hiram's derogatory query of v 13a.

15–23 We have been told about a freeman's corvée raised to prepare stone and timber for Solomon's temple (5:27–32; Eng. vv 13–18); now we learn of a permanent slave corvée that was raised for ongoing construction work in Jerusalem and throughout the land. Yahweh's house (= temple) and the king's house (= palace) are known from chaps. 6–7. The Millo (root מלא "fill") may have been a terrace or abutment between David's City and the temple complex. Reference to building "the wall of Jerusalem" can only be understood as with respect to a project of rebuilding and strengthening the walls already in place (cf. 2 Sam 5:9). Solomonic defense-works in Hazor, Megiddo, and Gezer, particularly the characteristic triple gateway, are known from archeological excavations. Each of these was an ancient Canaanite town from the Bronze Age, and had always been important in defense strategy. Hazor lay in the far north, near the Sea of Galilee. Megiddo guarded the Carmel pass from the valley of Jezreel. Gezer lay between the Shephelah and the coastal plain due west from Jerusalem. Thus each city was located on Israel's borders; so also Beth-Horon the Lower at the edge of the Benjaminite hill-country, guarding the strategic road to Jerusalem, Baalat southeast of Beersheba, and Tamar in the extreme southern Negeb. Also constructed by the corvée were an unspecified number of store-cities, chariot cities, and cities for horsemen, which together occasioned the sophisticated provisioning system described in 4:7–19, 5:6–8 (Eng. 4:26–28). To this list the writer adds, "anything whatsoever that Solomon desired to build," as though Solomon's accomplishments exceeded the writer's ability to record them. The reference to Lebanon in Hiram's territory surprises us but must have to do with structures involved in the cutting and transport of timber (cf. 5:20; Eng. v 6).

Solomon may indeed be admired for his energy and ambition, but hardly for any sensitivity to human values. Like every other ruler in the ancient world, he believed in the exploitation of his fellow human beings. Thus the expansion in vv 16–17a, relating how Pharaoh's army captured Gezer, exterminated its Canaanite inhabitants, and gave Solomon control of it as his daughter's dowry, implies that Solomon was quite willing to profit from the violent expropriation of other people's property. The various details of the slave corvée, which involved all the surviving native population, reflects not only inhumanity to unfortunate individuals but an attitude of permanent xenophobia, drawn upon to justify the wholesale exploitation of peoples. (Dtr's chauvinistic comments in vv 21a, 22 show that later Israelites generally shared this same attitude and approved of Solomon's harshness.) V 23's notice that only 550 bosses were required to supervise all this work suggests a much smaller work-force than that supervised by the 3300 of 5:30; Eng. v 16.

24–25 Although it is not in the list of v 15, Solomon is said to have built a new "house" for Pharaoh's daughter outside the city. Evidently this was long delayed, and it may very well have occurred because the queen grew tired of the hubbub of city life and demanded a quiet retreat somewhere else. Certainly her high position would preclude her being banished or in any way embarrassed, and it is likely that she continued to reside at least part time in her original palace adjacent to the king's. We can only speculate that her new residence would have stood on the Mount of Olives, to which she would have had to "go up" (cf. 11:7). On Solomon's "burnt-offerings" and "communion-offerings," see on 3:15. The reference to "three times in the year" indicates Solomon's personal participation in Israel's three great yearly feasts (Exod 23:14, 34:23), now held in Jerusalem. We read nothing elsewhere of Solomon's sacrificial altar except in the late expansion at 8:64. "Fire-offerings" is a restoration of a corrupt text; these were special offerings reserved for the priests (cf. Lev 6:12, Deut 18:1, Josh 13:14, 1 Sam 2:28).

Explanation

Solomon's defense works and monumental buildings drained the nation's wealth while providing only a temporary appearance of strength and grandeur. The harsh, ambitious Solomon of whom we read here is much closer to historical reality than the idealized figure of whom we read in chaps. 3, 5, 8, and 10.

Solomon's Wealth and Wisdom
(9:26—10:29)

Bibliography

Canciani, F., and **Pettinato, G.** "Salomos Thron, philologische und archäologische Erwägungen." *ZDPV* 81 (1965) 88–108. **Crown, A. D.** "Once Again I Kings 10:26–29." *Abr-Nahrain* 15 (1974/75) 35–38. **Ullendorff, E.** "The Queen of Sheba (I K. 10:1–13)." *BJRL* 45 (1963) 486–504.

Translation

26 *And Solomon* [a] *made a fleet in Ezion-geber—which* [b] *is adjacent to* [b] *Eilat* [c]*— on the shore of* [d]*the Sea of Reeds* [d] *in the land of Edom.* 27 *And Hiram sent as crew for the fleet his servants who were regular seamen experienced with the sea, accompanying the servants of Solomon.* 28 *And they went to Ophir and obtained from there gold in the amount of* [a]*four hundred and twenty* [a] *talents, and brought it to King Solomon.*

10:1 *Now the queen of Sheba had heard* [a] *Solomon's reputation,* [b]*redounding to the name of Yahweh,* [b] *and she came to try him out with hard problems.* 2 *And she arrived in Jerusalem with a large armed guard; camels* [a] *were bearing balsam with very much gold and precious gems. And she entered in to Solomon* [b] *and conversed with him about everything that was in her heart.* 3 *And Solomon* [a] *told her about every matter that she had; no single item was obscure to* [b]*the king* [b] *so as to prevent him from telling her.*

4 *When the queen of Sheba had observed all Solomon's wisdom and the house he had built* 5 *and the food for his table* [a] *and where his servants sat and where his ministers* [b] *stood, with their robes,* [c] *and his cup-bearers,* [d] *and his burnt-offerings* [e] *which he offered at Yahweh's temple, she was simply left breathless;* 6 *and she said to the king,* [a] *"True was the report that I heard in my own country concerning your words* [b] *and concerning your wisdom.* 7 *And I did not give credence to* [a]*those reporting this* [a] *until I came and my eyes actually saw it.* [b]*And behold, the half has not been told me!* [b] *You excel in prosperity* [c] *the report that I heard.* 8 *Happy are your wives!* [a] *Happy are these your servants who stand continually before you, listening to* [b] *your wisdom!* 9 *Let Yahweh your God be blessed, who delights in you, appointing you upon Israel's throne because Yahweh loves Israel* [a] *forever, and has made you king* [b] *for the performance of justice and right."* [c]

10 *Then she presented the king* [a] *with a hundred twenty talents of gold, along with very much balsam and precious gems. Never again did* [b]*such a quantity enter* [b] *as that balsam that the queen of Sheba gave King Solomon.* 11 *What is more,* [a]*Hiram's fleet* [a] *which carried gold* [b] *from Ophir brought* [c] *almug* [d] *timbers* [e]*in great abundance,* [e] *with precious stones.* 12 *And the king made the almug timbers into steps* [a] *for Yahweh's temple and the king's house, also into harps and lyres for the singers. Never again came such almug timbers,* [b] *and never again* [c] [d]*was it seen, up to this day.* [d]

13 *Then King Solomon presented the queen of Sheba with everything she desired, whatever she requested, in addition to what* [a]*he had already given her, in kingly* [b] *style.* [a] *And she departed to journey back to her country—she and* [c] *her servants.*

¹⁴*And the weight of the gold that came to Solomon in one year was six hundred sixty-six gold talents,* ¹⁵ *not counting the taxes* ᵃ *laid on travelers and the profits* ᵇ *of the merchants, all the Arab* ᶜ *kings, and the provincial governors.* ᵈ

¹⁶ *And Solomon* ᵃ *made two* ᵇ *hundred large shields out of beaten gold, six hundred weight-units going into a single shield;* ¹⁷ *also three hundred small shields of beaten gold, three minas of gold going into a single shield.* ᵃ *And the king placed them in the House of the Lebanon Forest.* ¹⁸ *And the king made a great ivory throne, covering it with fine* ᵃ *gold.* ¹⁹ *The throne had six steps; and the throne had a* ᵃ*calf's head* ᵃ *in back of it, with arms on either side alongside the place of the seat, and two lions standing next to the arms.* ²⁰ *Also twelve lions* ᵃ *were standing* ᵇ *upon the six steps, on either side. The like has not been made in* ᶜ*any kingdom.* ᶜ ²¹ *And all of Solomon's* ᵃ *drinking vessels were golden.* ᵇ *And all the vessels of the House of the Lebanon Forest were of refined gold. There was no silver; it had no esteem* ᶜ *in the days of Solomon.* ᵈ ²² *For the king had at sea a Tarshish-style fleet accompanying Hiram's fleet.* ᵃ *Once each three years the Tarshish-style fleet would arrive,* ᵇ *bearing gold and silver,* ᶜ*ivory, apes, and baboons.* ᶜ

²³ *And Solomon* ᵃ *was greater than all kings,* ᵇ *both in riches and in wisdom.* ²⁴ *And all the earth* ᵃ *sought Solomon's presence in order to listen to his wisdom which God* ᵇ *had put into his heart.* ²⁵ *These would bring each his own present:* ᵃ*silver articles;* ᵃ *gold articles; or garments,* ᵇ *armament* ᶜ *and spices; horses* ᵈ *and mules—in each year its proper item.*

²⁶ ᵃ*Also Solomon had* ᵃ ᵇ*fourteen hundred* ᵇ *chariots* ᶜ *with twenty* ᵈ *thousand horses;* ᵉ*he stationed them* ᵉ *in the chariot cities and with the king in Jerusalem.* ²⁷ *And the king* ᵃ *regarded* ᵇ*the gold and* ᵇ *the silver in Jerusalem as so many stones, and the cedars he compared to the sycamores which grow in profusion upon the Shephelah.* ²⁸ *Now the export of the horses that belonged to Solomon was from* ᵃ*Musri and Qewe.* ᵃ *The merchants of the king would receive them from Qewe at a certain price.* ²⁹ *And a chariot,* ᵃ*would come up for export* ᵃ *from Musri for a hundred* ᵇ *pieces of silver, or a horse for fifty* ᶜ *pieces of silver. Moreover, whatever was intended for any of the Hittite kings or the kings of Syria would be exported* ᵈ*through their entrepreneurship.* ᵈ

Notes

MT 9:26 = G 29; MT 9:27–29 = G 31–33; MT 10:23–25 = G 26–28.

26.a. Conjectured from versional disagreement: Gᴮ "Solomon the king"; MT, Gᴸ, Chr "King Solomon."

26.b-b. MT lit. "with" (אֵת), paraphrased in G τὴν οὖσαν ἐχομένην "has as property/dependency."

26.c. MT, Chr, read the rare "Eilôt"; elsewhere MT and G have "Eilat" (cf. MT's change of "Ramat Gilead" to "Ramoth Gilead," exemplifying a tendency to substitute pl forms for the fem sing.

26.d-d. Heb. סֽוּף־יַם "Sea of Reeds" figures prominently in the exodus tradition (e.g., Exod 15:22 P), hence Chr "the sea," Par "that which is alongside the sea," G "the last sea."

28.a-a. MT. G "one hundred twenty"; cf. 10:10.

10:1.a. Reading pf with G, Chr (Par) in place of MT's ptcp.

1.b-b. MT, G. Chr's and Tg's omission may be ideological. Cf. *HOTTP*, 311.

2.a. MT. G, Chr "and camels."

2.b. MT, G. MSS "King Solomon."

3.a. MT, Gᴮ. Gᴸ "King Solomon."

3.b-b. MT, G. Chr "Solomon."

5.a. MT. G "Solomon."

5.b. MSS, Q. K, G sing.

5.c. MT. G "and his robe."

5.d. MT, G. Chr adds "with their robes."

5.e. Par. MT, G, Chr sing. Cf. Syr, Vg.

6.a. MT. G^{BL} "King Solomon."

6.b. MT. G^{BL} sing.

7.a-a. G^{BL}. MT "words"; cf. v 6, sing.

7.b-b. MT. G^B "and behold, the half is not like what was told me"; similarly G^L.

7.c. G^{BL}. MT "wisdom and goodness" spiritualizes. Read עַל (G, Chr) for MT אֶל.

8.a. G, Syr. MT "men" is a tendentious alteration in view of 11:1ff.

8.b. MT. G adds pleonastic "all."

9.a. MT. G^{BL}, Chr "to make him stand" is pleonastic.

9.b. MT. G adds explicative "over these."

9.c. MT. G^{BL} add pleonastic "and in their/his right."

10.a. MT. G "Solomon."

10.b-b. MT, G. Chr "was there."

11.a-a. MT, G. Consistently with "the servants of Hiram and the servants of Solomon" as subject, Chr (Par) makes the grammar pl throughout.

11.b. MT, G, Chr. Par adds explicative "to Solomon."

11.c. G^{BL}, Chr, MT adds explicative "from Ophir."

11.d. MT. Chr "algum"; G^B πελεκητά "hewn"; G^L ἀπελέκητα "unhewn." So also in v 12 twice.

11.e-e. MT, G^B. G^L transposes; Chr omits.

12.a. Heb. מסעד is a h.l.; cf. Chr מסלות = Par.

12.b. MT. G^{BL} adds "upon the land/earth" (explicative).

12.c. MT. G^B adds "anywhere"; G^L adds "anywhere yet" (explicative).

12.d-d. MT, G (sing). Chr "were seen like them previously in the land of Judah" is characteristically paraphrastic.

13.a-a. MT, G. Chr (Par) has an ideological correction, "she had brought to the king (Solomon)."

13.b. MT כְּיַד הַמֶּלֶךְ "like the hand of the king," to which MT, G, Chr have added "Solomon"; Syr, Vg, A, Par "the/a king."

13.c. MT. G^{BL} add explicative "all."

15.a. G^{BL} φόρων, reading מֵעֹנְשֵׁי "fines," "taxes," for MT מֵאַנְשֵׁי "from the men of." Cf. *HOTTP*, 312.

15.b. Correcting MT וּמִסְחַר "traveler," "trafficker" (RSV; BDB) to וּמסחר "profits" because the groups mentioned are to be understood as agents of the king (Noth; Köhler-Baumgartner Lexicon).

15.c. Chr, Syr, Vg. MT "evening" is a misreading; cf. G.

15.d. MT, G. Chr adds pleonastic "bringing gold and silver to Solomon."

16.a. G^B. MT, G^L "King Solomon."

16.b. MT. G "three"; cf. v 17.b.

17.a. MT and G^L continue to read "small shields" (θύρεος = מגן) while G^B reverts to "large shield" (ὅπλον = צנה).

18.a. Heb. מופז is cognate to Ug. pd; it is reproduced neither by G δοκίμῳ nor by Chr טהור.

19.a-a. MT רֹאשׁ־עָגֹל is a pointing which avoids the word עגל "calf," which is supported by G "calves' heads." Chr is corrupt, having first substituted כבש "lamb" for עגל, which eventually became כבש "footstool."

20.a. Here alone in the Heb. Bible occurs the masc pl of אריה "lion"; n.b. the feminines.

20.b. G^{BL}, Syr, Vg. MT adds explicative "there."

20.c-c. G, Chr. MT pl.

21.a. G^{BL}. MT "King Solomon's."

21.b. MT. G^{BL} has pleonastic addition "and washing vessels were gold."

21.c. Chr eliminates the conflict with v 27 by removing the second negative, producing the reading, "There was no silver of esteem. . . ."

21.d. G^{BL}. MT, Chr have harmonistic addition "as anything"; cf. note 21.c.

22.a. MT, G. Chr "servants"; cf. 9:27.

22.b. MT. G^{BL} "came to (king) Solomon."

22.c-c. MT. G^{BL}'s substitution, "stones carved and hewn (^L unhewn)," is clearly tendentious.

23.a. G^BL. MT, Chr "king Solomon."

23.b. G^BL, Par. MT, Chr add explicative "of the earth" in the light of v 24.

24.a. MT. G^BL, Chr "kings of the earth" read מבקשים "seeking" as demanding a pl subject other than the collective כל־הארץ "all the earth."

24.b. MT, Chr. G κύριος "Lord" may translate the Tetragrammaton, though that is not the usual practice in 1 Kgs/3 Reigns; cf. chaps. 3, 8.

25.a-a. MT. G^BL omit (haplography?).

25.b. MT. G^BL sing.

25.c. Omitting the copula with G^B, Chr. Gr. στακτὴν presupposes Heb. נשק "kindle."

25.d. MT. G^BL "and horses."

26.a-a. G^BL, Chr. MT has the explicative addition, "and Solomon gathered chariots and horsemen, and he had. . . ."

26.b-b. G^BL, Chr "forty thousand"; cf. 1 Kgs 5:6 (Eng. 4:26).

26.c. Chr סוסים אריות "stalls," from 1 Kgs 5:6, is reflected in G^B θήλειαι ἵπποι "female horses," "brood-mares"; hence G^L's addition, τοῦ τίκτειν "for breeding."

26.d. MT. G^BL "twelve."

26.e-e. G^BL, Chr. MT "and he led them."

27.a. MT, G^B. G^L "King Solomon."

27.b-b. G, Chr. MT omits, perhaps tendentiously in view of v 21.

28.a-a. See *HOTTP*, 313, and the commentaries.

29.a-a. MT, G. Chr changes the verbal form to avoid MT's awkward syntax, making the merchants the subject.

29.b. G^BL. MT, Chr "six hundred"—probably an exaggeration (see below).

29.c. G^BL. MT, Chr "one hundred and fifty."

29.d-d. MT, Chr. G^BL κατὰ θάλασσαν "by sea" misreads MT בידם as בים.

Form/Structure/Setting

Annotation on Solomon's wealth and prosperity (1): Gold from Ophir, 9:26–28

The story of the queen of Sheba

1. The royal visit, 10:1–3
2. Praise of Solomon's wisdom, vv 4–9
3. The mutual exchange of gifts
   a. The queen's gifts to Solomon, v 10a

Annotation on Solomon's wealth and prosperity (2): Balsam and Almug timber, vv 10b–12

The story continued:

   b. Solomon's gifts to the queen, v 13

Annotation on Solomon's wealth and prosperity (3): The import of gold, vv 14–15

Annotation on Solomon's wealth and prosperity (4): The manufacture of golden shields, vv 16–17

Annotation on Solomon's wealth and prosperity (5): The ivory throne, vv 18–20

Annotation on Solomon's wealth and prosperity (6): The drinking vessels and the source of gold, vv 21a, 22

[Comment: Silver of little esteem, v 21b]

[Comment: All people come to hear Solomon and bring him gifts, vv 23–25]

Annotation on Solomon's wealth and prosperity (7): Solomon's chariotry, v 26

[Comment: The comparative commonness of gold, silver, and cedar, v 27]
Extract from the Book of Solomon's Acts (19): Solomon's commerce in horses
and chariots, vv 28–29

One single word dominates this entire section: gold. All of the original
materials together with all of the expansions, even including the story of
the Queen of Sheba, are held together by this single word, the sole exception
being three verses toward the end having to do with Solomon's horses (vv
26, 28–29). Unlike the late list of golden implements for the temple found
in 7:48–50, much of what is recorded here is factual. While we do not hesitate
to ascribe vv 28–29 to the Book of Solomon's Acts, it seems likely that the
seven annotations about Solomon's wealth come from some other written
source, perhaps a sort of treasury report. On the one hand, these annotations
are later than the Book of Solomon's Acts, and on the other hand, they are
earlier than Dtr's redaction, which apparently took them just as they stand,
enclosing the relatively late story of the Queen of Sheba. Their relative lateness
is revealed by such phrases as "never again did such a quantity enter" in v
10, "never again was it seen up to this day" in v 12, and "the like has not
been made in any kingdom" in v 20, all of which assume that a span of
time has transpired sufficient to make such comparisons possible. This relative
lateness is further attested by the fact that vv 10b–12 breaks into, and comments upon, the final scene of the Queen of Sheba story. It has become
customary for commentators to date this story very late, even postexilic, because it seems, like 5:9–14 (Eng. 4:29–34), to exaggerate Solomon's wisdom.
We may confidently date this story much closer to the actual time of Solomon,
nonetheless, because the wisdom that it praises is very similar to the early,
historically rooted concept of pragmatic, judicial wisdom (v 9: "the performance of justice and right").

The outline shows the simple structure of this story: the royal visit is fondly
described (1–3); the queen inspects Solomon's establishment and lavishly
praises his wisdom (4–9); the two monarchs exchange farewell gifts, Solomon
outdoing the queen (10a, 13). Although this narrative may be based on an
actual historical visit, the story as told has as its aim to exemplify Solomon's
paradigmatic virtues of wisdom and wealth. Its purpose is to depict Solomon
as the model king. In spite of v 3, the wisdom it ascribes to him is not the
encyclopedic wisdom of the postexilic Solomon figure. It probably gained
currency in circles close to the successive kings of the Davidic dynasty, blowing
up the image of what their exemplary forefather had been.

Late expansions are in v 21b, vv 23–25, and v 27. The first and the last
are very much in the same vein, though the latter directly contradicts the
former's statement that there was no silver. Vv 23–25 are inspired by the
Queen of Sheba story, but give Solomon a cosmic significance as does 5:9–
14 (Eng. 4:29–34); it displays a high level of artificiality in stating that a different gift would be brought each year, according to a prearranged schedule.

Comment

9:26–28 This annotation does not entirely harmonize with 10:11–12 or
10:22, but each may reflect a different situation or period of Solomon's reign.

Ezion-geber, with Eilat slightly to the west, lay at the head of the Gulf of Eilath/Aqaba, the eastern arm of the Red Sea. It is striking that this body of water is called "the sea of Reeds," יַם־סוּף, for that is also the sea of the Exodus crossing according to Exod 13:18, 15:4, etc. It is natural that Hiram's Phoenician seamen should accompany Solomon's, for they were accomplished sailors. Ophir is not southwestern Arabia, as many claim (cf. V. Christides, *RB* 77 [1970] 240–47), but Somaliland, the same as the land of Punt mentioned in Egyptian literature (cf. G. W. Van Beek, *IDB* III, 605–6). For "talent" see on 9:14.

10:1–10a, 13 Sheba and Havilah were important South Arabian trade centers. An eminent authority in the South-Semitic languages, E. Ullendorff, rejects this region as the homeland of this queen, choosing instead, because of the reference to timber, the horn of Africa (see on Ophir above). This queen has had a checkered history in religious tradition: in the NT and the apocryphal Acts she is Candace; the Talmud equates her with the demonic temptress Lilith; but Ethiopic tradition turns her into a most noble person, at the same time making Solomon her seducer (E. Ullendorff, *Ethiopia and the Bible*, London (1968) 131–45; cf. E. Ullendorff, *BJRL* 45 [1962–63] 486–504). All this is irrelevant to the biblical account. Coming from the heart of Africa (or possibly Arabia), she represents riches and glory. Characteristically, she comes to Jerusalem with a large armed guard. She and Solomon engage in a test of his wisdom. The queen is amazed, but extends her amazement through inspecting the minute details of how he runs his household and public affairs. She utters a glowing encomium that describes his wives and servants as happy, then praises Yahweh for delighting in Solomon ("Yahweh loves Israel forever" is, however, an Israelite touch). Then she gives him gold, balsam, and precious gems. He acts "in kingly style" by first giving her numerous presents and then adding whatever she desires or requests. She returns home, according to this story, never to meet Solomon again.

10b–12 V 10b is no late gloss, like vv 21b and 27, but a comment from the annotator, similar to v 12b. As has been said, the fact that vv 10b–12 interrupts the Queen of Sheba narrative and comments on it shows that the story was available to the annotator. Here it is Hiram's, not Solomon's, fleet that is in question. It brought Solomon almug-wood for the temple steps and for musical instruments; this was probably a hard reddish-brown wood (cf. J. C. Trever, *IDB* I, 88; W. E. Clark, *AJSL* 36 [1919–20] 103–19, J. C. Greenfield and M. Mayrhofer, VTSup 16 [1967] 83–89).

14–15 On the talent see 9:14. The number 666 looks schematic. This represents the gold obtained by trading with gold-exporting regions. The annotator goes on to specify two other ways of getting gold: (1) through the taxation of caravans and (2) through profits from state monopolies or franchises, viz., such as were held by local merchants, Arab vassals, and provincial governors.

16–17 Solomon's golden shields were essentially decorative, and as such were hung in the House of the Lebanon Forest (7:2–5), from where Shishak later plundered them during Rehoboam's reign (14:26). The "large shield," צִנָּה, was the rectangular buckler carried by heavy infantry, while the "small shield," מָגֵן, was the target, light and round and carried by light infantry or officers. A mina varied in weight from 500 to 1050 grams. The "weight-units" mentioned in v 16 represent an omission in the text, but shekels, from 8.33 to 16.74 grams, are probably intended.

18–20 Solomon's throne was a thing of grandeur, with decorations of ivory (A. Cohen, *BMik* 23 [1978] 237–38, claims it was a wood that looked like ivory) and "fine" or solid gold. The six (Gray, 266: seven) steps probably have no special symbolic significance, but the calf's —or bull's—head probably was borrowed from baalistic Canaanite models (instead MT has the improbable "round top," adopted as original by F. Canciani and G. Pettinato, *ZDPV* 81 [1965] 88–108). One of the Megiddo ivories (*ANEP* 332) shows a throne supported by sphinxes with lions' bodies, but Solomon's lions may have been no more than the traditional symbol of the tribe of Judah (Gen 49:9).

21–22 The import of gold was so prolific that Solomon's drinking vessels were made of it; and of specially refined gold, רוגס בהז, were the implements used in the House of the Lebanon Forest. V 22 tells of Solomon's own fleet which made a voyage every three years. Since the African-Arabian coast remained the region for obtaining gold, it is likely that Solomon employed ships similar in construction to the metal-carrying ships from faraway Tarshish (Spain), but his ships did not themselves sail the Mediterranean. Besides silver, the other products obtained on these voyages were typical of eastern Africa. Ivory came from elephants. W. F. Albright has identified the Hebrew for "apes and baboons" as cognates to the Egyptian words for these particular animals (Albright, *Archaeology and the Religion of Israel*, 212; cf. W. E. Clarke, *AJSL* 36 [1919–20] 103–19; G. Wörpel, *ZAW* 79 [1967] 360–61; K.-H. Bernhardt, *ZAW* 81 [1969] 100).

23–27 On the laudatory glosses in vv 23–25, 27, see above. Because the annotation in v 26 seems in disagreement with 5:6 (Eng. 4:26), the versions and Chr attempt harmonizing emendations, but this notice may be from a different time during Solomon's reign. Here it is expressly stated that some of the chariots and horses were assigned to guard the king in Jerusalem.

28–29 Musri has been misunderstood as Egypt in Deut 17:16, 2 Kgs 7:6; it was actually the Cappadocian seacoast in Asia Minor. Qewe was nearby, close to the Taurus mountains. This extract from the Book of Solomon's Acts relates that Solomon's merchants would buy horses in Qewe for fifty "pieces" (probably shekels) of silver and chariots in Musri for a hundred, supplying the Hittite and Syrian kings along the way with both as they brought their purchases home to Solomon (cf. A. D. Crown, *Abr-Nahrain* 15 [1974/ 75] 35–38).

Solomon's Numerous Wives and Their Influence (11:1-13)

Bibliography

Gooding, D. W. "The Septuagint's Version of Solomon's Misconduct." *VT* 15 (1965) 325–35.

Translation

[1a] Now *King Solomon loved many foreign wives* [ba] *alongside the daughter of Pharaoh:* [c] *Moabitesses, Ammonitesses, Edomitesses, Sidonianesses, Hittitesses,* [c] [2] *from the nations concerning which Yahweh had said to the Israelites, "Do not have dealings with them, and let them have no dealings with you; surely* [a] *they will seduce your heart to follow their gods." To them did Solomon attach himself in love.* [3] *And he had seven hundred wives of queenly rank, plus three hundred concubines; and his wives seduced his heart.* [4] *Now it was in the time of Solomon's old age* [a] *that his wives seduced his heart to follow other gods.* [a] *So his heart was not perfect with Yahweh his God, like the heart of David his father;* [5] *Solomon went after Ashtoreth the god of the Sidonians and after Milcom the filth of the Ammonites.* [a] [6] *So Solomon did what was wrong in Yahweh's eyes and did not fully follow after Yahweh the way David his father did.* [7] *Then Solomon built a country shrine to Chemosh the filth of Moab;* [ab] *also one to Molech the filth of the Ammonites.* [8] *And he did the same for all his foreign wives* [a] *who were burning incense and sacrificing to their gods.* [a]

[9] *So Yahweh was outraged over Solomon, since his heart had turned away from Yahweh the God of Israel, who had revealed himself twice to him* [10] *and had commanded him in this matter not to go after other gods;* [a] *but he did not keep* [a] *what Yahweh* [b] *had commanded him.* [c] [11] *So Yahweh said to Solomon, "Because this is the way it has been with you, and you have not kept my commandments* [a] *and my statutes which I commanded you, I will surely tear the* [b] *kingship out of your hand and give it to your servant.* [12] *Only, in your days I will not do it, for the sake of David your father;* [a] *out of the hand of your son I will take* [b] *it.* [13] *Indeed, not the entire kingdom do I intend to take.* [a] *One tribe will I give to your son, for the sake of David my servant and for the sake of Jerusalem* [b] *which I have chosen."*

Notes

Corresponding to MT 11:1–13 is the G verse sequence: 1–3a, 4, 3b, 10b, 6, 8, 5, 7, 9–10a, 11–13. G omits MT vv 3b, 5b, 7b for ideological reasons; see Gooding (bibliography).

1.a-a. MT. G[BL] "and King Solomon was a womanizer."

1.b. G places v 3a here.

1.c-c. MT. G[BL]'s list differs.

2.a. MT אך. G[BL] μή (prohibitive).

4.a-a. G places this material at the end of the verse, as if to limit the time when Solomon failed to be like David.

5.a. G[BL] aims to consolidate the material by transposing vv 5, 6, and by adding "and Astarte the abomination of the Sidonians."

7.a. See *HOTTP*, 314.
7.b. G[BL]. MT "on the mountain which faces Jerusalem" is a gloss from 2 Kgs 23:13; cf. *BHS*mg.
8.a-a. MT, G[BL]; G[L] MSS sing.
10.a-a. MT. G "and to keep and perform."
10.b. MT. G "Yahweh God."
10.c. MT. G inserts v 4b to secure a smoother reading in vv 4–5 and to state in the present context the reason for Yahweh's wrath.
11.a. G[BL] "commandments" preserves the normal Dtr locution over against MT "covenant."
11.b. MT. G[BL] "your" has been influenced by second-person readings in the sequel of this verse.
12.a. MT, G (normal Dtr terminology). Syr "my servant" is influenced by v 13.
12.b. G[BL]. MT "tear" has come into the text from vv 11, 31.
13.a. See note 12.b.
13.b. MT. G adds "the city."

Form/Structure/Setting

[Dtr: Foreign wives lead Solomon into idolatry
1. His marriages, 11:1–2]
Extract from the Book of Solomon's Acts (20): Solomon's harem, v 3a
[2. His idolatry, vv 3b–6, 8]
Extract from the Book of Solomon's Acts (21): Solomon builds heathen shrines, v 7
[3. The threatened punishment: loss of the kingship, vv 9–13]

Two more extracts from the Book of Solomon's Acts, the last, are employed by Dtr as an anchor for his final negative assessment of Solomon's reign. Yet Dtr cannot find it in himself to give this king the full blame for the idol worship that began to assert itself here in the very precincts of the temple: it was because of the many heathen women; it was because they led him astray. Yet "Yahweh was outraged over Solomon" (v 9). Speaking to him once again and for the final time, Yahweh threatens to tear the kingship away from him, mitigating this only by specifying (1) that this would actually happen during the reign of his son and (2) one tribe would be retained for David's sake.

Comment

Not only does Dtr say that Solomon "loved" many foreign women, but he stresses that he "attached" . . . ל דָּבַק himself to them in love (1–2), for by becoming attached to them he became slack toward Yahweh. "Many foreign wives" paraphrases the extract's specific number given in v 3. The daughter of Pharaoh is mentioned now once again, though not her Egyptian god(s). Counting her, Dtr specifies six different nationalities, all of them but hers representing peoples living within the borders of Solomonic Israel or immediately adjacent to it. V 2 shows us that Dtr is thinking of the prohibition in Deut 7:1–5, which likewise forbids Israel to marry (חתן hithp, stronger than our text's בוא, translated "have dealings with") foreign women lest they seduce their hearts into idolatry. If v 3 were part of Dtr's expansion, it would not mention concubines, for Dtr complains only that his wives seduced Solomon's heart. Thus it is definitely original archival material, and in this case records a popular ancient tradition about Solomon. This is not to say that the seven hundred and the three hundred are factually historical, for the two numbers are patently schematic (7x10x10 of queenly rank, 3x10x10 mere concubines), and the serious question will arise as to where so many women, with their numerous children, could have been accommodated. The number seemed beyond counting—of that we may be sure. Marrying the wives was part of Solomon's political strategy; taking the concubines demonstrated his wealth along with his lusty manhood. In any event, Dtr specifies (v 4) that these foreign women did not seduce Solomon into idolatry until old age had begun to descend upon him, intending by this to partially excuse him. But at last Dtr has to be blunt: "Solomon went after Ashtoreth . . . and after Milcom . . . Solomon did what was wrong . . . and did not fully follow after Yahweh" (vv 5–6). Here Dtr introduces his characteristic אז "then" for inserting his final extract, one that records that Solomon built a במה "country shrine" for Chemosh and another for Molech; as in v 5, the word "filth," שקץ, is scribally substituted for the original word, "god," אלהי. Reference to a במה suggests an urban shrine somewhat away from Jerusalem ("on the mountain which faces Jerusalem" is a tendentious gloss in MT not read by G), hence not very likely to have actually been the scene of idol worship on the part of Solomon's wives. Nonetheless, Dtr's comment in v 8 settles his point that it was their seduction of Solomon rather than Solomon's own waywardness that had led to this sad state of affairs.

Dtr is now finished saying what he thinks of Solomon; in vv 9–10 he tells also what Yahweh thinks. Yahweh is "outraged," אנף hithp. In Yahweh's eyes Solomon had turned away, apostasized—and this in spite of a double revelation commanding him not to do so (but neither 3:14, 6:12, nor 9:4 specifically mentions idolatry). So Yahweh speaks directly to Solomon for the last time (vv 11–13). The "because"-clause shows that, after all, idolatry amounts to not keeping Yahweh's commandments and statutes. Yahweh threatens as punishment to tear the kingdom from Solomon's hand and give it to his servant—an obvious reference to Jeroboam (v 26). But for David's sake this is to happen in Rehoboam's days, and for David's sake one tribe is to be retained. When all is said and done, this is what matters most: that the tribe of Judah should live on as the kingdom of Judah, that the Davidic (not Solomonic!) lineage should live on in permanent possession of the throne, and that Yahweh's chosen city, Jerusalem, should remain secure.

Explanation

It is a historical fact that Solomon built, or allowed to be built, pagan shrines near Jerusalem (See 2 Kgs 23:13). This was as much a part of his deliberate policy as his multiple marriages. The marriages and the pagan shrines may have had some direct connection, but not nearly so much as Dtr claimed. The marriages were mainly political alliances, securing sundry enclaves as vassals and powerful neighbor states (like Egypt) as allies. The pagan shrines represented the people belonging to their various entities, and their nearness to the Jerusalem temple symbolized their subjugation to Yahweh (see the *Introduction*). This was by no means the rigid monotheism that Dtr demanded, nor is it representative of biblical religion as a whole. At the very best, it expressed a faulty religious imperialism aiming at the advance of Yahwism through power and wealth. At the worst, it represented a perilous accommodation to sub-biblical impulses, constantly placing a stumbling block in the path of the weak and superstitious. If Solomon was not quite so poorly motivated as Dtr supposes, a level-headed evaluation based on sober criticism will mark him down as more a menace than a benefactor to authentic biblical faith.

Three Potential Rivals: Hadad, Rezon, and Jeroboam (11:14–43)

Bibliography

Bartlett, J. R. "An Adversary against Solomon, Hadad the Edomite." *ZAW* 88 (1976) 205–26. **Caquot, A.** "Aḥiyya de Silo et Jeroboam Ier." *Sem* 11 (1961) 17–27. **Eissfeldt, O.** "Protektorat der Midianiter über ihre Nachbarn im letzten Viertel des 2. Jahrtausends v. Chr." *JBL* 87 (1968) 383–93. **Gooding, D. W.** "The Septuagint's Rival Versions of Jeroboam's Rise to Power." *VT* 17 (1967) 173–89. **Klein, R. W.** "Jeroboam's Rise to Power." *JBL* 89 (1970) 217–18 (rejoinder by Gooding, *JBL* 91 [1972] 529–33; further rejoinder by Klein, *JBL* 92 [1973] 582–84). **Napier, B. D.** "The King Walks Before You: 1 Sam. 12—1 Kings 11." *From Faith to Faith. Essays on Old Testament Literature.* New York: Harper & Row, 1955. **Plein, I.** "Erwägungen zur Überlieferung von 1 Reg 11, 26–14, 20." *ZAW* 78 (1966) 8–24. **Seebass, H.** "Zur Teilung der Herrschaft Salomos nach I Reg 11, 29–39." *ZAW* 88 (1976) 363–76. ———. "Die verwerfung Jerobeams I. und Salomos durch die Prophetie des Ahia von Silo." *WO* 4 (1963) 163–82.

Translation

[14] *Now Yahweh raised up as an antagonist to Solomon Hadad the Edomite, from the seed royal.*[a] *He was in Edom;* [15] *and it so happened that when David was exterminating*[a] *Edom, while Joab general of the army was* [b]*going up*[b] *to inter the casualties of battle, he smote every male person in Edom;* [16] *indeed, it was six months that he remained there—Joab with all Israel*[a]*—as long as it would take to cut down every male person in Edom.* [17] *But Hadad fled, he and some Edomite men belonging among his father's servants who happened to be with him, heading for Egypt (now Hadad was just a young boy).* [18] *And they*[a] *left Midian*[b] *and came*[c] *to Paran; and they took men with them*[d] *and came*[e] *to Pharaoh king of Egypt.*[f] *And he*[g] *gave him a house, arranged provisions for him, and assigned him some land.* [19] *And Hadad found much favor in Pharaoh's eyes, so that he gave him as wife the sister of his own wife, even the sister of Tahpenes the queen mother.* [20] *And the sister of Tahpenes bore to him a certain Genubath to be his son; and Tahpenes had him weaned in the midst of* [a]*Pharaoh's household,*[a] *so that Genubath resided* [b]*at Pharaoh's palace*[b] *among Pharaoh's sons.* [21] *Now Hadad heard there in Egypt that David had slept with his fathers and that Joab, general of the army, was dead. So Hadad said to Pharaoh, "Dismiss me so that I may go to my country."* [22] *And Pharaoh said to him,*[a] *"But what do you lack from me, and here you are requesting to go to your own country!" and* [b]*he said,*[b] *"But by all means do send me away!"*[c]
[23] *And God raised up as an antagonist to him Rezon son of Eliada, who had fled from being with Hadadezer king of Zobah, his master.* [24] *And* [a]*he gathered*[a] *men to himself, to become captain of a marauding band* [b]*at the time when David was slaying them.*[b] *And they captured Damascus* [c]*and took up residence in it; and he*[d] *reigned in Damascus.*[c] [25] *And he was an antagonist to Israel all the days of Solomon,* [a]*adding to the harm done by Hadad.*[a] [b]*And he abhorred Israel,*[b] *and he reigned over Syria.*[c]

[26] *Now Jeroboam son of Nebat, an Ephraimite out of Zeredah, [a]whose mother's name was Zeruah (a widow woman),[a] served Solomon [b]but raised his hand against the king.[b]* [27] [a]*And this was the cause for which he raised his hand against the king. Solomon built the Millo; he closed up the gap in the city of David his father.* [28] *Now the man Jeroboam was a man of valor, and Solomon observed concerning the youth that he was somebody who could get work done, so he appointed him over the entire [a] porterage from the House of Joseph.* [29] [a]*And it happened at that time that Jeroboam had departed from Jerusalem, and Ahijah the Shilonite, the prophet, came upon him; [b] and he [c] was wrapped in a new mantle. And the two of them were [d] in the open,* [30] *when Ahijah grasped the new mantle that was on him and tore it into twelve pieces.* [31] *And he said to Jeroboam, "Take for yourself ten pieces, because thus says Yahweh the God of Israel, 'Behold I intend to tear the kingship out of Solomon's hand, and I shall give you the [a] ten tribes; * [32] *but the one [a] tribe shall remain his, on account of my servant David and on account of Jerusalem which I have chosen out of all the tribes of Israel* ([33] *because they [a] have forsaken me and have worshiped [b] Ashtoreth the god [c] of the Sidonians, Kemosh the god [d] of Moab, and Milcom the god [e] of the Ammonites), but he [f] has not walked in my ways, doing what is right in my eyes [g] like David his father.* [34] [a]*But I do not intend to take the kingship out of his hand,[a] but will appoint him as prince all the days of his life for the sake of David my servant whom I chose;[b]* [35] *but I will take the regal authority from the hand of his son and give it [a] to you—the ten tribes.* [36] *And to his son I will give [a]one tribe[a] so that there may continually be a lamp unto David my servant in my presence in Jerusalem, the city which I chose for myself, to put my name there.* [37] *And you I shall take, and you shall reign over what [a] your soul wishes, and you shall become king over Israel.* [38] *And it shall be, that if you will [a]listen to [a] all that I command you and will walk in my ways and will do what is right in my eyes, keeping my statutes and my commandments precisely as my servant David did, then I will be with you and will build you into a solid house, just as I built for David.' "* [b(39a)]

[40] [a]*So Solomon endeavored to kill Jeroboam; and he [b] arose and took flight to Egypt, to Shishak king of Egypt. And he remained in Egypt until the death of Solomon.* [41] *Now the rest of the deeds of Solomon, with all that he made and [a] his wisdom, are they not written in the Book of the Acts [b] of Solomon?* [42] *And the years during which Solomon reigned in Jerusalem [a] were forty years.* [43] [a]*And Solomon slept with his fathers and was buried in the city of David his father. [b] And his son Rehoboam reigned in his stead.*

Notes

14.a. MT lit. "seed of the king." G "seed of the kingdom."

15.a. G[BL]. MT בהיות "when he was . . ." is ideological and apologetic.

15.b-b. MT; the root עלה covers a variety of battle actions. Not understanding, G[BL] paraphrase with a specific action-verb, "marching" ($\pi o \rho \epsilon v \theta \tilde{\eta} v a \iota$).

16.a. MT, G[L]. G[B] "in Idumaea/Edom" is explicative and apologetic.

18.a. MT. G[BL] "men" (explicative).

18.b. MT, G[L]. G[B] "from the city of Midian" shows poor geographical knowledge.

18.c. MT, G[L], whose ἐρχονται has produced the auditory corruption of G[B], ἄρχοντες, "they come."

18.d. G[BL]. MT adds explicative "from Paran."

18.e. G[BL]. MT adds "into Egypt" as another explicative gloss.

18.f. MT. G[BL] embellish the account with "and Hadad went in to Pharaoh."

18.g. MT, G^B G^L. "Pharaoh" is explicative.
20.a-a. MT. G^BL "Pharaoh's sons" is a doublet from the end of the verse.
20.b-b. MT. G^BL omit.
22.a. MT. G^BL "Haded" (Ἀδὲδ).
22.b-b. MT. G^BL "Hadad said to him."
22.c. MT. G^BL create what is considered a satisfactory conclusion for this abrupt ending: "and he sent Hadad to his own country."
24.a-a. MT. G^BL, Syr "were gathered."
24.b-b. MT. G^BL have an ideological and apologetic omission.
24.c-c. MT, G^L. G^B omits.
24.d. G^L. MT "they."
25.a-a. Cf. *HOTTP,* 316.
25.b-b. Cf. *HOTTP,* 317.
25.c. MT. ארם "Aram." G^BL, Syr "Edom" =אדם.
26.a-a. MT. G^BL "son of a widow woman" is explicative.
26.b-b. MT. G^BL omit (haplography).
27.a. As parallel to vv 27–28, cf. LXX 12:24b.
28.a. MT. G^BL omit.
29.a. Cf. LXX 12:24°.
29.b MT. G^BL add explicative "on the road."
29.c. MT. G^BL have explicative "Ahijah."
29.d. G^BL. MT has explicative "alone."
31.a. MT, with determinative. G^BL indeterminate.
32.a. MT. G^BL "two" (cf. v. 36).
33.a. MT. G^BL make the grammar sing, referring to Solomon (see 11:1ff.).
33.b. MT. G^BL "made"; G^L "worshiped."
33.c. MT. G^BL "abomination."
33.d. MT. G^B corr; G^L "idol."
33.e. MT. G^BL "filth."
33.f. G^BL. MT "they."
33.g. G^BL. M adds "and my statutes and my ordinances."
34.a-a. MT. G^L transposes with the line, "but will appoint . . . of his life."
34.b. G^B. MT and G^L add "who kept my commandments and my statutes."
35.a. MT. G^BL omit.
36.a-a. MT. G "two tribes" (ideological correction); cf. v 32.
37.a. G^BL. MT "all that" is pleonastic.
38.a-a. MT. G^BL φυλάης = Heb. תשמר "keep," misread for MT תשמע "listen to."
38.b. G^B. MT and G^L add "and I will give you Israel."
(39.a.) G^B MSS. Weakly attested (MT, G^bc2) is the addition, "and I will afflict the seed of David because of this; however, not in all the days." This is numbered v 39 in the Heb. and Eng. Bibles.
40.a. Cf. LXX 12:24°.
40.b. G^BL. MT "Jeroboam" (explicative).
41.a. MT. G^BL "and all."
41.b. MT, G^B. G^L adds "of the days"; i.e., chronicles, cf. 14:19 etc.
42.a. G^BL. MT adds explicative "over all Israel."
43.a. Cf. LXX 12:24ᵃ.
43.b. G^BL add the tendentious gl: "And it came to pass that when Jeroboam son of Nebat heard it, being yet in Egypt, whither he had fled from Solomon's presence, and had abode in Egypt, he straightway came to his hometown in the district of Sareira in mount Ephraim; and King Solomon slept with his fathers, and his son Rehoboam reigned in his place."

Form/Structure/Setting

The history of Hadad
  1. The Israelite menace to Edom, vv 14–16
  2. Hadad's flight to Egypt, vv 17–18

3. Affiliation with Pharaoh's family, vv 19–20
4. Preparation for return, vv 21–22
The history of Rezon
  1. Formation of a fugitive band, vv 23–24a
  2. Seizure of the capital and the menace to Israel, vv 24b–25
The history of Jeroboam
  Introduction, v 26
  1. Jeroboam put in charge of a large work-force, vv 27–28
[Dtr: Transition to the Ahijah story, v 29a]
  2. The Ahijah story
    a. The symbolic act, vv 29b–30
    b. The interpretive command, v 31
[Dtr: Exception on the one tribe, v 32]
[Expansion: Comment on Israel's idolatry, v 33a]
[Dtr: Complaint against Solomon, v 33b]
    c. Explanation, vv 34–35
[Dtr: Perpetuation of David's lamp, v 36]
    d. The divine appointment, v 37
[Dtr: a conditional promise to Jeroboam, v 38]
  3. Jeroboam flees from Solomon, v 40
[Dtr: Stereotyped conclusion for Solomon: the source, length of reign, death and burial, successor, vv 41–43]

Dtr had at his disposal three "histories" of persons who eventually became a menace to Solomon: that of Hadad the Edomite, that of Rezon son of Eliada, and that of Jeroboam son of Nebat. A "history," as referred to here, is more than a mere report and less than a complete biography; it is an ordered selection of historical facts demonstrating the situation for which it is designed. Dtr is responsible for selecting this material and for expanding the history of Jeroboam. It is the last that claims the reader's special attention because it leads directly into chap. 12 and the story of the Northern Kingdom. It is characteristic of these narratives that they remain unconnected to one another; the Hadad story, in particular, simply ends with Hadad's request for permission to leave Egypt and does not narrate his actual return to Edom. Thus it is not surprising that the Jeroboam history, in its original form, never tells us just what Jeroboam did to make him "raise his hand against the king," v 26; we are simply told in v 40 that Solomon sought to kill him, so that he fled to Egypt. It seems logical to suppose that the original history told something roughly equivalent to what the Ahijah story, minus the Dtr additions, narrates, viz., that Jeroboam began to show disloyalty to King Solomon because a prophet had appeared to him speaking of his eventual succession. Dtr seems to have got hold of the Ahaziah legend and have substituted it for the original notice because it offered better opportunities for his own moralizing expansions.

In the writer's book, (de Vries, *Prophet against Prophet*, 54, 58) all the prophet stories (or legends) in Samuel and Kings are assigned to one of eleven distinct subgenres. This one, together with the one in chap. 14, belongs to the subgenre, "Succession oracle narrative," which is a story in which a prophetic oracle specifies the terms of regal succession (cf. also 2 Sam 7:1–12, 16–

17). The purpose of this subgenre is to demonstrate the transcendent authority of Yahweh in the transfer of regal power. The structure of this particular story is strikingly simple; all four parts, having to do with (a) the symbolic act, (b) the interpretive command, (c) the explanation, and (d) the divine appointment, are concerned with the prophetic oracle of succession. There is a minimum of narration. We are told only that Ahijah met Jeroboam (the place is not specified; v 29a is Dtr's transition), that he was wrapped in a new mantle, that he tore this into twelve pieces, and that he instructed Jeroboam to take ten of them. Ahijah then recites Yahweh's oracle, which first states that Ahijah's giving of ten pieces from the mantle symbolizes Yahweh's intent to give Jeroboam ten tribes now belonging to Solomon; it next explains that it is not from Solomon's own hand that Yahweh intends to take the kingship but from that of his son who shall succeed him; and finally it utters the official words of appointment (v 37). Here at the end the point becomes quite clear that the matter of regal succession is definitely Yahweh's prerogative. Yahweh has not accepted an automatic rule of primogeniture. Solomon is reigning, and will continue to reign, because Yahweh will appoint him as "prince" (נשיא; cf. 1:35) all the days of his life. V 34 might readily be assigned to Dtr, or at least the words, "for the sake of David my servant whom I chose," were it not for the recognition that the structure of the oracle requires a specific statement of Yahweh's will concerning Solomon's tenure as a contrast to the climactic declaration regarding Jeroboam. V 37 sets the direct object, "you" (Jeroboam) foremost for maximum contrast. The operative verb in vv 34, 35, and 37 is לקח "take": Yahweh will not "take" the kingship (הממלכה) from Solomon while he lives; but he will "take" the regal authority (המלוכה) from Solomon's son; he will also "take" Jeroboam and make him king. All of this is designed as interpretation for the initial declaration in v 31, where Yahweh's intent to tear, קרע, the kingship (הממלכה) out of Solomon's hand expresses Yahweh's sovereign prerogative to determine what is to happen with the tribes that Solomon now rules.

Although the prophet story explicitly allots no more than ten tribes to Jeroboam, Dtr states that one tribe shall remain to Solomon (v 32), i.e., to his son (v 36)—all for the sake of David and Jerusalem. A later interpolator, probably from the school of Dtr, added v 33. Accepting the validity of Jeroboam's divine appointment, Dtr appends words in v 38 making the longevity of this king's dynasty dependent on obedience to the divine commandments (MT v 39 is omitted in G^B and is probably not original).

In vv 41–43 we encounter Dtr's first regularly styled concluding notice. It tells us (1) that there is much more to tell about Solomon, but one should look in the Book of Solomon's Acts for this; (2) his length of reign; (3) his death and burial, and the succession of Rehoboam. The story of Solomon is now finished, and Dtr will go on to speak of the turbulent history that lies ahead.

Comment

14–22 "Now Yahweh raised up an antagonist": beginning in the same style as vv 23–25, where, however, the divine name is "God" אלהים; though nothing reveals a bias on the part of these two histories for or against Solomon, divine causation lies behind whatever good or evil is implied. Hadad ("The Thunderer") is a divine appellative common in northwest Semitic cultures, also the name of several Edomite kings (cf. Gen 36:35–36). To say that Hadad was of the royal seed indicates that he had not yet become king at the time of narration. The bloody war of extermination of which our text speaks may be the same as the one described in 2 Sam 8:13–14. We can judge from v 21 that David and Joab were equally dreaded. What happened to Hadad's father is not narrated, but some of the palace guard fled with Hadad first to Midian (south of Edom in northern Arabia), then to Paran (in western Sinai), and finally to Egypt. As often, Egypt proves hospitable to refugees from Asia (see the Joseph story). The reigning Pharaoh (probably from the twenty-first dynasty) gives him house, provisions, land, and even a wife from the royal family, who bears him a son to be reared with the Pharaoh's own sons (the names of mother and son, occurring only here, are historical but may have been garbled in transmission). When the report comes that both David and Joab are dead, Hadad moves to renounce security and luxury in order to return to Edom. It is not said that he did return, but since he was counted as one of Solomon's foremost "adversaries," we may assume that he became a troublesome guerrilla fighter during many years to follow (cf. J. R. Bartlett, *ZAW* 88 [1976] 205–26; O. Eissfeldt, *JBL* 87 [1968] 383–93).

23–25   In 2 Sam 3–8 it is stated that David defeated Hadadezer king of Zobah, an Aramaic kingdom probably located in the Biqaʿ valley between the Lebanon and Antilebanon ranges. Because the Arameans of Damascus tried to help Hadadezer, David defeated them too, took much plunder, exterminated great numbers of troops, and placed a garrison in Damascus. According to the present account, Rezon organized a guerrilla band and eventually recaptured Damascus, where he became king. He became Israel's implacable foe during the entire reign of Solomon. Although he could not have mounted any kind of invasion, his attitude foreboded much greater evils destined for future days.

26–28, 40   Although Jeroboam has a patronym, we would know that his father was dead not only from the fact that his mother is identified as a widow but also from the unusual fact that she is named. He was an Ephraimite (his town, Zeredah, is unidentified), hence could appropriately serve as boss over a corvée group from the "house of Joseph" (v 28), which designates the two tribes, Ephraim and Manasseh. As one of Solomon's officials ("he served him"), he used his power and prestige against him. V 27 promises to tell us how, and prepares for this by stating the following facts: in the work of building the Millo (cf. 9:15, 24), Solomon observed that he was a skilled and industrious worker; though but a youth, he proved also to be a man of valor, גבור חיל. So he appointed him over all the Josephite porters (סבל; cf. 5:29 [Eng. 15]). As has been said, we never learn what Jeroboam did next, for Dtr has substituted the Ahijah story and his own comments for what stood in the original account. Jeroboam may have used his position to sidetrack some of Adoniram's (4:6, 5:28 [Eng. 14]; cf. 12:18) harsher commands, thereby establishing himself as hero in the Josephites' eyes. Probably the Ahijah story has a historical core, so that there was also an oracle which stirred Jeroboam to open revolt. In any event, he was eventually forced to flee to Shishak (Shoshenq, founder of the twenty-second Egyptian dynasty; cf. 14:25–26) to avoid being killed by Solomon.

29–38 "And it happened at that time": בעת ההיא makes a temporal sequence more specific than with אז "then" (*YTT* 41). Dtr's temporal transition is coupled with his geographical transition, moving Jeroboam from Jerusalem to wherever Ahijah was. Though Ahijah (active also in 14:1–18) was from Shiloh, ancient seat of the ark (1 Sam 1–4), it is not said that the prophecy occurred there. The "new mantle" aptly symbolizes the new, unbroken nation of Israel. This is ripped into twelve pieces, the number of the tribes of Israel, and Jeroboam is instructed to take ten of them. Often the similarity between this event and that of 1 Sam 15:27–28 is observed, but there the person doing the tearing is the person for whom the symbol is interpreted (Saul), foreboding ill for him and not good, as here. Various details both in the prophet story and in the Dtr expansions have been discussed above; however, it is necessary to call special attention to v 36's promise of a continual lamp (ניר) to David, found also in 1 Kgs 15:4 and 2 Kgs 8:19, and possibly dependent on 2 Sam 21:17, where David is called "the lamp (נר) of Israel." From vv 31, 35 one learns that at least nominal authority over ten tribes is given to Jeroboam, but the climactic appointment of v 37 declares that he shall in fact rule only over what his soul (נפש) desires—which in any event makes him and not Solomon's son king over Israel. "Israel" does not mean here just the ten tribes, but the same "Israel" over which David and Solomon ruled. Dtr tries to clarify this in vv 32 and 36 by stating that Solomon or his son shall retain rule over one tribe. Twelve minus ten makes two, and that is the figure that G substitutes in both places for MT's "one," but MT faithfully reproduces Dtr's intent. In his time Benjamin (the twelfth) had long since been absorbed into the nation (hence tribe) of Judah. "A solid house" in v 38 echoes 2 Sam 7:13; cf. 23:5. Continually excoriating Israel for Jeroboam's sins, Dtr holds this out as a hypothetical promise, conditional on an obedience that in his own time he already knew the northern kings had not fulfilled.

41–43 The forty years of Solomon, like the forty years of David (2:11), may be schematic and hence not to be taken literally—a fact of which biblical chronologists have taken insufficient account. For the death and burial formulas in v 43, cf. on 2:10.

Explanation

David had indeed been a man of blood. His harshness toward Syria and Edom created implacable enemies even while Solomon (whose name means "peace") enjoyed the wealth and power created by that harshness. A few generations hence, Syria would become a threat to Israel's very existence. A few centuries hence, Edom would possess the desolate wastes of Judah (cf. Obad 11–14, Ezek 35:10–15). Josephites pressed into hard service for Solomon's works of grandeur would rise in revolt against his son. One day only a single "lamp" would remain to David in Jerusalem, and at last even that would gutter out. Thus does Yahweh raise up adversaries to those who rule falsely in his name.

Account of the Two Kingdoms up to Ahab
Chapters 12–16

The Rejection of Rehoboam   (12:1–24)

Bibliography

Aberbach, M., and **Smolar, L.** "Jeroboam and Solomon: Rabbinic Interpretations." *JQR* 59 (1968–69) 118–32. ———. "Jeroboam's Rise to Power." *JBL* 88 (1969) 69–72. **Alt, A.** "Das Königtum in den Reichen Israel und Juda." *VT* 1 (1951) 2–22 (=*Kleine Schriften* II, 116–34). ET, "The Monarchy in Israel and Judah." *Essays.* New York: Doubleday (1968) 239–59. **Debus, J.** *Die Sünde Jerobeams.* FRLANT 95 (Göttingen: Vandenhoeck und Ruprecht, 1967). Teil II: "Die Jerobeam-Geschichte in der Parallel-Version des Codex Vaticanus der Septuaginta," 55–92. ———. *Idem.* Exkurs 4: "Ein 'Zwei-Kammer System' im israelitischen Staatswesen (zur Auseinandersetzung mit den Thesen von A. Malamat)." 30–34. **Dubarle, A. M.** "Le Jugement des auteurs bibliques sur le schisme de Jéroboam." *Miscellanea Biblica A. Fernández.* Madrid, 1961. **Evans, D. G.** "Rehoboam's Advisers at Shechem and Political Institutions in Israel and Sumer." *JNES* 25 (1966) 273–79. **Galling, K.** "Die israelitische Staatsverfassung in ihrer vorderasiatischen Umwelt." *AcOr* 28/3–4 (Leipzig 1929). **Grønbaek, J. H.** "Er-wägungen zu 1 Kön xii 21–24." *VT* 15 (1965) 421–36. **Halpern, B.** "Sectionalism and the Schism." *JBL* 93 (1974) 519–32. **Johnson, A. R.** *The One and the Many in the Israelite Conception of God.* Cardiff: University of Wales Press, 1942. **Lipinski, E.** "Le récit de 1 Rois XII 1–19 à la lumière de l'ancien usage de l'hébreu et de nouveaux textes de Mari." *VT* 24 (1974) 430–37. **Malamat, A.** "Kingship and Council in Israel and Sumer: A Parallel." *JNES* 22 (1963) 247–53. **Seebass, H.** "Zur Königserhebung Jerobeams I." *VT* 17 (1967) 325–33. **Stamm, J. J.** "Zwei alttestamentliche Königsna-men." *Near Eastern Studies in Honor of William Foxwell Albright.* ed. H. Goedicke. Balti-more: Johns Hopkins Press, 1971. **Tournay, R.** "Quelques relectures bibliques antisamaritaines (I K 12)." *RB* 71 (1964) 524–31. **Weinfeld, M.** "King-People Relation-ship in the Light of 1 Kings 12, 7." *Leš* 36 (1971) 3–13.

Translation

[1] *Rehoboam* [a] *went to Shechem, for it was to Shechem that all Israel came* [b] *in order to make him king.* [2] *And when Jeroboam son of Nebat heard about it—now he was still in Egypt whither he had fled before King Solomon—then Jeroboam* [a] *re-mained in readiness in Egypt.* [a] [3] *And they sent and summoned him; and Jeroboam and all* [a] *Israel came* [b] *and* [c] *spoke to Rehoboam* [d] [e] *as follows:* [e] [4] *"Your father made our yoke hard;* [a] *but as for you,* [b] *make it lighter than the hard servitude of your father, with his heavy yoke which he imposed upon us, and then we will serve you."* [5] *And he* [a] *said* [b] *to them,* [b] *"Depart* [c] *for yet* [c] *three days, and then return to me."* *So they* [d] *departed.* [6] *And* [a] *the king* [a] *took counsel with the veterans, who had always*

stood in the presence of Solomon his father while he was yet alive; and this is what he said, "How would you be giving advice, [b]*so that I may give word back to this people?"* [b] [7] *And they spoke to him as follows, "If today* [a] *you will be a servant to this people, and will serve them* [b]*and humble yourself,* [b] *and will speak to them pleasant words, then they will become servants to you for always."*

[8] *But he ignored the advice of the veterans who counseled him and consulted instead the newcomers who had grown up with him and were now standing before him.* [9] *And he said to them, "What do you advise* [a]*us to return as our answer* [a] *to this people, who have spoken to me as follows, 'Lighten the yoke which your father put upon us'?"* [10] *And the newcomers who had grown up with him replied as follows: "Thus shall you say to this people, who speak to you, saying, 'Your father made our yoke heavy, but do you* [a] *lighten it!' Thus shall you say to them: 'My little finger is thicker than my father's waist.* [11] *So now: my father burdened you with a heavy yoke, but I will increase the yoke that is on you; my father chastised you with whips, but I will chastise you with scourges.'"*

[12] *And* [a]*all the people* [a] *came to Rehoboam* [b] *the third day in compliance with what the king had said:* [c] *"Return to me on the third day."* [13] *And the king answered the people harshly, ignoring the advice of the veterans, which they had offered him.* [14] *And he spoke to them in accordance with the advice of the newcomers, as follows: "My father made your yoke heavy, but I will increase your yoke; my father chastised you with whips, but I will chastise you with scourges."* [15] *So the king would not listen to the people, for it was a turn of events brought about by Yahweh, which Yahweh had spoken by means of Ahijah* [a] *the Shilonite to* [b] *Jeroboam son of Nebat.*

[16] *Thus* [a]*all Israel* [a] *perceived that the king did not intend to listen to them. And the people returned word to the king as follows:*

"[b]*What portion do we have* [b] *in David?*

[c]*There is no inheritance* [cd] *in the son of Jesse.*

To your tents, O Israel!

You [e] *go pasture* [f] *your own household, David!"*

So Israel went off [g]*to their* [g] *tents.* [17] *But* [a]*the Judahites and* [a] *the Israelites who were living in the cities of Judah caused Rehoboam to reign over them.* [18] *Then* [a]*the king* [a] *sent Adoniram,* [b] *who was in charge of the corvée, but all Israel stoned him with stones so that he died; and King Rehoboam had to struggle to get up into his chariot in time to flee to Jerusalem.* [19] *So all Israel has been in revolt against the house of David to this day.* [20] *And it happened that when all Israel heard that Jeroboam* [a] *had returned, they sent and called him to the assembly. And they made him king over all* [b] *Israel. There was no one who supported the house* [c] *of David apart from the tribe of Judah, all by itself.*

[21] *And Rehoboam came* [a] *to Jerusalem and assembled* [b]*the entire house of* [b] *Judah and* [c]*the tribe of* [c] *Benjamin, a hundred twenty* [d] *thousand choice men trained for battle, to fight with* [e] *the house of Israel in order to restore the sovereignty to Rehoboam son of Solomon.* [22] *And the word of Yahweh* [a] *came to Shemaiah, a man of God, as follows:* [23] *"Say to Rehoboam son of Solomon, king of Judah, and to* [a]*all the house of* [a] *Judah, and Benjamin, and the rest of the people, saying* [24] *'Thus says Yahweh: "You shall not go up and you shall not fight with your brothers the Israelites. Return each of you to his house, for from me came about this turn of events."'" And they listened to the word of Yahweh and turned back, in order to behave in accordance with the word of Yahweh.* [a]

Notes

1.a. MT. G^B "King Rehoboam" is pleonastic. G^L "the king" is premature in view of the verse's sequel.

1.b. MT (sing). Most witnesses (G^{BL}, Syr, Tg, Seb, Chr, Mss) treat the subject as a plural.

2.a-a. MT; cf. *HOTTP*, 318. Chr "returned from Egypt" puts Jeroboam at Shechem when Rehoboam is rejected. Cf. G 12:24^b.

3.a. Chr. MT "the assembly of Israel" is premature.

3.b. Chr. Q, Vrs. sing, corrected by K to agree with וידברו "and they spoke"; but see the sing in MT v 7.

3.c. MT. G^{BL} add "the people."

3.d. MT. G^{BL} "King Rehoboam."

3.e-e. MT. G^{BL} omit.

4.a. MT, G^L. G^B "heavy."

4.b. MT and G^{BL} add "now," which should be omitted as an auditory doublet; cf. v 14 and Chr (Par).

5.a. MT, G^B. G^L has explicative "the king."

5.b-b. MT, G^B, Chr. G^L's omission might seem original except that "the king" seems to fill a gap in a corrupt text.

5.c-c. MT (עֹד שְׁלֹשָׁה יָמִים "yet three days"). G^{BL} read עַד "until" (ἕως ἡμερῶν τριῶν "till three days"). The Heb. expression emphasizes the duration; the Gr. expression emphasizes the termination.

5.d. G^{BL}. MT "the people" is explicative.

6.a-a. G^{BL}. MT "King Rehoboam."

6.b-b. G^B is the closest to the original text. In the first clause of Rehoboam's query, G^{BL} follow MT except in substituting the indicative middle of βουλεύω for the niph pl ptcp of יעץ. The result or purpose clause that follows began in the original with a first personal sing *wāw*-consecutive of שׁוב "return" in G^B's rendering (καὶ ἀποκριθῶ), less effectively represented by a purpose clause introduced by the hiph inf of שׁוב in MT and by ἵνα "in order to" in G^L. Since דָּבָר "answer" is the verbal object, אֶת הָעָם "the people" in MT creates an awkward syntax that is certainly not original. G^{BL}, Chr read an indirect object, "to this people," which is what the sense requires.

7.a. G^{BL} "on this day"; Chr omits (*hab* Par).

7.b-b. MT. G^M omits; G^L corr.

9.a-a. MT. G^{BL} "and what shall I answer."

10.a. MT. G^{BL} σύ νῦν = אַתָּה עַתָּה, "you now," an auditory conflation. Without question the personal pronoun is to be read, for emphasis is on the contrast between Rehoboam and Solomon, not on points in time.

12.a-a. G^{BL}, reading a pl verb (καὶ παρεγένοντο = ויבאו "and they came" (MT is defective: ויבו). MT reads "Jeroboam and all the people" as subject; cf. Chr. See *HOTTP* 320.

12.b. MT. G^{BL} "King Rehoboam."

12.c. MT, G^L. G^B has explicative "to them."

15.a. MT, G^B. G^L adds "the prophet"; cf. 11:29 in G^{BL}.

15.b. MT. Cf. G^{BL}, both of which have a preposition (^Bπερὶ "about," ^Lἐπί "against") translating Heb. עַל "against," which implies denunciation in the Dtr spirit. MT אֶל is *lectio difficilior* because a lighter word would not likely be substituted for a harsher word.

16.a-a. MT and G^B. G^L, Vg, Ms "the people."

16.b-b. MT and G^B. G^L, Ms, Syr, Tg^{ms} "there is no portion"; cf. 2 Sam. 20:1.

16.c-c. MT, G^B. G^L "nor an inheritance" (cf. *BHK*mg).

16.d. MT, G^L. G^B "for us" is explicative.

16.e. G^{c}2. MT, G^{BL} *rell* "now." In spite of the weak attestation, σύ = אַתָּה, "you," is to be read (see Noth, 277) since the contrast lies between the rebellious people on the one side, and "David" on the other. It is understandable that the Heb. text-tradition readily became corrupted to read עַתָּה "now."

16.f. G^{BL}, Tg, reading Heb. רְעֵה. It is surprising that MT has become corrupted to רְאֵה "see" (with the meaning "see to," "care for").

16.g-g. MT, G begin with sing verb and sing subject, but in the prepositional phrase both adopt the pl.

17.a-a. G^L. MT omits these words (haplography); G^B omits the entire verse.

18.a-a. G^B. MT, G^L "King Rehoboam."

18.b. G^L. Cf. 4:6. MT "Adoram"; G^B "Aram" (corr or abbreviations).

20.a. MT, G^L. G^B "Rehoboam."

20.b. MT, offering the *lectio difficilior* in view of Judah's exemption from Jeroboam's rule mentioned immediately after. G^{BL}'s omission may follow a textual tradition correcting for this fact.

20.c. MT, G^L; G^B omits. This is a quaint old Heb. expression that the G^B translator may have found offensive to good style, yet its political overtones well suit it to this context, marking it as original.

21.a. K pl; Q, Chr, Vrs. sing.

21.b-b. MT (see note 20.c). G^{BL} "the congregation" (τὴν συναγωγὴν = Heb. עדה). Chr "the house of"; Par omits. One can read much text history in this text, the Gr. renderings showing the ideological interference of the late postexilic period.

21.c-c. MT, G. Chr omits.

21.d. G^{BL}. MT "eighty."

21.e. Chr (Par) omits.

22.a. G, Chr (Par). MT "God" is probably influenced by "man of God."

23.a-a. Chr "Israel in Judah"; Par "Judah." The tendency to avoid "house of" in the old political sense shows the degree to which the Chronicles tradition follows the late theocratic ideal.

24.a. G^{BL} MSS add vv 24^{a-z}.

Form/Structure/Setting

Narrative of Rehoboam's rejection
   Introductory, 12:1
[Expansion concerning Jeroboam, vv 2–3aα]
   1. "All Israel" demands a mitigation
      a. Their speech, vv 3aβb–4
      b. A request for delay, v 5
   2. Rehoboam consults the veterans
      a. His request, v 6
      b. Their reply, v 7
   3. Rehoboam consults the newcomers, v 8
      a. His request, v 9
      b. Their reply, vv 10–11
   4. Their decisive encounter
      a. The people return, v 12
      b. Rehoboam's reply
         (1) He ignores the veterans' counsel, v 13
         (2) He repeats the words of the newcomers, v 14
[Dtr: interpretive comment, v 15]
      c. "All Israel's" reaction
         (1) Perception of Rehoboam's ill-will, v 16aα א
         (2) A defiant reply, v 16aα ב β
         (3) Their dispersal, v 16b
[Expansion: Explanatory comment, v 17]
   5. Violence against violence
      a. Adoniram stoned, v 18a
      b. Rehoboam flees, v 18b
      c. Perpetual rebellion, v 19

6. Jeroboam the counter-king
   a. His coronation, v 20a
   b. Rejection of the house of David, v 20b
Religio-political propaganda for Rehoboam's inaction
  1. Preparation of a potent military force, v 21
  2. Shemaiah's prophetic prohibition, vv 22–24a
  3. The people's compliance, v 24b

The numerous titles in our *Bibliography* for this section show the high level of scholarly interest in the event recorded. Ancient Israel had come here to a hinge of its history. The dynastic state just recently established by David and consolidated by Solomon was in the vise, about to break up. From our vantage point it is tempting to wonder what a continually united Israel might have become. In this age of imperial vacuum, was there anything that could have kept a united Israel from becoming a world power, avoiding perhaps the eventual calamities of the Assyrian and Babylonian age?

Nowhere inside or outside the Bible has the division of Israel been recorded in a factual, straightforward fashion, not even here. Vv 1–20 comprise what is in effect a reproach, a negative report, had there been anyone to report to. Vv 21–24 constitutes a short piece of religio-political propaganda. The first emphasizes only the senseless obstinacy of Rehoboam and its calamitous effects, while the second makes an apologia for this same king's failure to move decisively to counteract these effects.

It is impossible to review here the lively recent debate concerning the various parties and persons involved in Israel's revolt, except to say that much interest has focused on A. Malamat's claim (*JNES* 22 [1965] 247–53) that "the elders" and "the youths" in vv 1–20 were in fact distinct, constituted assemblies comparable to the two houses of a legislature. Without ruling out apodictically that such "houses" may have actually existed in Israel, the present writer has translated "the veterans" and "the newcomers," to represent their actual functions, not their respective formal titles.

A decision as to who composed the reproach narrative depends on a number of subtle points. Certainly the author cannot be someone living in the north, as J. Gray claims in his commentary, for this person knows a great deal more about what went on among the Judahites present at Shechem than about what happened there after they had departed (v 20). Noth (272) is wrong in arguing from "to this day" in v 19 (this happens to be a familiar deuteronomistic phrase) that the narrative originated close to the time of Dtr, for it gives evidence of being in fact much earlier. One special point in the structure of the narrative that seems to betray the author's identity is the complaint in v 8, "But he ignored the advice of the veterans who counseled him. . . ." Coming as it does prior to the narration about Rehoboam's counseling with the newcomers and prior to this king's announcement of his decision three days later (v 13), this leads the reader to suppose that Rehoboam announced his negative reaction to the veterans immediately, which is improbable as a historical fact and inconsistent with the narrative's own obvious intent. It is therefore meant as a prejudgment on the king's counseling with the newcomers, which *ipso facto* constitutes a rejection of the veterans. Who could possibly represent such an attitude except someone from among the veterans? The author is a Judahite and loyal supporter of the house of David, perhaps even a functionary at Solomon's and Rehoboam's court. Yet he is no narrow tribal partisan, for his repeated reference to "all Israel" (the tribal union) shows that he aspires to the perpetual unification of this one people. We can understand then what pathos and disappointment lie in his conclusion, "So all Israel has been in revolt against the house of David to this day." He perhaps wrote this reproach narrative long after the event, probably after Rehoboam's death, as a testimony to his fellow Judahites of what might have been. An opportunity had come and been lost. It was as the veterans said to Rehoboam in v 7: one day of humility would have produced loyal servanthood on the part of "all Israel" for always (*YTT*, 226), but it was not to be.

It is possible to make a general rule that the conclusion of a narrative gives away what its message is. This is especially true of vv 21–24, which ends, "And they listened to the word of Yahweh and turned back, in order to behave in accordance with the word of Yahweh." Rehoboam had a hundred twenty thousand elite troops with which to whip the northern tribes back into submission, but he failed to use them. What is questionable is that Rehoboam chose not to fight merely because Yahweh's prophet told him not to. A "man of God" named Shemaiah may very well have delivered the discouraging oracle, but the likelihood is that there were also court prophets present who would have urged Rehoboam to proceed. Which Rehoboam listened to depended on the king's mood. Thus this little piece offers the reader just a tiny slice of what was probably a highly complex situation, and what it offers is designed to justify what the king chose to do.

These strongly slanted pieces are what Dtr found available for telling about the division of the kingdom. He adds his own statement in v 15 to the effect that Rehoboam's obstinacy was bringing to fulfillment the prophecy of Ahijah. Disregarding the original narrative which allows Jeroboam to appear only at v 20, an interpolator tells in vv 2–3a that this person returned in time to join in the assembly at Shechem. Another interpolator explains in v 17 that the Judahites as well as some Israelites accepted Rehoboam as king.

Comment

1–20 Shechem, between Mount Gerizim and Mount Ebal, at the boundary between the tribes of Manasseh and Ephraim, had long been a Canaanite enclave but became an important Israelite shrine-site when it was incorporated into David's realm. There is probably a historical kernel in Josh 24's narrative about the tribes coming there to make a covenant with Yahweh. The present passage is the most important evidence that it remained a central point of assembly for the former tribal league. This was reactivated at the death of Solomon (otherwise than at the death of David) and demanded recognition of the ancient right to approve—if not to choose—a new king. Rehoboam found himself obliged to travel there, but evidently he had inherited his parent's hard-headed despotism. The gloss in vv 2–3a manages to get Jeroboam all the way from Egypt just in the interval of Rehoboam's trip to Shechem, a journey of a day or two: Jeroboam in fact returned in some unreported

way after the revolt, following which he was made king at a new assembly
(v 20); hence he had no part in the revolt whatsoever.

"All Israel" stands for the entire tribal league, including Judah. The universal complaint was against Solomon's harshness (the corvée, taxation, etc.)
and the demand was for leniency. Rehoboam uses three days (a conventional
number meaning a short but adequate period of time) for deliberating his
reply, consulting first the veterans (lit., "elders") who had been his father's
counselors ("stood in his presence"), then the newcomers (lit., "the youths")
with whom he had grown up. The advice of the veterans is eminently reasonable, and not entirely devoid of craftiness. They want Rehoboam to "be a
servant" "today," meaning humble himself and speak pleasant (i.e., favorable)
words, so that "they will become servants to you for always" (v 7). It is as
if the veterans want Rehoboam to keep up only a temporary pretense, until
"all Israel" receives him as king, and he will be free to treat them as "servants,"
or slaves, from then on. But Rehoboam speaks harshly to "all Israel" instead,
quoting from the newcomers their cute little rhymes about his finger being
thicker than his father's waist, and chastising them with scourges in the place
of his father's whips. When "all Israel" hears this, they have their own ditty
to recite (v 16); it resurrects all the bitter feeling of past generations for
David's usurpations and deeds of violence, done to Saul and the northern
tribes. "So Israel went off to their tents" is proleptic in view of what happens
in v 18, which requires their presence, and echoes the ditty ("tents" is symbolic
for "houses," occurring in the usual formula, v 24). Rehoboam tries next
to get Adoniram, a stern man in charge of the corvée (cf. 4:6), to compel
them, but he is stoned, and the king barely manages to get into his chariot
and take off to Jerusalem. V 19 is the conclusion: perpetual revolt. V 20
adds an item about Jeroboam being made king over "all Israel," leaving no
support for Rehoboam except the single tribe of Judah.

21–24   Here the tribe of Benjamin joins the "house of Judah"; according
to 15:22, the kingdom of Judah managed to occupy Benjaminite territory
as far north as Ramah until the reign of Asa, Rehoboam's grandson. The
one hundred twenty thousand (12x10x100) is schematic and may not be factually accurate. These were choice men trained for battle, בחור עשה מלחמה;
the Benjaminites especially were renowned for their prowess in battle (e.g.,
Saul, Jonathan, Shimei, etc.). Shemaiah is not mentioned elsewhere in Kings
(cf. 2 Chr 12:5–15); he is here called "man of God," meaning a charismatically
endowed person, at least potentially a prophet. When he speaks he first reports
Yahweh's initial instructions to himself; among his addressees are "the rest
of the people," suggesting that others besides Judahites and Benjaminites
intended to fight for King Rehoboam. "Thus says Yahweh" is the familiar
herald formula with which oracles ordinarily began. The divine command
is to return, and the explanation is that Yahweh himself intended the revolt
to happen.

Explanation

1 Kgs 12:1–24 is no direct apologia for democracy and self-determination;
one notes that "all Israel" demanded leniency, but not independence. Nor

is it a moralizing admonition to heed one's elders and respect the old. These attitudes and aspirations may have been present in the participants' minds, but they are not advocated by the biblical text. It does indeed have a message about how monarchical willfulness may adversely affect the destiny of entire nations. Rehoboam is harsh, despotic, and autocratic, but the worst part is that he is also stupid and incompetent. If we interpret v 7 correctly, the veterans were not actually advising leniency as a permanent policy, but only as a sham concession designed to get "all Israel's" formal approval. According to the traditions of the tribal league, the king was supposed to be the people's "servant," and this is what the veterans counseled him to pretend to be so that the people might become his "servants" permanently. One of those veterans wrote up what happened as a reproach, and his complaint is not so much that Rehoboam heeded the advice of the newcomers as that he scorned to follow the veterans' ploy for one single day. Surely Rehoboam was a weak and fragile personality, disguising this for the moment with a show of harshness and bravado. The reader is not surprised to learn in vv 21–24 that he was also cowardly and indecisive when the time came to fight.

Possibly this passage's most important lesson is how much easier it is to break up what belongs together than it is to restore what is broken. How profoundly true are Jesus' words "Blessed are the peacemakers, for they shall be called sons of God" (Matt 5:9)!

Jeroboam's Religious Innovations
(12:25–32)

Bibliography

Aberbach, M., and **Smolar, L.** "Aaron, Jeroboam and the Golden Calves." *JBL* 86 (1967) 129–42. **Allan, N.** "Jeroboam and Shechem." *VT* 24 (1974) 353–57. **Bailey, L. R.** "The Golden Calf." *HUCA* 42 (1971) 97–115. **Danelius, E.** "The Sins of Jeroboam Ben-Nabat." *JQR* 58 (1967–68) 95–114, 204–23. **Donner, K.** "'Hier sind deine Götter, Israel!'" *Wort und Geschichte, Festschrift für K. Elliger zum 70. Geburtstag.* AOAT 18. Neukirchen-Vluyn: Verlag Butzon & Becker Kevelaer, 1973. **Dus, J.** "Die Stierbilder von Bethel und Dan und das Problem der 'Moseschar'." Instituio Orientale di Napoli 28/18. *AION* 18 (1968). **Morgenstern, J.** "The Festival of Jerobeam I." *JBL* 83 (1964) 109–18. **North, R.** "Jeroboam's Tragic Social-Justice Epic." *Homenaje a Juan Prado,* Madrid, 1975. **Obbink, H. T.** "Jahwebilder," *ZAW* 47 (1929) 264–74. **de Vaux, R.** "Le schisme religieux de Jéroboam Ier." *BibOr-Vosté.* Rome: "Angelicum," (1943) 77–91.

Translation

[25] *And Jeroboam built Shechem[a] in Mount Ephraim and resided there; and he went out from there and built Penuel.*

[26] *And Jeroboam thought in his heart, "Now[a] the sovereignty will return to the house of David* [27] *if this people are allowed to perform sacrifices at Yahweh's temple in Jerusalem. In that case the[a] people's heart will go back to[b] their masters, including Rehoboam king of Judah, [c]and they will slay me."[c]* [28] *So the king took counsel. And he[a] made two calves of gold. And he said to them,[b] "You have had enough of going up to Jerusalem:*

> *Behold thy gods, O Israel,*
> *who brought thee up from the land of Egypt!"*

[29] *And he placed the one in Bethel and the other in Dan.* [30] *And this matter became an error.[a] And the people processed before the one unto Dan.[b]* [31] *And he[a] made temples[b] for the country shrines. And he made priests from the masses of the people, even though they might not belong among the Levites.* [32] *And Jeroboam made a festival in the eighth month, on the fifteenth day of the month, similar to the festival [a]in Judah.[a] And he approached the altar; [b]thus he did[b] in Bethel in order to sacrifice to the calves which he had made. And he appointed to serve in Bethel the priests of the country shrines which he had made.*

Notes

25.a. MT. G[BL] add explicative "which is."

26.a. MT, G[L]. G[B] "behold now" is not likely to be original since the particle, הנה, normally precedes nouns and verbs.

27.a. G[BL]. MT "this" is explicative.

27.b. MT and G[L]. G[B] inserts a mitigating "the Lord (κύριον) and. . . ."

27.c-c. G[B]. G[L] omits; MT adds the dittography "and they will go back to Rehoboam king of Judah."

28.a. MT. G^BL add "went and," for some reason supposing that the fabrication of the calves would have to occur elsewhere than in Shechem.

28.b. MT. G^BL πρὸς τὸν λαόν = Heb. אֶל הָעָם "to the people" is a corruption of אלהם "to them."

30.a. MT, G^B. G^L adds explicative "for Israel."

30.b. MT, G^B. G^L corrects what it thinks to be an erroneous omission with the phrase "and before the other unto Bethel."

31.a. MT, G^B. G^L has explicative "Jeroboam."

31.b. G^BL οἴκους. Noth (268) would read the apparent Heb. sing (MT בֵּית "house") as pl in function within the construct chain with בָּמוֹת "country shrines." It seems more likely that בָּתֵּי "houses of," construct pl, has been corrupted to בֵּית "house of."

32.a-a. MT. G^BL "in the land of Judah" is explicative.

32.b-b. MT. G^BL "which he made"—the best that the Gr. translators were able to do with the Heb. as it stands in the MT; but the Gr. substitutes the connective אשׁר = Gr. relative pronoun, of which there is no trace in the Heb.

Form/Structure/Setting

Extract from the Book of the Chronicles of the Israelite Kings: Jeroboam's building activities, v 25
Report concerning the golden calves
  1. Resolve to prevent travel to Jerusalem, vv 26–27
  2. Fabrication and dedication of the golden calves, v 28
[Expansion: The two calf shrines, v 29]
  3. Concluding censure, v 30a
Complaints against Jeroboam's religious innovations
  1. Procession to Dan, v 30b
  2. New shrines, v 31a
  3. New priests, v 31b
  4. A new festal calendar, v 32aα
  5. Sacrifice to the Bethel calf(ves), v 32aβ
  6. New priests at Bethel, v 32b

V 25 is the first of a number of extracts from a new archive known as the Book of the Chronicles of the Israelite Kings (14:19, 15:31, etc.). The report that follows (vv 26–30a) contrasts with this in being markedly subjectivistic, presuming first to know Jeroboam's thoughts and in the conclusion rendering an apodictic judgment on that king's religious innovations. It contains this section's only literary expansion (v 29), correcting the possible misconception that both the golden calves remained in Bethel (see v 32). All that can be said about the possible authorship of this report is that it surely comes from Judah and reflects a strong Jerusalemite bias. With respect to the series of complaints listed in vv 30b–32b, it can be conjectured that they were not only from Judah but from a definite group of sacral functionaries known as the Levites. Levites lived in a number of special cities (Josh 21), including some in Judah and Benjamin, but also many among the northern tribes, including Shechem. We take note of B. Mazar's thesis, presented in "The Cities of the Priests and Levites," (VTSup 7 [1960] 193–205) that the Levites were agents of David. V 31's complaint that Jeroboam made priests of some who were not Levites reveals quite clearly that it was this group

that was responsible for preparing the whole list. This constitutes a report
passed from one Levite to another Levite over the border, and destined for
the high-priesthood at the temple.

Comment

25 Respecting Shechem, see on 12:1. It lay in the territory of the tribe
of Manasseh, but the mountain range where it was located was known as
Mount Ephraim. Having been made king there, Jeroboam did some rebuilding
of the city in order to make it his royal residence. For some unstated reason
(N. Allan, *VT* 24 [1974] 353–57, argues that David-loyal Levites in this Levitical
city intrigued against him), he changed his mind and rebuilt Penuel, a sacred
city on the Jabbok, across the Jordan (cf. Gen 32:31 [Eng. 30]), from which
he eventually moved in order to take up residence at Tirzah (cf. 14:17).

26–30a Jeroboam's act of installing Yahweh-symbols in the ancient shrines
of Bethel and Dan was rightly interpreted by the maker of the report as
having a political purpose. So long as Israelites from north of the border
continued their thrice-annual pilgrimages to Yahweh's temple in Jerusalem,
they were likely to run away, or at least become disloyal and ready to foment
revolution. The writer puts words into Jeroboam's mind that must have been
close to actuality: "They will slay me." Jeroboam would have thought that—
but hardly the writer's biased notion that the rebels would have been returning
to their proper masters. Jeroboam did see the necessity of sealing off the
border—a political concern. But his concern was also religious, for he needed
holy places that the people would accept as authentic Yahweh shrines. It
was not enough that Dan (cf. Judg 18:27–31) and Bethel (cf. Gen 28:16–
22, 35:1–4) had long been reconsecrated as Yahweh shrines. One or both
(preferably both) needed a special sacred object similar to the ark to signify
Yahweh's real presence. Jeroboam and his counselors decided to make a
calf (or bull) for each shrine and install these in the most holy place, the
innermost adytum. Much controversy has arisen as to the function of these
calves, but the present consensus is that they were not idols but ornaments
or pedestals.

All the same, such a symbol had to create problems for those who were
just progressing in the biblical understanding of God. All around Israel, and
in the numerous Canaanite enclaves within its territory, were half-Yahwists
to whom the calf or bull was the symbol of male fecundity. Officially or unoffi-
cially, Baalism was in the land; it was destined in the days of Ahab to gain
the mastery. Thus the golden calves could have done nothing but confuse
and mislead. Perhaps Jeroboam did not intend it so, but that he should have
chosen such a symbol to represent Yahweh shows that he may have been
but a half-Yahwist himself. This did not, however, prevent him from reciting
words of solemn acclamation reflecting Israel's Exodus tradition, "Behold
thy gods, O Israel, who brought thee up from the land of Egypt!" Exod
32:1, 4 has exactly these same words, but Jeroboam did not get them from
there. Jeroboam undoubtedly intended the occasion to be good and happy
and holy. The Exodus account of the golden calf understands it as a wicked
act. The reporter who composed the account in 1 Kgs perhaps interjected

a bit of this censorious attitude, for he uses the plural form of "brought" where the original formula should have had the singular, in order to ensure that אלהיך is not read as "thy God" (a common equivalent to Yahweh) but as "thy gods." At the conclusion, the reporter delivers his assessment: Jeroboam's innovation is an error (חטאת), something that violates the standards of religious orthodoxy.

30b–32 Here are six complaints, gathered from Levitical spies scattered around the country. (1) Since the two golden calves were made at the same place—probably Bethel—there was a religious procession with one of them to Dan in the far north. (2) Open-air altars were upgraded by the addition of walled and roofed shrines. (3) Anybody, not just Levites, could become a priest. (4) The religious calendar was changed. (5) Jeroboam ventured to approach the altar, something only priests may do. (6) Priests from the country shrines were brought in to serve in Bethel. The only one of these that calls for special comment is the one about the calendar. There seems to be no consensus about what happened. To this writer the most plausible suggestion is that Jeroboam, just returned from Egypt, was observing a different new year from the one proclaimed by the Jerusalem priesthood. This was quite possible, for the Hebrew lunar-solar calendar (with 355 days) got out of synchronism every two or three years, requiring the addition of an intercalary month. Thus it could have happened that Jeroboam actually did observe the feast of tabernacles in his seventh month, as required by Num 29:12–39, but this may have been the eighth month according to Jerusalemite reckoning. Thus this was no innovation, just an expression of Jeroboam's independence of Jerusalem.

Explanation

Serious religious issues are at stake in this passage. One is the question of religious tolerance. Since only Judahite documents are represented, everything is stated from a Judahite point of view. Continually the innovations of Jeroboam are placed in a bad light. His calendar was misunderstood; his liberalizing of access to clergy status, his upgrading of the local shrines, and his reason for adorning the Bethel shrine were misrepresented. He may have been misquoted in his acclamation of the calf, making it seem that he was worshiping the calf itself, and that it represented a plurality of gods. Jeroboam may have been unaware of baalistic associations respecting the calf, which after all had adorned the throne of Solomon (10:19), and which certainly did not offend the Judahite man of God who cries out against the altar (not the calf) of Bethel in chap. 13! Another serious problem is the dominance of civil authority over religion, about which we shall have opportunity to comment in another context.

The Prophecy against the Bethel Altar (12:33—13:34)

Bibliography

Barth, K. *Exegese von 1. Könige 13.* Neukirchener Verlag, 1955. **Gross, W.** "Lying Prophet and Disobedient Man of God in 1 Kings 13: Role Analysis as an Instrument of Theological Interpretation of an Old Testament Narrative Text." *Semeia* 15 (1979) 97–135. **Hossfeld, F. L.,** and **Meyer, I.** *Prophet gegen Prophet; eine Analyse der alttestamentlichen Texte zum Thema: Wahre und falsche Propheten.* BibB 9. Fribourg: Schweizerisches Katholisches Bibelwerk, 1973. **Jepsen, A.** "Gottesmann und Prophet. Anmerkungen zum Kapitel 1. Könige 13." *Probleme biblischer Theologie. Gerhard von Rad zum 70. Geburtstag.* Munich: Chr. Kaiser (1971) 171–82. **Klopfenstein, M. A.** "1. Könige 13." *Parrhesia. Karl Barth zum 80. Geburtstag.* Zürich: EVZ-Verlag (1966) 639–72. **Lemke, W. E.** "The Way of Obedience: I Kings 13 and the Structure of Deuteronomistic History." *Magnalia Dei. The Mighty Acts of God. Essays on the Bible and Archaeology in Memory of G. Ernest Wright.* Garden City, N.Y.: Doubleday (1976) 301–28. **Würthwein, E.** "Die Erzählung vom Gottesmann aus Juda in Bethel. Zur Komposition von 1 Kön 13." AOAT 18. *Wort und Geschichte,* K. Elliger Fs. Neukirchen: Verlag Butzon & Bercker Kevelaer (1973) 181–89.

Translation

[33] *And he* [a] *approached the altar he had made* [b] *on the fifteenth day of the eighth month, the month* [c] *which he devised out of his own heart; and having made a festival for the Israelites, he approached the altar to make sacrificial smoke.*

[13:1] *Now behold, a man of God came from Judah by the word of Yahweh to Bethel while Jeroboam was standing on the altar about to make sacrificial smoke,* [2] *and he declaimed against the altar by the word of Yahweh:* [a] *"Altar, altar, thus says Yahweh, 'Behold, a son shall be born to the house of David, Josiah by name; and he shall sacrifice upon you the priests of the country shrines* [b] *who have been making sacrificial smoke on you, and they* [c] *shall burn upon you human bones.* [3] *And he will offer on that day a sign, as follows: "This is the sign* [a] *which Yahweh spoke,* [b] *'Behold, the altar shall be split open and the fat that is upon it shall be spilt out.'"'"*

[4] *And it happened that when* [a] *the king* [a] *heard the word* [b] *of the man of God which he declaimed against the altar of Bethel, he* [c] *extended his hand from upon the altar saying, "Arrest him"; but* [d] *his hand which he reached out toward him withered so that he was unable to draw it back to himself.*

[5] *And the altar was split open, and the fat from the altar was spilt out, according to the sign which the man of God gave by the word of Yahweh.*

[6] *And the king* [a] *said* [b] *to the man of God, "Implore the presence of Yahweh your God* [c] *that my hand may be restored unto me." So the man of God implored the presence of Yahweh, and* [d] *the king's hand was restored to him* [d] *and became just as it was at first.* [7] *And the king said to the man of God, "Come home with me and I will give you a present."* [8] *But the man of God said to the king, "If you should give me half of your house I would not go with you, nor will I eat bread or drink*

water in this place. ⁹ *For thus* ᵃ*was it commanded me by the word of Yahweh,* ᵃ *'You shall not eat bread and you shall not drink water; and you shall not return on the road on which you traveled.' "* ¹⁰ *So he departed by another road and did not return on the road by which he had come to Bethel.*

¹¹ *Now a certain old prophet was living at Bethel. And a son* ᵃ *of his came* ᵃ *and told* ᵃ *him the entire deed that the man of God had done* ᵇ*this day* ᵇ *in Bethel, with* ᶜ *the words which he had spoken to the king.* ᵈ*And when they told their father,* ᵈ ¹² *their father said to them, "Which way did he go?" And his sons* ᵃ*had observed* ᵃ *the road on which the man of God who had come from Judah* ᵇ*had gone away.* ᵇ ¹³ *And he said to his sons, "Saddle the ass for me." So they saddled the ass for him, and he got up on him* ¹⁴ *and went after the man of God. And he found him sitting beneath an oak. And he said to him, "Are you the man of God who has come from Judah?" And he said, "I am he."* ¹⁵ *Then he said to him, "Come* ᵃ *with me and eat some bread."* ¹⁶ *But he said, "I am unable to return with you,* ᵃ *and I will not eat bread or drink water* ᵇ *in this place,* ¹⁷ *for it was commanded me by the word of Yahweh, 'You shall not eat bread there* ᵃ *and you shall not drink water. You* ᵇ *shall not return* ᶜ *by traveling on the same road on which you first traveled.' "* ¹⁸ *But he* ᵃ *said to him, "I too am a prophet, just like yourself, and an angel has spoken to me by the word of Yahweh as follows, 'Bring him back with you to your house and let him eat bread and drink water.' " He lied to him.*

¹⁹ *So he returned with him, and ate bread in his house and drank water.* ᵃ ²⁰ *And it happened while they were sitting* ᵃ *that the word of Yahweh came to the prophet who had brought him back.* ²¹ *And he cried out to the man of God who had come from Judah: "Thus says Yahweh, 'Because you rebelled against Yahweh's express order* ᵃ *and have not observed the instruction which Yahweh your God imposed upon you,* ²² *but have returned and have eaten bread and drunk water in the* ᵃ *place concerning which he said to you, "Do not eat bread and do not drink water," your corpse shall not come to the grave of your fathers.' "*

²³ *And it happened that* ᵃ*after he had eaten bread* ᵇ *and after he had drunk,* ᵃ *he* ᶜ *saddled the ass for him,* ᵈ*the one belonging to the prophet who had brought him back,* ᵈ ²⁴ ᵃ*and he went away.* ᵃ *And a lion came across him on the road and killed him. And his corpse lay tossed in the road while the ass remained standing alongside him; and the lion continued to stand alongside the corpse.* ²⁵ ᵃ*And they* ᵇ *came and told it in the city in which the old prophet was living.*

²⁶ *And the prophet who had turned him from the road heard it and said, "He is the man of God who rebelled against Yahweh's express order."* ᵃ ²⁸ *And he went and found his corpse tossed in the road, and the* ᵃ *ass and the lion standing beside the corpse. The lion had not eaten the corpse, and he had not mauled the ass.* ²⁹ *And the prophet lifted up the corpse of the man of God* ᵃ*and placed him upon* ᵇ *the ass and came back with him* ᶜ*to the* ᵈ *prophet's city* ᵃ *in order to bury him.* ³⁰ ᵃ*And he deposited his corpse* ᵃ *in his own grave; and they lamented over him, "Alas, O brother!"* ᵇ ³¹ *And it happened after they had buried him that he spoke to his sons as follows, "When I die, you shall bury me in the* ᵃ *grave in which the man of God has been buried; alongside his bones shall you deposit* ᵇ*my bones.* ᵇ ³² *For the word shall most assuredly come to pass that he declaimed by the word of God against the altar* ᵃ *in Bethel and against* ᵇ *the temples of the country shrines which are in* ᶜ *Samaria."*

³³ *After this event Jeroboam did not return from his* ᵃ *way, but went back and*

made priests for the country shrines from the masses of the people; whomever had the desire, he ordained, and he became a priest **b** *of the country shrines.* **34** *And this* **a** *thing became an error for the house of Jeroboam, both to efface and to demolish it from the face of the ground.*

Notes

33.a. MT and G**B**. G**L** has explicative "Jeroboam."

33.b. G**BL**. MT has explicative "in Bethel."

33.c. MT. G**BL** "festival" copies the following reference; it has a sharpened polemic ring in comparison with "month."

13:2.a. G**B**. MT and G**L** add "and he said" in order to direct the verb קרא "declaimed" to the following citation.

2.b. MT, G**B**. G**L** adds interpretive "and."

2.c. MT is *lectio difficilior* and clearly has the historical scene of 2 Kgs 23 in mind. G, Syr, Vg correct to the sing, with reference to Josiah.

3.a. MT. G**BL** "word." Though MT repeats the word מופת "sign," this is no dittography, and MT deserves to be retained as *lectio difficilior*. The Gr. translators made their change because they had no idea of the explanation for its use here, as discussed in *Comment.*

3.b. MT and G**L**. G**B**'s insertion "saying" is pleonastic, though the pleonasm was likely in the Heb. *Vorlage* (לאמר).

4.a-a. MT and G**L**. G**B** has explicative "King Jeroboam."

4.b. MT and G**L**. G**B** pl.

4.c. G**L**. Both MT "Jeroboam" and G**B** "the king" are explicative.

4.d. MT, G**L**. G**B** is again pleonastic in copying the old Heb. "and behold."

6.a. MT and G**L**. G**B** has explicative "King Jeroboam."

6.b. G**B**. MT and G**L** have pleonastic "answered . . . and said."

6.c. G**BL**. MT has pleonastic addition "and pray on my behalf."

6.d-d. MT. G**BL** are more explicit with "and he restored the king's hand to him."

9.a-a. MT, G**L**. Again preferring the active voice, G**B** paraphrases "Yahweh commanded me in a word."

11.a,a,a. In agreement with vv 12ff., MT, which speaks of "sons" (pl), G and the Vrs. use the pl styling also in v 11, but MT's sing is probably original (*lectio difficilior*).

11.b-b. MT היום "the day" is unparalleled in this usage; cf. *YTT,* 227. The time reference remains present, not past, as implied by G**B** ἐν τῇ ἡμέρᾳ "in the day," G**L** ἐν τῇ ἡμέρᾳ ἐκείνῃ "in that day."

11.c. את is read as a preposition rather than as the sign of the definite object, as in MT and G.

11.d-d. MT. G "and they turned their father" (corr?).

12.a-a. MT, G, Vrs "made him see" = "pointed out to him"; cf. *HOTTP,* 321.

12.b-b. MT, G**L**. G**B** ἀνῆλθεν reads Heb. הלך as "come up," "approach"; correctly, G**L** reads ἀπῆλθεν, "went away."

15.a. G**BL**. MT הביתה "to the house" is explicative; cf. v 19.

16.a. G**BL**. MT has pleonastic addition "and to go with you."

16.b. G, Vg. MT adds explicative "with you."

17.a. G**BL**. MT inserts this word after "drink."

17.b. MT. G**BL** "and you" endeavors a more syndetic syntax.

17.c. MT and G**L**. G**B** "thither" is pleonastic.

18.a. MT. G**BL** "and he," interpreting the lying as separate from the preceding report of revelation.

19.a. MT and G**B**. G**L** adds explicative "in his house."

20.a. MT. G**BL** add explicative "at the table."

21.a. MT פי יהוה lit. "Yahweh's mouth"; G**BL** normalizes this anthropomorphic expression to "the word (ῥῆμα) of Yahweh."

22.a. MT, G**L**. G**B** has explicative "this."

23.a-a. MT. G**BL** substitute the impersonal expression "the (**L** his) eating of bread and drinking of water."

23.b. MT, G. Vg omits.

23.c. MT, G. MSS pl.

23.d-d. The parenthesis in MT is justified by emphasis on the identity of the ass, which was destined to encounter the lion and to bear the corpse of his master, the Judahite man of God. G^BL omit by haplography. Cf. *HOTTP*, 322.

24.a-a. MT. G^BL "and he turned and went away" is pleonastic.

25.a. Omit with G^L: "And behold, men were passing by and saw the corpse tossed in the road and the lion standing beside the corpse" (so MT, G^B). That this is the explicative gloss of a later hand may be argued from the fact that twice G^BL offers παρά as the translation of Heb. אצל "beside (him)," whereas in v 25 ἐχόμενα translates this same Heb. word (cf. Lev 6:10; Judg 19:14; 1 Kgs 1:9; Neh 2:6, 3:23, 12, 18; Ezek 1:15, 19, etc.). This sudden shift in translation equivalence is a clear clue to the lateness of the addition.

25.b. MT, G^B. G^L has explicative "men."

26.a. Lit. "mouth"; cf. note 21.b. We omit with G^B the remainder of v 26 and all of v 27: "And Yahweh gave him to the lion and he mauled him and killed him, according to the word of Yahweh which he spoke to him. And he said to his sons as follows, 'Saddle me the ass,' and they saddled him." MT reads this, with some late Gr. MSS (^b), but certain details, such as the addition that the lion "mauled" (שבר) the man of God, mark it as secondary.

28.a. G^BL, Syr, Tg. MT omits the determinative.

29.a-a. MT. G^BL "and the prophet placed him upon the ass and came back with him to the city." "The prophet" is nominative and serves as subject, but its position at the very end of this sequence shows that MT's עיר הנביא "city of the prophet" stood in the Gr. *Vorlage*.

29.b. G^BL. MT "unto" (אל).

29.c. G^BL. MT has pleonastic "and he came."

29.d. G^BL. MT adds explicative "old."

30.a-a. MT, G^L. G^B omits (haplography).

30.b. G^BL. MT "O my brother."

31.a. MT and G^L. G^B has explicative "this."

31.b-b. MT. G^BL have pleonastic "me, in order that my bones may be saved along with his bones."

32.a. G^BL. MT inserts "that is," perhaps implying that the altar did not properly belong in Bethel, but just happened to be there.

32.b. G^BL. MT's addition, "all," is ideological and pleonastic.

32.c. G^BL. MT's addition, "the cities of," distinguishes between the region of Samaria and certain apostate cities located in it.

33.a. G^BL. MT "evil" is interpretive and ideological.

33.b. G^BL, Syr, Vg. MT is pl, in disagreement with its singularistic syntactical contexting.

34.a. MSS, G, Syr, Tg. MT "by the thing/word."

Form/Structure/Setting

A Bethelite prophet narrative

[Dtr transition: Jeroboam at the Bethel altar, 12:33]

    1. The word against the Bethel altar

        a. An oracle uttered and substantiated

            (1) A Judahite man of God denounces the altar, 13:1a, 2aα

[Editorial expansion, v 1b]

[Dtr: Prediction of Josiah's purges, vv 2aβb–3]

            (2) The king's reprisal frustrated

                (a) His hand stretched out, v 4a

                (b) His hand withered, v 4b

[Dtr: The prophecy fulfilled, v 5]

                (c) His hand restored, v 6

        b. The communication of attendant revelation

            (1) The king's invitation, v 7

      (2) The man of God's refusal and its explanation, vv 8–9
      (3) Narrative of compliance, v 10
   2. The testing of the attendant revelation
     a. The violation
      (1) The Bethel prophet finds the man of God, vv 11–14
      (2) His invitation refused
        (a) The invitation, v 15
        (b) The refusal, v 16
        (c) The explanation, v 17
      (3) His invitation accepted
        (a) The countering revelation, v 18a
[Gloss, 18b]
        (b) The man of God complies, v 19
     b. The punishment
      (1) An oracle of imminent death
        (a) Narrative introduction, vv 20–21a
        (b) Invective, vv 21b–22a
        (c) Threat, v 22b
      (2) Its fulfillment
        (a) The man of God's departure, v 23
        (b) His death by a lion, v 24
        (c) Report to the Bethel prophet, v 25
   3. Confirmation of the prophetic power of the Judahite man of God
     a. The Bethel prophet disposes of the body
      (1) Interpretive identification, v 26
      (2) Recovery and burial of the man of God's body, vv 28–30
     b. The Bethel prophet prepares for his own burial
      (1) Instructions to his sons, v 31
      (2) Explanation, v 32a
[Dtr expansion, v 32b]
[Dtr: Further complaints against Jeroboam's cultic practices, vv 33–34]

In the writer's book *Prophet against Prophet* (59–61, 86, 101, 109–10, 147–48) this strange story has received extensive discussion. It has been a puzzle to exegetes as well as to theologians. The latter have asked, Does God actually give conflicting revelation to opposing prophets? The former have asked, Is it early or late? Is it one story or two? Does it come from Judah or the north? What is its central theme: revelation, obedience, or what? Most exegetes say it is early; the present writer says it is very early, perhaps before Jeroboam introduced the golden calf because the Judahite man of God denounces only the altar; so also W. Dietrich, *Prophetie und Geschichte*, FRLANT 108, Göttingen: Vandenhoeck & Ruprecht (1972) 114–20, 138. But A. Jepsen, *Nabi* (Munich: Beck, 1934) 178, and "Gottesmann und Prophet," *Probleme biblischer Theologie*, von Rad Fs., says it is postdeuteronomistic. Some critics make two narratives of it; so J. Gray, 324–32, E. Würthwein, "Die Erzählung von Gottesmann," *Wort und Geschichte*, Elliger Fs. But several recent commentators recognize that it is truly a single story in spite of the apparent new beginning at v 10 (M. Noth, in loco; F. L. Hossfeld and I. Meyer, *Prophet gegen Prophet,* 21–27; Dietrich, *Prophetie und Geschichte;* W. Lemke, "The Way of Obedience," *Magnalia Dei.*) Most critics say the provenance of this story is Judah, but the present writer has argued in the above-mentioned work that it must have come from a circle of Bethel prophets since the only Judahite witness to what happened (the slain man of God) never returned to tell about it. To many interpreters the main theme is the criterion of revelation. Lemke stresses the test of radical obedience. While it is true that these are both prominent themes, this writer has argued that the major concern is for the authority, and hence authenticity, of the Judahite man of God. In the listing of subgenres for the collection of prophetic legends, he has placed this narrative among "prophetic authorization narratives" of the word-fulfillment type (*Prophet against Prophet,* 55, 59–61).

It is rather obvious that Dtr has intruded at awkward points. In 12:33 he makes the transition from 12:25–32, then creates a speech to be placed in the mouth of the man of God, 13:2aβb–3, adding a fulfillment to it in v 5. In v 32b he carelessly appends to the narrative's conclusion a statement that the man of God had also declaimed against the temples of the country shrines. Some person from within the deuteronomistic school (see Lemke) then adds a separate statement in vv 33–34 to the effect that Jeroboam's practice of ordaining priests from the masses became the error (or "sin") for which his house was ultimately judged (directly conflicting with 12:30, which identifies the golden calves as the primal sin).

As he has redacted it, this narrative certainly does express the driving hostility of Dtr against rival shrines. This same redactor was responsible for the narrative report of Josiah's reforms appearing in 2 Kgs 23–24. One feature of that king's reforms as reported there was to demolish the shrine at Bethel, which lay just north of Judah's boundaries. Assyria was too weak to prevent Josiah's incursions. In 2 Kgs 23:15–20 we are told that he destroyed the Bethel altar, hauled bones from nearby tombs in order to burn them on the ruins of that altar, demolished all the country-shrines (RSV "high places") throughout Samaria, and slew the priests in charge of these establishments. In vv 16–18 this account makes explicit reference to 1 Kgs 13, leading some writers to suppose that the latter was created by the deuteronomistic school. It is certainly true that the event recorded in 2 Kgs 23:15–20, applauded by Dtr, was responsible for the preservation of 1 Kgs 13, but this does not substantiate the notion that Dtr composed it. Had he done so, he never would have referred to the Bethel prophet as "the prophet who came out of Samaria"; Josiah's recollection as reported by Dtr is markedly more vague on details than 1 Kgs 13 itself. A further consideration is that Dtr would certainly have written this narrative in such a way as to have brought condemnation, not just against Bethel's altar, but against the golden calf which he had found so atrocious, and for which he constantly condemns the kings of Israel.

It is really hard to understand how anyone could think of dividing this prophet story into two parts. True, v 10 does mark the major break within the narrative. But vv 1–10 are pointless without a continuation, while vv 11–32a extend the narrative about the man of God's trip to Bethel and his return. The key unifying elements are (1) the thrice-repeated statement that the man of God had been forbidden to eat, drink, or return by the same road (vv 9, 17, 22); (2) the demonstration that the divine prohibition was authentic in the man of God's death by the lion (v 24), explicitly acknowledged in v 26 by the Bethelite prophet; and (3) the action of the latter in burying the man of God in his own grave (v 30), instructing his sons to bury him next to him (v 31), and explaining cryptically at the conclusion (v 32a), "For the word shall most assuredly come to pass that he declaimed by the word of God against the altar in Bethel." The authenticity of the revelation against the altar was guaranteed by the fact that the attendant instructions could not be violated without risk of divine retribution. Therefore the man of God was a holy man and a true prophet.

Comment

33 Dtr garbles the syntax of this transitional comment, repeating the complaint about Jeroboam venturing to approach the altar, then emphasizing his willfulness in "making" the altar, in "devising" a date "out of his own heart," and in "making" a festival. "To make sacrificial smoke," להקטיר, means to offer burnt offerings.

13:1–10 "Man of God": cf. Shemaiah in 12:22, which shows that such a person might also prophesy. In the present chapter it is clear that this term expresses the provisional acknowledgment of prophetic status. A prophet could not be hindered by political boundaries, in spite of the efforts of despotic officials (cf. Amos 7:10–17). Bethel was connected to Jerusalem by a major highway. To return from it by another route would mean following perilous pathways through fields and thickets. In v 2 the man of God declaims against the altar "by the word of Yahweh" (a peculiar Bethelite locution?), but his actual words are not reported in the original narrative, only the daring act of speaking, for Bethel was a prestigious Yahweh shrine of great antiquity. Dtr phrases a judgment oracle (v 2) predicting the birth of King Josiah almost three centuries later and adding that that king would desecrate the Bethel altar by sacrificing on it the priests of the country shrines and by burning human bones on it; this prediction actually constitutes a misreading of 2 Kgs 23:19–20, which mentions that Josiah slew the priests of all the Samaritan high places but says nothing about sacrificing them. 1 Kgs 13:3 continues with the prediction (on its futuristic bearing see M. Noth *in loco* and *YTT*, 290–91) that Josiah would set a confirmatory sign to the effect that the altar would split open and pour out its residue of fat. This is not mentioned in 2 Kgs 23, and it is not clear whether Dtr intends the statement of its fulfillment in v 5 to have occurred in Josiah's time or at the moment when our narrative's king's arm withered. To say the least, this seems irrelevant to the narrative and shows a blind fury on Dtr's part.

The entire episode in which the man of God causes the king's arm to wither and then, at his plea, restores it (vv 4, 6) is meant as provisional proof of the man of God's authenticity. At the same time, it motivates the king's invitation (v 7), leading in turn to the climax of part one, the man of God's refusal and return (vv 8–10). Yahweh's command not to eat, drink or return by the same road certainly seems arbitrary and irrational, but that is precisely the point: the man of God's complete subjection to the divine purpose can only be tested through laying on him conditions that may seem unreasonable and burdensome to him.

11–25 That the Bethel prophet was old explains two things: why he was staying at home when the king (not named in the prophet story as Jeroboam) came to offer sacrifices and why, at the end, he should have laid the man of God to rest in his own tomb. The text of vv 11–12 is either corrupt or simply confused in speaking first of a single son and then of several. The old man is told what the man of God had said. This alarms him so much that he resolves to find him and determine whether he has authentic, authoritative revelation. Following him, he finds him resting under an oak (on האלה, "the terebinth," see G. Dalman, *JBL* 48 [1929] 359–60) and asks him to return with him and eat bread. The man of God repeats his complete instructions from Yahweh (vv 15–17), yet allows himself to be persuaded by the claim of countering revelation in v 18, whose authority is underscored by the statement that a direct intermediary, an angel, had spoken. The gloss, "He lied to him," is a late attempt to rationalize the Bethel prophet's words; in terms of the story's own self-understanding, the latter was equally inspired, but with a divine command to bring the man of God to the test respecting the authority of his own inspiration. After sharing table hospitality, the Bethel prophet cries out with a passionate word of new revelation; he speaks an oracle charging rebellious noncompliance and threatening immediate death (vv 21–22). This last is so phrased, however, as to make it possible for the Bethel prophet himself to bring it to fulfillment ("Your corpse shall not come to the grave of your fathers"). The Bethel prophet gives the man of God his ass, knowing that he would soon have it back, and sends him away. A lion comes and kills him, but does not eat him, which is clearly the act of God, for otherwise lions kill in order to eat.

26–34 Travelers report this spectacle to the old Bethel prophet, who identifies the dead man of God while interpreting his death as a fulfillment of the threat. Immediately he moves to bring the threat to even greater realization. He picks up the corpse, brings it to his own city (v 29, like v 25, mentions the city anonymously), and lays it in his own grave. The mourners lament, "Alas, O brother," thereby acknowledging a bond of spiritual kinship. In instructing his sons, the Bethel prophet expresses the wish to be buried in close contact with the body of the Judahite man of God. The apparent reason is that he wishes to be sanctified in his death through contact with one who has proven to be holy; and because that person's revelation definitely came straight from God, it is certain that his oracle against the altar must come to pass.

Explanation

The present writer has argued in *Prophet against Prophet* (101) for the essential historicity of the event narrated in this Bethelite prophet narrative. This is in spite of remarkable elements of wonder, such as the miracle of withering and restoring the king's hand, the outburst of revelational fervor on the part of the Bethel prophet, and the very unlionlike lion. There is also a sub-biblical element of superstition in the Bethel prophet's motive for burying the man of God in his own grave. This remarkable fact provides the etiological link that accounts for the preservation of the story (2 Kgs 23:17–18); the grave with its monument remained in place to remind every passerby of the event. But the grave in itself does not guarantee the story's historicity. It is rather the remembrance of the oracle against the Bethel altar, inimical to the essential loyalties of the Bethel prophets, that demands a historical basis, for their tradition would certainly have discarded this element if (1) it had not actually happened and (2) its authenticity had not been guaranteed by the death of the man of God. After the Northern Kingdom was destroyed in 723/22 B.C., some of the Bethel group of prophets may have drifted south across the border into Judah, and eventually their striking narrative became part of the Jerusalem heritage, ready to be used by Dtr for his redaction. Of course, the original narrators never would have approved of the way in which Dtr used their holy narrative, but it was due to Dtr, nonetheless, that it was preserved as part of the Bible.

This narrative can instruct us, if we will listen, because our generation is as confused as any other about the marks of authentic revelation. The complexities of its exegesis are so formidable that, as we have seen, even biblical specialists do not agree on many essential points. This lack of perfect agreement is no excuse, however, for the theologians to set criticism aside and allow their personal principles of religious philosophy to take over. This is precisely what the famous Swiss scholar Karl Barth once did, but with results that can scarcely produce fruit in terms of a richer exegetical understanding. Barth wrote about the opposing prophets of 1 Kgs 13 in his *Kirchliche Dogmatik* II/2, 434–53. According to Barth, the clue to this chapter is the doctrine of election as he has expounded it. Following his well-known dialectical method, Barth first identifies the Judahite man of God, with the kingdom of Judah, as Yahweh's true elect, standing over against the reprobate Bethel prophet and his Northern Kingdom. As Barth coins it, the latter represents "profession" while the former represents "confession"; the Northern king and his professionalistic prophet are like the formalistic Amaziah of Amos 7:10–17, and the Judahite man of God is another Amos. Having made these identifications, Barth proceeds to show how elements of the reprobate repeatedly compromise the elect one at crucial points in the story—as when the man of God turns back to dine with the Bethel prophet. Contrariwise, elements of election mark the reprobate Bethelite's behavior, as when he goes out to find the slain man of God and when he buries him in his own grave. The lion is for some reason the "lion of Judah," hence a symbol of true religion's denunciation of the false, formalistic religion to which the elect man of God has momentarily succumbed. The epitome of false, formal religion is found in the behavior of the Bethel prophet in first inviting the man of God to his house and then professing (or pretending) to denounce him through angelic inspiration.

Martin A. Klopfenstein, "1. Könige 13" (Barth Fs) 639–72, subjected Barth's interpretation to a searching criticism. While finding the categories of "elect" and "reprobate" helpful, Klopfenstein found no justification for numerous details in Barth's exposition, and for the treatment as a whole.

The identification of the lion as the elect "lion of Judah" is completely arbitrary. The story is not based on a constant interchange of roles, as Barth thought, but works up to and flows out from the one crucial moment (v 20) when, according to the text, an actual "word of the Lord" occurred.

Even though the Judahite man of God is elect, says Klopfenstein, it is the non-elect Bethelite who receives authentic revelation. What he says through prophetic revelation happens: the man of God does not get buried in his own tomb since he is killed by the lion and then buried in the tomb of the Bethel prophet. What the story is aiming to teach, then, concludes Klopfenstein, is that Yahweh can work his purpose even through disobedient men, and that the divine light cannot be extinguished even when entrusted to the unfaithful.

Klopfenstein has not effectively refuted Barth because his thinking has been too much dominated by the dialectic between "elect" and "non-elect." The problem is that strange fire has been brought to the altar. An antique text has been made to bear all the systematic logic of a modern philosophy of religion. True, "election" is an OT idea, but it is not an issue in this story. As we have tried to explain it, the story is about the marks of authentic prophecy—to be specific, the degree of obedience to which a genuine bearer of revelation is willing to commit himself. We again call the reader's attention to the thrice-repeated instructions that were given the man of God along with his commission to declaim against the Bethel altar. The section in which the king invites him to his house concludes with the Judahite's firm refusal, explained in the words, "So it was commissioned me by the word of Yahweh, saying, 'You shall neither eat bread, nor drink water, nor return by the way that you came'" (v 9). When the Bethelite finds this man resting under the tree and invites him to his house, he replies in similar words, "I may not return with you, or go in with you; neither will I eat bread nor drink water with you in this place; for it was said to me by the word of Yahweh, 'You shall neither eat bread nor drink water there, nor return by the way that you came'" (vv 16–17). Then, as the word of Yahweh comes to the Bethelite prophet, he accuses the Judahite of disobedience to the word of Yahweh; he has not kept the commandment "which Yahweh your God has commanded you, but have come back, and have eaten bread and drunk water in the place of which he said to you, 'Eat no bread and drink no water'" (vv 20–21).

Who can miss the point that this attendant revelation is absolutely structural? It explains the king episode, it creates the point of tension in the Bethelite's hospitality episode, and it provides the hinge for the climactic oracle of judgment. Very clearly and emphatically, the Judahite man of God has been instructed what not to do. Because he is unable to discern that the Bethelite prophet is only trying to test the authenticity of his inspiration, but trusts that prophet's assurance that it is all right to disregard the divine instruction in this one instance, the man of God actually disobeys Yahweh. Through inspiration, the Bethel prophet denounces him for his sin and then announces the penalty. Now all that has to happen is that Yahweh will actually punish him, as he has said through the Bethel prophet. If the Judahite actually does die for his disobedience, the Bethel prophet will know that he did indeed have authority to denounce the holy altar at Bethel. And so it is: the lion kills him; the old prophet buries him. And the old prophet tenderly places his body in his own tomb, instructing his sons to bury him alongside himself, for truly this was a holy man, a man in whom was the very word of God. Had the prophecy not come true and the man of God come safely home to Judah, the message of the Bethel prophet would have been proven false, but not it alone. Most important, nonfulfillment would have proven the man of God false, a presumptuous liar who pretended to obey the word of God when he had received no true word from God.

In every age there are those who presume to speak for God. Sometimes it is a word of praise, sometimes it is a word of denunciation. How will the people know to whom to listen, which prophet to fear (Deut 18:22)? Does a word of praise or denunciation truly come from above, or merely from the imaginings of the preacher's mind? Scripture offers many different tests, but 1 Kgs 13, once properly interpreted, offers the clearest test of all. That test is radical obedience. The preacher-prophet must be so committed to the transcendent truth of what he proclaims that his very own life is affected by it.

The Judahite man of God had to believe in his own stern word of denunciation against the Bethel altar so intensely that his whole behavior would be determined by it. It was not enough to demonstrate his spiritual power by restoring the shrunken arm of a king; it had to be demonstrated by a tenacity in such "little things" as not eating, not drinking, not returning by the same road.

Did the man of God understand the reasons for these strange prohibitions? Undoubtedly not. They seemed trivial, and in the case of refusing the king's hospitality he refused them out of a naïve obedience that had not yet been put to the sorest test. Somehow, his obedience was not carried out simply because Yahweh had said so. So what if Yahweh should speak through a colleague, some other man of the Spirit, to set these rules aside? Would it not make more sense to follow this new word than to adhere stubbornly to a set of arbitrary and aimless rules? Being of such a mind, the Judahite man of God was bound to fall for the Bethelite's trick. So he failed, and failing he perished. But let us observe that, though he failed, God's word did not fail. His very failure was the proof, in the Bethelite's interpretation, that the Judahite was inspired after all—inspired in spite of his stupidity, waywardness, and disobedience. Thus today we look for radical obedience in the way of life to which God's servants commit themselves. If they stumble—and stumble they will—their very weakness may confirm the word of God which they preach.

In all of history there was only one Prophet who kept God's rules in every minutia. He would not be distracted from God's stern pathway, not even by religion's greatest authorities. He too was doomed to die, but for the sins of others rather than for sins of his own. In his grave he sanctified the death of many others—of all those who call him not just "man of God" but "Son of God." The paradox of the Judahite man of God, compelling as it is, is but a faint illumination of that greater paradox, the absolute obedience and the saving death of Jesus Christ.

The Death of Jeroboam's Child   (14:1-20)

Bibliography

Seebass, H. "Tradition und Interpretation bei Jehu ben Chanani und Ahia von Silo." *VT* 25 (1975) 175–90.

Translation

¹ *At that time Abijah the son of Jeroboam became ill.* ² *And Jeroboam said to his wife, "Get up, please, and disguise yourself so they won't know that you are wife to Jeroboam, and go off to Shiloh. Behold, that is where Ahijah the prophet is—the one who spoke to me* ᵃ*about reigning* ᵃ *over this people.* ³ *And take in your hand ten loaves of bread, with cakes and a jar of honey, and come to him. He will tell you what is to happen with the boy."* ⁴ *So Jeroboam's wife did so: she arose, went off to Shiloh, and came to the house of Ahijah.*

Now Ahijah was unable to see because his eyes could not focus for old age. ⁵ *So Yahweh said to Ahijah, "Behold, Jeroboam's wife is coming* ᵃ *to seek an oracle from you concerning* ᵇ *her son, because he is ill. So and so shall you say unto her. And it will be that, when she enters, she will appear as another person."* ⁶ *So when Ahijah heard the noise of her feet approaching* ᵃ *the door, he said, "Enter, wife of Jeroboam. Why are you pretending to be another person? As for me, I am sent to you heavily burdened.* ⁷ *Go, say to Jeroboam, 'Thus says Yahweh God of Israel, "Because I exalted you from the midst of the people, appointing you as prince over my people Israel,* ⁸ *and tearing the kingship from the house of David and giving it to you; but you have not behaved like my servant David, who kept my commandments and who walked after me with all his heart, doing exclusively* ᵃ *what is right in my eyes;* ⁹ *and you have behaved worse than any who preceded you, going and making yourself other gods and molten images to infuriate me, casting me behind your back;* ¹⁰ *therefore I am about to bring disaster upon* ᵃ *the house of Jeroboam:*

"And I will cut off the one belonging to Jeroboam
  who urinates against the wall,
    helpless and abandoned in Israel;
and I will burn up after the house of Jeroboam
  as one burns dung until it is gone!

¹¹ *Whoever belonging to Jeroboam dies in the city*
  the dogs will devour,
and whoever dies in the open field
  the birds of the heaven will devour."

For Yahweh has said it!'

¹² *"Now you, arise; go to your house. Just as your feet enter* ᵃ *the city the child shall die.* ¹³ *And all Israel shall mourn for him and shall bury him, for this one alone of those belonging to Jeroboam shall enter a grave, inasmuch as there has been found*

in him something good in the consideration of Yahweh, God of Israel, with respect to the house of Jeroboam. ¹⁴ And Yahweh will raise him up a king over Israel who will cut off the house of Jeroboam. ᵃ This today? And what indeed next? ᵃ ¹⁵ And Yahweh will smite Israel just as a reed is battered in the water; and he will uproot Israel from this good ground which he gave to their fathers, and will scatter them beyond the Euphrates because they made their Asherim, infuriating Yahweh. ¹⁶ So he will give up on Israel on account of Jeroboam's errors, by which he sinned and by which he made Israel to sin."

¹⁷ So Jeroboam's wife arose, took her journey, and entered Tirzah. She entered the city gate just as the lad died. ¹⁸ And all Israel buried him and mourned for him, according to the word of Yahweh, which he spoke by means of his servant Ahijah the prophet. ¹⁹ Now the rest of the acts of Jeroboam, how he fought and how he ruled, behold they are written in the Book of the Chronicles of the Israelite kings. ²⁰ And the years ᵃ during which Jeroboam reigned were twenty-two years, and he slept with his fathers. And his son Nadab reigned in his stead.

Notes

14:1–20 MT are omitted in G^BL.

2.a-a. G⁰, Syr, Tg, Vg, reading Heb. לִמְלֹךְ "to reign." This same *Vorlage* is misread by MT לְמֶלֶךְ "to a king," which makes no sense in this context.

5.a. Reading בָּאָה (ptcp fem) "coming" for MT's inappropriate qal fem sing (בָּאָה.) "she came."

5.b. Reading עַל "upon" for MT אֶל "to."

6.a. Reading pl for MT fem sing; MT wrongly takes "noise" (קֹל) as subject.

8.a. MT (רַק) "only." Mss, Syr, Vg omit.

10.a. Reading עַל "upon" for MT אֶל "to."

12.a. MT בְּבֹאָה, intended as a prepositional phrase with infinitive (בְּבוֹא "in coming"; cf. *BH*mg), is corrupt.

14.a-a. On restoring this severely garbled line, cf. *HOTTP*, 322; *Prophet against Prophet*, 85.

20.a. Lit. "days," a Heb. idiom for "year, years."

Form/Structure/Setting

Another Ahijah story
[Dtr transition, 14:1aα]
1. Jeroboam seeks a revelation of healing
   a. Exposition: Jeroboam's ill son, v 1αβb
   b. Jeroboam instructs his wife
     (1) A trip to Shiloh, v 2
     (2) Gifts for Ahijah, v 3a
     (3) The anticipated oracle of wellbeing, v 3b
   c. Narrative of compliance, v 4a
2. Ahijah reveals doom on Jeroboam's house
   a. A symbolic display of perspicacity
     (1) Yahweh informs Ahijah
       (a) Ahijah's blindness, v 4b
       (b) Yahweh apprises and instructs, v 5
     (2) Ahijah's challenging welcome, v 6a

    b. A grim announcement
    Transitional introduction, v 6b
[Dtr: Oracle against the house of Jeroboam
  1. Invective
    a. Failure to live up to the privilege of replacing David's house, vv 7–8
    b. Provoking Yahweh by making idols, v 9
  2. Threat (two ancient tirades against Jeroboam's house), v 10aα
    a. Destruction amid disgrace, v 10aβb
    b. Desecration of the dead, v 11]
The story continued
        (1) Command for her portentous return, v 12
        (2) Announcements
            (a) of the child's symbolic funeral, v 13
            (b) of an ordained instrument of destruction, v 14aα
[Gloss, v 14aβb]
[Expansion: An anti-Jeroboam theology of the exile, vv 15–16]
    c. Narrative of compliance
        (1) The wife's return and the child's death, v 17
        (2) His funeral as prophetic fulfillment, v 18
[Dtr: Closing summary for Jeroboam, vv 19–20]

For some uncomprehended reason, G^{BL} do not have these verses, but paraphrase parts of them in 12:24$^{g\text{-}n}$. The content is another heavily redacted prophet story, as in 11:29–40 from the school of Ahijah, and belonging to the succession-oracle subgenre. The story has a simple, two-part structure. In the first part, Jeroboam seeks a favorable oracle concerning his sick son, the heir apparent, instructing his wife in such a way as to obtain a more sympathetic revelation. In the second part, Yahweh frustrates Jeroboam's stratagem through direct revelation to Ahijah, who then follows Yahweh's instructions by announcing to Jeroboam's wife that the child is to die as soon as she returns home, explaining also that the people's mourning is to be not only for the child but for the entire house of Jeroboam, since the child alone will be found worthy to receive burial. The narrative of compliance at the end states simply that the child does die as predicted, and that this occurs as the fulfillment of Ahijah's word.

    Like 11:29–40, this narrative claims for Yahweh the right to specify who shall succeed to the kingship. It looks as if it may not be the sick young child, Abijah. Jeroboam tries to remedy the deadly illness by deceiving Ahijah into a generous oracle of restoration. It does not work; the oracle is for immediate death. But this death is symbolic of the death of Jeroboam's entire household. Jeroboam has attempted to manipulate the supernatural in the interests of his own dynasty, but Yahweh strikes down the earliest claimant of this line, announcing (v 14a) that other heirs of Jeroboam's line would be cut off by a new king, one who would be raised up by Yahweh for this very purpose.

    The untutored reader finds it difficult to read the prophet story this way because of the numerous interpolations that have cluttered the text. The worst of these is Dtr's own oracle against the house of Jeroboam, including invective and threat in the pattern of the classical judgment oracle, in vv 7–11. The prophet story does not deliver any specific charge against Jeroboam; Yahweh does not need an excuse for what he does. But Dtr supplies two good reasons: (1) the failure of Jeroboam to keep the commandments as David did; (2) his fabrication of "other gods" and "molten images," evidently the golden calves. Dtr is quite furious in his denunciation, declaring that Jeroboam is worse than all who preceded him (v 9), which must mean David as well as Solomon in light of the plural verb in the relative clause. He then announces Yahweh's severe judgment by quoting two scurrilous ditties deriding the house of Jeroboam (vv 10–11). Each is a poetic couplet, the first with a tricolon and a bicolon, the second with two bicolons. The first is ribald and flagrantly offensive, going out of its way to refer to a male person as one who urinates against the wall and comparing Jeroboam's house to dung. It and the second ditty are quoted by Dtr once again in 21:21, 24; the second is quoted by him in 16:4.

Dtr is responsible for the introductory transition at the beginning of v 1 (cf. 11:29), loosely linking this story with the preceding. He is also responsible for the closing summary for Jeroboam in vv 19–20. This passage also contains a post-deuteronomistic expansion in vv 15–16 that blames Jeroboam for the exile; also a scribal gloss in v 14 (see *Notes*).

Comment

1–6 Jeroboam's residence at this time is at Tirzah (cf. v 17), westward from Penuel and close to Shechem on the wadi Fariah. From Jeroboam's instruction to his wife we are to suppose that he dreads Ahijah's condemnation and wants her to appear as an ordinary woman. She is to go to Shiloh, in Ephraim, off the main Shechem-Jerusalem road. Since Ahijah brought him his original oracle of appointment, Jeroboam hopefully looks to him now for another favorable prophecy, an oracle of healing. His wife is to present the prophet with a modest gift (cf. 2 Kgs 5:22–23), her token of respect. Ahijah can no longer see well, but he is forewarned by Yahweh's revelation. To show his prophetic perspicacity, he identifies her before she enters his house, rebuking her for pretending to be someone else. "I am sent to you heavily burdened" sounds strange on the lips of a man almost blind, who cannot move from his house. These are technical phrases used by prophets to describe themselves: as messengers of Yahweh they are sent; the oracles they bring constitute a heavy burden. These phrases immediately alert Jeroboam's wife to the fact that the prophet's message cannot bode well for her.

7–11 Dtr has Ahijah repeat the language of Jeroboam's appointment from original material at 11:34. As there, the term "prince," נָשִׂיא, here נָגִיד, seems to imply the predynastic element of divine appointment (1 Sam 10:1, 2 Sam 5:2). Although the Ahijah story of chap. 11 had not made emulation of David's obedience a condition (this appears only in Dtr material in vv 38–39), Dtr here makes Jeroboam's failure to keep this condition the reason for his condemnation. As has been observed, in v 9 Dtr goes a bit overboard in comparing

Jeroboam with his predecessors, since David has to be included in the comparison, and he had not done any evil at all. The making of the golden calves constituted, for Dtr, infuriating Yahweh, casting him behind one's back. The phrase in v 10, עצור ועזוב, has been much discussed (cf. P. Saydon, *VT* 2 [1952] 371–74). It apparently means "helpless and abandoned," in Heb. an alliterative phrase of utter loathing. V 11 predicts, with v 13, the nonburial of Jeroboam's heirs, which is for Jews always the ultimate horror and humiliation.

12–16 Jeroboam's wife is instructed to depart. So pervasive is the power of Yahweh's control that the child is set to die at the very instant her feet enter the city. Israel shall then mourn, giving him a burial that shall be denied others of his family; because Abijah is still a child he has a fragment of good that is altogether absent in the others. As v 14 says, Yahweh will not leave the downfall of Jeroboam's house to others, but will take direct charge by raising up for himself a new king to perform it. Vigorous language is used in v 15 to depict a late commentator's concept of Israel's doom: she will be smitten, uprooted, scattered beyond the Euphrates (the Babylonian exile), simply because she infuriated Yahweh by making Asherim, i.e., representations of the Canaanite goddess of fertility. V 16 is drastic: Yahweh will give up on Israel, i.e., renounce their election, just because of Jeroboam's sins.

17–18 The story's conclusion is strikingly anticlimactic, reporting Jeroboam's wife's conformity to her instructions, the child's death and burial, and the instrumental cause of it all—Yahweh's word through Ahijah his servant.

19–20 The final notice for Jeroboam makes special mention of what must have been great feats of "fighting" and "ruling." According to the usual pattern, the annals are mentioned for further reference, then the length of Jeroboam's reign, together with the customary formulas for death and burial, and his succession by Nadab.

Explanation

Dtr's derision seems unworthy of those who claim to cherish a biblical attitude of patient understanding in the midst of judgment. It is rather from the primitive prophet story that moderns can best learn, for it is as true today as ever that spiritual power must prevail over the secular, not in theocratic imperialism but in the free, democratic attitude of severe, yet loyal, criticism.

THE CHRONOLOGY OF THE HEBREW KINGS

Our discussion has come now to the point where it is necessary to offer some explanations concerning the chronology of the reigns mentioned in this book. We have encountered the figure of forty years for Solomon's reign (11:42) and of twenty-two years for the reign of Jeroboam (14:20). As we read further we shall find that a length of reign is given for each Judahite and Israelite ruler. We shall further discover that the accession dates for the various kings are given in terms of the opposite king's tenure. Mainly, the Greek recensions agree with the Hebrew figures, but toward the end of the book serious discrepancies begin to arise.

It is not our intent to provide the user of this commentary with the complete discussion that this difficult subject requires. This may be sought in the works listed in the *Bibliography*. For a fairly comprehensive summary of opposing views and probable solutions, the reader may refer to the writer's articles, "Chronology of the Old Testament," in *IDB* I, 580–99; also a supplemental article in *IDBSup* 161–66. Here we present only what is absolutely essential for the intelligent use of the commentary.

The Book of 1 Kgs falls roughly into the period from David's death to the end of the Omride dynasty. We know that Rehoboam of Judah and Jeroboam of Israel began their respective reigns at the same time, but we do not know the date. We can discover the absolute date of Ahab's death and of Jehu's accession, however, from two separate records of the Assyrian king, Shalmaneser III (859–824 B.C.). In this king's Monolith Inscription (*ANET* 278) he describes his battle at Qarqar against Ahab and his Syrian allies, an event that took place in his sixth year of reign, 853. In his annals (*ANET* 280), he claims to have received tribute from Jehu in his eighteenth year, 841 B.C. (see also a carving of Jehu cringing before him on the Black Obelisk, *ANEP* 122). Now, it is stated in 1 Kgs 22:51 that Ahab's son Ahaziah reigned two years, and in 2 Kgs 3:1 that his second son, Joram, reigned twelve years. Joram was the Israelite king who was murdered by Jehu together with Judah's Ahaziah (2 Kgs 9:24, 27). We have a problem here because two Israelite kings who together reigned for fourteen years must be fitted between the 853 of the Ahab inscription and the 841 of the Jehu inscription. The solution lies in the recognition that the Northern Kingdom was counting reigns by a method (called antedating or nonaccession year) that ascribed the last year of reign to the dying king but at the same time counted it for his successor, thus producing one year too many in each reign. That is clearly what happened here; Ahaziah actually reigned only one year, and Joram eleven years, making a total of the twelve years required for the interval between 853 and 841, assuming that Ahab died in 853.

It should be possible on this basis to count backward and find the date for the disruption—also the accession of Rehoboam and Jeroboam. As we make this tally we discover that the parallel sums do not agree. In Judah we have Rehoboam (17), Abijam (3), Asa (41), Jehoshaphat (25), Jehoram

(8), and Ahaziah (1), a total of 95 years. In Israel we have Jeroboam (22), Nadab (2), Baasha (24), Elah (2), Omri (12), Ahab (22), Ahaziah (2), and Joram (12), a total of 98 years, plus the seven days of Zimri. True, two of the excess Israelite years have already been accounted for in the antedating method used for Ahaziah and Joram, and as we test further we find evidence that Israel used this method from the very beginning, as in the notices that Nadab acceded in Asa's second year, reigning for two years (15:25), while his successor began to reign in Asa's third year (15:28). On close inspection it appears, however, that the Judahite scribes employed a different method of reckoning (postdating or accession year), in which a new reign was not counted until the following new year, thus producing an accurate year-count from reign to reign. It seems also that the Judahites switched to the Northern method under the influence of the house of Ahab and dropped it later in favor of the original method. We discover also that the Israelite kings counted their years from a new year in the spring while the Judahites counted from a new year in the fall. Also, there is evidence that Jehoshaphat may have been coregent with his father Asa, counting his reign from that date, and that his son Jehoram may have been coregent with him, the basis in 2 Kgs 1:17 of Joram of Israel's synchronism. Despite all these complexities, it is possible to bring all the reigns and synchronisms into a meaningful pattern, following the methods particularly of Edwin R. Thiele. His assumption has been that the Hebrew scribes knew what they were doing and were reasonably consistent about doing it; also that the MT has carefully guarded these figures against corruptions, providing the basis for a consistent and accurate chronology if one only respects the methods that were followed by the scribes. In other words, the complexity of these figures shows neither stupidity, nor tendentious tampering, nor careless error.

Though the number of scholars who accept Thiele's method is growing, it clearly does not satisfy all. Among Thiele's critics are those who would emphasize the numerous discrepancies between the MT and the LXX. Thus: 1 Kgs 15:2, Abijam reigns 3 years (G 6); 15:9, Asa accedes in 20 Jeroboam (G 24); 16:8, Elah accedes in 26 Asa (G 20); 16:10, Zimri accedes in 27 Asa (G^B om, G^L 22); 16:15, Zimri reigns 7 days (G^B years, G^L days); 16:29, Ahab accedes in 38 Asa (G 2 Jehoshaphat); 22:41, Jehoshaphat accedes in 4 Ahab (G^B *Kaige* = MT; G^L om; G^{BL} 16:28⁻ 11 Omri); 22:51, Ahaziah accedes in 17 Jehoshaphat (G^L 24); 2 Kgs 1:17, Joram accedes in 2 Jehoram (G^L 1:18 = MT, G^B 1:18, 18 Jehoshaphat); 3:1, Joram accedes in 18 Jehoshaphat (G^B = MT; G^L om); 8:25, Ahaziah accedes in 12 Joram (G^B = MT, G^L 11).

It would not be possible to rely upon the LXX for the entire period of the Hebrew kingdoms, because after the account of the early reigns the discrepancies disappear from the major recensions. This is not simply because the *Kaige* text prevails in G^B, for that reappeared already in 1 Kgs 22, in and after which some serious disagreements continue to emerge. This ought to forewarn the Bible student that the LXX differences may have been produced by an attempt to correct the underlying Hebrew text. One scholar, J. D. Shenkel, has recently argued, nonetheless, that although G^B is badly mixed up, G^L does preserve the original figures in those passages where it differs from MT (*Chronology and Recensional Development in the Greek Text of Kings*

[Cambridge, Mass.: Harvard University Press 1968]). Shenkel argues that "Jehoshaphat" does not belong in 2 Kgs 3, after the notice of his death in 1 Kgs 22:50; therefore G^L is correct in substituting "Ahaziah." All the preceding figures for the respective kings have to be adjusted accordingly; MT has been tendentious in changing them in the first place. But the present writer has strong objections to this procedure. When G^L omits Joram's synchronism for Jehoshaphat's eighteenth year in 2 Kgs 3:1, it disrupts the regular pattern of the deuteronomistic introduction, and hence shows that it is he who is tendentious. In *JTS* 21 (1970) 118–31, D. W. Gooding showed that 1 Kgs 16:28[+], drawing Jehoshaphat's reign forward, is a doctrinaire adaptation of 22:41–51. The obvious explanation for G^L's revision is that it is a misguided attempt to make sense out of apparently conflicting evidence for Omri's reign in 16:23. The MT meant the synchronism with Asa's thirty-first year to mark Omri's victory over Tibni, and the length of Omri's reign to begin with his seizure of power from Zimri. It is only by following the MT and applying all the methods of the Hebrew scribes, not by adopting G^L, that this fits into the overall chronology of the various kings.

To conclude, we have reason to believe that the following dates for the kings are correct; (1) of *Judah:* Rehoboam, 931–913; Abijam, 913–911; Asa, 911–870; Jehoshaphat, 870–848; Jehoram, 848–841; Ahaziah, 841. (2) of *Israel:* Jeroboam, 931–910; Nadab, 910–909; Baasha, 909–886; Elah, 886–885; Zimri, 885; Omri, 885–874; Ahab, 874–853; Ahaziah, 853; Joram, 852–841.

The Reign of Rehoboam   (14:21-31)

Bibliography

Beyer, G. "Das Festungssystem Rehoboams." *ZDPV* 54 (1931) 113–34. **Blau, O.** "Sisaqs Zug gegen Juda aus dem Denkmal bei Karnak erläutert." *ZDMG* 15 (1861) 233–50. **Elizur, Y.** "The Biblical Account of Shishak's Invasion: Prophetic Historiosophy versus Reality" (Heb.). *Fourth World Congress of Jewish Studies,* I. Jerusalem 1967. **Mazar, B.** "The Campaign of Pharaoh Shishak to Palestine." VTSup 4 (1957) 57–66.

Translation

[21] *And Rehoboam son of Solomon reigned in Judah.[a] Rehoboam was [b]forty-one[b] years old at his accession, and he reigned seventeen[c] years in Jerusalem, the city which Yahweh chose, to place his name there, out of all the tribes of Israel. And the name of his mother was Naamah[d] the Ammonitess.* [22] *And Rehoboam[a] did what was evil before Yahweh. And they provoked him to jealousy, more than all that their fathers had done, by their sins which they committed.* [23] *And [a]even they too[a] built themselves country shrines and standing stones and Asherim, upon every high hill and beneath every green tree.* [24] *And even the [a]sacred prostitute[a] existed in the land. They behaved [b]according to[b] every abomination of the nations which Yahweh had driven away before the Israelites.*

[25] *In King Rehoboam's fifth year Shishak[a] king of Egypt came up against Jerusalem* [26] *and seized[a] the treasuries of Yahweh's temple and the treasuries of the king's house; and he took everything;[b] he even took all the golden shields which Solomon had made.* [27] *So [a]the king[a] made to replace them bronze shields, entrusting them to the care of the chief retainers guarding the entranceway to the king's house.* [28] *It was customary whenever the king entered Yahweh's temple for the retainers to carry them, and to return them again to the retainer's armory.*

[29] *Now the rest of the acts of Rehoboam, and all that he did, are they not written in the Book of the Chronicles of the Judahite Kings?* [30] *And there was hostility between Rehoboam and Jeroboam continually.* [31] *And Rehoboam slept with his fathers and was buried with his fathers in the city of David. (And the name of his mother was Naamah[a] the Ammonitess.) And Abijam[b] his son reigned in his stead.*

Notes

21.a. MT and G[B]. G[L] adds "and Benjamin," consistently with the ideology of G in 11:32, 36.

21.b-b. LXX 12:24[a] "sixteen."

21.c. *Idem* "twelve."

21.d. MT and G[L]. G[B] corr. Cf. 15:2, 10.

22.a. G[BL]. MT "Judah"; Chr omits. MT is explicable as a harmonization toward the second part of the verse, in which an undefined plurality sin, but G probably deserves preference as *lectio difficilior.*

23.a-a. MT. G[BL] "they."

24.a-a. MT. G[BL] σύνδεσμος = Heb. קשר, "conspiracy," involving transposition and misreading of ד as ר, from MT קדש "prostitute."

24.b-b. MT. G^{BL} "some of" (from Heb. מִכָּל).
25.a. Q; K "Sho/ushak." G^{BL} Σουσακείμ = Heb. ששכים.
26.a. MT. G^{BL} has pleonastic "all."
26.b. MT. G^{BL} "the golden spears which David had taken from the hand of the servants of Hadad-ezer king of Zobah and had brought to Jerusalem." This appears to be an independent midrash on 2 Sam 10.
27.a-a. MT "King Rehoboam"; G^{BL} "Rehoboam the king." Consistently with our previously articulated text-critical rule, where proper names are transposed in the major witnesses with the title, the former is of doubtful originality and should be omitted.
31.a. Cf. v 4 (see *Comment*).
31.b. MT. G^{BL}, Chr consistently change this to the Yahweh-name "Abijah."

Form/Structure/Setting

[Dtr: Introductory summary for Rehoboam, vv 21–22a]
[Expansion: Theological condemnation of Judah's cultic sins, vv 22b–24]
Extract from the Book of the Chronicles of the Judahite Kings, vv 25–26
Memorandum from the temple archives, vv 27–28
[Dtr: Closing summary for Rehoboam, vv 29–31]

Original material in the Rehoboam section consists of our first extract from the Book of the Chronicles of the Judahite Kings (mentioned for the first time in v 29), a memorandum on the bronze shields from the temple records, and the date used for Dtr's opening and closing summaries. The introductory summary gives us Rehoboam's age at his accession together with his length of reign (41 actual years), the name of his mother, and a brief statement to the effect that he did evil before Yahweh. This is expanded by a late member of the deuteronomistic school (vv 22b–24) to specify the various iniquities and place the blame on the entire nation. The closing summary mentions the archives, emphasizing the continual hostility that existed toward Jeroboam; it then gives notice of Rehoboam's death and burial, repeats the name of his mother, and states the fact of Abijam's succession.

Comment

21–24 As usual, the opening summary mentions that Jerusalem is the place of Rehoboam's reign, but Dtr shows us clearly in this instance that he is the author by throwing in his honorific descriptions of that city (cf. 11:13, 26). Rehoboam's mother Naamah is mentioned because she automatically became queen mother; that she was an Ammonitess is no surprise in view of Solomon's practice of marrying foreign women. Dtr does not rate Rehoboam as a righteous king; he is blamed instead for doing what Yahweh considers evil. Dtr himself does not say what evil he did; this is reserved for the expansion beginning in v 22b, which is motivated by specific information needed for filling out this word of summary condemnation. The supplementer begins and ends with a theological judgment. He states that Yahweh had been provoked to jealousy, that Rehoboam's subjects did worse sins than all previous generations. They actually did what the northerners were being condemned for: built country-shrines. To this is added the questionable practice of erecting מצבות, "standing stones," and the baalistic Asherim.

This occurred at every suitable place, "upon every high hill and beneath every green tree" (Deut 12:2, 2 Kgs 16:4, 17:10, Jer 2:20, 3:6, 17:2, Ezek 6:13). But worst of all, the people tolerated the odious Canaanite rite of sacred prostitution, male and female (קדש, a collective, stands for both); cf. 15:12. These are expressly forbidden in Deut 23:18. In sum, the Judahites followed the "abominations." התועבת (a frequent term in Deut, Dtr, and the prophets), of the dispossessed nations.

25–28 Rehoboam's fifth year was 926/25 B.C. Shishak or Shoshenq ruled Egypt from *ca.* 940 to *ca.* 915 B.C. The Amon temple in Karnak sheds invaluable light on this text's laconic report about Shishak's raid in this year. An inscription on its walls lists more than one hundred fifty cities in Judah and Israel that this pharaoh claims to have captured. At most this means that he took plunder from towns which he was able to overwhelm, and tribute from stronger cities, such as Jerusalem. It may have been under siege and finally yielded to the point of agreeing to be his vassal and pay him tribute. This is the evident meaning of our text's statement about handing over the content of the two treasuries—that of the temple and that of the royal palace—together with the golden shields of Solomon. Although the kingdom of Judah and city of Jerusalem were thereby drastically impoverished, they did not continue to suffer significantly under Shishak's control. This Egyptian monarch was unable to set up a permanent empire in Palestine. In fact, two centuries were to pass before formidable Egyptian attacks on Palestine would resume. As the temple report in vv 27–28 indicates, bronze shields were cast to replace the gold ones. They were used by the palace guards on ceremonial occasions, as when the king would enter Yahweh's temple.

29–31 Since there is no mention of actual fighting between Rehoboam and Jeroboam, v 31 chooses the translation, "hostility." There would have been continual border incidents, and the kings would have refused to exchange ambassadors. For no apparent reason, v 31 repeats v 21's item about the name of Rehoboam's mother. This may be a secondary gloss since the introductory formula is the normal place for this information.

The Reign of Abijam (15:1-8)

Translation

¹ Now in the eighteenth year ᵃof the reign ofᵃ Jeroboam son of Nebat, Abijam became king over Judah. ² Threeᵃ years he reigned.ᵇ And the name of his mother was ᶜMaacah daughter of Abishalom.ᶜ ³And he walked in allᵃ the sins of his father which he committed prior to him; and his heart was not wholly loyal to Yahweh in the way his father David'sᵇ was. ⁴Indeed, it was because of David ᵃthat Yahweh appointed him as a lamp,ᵃ in order to raise up his sonᵇ after him and to establish Jerusalem; ⁵that is, David performed what was right in Yahweh's eyes, not departing from anything that he commanded him all the days of his life.ᵃ ⁶ᵃAnd hostility had existed between Rehoboam and Jeroboam all the days of his life.ᵃᵇ ⁷Now the remainder of Abijam's actions, and all that he did, are they not written ᵃin the Book of the Chronicles of the Judahite Kings?ᵃ And hostility existed between Abijam and Jeroboam. ⁸And Abijam slept with his fathers,ᵃ and they buried him in the city of David. And Asa his son reigned in his place.

Notes

1.a-a. Gᴮᴸ. MT "of king." Most modern translations follow MT because this is the regular form and is translated accordingly in the Gr. of other passages. Nevertheless, it is better to follow the Gr. here: βασιλεύοντος ᾽Ιεροβοάμ = Heb. ירבעם למלך "of the reign of Jeroboam"; v 9, introducing Asa, offers the normal formula for a southern king's synchronism with a king of the north, in this case the same Jeroboam. The order of the Heb., copied exactly by the Gr., has (1) "in the year," (2) numeral, (3) "belonging to" (ל), with proper name "Jeroboam," (4) title: king of Israel. In other words, the proper name appears prior to the title—not as in 15:1, where the author in fact denies Jeroboam the title "king" and only identifies him by his father. The intent here, then, is to accredit Jeroboam with a reign (by which to count Judahite kings!) but to deny him the title "king."

2.a. MT. Gᴮᴸ "and six."

2.b. Gᴮ, here writing the aorist in place of OG's historical present βασιλεύει in v 1. MT and Gᴸ add explicative "in Jerusalem" (the usual Dtr formulation for southern kings).

2.c-c. Cf. v 10. Chr "Micaiah daughter of Uriel from Gibeah" (Par "Gibeon") fabricates names for the purpose of exegetical harmonization.

3.a. MT. Gᴮᴸ omit; this may be ideological or through haplography.

3.b. MT, Gᴮ omits (haplography from previous occurrence in this verse).

4.a-a. Gᴮ is preferred in its omission of MT, Gᴸ "in Jerusalem," but its word κατάλειμμα, normally = שארית "remnant," cannot render MT ניר "light" (Gᴸ = Gᴮ).

4.b. MT, sticking to the old Dtr ideology. Gᴮᴸ "sons" views the Davidic dynasty historically, as composed of numerous individual kings.

5.a. Gᴮ. MT and Gᴸ add the explanatory comment, "except in the matter of Uriah the Hittite." Cf. HOTTP, 323.

6.a-a. MT. Gᴮᴸ omit through haplography. Cf. 14:30 (see HOTTP, 323).

6.b. Chr inserts a long passage.

7.a-a. Chr "in the interpretation (Par "book") of the prophet Iddo?"

8.a. Gᴮᴸ "in Jeroboam's twenty-fourth year" is erratic both in its numerology and in its placement of a synchronism in a closing formula.

Form/Structure/Setting

[Dtr: The reign of Abijam
1. Introductory summary, 15:1-2

2. Theological assessment, vv 3–5]
Extract from the Book of the Chronicles of the Judahite Kings, v 6
[3. Dtr: Closing summary, vv 7a, 8]
Extract from the Book of the Chronicles of the Judahite Kings, v 7b

In v 6 an extract is repeated from the archives concerning hostility under
Rehoboam and Jeroboam (cf. 14:30), and v 7b presents a similar extract
concerning Abijam and Jeroboam. Otherwise, the notice on Abijam comes
entirely from Dtr. His introductory summary offers a theological assessment
that goes to unusual lengths in explaining why Yahweh tolerated this king.
Otherwise it and the closing summary follow the customary pattern.

Comment

The name of Rehoboam's successor is given as Abijam in Kgs and Abijah
in Chr. The latter is found fairly frequently and has the additional advantage
of reflecting late concepts of orthodoxy. Its meaning is, "My Father is Yah-
(weh)," whereas "Abijam" must mean "My Father is Yam," the mythical
Sea-god known from Ugaritic literature. This, however, only argues for the
probable originality of "Abijam," which was undoubtedly interpreted meta-
phorically in the early Judahite court. For the name of Abijam's mother,
Chr has an entirely different name (see *Notes*), which may be original in light
of the fact that Asa is given the same mother (vv 10, 13). Alternatively, because
Abijam's reign was so short, Maacah may simply have continued as גְּבִירָה,
"queen mother," a position of power and influence. Her father, "Abishalom,"
may be the same as Solomon's dead brother (but see 2 Sam 14:27). Abijam
is blamed for committing all his father's sins, hence not wholly following
David's loyalty. Dtr explains that Yahweh used him as a lamp (נִיר; cf. 11:36)
by which to raise up a son who would "establish" Jerusalem. V 6 is virtually
identical to 14:30 and must be given a pluperfect translation; both notices
probably go back to the same archival item. In his concluding summary,
Dtr is not able to mention any particular notable feature of Abijam's reign.
Just prior to the usual death notice, he inserts another archival item stating
that Abijam continued his father's policy of hostile relationships with Jeroboam.

The Reign of Asa (15:9-24)

Bibliography

Barrick, W. B. "On the 'Removal of the "High-Places"'" in 1–2 Kings." *Bib* 55 (1974) 257–59. **Malamat, A.** *The Aramaeans in Aram Naharaim and the Rise of their States* (Heb). Diss. Hebrew University, 1952. **Melin, G.** "Die Stellung der Geᵇira im Staate Juda (1 K 15:13)." *TZ* 10 (1954) 161–75. **Unger, M. F.** *Israel and the Aramaeans of Damascus.* London: J. Clarke & Co., 1957.

Translation

[9] *Now in the twentieth[a] year of Jeroboam king of Israel [b]Asa king of Judah began to reign,[b] [10] and for forty-one years he reigned in Jerusalem. And the name of his mother was Maacah[a] daughter of Abishalom. [11] And Asa performed what was right in the eyes of Yahweh, like David his father. [12] And he dismissed the [a]cult prostitutes[a] from the land, and removed all the idols which his fathers,[b] [13] even Maacah his mother, had made, so that he deposed her from the office of queen mother. She had made a detestable cult object for Asherah, so that Asa had to cut down her cult object and burn it in [14] the wadi Kidron. But they[a] did not remove the country shrines; nevertheless, Asa's own heart was continually loyal toward Yahweh. [15] And [a]he brought[a] the sacral booty[b] of his father, with the sacral booty [c]of his own,[c] into the temple of Yahweh, silver and gold and artifacts. [16] And hostility existed between Asa and Baasha[a] throughout all their days. [17] Now Baasha king of Israel came up against Judah. And he constructed Ramah [a]so as to prevent anyone wishing to depart from or enter in[a] to Asa king of Judah. [18] Then Asa took[a] the silver and the gold that [b]were still left[b] in the treasure-rooms [c]of Yahweh's temple [d]and in[d] the treasure-rooms[c] of [e]the king's[e] house, and entrusted them into the hand[f] of his servants. And King Asa sent them to Ben-Hadad, the son of Tabrimmon, son of Hezion, the king of Syria who was dwelling in Damascus, with the following message: [19a]"There is[a] a treaty between me [b]and you,[b] between[c] my father and your father. Behold, I have sent you a gift of silver and gold; come, break your treaty with Baasha king of Israel so that he will withdraw from me." [20] And Ben-Hadad hearkened to King Asa, dispatching whatever officers of [a]the armed forces[a] were available to him against the cities of Israel. And he[b] attacked Iyyon, Dan, and Abel-beth-maacah;[c] also all of Kinneroth[d] adjoining the entire territory of Naphtali. [21] So when Baasha heard of it, he left off building Ramah, and [a]stayed in[a] Tirzah. [22] Then King Asa made a proclamation to entire Judah, leaving nobody free, that they should carry away the stones of Ramah, with its timbers, with which Baasha had been building. And [a]King Asa[a] built Geba of Benjamin and Mizpah with them.[b] [23] Now the remainder of[a] Asa's acts, including all his works of greatness[b] which he did [c]and the cities that he built,[c] are these not written in the Book [d]of the Chronicles of the Judahite Kings?[d] However, at the time of his old age[e] he suffered with his feet. [24] And Asa slept [a]with his fathers[a] and was buried with his fathers in the city of David his father. And Jehoshaphat his son reigned in his place.*

Notes

9.a. MT. G^BL "twenty-fourth"; cf. v 8 LXX.
9.b-b. MT. G^BL "Asa became king over Judah."
10.a. MT. G^BL "Hannah"; cf. v 13.
12.a-a. MT (הקדשים, translated σύνδεσμος in 14:24). Here G^B renders τελετὰς "priests," while G^L renders στήλας = Heb. מַצֵּבוֹת "standing stones." Since the problem of translation cannot have been linguistic, these variations can only be ideological and apologetic.
12.b. Chr inserts a long passage.
14.a. MT. G^BL, Syr, Vg have "he," making Asa the antecedent.
15.a-a. MT, G^B. G^L has paraphrastic "Asa brought into Yahweh's temple."
15.b. MT (קדשי "holy things"; cf. 7:51). Not understanding the word, the Gr. translators offer κίονας "pillars," which does not appear to have a regular Heb. equivalent.
15.c-c. K, G, Syr, Tg, Chr. Q makes the pious correction, "of Yahweh's temple."
16.a. MT, G^L. G^B adds explicative "king of Israel"; cf. v 17.
17.a-a. לבלתי תת יעא רכא) "to prevent departing from or entering in." G^BL τοῦ μὴ εἶναι = היות לבלתי "so it is not."
18.a. G^BL. MT adds pleonastic "all."
18.b-b. MT. G^BL "was found" (sing).
18.c-c. MT, G^L. G^B omits (homoioteleuton).
18.d-d. G^L, Syr. MT "and the"; G^B corr.
18.e-e. MSS, Q. K corr.
18.f. MT. G^BL pl.
19.a-a. MT, noun-clause. The Gr. translators are puzzled by this unusual construction: G^B offers διαθήκη for Heb. בְּרִית "covenant," "treaty," preceded by the impv of διατίθημι "arrange," as though the two were from the same root, but there is no reason to suppose that the Heb. *Vorlage* had a verb. G^L Διαθήκη ἔστω "let there be a treaty" might be a legitimate paraphrase except for the fact that a subjunctive is not suitable when referring to something that occurred in the past—the forefathers' treaty.
19.b-b. MT, G^L. G^B omits (haplography?).
19.c. MT. G^BL "and between" is syndetic, giving better Gr. style.
20.a-a. MT (pl). G^BL have sing with pl gen and the possessive pronoun.
20.b. MT, Par (sing, referring to Ben-hadad). Chr, G pl, choosing "armed forces" as the subject.
20.c. MT. G^BL corr; cf. Chr.
20.d. MT. G^BL corr. Chr מסכנות "storage places"; Par reads Heb. ככרות "surroundings."
21.a-a. MT. G^BL "returned to." MT uses root ישׁב "dwell," G reads root שׁוּב "return." MT is *lectio difficilior*, but makes good sense when understood with reference to Baasha's behavior subsequent to the Syrian invasion.
22.a-a. MT, G^B. G^L "Asa"; Chr omits. A mention of Asa's regal office is to be expected here.
22.b. Chr inserts a long passage.
23.a. G^BL. MT "of all" is not only pleonastic, but clearly enters the text from the two occurrences of וכל "and all" in the immediate sequel.
23.b. G^BL. MT adds "and all" (see above).
23.c-c. MT. G^L "and cities . . ."; G^B omits (haplography?).
23.d-d. Chr "of the kings of Judah and Israel."
23.e. MT and G^B. G^L has interpretive gloss "Asa did what was evil."
24.a-a. MT, G^L. G^B omits (haplography).

Form/Structure/Setting

[Dtr: The reign of Asa
   1. Introductory summary, vv 9–10
   2. Cult reforms and theological assessment, vv 11–14]
Memorandum from the temple archives, v 15

Extract from the Book of the Chronicles of the Judahite Kings, v 16
Narrative of Asa's alliance with Ben-Hadad
  1. The proposal
    a. Baasha's threat: a fort at Ramah, v 17
    b. Asa's embassage to Damascus
      (1) The gift, v 18
      (2) Bribery to betrayal, v 19
  2. The compliance
    a. Preparations for Syrian aggression, v 20a
    b. The campaign, v 20b
  3. The result: favorable conditions for Asa
    a. Baasha withdraws, v 21
    b. Asa builds counterfortresses, v 22
[Dtr: Closing summary for Asa, vv 23–24]

The account of Asa's reign begins with an unusually expansive summary
from Dtr, picking up from the archives a detail of how idolatry affected the
king's own household. Following brief extracts from the temple archives and
the Judahite chronicle, Dtr inserts a detailed political narrative from Asa's
court, telling of his treaty with Syria and of his border defenses. At the conclusion, the Asa account receives a somewhat expanded closing summary in
the usual Dtr format.

Comment

9–15 Jeroboam was still king in Israel when Asa began to reign, but it
would be with Baasha, the leader of a new dynasty, that Asa would have
serious trouble. According to our chronology, Asa appointed Jehoshaphat
to serve as coregent with him during his final three years (his foot trouble
reported in v 23 may have been the cause of this). On the identity of his
"mother," see above on v 2. Dtr finds him to be the first Judahite king to
deserve high praise: he did "what was right in the eyes of Yahweh, like David
his father" (11), and his "heart was continually loyal toward Yahweh" (14).
In particular, he exiled the cult prostitutes, הקּדֵשִׁים, a masc pl, but functioning
as common gender to include both sexes. He also "removed" (i.e.,
destroyed) all the idols (הגלּלים, vocalized for the word "filth," which syna-
gogue-readers were supposed to pronounce) made by his fathers, i.e., "ances-
tors," meaning primarily Solomon. He had to depose Maacah (his grand-
mother), from being גבירה because she had installed a cult object, probably
a wooden plaque, of Asherah (see the pl in 14:23), Canaanite goddess of
fertility (the Earth Mother). He did not suppress the country-shrines, but
Dtr is in no mood to blame him for that. The temple extract in v 15 mentions
without comment that Asa also deposited sacral booty in the temple treasury
(cf. 7:51b), something which Abijam had evidently neglected.
16–22 A summary statement from the Book of the Chronicles of the Judahite Kings introduces the political narrative of vv 16–22. Baasha "came
up," i.e., attacked Judah, apparently without encountering effective resistance.
Most of Benjamin's ancestral territory had been under Jerusalem's control

(see 12:21), but now Baasha fortified Ramah (Samuel's residence, 1 Sam 7:17), about three miles south of the traditional border. As the narrator sees it, this was to prevent northerners from having contact with Asa (that the title, "King Asa," predominates in these verses suggests that the writer is a loyal partisan of this king), though Baasha's true purpose may have been to defend against Judahite aggression. Shishak had pretty well cleaned out the temple's and the palace's treasuries (14:26), but Asa sent what was left to bribe Ben-Hadad to attack Baasha. Since this Syrian king's father and grandfather are mentioned, his relationship to the Rezon of 11:23–25 is problematical. Upon arriving in Damascus, Asa's emissaries ("servants") present a message which (1) calls attention to a treaty between Asa's and Ben-Hadad's respective "fathers" (otherwise unmentioned; there is no solid basis for Noth's proposal [339] to read the noun-clause as a wish); (2) calls attention to the gift; and (3) requests Ben-Hadad to break his treaty with Baasha (also unmentioned elsewhere).

V 20 reads as if the bulk of Ben-Hadad's army may have been occupied elsewhere, but he sent the forces that were available into a raid of three towns in the upper Jordan valley, together with the fertile plain adjacent to the Sea of Galilee and the Galilean uplands as far inland as the border of Naphtali. As our narrator tells it, Baasha left off building Ramah when he heard of this raid and returned to Tirzah, but he is probably ignorant of what probably did happen, viz., that Baasha sent a strong force to drive Ben-Hadad away. In any case, Asa's design was met. Since there were no more Israelite soldiers to defend Ramah, Asa was able to effectuate a universal conscription for taking Ramah down and using its timbers to build his own forts at Geba and Mizpah.

23–24 In Asa's closing summary, Dtr is moved to make special mention of unnamed "works of greatness" and certain cities that were built (or rebuilt). Asa did become old; subsisting on a rich diet, he probably contracted gout, "the ailment of kings." With his approving attitude toward Asa, Dtr is not inclined to judge this illness as some kind of punishment sent from Yahweh.

The Reign of Nadab (15:25–31)

Translation

25 Now Nadab son of Jeroboam began to reign over Israel in the second[a] year of Asa king of Judah. And he reigned over[b] Israel for two years. **26** And he did what was evil in Yahweh's eyes, walking in the way of his father, even in the sin[a] with which he caused Israel to sin. **27** Then Baasha son of Ahijah, [a]belonging to the house of Issachar,[a] formed a conspiracy against him, and he[b] struck him down at Gibbethon belonging to the Philistines while Nadab and all Israel were besieging Gibbethon. **28** And Baasha killed him in the third[a] year of Asa king of Judah [b]and reigned in his place.[b] **29** And it so happened that, [a]as soon as he became king,[a] he struck down the[b] house of Jeroboam. He did not allow to survive a single breathing soul to Jeroboam without destroying it, according to the word of Yahweh which he spoke by means of his servant Ahijah the Shilonite, **30** on account of Jeroboam's sins, [a]which he himself sinned[a] [b]and which[b] he caused Israel to sin[c] in his provocation with which he enraged Yahweh the God of Israel. **31** Now the remainder of Nadab's acts, and all that he did, are these not written in the Book of the Chronicles of the Israelite Kings?[a]

Notes

25.a. G MSS "third," "tenth."
25.b. MT, G^L. G^B "in."
26.a. MT, accurately expressing Dtr theology. G^{BL}, Syr, Vg pl.
27.a-a. MT. G^L "over the house of Bellama/Beddama belonging to Issachar"; G^B *similiter* (corr).
27.b. G^B (cf. v 28). MT and G^L pl.
28.a. G^{MSS} "fourth."
28.b-b. MT, reproducing Dtr terminology. G^B "and he reigned" and G^L "and Baasha reigned over Israel" are paraphrastic.
29.a-a. MT and G^{BL}. MSS, Tg^{MSS} "during his reign" perhaps intend to deny the legitimacy of Baasha's kingship.
29.b. G^B. MT, G^L add interpretive "entire."
30.a-a. MT, G^L. G^B omits (haplography?).
30.b-b. MT. G^{BL} "just as."
30.c. MT and G^L. G^B "and in . . ." differentiates between Jeroboam's causing Israel to sin and his provoking of Yahweh.
31.a. G^{BL} omit the entire v 32. MT adds a gl reading, "and hostility existed between Asa and Baasha throughout all their days" (cf. v 16).

Form/Structure/Setting

[Dtr: The reign of Nadab
1. Introductory summary, v 25
2. Theological assessment, v 26
3. Notice of Baasha's conspiracy, vv 27–28
4. Interpretation as fulfillment of prophecy against Jeroboam's house, vv 29–30
5. Closing summary, v 31]

We know nothing whatever about Nadab except what Dtr has provided in his short statement. There is an opening summary in the usual style, a theological assessment, and a closing summary. In addition, Dtr paraphrases an independent notice about Baasha's conspiracy, incorporating this into his overall statement as in 16:9–10 (compare independent notices in 16:21–22, 24, 34). He of course makes a special point of arguing (vv 29–30) that this event fulfills the prophecy of 14:10–11, 14–16.

Comment

The two years of Nadab's reign really amount to somewhat more than one. Dtr has said that Judah did what was evil (14:22), but has withheld such blame from its kings. Of the northern kings, however, he will have no good to say; Nadab is only the first who will be named evil. This is because he walks in his father's ways, which means not suppressing the golden calves. Because the principle of succession from father to son is not well established in Israel, Baasha son of Ahijah makes a conspiracy and kills him while he is engaged in reducing Gibbethon, a Philistine town on the coastal plain near Gezer. Dtr quotes his entire notice, including a synchronism for Baasha's reign which he will copy from his usual sources in v 33. Dtr goes on to mention that Baasha immediately carried out a blood-purge against Jeroboam's entire "house," i.e., family, fulfilling Ahijah's prophecy (the prophet, from Shiloh in Ephraim, cannot be Baasha's father, since the latter is from Issachar, v 27). Jeroboam's sins are specified as (1) those that he himself committed, and (2) those that he caused Israel to sin, a striking expression of the principle of corporate guilt. One should note that the summary conclusion for Nadab (v 31) lacks a death notice; Nadab did not "sleep with his fathers" because he was struck down by an act of treason and bloody riot.

The Reign of Baasha (15:33—16:7)

Bibliography

Brueggemann, W. "From Dust to Kingship." *ZAW* 84 (1972) 1–16. **Seebass, H.** "Tradition und Interpretation bei Jehu ben Chanani und Ahia von Silo." *VT* 25 (1975) 175–90.

Translation

[33] *In* [a] *the third year of Asa king of Judah, Baasha son of Ahijah began to reign over* [b] *Israel in Tirzah for twenty-four years.* [34] *And he* [a] *did what was evil in Yahweh's eyes, walking in the way of Jeroboam* [b] *and in his sin* [c] *by which he caused Israel to sin.* [16:1] *And it so happened that the word of Yahweh came to* [a] *Jehu son of Hanani against Baasha,* [b] [c] *as follows:* [c] [2] *"In view of the fact that I raised you from the dust and appointed you as leader over my people Israel, and yet you have walked in the way of Jeroboam, causing my people Israel to sin, so as to enrage me through their sins,* [3] *behold, I will* [a] *make it flame up* [a] *behind Baasha and behind his house, equating your* [b] *house with the house of Jeroboam son of Nebat.* [4] *Anyone belonging to Baasha who dies in the city, the dogs shall devour, and anyone of his who dies in the open, the birds of the heaven shall devour."* [5] *Now the remainder of Baasha's acts, and* [a] *whatever he did, and his works of greatness, are these not written in the Book of the Chronicles of the Israelite Kings?* [6] *And Baasha slept with his fathers and was buried in Tirzah. And Elah his son reigned in his place.* [a]

[7] *What is more, by means of Jehu son of Hanani, the prophet, the word of Yahweh came to* [a] *Baasha and to* [b] *his house,* [c] *both concerning* [c] *all the evil that he did in Yahweh's eyes, enraging him through the works of his hands so as to become like the house of Jeroboam, and concerning the way in which he did demolish it.*

Notes

33.a. MT. G[BL] have syndetic "and in."

33.b. MT. G[BL] have interpretive "all Israel."

34.a. MT, G[B]. G[L] has explicative "Baasha."

34.b. MT. G[BL] insert pleonastic "son of Nebat."

34.c. MT. G[BL] pl.

16:1.a. MT. G[BL], ἐν χειρί = Heb. בְּיַד "by the hand" (cf. 16:7).

1.b. MT, G[B]. G[L] adds explicative "king of Israel."

1.c-c. MT, G[L]. G[B] omits (stylistic).

3.a-a. MT. G[BL] ἐξεγείρω = Heb. מֵעִיר "rousing up," a corruption of MT מַבְעִיר "causing to burn."

3.b. MT. G[BL] "his" takes Jeroboam as the antecedent.

5.a. MT. G[BL] have pleonastic "all."

6.a. MT. G[BL] add the chronological gloss, "in the twentieth" (G[c2] "ninth") "year of King Asa."

7.a. MT. G[BL] "against" (= Heb. עַל).

7.b. Idem.

7.c-c. MT, G[L]. G[B] omits. MSS, Syr, Tg[b] "concerning."

Form/Structure/Setting

[Dtr: The reign of Baasha
1. Introductory summary, v 33
2. Theological assessment, v 34
3. Report of Jehu's condemnation
   a. Narrative introduction, 16:1
   b. Invective, v 2
   c. Threat, vv 3–4
4. Closing summary, vv 5–6]
[Expansion, 7]

The reign of Baasha is entirely told in the words of Dtr, who has an abbreviated introduction and theological assessment (15:33–34), and then a prophetic oracle, with invective and threat (16:1–4) followed by the usual concluding summary (vv 5–6). Although ascribed to a certain Jehu ben Hanani, the oracle is an attempt to provide for Baasha something similar to Ahijah's oracle to Jeroboam's wife in 14:7–11. The situations are parallel, for Baasha's son Elah is to die in the same way Nadab did (vv 8–14), in fulfillment of prophecy. This is a point that will be emphasized in v 12, but a postdeuteronomistic expansion in v 7 already drives it home.

Comment

Since the Israelite scribes counted the Judahite reigns according to their own kings' antedating method, it was actually in Asa's second year that Baasha gained the throne. His actual reign was twenty-three years. His evil is judged, as always, by Jeroboam's sin. Nothing is known about Jehu the son of Hanani; Chr mentions him in 2 Chr 19:2, 20:34. Such a prophet may have existed and may have declaimed against Baasha, but Dtr has no other record of this and the oracle is cast entirely in his own customary language. "I raised you from the dust" is melodramatic, and in any case theologically problematic in Yahweh's mouth to someone who murdered his master. "Appointed as leader (נָגִיד)" is borrowed from 14:7. The accusation of sinning like Jeroboam is sharpened by a reference to "enraging" Yahweh (v 2; cf. 14:9, 15:30, 16:7). In the threat, the metaphor of a flame is borrowed from 14:10. As he says, Dtr is equating Baasha's house with the house of Jeroboam. Thus he goes on to cite the grisly ditty of 14:11 (the fulfillment in v 11 quotes the vile ditty of 14:10). In the concluding summary Dtr seems exasperated and quite indifferent in referring vaguely to "whatever he did," but a second glance at the archives reminds him that the reader may also be interested in certain "works of greatness." V 6's death notice is the first to specify the place of burial for a northern king (Tirzah).

The Reign of Elah (16:8–14)

Translation

⁸ᵃ*In the twenty-sixth year of Asa king of Judah*ᵃ *Elah son of Baasha began to reign over Israel* ᵇ*in Tirzah for two years.*ᵇ ⁹*And his servant Zimri,*ᵃ *commander of half his chariotry, conspired against him. Now he was in Tirzah, drinking strong drink in the house of Arza, custodian of the palace property in Tirzah.* ¹⁰*And Zimri got in and struck him down and killed him* ᵃ*(it was the twenty-seventh year of Asa king of Judah),*ᵃ *and he became king in his place.* ¹¹*And it so happened during his reign that,* ᵃ*as soon as he sat on his throne* ᵃ*he struck down the entire house of Baasha,* ᵇ*leaving to him not a single one who urinates against the wall; also his kinsfolk and his friends.* ¹²*So did Zimri demolish the entire house of Baasha,*ᵃ *according to Yahweh's word which he had spoken against him* ᵇ ᶜ*by means of*ᶜ *Jehu* ᵈ *the prophet,* ¹³*on account of all the sins of Baasha and* ᵃ*the sins of*ᵃ *Elah his son,* ᵇ*which they themselves sinned*ᵇ *and by which they caused Israel to sin, enraging Yahweh the God of Israel through their vain things.* ¹⁴*Now the remainder of Elah's acts, and all that he did, are these not written in the Book of the Chronicles of the Israelite Kings?*

Notes

8.a-a. MT. Gᴮ omits; Gᴸ "in the (reign) of Asa of Judah." Gᴸ attempts awkwardly to supply the omission seen in Gᴮ, which cannot be regarded as original vis-à-vis MT because its aorist rendering (ἐβασίλευσεν "reigned") for MT מלך is not in conformity with Gᴮ's normal and undoubtedly original Gr., the OG historical pres, seen in 15:1, 9, 25, 33, 16:28 (βασιλεύει "reign").

8.b-b. MT, Gᴸ. Gᴮ "for two years in Tirzah."

9.a. MT. Gᴮᴸ "Zambrei"; *sic* passim.

10.a-a. MT. Gᴮᴸ omit, possibly out of consideration of the numerical disagreement between the two synchronisms and the two-year length of reign mentioned in v 8 (but see pp. 180–82, "The Chronology of the Hebrew Kings").

11.a-a. MT (בשבתו על־כסאו). Gᴮᴸ ἐν τῷ καθίσαι αὐτὸν ἐπὶ τοῦ θρόνου αὐτοῦ "when he sat on his throne." Although G may be misreading Heb. כ as ב, it may be deliberately broadening the time-period for Zimri's program of extermination.

11.b.–12.a. MT. Gᴮᴸ omit by homoioteleuton.

12.b. Gᴮᴸᴼʳ. MT "unto."

12.c-c. MT, Gᴸ. Gᴮ "and unto" corr.

12.d. MT, Gᴮ. Gᴸ adds explicative "son of Hanani."

13.a-a. MT. Gᴮᴸ omit for stylistic reasons.

13.b-b. MT. Gᴮᴸ omit, a haplography perhaps occasioned by adherence to Dtr's stereotyped formulation.

Form/Structure/Setting

[Dtr: The reign of Elah
1. Introductory summary, v 8
2. Notice of Zimri's conspiracy, vv 9–10
3. Interpretation as fulfillment of prophecy against Baasha's house, vv 11–12

4. Theological interpretation, v 13
5. Closing summary, v 14]

Dtr's report about Elah is styled very much like that about Nadab (15:25–31). There is a very brief introductory and closing summary, the latter without reference to death and burial. In a position of central importance is a notice about Zimri's consipracy (vv 9–10), followed by a didactic statement about this being the fulfillment of prophecy, and then the usual theological assessment.

Comment

Elah reigned in Tirzah for an accredited two years, which was somewhat more than an actual one year. In terms of Judahite reckoning, his accession was actually in Asa's twenty-fifth year, and his death occurred in Asa's actual twenty-sixth year (vv 10, 15). Zimri has a Semitic name but, like Omri, appears without a patronym. He is, however, identified as commander of half the chariotry. Elah is apparently dissipated, a fact of which the conspiracy takes advantage. Perhaps Arza, in whose residence the king is drinking, and who occupies an office similar to that of Ahishar (4:6), is in the conspiracy and lets Zimri get inside to do his bloody deed. So Zimri takes over, wiping out every member of Baasha's line and again showing that "he who takes the sword shall die by the sword." Having supplied this notice, Dtr makes his moralizing application, emulating his previous observations about the house of Jeroboam (15:29–30). In his theological interpretation Dtr departs from his usual habit of attributing all of a king's evil-doing to Jeroboam, this time mentioning the sins of Baasha and the sins of Elah (v 13). "Vain things" is a new term of derision for the heathen gods (cf. v 26). Dtr's intent is to accentuate the parallelism between Jeroboam-Nadab and Baasha-Elah.

The Reign of Zimri (16:15–22)

Bibliography

Miller, J. M. "So Tibni Died (I Kings xvi 22)." *VT* 18 (1968) 392–94. **Soggin, J. A.** "Tibni, re d'Israele nella prima meta del IX sec. av. Cr." *RSO* 47 (1972) 171–76.

Translation

[15a]*In the [b]twenty-seventh[b] year of Asa king of Judah[a] Zimri reigned[c] for seven days[d] in Tirzah. Now [e]the people were encamped[e] against Gibbethon,[f] which belongs to the Philistines.* [16]*And the encamped people heard[a] the following: "Zimri has made a conspiracy, and has actually struck down the king!"[b] So [c]all Israel[c] made Omri, general of the army, king over Israel that day in the camp.* [17]*And Omri[a] went up, and all Israel with him, from[b] Gibbethon. And they laid siege to Tirzah.* [18]*And it so happened that, when Zimri saw that the[a] city was captured, he[b] went to the pinnacle of the king's house and, burning the king's house with fire on top of himself, he[c] died;* [19]*on account of his sin[a] that he sinned, doing what was evil in Yahweh's eyes, walking in the way of Jeroboam[b] and in the sin[c] that he committed, causing Israel to sin.* [20]*Now the remainder of Zimri's acts, including his conspiracy that he conceived, are these not written in the Book of the Chronicles of the Israelite kings?* [21]*Then the people of Israel were split [a]into halves.[a] One half of the people were in support of Tibni[b] son of Ginath for king, while the other half were in support of Omri.[c]* [22a]*But the people who were supporting Omri got the better of[a] the people who were supporting Tibni son of Ginath.[b] Tibni died,[c] and Omri became king.[d]*

Notes

15.a-a. MT, G[L]. G[B] omits in consideration of his chronological reconstruction.

15.b-b. MT. G[L] "twenty-second"; G[L] MS "thirty-first."

15.c. G[B]'s aorist (ἐβασίλευσεν) again betrays his omission of the date and the beginning of a new sentence as arbitrary and ideological (see above on v 8).

15.d. MT and G[L], following the normal sense of יָמִים "days." Although it is שָׁנָה that stands for "year" in this context, G[B] takes advantage of the fact that since the pl of יוֹם "day" may also mean "year" (e.g. at 1 Sam 1:3), it is susceptible to being rendered here, in the pl, as "years." This is clearly a tendentious mistake, and has become the source of much confusion in G[B]'s entire scheme of chronology.

15.e-e. MT. G[BL] "Israel's encampment was . . ." (stylistic?).

15.f. MT. G[BL] "Gibeon." Cf. 15:27.

16.a. MT. G[BL] add explicative "in the camp."

16.b. MT, G[B]. G[L] has explicative "King Elah."

16.c-c. MT, G[B]. G[L] "the people" is a repetition from the first part of the verse. G[B] arranges the syntax to read, "And they made Zimri king in Israel." G[B] calls Omri "Zimri" in vv 16–17, 21–28.

17.a. MT, G[L]. G[BL] MSS "Zimri"; see above.

17.b. MT, G[L]. G[B] "in."

18.a. MT. G[BL] have explicative "his."

18.b. MT, G[L]. G[B] "they" (interpretive).

18.c. MT, G[L]. G[B] has explicative "the king."

19.a. K. Q and G pl (ideological).
19.b. MT. G^BL have pleonastic "Jeroboam son of Nebat."
19.c. MT. G^BL pl.
21.a-a. MT. G^BL omit (haplography).
21.b. MT. G^BL "Thamnei"; *sic* passim.
21.c. G^B "Zambrei" (see note 16.c-c).
22.a-a. MT. G^BL omit.
22.b. MT. G^Arell add ὑπερίσχυσεν "prevailed"; G^BL omit.
22.c. MT. G^BL add from an independent tradition: "and Joram his brother at that time."
22.d. MT. G^BL add interpretive "after Tibni."

Form/Structure/Setting

[Dtr: The reign of Zimri
  1. Introductory summary, v 15a]
Narrative of Omri's rebellion and Zimri's death
  1. Omri besieges Tirzah
    a. Encampment before Gibbethon, v 15b
    b. Omri acclaimed at the report of Zimri's conspiracy, v 16
    c. The march of Tirzah, v 17
  2. Zimri's despair and suicide, 18
  [2. Dtr cont.: Theological assessment, v 19
  3. Concluding summary, v 20]
Notice of rivalry between Tibni and Omri
  1. The people divided, v 21
  2. Omri's ultimate supremacy, v 22

The section on Zimri has a most unusual structure. There is a brief introductory summary, but Dtr's theological assessment comes at the end (v 19), just before the concluding summary, without death notice, referring the reader to the archives. In between is a brief narrative, not just a notice because it describes action, about how Zimri died. But before he can go on to relate the story of Omri's reign (vv 23–28), Dtr makes use of another notice from his special source (vv 21–22), indicating that Omri was not free to take immediate possession of the throne, like Baasha and Zimri, but had to share power for a while with his rival, Tibni.

Comment

It was in the actual twenty-sixth year of Asa that Zimri seized the throne. His tenure was brief (see *Notes* on "seven days") because the army ("all Israel"), encamped once again at Gibbethon (cf. 15:27), reacted negatively when they heard of Zimri's treacherous deed. Omri (also without patronym, but more famous and powerful than the Bible suggests because the Assyrians subsequently referred to Israel as *Bit-Ḫumri*, "House of Omri") is Zimri's commanding officer ("general of the army" over against "commander of half of the chariotry") and may for this reason have taken special offense at what Zimri had done. Because of the unusual "that day," ביום ההוא, in v 16, this writer has argued in *YTT*, 110–12, that Omri's coronation amounted to acclamation by the sacral union, authorizing him to strike Zimri down as an act of loyalty and charismatic entitlement. It is important to note that Omri was made king and that he did not simply seize power in a conspiracy. Quickly the army marched to Tirzah and besieged it. Before long the city fell. Zimri showed bravado in his death, burning to death, where all could see, in the fire he himself had set. In v 19 Dtr hastens to level his censure and to offer his concluding summary. With the usual אז, "then," he appends the notice about Tibni and Omri. We know little more about Tibni than we do about Omri, except that his father's name is given. The halves mentioned may not have been equal halves. There is no mention of fighting between them; "got the better of" means simply "became stronger than." Thus Omri eventually had more support than Tibni. Somehow, somewhere Tibni died, and then Omri ruled without a rival, ready to establish the strongest administration Israel had yet seen.

The Reign of Omri   (16:23-28)

Bibliography

Alt, A. "Der Stadtstaat Samaria." *Berichte über die Verhandlungen der sächsischen Akademie der Wissenschaften zu Leipzig, Phil.-hist. Klasse*, Band 101, Heft 5, 1954 (= *Kleine Schriften* III, 258–302). **Whitley C. F.** "The Deuteronomic Presentation of the House of Omri." *VT* 2 (1952) 137–52.

Translation

[23] *In the thirty-first year of Asa* [a]*king of Judah*[a] *Omri began to reign over Israel for twelve years; he reigned in*[b] *Tirzah for six years.* [24] *And he*[a] *bought the hill of Samaria from Shemer*[b] *for two silver talents, and built up the hill. And he called the name of the city*[c] *which he built after the name of Shemer, owner of the hill: Samaria.*
[25] *And Omri did what was evil in Yahweh's eyes, being more perverse than all who preceded him.* [26] *And he walked in every way of Jeroboam son of Nebat and in his sin*[a] *by which he caused Israel to sin, enraging Yahweh the God of Israel by their vain things.* [27] *Now the remainder of the acts of Omri,* [a]*and all*[a] *that he did, and his works of greatness,*[b] *are these not written in the Book of the Chronicles of the Israelite Kings?* [28] *And Omri slept with his fathers and was buried in Samaria. And Ahab his son reigned in his place.*[a]

Notes

23.a-a. MT, G[L]. G[B] omits (haplography).
23.b. MT, G[BL]. MS[b] "and in."
24.a. MT, G[L]. G[B] "Zambrei" (explicative); see on v 16.
24.b. MT. G[BL] add explicative "the owner of the mountain/hill."
24.c. MT. G[BL] "mountain" (ὄρος) may have come into the text under the influence of the two foregoing occurrences.
26.a. Q (= the standard Dtr terminology). K, G[BL] pl.
27.a-a. MSS, G[BL], Syr. MT omits (perhaps corr; see below).
27.b. G[BL]. MT's addition "that he did" is a probable dittography.
28.a. In LXX, vv 28[a-h] follow (see 22:41–53).

Form/Structure/Setting

[Dtr: The reign of Omri
  1. Introductory summary, v 23]
Notice of Omri's purchase of Samaria, v 24
  [2. Dtr cont: Theological assessment, vv 25–26
  3. Concluding summary, vv 27–28]

Again in the case of Omri, we are almost entirely dependent for information on Dtr, whose theological assessment is severed from its usual position by the insertion of a notice concerning the way in which this king acquired Israel's future capital, Samaria.

Comment

The synchronism for Omri is reckoned from his sole rule, but his total length of reign counts the years during which he contended with Tibni, designating the first part of this period as years spent in Tirzah. The twelve and the six are accredited years, and represent an actual eleven and five, respectively. Evidently Omri departed from Tirzah as soon as Tibni died. His rival's death left him free to do as he pleased, and he saw the wisdom of exchanging an eastward-facing, fairly low hilltop for a westward-facing, high and isolated eminence. For strategic location, Samaria can hardly be praised too much. It stands entirely alone, with rich fields on every side. It can be reached directly from Shechem on the east, but looks out over the westernmost Manassite hills toward the coastal highway. The notice in v 24 was probably in written form as Dtr received it, but it evidently reproduces a popular oral tradition. Since a new capital city would hardly be named after a previous owner, we would agree with Gray and Noth that the ascription to Shemer is imaginative folk-etymology, although Gray (367) may be right in pointing to the pl אדני "lord" as evidence that Shemer was a clan or tribe. The actual name of the site was "Mount Shomron" (for the form, cf. Sirion, Hermon, Lebanon, Zion), and hence Omri called his city Shomron (Greek: Samaria). That he paid money for it (the amount may be legendary) and built it suggests that it had not been previously occupied. Although some traces of Early-Bronze occupation have been found, the Harvard expeditions of 1924 and following years has confirmed that Omri's city was indeed the first on this site.

Dtr's theological assessment singles out Omri for special blame. He did all that Jeroboam did and more. As in v 13, Yahweh is said to have been enraged by Israel's "vain things," i.e., heathen idols. The concluding summary follows the usual pattern, alluding to Omri's "works of greatness," such as building Samaria, without naming them.

The Reign of Ahab (16:29-34)

Bibliography

Eissfeldt, O. "Die Komposition von I Reg 16,29–II Reg 13,25." *BZAW* 105 (1967) 49–58. **Jack, J. W.** *Samaria in Ahab's Time. The Harvard Excavations and their Results, with Chapters on the Political and Religious Situation.* Edinburgh: T. & T. Clark, 1929. **Muszynski, H.** "Sacrificium fundationis in Jos 6,26 et I Reg 16,34?" *VD* 46 (1968) 259–74. **Parrot, A.** *Samaria the Capital of the Kingdom of Israel.* Tr. S. H. Hooke. New York: Philosophical Library, 1958. **Reisner, G. A., Fisher C. S.,** and **Lyon, D. G.** *The Harvard Excavations at Samaria 1908–1910,* 2 vols. Cambridge, Mass.: Harvard University Press, 1924. **Yadin, Y.** "The 'House of Baal' in Samaria and in Judah" (Heb). *Eretz-Shomron. The 30. Archaeological Convention, September 1972.* Jerusalem: Israel Exploration Society, 1973.

Translation

[29] *And Ahab son of Omri reigned over Israel* [a]*in the thirty-eighth year of Asa* [a] [b]*king of Judah.* [b] *And* [c] [d]*Ahab son of Omri* [d] *reigned over Israel in Samaria for twenty-two years.* [30] *And Ahab son of Omri did evil in Yahweh's eyes* [a] *beyond all who preceded him.* [31] [a]*And it seemed to be that, if it was too slight a thing* [a] *simply to walk in the sins of Jeroboam son of Nebat, he took to wife Jezebel daughter of Ittobaal,* [b] *so that he went and served Baal and did homage to him.* [32] *And he erected an altar to Baal for* [a] *the temple of Baal* [b] *which he built in Samaria.* [33] *And Ahab made an Asherah. So Ahab excelled in doing things* [a] *to enrage* [b]*Yahweh, the God of Israel,* [b] *more* [c] *than all the kings who preceded him.* [34] [a]*And in his days* [a] *Ahiel* [b] *the Bethelite built Jericho. With Abiram his firstborn he laid its foundation and with Segub* [c] *his youngest he set its gates, according to the word of Yahweh which he spoke by means of Joshua the son of Nun.*

Notes

29.a-a. MT. G[BL] "in the second year of Jehoshaphat" is in support of erroneous chronologies.
29.b-b. MT, G[L]. G[B] omits (paraphrastic).
29.c. MT, G[L]. G[B] omits (stylistic).
29.d-d. MT. G[BL] omit (paraphrastic).
30.a. MT. G[B] adds parenthetically "he did evil"; G[L] "and he did evil."
31.a-a. MT. G[BL] paraphrase with "and it was not enough for him."
31.b. Josephus (= G[BL] "Iet(e)baal"). The Heb. Bible has the correct consonants but ignorantly vocalizes "Ethbaal" (MT).
32.a. MT (לבעל בית הבעל) "to Baal (for) the house of Baal". G[BL] "in" reads a superfluous ב "in" before בית "house."
32.b. MT. G[BL] τῶν προσοχθισμάτων αὐτοῦ "his offenses," the usual translation for Heb. תועבה "abomination" (1x) and שקוץ "filth" (5x), terms of derision for heathen deities. The Gr. *Vorlage* must have had one of these words (in the pl), showing the MT to be relatively conservative in this reading.
33.a. MT. No noun stands in the Heb. as a basis for G[BL] παροργίσματα "offensive things."
33.b-b. MT. G[BL] "his soul."
33.c. MT. G[B] "he did evil beyond" (paraphrastic); cf. G[L].

34.a-a. MT. G^B omits. G^L lacks the entire verse.

34.b. G^B ʾΑχειηλ = Heb. אחיאל "Ahiel," a theophoric name in the traditional style. MT חיאל "Hiel" is an abbreviation, or shows mutilation.

34.c. K (cf. 1 Chr 2:21f.). Q, G^B, MSS, Vrs "Segib."

Form/Structure/Setting

[Dtr: The reign of Ahab
  1. Introductory summary, v 29
  2. Theological assessment, vv 30–33]
Notice of the rebuilding of Jericho, v 34abα
[Dtr: Interpretation as the fulfillment of prophecy, v 34bβ]

Comment

What Dtr has here to tell us of Ahab is meant only as a preface to the sizeable collection of prophet stories that follow in chaps. 17–22. The synchronism of Ahab's accession is again one year too long; it was actually in Asa's thirty-seventh year that Ahab came to the throne, and he reigned for somewhat more than twenty-one years. Together with Omri's eleven years and Ahab's sons' one and eleven years, this makes forty-four years for the entire Omride dynasty, the longest to remain in power in Israel up until this time. This was a rich, powerful, and influential dynasty, giving its name permanently to the country, as we have seen. It was also the most corrupt and apostate dynasty to date, one that provoked the rise of northern prophecy and that earned the most violent reproof on the part of Dtr. The latter can hardly find language harsh enough to express his disdain. Ahab does evil "beyond all who preceded him" (v 30); "Ahab excelled in doing things to enrage Yahweh . . . more than all the kings who preceded him" (33). Ahab is even worse than his father Omri (cf. v 25). Dtr is explicit, accusing Ahab of four heretofore unthinkable sins: (1) marrying the baalist daughter of a baalist king, (2) worshiping Baal and bowing down to him, (3) building a Baal temple in Samaria with its public altar, and (4) making an image of the Earth-Mother, Asherah. In the days of David and Solomon, Israel had enjoyed good commercial relations with the Phoenicians, but Ahab makes a Phoenician princess his queen. Solomon had made Pharaoh's daughter his queen, but the difference is that Jezebel was extremely assertive and intolerant. Her name is vocalized in Heb. to suggest the meaning, "No dung," but the original Phoenician evidently meant "Where is the prince?" Her father, Ethbaal or Ittobaal, mentioned by Josephus and dated by E. Meyer ca. 887–856, had a name that actually celebrated the Phoenician religion. It means "Baal exists." The name "Baal," which means "lord" or "husband," was known throughout the Levant and was used even in Israel as an appellative for Yahweh (see the names of Saul's sons, Ishbaal, Meribaal, etc.). Here the specific Baal worshiped at Tyre intruded into the public worship structure of the Northern Kingdom, bringing with him a whole pantheon of Phoenician deities and the ritual for worshiping them.

In v 34 Dtr copies a notice about Jericho to suggest that the wickedness introduced by Ahab encouraged a certain man to violate the taboo placed on that city according to Josh 6:26. The facts as stated are only that a Bethelite named Ahiel "built" Jericho, but sacrificed Abiram, his firstborn, in its foundation and Segub, his eldest, at its gates. The foundation sacrifice, revealed by modern archeology, is probably what was involved. The children named were probably infants, dead or alive, placed in jars and inserted into the masonry, propitiating the gods and warding off evil.

Narratives of the Prophets in Elijah's Time 17:1—22:40

THE ELIJAH NARRATIVES: COMPOSITION AND REDACTION

Bibliography

Alcaina Canosa, C. "Panorama crítico del ciclo de Eliseo." *EstBib* 23 (1964) 217–34. **Bottini, G. C.** "Il racconto della siccità e della pioggia (1 Re 17–18)." *LASBF* 29 (1979) 327–49. **Bronner, L.** *The Stories of Elijah and Elisha as Polemics against Baal Worship.* Leiden: E. J. Brill, 1968. **Carroll. R. P.** "The Elijah-Elisha Sagas: Some Remarks on Prophetic Succession in Ancient Israel." *VT* 19 (1969) 400–415. **De Vries, S. J.** *Prophet against Prophet. The Role of the Micaiah Narrative (I Kings 22) in the Development of Early Prophetic Tradition.* Grand Rapids: Eerdmans, 1978. **Eissfeldt, O.** "Die Komposition von I Reg 16,29—II Reg 13,25." *BZAW* 105 (1967) 49–58. **Élie: le prophète.** Les études Carmélitaines. 2 vols. Desclée de Brouwer, 1956. **Fohrer, G.** *Elia.* ATANT 31. Zürich: Zwingli Verlag, 1957; 2nd ed., 1968. **Jaros, K.** "Der Anspruch Gottes in der Politik." *BLit* 2 (1976) 87–95. **Jepsen, A.** *Nabi; soziologische Studien zur alttestamentliche Literatur und Religionsgeschichte.* Munich: Beck, 1934. **Keller, C. A.** "Wer war Elia?" *TZ* 16 (1960) 298–313. **Koller, Y.** "Chronological Order in the Elijah Narrative" (Heb). *BMik* 55 (1973) 471–81. **Long, B. O.** "2 Kings III and Genres of Prophetic Narrative." *VT* 23 (1973) 337–48. **Michaux, W.** "Les cycles d'Elie et d'Elisee (1 Rois 17 à 2 Rois 13,22)." *BK* 2 (1953) 76–99. **Plöger, O.** *Die Prophetengeschichten der Samuel- und Königsbücher.* Diss. Greifswald, 1937. **Rofé, A.** "The Classification of the Prophetical Stories." *JBL* 89 (1970) 427–40. **Smend, R.** "Der biblische und der historische Elia." VTSup 28 (1975) 167–84. ———. "Das Wort Jahwes an Elia. Erwägungen zur Komposition von 1 Reg. XVII–XIX." *VT* 25 (1975) 525–43. **Steck, O. H.** *Überlieferung und Zeitgeschichte in den Elia-Erzählungen.* WMANT 26. Neukirchen-Vluyn: Neukirchener Verlag, 1968.

In the *Introduction* pains were taken to explain the function of prophet stories among other kinds of legend. It was emphasized that their concern for literal history is tangential since their essential aim is didactic and exemplary. Their intent is not to record what *has* happened, but what happens and can happen. The exaggerated supernatural element in some of them is a metaphor for God's power and the power of God-filled men.

In *Prophet against Prophet,* the writer distinguishes the various subgenres of prophet story (or legend) on the basis of their respective functions. It will be useful for the user of this commentary to have a summary listing of these subgenres:

  1. Power-demonstration narrative: a marvelous story exemplifying charismatic power, offering edifying illustrations of what a model prophet can do (subtypes: marvelous act stories, interpreted act stories, prophetic word stories).
  2. Prophetic call narrative: the story of a prophet's designation and empowerment, identifying the source of a particular prophet's charismatic gift.

3. Prophet-legitimation narrative: a marvelous story demonstrating the scope and nature of a prophet's empowerment, identifying that prophet as genuine.

4. Charismatic designation narrative: a story in which the gift of charismatic power confirms the anointing of a king, demonstrating the authority of a prophet to impart his spirit to a secular leader.

5. Historical demonstration narrative: a modified holy-war story in which a prophet identifies a coming event as an exercise of divine power, enhancing belief that Yahweh is in control of history.

6. Succession oracle narrative: a story in which a prophetic oracle specifies the terms of regal succession, demonstrating the transcendent authority of Yahweh in the transfer of regal power.

7. Prophet-authorization narrative: a marvelous story demonstrating the power of a prophet to prevail over institutional rivals, enhancing belief in prophetic authority to challenge usurpations of Yahweh's supremacy (subtypes: word-fulfillment stories, supplicatory power stories, theophanous commission stories).

8. Regal self-judgment narrative: a story in which a king's word or act determines his own judgment, enhancing the belief that Yahweh's supreme authority comes to paradoxical expression in the responsible deeds of the institutional holders of political power (subtypes: oracle-manipulation stories, abusive action stories).

9. Superseding oracle narrative: a story in which a superseding oracle to a king is fulfilled in preference to one that it follows, demonstrating how Yahweh's ultimate purpose in historical events takes priority over his mediate purpose (subtypes: evil over good stories, good over evil stories).

10. Instrumental fulfillment narrative: a story in which the fulfillment of one element in a complex oracle is instrumental toward the oracle's ultimate fulfillment, demonstrating that Yahweh ordains instrumental causes in the realization of his historical purposes.

11. Word-controversy narrative: the story of a contest between rival claimants to prophetic revelation, demonstrating that Yahweh has power to counteract conflicting prophecy for the fulfillment of his historical purposes.

The reader is invited to consult *Prophet against Prophet* (53–56) for a complete listing of the passages belonging in these various categories, which are elucidated on 56–72. Of the prophet stories already encountered in 1 Kgs, the Ahijah narratives in chaps. 11 and 14 belong to subgenre 6 while the Bethelite story of chap. 13 belongs to the word-fulfillment subtype of subgenre 7. The narratives in chaps. 17–22 will be found to belong among several of the subgenres listed above. 1 Kgs 17:1–16, 18:1–18, 41–46 and 1 Kgs 18:21–39 are supplicatory power narratives belonging to subgenre 7. 1 Kgs 17:17–24 belongs to subgenre 3. 1 Kgs 19:1–18 represents the theophanous commission subtype of the subgenre 7. 1 Kgs 19:19–21 is the sole representative of subgenre 2. 1 Kgs 20:1–21 and 1 Kgs 20:26–29 belong to subgenre 5. 1 Kgs 20:30–43 is an oracle manipulation narrative in subgenre 8. 1 Kgs 21:1–

29 belongs to subgenre 8, abusive action subtype. 1 Kgs 22:1–37 is the literary combination of two independent prophet stories, one of which is an evil over good story of subgenre 9, and the other of which represents subgenre 11.

The life-setting (*Sitz im Leben*) of the various narratives is a clue to their origin and redaction. The prophetic call narrative and the prophet-legitimation narrative each have their setting (and hence their origin) in the schools of the particular prophets (thus 1 Kgs 19:19–21 belongs to the Elisha school, 1 Kgs 17:17–24 to the Elijah school). The historical demonstration narrative exalts prophetic power but also supports regal authority; the examples that we have (1 Kgs 20:1–21, 26–29) do not name the prophets involved, and hence arise from some undetermined source within the prophetic movement. All of the prophet-authorization narratives in 1 Kgs were composed and preserved within the Elijah school, reflecting, no doubt, the extreme tension and hostility that characterized relationships between the house of Ahab with the Baal establishment on the one side, and Elijah and his disciples on the other side. The regal self-judgment story in 1 Kgs 20:30–43 is anonymous but puts the Israelite king under sharp judgment; so likewise the regal self-judgment story of chap. 21, except that here king and prophet are both named, although it is probable that the Elijah of this story functions entirely as a late stereotype. The Micaiah of the interwoven stories in chap. 22 is definitely a pious stereotype, but especially so in the very late (*ca.* 700 B.C.) word-controversy narrative, the earliest composition to draw attention to direct competition between contending groups of prophets.

In a separate chapter of *Prophet against Prophet* (112–27), the writer has reconstructed the redaction history of this material. It is shown that there are three distinct literary complexes: (1) the Elijah cycle; (2) the Elisha cycle; and (3) the Omride-war cycle. The Elijah cycle grew out of an early collection of prophet-authorization narratives (the drought story in 1 Kgs 17–18, the fire on the altar story in 18:21–39, the Elijah on Horeb story in 1 Kgs 19, and the Ahaziah story of 2 Kgs 1:2–17), together with the prophet-legitimation story in 1 Kgs 17:17–24. This was heavily redacted by someone sympathetic with Jehu's revolt. Somewhat later Jehuite propaganda is the Naboth story in chap. 21. 1 Kgs contains only a single fragment from the Elisha cycle, viz., the story of Elisha's call in 19:19–21, which the editor who combined all three cycles brought to a forward position because of the mention of Elisha in 19:17. The rest of the material in 1 Kgs belongs, then, to the Omride-war cycle. It contains the three anonymous narratives of 20:1–21, 20:26–29, and 20:30–43, plus the early Micaiah story in 22:2–9, 15–18, 26–37 (the second Micaiah story was inserted very late into an already complete book of the prophets). Like the early Elijah collection, this material was redacted and expanded by a Jehuite editor. The original king in these prophet stories of chaps. 20 and 22 was not Ahab but one of his sons, probably Joram. The key to understanding the Jehuite redaction lies in the words of the anonymous prophet spoken to "the king of Israel" in 20:42: "Because you have let go out of your hand the man whom I had devoted to destruction, therefore your life shall go for his life, and your people for his people." The reference is to Ben-hadad, who had been causing Israel much trouble, but whom the

Israelite king had let go. The Jehuite editor had lived to see how much sorrow the Syrians, especially under Hazael, could cause, and he blamed this all on the Israelite king's lenience. It is probably the same king, Joram, whose death has inspired chap. 22, although the details have here been imaginately altered with respect to the literally historical account in 2 Kgs 9. All the bitterness felt by this redactor comes to the surface in the words that he adds to the account of the king's death in 22:38, words about dogs licking Ahab's blood and harlots washing themselves in the water with which his chariot had been washed. Later levels of redaction have made Ahab, not Joram, the referent throughout chaps. 20 and 22, probably because Ahab had grown into a symbol of utter and ultimate wickedness.

Altogether, the prophet stories of 1 and 2 Kgs bear eloquent testimony to a time of extreme crisis in Israel. Ahab and his sons, but especially his wife Jezebel, were actively fostering Baalism. Hostilities with Syria were on the rise, and hostilities with Hazael would result in the nation's humiliating subjugation. The prophets about whom these stories were told strove for recognition and legitimacy, which inevitably could come only as they stood up, in Yahweh's name, to resist the abominations of Baalism and the menace of Syrian aggression.

We are indebted to O. H. Steck, *Überlieferung und Zeitgeschichte*, for showing how a redactor in Jehu's reign shaped these prophet stories as a propaganda tract against the house of Ahab. It is he who provided the transition at the beginning of 17:17 for incorporating the story of the sick child (v 20, anticipating the prayer of Elijah in v 21, is a later gloss raising a theological question not contemplated by the original narrative). It is he also who inserted expansions at 18:3b–4, 10–11, and 13–14. In 18:19–20 and 18:40 he also provided linkages to the drought story, bringing the Baal prophets on the scene and then disposing of them. The one remaining prophet story in this early Elijah collection, that of 19:1–18, had an independent existence before a Jehuite redactor went to work on it, but its introduction was altered in such a way as to show acquaintance with the redactional additions already made in 18:19–20, 40.

It is important that the reader be reminded of how very much these Elijah narratives depend on the model of Moses. H. Gese ("Bemerkungen zur Sinaitradition," *ZAW* 79 [1967] 137–54), G. Seitz (*Redaktionsgeschichtliche Studien zum Deuteronomium* [BWANT 93, Stuttgart: W. Kohlhammer, 1971] 306), and R. P. Carroll (*VT* 19 [1969] 400–415), are among recent writers who have emphasized this affinity. The only writing prophet from the North, Hosea, claims in 12:13 that Moses was himself a prophet: "By a prophet Yahweh brought Israel up from Egypt"; this is seconded in Deut 18:15, where a typological "Moses" says, "Yahweh your God will raise up for you a prophet like me from among you, from your brethren—him you shall heed." The reference is to the model prophet, any and all prophets who are like Moses. The similarity of Elijah to Moses is not only seen in the narrative of Elijah traveling to the Mountain of God (chap. 19), but also in a heretofore undetected similarity between the Yahwist's story (J) of Moses in the Pentateuch and this entire collection of Elijah narratives, which, together with 2 Kgs 1:2–17, all fall into the subgenre "prophet-authorization narrative." J materials in Exod 3–4, 33:7–11, Num 11:16–17, 24–30, 12:1–15a feature Moses as a prophet, but J's story of the plagues and of Israel's deliverance in Exod 5–14 has a schema, or pattern, that is strikingly like that of these prophet stories. This schema has five points of tension and resolution: (1) the prophetic challenge, (2) a threat or rebuke to the prophet, (3) a definition of the terms for the decisive struggle, (4) a description of the divine intervention, and (5) confirmation of the prophet's authority. The following chart places Exod 5–14 and four Elijah stories in parallel, showing where in each the five elements are manifest.

	Exod	1 Kgs	1 Kgs	1 Kgs	2 Kgs
Challenge	5:1	17:1	18:21a	19:1	1:3–4
Rebuke	5:20–21	18:17–18	18:21b	19:2	1:9, 11
Terms	6:1	18:41	18:22–24	19:9b–10, 13b–14	1:10a, 12a
Intervention	7:14—14:30	18:43–45	18:38	19:11–12	1:10b, 12b
Confirmation	14:31	18:46	18:39	19:15–18	1:13–17

Supportive argument for the above analysis must by all means give due allowance to individual differences among the various narratives. Enough has been said, however, to illuminate the prophetic ideology represented in the Elijah tradition. Like Moses, Elijah saw himself in a great contest with the forces of apostasy. Like Moses, he did not refrain from leveling monumental challenges, confident that Yahweh would fulfill his expectations. The explanation for Elijah's confidence lay in the fact that, like Moses, he was a man of prevailing, powerful prayer (1 Kgs 18:36–37, 42). When Jesus, the greatest of all the prophets, went up into a high mountain to be reimpowered of God (Mark 9:2–8 and parallels), Elijah was there, with Moses, to teach him how to face his last deadly contest, and win. Once Elijah despaired of his life, believing that Yahweh could do nothing more with only one prophet left (1 Kgs 19:10, 14), but God showed him that all the power of heaven and earth could be concentrated in a quiet little breeze; and if so, how much more in the winds and the earthquakes and the fires that hasten to perform his will?

Elijah Challenges Baal
(17:1–16; 18:1–18, 41–46)

Bibliography

Bobichon, M. "Jézebel au pays des prophètes." *BTS* 120 (1970) 7. **Cohen, M. A.** "In All Fairness to Ahab. A Socio-political Consideration of the Ahab-Elijah Controversy." *EI* 12 (1975) 87–94. **Heising, A.** "Exegese und Theologie der alt- und neutestamentlichen Speisewunder." *ZTK* 86 (1964) 80–96. **Patai, R.** "The Control of Rain in Ancient Palestine." *HUCA* 14 (1939) 251–86.

Translation

[1] *Now Elijah* [a] *the settler (from the settlers in Gilead) said to Ahab, "By the life of Yahweh* [b] *[c]God of Israel,[c] [d]whose minister I am,[d] [e]there shall be neither dew nor rain throughout these years* [e] *except at my express word!"* [2] *Then the word of Yahweh came to him:* [a] [3]*"Go hence and head* [a] *eastward. And you shall conceal yourself in the wadi Kerith which lies on the opposite bank of the Jordan.* [4] *Now it is arranged for you to drink* [a] *from the wadi; and I have appointed ravens to provide for you there."* [5a]*So he went and did* [a] *according to the word of Yahweh:* [b]*he stayed* [b] *in the wadi Kerith which* [c] *lies on the opposite bank of the Jordan.* [6] *And the ravens would bring him bread* [a]*and meat* [a] *in the morning,* [b]*and bread* [b] *and meat in the evening. And he drank* [c] *from the wadi.*

[7] *Now it happened at the end of a considerable time that the wadi ran completely dry because there was not a drop of rain in the land.* [8] *Then the word of Yahweh came to him:* [a] [9]*"Arise, go* [a] *to Zarephath belonging to Sidon.* [b] *Behold, I have appointed there a widow woman to provision you."* [10] *So he arose and went to Zarephath. And he came to the gate of the city, and right there was a widow woman collecting twigs. And he* [a] *called to her and said,* [b] *"Fetch me* [c] *please a little water in a cup so that I may drink."* [11] *So she went to fetch it, but he* [a] *called to* [b] *her and said, "Fetch* [c] *me please a bit of bread in your hand."* [12] *And she* [a] *said, "By the life of Yahweh your God,* [b]*I have nothing to bake with,* [b] *except just enough flour in a jar to fill one's palm and a bit of oil in a cruse. And behold, I am just in the process of gathering two twigs so that I may go in and prepare this for myself and my sons.* [c] *We will eat this,* [d] *and then we will die."* [13] *But Elijah said to her, "Do not be afraid; go* [a] *make preparations just as you said, but first make me a small cake out of it and bring it out to me. And you shall then provide for yourself and your sons.* [b] [14] *For thus says Yahweh,* [a] *'The jar of flour shall not be used up, and the cruse of oil shall not run out, until such a day as Yahweh shall give rain upon* [b]*the ground.'"* [b] [15] *And she* [a] *went and did* [b]*according to Elijah's word;* [b c] *and* [d]*she ate, and her children,* [d]*[e]for many days.* [e] [16] *The jar of flour was not used up and the cruse of oil did not run out, according to the word of Yahweh which he spoke by means of Elijah.*

* * * * * *

18:1 *Now it happened after* [a] *many days that Yahweh's word came to Elijah (in the third year), as follows: "Go, appear before Ahab, and I will give rain upon the face of the ground."* [2] *So Elijah went to appear to Ahab.*

Now the famine was severe in Samaria. [3] *And Ahab summoned Obadiah, who was in charge of the royal property. Now Obadiah was exceedingly reverential toward Yahweh.* [4] *And it so happened, when Jezebel cut off Yahweh's prophets, that Obadiah took a hundred prophets* [a] *and hid them, fifty men in* [b] *a cave.* [b] *And he provided them with bread and water.* [5] *And Ahab said to Obadiah, "Go* [a] *into the land, to* [b] *the springs of water and to* [c] *the wadis. It may be that we will find grass sufficient to save the horses and the mules,* [d] *and we will not be deprived of any of the animals."* [d] [6] *And they split up* [a] *the land* [a] *between them, to pass through it. Ahab traveled on the one road,* [b] *and Obadiah traveled on the one road by himself.* [7] *And it happened that Obadiah was on the road* [a] *when behold,* [b] *here was Elijah coming to meet him!* [c] [d] *And he recognized him.* [d] *And he fell on his face and said, "Is it you, O lord Elijah?"* [8] *And he* [a] *said to him,* [b] *"Go, say to your lord, 'Behold Elijah!'"* [9] *But he* [a] *said, "How have I sinned, that you place your servant into the hand of Ahab, to have me killed?* [10] *By the life of Yahweh your God,* [a] *there is no people or kingdom whither my lord has not sent to inquire for you, and when they said no he would adjure* [b] *the kingdom or people in question that they had indeed not found you.* [11] *And now you are saying, 'Go, say to your lord,* [a] *"Behold Elijah!"'* [a] [12] *And what will happen is, I will go from you and Yahweh's spirit will take you off to* [a] *I know not where. And I will come to tell Ahab about it, and* [b] *when he cannot find you* [b] *he will kill me, even though your servant has revered Yahweh from my* [c] *youth.* [13] *Has it not been told* [a] *my lord what I did? When Jezebel slew Yahweh's prophets,* [b] *I hid some of Yahweh's prophets, a hundred men,* [b] *fifty men* [c] *by fifty* [c] [d] *in a cave,* [d] *and provided them* [e] *with bread and water.* [14] *And here you are saying,* [a] *'Go, say to your lord, "Behold Elijah!"';* *and he will kill me."*

[15] *Then Elijah said, "By the life of Yahweh of Hosts, whose minister I am,* [a] *today I will appear to him!"* [b] [16] *So Obadiah went to meet Ahab and told him, and Ahab went* [a] *to meet Elijah.* [17] *And it so happened that, when Ahab saw Elijah, Ahab said to him,* [a] *"Is that you, O Israel's hex?"* [18] *And he* [a] *said, "It is not I who have put the hex on Israel, but you and your father's house, through* [b] *your collective* [b] *abandonment of* [c] *Yahweh's commandments.* [c] *And* [d] *you yourself* [d] *have gone after the baals.*

* * * * * *

[41] *And Elijah said to Ahab, "Go up, eat and drink, for there is the noise of the tumult* [a] *of rain."* [42] *So Ahab went up to eat and drink while Elijah went up on* [a] [b] *the summit* [b] *of Carmel. And he crouched down on the ground, putting his face between his knees.* [c] [43] *And he said to his lad, "Please go up, look in the direction of the sea."* [a] *So he went up* [a] *and* [b] *looked. And he said, "Nothing!" And he* [c] *said,* [d] *"Return," seven times.* [e] [44] *And it so happened at the seventh time that he said,* [a] *"Behold, a cloud small as a man's hand is rising up out of the sea!"* [b] *Then he said, "Rise up, say to Ahab, 'Hitch up* [c] *and get on down, lest the rainstorm bog you in!'"* [45] *And it did happen that here and there the sky began to grow dark with clouds and wind. And pretty soon there was an enormous rainfall, with Ahab riding* [a]

to get back to Jezreel.^b ⁴⁶*And the hand of Yahweh came*^a *upon Elijah. And, girding up his loins, he ran in front of Ahab* ^b*as far as the approach to*^b *Jezreel.*

Notes

1.a. MT, G^L. G^B has explicative "the prophet."
1.b. MT, G^L. G^B adds a doublet, "the God of hosts," in which "God" may be a corruption of "Yahweh" through the influence of the following clause.
1.c-c. MT, G^B. G^L omits (haplography?).
1.d-d. Lit., "before whom I stand"; cf. 18:15.
1.e-e. Paraphrase of an oath-clause ("if there will be, etc.") resistant of literal English translation.
2.a. MT adds לאמר "to wit," "as follows"; this is not only missing in the *Vorlage* of G^{BL} but is usually lacking in the Heb. (MT) of this pericope. G^{BL} "to Elijah" for MT "to him" involves a translational corruption, as in v 8 (אֶל אֵלִיָּהוּ "to Elijah" from אֵלָיו "to him").
3.a. MT, lit., "turn yourself"; G^{BL} omit (haplography).
4.a. MT. G^{BL} add explicative "water."
5.a-a. MT. G^B omits "so he went"; G^L omits "and did."
5.b-b. G^{BL}. MT "and he went and stayed" involves a dittography from v 5a.
5.c. MT, G^L. G^B omits the relative particle, as in v 9 (stylistic?).
6.a-a, b-b. MT. G^{BL} omit, aiming perhaps for better stylistic parallelism.
6.c. MT. G^{BL} add explicative "water."
8.a. MT. G^B "Elijah" and G^L "Elijah the Tishbite" are explicative. G^{BL} omit לאמר "as follows" (cf. v 2).
9.a. MT. G^{BL} add pleonastic "and go."
9.b. G^{BL}. MT adds "and stay there" under the influence of v 5.
10.a MT. G^{BL} have explicative "Elijah."
10.b MT. G^{BL} have explicative "to her."
10.c. MT. G^{BL} omit (haplography).
11.a. MT. G^{BL} have explicative "Elijah."
11.b. MT. G^{BL} ὀπίσω = Heb. אַחֲרֵי "after" is interpretive since the narrative assumes that she had already departed Elijah's presence, though she was still within calling distance.
11.c. MT לִקְחִי is abnormal as an impv fem sing alongside the regular form קְחִי in v 10. קְחִי לָהּ "fetch to her" has been suggested as an emendation (*BHS*mg), but a personal object after "said" is read only by G^L, which freely interpolates explicative material. Perhaps v 11 preserves an authentic North-Israelite form.
12.a. MT. G^{BL} has explicative "the woman."
12.b-b. The usual oath formula: "if . . . ."
12.c. G^{BL}. The sing in MT shows contamination from vv 17–24.
12.d. MT. G^{BL} omit (haplography).
13.a. MT. G^{BL}, avoiding asyndetic structures, add "and."
13.b. G^{BL}. MT sing (see note 12.c.).
14.a. G^{BL}. MT adds "the God of Israel" by contamination from v 1.
14.b-b. G^{BL}. MT borrows "the face of the ground" from 18:1.
15.a. MT. G^{BL} have explicative "the woman."
15.b-b. MT and G^L MS. G^{BL} omit (haplography).
15.c. MT, G^B. G^L adds interpretive "and he (someone) gave to him."
15.d-d. Q, G^{BL} "and she ate, and he, and her household (G children = וּבָנֶיהָ)"; K "and he ate, and she, and her household." The ideological problem is the position of Elijah as guest. Very likely he was not originally in this line of narrative at all, as is shown by the fem narrative verb at the beginning; hence our translation, which makes no mention of him.
15.e-e. MT. G^{BL} omit (haplography).
18:1.a. There is no need to emend the lapidary Heb.; cf. G^{BL}.
4.a. MT. G^{BL} "prophetic men" may represent the doublet אֲנָשִׁים "men" and נְבִאִים "prophets."

4.b-b. MT, G^B. G^L*rell* "in two caves"; cf. v 13.

5.a. MT. G^BL add a pleonastic "and let us traverse."

5.b. G^BL. MT adds pleonastic "every."

5.c. Idem.

5.d-d. Reading a niph from נכד with Gray; cf. *BHS*mg. KBL reads a hiph impf with the meaning "have to kill," which is supported here by G^BL ἐξολοθρευθήσονται. Gr. σχηνών = המחכות misreads הבהמת "animals."

6.a-a. MT. G^BL "the road."

6.b. G^BL. MT adds explicative "alone."

7.a. MT. G^BL adds explicative "alone."

7.b. MT, G^L. G^B*rell* "and came."

7.c. MT. G^BL add explicative "alone."

7.d-d. MT. G^BL καὶ Ἀβδειου ἔσπευσεν "and Obadiah hastened" = ע רימהר' corr from MT ויכרהו.

8.a. MT. G^BL have explicative "Elijah."

8.b. G^L. MT, G^B add interpretive "it is I."

9.a. MT. G^BL have explicative "Obadiah."

10.a. Oath formula; lit., "if . . . ."

10.b. MT. G^BL ἐνέπρησεν is a corruption of ἐνέπλησεν = הַשְׁבִּיעַ "adjure" (so Klostermann; cf. Burney, 221).

11.a-a. MT, G^L. G^B omits (haplography).

12.a. MT. G^BL add pleonastic "a (the) country."

12.b-b. MT, G^L MSS. G^B omits; cf. v 14.

12.c. MT. G^BL MSS, Syr, Vg substitute "his" as a stylistic improvement.

13.a. MT. G^BL add pleonastic "you" before "my lord."

13.b-b. MT, G^B. G^L "and I took from Yahweh's prophets a hundred men and hid them."

13.c-c. MT. G^BL "by fifty."

13.d-d. MT, G^B. G^L "in two (the) caves."

13.e. MT, G^L. G^B omits "them."

14.a. MT, G^L. G^B adds explicative "you."

15.a. See on 17:1.

15.b. Oath formula, lit., "if . . . ."

16.a. MT. G^BL have interpretive "ran and went."

17.a. MT. G^BL have explicative "Elijah."

18.a. MT. G^BL have explicative "Elijah."

18.b-b. This paraphrase brings out the force of the Heb. 2nd pers pl, contrasted emphatically to the sing of the sequel.

18.c-c. MT. G^BL "Yahweh your God."

18.d-d. MT and G^B (sing). G^min, Syr, Tg, Vg pl. G^L inf (paraphrase?).

41.a. MT. G^BL τῶν ποδῶν "of the feet" may be intended as a paraphrastic simile equivalent to Heb. קוֹל "noise."

42.a. MT, G^B. G^L εἰς = "into."

42.b-b. MT. G^L omits; G^B ἐπὶ τὸν κάρμηλον "to Carmel" may paraphrase MT אֶל־רֹאשׁ הַכַּרְמֶל.

42.c. Q, G^BL. K sing.

43.a-a. MT. G^BL omit. The omission may be exegetical in view of the foregoing statement that Elijah was already atop the mountain.

43.b. MT. G^BL substitute explicative "the lad."

43.c. MT. G^BL have explicative "Elijah."

43.d. MT, G^L. G^B inserts "and you" = Heb. וְאַתָּה, a possible corr from וְעַתָּה "so now," which would make good Heb. syntax in this context.

43.e. MT. G^BL add the epexegetical gl "And he returned (^L took a look) seven times (^L more); and the lad returned seven times."

44.a. MT. G^BL omit.

44.b. G^L. MT and G^B "the water."

44.c. MT. G^BL add explicative "your chariot."

45.a. MT. G^BL καὶ ἔκλαεν/ἔκλαιεν "and he wept" reads וַיֵּבְךְ, a corr of MT וַיִּרְכַּב.

45.b. MT, G^L. G^B regularly reads a corr (so v 46), "Israel" for "Jezreel."

46.a. MT; lit., "was/became"; so G^L ἐγένετο. G^B omits.

46.b-b. MT; lit., "until you come to." G^BL "unto" (stylistic).

Form/Structure/Setting

Thematic announcement to Ahab, 17:1
1. Demonstrations of Yahweh's power to provide
    a. In the summoning of nature's creatures
        (1) The divine instruction, vv 2–4
        (2) Narrative of compliance, vv 5–6
    b. In the renewal of human sustenance
        (1) The divine instruction, vv 7–9
        (2) Interview: the Zarephath widow's extremity, vv 10–12
        (3) Oracle of abundance, vv 13–14
        (4) Narrative of compliance, v 15
        (5) Interpretation as the fulfillment of prophecy, v 16
2. Elijah's confrontation with Ahab
    a. The preparation
        (1) Elijah comes to Ahab, 18:1–2a
        (2) Obadiah searches for water
            (a) The desperate situation, v 2b
            (b) Ahab's instructions, vv 3a, 5
[Expansion, vv 3b–4]
            (c) The search, v 6
        (3) Elijah instructs Obadiah
            (a) The unexpected encounter, v 7
            (b) Obadiah protests Elijah's instruction, vv 8–9, 12
[Expansion, vv 10–11]
[Expansion, vv 13–14]
            (c) Elijah promises an immediate appearance, v 15
    b. The encounter
        Narrative transition, v 16
        (1) Ahab's accusation, v 17
        (2) Elijah's counteraccusation, v 18
3. Resolution: Elijah's prayer brings rain
    a. The disposition of Ahab
        (1) Instruction to symbolic preparation, v 41
        (2) Narrative of compliance, v 42a
    b. Elijah's supplication
        (1) The disposition of prayer, v 42b
        (2) The search for Yahweh's answer, v 43
    c. Yahweh's answer and Elijah's vindication
        (1) The sign of rain and instructions to Ahab, v 44
        (2) A torrent of rain sends Ahab fleeing, v 45
        (3) Elijah runs before Ahab, v 46

The opening verse defies classification as to genre. It has no parallels in prophetic literature. It is an oath in Yahweh's name that no rain will fall until the prophet announces it.

The stories that follow (17:2–6 and 7–16) conform to classic standards for "word fulfillment" narratives. They begin with the reception of a word from God which contains a command and a promise. They then recount

obedience to the command followed by fulfillment of the promise. They close
by noting that this all occurred according to the word of God.

The other narrative units are much more difficult to classify. The climax
of the story occurs in the encounter between king and prophet (18:16–18)
and the successful prayer for rain (18:41–46).

The first prophet narrative in this collection has a most unusual structure;
its meaning is summed up in a motto verse at the beginning, the words
that Elijah swears by Yahweh: "There shall be neither dew nor rain throughout
these years except at my express word!" This is meant as Yahweh's challenge
to Baal, represented by Ahab. If Yahweh withholds rain so that Baal is not
able to do anything about it, and then brings it through Elijah's word, he
will prove himself to be the one true God. But this is meant also as a test
of whether Elijah is Yahweh's minister. Elijah next disappears. While the
whole land languishes, Yahweh shows his power to provide by making the
wadi Kerith flow and appointing the ravens to bring food, next by making
the Zarephath widow's jar and cruse remain full "until such a day as Yahweh
shall give rain upon the ground" (17:14). The second episode (18:1–18) shows
an ephemeral Elijah committing himself to a promise to come face to face
with Ahab; the challenge is drawn as the two exchange accusations as to
who it is that has actually put the hex on Israel. This story proceeds to its
third and climactic episode at 18:41, placing Elijah and Ahab on Mount Carmel. While the latter engages in symbolic feasting, Elijah prays repeatedly
to the brazen heavens. With onrushing suddenness his prayer is answered,
and the rains descend. As Ahab drives madly homeward, the prophet runs
before him, triumphant in Yahweh's spirit.

Comment

17:1–16 Elijah's name seems to be symbolic of his special mission, which
is to confess that Yahweh (Jah) is his God (Eli). In eight passages, including
21:17, he is identified as "the Tishbite," but since it is very doubtful that
there was a place Tishbe in Gilead, as many commentators have claimed, it
is perhaps best to follow the suggestion (see S. Cohen in *IDB* IV, 653–54)
that the "i" should be revocalized as an "o", giving us the meaning "settler."
Gilead, east of Jordan and south of the Yarmuk, was wild, forested, and
largely unsettled at this period. Suddenly Elijah stands before Ahab (in Samaria?) and quotes Yahweh's oath to withhold moisture indefinitely, until
Yahweh says otherwise. Baal claims to be god of storm and fertility, present
in the dew and rain, but Yahweh directly challenges him. Yahweh's word
immediately directs the prophet to head eastward, not so much to escape
Ahab's vengefulness as to demonstrate the immediate effects of Yahweh's
threat. In spite of the endeavor of Eusebius and some modern interpreters
to identify the wadi Kerith (RSV "Cherith"), its location is unknown. Yahweh
will provide water from the wadi, and bread and meat from the ravens. Elijah
goes and does as Yahweh commands in order to demonstrate that Yahweh
can provide for his prophet even while the land sinks into famine and drought.

But this demonstration takes a more dramatic form when eventually even
this wadi dries up. Yahweh directs Elijah to leave Israelite territory and travel

to Zarephath, on the Mediterranean about seven miles south of Sidon, where he promises that a widow woman (the poorest of all society) will feed him. What he sees when he arrives there is in every way a challenge to faith. At the prophet's request the widow woman is willing to fetch him water, but when her willingness encourages him to request food as well, she piteously replies that she is only preparing a last frugal meal for herself and her sons before she resigns herself to starvation. In words of assurance borrowed from the theophany ("Do not be afraid"), he challenges her faith by demanding that she first make him a little cake. To this he adds his salvation oracle (v 14) promising that the flour and the oil will be wondrously renewed until Yahweh gives the rain needed for growing these elements from the parched soil. Vv 15–16 are almost anticlimactic, telling us that she acted according to the prophetic word, and that this prophetic word proved true "for many days."

18:1–18 Many more days pass ("in the third year" is considered a gloss) before the provisional demonstration of Yahweh's power over Baal is concluded. At Yahweh's right time he instructs Elijah to appear once more to Ahab, informing him that he will now give rain. Next comes an involved episode (complicated by lengthy additions) in which Elijah arranges for this meeting through Obadiah. This person has the same office referred to in 4:6. He and Ahab are on separate roads, searching for pasturage for their animals. Mysteriously, Elijah appears to Obadiah. When Elijah tells him to inform Ahab that he is here, he protests that Elijah will likely disappear again, leaving his life in danger when Ahab comes to find the prophet. In v 15 Elijah swears most solemnly ("By the life of Yahweh of Hosts") that "today" he will definitely appear to Ahab (cf. *YTT*, 227–30). Elijah has been away so long that Ahab can scarcely believe that the person he beholds is really Elijah; as he asks for identification, his question becomes a defamatory accusation, "Is that you, O Israel's hex (עכר)?" RSV "troubler" is not strong enough; the Hebrew suggests one who is consorting with dark supernatural forces in order to render harm. Elijah throws the accusation back in Ahab's face, charging the entire house of Omri with abandoning Yahweh's commandments, then specifically blaming Ahab for serving the baals (the plural reflects the presence of numerous Baal-shrines in the land). This episode is now interrupted by the insertion of the fire-on-the altar narrative; the Jehuite redactor prepares for this, but also for the conclusion of the drought narrative in vv 41–46, by demanding that Ahab assemble the prophets of Baal (also the prophets of Asherah, of whom nothing is said in vv 21–39) at Mount Carmel.

41–46 The drought story continues in v 41 as Elijah instructs Ahab (not present in the altar narrative) to ascend (from where to where?) and to engage in what must be a symbolic eating and drinking, appropriate to this moment since Elijah ecstatically hears the tumult of rain under an as yet cloudless sky. Climbing to the very summit of Carmel, Elijah crouches in a profound prayer of supplication. His patience and persistence are demonstrated as he sends his young servant seven times to look toward the sea. Seven is, of course, the number of completion and perfection. The servant reports a tiny cloud rising from the horizon; so certain is Elijah that this is Yahweh's answer that he tells his servant to urge Ahab to make haste in order to escape the coming downpour. Darkness and clouds quickly gather. The wind begins to blow. As Ahab mounts to ride back to Jezreel (the summer residence of the Omride kings), a torrent descends. The "hand of Yahweh" (a term for the overwhelming power of the divine spirit; cf. Ezek 8:1) enables Elijah to run before Ahab in triumph to the very gates of Jezreel.

Explanation

17:1 is a motto verse, epitomizing the central theme of this digressive story. About Elijah it can be said that he "stood before Yahweh," i.e., served as one of his intimate counselors and obedient ministers. About Yahweh it can be said that he is the God of Israel—a point on which Ahab vacillates— but also that *he lives*. Yahweh differs from all the other gods in that he actually lives, acts, and responds to his people's need. Ahab with his Phoenician in-laws may believe all their myths about Baal and may participate with fervor in his rites, but he is no living God in the sense that Yahweh is. Can he truly guarantee fertility? Can he give life the way Yahweh does? As Yahweh's minister, Elijah delivers a challenge, actually framed as a threat, to the effect that Yahweh, and he alone, can withhold the water on which all growing things depend, and will bring it back again only when he tells his prophet to say so.

Immediately the prophet goes off to hide. Many commentators have inferred from chap. 19 that he did this to save his skin, but episode 2, in which Elijah reappears, suggests that this hiding has a symbolic intent. As furtive and ephemeral as Elijah is, so evasive is the rain that regularly occurs, and that the Baalists confidently expect. The prophetic threat is fulfilled. The land of Israel and all the lands nearby undergo a dreadful drought. All the brooks and rivers dry up. There is little water and almost no food. But Yahweh secretly feeds his prophet at the brook Kerith.

When even this brook dries up, Elijah goes at the command of Yahweh to the very country of the baalists, Phoenicia, to beg food from one of Zarephath's lowliest and poorest, a widow gathering sticks with which to prepare a last meal for herself and her family. One who listens to this tale will say, No wonder she refused to give Elijah the food and water he requested. The marvel is that God gave her faith sufficient to believe his assurance and his prophecy—but the God who can direct ravens to bring food in a desolate wadi can surely create faith in this widow's heart. To the miracle of faith Yahweh adds the miracle of a never-empty jar of meal and a never-failing cruse of oil. That the prophet with the widow and her sons are fed, while the heavens withhold rain and dew, foretells a great divine work to come— the giving of rain on the day that Yahweh has chosen.

When the judgment for sin comes, it may strike the pious along with the wicked; thus the devout Obadiah is as much concerned for finding fodder as is his master, Ahab. We may be sure that Ahab and his court will be the last to experience actual hunger, but in our story he has been reduced to sorry straits. He and Obadiah are searching every ravine and every gully for a few blades of grass. We may wonder whether Ahab would do as much for his people. Probably his worry is more for his stable than for the masses of human beings over whom he has been placed. Mysteriously, Elijah appears to Obadiah, and on the promise that Elijah will definitely confront Ahab this very day (הֹיּוֹם), 18:15, he goes off to find Ahab and bring him to Elijah. Thus for the first time in several years the representative of institutional power—the baalizing king—and the representative of spiritual power—the humble, spirit-filled prophet—meet. Assuming the stance of overbearing royalty, Ahab turns his question of identification into a reproach: "Is it you, you who have put the hex on Israel?" We may ask, Is it the instrument of divine judgment who causes the pain, or those who have provoked that judgment? It is easy to blame God for our suffering when we have caused it ourselves. Elijah's answer is blunt and clear: by disobeying Yahweh's commandments and following Baal, Ahab has made himself the hex.

The confrontation scene is assuredly the climax of the entire account, but it drives toward a resolution in the actual giving of rain. Having invited Ahab to symbolic feasting, Ahab climbs to Mount Carmel's height. This impressive topographical feature is referred to in Scripture as the very epitome of vegetative fertility, no doubt because it is crowned by a dense and beautiful forest. To go to such a place is to go into the pit, into the bull ring, for both Baal and Yahweh claim it. But it has more than symbolic significance, for it brings the prophet near to heaven while placing him at an excellent vantage-point from which he may immediately espy what answer Yahweh will give to his prayer. It is a prayer—repeated seven times—that constitutes the equivalent of "my word" in 17:1. Elijah does not command; Yahweh commands. Elijah does not command; he prays. But in such a spirit-empowered man, prayer has the force of a command. Elijah has completely identified himself with Yahweh, so Yahweh will not forsake him now. The persistent, sevenfold prayer symbolically rehearses the long, persistent drought that Yahweh had ordained through the prophet's mouth. Now as Yahweh answers, there first appears "a little cloud like a man's hand . . . rising out of the sea." (18:44). The prophet does not wait until the tiny cloud becomes a torrent in order to warn Ahab, for a true prophet knows how to discern the signs of the times. Elijah can interpret this sign of God's coming; 17:1 is fulfilled.

At the very end of the story, Ahab rides furiously toward Jezreel while Elijah, driven by "the hand of Yahweh," runs before him, triumphantly demonstrating the right of spiritual power to dominate over the claims and pretensions of earthly institutions. But paradoxically this running shows that spiritual power does not usurp the place of earthly institutions. To run before a king is to serve him still. Thus in the end the judgment on Ahab is intended for making him a better king over the covenant people. He is being chastened and instructed, not destroyed. Whether repentance will come before a final punishment, is left untold. Ahab may not repent, but he now surely knows who is true God in Israel.

Reviving the Sick Lad   (17:17–24)

Bibliography

Bobichon, M. "Une païenne reconnaît l'homme de Dieu." *BTS* 157 (1974) 15. **Driver, G. R.** "Ancient Lore and Modern Knowledge.—2. Resuscitation." *Hommages à A. Dupont-Sommer.* Paris: Adrien-Maisonneuve, 1971. **Kilian, R.** "Die Totenerweckungen Elias and Elisas—eine Motivwanderung?" *BZ* n.F. 10 (1966) 44–56.

Translation

[17] *And it so happened after these things—now* [a] *the son of the woman who was mistress of the household got sick. And, as it happened, his sickness grew very severe, to the point where breath was scarcely left in him.* [18] *And she* [a] *said to Elijah, "What is the quarrel between me and you, O man of God? Have you come to me to make public my transgression and kill my son?"* [19] *And Elijah said,* [a] *"Give me your son."* *And he took him from her bosom and carried him to the upper room where he was staying, laying him on his bed.* [20] *And he* [a] *cried to Yahweh and said,* [b] *"O Yahweh* [c] *my God,* [c] *hast thou in very fact brought evil on the widow with whom I am sojourning, causing her son to die?"* [21] *And he* [a] *stretched himself out* [a] *over the lad three times. Then he cried to Yahweh and said, "O Yahweh my God, please cause the life of this lad to come back inside him!"* [b] [23] [a] *And so it was: the lad cried out,* [a] *and he brought him down from the upper chamber into the house and presented him to his mother. And Elijah said, "Look, your son is alive."* [24] *And the woman said to Elijah,* [a] *"Now for sure* [a] *do I know that you are a man of God, and that the word of Yahweh is truly in your mouth."*

Notes

17.a. G[BL]. MT omits. We read the second καί in this verse as a conjunction representing what was originally found in Heb., but sacrificed to the preceding redactional line, "And it happened after these things. . . ."

18.a. MT. G[BL] have explicative "the woman."

19.a. MT. G[BL] add explicative "to the woman."

20.a. MT. G[BL] add explicative "Elijah."

20.b. MT. G[BL] improve the style with introductory οἴμοι "alas" (Heb. הוי).

20.c-c. MT. G[BL] omit (haplography).

21.a-a. MT (hithp of מדד, only here). G[BL], not understanding the rare Heb. form, offer ἐνεφύσησεν "he breathed upon."

21.b. G[B]. MT and G[L] accentuate the element of the miraculous in their long insertion: [22] and Yahweh listened to the voice of Elijah, and the lad's life went back inside him and he lived. [23] And Elijah took the lad. . . ."

23.a-a. G[BL]. MT omits.

24.a-a. MT (זה עתה). G[BL], not understanding the unusual expression, offer "behold."

Form/Structure/Setting

[Redactional introduction, v 17aα]
    Exposition: Illness occurs in a place of hospitality, v 17aβ

1. The mistress's complaint
   a. An illness robs her son of breath, v 17b
   b. She draws false implications concerning Elijah's power, v 18
   c. Elijah confronts the challenge, v 19a
2. The prophet's action
   a. Transport to his own bed, v 19b
   [Gloss, v 20]
   b. A symbolic act, v 21aα
   c. A prayer, v 21aβb
3. The marvelous restoration
   a. The lad cries out, v 23aα
   b. Elijah presents him to his mother, v 23aβb
4. Interpretive conclusion: her testimony, v 24

Elijah's dealing with the widow of Zarephath in the introductory section of the first story provided an ideal place for a redactor to attach this quite extraneous prophetic legitimation narrative. Here the theme is the restoration of a sick or dying lad (cf. 2 Kgs 4). In 17:18 his mother challenges Elijah's character as a "man of God," hinting that the sickness may have come from a demonic power for evil. But Elijah exposes the lad to Yahweh's attention in supplicatory prayer, and he revives. When he presents him to his mother, she exclaims that he is indeed a "man of God," having the true word of Yahweh in his mouth. This is a declaration of formal legitimation, a confession that Elijah's manifest numinosity comes not from the realm of darkness and death, but of life and truth.

Comment

"After these things" (אחר הדברים האלה) is a useful, often-employed device for attaching extraneous material. The verb חלה can refer to wounds received in battle or to any kind of serious sickness. Apparently no man is present to take his role as master of the household, for the sick boy is referred to simply as "son of the woman who was the mistress of the household." Since the house inhabited by the Zarephath widow is not in question, the reader asks, "What house is it?" It is apparently not the house of a friend or relative, for Elijah finds himself there as a stranger as well as a guest. We cannot be seriously mistaken in thinking of it as a kind of boarding house, a temporary refuge for travelers.

The story hastens on its way: the woman addresses Elijah in words of high emotion. Though she knows his reputation as a "man of God," she does not hesitate to complain that he has brought this sickness on her son. He has had a sinister purpose: to bring her sins to remembrance! What sins, and how does sickness bring them to remembrance? Her sins must remain her own secret, but her theology of divine judgment is so erroneous that Elijah must act to refute it. Yahweh, the God of Israel, has established no cause and effect relationship between a person's sin and the calamities of life (contra Job's "friends"!). If words could be borrowed from the NT, the purpose of this lad's sore sickness would rather be "that the works of God might be made manifest in him" (John 9:3). Elijah does not argue with this overwrought woman, but simply asks her, "Give me your son." He takes him unconscious upstairs and lays him on his own bed (v 19). V 20 might fit in, but the story's original prayer in v 21 shows that this must be a secondary addition; it makes three mistakes: (1) calling the woman a widow, (2) saying that the boy is dead, and (3) allowing Elijah to voice the woman's bad theology to the effect that Yahweh might actually kill little boys. Then Elijah stretches himself three times "out over" or "upon" the lad; it is not magic, but a typical symbolic act familiar to the prophetic movement in Israel. It is an "acted out" way of saying, "Let his lifeless body be as my lively body," and the prayer that accompanies it fortifies this symbol: "O Yahweh my God, please cause the life (נֶפֶשׁ)of this lad to come back inside him!"

Since Elijah is a man of prevailing prayer, Yahweh answers as he is asked. The lad comes to; Elijah carries him downstairs and hands him to his mother. His words of presentation, "Look, your son is alive," call on her to witness not only that a mighty act of God has been performed, but also that she has been drastically mistaken in taking the boy's apparent death as an act of evil intent. Her response is eloquent and altogether appropriate (v 24). The woman has called Elijah "man of God" out of reverence and respect, but now she knows him to be a "man of God" whose word from God is truth.

Explanation

It is vastly different when religion is a mere *profession* rather than a true, lifelong *confession*. Lay people have trouble discerning the distinction, but ministers may have even more trouble, especially when it is a question about themselves. Was Elijah merely a professional "man of God"—one who knew all the words and went through all the rituals—or was he the kind of "man of God" whom God has completely taken over, filling him with love and truth? This is a question all religious people need to direct to themselves, for how many deeds of darkness have been done by those who have disguised themselves as "men of God"! The perfect model of a "man of God," with the true word of God in his mouth, is not this Elijah, exemplar of authentic prophetism, but one whom he was destined one day to meet on a Mount of Transfiguration, Jesus Christ (Mark 9:4 and parallels). How ironic it is that the professional "men of God" of his day—the Pharisees and the doctors in the temple—put him to death because he raised the dead to life and told the people the word of true prophecy. This brief, charming narrative retains its power, then, for it expresses the perpetual paradox of something good that can also perform evil. Let us be warned by this Scripture: the dark and the demonic lurk in holy places; only deeds of love and deeds of integrity can demonstrate that they have no power to delude us.

The Contest with the Baal Prophets
(18:19–40)

Bibliography

Alt, A. "Das Gottesurteil auf dem Karmel." Festschrift Georg Beer (1935). **Ap-Thomas, D. R.** "Elijah on Mount Carmel." *PEQ* 92 (1960) 145–55. **Burmester, O. H. E.** "The Bohairic Pericope of III Kingdoms xviii 36–39." *JTS* 36 (1935) 156–60. **Eissfeldt, O.** *Der Gott Carmel. SAB* (1953) Nr. 1. **Galling, K.** "Der Gott Karmel und die Ächtung der fremden Götter." *Geschichte und Alte Testament.* BHT 16. Tübingen: Mohr, 1953. **Jepsen, A.** "Elia und das Gottesurteil." *Near Eastern Studies.* (Albright Fs.) Baltimore: Johns Hopkins, 1971. **Junker, H.** "Der Graben um den Altar des Elias. Eine Untersuchung über die kultische Uberlieferung von I Kg 18, 29–38." *Miscellanea Biblica A. Fernandez.* = *EstEccl* 34 (1960) 547–56 = *TTZ* 69 (1960) 65–74. **Kopp, C.** "Il sacrificio di Elia sul Carmelo." *BibOr* 2 (1960) 11–13. **Rowley, H. H.** "Elijah on Mount Carmel." *BJRL* 43 (1960) 190–219. **Seebass, H.** "Elia und Ahab auf dem Karmel." *ZTK* 70 (1973) 121–36. **Tromp, N. J.** "Water and Fire on Mount Carmel. A Conciliatory Suggestion." *Bib* 56 (1957) 480–502. **de Vaux, R.** "Les prophètes de Baal sur le Mont Carmel." *BulMusBeyrouth* 5 (1941) 7–20 = *BibOr* (1967) 485–97. **Vigouroux, P.** "Les pretres de Baal (III Reg. xviii, 23–28) et leurs successeures dans l'antiquités et dans les temps présent." *RB* 7 (1896) 227–40. **Würthwein, E.** "Die Erzählung vom Gottesurteil auf dem Karmel." *ZTK* 59 (1962) 131–44.

Translation

[19] *So now send; gather to me all Israel at Mount Carmel; also the prophets of Baal,*[a] *four hundred and fifty, plus the prophets of Asherah, four hundred, those dining at Jezebel's table.* [20] *So Ahab sent to all Israel.*[a] *And he assembled*[b] *the prophets at Mount Carmel.*

[21] *And Elijah drew near to all* [a]*the people*[a] [b]*and said*[b], *"For how much longer are you going to hobble about on two crutches? If Yahweh is God, go after him, and if Baal is, go after him."* *But the people answered*[c] *not a word.* [22] *And Elijah said to the people, "I survive all by myself as a prophet belonging to Yahweh, while the prophets of Baal number four hundred fifty men.*[a] [23] *Now let them give us two oxen, and let these choose one of the oxen for themselves, cut it up, and place it upon the logs, but let them not put fire to it. And I will prepare one*[a] *of the oxen and will place it on the logs, but will not put fire to it.* [24] *Then you shall call on the name of your god*[a] *while I call on the name of Yahweh.*[b] *And it will be that the god who answers by fire,*[c] *he is God."* *And all the people answered and said, "The word*[d] *is good."*

[25] *Then Elijah said to the prophets of Baal, "Choose for yourselves the one ox and prepare it first, since you are in the majority. And call on the name of your god. But put no fire to it.* [26] *And they took the ox*[a] *and prepared it. And they called on the name of Baal from morning to midday, as follows,*[b] *"O Baal, hear us,"* *but there was no sound and no answer. And they leaped around the altar which they*[c] *had made.* [27] *And at midday Elijah*[a] *began to ridicule them, and he said, "Call in a loud voice, for he is a god! Perhaps he has business*[b] *and perhaps he has a trip to make. Or it could be that he is asleep and needs to be awakened!"* [28] *So they*

called with a loud voice and slashed themselves, according to their ritual, with swords and lances, until the blood poured out upon them. [29] *And it turned out that, although they raved on from about noon until it was time to offer the oblation, there was no sound, nobody giving answer, and no one paying attention.* [a]

[30] *And Elijah said to* [a] *the people, "Draw near to me"; and all the people drew near to him.* [b] *And he repaired the altar of Yahweh that had been overturned.* [b] [31] *And Elijah took twelve stones, signifying the number of the tribes of Israel,* [a] *which accords with Yahweh's word to him that says, "Israel shall be your name."* [32] *And he constructed the stones* [a] *into an altar dedicated* [a] [b] *to the name of Yahweh.* [bc] *And he* [d] *constructed a ditch* [e] *to hold the equivalent of two seahs of seed, encircling the altar.* [33] *Then he arranged the logs,* [a] *cut up the ox, and placed it on the logs.* [b] *And he* [a] *said, "Fill* [b] *four* [c] *jars with water." And they poured it over the sacrifice* [d] *and over the logs.* [de] [34] *And he said, "A second time," and they did it a second time. And he said, "A third time," and they did it a third time.* [35] *And the water ran all around the altar, and even the ditch he* [a] *filled with water.*

[36] [a] *And when it was time to offer the oblation* [a] *Elijah* [b] [c] *drew near* [c] *and said, "O Yahweh, God of Abraham, Isaac, and Israel, today* [d] [e] *let it be known* [e] *that thou* [f] *art* [g] *God in* [h] *Israel, and that I am thy servant, that* [i] *by thy word* [i] *I have performed* [j] *these things.* [37] [a] *Answer me, Yahweh, answer me, so that this people may know that thou, Yahweh, art God,* [a] *and that thou hast turned* [b] *their heart* [b] *in the opposite direction!"* [38] *And* [a] *Yahweh's fire* [a] *fell* [b] *and consumed the sacrifice and the logs,* [c] *the stones and the dust;* [c] *and* [d] *it even licked up* [d] *the water that was in the ditch.* [e] [39] [a] *And all the people saw it. And they fell* [a] *on their faces and said,* [b] [c] *"Yahweh, he is God! Yahweh, he is God!"* [c] [40] *And Elijah said to them,* [a] *"Seize the prophets of Baal, let not one of them escape!" So they seized them and brought them down to Elijah at the river Kishon, and they slaughtered them there.*

Notes

19.a. MT. Gr. αἰσχύνης "shame" translates the mock-name בֹּשֶׁת in the Heb. *Vorlage;* cf. vv 25, 26.

20.a. G[BL]. MT "the children of Israel"; MSS: "the territory of Israel" are pleonastic.

20.b. MT. G[BL] adds pleonastic "all."

21.a-a. MT, G[L]. B[B] omits (haplography).

21.b-b MT. Pleonastic additions are G[B] "and Elijah said to them" and G[L] "and said to them."

21.c. 2 MSS and G[B]. MT and G[L] MS add explicative "him."

22.a MT. 2 MSS and G[BL] add a corruption from v 19, "and the prophets of Asherah are four hundred."

23.a. MT, G[L]. 2 MSS and G[B] have explicative "the second/other."

24.a. MT. G[BL] θεῶν read Heb. אֱלֹהִים as "gods"; but cf. v 25.

24.b. MT. G, Syr, Vg MSS add explicative "my god."

24.c. MT, G[B]. G[L] adds interpretive "today" under the influence of v 36.

24.d. MT. G[BL] insert "which you speak" as a stylistic improvement.

26.a. G[BL]. MT's addition, "which someone gave him," is interpretive.

26.b. MT. G[BL] add "hear us" as a stylistic improvement.

26.c. MSS, G[BL], Vrs, Seb. MT has an inexplicable sing, intended as a passive or indefinite active; cf. *HOTTP,* 327.

27.a. MT. G[BL] add explicative "the Tishbite."

27.b. G[BL]. MT adds the scurrilous gloss, "and perhaps he is defecating."

29.a. MT. G[B] (cf. [L]) has the long interpretive gloss, "and Elijah spoke to the prophets of wrath (προσοχθισμάτων = Heb. שִׁקּוּץ "filth"?) as follows, 'Cease (from) now on, and I will prepare my sacrifice.' And they ceased and departed."

30.a. G^{BL}. MT adds interpretive "all."

30.b-b. MT. G^{BL} omit, but restore it in LXX v 32.

31.a. G^{BL}; see second part of the verse. MT "sons of Jacob" may be a late ideological alteration.

32.a-a. MT. G^{BL} omit.

32.b-b. MT, G^B. G^L omits.

32.c. MT. G^{BL} add v 30b (MT).

32.d. MT. G^{BL} pl intends to correct a palpable error.

32.e. MT. Heb. תעלה "ditch" is transliterated in G^L to get θααλα, corrupted in G^B to θάλασσα(ν) "sea."

33.a. MT, G^B. G^L καὶ ἐπέθηκε(αν) = Heb. וַיָּשֶׂם "and he placed."

33.b. MT. G^{BL} are pleonastic and appear to have a double reading; so G^B: "And he arranged the logs on the altar that he had made and prepared the burnt-offering, and placed the logs, and arranged (them) on the altar."

34.a. MT, G^B. G^L has explicative "Elijah."

34.b. MT. G^{BL} "take me."

34.c. MT, G^B. G^L "two."

34.d-d. MT, G^B. G^L omits.

34.e. MT, G^L. G^B adds pleonastic "and he did so."

35.a. MT, G^L. G^B pl; cf. note 32.d.

36.a-a. MT and G^{Lmin}. G^B omits (ideological and exegetical in view of v 29).

36.b. G^{BL}. MT adds explicative "the prophet."

36.c-c. MT. G^{BL} "called to heaven" (interpretive and corrective).

36.d. MT. G^{BL} paraphrase in the light of v 37a: "Hear me, Yahweh, in fire."

36.e-e. MT. Avoiding passives, G^{BL} substitute "and let all this people know."

36.f. MT, G^B. G^L adds interpretive "alone."

36.g. MT, G^L. G^B adds explicative "Yahweh."

36.h. MT. G^{BL} "of."

36.i-i. Q, MSS, Syr, Tg, Vg. K pl. G^{BL} "by thee."

36.j. G^B. MT and G^L add pleonastic "all."

37.a-a. MT. G^{BL} omit, perhaps because of seeming repetition.

37.b-b. MT. G^{BL} "the heart of this people" (stylistic).

38.a-a. MT. G^{BL} "fire near Yahweh" reflects late Jewish piety.

38.b. MT. G^{BL} "from heaven" is an explicative addition.

38.c-c. MT. G^{BL} omit.

38.d-d. MT. G^{BL} omit.

38.e. MT. G^{BL} have paraphrastic "and the fire licked up the stones and the dust."

39.a-a. MT. G^{BL} shorten paraphrastically with "and all the people fell."

39.b. MT. G^{BL} add "truly" (stylistic).

39.c-c. MT. G^{BL} "Yahweh (the) God, he is (the) God" (ideological and interpretive).

40.a. MT. G^{BL} has explicative "the people."

Form/Structure/Setting

[Redactional transition, vv 19–20]
1. The contest arranged
   a. Elijah endeavors to force the people's decision
      (1) His demand, v 21a
      (2) The people's non-answer, v 21b
   b. The agreement to elicit a divine resolution
      (1) Elijah's proposal
         (a) The inequality of the contending forces, v 22
         (b) Equivalent sacrifices, v 23
         (c) The decisive appeal to Deity, v 24a
      (2) The people's approval, v 24b

2. The failure of Baal and his prophets
   a. An unsuccessful morning, vv 25–26
   b. Ridicule at noonday, v 27
   c. An unsuccessful afternoon, vv 28–29
3. The handicapping of Yahweh
   a. The preparation of Elijah's sacrifice
     (1) The summons to witness, v 30a
[Gloss, 30b)
     (2) Elijah builds a symbolic altar, vv 31–32a
     (3) Further preparations, vv 32b–33a (Eng. 33)
   b. The spoiling of Elijah's sacrifice, 33b (Eng. 34)–35
4. The triumph of Yahweh and Elijah
   a. Elijah's prayer
     (1) An appeal for decisive proof and vindication, v 36
     (2) A plea for the people's conversion, v 37
   b. Yahweh's awesome response, v 38
   c. The people witness, worship, and confess, v 39
[Redactional conclusion, v 40]

The theme of prophet authorization characterizes the material which the Jehuite redactor next inserts. In 18:21–39 Elijah has a contest with the prophets of Baal. The thematic word in this narrative is עָנָה, "answer," "respond." The people will not *answer*, v 21; Elijah proposes two sacrifices with the explanation, "the god that *answers* by fire, he is god"—to which the people *answer*, "The word is good" (v 24); when the Baalists call on their god, there is no *answer* (v 26, strengthened in v 29); when Elijah makes his climactic prayer he cries, *"Answer* me, Yahweh, *answer* me!" (v 37). As the writer has shown on pp. 231–33 in *YTT*, Elijah's prayer in vv 36–37 with foremost הַיּוֹם "today,"epitomizes the entire narrative as a demonstration that (1) Yahweh is truly God in Israel and (2) Elijah is his true servant. In the final analysis, therefore, this is not so much a story about a contest between Yahweh and Baal as a story demonstrating that Elijah is Yahweh's true, authorized prophet. The people have doubted that authority, but in the end their witness, worship, and confession show that they accept it.

Gratefully we turn to the work of the present generation of scientifically oriented exegetes, whose methodology is proving more and more productive in delivering us from naïve literalism and from sterile, rationalistic historicism. Though these interpretations may seem opposite to each other, they each commit the error of assuming that the only possible reading of the "Carmel" narrative is as the literal (though perhaps incomplete) report of an actual historical event. Only, what literalism attributes directly to the supernatural, historicism is likely to attribute to a scheming charlatan with a hidden barrel of naphtha and burning-glass (so Montgomery-Gehman, *Kings*, ICC 1951, *in loco*), or the like. More recent interpretations have sought to deliver us from this impasse by treating the story as a holy legend. Legend, yes; but *holy* legend. In this view, what is recounted in this story may never have literally happened, but this hardly matters, for if it is holy legend we are invited to respond to it not just as history but as witness and appeal.

Actually, there has been a flurry of discussion in recent years about this passage in the context of the other Elijah narratives and the whole corpus of prophet stories. Among titles listed in our *Bibliography,* we mention the writings of Alt, de Vaux, Eissfeldt, Fohrer, Ap-Thomas, Rowley, Würthwein, Steck, Bronner, and Jepsen as the most important. A major concern in all this discussion has been to determine precisely what kind of story this is, since it is possible to conjecture from this its central concerns: setting, purpose and message. Scholars such as Alt and Würthwein have opined that this is the *hieros logos* (legitimizing cult-recital) for an actual shrine on Mount Carmel taken over in the days of Ahab by the zealots of Yahweh from its previous custodians, the adherents of Baal. One problem with this hypothesis is that there is no biblical tradition of such a shrine, and no remains of it have ever been found (traditions of a temple on Carmel in the Hellenistic period are more likely the effect than the cause of our biblical account). Another problem is the question why the Yahwists should have used force to drive out the Baalists when they had plenty of places to build a shrine of their own. Anyway, the text says that Elijah built a new altar. That he would have built an altar for Yahweh alongside an established Baal altar is in itself highly unlikely.

The close parallel in 2 Kgs 1:1–16 suggests affinities with that account. In matter of fact, both are prophet-authorization narratives. In neither account is the sending of the heavenly fire a matter of ultimate concern—as it would have been in a *hieros logos* legitimating a shrine. There the fire shows the three troops that Elijah is indeed a "man of God" authorized to pronounce judgment on an apostate king. Here the fire answers Elijah's prayer, proving Yahweh to be God in Israel and Elijah to be his true prophet. And, as we have stated, this story has the further purpose of enabling the people to answer which god is truly God.

The structural and redactional analysis that we have been following enables us to avoid certain pitfalls into which exegetes continue to fall. We find, for instance, that Eissfeldt's Introduction, J. Gray's commentary on Kings, and the articles of Ap-Thomas and Rowley take the entirety of chaps. 17–19—perhaps with minor glosses—as one literary piece. The most immediate consequence of this misconception is that the drought story and the fire-on-the-altar story belong together within the same exegetical context. But then we are forced to ask with numerous critics what the sending of fire has to do with the question of whether Yahweh will give rain to end the drought; also where Elijah got his twelve "barrels" of water to pour so profligately over his altar. If the Baal contest is taking place on the summit of Mount Carmel, how do they manage to haul so much water up several thousand feet from the nearest good source, the river Kishon at its foot? In matter of fact, there remains no reason to place the Baal contest on Mount Carmel since it is an originally independent story, taking place at some unspecified site. We note that King Ahab is never mentioned in this story, as he surely would have been had chaps. 17–19 been one continuous story.

Comment

21–24 "And Elijah drew near to all the people": throughout the narrative Elijah takes the initiative. Already at the beginning, the question arises, Where did Elijah come from? We do not know, nor do we know where this event is taking place, except that it is in the near vicinity of a Baal shrine. "Draw near" (נגשׁ qal and niph) often means opening a controversy or demanding a decision (Gen 18:23, 27:21, 45:4; Josh 14:6, 21:1; 1 Sam 14:38; Isa 41:1, 50:8; Joel 4:9); hence it sometimes means to prepare to deliver or receive a prophetic oracle (1 Kgs 20:22, 28; 2 Kgs 2:5; Jer 42:1). Our narrator uses it to introduce action in scenes 1, 2, and 4. "How much longer . . . ?": often in controversy contexts, introducing an appeal, charge or grievance (e.g., Ps 82:2, 94:3; Jer 4:14). "Hobble about": Heb פסח "passing over" may also mean "be lame" (cf. 2 Sam 4:4); here it apparently means "limp" or "hobble" (cf. Fohrer, *Elia* 9–11), though in v 26 it refers to a ritual dance (cf. 2 Sam 4:4). "Two crutches": this translates a Heb. word, found only here, whose related forms mean "boughs of trees," "lop off branches," hence perhaps the idea of being on crutches. In any event, the allusion is to wobbling, indecisive action, in which the people "walk" (= moral behavior) neither one way nor the other. "If Yahweh is God, go after him; if Baal is, go after him": the prophet demands action consistent with belief. (Better one way or the other—even the wrong way!—than in between; cf. Rev 3:15). "But the people answered not a word": the first occurrence of the thematic word "answer" (Heb. ענה); see above. "I survive all by myself as a prophet belonging to Yahweh, while the prophets of Baal number four hundred fifty men"; compare the redactor's addition in v 19. Nowhere in the OT does the four hundred fifty figure reappear, though we do have the four hundred prophets of 1 Kgs 22:6 and the fifty sons of the prophets in 2 Kgs 2:7, 16–17. Elijah is not expressing self-pity but is accentuating the scope of his ultimate victory in the light of overwhelming odds. Baal's prophets are mentioned again in 2 Kgs 10:19, and nonbiblical records tell us of prophets outside Israel (Mari). Like some of Israel's prophets, the Baal prophets of our passage seem to be functionaries of the cult.

In v 23 Elijah proposes equal unlit sacrifices. The legitimacy of nonpriests doing this reflects a situation earlier than that envisaged in the Levitical legislation. All is to be done in preparation, but the sacrifice will remain incomplete (hence ineffective and meaningless) until fire is put to it. We are here moving outside the proper realm of the cultic institution, where the officiant has strict jurisdiction, controlling the fire which is the powerful instrument to make a sacrifice out of a nonsacrifice. The issue is to be left entirely up to the rival gods, eliminating the confusing element of propaganda and ecclesiastical hocus-pocus. "Call on the name of your god . . . of Yahweh": to get an answer, one must call one's god by his correct name (cf. Gen 28:13, 33:29; Exod 3:14–15). "The god who answers by fire, he is God": early Israel believed not in a theoretical but in a practical monotheism, i.e., that the only god who counts as real is the one who acts, who has power to help his people. The rest is idle speculation. Here the issue is especially sharp because both Baal and Yahweh claimed the power of fire (for Yahweh, see Gen 15, 19; Exod 3, 19; Judg 6, 13; Amos 1:4, 7, 10, 12, 14; 2:2, 5; Zech 2:5; Mal 3:2). The power actually to send fire will decide which of the two is really God. "It is well spoken": literally, "Good is the word"; cf. v 21. The people who would not or could not answer the prophet's demand now agree to let another answer for them.

25–29 "Prepare it first, since you are in the majority." Continuing the theme of insuperable odds, the narrative shows that Elijah has utter confidence that Baal will not or cannot answer. "From morning to midday"; cf. "at midday," v 27; "noon," v 29; "time to offer the oblation," vv 29, 36. The prominent time-factor is another element of suspense, emphasizing the odds against Elijah. The Baalists take practically the whole day, leaving hardly any time for Elijah to procure Yahweh's answer. "They leaped": Heb. פסח, a pun on v 21. Orgiastic dancing is evidenced from various sources as characteristic of Phoenician-Canaanite religion. To our narrator it is explicable only as an act of desperation occasioned by Baal's failure. "Elijah . . . ridicule[d]": Heb. תלל. This is the sole biblical occurrence of the word, but its meaning is evident from the context (see the LXX). "Call in a loud voice"—the same as above, only more so. "He is musing (Heb. שיח) . . . gone aside (Heb. שיג) . . . gone on a journey." The interpretation is somewhat conjectural. It is tempting to go along with some Jewish exegetes in taking this as a racy, sly sarcasm meaning "busy at the privy." "He is asleep and needs to be awakened": various ancient religions conceived of their gods going to sleep at night—but this is noonday! "Slashed themselves": Heb. גדד hithp, (cf. Deut 14:1). This corresponds to another extrabiblical report, one concerning the Phoenicians and Canaanites. It strikes our narrator as extremely outlandish ("according to their ritual"), a sign of the wildest desperation. "They raved on": an overtranslation of Heb. נבא hithp (cf. 1 Kgs 22:10). "No sound, nobody giving answer, no one paying attention": a cumulative conclusion; cf v 26. We are to understand v 29 as referring to a continuous effort going on while scene 3 (vv 30–35) transpires.

30–35 "Draw near to me": see above. "All the people" are to help, but their very help (pouring the water) is to underscore the eventual witness for which they have been summoned. "Repaired the altar, etc.": an ideological gloss that preempts v 31. "Twelve stones, signifying the number of the tribes . . .": a meaningful symbol, based on an old convention (cf. Josh 4:5ff.); this is to be *Israel's* altar, *Yahweh's* altar. "Constructed the stones into an altar . . . constructed a ditch . . ."; enigmatic, seemingly contradictory. On the interpretation of "to hold the equivalent of two seahs of seed" there are various possibilities, but no doubt this expression conveyed a precise notion to the original hearers. Next comes the command to pour four jars of water again and again (= twelve jars corresponding to the twelve stones), seemingly nullifying all that had been done. "He filled the ditch": the final element of the superlative handicapping of Yahweh; cf. v 38.

36–39 "And when it was time to offer the oblation. . .": Heb. בעלות המנחה. This is the climactic moment, for which all else had been preparation. It would be supposed that the sacrifice meant here was the one offered from ancient times in the evening, just before sunset (cf. Exod 29:38ff., Num. 28:3 ff., 2 Kgs 16:15, Ezra 9:4–5, Dan 9:21). But Josephus and the Mishnah, following a tradition that evidently misunderstood our text, speak of a sacrifice in the midafternoon. This has been taken as justification for setting the time of Elijah's prayer several hours before sunset, early enough to allow for the further actions of vv 40–46 on the same day. But this consideration is removed when these verses are identified as from another source. Since the action of vv 30–35 is to be understood as contemporaneous with that of v 29, no reason remains for fixing any other time than evening as the moment of Elijah's prayer. Actually, it is this that gives meaning to the time-word "today," in emphatic foremost position. Today has been all but consumed by the Baal prophets, but Yahweh is able to act yet—all in one short moment. "God of Abraham, Isaac, and Israel": the old familiar formula, but with "Israel" deliberately substituted for "Jacob" as a basis for the punning sequel, "Thou art God in Israel." "Let it be known that . . . I am thy servant" (cf. Exod 14:31); this is parallel to "by thy word [foremost in Heb.] I have performed these things." The revelation Elijah seeks is to demonstrate (1) the answer to the contest (Yahweh is God in Israel) and (2) the answer to the controversy with the people (v 21), who by their nonanswer have shown that they doubt Elijah's prophetic credentials, and hence the power of his word. "Answer me, Yahweh, answer me!": the final, impassioned plea; Elijah can do or say no more. If Yahweh will not now respond, all is lost. "That thou, Yahweh, art God": more absolutely than in v 36 because if Yahweh is God in Israel he is God *par excellence.* "Hast turned their heart in the opposite direction": enigmatic unless emended. Is Elijah saying that Yahweh has caused Israel's apostasy in some way? Unwelcome as this notion may be to us moderns, it may have support in such passages as 1 Sam 16:14, 2 Sam 24:1, 1 Kgs 22:22–23, Amos 3:6, etc.

Finally, in the words of vv 38–39, the fire falls, resolving the contest: the people fall on their faces, settling the controversy. The dramatic climax is so simple, so abrupt, as to astound us. But this is just the effect intended. All the preceding has been devised to build suspense as to whether Yahweh would actually answer in fire, yet for the narrator there had never been the slightest doubt that he really would. "All the people saw": i.e., witnessed (cf. Exod 14:13, 30–31). "Yahweh, he is God; Yahweh, he is God"; so the Heb. text. The LXX, perhaps aiming at stylistic improvement (!) by avoiding exact repetition, reads, "Yahweh is God, he is God!"

Explanation

The Israelite people had been so confused by countering claims that they had been unable to decide. "The people answered not a word." They *would* not answer Elijah because they *could* not answer. Yahweh was their ancestral God, but the naturalistic appeal of the vegetative Baal religion had confused them. Elijah was right: "If Yahweh is God, follow him; if Baal, follow him." Belief must produce action—a committed, consistent life. If one believes in Baal, one should live a luxuriant, materialistic life; if one believes in Yahweh, one must live according to the high spirituality of his noble, austere commandments. Since the people cannot respond, Yahweh responds for them. What four hundred fifty Baal prophets could not get Baal to do by dancing and slashing all day, Yahweh did in a last brief moment before sunset, and he did this in response to the simple but powerful supplication of his true servant, Elijah. While Baal was away on a journey, or on business, or sound asleep, Yahweh was alert and attentive, only waiting until the impotency of Baal should be fully demonstrated. Repeatedly the Baal prophets had cried, "Baal, hear us!"—but there had been no answer, no voice, no one to take heed.

Contrariwise, one brief, urgent prayer moves Yahweh to action. Baal may claim to be a god of fire, but he has no fire when it is needed. It is Yahweh who has a fire that leaps out to perform his will. But let us be assured that Yahweh sends his fire not just to subdue Baal and refute the baalists, but to confirm his prophet and convince his people. The story, after all, is about them, for they are the only ones concerning whom there has been any doubt. The denouement comes not when Baal fails, or even when Yahweh succeeds, but when the people who have been limping on two opinions worship and confess, "Yahweh, he is God! Yahweh, he is God!"

Moderns may ask, Is one to demand fire from heaven as a resolution to doubting? The answer is no, because this age has outgrown the conception of that spectacular kind of irruptive supernaturalism. We would not belittle that belief, but should measure our thought-world against the thought-world of the ancients. The ancient Hebrews expected God to answer them by fire because to them he was a God of fire. But that was only the peculiar coloring of an essence that lay much deeper. What gave Yahwism its intense vitality was the conviction that the God of Israel was alive, was real, was imminently available, was both able and willing to act.

They believed that he was completely committed to the well-being of his covenant people, unlike the pantheizing gods of the heathen environment. The heathen gods were notoriously capricious and grossly self-interested; they could never be counted on to act on behalf of their essentially self-seeking devotees, unless forced in one way or another to do so. The ancient world of myth and ritual had precisely this purpose: *cultivare deorum*, "cultivating the gods"—from which comes our English "cult." The caricature in Elijah's sarcastic words is basically accurate: Baal truly was the kind of god who could never be counted on. He might answer, but he might not. In any contest with him—or all the gods of heathendom put together—Yahweh would win hands down. When it came to answering his people, there was no uncertainty. He could answer. He would answer. Perhaps not by fire, but then in so clear and powerful a way that his people would know that he had heard and that his purpose was sure to come to pass.

Yahweh Renews Elijah's Authority (19:1-18)

Bibliography

Allen, R. B. "Elijah the Broken Prophet." *JETS* 22 (1979) 193–202. **Carlson, R. A.** "Élie à l'Horeb." *VT* 19 (1969) 416–39. **Hossfeld, F.-L.** "Die Sinaiwahlfahrt des Propheten Elia." *ErbAuf* 54 (1978) 432–37. **Lust, J.** "Elijah and the Theophany on Mount Horeb." *BETL* 41 (1976) 91–100. **von Nordheim, E.** "Ein Prophet kündigt sein Amt auf (Elia am Horeb)." *Bib* 59 (1978) 153–73. **Seybold, K.** "Elia am Gottesberg. Vorstellungen prophetischen Wirkens nach 1. Könige 19." *EvT* 33 (1973) 3–18. **Stamm, J. J.** "Elia am Horeb." *Studia biblica et semitica Theodoro Christiano Vriezen . . . dedicata.* Wageningen: Veenman, 1961. **Weissman, S.** "Die Erzählung von der Theophanie am Horeb (I Reg 19)." *BMik* 11 (1965) 140–43. **Würthwein, E.** "Reflections on I Kings 19:9–18." *Proclamation and Presence. Old Testament Essays in Honour of G. H. Davies.* London: SCM Press (1970) 152–66.

Translation

[1] *And Ahab told Jezebel[a] everything Elijah had done, [b]including the way[b] he had killed[c] the prophets with the sword.* [2] *Then Jezebel sent[a] to Elijah saying, "[b]If you are Elijah, I am Jezebel.[b] Thus may the [c]gods do,[c] and even more, if by this time tomorrow I do not make your life like the life of one of them!"* [3] *And he[a] was frightened;[b] he arose and went for his life, arriving at Beersheba, [c]belonging to[c] Judah. And he dismissed his lad there,* [4] *while he himself went on into the desert for a day's journey. And he came and sat down beneath a certain[a] broom tree. And he asked for his life, so that he might 'die; and he said, "Enough now, Yahweh,[b] take my life,[c] for I am no better than my forefathers!"* [5] *Then he lay down and slept[a] beneath the broom tree.[b] And behold, someone[c] was prodding him and saying to him, "Get up and eat!"* [6] *And he[a] looked, and behold, near his head was a cake made on heated stones, as well as a cruse of water.[b] So he ate and drank,[c] then went back to sleep.* [7] *And the angel of Yahweh came back a second time and prodded him, saying, "Get up and eat, for the trip is too far for you."* [8] *So he arose, ate and drank,[a] and walked on in the strength of that food for forty days and forty nights, as far as the mountain of God.[b]*

[9] *And at that place he entered a certain cave, and there he lodged. And behold, the word of Yahweh occurred to him, saying,[a] "What is it with you here, Elijah?"* [10] *And he[a] said, "I have been furiously zealous for Yahweh, God of Hosts; for the Israelites have forsaken [b]thy covenant,[b] thine altars they have overturned, and thy prophets they have slain with the sword. And I survive—I alone—but they are attempting to take my life."* [11] *And he said, "Go out and stand [a]on the mountain[a] before Yahweh."[b] And behold, Yahweh was passing by, and a wind great and strong was tearing up the mountains, shattering the rocks before Yahweh. Yahweh was not[c] in the wind. And after the wind came an earthquake; Yahweh was not in the earthquake.* [12] *After the earthquake came a fire; Yahweh was not in the fire. And after the fire came a gentle little breeze.* [13] *And it so happened that, when Elijah heard it, he wrapped his face in his mantle, and going outside, he stood [a]at the entrance to[a] the*

cave. And behold, a voice came to him and said, "What is it with you here, Elijah?" [14] And he[a] said, "I have been furiously zealous for Yahweh, God of Hosts; for the Israelites have forsaken [b] thy covenant,[b] thine altars they have overturned, and thy prophets they have slain with the sword. And I survive—I alone—but they are attempting to take my life."

[15] And Yahweh said to him, "Go, retrace your trip. [a]And you are to go[a] through the wilderness to Damascus[b] and are to anoint Hazael king over Syria. [16] Also Jehu son of Nimshi you are to anoint as king over Israel; and Elisha son of Shaphat[a] you are to anoint[b] as prophet to take your place. [17] And him who escapes from the sword of Hazael, Jehu will kill, while him who escapes from the sword of Jehu, Elisha will kill. [18] Also, I[a] have left in[b] Israel seven thousand—all the knees that have refused to bend for Baal and every mouth that has refused to kiss[c] him."

Notes

1.a. MT, G[L]. G[B] adds explicative "his wife."

1.b-b. G[BL] (καὶ ὡς = Heb. וַאֲשֶׁר "and which," the probable original). MT made this the basis for a dittography, וְאֵת כָּל אֲשֶׁר "and everything which," from the foregoing context.

1.c. G[BL]. MT adds pleonastic "all."

2.a. G[BL]. MT adds explicative "a messenger."

2.b-b. G[BL]. MT omits (ideological?).

2.c-c. MT (אֱלֹהִים "the gods," with pl verb). G[BL] sing subject and verbs. Of the two textual traditions, it is more likely that G has been affected by ideological considerations.

3.a. MT. G[BL] have explicative "Elijah."

3.b. MSS, G, Syr, Vg, reading Heb. וַיִּרָא. MT "saw" (וַיַּרְא) may be ideological. Cf. BHSmg; HOTTP, 327.

3.c-c. MT. G[BL] "in the land of" reads MT אֲשֶׁר לִיהוּדָה "which belongs to Judah" as "the land of Judah" אֶרֶץ לִהוּדָה.

4.a. MT. G[BL] omit (paraphrastic?).

4.b. MT and G[LMS]. G[B] transposes the vocative to the end of the clause.

4.c. MT. G[BL] add explicative "from me."

5.a. MT. G[BL] add explicative "there."

5.b. G[BL]. MT adds explicative "a certain."

5.c. G[BL] (τις). MT "an angel" is ideological and interpretive.

6.a. MT, G[L]. G[B] has explicative "Elijah."

6.b. MT. G[B] "and he arose"; G[L] "and Elijah arose."

6.c-8.a. MT, G[B]. G[L], Syr omit (homoioteleuton).

8.b. MT adds an interpretive gl "Horeb," while G[BL] read "as far as Mount Horeb," omitting "of God." The MT reading is likelier to be original than the Gr. because the latter drops out a less definite word for a more specific one, but it is more probable that the less definite word, chosen by MT, was original, the more specific word (Horeb) being added later.

9.a. G[BL]. MT adds explicative "to him."

10.a. MT. G[BL] add explicative "Elijah."

10.b-b. MT. G[BL] "thee." See v 14. Cf. HOTTP, 328.

11.a-a. MT. G[BL] αὔριον = Heb. מָחָר "tomorrow" is a corruption of MT בָּהָר "on the mountain."

11.b. MT. G[BL] add explicative "on the mountain."

11.c. MT, G[L]. G[B] omits the negative (ideological?).

13.a-a. MT. Since the Heb. idiom makes no use of prepositions, these are supplied imaginatively by G[B] (ὑπὸ "inside") and G[L] (παρὰ "next to").

14.a. MT. G[BL] add explicative "Elijah."

14.b-b. MT. As in v 10, G[BL] substitute "thee."

15.a-a. G[BL]. MT omits (corr?).

15.b. G[L]. MT, G[B] add a superfluous "and you are to go" (dittography).

16.a. G[BL]. MT adds explicative "from Abel-Meholah." Cf. BHSmg (gl).

16.b. MT, G^L. G^B inserts "from Abel-Meholah" in an awkward place.
18.a. MT, G^L. G^BMSS 2nd person. Cf. Rom 11:4 (see *BHS*mg).
18.b. MT, G^B. G^L "out of" (ideological?).
18.c. MT. G^BL "worship/do obeisance to" (ideological).

Form/Structure/Setting

1. Return to the site of theophanous empowerment
   a. Elijah resigns prophetic responsibility
      (1) The threat of abusive political force, 19:1–2
      (2) Elijah's flight to the desert
          (a) Abandonment of Yahweh's land, vv 3–4a
          (b) Relinquishment of life, v 4b
   b. Elijah's transportation
      (1) His strengthening
          (a) The first angelic visit, vv 5–6
          (b) The second angelic visit, v 7
      (2) His fantastic journey, v 8
2. A revelatoin of human and divine possibilities
   Transition: Arrival at the mountain of God, v 9a
   a. The first inquest
      (1) Yahweh's challenge, v 9b
      (2) Elijah's despondent reply
          (a) His superabundant zeal, v 10aαℵ
          (b) The prevailing power of apostasy, v 14aαℶβb
      (3) The summons to new revelation, v 11aαℵ
   b. The second inquest
      (1) The theophanic revelation
          (a) The three violent forces and the quiet sound, vv 11aαℶβb–12
          (b) Elijah's worship, 13a
      (2) Yahweh's challenge, v 13b
      (3) Elijah's despondent reply
          (a) His superabundant zeal, v 14aαℵ
          (b) The prevailing power of apostasy, v 14aαℶβb
3. The commission to instigative action
   a. Intervention in Syria
      (1) The journey to Damascus, v 15a
      (2) The anointing of Hazael, v 15b
   b. Intervention in Israel
      (1) The anointing of Jehu, v 16a
      (2) The anointing of Elisha, v 16b
   c. Yahweh's purpose
      (1) The threefold scourge, v 17
      (2) The faithful residue, v 18

We are indebted to O. H. Steck, *Überlieferung und Zeitgeschichte*, for demonstrating how a redactor in Jehu's reign, beginning in 841 B.C., shaped these four Elijah stories as a propaganda tract against the house of Ahab. It is this redactor who provided the transition at the beginning of 17:17 for incorporating the story of the sick child (v 20, anticipating the prayer of Elijah in v 21, is a later gloss raising a theological question not contemplated by the original narrative). It is he also who inserted expansions at 18:3b–4, 10–11, and 13–14. In 18:19–20 and 18:40 he also provided linkages to the drought story, bringing the Baal prophets on the scene and then disposing of them. The one remaining prophet story in this early Elijah collection, that of 19:1–18, had an independent existence before a Jehuite redactor went to work on it, but its introduction was altered in such a way as to show acquaintance with the redactional additions already made in 18:19–20, 40. 19:1–18 is distinctive in making thematic the prophet's return to the scene of the theophanous commissioning. It features a contrast between the "there" of where Elijah should have been (Palestine) and the "here" of Horeb, his present place of refuge. It also features the strong contrast between Elijah's utter despondency (v 4) and Yahweh's immeasurable, incomprehensible power, symbolically revealed in the seeming nonpower of the gentle little breeze (v 12). It ends with a boldly ambitious commission (vv 15–16) to be realized through Yahweh's power, manifest still in humble and unlikely places.

Comment

1–8 Jezebel's message to Elijah is meant as a challenge, perhaps symbolically pitting her name "Where is the Prince?" against his name "Yahweh is my God" (cf. O. Eissfeldt, VTSup 16 [1967] 65–70). "By this time tomorrow," כעת מחר, is a threat formula; cf. Exod 9:18. The threat is a convention because if Jezebel had actually intended to arrest Elijah she would have sent her bailiffs and not her messenger, giving him a day's head start. Psychologizing interpretations of this narrative have been hard put to explain how the triumphant, high-flying Elijah of 18:46 could suddenly become so frightened (19:3) and despondent (vv 4–9), but of course this question does not arise for those who recognize the original independence of these passages. The point is that Elijah interprets Jezebel's personal attack on him as the end of his ministry. The prophet's dismissal of his servant at Beersheba, the southernmost limit of Yahweh's land, signifies that he is abandoning it altogether. A day's journey into the Negeb is as far as he intends to go; he lies down weary unto death and prays for Yahweh to let it be enough; his forefathers are in their graves, let him be as they are, for he is no better than they (v 4). But he must travel further, physically and spiritually; so twice an angelic visitor (v 7, "angel of Yahweh" means Yahweh's emissary, a hypostatic extension of his own being) feeds him, on the second occasion explaining that the trip that Yahweh intends for him requires all the strength that this food can bring. Marvelously, Elijah travels on that morsel of heaven-provided food for forty days and nights, and thus comes to the mountain of God. Although the probable original text does not identify this mountain (see the *Notes*), it is clearly the mountain of revelation and of theophanous empowerment, Mount Horeb, where Moses saw God (Exod 24:11).

9–14 This section emphasizes the locale with adverbs of place ("there," שם; "here," פה). Either on or near the mountain, Elijah hides in a cave.

When Yahweh's word challenges him, the prophet explains that all his furious zeal for Yahweh, "God of Hosts," has been in vain. The Israelites have devoted themselves to (1) forsaking the covenant, (2) overturning the altars, and (3) killing the prophets, so that Elijah alone survives (v 10, repeated for effect in v 14). Directing him to stand outside on the mountain, Yahweh passes by (cf. Exod 33:22, 34:6). With great dramatic power, the narrative mentions wind, earthquake, and fire, the familiar symbols of the theophanic presence (cf. Exod 19:16–19), as potential manifestations of Yahweh's power. Then is mentioned a קול דממה דקה (v 12), which has been variously translated but apparently means nothing more than "a gentle little breeze" (cf. J. J. Stamm, "Elia am Horeb," *Studia biblica*). To interpret v 13 in view of v 11, we are to suppose that the tumult frightened Elijah back into his cave and the gentle breeze drew him out. His repeated complaint in v 14 is an implicit confession that no strength for ministry remains in him and must therefore come from God himself.

15–18 The interpretation of this section, and of the entire narrative, depends for its understanding on the climax in v 18. Elijah must reverse his retreat, returning to the land of ministry and there accomplishing mighty acts of prophetic power, anointing Hazael (cf. 2 Kgs 8:7–15), Jehu (cf. 2 Kgs 9:1–13), and Elisha (cf. 1 Kgs 19:19–21, which records a competing tradition, to the effect that Elijah threw his mantle over Elisha). Each of these is to wield the sword, personally or by proxy, against the baalists. Yahweh will see to it that the one follows up on the other. And if this is not enough, Yahweh still depends upon his quiescent seven thousand, who may at this moment be unknown, but will do Yahweh's work when they are needed. (On vv 10, 14, 18, cf. Rom 11:3–4.)

Explanation

In the three Elijah legends of chaps. 17–18, the prophet was depicted in power and strength, but here it is in weakness and resignation. Elijah had defied every enemy, whether mighty Ahab or the four hundred fifty Baal prophets and apostate Israel, or simply the superstitious mother with her dying child. Elijah had performed mighty works—though always through prayer and not through deeds of magic. He brought food to the starving widow of Zarephath, rain to end the drought, fire to consume the sacrifice, and—in kindly reassurance—life and healing to the sick boy. It is altogether different in 1 Kgs 19:1–18. Here he who was strong has become weak. He cowers before his new enemy, Jezebel. Far from performing another mighty work, he flees into the desert, abandoning life itself.

The reader should not overlook how often this narrative mentions Elijah's life: in v 2 Jezebel threatens to take it; in v 3 he flees for his life; in v 4 he surprisingly surrenders the life he has seemed so anxious to save; in his twofold complaint of vv 10, 14, he states that his enemies seek his life, to take it away. There can be little doubt but that the Elijah of our narrative is so weak and filled with despair because he has suddenly cut himself off from the fountain of his strength, the God of Israel, who is also the God of heaven and earth. All that he can remember that is positive is his own prophetic authority and authenticity: "I have been furiously zealous for Yahweh, God of Hosts." Any prophet who sees things going badly in his ministry and as a result wants to abandon it and perhaps surrender his very life must assuredly have forgotten from whom his real strength comes.

Because Yahweh still has work for Elijah to do, he gives him heavenly food for the long trek to Horeb, and there he reimpowers him to mighty deeds by showing him that he is present not only in the "earthquake" and "fires" and "winds" that have heretofore supported Elijah's labors, but also in so still a silence of God's apparent absence as to seem no more than a quiet murmur. This is a rebuke not only for the biblical prophet, but for all religionists who rely on shoutings and flurries of action, while neglecting the way of quiet love, simple piety, and persuasive kindness. God is more likely to have his "seven thousand whose knees have not bowed to Baal and whose mouths have not kissed him" among those who practive these virtues than among those who make a great show of their religion.

In the structure of this prophet story, place is crucial. We are not told where Elijah is at the beginning, although it is apparent that he is within the land of Israel. In fright and despair, the prophet flees southward, coming to Beersheba at the very southern border of Judah. In Judah he is beyond Jezebel's reach, but still within Yahweh's land. Dismissing his servant signifies leaving his ministry, but departing Beersheba and traveling for a day further into the desert signifies abandoning the covenant people, who live in Yahweh's land. Under the broom tree in the Negeb Elijah prays Yahweh to take his life, for all that he has lived for—his prophetic ministry and Yahweh's people—are gone. It is there that God takes over, feeding him with angelic food and bringing him in forty days and nights to the mountain of God. V 9 is a clue to the meaning of the entire account. It twice uses the adverb "there" and then has God say, "What are you doing *here*, Elijah?" Assuredly, the Negeb was no proper place for this mighty man of God, but Horeb still less, unless it were to receive a new theophanous commission. Our narrative is also fond of putting things in twos. As Elijah had to eat the heavenly food and water twice before he could gain strength to go onward to the mountain (vv 5–8), Elijah answers Yahweh's challenge of v 9 with a first complaint and then, when again asked, "What are you doing *here*, Elijah?" (v 13), he replies with a second complaint that is phrased identically to the first (vv 10, 14). Thus it is not the theophany in itself that is able to relieve the prophet of his complaint, for that complaint remains true. Elijah has been furiously zealous; the people of Israel have forsaken the covenant; they have thrown down Yahweh's altars and killed his prophets; they are indeed seeking to take the life of Yahweh's last living prophet. What now? We are told nothing of a change of Elijah's psychological state. We are not even told whether he actually did carry out the anointing of Hazael, Jehu, and Elisha. Elijah's abandonment of ministry and surrender of life is overcome by the straightforward commission with which this narrative ends. Doubts will cease and misgivings vanish when God puts him to work.

Elisha's Call (19:19–21)

Bibliography

Alcaina Canosa, C. "Vocación de Eliseo (1 Re 19, 19–21)." *EstBib* 29 (1970) 137–51. **Alt, A.** "Die literarische Herkunft von I Reg 19, 19–21." *ZAW* 32 (1912) 123–25. **Böklein, E.** "Elisas 'Berufung' (1 Reg 19, 19–21)." *ZAW* 32 (1912) 41–48, 288–91. **del Olmo Lete, G.** "La Vocación de Elisea." *EstBib* 26 (1967) 287–93. **Reiser, W.** "Eschatalogische Gottespruche in den Elisa-Legendeń." *TZ* (1953) 321–38.

Translation

[19] *And he* [a] *went from there; and he came upon Elisha son of Shaphat while he was plowing, with twelve yokes of oxen preceding him. And he was with the twelfth, so Elijah* [b] *crossed over to him and tossed his mantle over him.* [20] *And he* [a] *left the oxen, to run after Elijah. And he said, "Please, I want to kiss my father* [b] *and mother* [b] *goodbye; then I will go after you." And he* [c] *said, "But what* [d] *do I have to do with you?"* [21] *Turning away from him, he took the yoke of oxen and sacrificed them, boiling them with the oxen's equipment.* [a] *And he gave it to the people, and they ate. Then he arose and went after Elijah. So he became his minister.*

Notes

19.a. MT, G[B]. G[L] has explicative "Elijah."
19.b. MT and G[LMSS]. G[B] omits through haplography with following אֵלָיו "to him."
20.a. MT. G[BL] has explicative "Elisha."
20.b-b. MT. G[BL] omit through haplography caused by the similar forms, לְאָבִי "to my father" and לְאִמִּי "to my mother."
20.c. MT. G[BL] have explicative "Elijah."
20.d. MT. G[BL] omit (haplography from misunderstanding?).
21.a. G[BL]. MT adds the explanatory gloss "the flesh."

Form/Structure/Setting

A story from the Elisha cycle: "Elisha's call"
1. The charismatic designation
   a. The situation, v 19a
   b. The act of empowerment, v 19b
2. The test of irresolution
   a. Elisha's request (= repudiation of the call?), v 20a
   b. Elijah's challenge, v 20b
3. The act of consecration
   a. A farewell feast, v 21a
   b. Entry into lifelong ministry, v 21b

The introductory words "And he went from there" are from the editor who joined the three major collections of prophet legends into a single prophet history (see De Vries, *Prophet against Prophet*, 112–13), bringing forward the first story from the Elisha cycle because of 19:16 (the next story in this cycle is at 2 Kgs 2:1–18). The present narrative is, we have said, "a prophetic-call legend," identifying the charismatic source of Elisha's power. Like other call narratives (e.g., Exod 3:9–15 [E]; Isa 6:1–8; Jer 1:4–10), it moves from empowerment to irresolution to confirmation. Elisha's request to be allowed to go home to kiss his parents farewell is clearly a delaying element, provoking Elijah's challenge that Elisha make up his mind (v 20). This then happens not through some special sign from God but through Elisha's consecrative act, showing that he is already filled with the divine spirit.

The prophets employed no idle embellishment to narrate their stories. Every word counted, and every word had power. Because of this story's extreme brevity, moderns may have difficulty in understanding it, but we may be sure that those who first told and heard it were attuned to the implications of every word.

Comment

Elisha is identified as Shaphat's son in 1 Kgs 19:16, 19; 2 Kgs 3:11; and 6:31. In 2 Kgs 5:8 he is called a "man of God," and in 2 Kgs 9:1, a prophet. Nothing is known about his father, Shaphat, and his birthplace, given as Abel-Meholah in the MT of 1 Kgs 19:16 (see also Judg 7:22, 1 Kgs 4:12), has not been identified with certainty. Like Saul in 1 Sam 11:5, Elisha is in the field plowing. Though the number twelve is certainly symbolic of the tribes, it also suggests a communal venture in which all the ox-teams from the village joined in cultivating a common field. Dramatically, Elijah lets eleven ox-teams pass him and then casts his mantle—the token of spiritual power (cf. 2 Kgs 2:8, 13–14)—over Elisha. One carefully notes the disparity with 1 Kgs 19:16, which is from a different tradition. Elisha immediately recognizes what the mantle means and runs after Elijah. He has a request to make, however—one that is met with skepticism on Elijah's part. Elisha only wants time to kiss his father and mother farewell. This sounds reasonable enough, but Elijah's response suggests that Elisha may be vacillating and will use the moment at home to drop out or hide away. The question, "But what do I have to do with you?" is therefore a challenge: it is up to Elisha to decide whether or not he will belong to Elijah permanently. Elisha more than accepts the challenge, however, for the text tells not of his kissing his parents but of slaughtering his oxen and chopping up their yoke in order to make a sacrificial feast dedicating himself to the prophetic ministry. The fellow-villagers who share the feast with him are witnesses to his ordination. This done, Elisha quits Abel-Meholah forever and become Elijah's apprentice until the end.

Explanation

The best commentary on the Elisha call-story is Jesus' word recorded in Luke 9:61–62: "Another said, 'I will follow you, Lord; but let me first say farewell to those at my home.' Jesus said to him, 'No one who puts his hand to the plow and looks back is fit for the kingdom of God.'"

Following God involves strenuous demands. Though a disciple of Christ, like a disciple of Elijah, must continue to live *in* this world, he can no longer be *of* it. There is only one direction for a disciple to go: forward—and that without misgivings and regrets. If he cannot make this commitment, it is better that he should stay home with his oxen.

Three Narratives from the Omride-War Cycle (20:1–43a)

Bibliography

Lipinski, E. "Le Ben-Hadad II de la Bible et l'Histoire." *Fifth World Congress of Jewish Studies,* 1969. Jerusalem: World Union of Jewish Studies, 1969. **Mazar, B.** "The Aramean Empire and its Relations with Israel." *BA* 25 (1962) 98–120. **Meek, T. J.** "I Kings 20:1–10." *JBL* 78 (1959) 73–75. **Miller, J. M.** "The Rest of the Acts of Jehoahaz (I Kings 20; 22, 1–38)." *ZAW* 80 (1968) 337–42. **Schwally, F.** "Zur Quellenkritik der historischen Bücher.—III. I Kön. 20, 13ff." *ZAW* 12 (1892) 157–59. **Weil, H. M.** "Le chapitre II de Michée expliqué par le Premier Livre des Rois chapitres XX–XXII." *RHR* 121 (1940) A 146–61. **Yadin, Y.** "Some Aspects of the Strategy of Ahab and David (I Kings 20; II Sam 11)." *Bib* 36 (1955) 332–51. **Zimmerli, W.** "Das Wort des göttlichen Selbsterweises (Erweiswort), eine prophetische Gattung." *Melanges bibliques A. Robert.* Paris: Bloud and Gay 1957 (=*Gottes Offenbarung* [Munich: Chr. Kaiser, 1963] 120–32).

Translation

¹ Now Ben-Hadad ᵃking of Syriaᵃ gathered all his forces;ᵇ and thirty-two kings were with him withᶜ cavalry and chariotry. Then he went up and besieged Samaria,ᵈ threatening battle against it. ² And he sentᵃ to Ahab the king of Israel inside the city ³ and said to him, "Thus says Ben-Hadad, 'Your gold and your silver all belong to me, also yourᵃ wives and your children belong to me.'" ⁴ And the king of Israel gave answer and said, "Just as you say, O my lord king! To you do I belong, with all that is mine." ⁵ But he sent the messengers back to say, "Thus says Ben-Hadad,ᵃ 'To be sure, I sent ᵇto youᵇ as follows, "Your silver and your gold and your wivesᶜ belong to me; ⁶ nevertheless, tomorrow about this time I am going to send my servants to you to search ᵃyour own houseᵃ and the houses of your servants, and what will happen is that everything that is valuable in yourᵇ eyes ᶜthey will seize with their hands and confiscate!"'"ᶜ ⁷ Then the king of Israel summoned all the elders of the landᵃ and said, "Now know and take notice that it is simple trouble that this one is looking for, for he sent to me for my women and my children,ᵇ for my silver and my gold, ᶜand I have not refused it to him."ᶜ ⁸ And all the elders and all the people said to him, "Do not obey, nor give in!" ⁹ So he said to the messengers of Ben-Hadad, "Say to myᵃ lord ᵇthe king,ᵇ 'Everything that you mentioned to your servant at first I will perform, but this thing I am unable to do.'" And the menᶜ departed and brought back word. ¹⁰ And Ben-Hadad sent to him and said, "Thus may the gods do to me and more if the dust of Samaria shall suffice for handfuls for all the troops who follow me!" ¹¹ But the king of Israel gave answer and said, ᵃ"You say,ᵃ 'Let not the one who binds on his armor boast as he who takes it off!'" ¹² And it happened, when this word was heard, while he was drinking—he and his kings—in booths, that he said to his servants, ᵃ"Get ready!"ᵃ And they got readyᵇ against the city.

¹³ And behold, a certain prophet came up toᵃ the king of Israel and said, "Thus says Yahweh, 'Have you seenᵇ this great mob? Behold, I am about to give them

into your hand today, so that you will know that I am Yahweh." [14] *And Ahab said, "By whom?" And he said, "Thus says Yahweh, 'By the youths of the governors of the provinces.'" And he* [a] *said, "Who will commence the combat?" And he answered, "You."* [15a] *Then he* [b] *mustered the youths of the governors of the provinces,* [a] *and they numbered two hundred thirty-two.* [c] *And after them, he mustered* [d] *the troops; and the* [e]*armed men* [e] *were seven* [f] *thousand.* [g] [16] *And he* [a] *went out* [b]*at noon,* [b] *just when Ben-Hadad was drinking himself drunk in the booths, he and the kings, the thirty-two kings helping him.* [17a]*And the youths of the governors of the provinces went out as the first contingent.* [a] [b]*Then Ben-Hadad sent;* [b] *and they reported to him* [c] *as follows, "Men are coming out from Samaria."* [18a]*And he said,* [a] *"If* [b]*they are coming* [b] *out to sue for peace, take them alive. And if it be to fight,* [c] *take them alive just the same."* [19] *And these* [a] *came out from the city* [b]—*the youths of the governors of the provinces and the army* [c]*that was* [c] *behind them.* [20] *And each man struck his opposite number,* [a] *so that Syria took flight with Israel pursuing them. And Ben-Hadad, king of Syria, escaped on horse and by steeds.*

[21] *This is the way in which the king of Israel went out and smote* [a] *the cavalry and chariotry; he delivered Syria a mighty blow.*

[22] *And the prophet approached the king of Israel* [a]*and said,* [a] [b]*"Strengthen yourself, and take intelligence, and make plans for what you intend to do, for at the turn of the year the king of Syria is going to come up against you."* [23] *And the servants of the king of Syria said* [a]*to him,* [a] *"A god of the mountains is their god.* [b] *For this reason they have beaten us. But if we should perhaps fight with them on the plain, it is likely that we would beat them.* [24] *Now this is what you should do: dismiss each of the kings from his position and appoint commanders in their places.* [25] *And you should recruit for yourself an army similar to the army that is fallen,* [a] *with horse to replace horse and chariot to replace chariot. Then let us fight with them on plain ground and we will surely beat them." And he hearkened to their voice and acted according to it.*

[26] *And it so happened, at the turn of the year, that Ben-Hadad mustered Syria and went up to Aphek for battle with Israel.* [27] *And the Israelites were mustered* [a] *and marched out to meet him.* [b] *And the Israelites* [c] *went into formation opposite them like two little bunches of goats, while Syria filled the land.* [28] *Then a man of God came near and said* [a] *to the king of Israel,* [b] *"Thus says Yahweh, 'Just because Syria says,* [c] *"Yahweh* [d] *is a god of the mountains, but he is not a god of the valleys," I will give* [e] *this mob into your hand, so that you* [f] *will know that I am Yahweh.'"* [29] *And these were arrayed opposite those for seven days. And it happened on the seventh day that battle was joined, and the Israelites* [a] *struck Syria down,* [b]*one hundred thousand* [b] *infantrymen on a single day.* [30] *So the survivors fled toward Aphek, into the city, but the wall fell on twenty-seven thousand individuals among the survivors.*

Now Ben-Hadad was fleeing, and he entered into the inner chamber of a house. [a] [31a]*And his servants said to him,* [a] [b]*"Please notice, we have heard* [b] *that the kings of the House of Israel are certainly* [c] *kings who honor treaties. Please let us put sackcloth on our loins and coils of rope on our heads,* [d] *then we shall go out* [e] *to the king of Israel. It is possible that he may spare your life."* [32] *So they bound* [a]*sackcloth on* [a] *their loins, with rope-coils* [b]*on their heads,* [b] *and* [c]*came to* [c] *the king of Israel* [d]*and said,* [d] *"Thy servant Ben-Hadad says, 'Allow my* [e] *life to be spared.'" And he said, "Is he still alive? He is my brother."* [33] *And the men were observant and quick-witted, and* [a]*took it as settled in his intent;* [a] *so they said, "Your brother Ben-Hadad."*

And he said, "Come and bring him." And Ben-Hadad came out to him; and he caused him to ᵇmount upᵇ into his chariot. ³⁴*And he* ᵃ *said to him,*ᵇ *"The cities which my father took from your father I shall return. And you shall establish bazaars for yourself in Damascus, just like my father established in Samaria. And I shall release you from* ᶜ *the vassal-treaty." So he made a treaty with him and sent him away.* ᵈ

³⁵ *Now a certain man belonging among the prophetic guilds said to his companion through Yahweh's word, "Fall upon me, please"; but the man refused to fall upon him.* ³⁶ *So he said to him, "Just because you would not obey Yahweh's voice, behold, as you are departing from me, a lion shall fall upon you." And as he departed his company, a lion did come at him and fall upon him.* ³⁷ *Then he found another man and said, "Fall upon me, please." So the man fell upon him, striking and bruising him.* ³⁸ *Then the prophet went and stood waiting on the road for the king,*ᵃ *having* ᵇ*disguised himself with a mask*ᵇ *over his eyes.* ³⁹ *And it so happened that, as the king was going by, he shouted to the king and said, "Your servant came away from the midst*ᵃ *of the battle, when behold, a certain man had* ᵇ*turned away*ᵇ *and was bringing a man to me. And he said, 'Guard this man!*ᶜ *If he should* ᵈ*turn out to be missing,*ᵈ *it will be your life for his life, or else you must* ᵉ*weigh out*ᵉ *a talent of silver.'* ⁴⁰ *But it happened, while your servant* ᵃ*was occupied*ᵃ *here and there, that*ᵇ *he was not there." And the king of Israel said to him, "Thus* ᶜ *shall be* ᵈ*your penalty;* ᵈ *you* ᵉ*have determined it."* ᵉ ⁴¹ *Then he hastened to remove the mask from his eyes, and the king of Israel recognized him, that he was one of the prophets.* ⁴² *And he said to him, "Thus says Yahweh, 'Because you dismissed my man destined for destruction when you had him in your hand,*ᵃ *your own life shall substitute for his life, and your people for his people."* ⁴³ *And the king of Israel went to his house resentful and fuming.*

Notes

1.a-a. MT. G^{BLmin} omit (haplography).

1.b. MT. G^{BL} adds the dittography "and he went up and besieged Samaria."

1.c. MT, G^{L}. G^{B} adds pleonastic "every."

1.d. MT, G^{B}. Because Samaria is mentioned in the foregoing dittography, G^{L} substitutes object "it."

2.a. G^{B}. MT, G^{LMSS} add explicative "messengers."

3.a. G^{B}. MT, G^{L} add interpretive "who are well favored."

5.a. G^{BL}. MT adds "as follows" (dittography).

5.b-b. MT, G^{L}. G^{B} omits (haplography).

5.c. G^{BL}. MT adds "and your children" (pleonasm from v 3).

6.a-a. MT, G^{B}. G^{L} "your houses."

6.b. MT, G^{L}. G^{B} "their" is interpretive. Cf. *HOTTP*, 327a.

6.c-c. MT. G^{BL} add pleonastic "which their hand will seize."

7.a. MT. G^{L} "Israel"; G^{B} omits.

7.b. MT, G^{L}. Reading ולבני as "and my sons." G^{B} adds interpretive "and my daughters."

7.c-c. Cf. *HOTTP*, 327a.

9.a. MT. Not recognizing that the Israelite king maintains his formal fealty, G^{BL} substitute "your."

9.b-b. MT. G^{BL} omit.

9.c. G^{BL}. MT substitutes interpretive "messengers."

11.a-a. MT(impv pl). G^{BL} ἱκανούσθω "enough now" probably reads דַּבֵּר "you say" as דַּי דַּבּ "enough now."

12.a-a. MT (שִׂימוּ). G^{BL} substitute pleonastic interpretation, "build defense walls."

12.b. MT. G^{BL} add "defense walls."

13.a. G^{BL}. MT adds explicative "Ahab."

13.b. G^{BL}. MT adds pleonastic "all."

14.a. MT. G^{BL} have explicative "Ahab."

15.a-a. MT, G^B. G^L has a double reading here and in v 17.

15.b. MT. G^{BL} have explicative "Ahab."

15.c. MT. G^B omits "two"; G^L adds the pleonastic gl "and the king (of) Ezer was with them."

15.d. G^{BL}. MT adds pleonastic "all."

15.e-e. G^{BL}. MT "Israelites" (corr).

15.f. MT. G^{BL} "sixty."

15.g. MT, G^L. G^B omits (haplography).

16.a. G^B. G^L has explicative "the king"; MT pl (corr from v 17).

16.b-b. MT, G^B. G^L "with them" corr.

17.a-a. MT, G^B. G^L corr (double reading).

17.b-b. MT. G^{BL} omit (cf. *HOTTP,* 328a).

17.c. MT. G^{BL} have explicative "the king of Syria."

18.a-a. MT. G^B "say to them"; G^L "and the king of Syria said" (explicative).

18.b-b. MT, G^L. G^B οὐ γάρ = Heb. כִּי לֹא "for not," a corr of MT יָצָאוּ "they went out."

18.c. G^{BL}. MT adds interpretive "they are coming out."

19.a. MT. G^B "and not" is a corr from Heb. וְאֵלֶּה "and these" = MT; G^L omits.

19.b. MT. G^B offers as subject explicative ἄρχοντα "the governors," corrupted in G^L to ἄχχονται, "they come."

19.c-c. MT. G^{BL} omit.

20.a. MT. G^{BL} add "and each man did it again to his opposite number."

21.a. MT. G^L "took"; G^B "took all."

22.a-a. MT, G^B. G^L adds "as follows" (stylistic).

22.b. G^{BL}. MT adds explicative "to him, 'Go.'"

23.a-a. MT, G^L. G^B omits (haplography).

23.b. MT. G^{BL} add "and not a god of the valleys" from v 28.

25.a. G^B. MT, G^L add explicative "from you."

27.a. G^{BL}. MT adds "and were provisioned" (וְכָלְכְּלוּ), a corr from the following וַיֵּלְכוּ "and they marched."

27.b. G^{BL}. MT substitutes interpretive "them."

27.c. MT. G^{BL} substitute "Israel" as a gentilic to agree with following "Aram."

28.a. MT, G. MS, G^A, Syr omit.

28.b. MSS, G^{BL}, Vg. MT inserts "and he said."

28.c. MT, G^B. G^L adds "that," avoiding the Hebrew's asyndetic style.

28.d. MT. G^{BL} add "the God of Israel."

28.e. G^{BL}. MT adds pleonastic "all."

28.f. Read sing (G) rather than MT's pl. As Zimmerli's study of the "historical demonstration formula" (my term) shows, the tendency of late literary levels is to move from the primitive sing to the pl; hence the MT reading here is the product of late scribal activity.

29.a. MT. G^{BL} substitutes the gentilic "Israel" to agree with "Aram," as in v 27.

29.b-b. MT, G^B. G^L, Vrs, "one hundred twenty thousand" (perhaps understood as a symbolic number, 12 × 10 × 1000).

30.a. G^{BL}. MT "the city" (corr from reference to "city" just previously in this verse).

31.a-a. MT. G^{BL} "and he said to his servants," an ideological change due to the higher level of despotic authority in the hellenistic world.

31.b-b. MT. G^{BL} "know," a paraphrastic adjustment to the preceding.

31.c. MT (כִּי asseverative). G^{BL} omit, probably out of lack of comprehension.

31.d. MSS, G, Syr, Vg. MT sing, probably through misspelling.

31.e. MT, G^L. G^B adds explicative "again."

32.a-a, b-b. MT, G^B. G^L puts "sackcloth" at the end of the clause, omitting "on" (περί), and it omits "on their heads." This appears to be a stylistic paraphrase.

32.c-c. MT. G^{BL} "said."

32.d-d. MT. G^{BL} omit.

32.e. MT, G^L. G^B "our" (interpretive correction).

33.a-a. MSS representing the Occidental tradition (K) read the ה as a pronominal suffix attached to the preceding word (G^BL τὸν λόγον "the word/matter" is explicative addition), while the Oriental tradition (Q) reads it as the interrogative particle with the following word. The root חלט occurs only here, and apparently means "declare valid" (Baumgartner, *Hebräisches und Aramäisches Lexikon*, I, 305). G ἀναλέγω, "reckon," is probably no more than a good guess.

33.b-b. MT. G^BL add explicative "unto him."

34.a. MT, G^B. G^L adds explicative "the king of Syria."

34.b. MT, G^B. G^L adds explicative "Ahab."

34.c. MT, G lit. "in."

34.d. MT, G^B. G^L adds the rather thoughtless interpretation, "from his house, and he departed from him."

38.a. MT. G^BL add explicative "of Israel."

38.b-b. MT. G^BL "bound with a bandage."

39.a. MT. G^BL substitutes interpretive "place of fighting."

39.b-b. MT. G^BL omit (haplography).

39.c. MT, G^B. G^L adds the transition, "and it will happen."

39.d-d. MT. G^BL add interpretive "happen to leap away."

39.e-e. MT. G^BL "come up with" (στήσεις = תָקוּם, corr of MT תִּקְשׁוֹל).

40.a-a. MT. G^BL "looked around" is interpretive.

40.b. MT, G^B. G^L adds "behold."

40.c. MT. G^BL "behold (^B and)."

40.d-d. MT, G^L. G^B τὰ ἔνεδρα "the ambush"? G^BL add interpretive "from me."

40.e-e. MT. G^BL "you murdered."

42.a. MT, G^BL, Vg. Vrs "my hand." MT implies but does not write the pronominal suffix.

Form/Structure/Setting

A story from the Omride-war cycle (1): "The holy war at Samaria"
1. The crisis
   a. Initial negotiation
      (1) The military situation, 20:1
      (2) The sharpened demand, vv 2–6
      (3) Rejection and defiance, vv 7–9
   b. Subsequent confrontation
      (1) The threat, v 10
      (2) The counter-threat, v 11
      (3) Order for attack, v 12
2. The encouraging oracle
   a. The oracle delivered
      Narrative introduction and herald formula, v 13aα
      (1) Situational query (= invective), v 13aβ
      (2) Announcement, v 13bα
      (3) Historical demonstration formula, v 13bβ
[Gloss, 14a]
   b. Interpretive instruction, v 14b
3. The fulfillment
   a. The preparation
      (1) Mustering, v 15
      (2) The approach, vv 16–17a
      (3) The Syrian strategy, vv 17b–18
   b. The battle
      (1) The approach (resumptive), v 19
      (2) Slaughter and pursuit, v 20a

[Redactional: Ben-Hadad's escape, v 20b]
  c. Epitomizing conclusion, v 21

A story from the Omride-war cycle (2): "The holy war at Aphek"
[Redactional: Preparations for renewed warfare
    a. Advice to the king of Israel, v 22
    b. Advice to the king of Syria, vv 23–25]
  1. The crisis
    a. Syrian aggression, v 26
    b. Israelite preparation, v 27a
    c. Unequal strength, v 27b
  2. The encouraging oracle
    Narrative introduction and herald formula, v 28a$\alpha$$\aleph$
    a. Invective, v 28a$\alpha$$\beth$$\beta$
    b. Threat (announcement), v 28bα
    c. Historical demonstration formula, v 28bβ
  3. The fulfillment
    a. A seven-day encampment, v 29a
    b. A single-day victory, v 29b

A story from the Omride-war cycle (3): "The release of Ben-Hadad"
[Redactional: Aphek proves unsafe for the Syrian survivors, v 30a]
  1. The king of Israel's word establishes Ben-Hadad's release
    a. Ben-Hadad treats for negotiation
      (1) His predicament, v 30b
      (2) The entreaty
        (a) The proposal, v 31
        (b) The approach, v 32a
      (3) The identification of affinity
        (a) The king's query, v 32b
        (b) The servants' response, v 33aα
        (c) The invitation, v 33aβ
    b. The negotiation of the treaty
      (1) Ben-Hadad's approach, v33b
      (2) The offer of concessions, v 34a
      (3) The acceptance of terms, v 34b
  2. The king's word establishes Israel's judgment
    a. A prophet prepares himself for announcing judgment
      (1) The validation of attendant revelation
        (a) A command refused, v 35
        (b) The refusal punished, v 36
      (2) The preparation for a symbolic role, v 37
    b. Symbolic judgment on the prophet
      (1) His disguise, v 38
      (2) His address to the king
        (a) The fictitious charge, v 39
        (b) The fictitious delinquency, v 40a

(3) The king's delinquency, v 40b

c. Interpretation: judgment on the king and on Israel
    (1) The prophet's self-disclosure, v 41
    (2) The oracle
        (a) Invective, v 42a
        (b) Threat, v 42b
    (3) Narrative sequel, v 43aα

[Gloss, v 43aβ]

On the structure, genre identification, and redaction of the above narratives, see the writer's discussion in *Prophet against Prophet,* 57–58, 63, 123–25. The first two stories are modified holy-war stories (cf. G. von Rad, *Der heilige Krieg im alten Israel,* 3rd ed., 1958) that share the prophet-story subgenre, "historical demonstration narrative." Although the second of them has the simpler outline, it is apparent that their basic structure is identical, moving from (1) the crisis to (2) the encouraging oracle to (3) the fulfillment. Except in the oracle, the second story lacks discourse. The first story gives the oracle a central place but embellishes the confrontation of the kings at the beginning (vv 2–12) and the Syrian preparation for the battle at the end (vv 17–18) with lively and colorful discourse. It is natural to assume, therefore, that the first narrative became a favored story among the people and was used for entertainment as well as for edification. In any event, the exegete must be aware that the prophet (or man of God) in vv 13 and 28 plays the decisive role in each of the two stories, and that the oracles promise victory as coming not from men but from God, viewing historical event as a revelatory showpiece for how Yahweh manages history to his purpose. In recognition of W. Zimmerli's work on the so-called "Erweiswort" in *Gottes Offenbarung* (Munich 1963) 54–56, 122–31, the present writer has thoroughly discussed v 13 in *YTT,* 231–33.

The narrative in vv 30b–43a has been assigned to the subgenre the regal self-judgment narrative. It is unusual in having a two-part structure. The two parts stand in striking contrast to each other. The king of Israel is the responsible actor in both, first pronouncing a word of brotherhood on the dangerous Ben-Hadad and, second, pronouncing on the sham-soldier prophet a word of judgment ("your life for his life," vv 39, 42) that the prophet reinterprets as a word of judgment on the king and his people.

These three stories have been edited by a Jehuite redactor for the purpose of being joined directly to chap. 22, which at one time immediately followed chap. 20. In vv 20b and 22–25 he added other expansions in order to tie the two historical-demonstration narratives together, and in v 30a he added words to connect the second of these narratives to the regal self-judgment narrative. A later glossator added "Ahab" in v 2 and in a gloss at v 14; also the words, "resentful and fuming" (see 21:4), in v 43; also the remaining words of this verse and the first clause of 21:1 in order to make a transition to chap. 21, once it had been transferred here from its original position following chap. 19.

Comment

1–12 The historical-demonstration narrative of vv 1–21 is definitely a prophet story in which an anonymous prophet plays the decisive role. The story has been dressed up for dramatic effect and for maximum entertainment value, yet it retains an essentially theological purpose. Though it is replete with detail, it also displays a number of highly schematic elements. One element that is certainly historical is the name of the hostile king, Ben-Hadad, whose identification presents this passage's first serious problem of interpretation. The king in question can hardly be the Ben-Hadad, son of Hazael, who is mentioned in 2 Kgs 13:24–25 because 1 Kgs 20:30–43 predicts military disasters for Israel, not the glowing successes with which Jehoash is credited. On the other hand, it is hard to imagine that he can be the Ben-Hadad, son of Tab-Rimmon and grandson of Hezion, who came to Asa's aid *ca.* 886 B.C. (1 Kgs 15:18–20), for the present story must be dated somewhere in the Omride era, probably toward its very end, *ca.* 845 B.C. It is possible that there was another Ben-Hadad between the two that have been mentioned, but we should probably take seriously the possibility that "Ben-Hadad," lit., "Son of Hadad" (with Heb. בן substituting for Aram. בר), was a throne-name rather than the personal name of these individual kings. As for Ben-Hadad's Israelite counterpart: this is certainly not Ahab, in spite of the glosses in vv 2 and 14; and because Joram is elsewhere identified as active in warfare against Syria (2 Kgs 8:28–29), the predictions of coming disaster in 1 Kgs 20:43, realized in the actions of Hazael, make this last Omride king the most likely candidate. Such, in any case, was the understanding of the Jehuite redactor, who also viewed 22:1–38 as referring to Joram, and accordingly attached that passage directly to this (see above).

"All of Ben-Hadad's forces" probably excludes the "thirty-two kings" (cf. v 16; it is a schematic number, used also in a gloss at 22:31), who represent territorial chieftains allied with him (cf. *ANET* 501). This army, equipped with cavalry and chariotry, comes upon Samaria with clearly hostile intent. The Israelite king recognizes that a gesture of subservience will be extracted from him but he is scarcely prepared for the harshness of Ben-Hadad's demands. The two kings converse through messengers who fly back and forth. In v 3 the Syrian makes his rude and peremptory demand, claiming ownership over monetary wealth and over precious human souls. The Israelite immediately agrees, but takes this interchange as a mere formality. The Syrian answers that a formal subservience is not enough; he demands the liberty to test it by sending his servants "about this time tomorrow" (threat form, cf. 19:2) to seize anything they may fancy (v 6). Seeing now the full gravity of the situation, the Israelite king next summons "all the elders of the land"—evidently the territorial leaders from throughout the realm, gathered to Samaria for some unspecified purpose—explaining that he has offered formal vassalage but now dreads the plunder and humiliation that the Syrian plainly intends. Acting on the elders' advice, the Israelite king rejects the new demand, whereupon Ben-Hadad utters a boast in the form of an oath, threatening to make mere handfuls of dust of Samaria. The Israelite king's response is truly classic: "Let not the one who binds on his armor boast as he who takes it off!"

His messengers are directly instructed ("you say," imperative) to speak exactly these words. The half-drunken Ben-Hadad (cf. v 16) is sufficiently enraged by this insolent reply that he issues the order to prepare to attack the city.

13–21 The oracle of a "certain prophet," introduced by the herald formula, directs to the king an accusatory question, "Have you seen this great mob (ההמון הגדול הזה)?" The root המם, from which "mob" comes, means "bewilder," "throw into confusion," and is technical terminology in the holy-war schema; cf. Judg 4:15, 1 Sam 14:20. This question substitutes for the usual invective and is followed by an announcement (threat) beginning with the imminent-action formula, "Behold, I am about to give them into your hand." "Today" is epitomizing, and introduces what Zimmerli calls the "Er-weiswort," or "word of proof," but which the present writer prefers to name "the historical demonstration formula" because it calls attention to the way in which a historical event demonstrates that Yahweh is who he says he is. V 14 is revealed as an addition not only by the name "Ahab," but especially by a new herald formula, inappropriately introducing the answer to a simple query. "The youths of the governors of the provinces," borrowed for this expansion from three original occurrences in this passage, probably refers to a special elite guard, composed of young men, normally attached to the various provincial governors. The king of Israel is instructed to commence (lit., "tie on," "engage") the fighting. He first musters the 232 elite corpsmen and the 7000 ordinary troops. Ben-Hadad is already scandalously drunk at noon. When the coming attack is reported to the bleary-eyed king, he seems more muddled than blood-thirsty, for the Israelites are to be taken alive whatever their intent (v 18). The Israelites are not so laconic, for each of them kills his own enemy soldier, driving the Syrian army into headlong flight. V 21 is a summation: what the king's soldiers did is what he did; the cavalry and the chariotry were symbolic of all the army because they were feared the most. In sum: "he delivered Syria a mighty blow."

22–30a Vv 22–25 is an elaborate redactional transition, preparing for vv 26–29. V 28 does not refer back to v 23 because the latter does not accurately reproduce "he is not a god of the valleys" (עמקים), substituting instead "the plain" (מישור), more appropriate to the actual terrain at Aphek (*Al-Fīq*, on a plateau some miles east of the southern end of the Sea of Galilee). The expansion has the prophet of v 13 advising the Israelite king to prepare for next year's campaign. תשובת השנה "at the turn of the year" refers to spring-time (cf. 2 Sam 11:1), when the new year was observed in the Northern Kingdom (see "The Chronology of the Israelite Kings"). What the Syrians said about the Israelites' fighting superiority in mountainous terrain was certainly true; it is their theological interpretation that was obnoxious. The glossator explains, however, that the old Syrian army has been completely replaced, civilian commanders (פחות) have been substituted for the ineffective "kings," and flat ground has been chosen. Then in v 26b he takes up the original historical-demonstration narrative about the battle at Aphek. One should note a linguistic peculiarity: the Israelites are consistently called בני ישראל, lit., "sons of Israel." One observes also the striking sobriety of this narrative as compared with that of vv 1–21. The Israelites seem pitiable in their relative weakness: "two little bunches of goats." The Syrians "fill the land." Reminding us of v 13, v 28 has a "man of God" announce, with accusatory quotation ("he is not a god of the valleys") and threat ("I will give this great mob into your hand"), followed by the historical-demonstration formula, "You will know that I am Yahweh." The conclusion is highly stylized: for seven days the opposing armies face each other (cf. Josh 6:12–21); then on one single day of battle (cf. "today," v 13) 100,000 Syrians are struck down. As though this were not sufficiently amazing, the Jehuite redactor summons Aphek's wall (like Jericho's ?) to annihilate 27,000 more (v 30a).

30b–34 "Now Ben-Hadad was fleeing," נס דדֿח־ןֿבו, is introductory exposition. As he hides in a house his retainers remind him of the reputation of the kings of the "House of Israel" (the kingdom as a political entity), to the effect that they are חסד מלכי "kings who honor treaties"; the writer has recently defended the traditional meaning for the word חסד ("A Reply to G. Gerlemann on *Malkê Ḥesed* in 1 Kings XX 31." *VT* 29, 359–62), arguing the validity of the present translation. Syria and Israel have been bound in a treaty, involving the oath of brotherhood, so the hope of Ben-Hadad's counselors is that the Israelite king may give some weight to it in spite of the present hostilities. The following action is simple and straightforward. The counselors approach the Israelite king with tokens of contrition (on the ropes, see Gray, 429–30); they take advantage of the king's references to "my brother" to obtain an invitation to parley. V 34 records the concessions that Ben-Hadad makes in exchange for his life: the return of captured cities; the establishment of bazaars in Damascus; release from the vassalage that had been imposed. On these conditions the Israelite king releases Ben-Hadad and sends him away.

35–43 It is little wonder that some commentators have thought that these verses constitute a new and separate story, but in fact they provide the indispensable conclusion to the foregoing episode. They do have marked peculiarities and a strange paradox; in matter of fact, the locution, "through Yahweh's word" and the miraculous lion seem to be taken directly out of the Bethelite story of 1 Kgs 13. The point of it all is, however, that just as the king's word, "He is my brother," determined the outcome of episode 1, the same king's word, "Your life for his life," determines the outcome of episode 2. A member of one of the prophetic guilds (הנביאים בני) was actually inspired by God when he demanded of a fellow that he strike him, and when the latter refused, failing to recognize "Yahweh's voice," he was threatened with an attack by a lion, and the threat came true. A second person did strike this "son of the prophets," so that he appeared bruised and wounded as he waited for the king beside the road. The king did not recognize him as a prophet because he wore a bandage over his eyes, so that he was not on his guard with respect to a possible prophetic denunciation. This came, strangely, in the king's reaction to a fiction the prophet told him, to the effect that he had not taken adequate care of a prisoner when warned that his life would go for the prisoner's life, or else that he would pay a heavy fine. Believing everything that the man had told him, the king decreed, "Thus shall be your penalty; you have determined it." Then the prophet removed his disguise, revealing that he was one of the prophets, and delivered Yahweh's oracle (v 42) to the effect that he, the king, had done just as the fictitious delinquent soldier had done, and must suffer accordingly. The invective clause is "Because you dismissed חֶרְמִי אִישׁ (the man whom I devoted to destruction)"; the threat is "your life for his life; your people for his people."

Explanation

Our foregoing genre analysis of the above material already provides the necessary explanation, to the extent that identification has been based on function rather than mere content. The function of the two historical-demonstration narratives is to show how God intervenes to control historical events. The weaker Israel seems, and the louder the enemy boasts, the more certain is the prophetic word that *this very day* will be a day when God hands the latter over to the former. Here is a drastic articulation of the transcendental element in history; for us the saying is still true, whether or not a "man of God" appear to utter it, that each day God is present in human experience, that each day potentially presents itself as his decisive moment. The function of the regal self-judgment narrative is to affirm that the holders of secular power may determine through the misuse of that power their own fate. The story tells us that there is a time for making treaties and a time for pursuing an enemy to destruction. As King Saul was condemned for neglecting to carry out the חֵרֶם (the ritual dedication to destruction) on Agag the Amalekite in 1 Sam 15, the Israelite king of this story (probably Joram, the last of the Omrides) is condemned for neglecting Yahweh's חֵרֶם on Ben-Hadad. His punishment—to be shared by the entire people of Israel—would come to pass when the Syrians under Hazael would tear up the treaty, repaying Israel's kindness with heedless violence and heartless greed.

The Narrative of Naboth's Judicial Murder (20:43b—21:29)

Bibliography

Andersen, F. I. "The Socio-Juridical Background of the Naboth Incident." *JBL* 85 (1966) 46–57. **Baltzer, K.** "Naboths Weinberg (1 Kön 21). Der Konflikt zwischen israelitischem und kanaanäischem Bodenrecht." *WuD* 8 (1965) 73–88. **Baumann, A.** "Naboths Fasttag und Josephus." *Theokratia, Festgabe für K. H. Rengstorf* (1973), II. **Bohlen, R.** "Alttestamentliche Kunstprosa als Zeitkritik." *TTZ* 87 (1978) 192–202. **Gooding, D. W.** "Ahab According to the Septuagint." *ZAW* 76 (1964) 269–80. **Jepsen, A.** "Ahabs Busse. Eine kleiner Beitrag zur Methode literarhistorischer Einordnung." *Archäologie und Altes Testament.* Festschrift für Kurt Galling, ed. A. Kuschke and E. Kutsch. Tübingen: J.C.B. Mohr, 1970. **Napier, B. D.** "The Inheritance and the Problem of Adjacency. An Essay on 1 Kings 21." *Int* 30 (1976) 3–11. ———. "The Omrides of Jezreel." *VT* 9 (1959) 366–78. **Poggioli, R.** "Naboth's Vineyard of the Pastoral View of the Social Order." *JHI* 24 (1963) 3–24. **Seebass, H.** "Der Fall Naboth in 1 Reg. XXI." *VT* 24 (1974) 474–88. **Weitemeyer, M.** "Nabots vingård" (1 Kong. 21:1–16). En traditionshistorisk kommentar. (Danish) *DTT* 29 (1966) 129–43. **Welten, P.** "Naboths Weinberg (1. Könige 21)." *EvT* 33 (1973) 18–32.

Translation

[43b] *And he entered into Samaria.* [21:1a] *And after these events it so happened that*[a] *a*[b] *vineyard belonged to Naboth the Jezreelite,*[cd] *next to the palace*[e] *of Ahab, king of Samaria.* [2] *And Ahab spoke to Naboth as follows, "Give me your vineyard so that it may become my vegetable garden, for it lies close*[a] *to my house. And I will give you in compensation a superior vineyard or, if that is better in your eyes, I will give you money equal to its*[b] *value."*[c] [3] *But Naboth said to Ahab, "It is forbidden me by Yahweh*[a] *to give you the inheritance of my forefathers."* [4a] *And Ahab entered his house resentful and fuming.*[ab] *And he lay down upon his bed and turned away his face, refusing to eat any food.* [5] *And Jezebel his wife came to him and said to him, "What is this, that your spirit is troubled, and that you are not eating food?"* [6] *And he said to her, "When I spoke to Naboth the Jezreelite* [a]*and said to him,*[a] *'Give me your vineyard for money; or if it pleases you I will give you a*[b] *vineyard in its place,' then he said, 'I will not give you my vineyard.'"* [7] *And Jezebel his wife said to him, "You now: you are going to perform majesty over Israel. Get up, eat food, and let your heart by happy. I will give you the vineyard of Naboth the Jezreelite."* [8] *And she*[a] *wrote letters*[b] *in*[c] *Ahab's name and sealed them with his seal, sending the letters*[d] *to the*[e] *elders and the freemen*[f] *who were living with Naboth.* [9] *And she wrote in the letters as follows: "Call a fast and seat Naboth at the head of the people;* [10] *also seat two men, scoundrels,*[a] *opposite him, and have them testify against him as follows,* [b]*'You have*[b] *cursed*[c] *God and the king.' Then take him out and stone him so he dies."* [11] *And the men of the city—the elders and the freemen who were living in his city—did just as Jezebel had instructed them.*[a] [12] *They called a fast and seated Naboth at the head of the people.* [13] *And two men, scoundrels, entered and sat opposite him. And they*[a] *testified against him*[b] *as follows,* [c] *"Naboth*

has ^c *cursed* ^d *God and the king.''* So they took him outside the city and stoned him with stones until he died. ¹⁴ *And they sent to Jezebel as follows: "Naboth has been stoned to death.''* ¹⁵ *And it happened, when Jezebel heard it,* ^a *that she* ^b *said to Ahab, "Get up, confiscate the vineyard of Naboth the Jezreelite, the one who refused to give it to you for money. For Naboth is no longer living, but is dead.''* ¹⁶ *And it happened, when Ahab heard that Naboth* ^a *was dead,* ^b *that Ahab arose to go down to the vineyard of Naboth the Jezreelite in order to confiscate it.*

¹⁷ *And* ^a *Yahweh spoke* ^a *to Elijah the Settler as follows:* ¹⁸ *"Arise, go down to meet Ahab, king of Israel, who is in Samaria.* ^a *Behold, he* ^a *is in the vineyard of Naboth whither* ^b *he has gone down in order to confiscate it.* ¹⁹ *And you shall speak to him* ^a *as follows:* ^a *'Thus says Yahweh, "Have* ^b *you murdered, and actually taken possession?''* *Therefore,* ^c *thus says Yahweh, "In the* ^d *place where* ^e *the dogs licked Naboth's blood, the dogs shall lick your blood* ^f —*even yours!'* ''' ²⁰ *And Ahab said to Elijah, "Have you found me, my enemy?''* And he ^a *said, "I have found you, because you have sold yourself* ^b *to perform what is evil in Yahweh's eyes.* ^c ²¹ *Behold, I am about to bring disaster on you, and will pursue you with fire. And I will cut off from Ahab anyone urinating against the wall, helpless and abandoned in Israel.* ²² *And I will make your house like the house of Jeroboam, son of Nebat, and like the house of Baasha, son of Ahijah, because of the anger to which you provoked me, causing Israel to sin.* ²³ *And also concerning Jezebel Yahweh spoke, as follows: 'The dogs shall eat Jezebel* ^a *within the bounds of Jezreel.'* ²⁴ *The one belonging to Ahab who dies in the city, the dogs shall eat, and the one belonging to Ahab who dies in the open, the birds of the heaven shall eat.''*

²⁵ *Moreover, there has been none like Ahab, who sold himself to do what was evil in Yahweh's eyes—whom Jezebel his wife misled.* ²⁶ *And he behaved very abominably in going after idols, just like everything that the Amorites did, whom Yahweh dispossessed before the Israelites.*

²⁷ᵃ *And it so happened, when Ahab heard these words,* ^a *that he tore his clothing and put sackcloth on his body. And he fasted and* ^b *lay down* ^b *in sackcloth.* ^c *And he went about dejected.* ^d ²⁸ *And the word of Yahweh came* ^a *to Elijah* ^b *the Settler* ^b *as follows:* ^c ²⁹ *"Have you observed how contrite Ahab is before me?* ^a *Because he is contrite before me,* ^a *I will not bring the disaster in his own days; in the days of his son I will bring the disaster.''* ^b

Notes

1.a-a. MT, G^L. G^B omits (perhaps lost with transposition to chap. 20).

1.b. MT. G^{BL} add "certain" (stylistic).

1.c. G^B "Israelite," as in chap. 18 (*sic* passim).

1.d. G^{BL}. MT adds interpretive gloss, "which was in Jezreel."

1.e. MT, G^B. G^L "house," a corruption from v 2.

2.a. G^{BL} ἐγγίων = MT קרוב, which has been scribally glossed with the addition of אֵצֶל "next to" from v 1.

2.b. MT. G^{BL} "your vineyard."

2.c. MT. G^{BL} add interpretive "and it will become my vegetable garden."

3.a. MT. G^B "my God"; G^L Yahweh my God."

4.a-a. MT. G^{BL} "and Ahab's spirit became troubled" is an interpretive substitution in view of v 5.

4.b. G^{BL} omit a long explanatory gloss in MT: "because of the word that Naboth the Jezreelite had spoken to him; and he said to him, 'I will not give you the inheritance of my forefathers.'"

6.a-a. MT. G^{BL} "saying" (stylistic).

6.b. MT, G^L. G^B "another."

8.a. MT, G^B. G^L adds explicative "Jezebel."

8.b. MT. G^{BL} sing is interpretive in light of the fact that only one letter is cited.

8.c. MT. G^{BL} ἐπί "upon" or "over" is interpretive in view of the fact that the signature would be "under" the body of the letter on the page.

8.d. K pl. Q, G^{BL} sing (see v 8).

8.e. MT, G^L. G^B omits.

8.f. G^{BL}. MT adds interpretive "who were in the city."

10.a. G^B omits to בְּנֵי בְלִיַּעַל "scoundrels" in v 13 (homoioteleuton).

10.b-b. MT. G^L, Syr, Vg "he has."

10.c. MT, G^L "blessed" (ideological alteration).

11.a. G^L. MT adds the double reading "just as she wrote in the letters she has sent them."

13.a. G^{BL}. MT "the scoundrels."

13.b. G^{BL}. MT adds "opposite the people," interpretive from "opposite him," vv 9, 13.

13.c-c. MT. G^{BL} "you have"; cf. v 10.

13.d. MT, G "blessed"; cf. v 10.

15.a. G^B. MT has pleonastic addition, "that he had been stoned to death"; cf. G^L.

15.b. G^B. MT, G^L have explicative "Jezebel."

16.a. MT, G^L. G^B adds "the Israelite."

16.b. MT. G^{BL} add the interpretive gl, "and he tore his cloak and put on sackcloth. And it happened after this . . ."; cf. v 27.

17.a-a. G^{BL}. MT "and the word of Yahweh came . . ." is influenced by the language of later prophetism.

18.a-a. MT. G^{BL} "for he."

18.b. MT. G^{BL} "because."

19.a-a. MT, G^B. G^L omits (stylistic).

19.b. MT, G^{BL} "because."

19.c. G^{BL}. MT "and you shall say to him as follows" is paraphrastic.

19.d. MT, G^L. G^B inserts pleonastic "every."

19.e. MT. G^{BL} add pleonastic "the swine and . . ." (cf. 22:38).

19.f. MT. G^{BL} have pleonastic addition, "(but) also the harlots shall bathe in your blood."

20.a. MT, G^B. G^L has explicative "Elijah."

20.b. MT. G^{BL} add interpretive "in folly."

20.c. MT. G^{BL} add interpretive "to enrage him."

23.a. MT. G^{BL} substitute "her" (stylistic).

27.a-a. MT. G^{BL} "and concerning the word just as Ahab repented before Yahweh's face, and he departed weeping" (stylistic).

27.b-b. MT. G^{BL} "put on."

27.c. MT. G^{BL} add "on the day when he (^L Jezebel) smote Naboth the Israelite (Jezreelite)" (interpretive).

27.d. G^B. G^L adds "with his son," with a view to v 29. MT omits.

28.a. MT. G^{BL} add "by the hand of his servant. . . ."

28.b-b. MT. G^{BL} omit.

28.c. MT. G^{BL} "and Yahweh said."

29.a-a. MT. G^{BL} omit (haplography).

29.b. G^{BL}. MT adds interpretive "upon his house."

Form/Structure/Setting

A legend from the Jehuite prophets: "Jezebel usurps Naboth's vineyard" [Editorial transition, 20:43b—21:1]

1. The problem of Naboth's reticence
   a. The unsuccessful negotiation
      (1) The situation, v 1aβ b
      (2) Ahab's offer, v 2
      (3) Naboth's refusal, v 3

b. The prospect of successful intervention
(1) Ahab's dejection, v 4
(2) Jezebel's resolution
(a) Ahab recounts his failure, vv 5–6
(b) Jezebel proposes regal usurpation, v 7
2. The problem resolved through the abuse of authority
a. Jezebel engineers Naboth's judicial murder
(1) Her forged letters, vv 8–10
(2) Narrative of compliance, vv 11–13
(3) The report to Jezebel, v 14
b. Jezebel disposes of her prize
(1) Her offer to Ahab, v 15
(2) Ahab prepares to take possession, v 16
3. Prophetic judgment on the abuse of authority
a. Elijah condemns Ahab
(1) The divine instruction
Introduction, v 17
(a) The command, v 18
(b) The accusatory question, v 19a
(c) The threat, v 19b
(2) The confrontation, v 20
[Dtr: Ahab's house to become like those of Jeroboam and Baasha, vv 21–22, 24]
[Expansion: Note concerning Jezebel's death, v 23]
[Dtr: Final assessment of Ahab's sins, vv 25–26]
b. Reinterpretation: The judgment deferred
(1) Ahab's contrition, v 27
(2) An oracle of reapplication
Narrative introduction, v 28
(a) Divine appeal respecting Ahab's contrition, v 29a
(b) Transfer of the judgment to Ahab's son, v 29b

The editorial transition at the beginning was required when the Naboth story was transferred here from its original position. There is no other secondary material except for the extensive deuteronomistic expansions toward the end (vv 21–26). It is not necessary to accept the opinion of those scholars who claim that vv 27–29 constitute a late addition; it is the structure of the original narrative according to the schema of the regal self-judgment subgenre that explains the abrupt change at this point, not the attempt of a redactor to revise the original.

This narrative has received extensive evaluation in the writer's book, *Prophet against Prophet*, 90, 115–16, 130–32. It has been assigned to the subgenre regal self-judgment narrative, type 2, abusive-action story. Other examples of this special type may be found at 1 Sam 15:1–35 (Saul's neglect of the חרם "ban"), 1 Sam 28:4–25 (Saul's appeal to the occult), and 2 Kgs 20:12–19 (Hezekiah's boasting to the Babylonians). The oracle-manipulation narrative (cf. 1 Kgs 20:30–43) features a king bringing judgment on himself through his own official declaration, reinterpreted by the prophet; but the king's violation of responsible behavior is what condemns him in the abusive-action narrative. In both types, Yahweh retains the prerogative of reinterpreting the terms of the king's punishment, and precisely that is what is happening here at vv 27–29.

There are three things in particular that reveal this narrative to be relatively late; i.e., from sometime during the reign of the Jehuite kings: (1) an awareness on the writer's part that the historical Ahab had not died violently, as v 19 decrees, but in peace and honor (see below on chap. 22), whereas it was Ahab's son Joram who actually experienced the oracle's direct fulfillment (see 2 Kgs 9:24–26); (2) a harsh and judgmental portrayal of Jezebel, typical of Jehuite polemic against her (1 Kgs 19:2, 2 Kgs 9:10, 30–37); and (3) the fact that this narrative had no fixed position within the original Elijah cycle (even though it allows that prophet, stiff and rather colorless as he is here, a role in it), which probably influenced the redactor/editor who eventually moved it to its present position. Thus it may confidently be said that it was composed considerably later than the time of Elijah's struggle with Ahab over the intrusion of baalism. That challenge was settled once for all in Jehu's coup of 841 B.C. 1 Kgs 21 is late propaganda aiming to condemn Jezebel for all of Ahab's aberrations, thereby justifying Jehu's bloody deed against Jezebel, her son, and her nephew at Jezreel (2 Kgs 9). To judge from Hos 1:4, such propaganda was necessary.

Comment

1–16 That Ahab and Jezebel are in Samaria is not to be deduced from 20:43, an editorial transition, but from Yahweh's explanation to Elijah in v 17. Some critics argue that "who is in Samaria" is a gloss, but the versions support MT in this reading. Internal evidence indicating the Samaria locale is the fact that Jezebel has to send letters to the leading men of Naboth's city, and receive word back from them by messenger (vv 9, 14). Naboth is of course said to be a Jezreelite, and 2 Kgs 9:25–26, part of a highly historical piece in support of Jehu's coup (cf. De Vries, *Prophet against Prophet*, 102–3), identifies a certain "plot of ground" near Jezreel as Naboth's property. Furthermore, it is clear that Ahab did have a palace in Jezreel (1 Kgs 18:46, 2 Kgs 8:29, 9:5–37). The title given him in v 1, "king of Samaria," pertains to his entire realm, which would have included the city of Jezreel. This evidence, plus the supposed unlikelihood that a Jezreelite would have possessed ancestral property adjacent to the royal palace in Samaria, led some critics to argue that everything must have taken place in Jezreel. To the present writer these apparent contradictions signify simply that the narrator was confused. He knew the main details of the Naboth story, but could not get everything straight, which is another item of evidence for relative lateness. It is best, in any case, to take the story on its own terms, interpreting the sending of the letters to imply what they must, viz., the geographical separation of Ahab/Jezebel and Naboth.

Ahab offers money or compensation in kind for Naboth's vineyard, but Naboth refuses on the grounds of ancestral law (cf. Lev 25). With the loss of land would have gone the loss of position, and before long Naboth and his posterity would have been reduced to the status of royal pensioners.

Autocratic as he is, Ahab dares take no direct action against Naboth. But not so Jezebel, who has been trained in the absolutistic traditions of the Phoenician city-states. To her Ahab seems a weakling. She means her enigmatic saying, "You now: you are going to perform majesty over Israel," as an explanation for what she directly performs in his name and with his authority (she signs the letters with his name and uses his seal, evidently with his acquiescence). She instructs two classes, viz., the supervising elders and the freemen who have a voice in judicial procedures, to hold a solemn fast and also arrange for two "scoundrels," בני־בליעל, to swear that Naboth has cursed God and the king, after which they are to execute him. It is certainly a sad spectacle that Israel's most powerful and revered classes could thus be instructed by royal edict to arrange for corrupt witnesses to destroy a righteous man in their midst, but so it was. The letter is read and obeyed. Jezebel receives word. She boastfully reports to Ahab that Naboth is dead, inviting him now to possess Naboth's vineyard for nothing. The alleged legal authority for confiscating it is, of course, the "scoundrels'" fictitious charge of cursing the king.

17–20 Here for the first time the transcendental element emerges. Yahweh instructs "Elijah the Settler" (cf. 17:1) to "go down" (from where?) to confront Ahab in Samaria. One should note not only that Elijah is introduced as someone unknown, but also that he is not acquainted with Ahab, who has to be described to him as "king of Israel." This hardly accords with historical actualities, and we take it as a token of late stylizing. Elijah must be near Samaria, for the king would not tarry long in the vineyard. After instructing Elijah concerning the situation, Yahweh gives him a characteristic oracle of judgment, with an accusatory question amounting to an invective, followed by a threat. It is rare to see the invective and the threat each introduced by the herald formula, "Thus says Yahweh" (Amos, the earliest of the writing prophets, has it before the threat, while most of the writing prophets have it at the beginning of the oracle, before the invective). The present threat has been influenced by 2 Kgs 9:26, but especially by the Jehuite redactor's derisive words in 1 Kgs 22:38, so obvious a parallel that G in the present passage directly interpolates details from that passage (see *Notes*). But of course Naboth died in Jezreel, while the king of 1 Kgs 22 (not Ahab) died at Ramoth-Gilead and was buried in Samaria. So we know that the threat was designed from the very beginning to apply to Ahab's son, Joram, not to Ahab himself. Although the styling of v 17 suggests that Ahab and Elijah were unacquainted, v 20 has Ahab address Elijah familiarly as his well-known nemesis. The reference to the "finding" expresses the narrator's notion that God unerringly discovers sin; Elijah's explanation that this is because Ahab has "sold himself" to do what Yahweh considers evil (copied by Dtr in v 25) is the narrator's interpretation of what Naboth's judicial murder actually amounted to.

21–26 Drawing an explicit parallel to what had happened to the house of Jeroboam and the house of Baasha, Dtr repeats from 14:10–11, 16:4, the imagery of a pursuing fire, the crude saying about helpless and abandoned males, and the harsh prediction about bodies being eaten by dogs and birds. A late member of the deuteronomistic school makes sure that Jezebel receives her proper share of scorn (v 23; cf. 2 Kgs 9:10, 33–37). From his hyperbolic denunciation of Ahab in 16:30, Dtr adds in vv 25–26 a second hyperbole, mentioning Jezebel's role in misleading Ahab, not to minimize, but to accentuate, his guilt, adding also the specific charge that he had reintroduced the idol-worship of the abominable Amorites.

27–29 Here is the surprise ending of the original regal self-judgment narrative. Ahab repents; and to show his repentance he dons sackcloth, fasts, sleeps in his sackcloth, and goes about dejected (cf. David in 2 Sam 12:13, 16). Yahweh speaks a new word to Elijah, but this time without a summons to action. What Yahweh says is, paradoxically, an oracle of salvation for Ahab, but also an oracle of judgment for his son. V 29 has no accusatory question, only a question of commendation: "Have you observed how contrite Ahab is before me?" This is followed by the concluding announcement/threat, to the effect that the disaster of v 19 shall not occur in Ahab's days but in the days of Joram.

Explanation

The genre-identification of this passage is its explanation. The lesson is that power corrupts, and that absolute power corrupts absolutely; but especially that God checks that power and calls it to account. If divine judgment seems slow in coming, wait; the announcement may have been designed for a generation still to come.

Two Narratives of Micaiah's Unfavorable Oracle (22:1–40)

Bibliography

De Vries, S. J. *Prophet against Prophet. The Role of the Micaiah Narrative (I Kings 22) in the Development of Early Prophetic Tradition.* Grand Rapids: Eerdmans, 1978. **Schwally, F.** "Zur Quellenkritik der historischen Bücher.—V, 1 Kön. 22, 19–25." *ZAW* 12 (1892) 159–61. **Seebass, H.** "Zu 1 Reg XXII, 35–38." *VT* 21 (1971) 380–83. **Würthwein, E.** "Zur Komposition von I Reg 22, 1–38." *Das ferne und nahe Wort.* Festschrift Leonhard Rost. Berlin: A. Töpelmann, 1967.

Translation

[1] So they[a] remained for three years: no warfare between Syria and Israel. [2] And it so happened in the third year that Jehoshaphat king of Judah went down to[a] the king of Israel. [3] And the king of Israel said to his servants, "Do you know that Ramoth[a]-Gilead belongs to us, yet we refrain from seizing it from the hand of the king of Syria?" [4] And he[a] said to Jehoshaphat, "Will you go with me[b] to Ramoth-Gilead?"[c] And Jehoshaphat said,[d] [e]"As you act, so shall I; [f]as your army acts, so shall my army act."[efg] [5] And Jehoshaphat[a] said to the king of Israel, "Inquire, please,[b] [c]of Yahweh."[c] [6] So the king of Israel assembled[a] the prophets, about four hundred persons, and[b] said to them, "Shall I go up to Ramoth-Gilead to fight, or shall I desist?" And they said, "Go up, and Yahweh[c] will[d] deliver it into the king's hand." [7] But Jehoshaphat said,[a] [b]"Is there not one other prophet of Yahweh here,[b] that we may inquire of him?" [8] And the king of Israel said to Jehoshaphat, "There is yet[a] a certain man from whom one may inquire of Yahweh, but I reject him because he does not prophesy[b] good concerning me, but evil: Micaiah son of Imlah."[c] And Jehoshaphat[d] said, "Let not the king say that!" [9] And the king of Israel summoned a certain officer and said, "Quickly, Micaiah son of Imlah!"

[10] [a]Now the king of Israel and Jehoshaphat king of Judah[a] were sitting each upon his throne, clad [b]in robes,[bc] [d]in the open place at the doorway of the gate[d] of Samaria, while all the prophets were prophesying before them. [11] And Zedekiah son of Kenaanah made himself iron horns and said, "Thus says Yahweh, 'By these[a] shall you push Syria to their destruction.'" [12] And all the prophets were prophesying the same, saying, "Go up to Ramoth-Gilead and succeed, and Yahweh shall deliver [a]into your hand even the king of Syria."[a] [13] And the messenger who had gone to summon Micaiah said to him, "Look now,[a] [b]the prophets have spoken[b] good to[c] the king with one[d] mouth. [e]Let your words[e] be like the word of one of them, and speak what is good!"

[14] But Micaiah said, "By Yahweh's life, I swear that whatever [a]Yahweh says to me,[a] that is what I will speak!"

[15] And he[a] came to the king. And the king said,[b] "Micaiah, shall I[c] go up to Ramoth-Gilead to fight, or shall I[d] desist?" And he said,[e] [f]"Go up and succeed,[f] and Yahweh [g]shall deliver it[g] into the king's hand." [16] And the king said unto him,[a] "How often must I adjure you that you are not to speak to me in Yahweh's

name except in truth?'' [17] Then he said,[a]

"I saw all Israel[b]
scattered on the mountains,
like sheep for whom there is no shepherd.
Also Yahweh said,
[c]They have no masters,[c]
they shall each return home in safety.'"

[18] And the king of Israel said to Jehoshaphat,[a] "Did I not say to you that he does not prophesy good concerning me, but only evil?"

[19] And he[a] said, "Therefore[b] hear the word of Yahweh![c] I saw Yahweh[d] sitting on his throne, with all the host of heaven standing beside him, to his right and to his left. [20] And Yahweh said, 'Who shall deceive Ahab,[a] [b]so that he may go up and fall at Ramoth-Gilead?'[b] And one said this and another said that.[c] [21] Then the[a] Spirit came forth and stood before Yahweh; and he said, 'I will deceive him.' And Yahweh said,[b] 'How?' [22] And he said, 'I will go forth and become a lying spirit in the mouth of all[a] his prophets.' And he said, 'You shall deceive him; indeed, you shall succeed! Go and do it!' [23] So now behold,[a] Yahweh has appointed a lying spirit in the mouth of[b] these your prophets. Thus Yahweh has spoken evil against you." [24] Then Zedekiah son of Kenaanah approached and struck Micaiah on the cheek, and said, [a]"In what manner[a] did Yahweh's spirit pass[b] [c]from me[c] to speak with you?" [25] And Micaiah said, "Behold, you shall be an observor of it on that day, when you shall enter an inner chamber to hide!"

[26] And the king of Israel said, "Take Micaiah and bring him back to Amon,[a] the city governor,[b] and to Joash the king's son, [27] and say,[a] 'Keep this person in jail and feed him with scant bread and scant water until I come[b] in safety.'" [28] And Micaiah said, "If you do indeed return in safety, Yahweh has not spoken through me."[a] [29] Then the king of Israel and Jehoshaphat king of Judah went up[a] to Ramoth-Gilead. [30] And the king of Israel said to Jehoshaphat,[a] "With respect to girding for combat and entering into battle: you dress in your[b] robes." But the king of Israel girded himself for combat and so went[c] into battle. [31a] And the king of Syria ordered[a] the chariot commanders [b]who were with him[bc] as follows: "Fight neither with the small nor the great, but solely with the king of Israel." [32] And it so happened, when the chariot commanders saw Jehoshaphat,[a] that they said, [b]"Surely he is[b] the king of Israel!" So they turned[c] to fight against him, and Jehoshaphat cried out.[d] [33] And it happened that, when the chariot commanders saw that he was not the king of Israel, they turned away from him. [34] But someone drew the[a] bow at a chance and struck the king of Israel between the scale armor and the breastplate. And he[b] said to his[c] charioteer, "Turn your hand[d] and bring me away from the battle line,[e] for I have been wounded!" [35] So the battle intensified that day, while the king[a] [b]remained propped up[b] in the chariot facing toward Syria.[c] [d]But he[e] died at evening.[d] [f]And the blood from his wound seeped into the bottom of the chariot.[f]

[36a] And the alarm spread[ab] just as the sun went down, "Each man to his city, and each man to his land!" [37] So the king died. And he came to Samaria, and they buried the king[a] in Samaria. [38] And they[a] washed the chariot at the pool of Samaria;[b] and the dogs licked the[c] blood and the harlots washed in it,[d] according to the word of Yahweh.[e] [39] Now the remainder of Ahab's acts, and all that he did, and the ivory house which he built; also all the cities which he built,[a] [b]are these not[b] written

in the Book of the Chronicles of the kings of Israel? ⁴⁰ *And Ahab slept with his fathers. And Ahaziah his son reigned in his place.*

Notes

1.a. MT. G^BL, following from chap. 20, have sing (referring to Ahab).
2.a. MT, G^B (*Kaige*). G^L adds explicative "Ahab."
3.a. MT. G^BL *passim* "Ramath."
4.a. MT. G^BL have explicative "the king of Israel."
4.b. MT, G^L, Chr, G^B "us."
4.c. The addition "to fight" (MT, G^BL, Chr is a corr from v 6).
4.d. G^BL. MT adds explicative "to the king of Israel"; Chr has explicative "to him."
4.e-e. G^L (omits "and" before the second "as"). MT, G^B (*Kaige*): "As I act, so shall you; as my army shall act, so shall yours." Cf. 2 Kgs 3:7.
4.f-f. Chr "and as your army shall act, my army will also be with you in the battle"; Par "and as my army, your army shall be with you in the battle."
4.g. MT, G^B (*Kaige*) add "as my horses act, so shall your horses act."
5.a. MT. G^BL add explicative "king of Judah."
5.b. G^L. MT, G^B (*Kaige*) add interpretive "first/today."
5.c-c. G^BL. MT "for Yahweh's word."
6.a. MT. G^BL add pleonastic "all" without regard to vv 7–8.
6.b. MT. G^BL add explicative "the king (^L of Israel)."
6.c. MT אדני. G κύριος = Yahweh.
6.d. MT. G^BL add pleonastic "surely."
7.a. MT. G^BL add explicative "to the king of Israel."
7.b-b. MT. G^BL "there is not a prophet of Yahweh here" (ideological).
8.a. MT. G^B omits (interpretive).
8.b. MT. G^BL "speak."
8.c. G^L *passim* "Namalei" (corr).
8.d. MT. G^BL add explicative "king of Judah."
10.a-a. MT, G^B G^L "Now Jehoshaphat king of Judah and Ahab king of Israel."
10.b-b. MT. G^BL omit (corr).
10.c. Chr adds "and sitting."
10.d-d. MT. G^B "in the gates"; G^L "on the road of the gate."
11.a. MT. G^BL add explicative "horns."
12.a-a. G^BL. MT "into the hand of the king" (interpretive from v 6).
13.a. MT. G^BL add "all."
13.b-b. G^BL. MT "the words of the prophets are" cannot be correct because "good" and "with one mouth" (פֶּה־אֶחָד) are singular.
13.c. MT. G^BL "concerning" (reading עַל for אֶל).
13.d. MT, G^L. G^B inserts ἐπί between "mouth" and "good," his substitute for "one," producing a highly paraphrastic rendering.
13.e-e. MT. G^BL "Let also you be in your words one" (paraphrastic).
14.a-a. MT, G. Chr "my God shall say"; Par "he shall say to me."
15.a. MT, G^B. G^L has explicative "Micaiah."
15.b. G^BL. MT adds explicative "to him."
15.c,d. G^BL, Par. MT, Chr "we."
15.e. G^BL. MT, Chr add explicative "to him."
15.f-f. MT, G, Par sing. Chr pl.
15.g-g. MT. G^BL omit (text corrupt from literary redaction).
16.a. MT, G^B. G^L adds "again" (stylistic).
17.a. MT. G^BL insert οὐχ οὕτως = Heb. ל(א)כן "therefore"; cf. v 19.
17.b. MT, G, Chr. Par omits.
17.c-c. MT. G^B "Yahweh is no God to them; G^L "if Yahweh they are toward God" (both corr).
18.a. MT. G^BL add explicative "king of Judah."
19.a. MT. G^BL add explicative "Micaiah."

19.b. MT. G^BL add "not I."

19.c. MT. G^BL add "not so" (= לֹא כֵן); cf. v 17.

19.d. MT, G^L. G^B "the God of Israel."

20.a. MT. G^BL, Chr (Par) add explicative "king of Israel."

20.b-b. MT, G^B (Kaige). G^L "and he shall go up to Ramoth-Gilead and fall there."

20.c. MT, G^B. G^L adds interpretive "and he said, 'You will not be able.' And he said, 'By you.'"

21.a. MT. G^BL omit (ideological?).

21.b. Chr (Par). MT, G^BL add explicative "to him."

22.a. MT, G^B (Kaige). G^L adds "these."

23.a. MT, G^B (Kaige). G^L omits.

23.b. Chr (Par). MT, G add "all."

24.a-a. MT, G. Chr (Par) "what is the road."

24.b. MT, G^L, Chr. G^B, Par omit.

24.c-c. MT, G^L. G^B omits.

26.a. MT. G^BL Σεμ(μ)ηρ. BHS derives from Εμ(μ)ηρ reading אמר for MT אמן.

26.b. MT, G^L. G^B substitutes interpretive "king."

27.a. G^BL. MT adds "thus says the king" (interpretive).

27.b. MT. G, Chr (Par) have "return," a corruption from v 28.

28.a. G^BL. MT adds a scribal gloss, "and he said, 'Hearken, O peoples, all of them'": cf. Mic 1:2. See HOTTP, 329.

29.a. MT. G^BL add explicative "with him."

30.a. MT. G^BL add explicative "king of Judah."

30.b. MT. G^BL "my" is interpretive.

30.c. MT, G. Chr pl; Par sing.

31.a-a. MT וּמֶלֶךְ אֲרָם צִוָּה; 6QK ויצו מלך ארם.

31.b-b. MT. G^BL omit (haplography).

31.c. Chr (Par). MT, G add "the thirty-two"; cf. 20:1, 16 (HOTTP, 329).

32.a. MT. G^BL add explicative "king of Judah."

32.b-b. MT. G^BL "he appears to be" (interpretive).

32.c. MT, G. Chr "surrounded."

32.d. MT, G^B. G^L adds interpretive "and Yahweh saved him"; Chr (Par) adds "and Yahweh helped him, and God turned them away from him."

34.a. MT, G^B (Kaige). G^L "his."

34.b. MT, G^B. G^L adds explicative "the king."

34.c. Chr (Par) "the."

34.d. Q, Chr (Par), G^L sing. G^B, K pl.

34.e. MT. G^BL τοῦ πολέμου "the battle"; cf. v 35.

35.a. MT, G. Chr adds explicative "of Israel."

35.b-b. MT, Chr "kept himself standing"; so G^BL, Par, adding "upon the chariot" (ἑστηκὼς ἐπὶ τοῦ ἅρματος).

35.c. MT. G^BL have a long ideological gloss: "and the blood (^L of the wound) poured (^L flowed) out of the wound into the bottom of the chariot."

35.d-d. Chr "until evening, when he died."

35.e. MT, G^B. G^L has explicative "the king."

35.f-f. MT and G^B. G^L, Chr (Par) omit.

36.a-a. MT. G^BL "and the battle-herald stood" (illustrative of hellenistic times, but hardly suitable to the Israelite battle scene).

36.b. G^BL. MT adds interpretive "in the camp/battle-line."

37.a. MT, G^B. G^L adds explicative "Ahab."

38.a. G^BL. MT sing.

38.b. MT, G^B. G^L adds "and the pigs"; cf. 21:19 (G 20:19).

38.c. G^BL. MT has explicative "his."

38.d. MT. G^B "in the blood"; G^L "in his blood."

38.e. G^L. MT, G^B add interpretive "which he spoke."

39.a. MT. G^BL "made."

39.b-b. MT. G^B "and behold these are written"; cf. G^L.

Form/Structure/Setting

[Redactional: Transition from chap. 20, 22:1–2a]
Narrative A: "An unfavorable oracle supersedes a favorable oracle"
  1. The problem: need for supporting revelation
    a. The proposal of "holy war" against Syria
      (1) The setting, v 2b
      (2) The political/military problem, v 3
      (3) The invitation to Jehoshaphat
        (a) The question, v 4a
[Gloss, v 4b]
        (b) The motivation, v 4b
    b. The search for divine approval
      (1) The demand for an oracle, v 5
      (2) The favoring oracle
        (a) The prophets summoned, v 6aα
        (b) The question, v 6aβ
        (c) The reply, v 6b
    c. An arrangement for confirmation
      (1) Jehoshaphat's demand, v 7
      (2) Characterizing identification of Micaiah, v 8a
      (3) The summoning
        (a) Jehoshaphat's rebuke, v 8b
        (b) The king of Israel's command, v 9

Narrative B: "The court of heaven prevails over the court at Samaria"
  1. The revelatory confrontation at Samaria
    a. The situation
      (1) The two kings sitting for consultation, v 10a
      (2) All the prophets prophesying, v 10b
    b. Zedekiah's favorable oracle
      (1) His symbolic act, v 11a
      (2) His interpretive announcement, v 11b
      (3) Confirmation by the assemblage, v 12aα
[Redactional: Editorial transition
    a. Citation of the confirming oracle, v 12aβb
    b. The messenger's advice to Micaiah, v 13]
  2. The revelatory confrontation in heaven
    a. Announcement of independent revelation, v 14

Narrative A continued
  2. The confrontation: conflict between a favoring and an unfavorable oracle
    a. The initial favoring oracle
      (1) The inquiry, v 15a
      (2) The reply, v 15b
      (3) The rebuke, v 16

    b. The superseding unfavorable oracle
      (1) The vision, v 17a
      (2) Oracular interpretation, v 17b
      (3) The king's confirmatory characterization, v 18

Narrative B continued
[Redactional transition, v 19aαא]
    b. Micaiah's unfavorable oracle
      Formal introduction, v 19aαבβ
      (1) The vision
        (a) The situation
          1) Yahweh sitting for consultation, v 19bα
          2) The heavenly host attending, v 19bβ
        (b) The consultation
          1) Yahweh's challenge, v 20aαb
[Redactional gloss, v 20aβ]
          2) The Spirit volunteers, v 21a
          3) Establishment of the means, vv 21b–22a
          4) Yahweh's commission, v 22b
      (2) Interpretive announcement
        (a) Explanation of the favorable oracle, v 23a
        (b) Declaration of its implication, v 23b
  3. Resolution: The diatribe between Zedekiah and Micaiah
    a. Zedekiah's rebuke
      (1) The blow, v 24a
      (2) The challenge, v 24b
    b. Micaiah's rejoinder
      (1) Zedekiah as witness to fulfillment, v 25a
      (2) Zedekiah as object of wrath, v 25b

Narrative A continued
    c. The interpretive diatribe
      (1) Instructions for Micaiah's confinement, v 26
      (2) The accompanying message, v 27
      (3) Micaiah's repartee, v 28a
[Gloss, 28b]
  3. Resolution: Fulfillment of the unfavorable oracle
    Transition: The scene shifted to Ramoth-Gilead, v 29
    a. A subterfuge frustrated
      (1) Dialogical instructions
        (a) For disguise, v 30
        (b) For attack, v 31
      (2) Narrative sequel
        (a) The attack on Jehoshaphat ends with his recognition
          1) Attack, v 32
          2) Withdrawal, v 33
        (b) An accidental arrow-shot strikes the king of Israel, v 34a
      (3) Confirmatory instruction for withdrawal, v 34b

b. Denouement: The battle ends with the death of the king of Israel
   (1) The fighting intensifies, v 35aα
   (2) The final subterfuge of seeming life, v 35aβbα
[Redactional gloss, v 35bβ]
   (3) The armies scatter, v 36
c. Resumptive conclusion, v 37
[Redactional conclusion, v 38]
[Dtr: Concluding summary for Ahab, vv 39–40]

This is one of the very few prophet narratives that is best explained as the interweaving of two independent sources (cf. De Vries, *Prophet against Prophet*, 1–51). Critics have long been in a quandary as to whether vv 1–38 is a historical report or some kind of prophet narrative, but the special source analysis which the writer has been able to give it shows clearly that this is indeed prophetic material, although from two independent narratives. Evidence that we actually do have distinct sources is as follows: (1) vv 4b–5 twice introduce Jehoshaphat as speaking, but in a self-contradictory way; (2) the scene shifts inexplicably at v 10; (3) the subject changes unaccountably at v 19, leading to Micaiah's second vision-oracle; (4) Micaiah is rebuked in v 24, then punished in vv 26–27; (5) climactic repartees appear at v 25 and v 28, respectively; (6) "put on your robes" in v 30 is inconsistent with v 10, where Jehoshaphat is described as robed; (7) the singular address in vv 10, 15 is inconsistent with the two kings as addressees; (8) reference to "all the prophets prophesying" in v 10 is redundant after v 6, and inconsistent with the wording of v 12b; (9) in v 9 the king of Israel dispatches a סריס "officer," but in v 13 a מלאך "messenger" fetches Micaiah; (10) in v 14 Micaiah swears by Yahweh's life to speak what Yahweh tells him, yet in v 15 he tells a lie, for which the king of Israel scolds him in v 16 (Micaiah is doing what he criticizes the king's prophets for doing in v 22); (11) לכן "therefore," in v 19 presupposes something Micaiah himself had just said, not someone else's comment; (12) the futuristic "that day" of v 25 is structurally inconsistent with the past "that day" of v 35 (cf. *YTT*, 112–13, 292–95). Add to this mass of detail the facts that the story has no meaningful structure as it now stands, and that the separate narratives that we have been able to disentangle do have meaningful structures in and of themselves, and we have a compelling case for the acceptance of this literary hypothesis.

The story that has been labeled "Narrative A" is a superseding oracle narrative whose only close parallel is in 2 Kgs 8:7–15. In this subgenre of prophet story a superseding oracle to a king is fulfilled in preference to one that precedes it; its purpose is to demonstrate how Yahweh's ultimate purpose in historical events takes priority over his preliminary or mediate purpose. (Cf. *Prophet against Prophet*, 63–65). Our Narrative A has to do not with the historical Ahab but with his son Joram, and comes from prophetic circles friendly to the Jehu dynasty. Its most probable date is toward the end of the ninth century B.C.

The story that has been labeled "Narrative B" is a word-controversy narrative, with a close parallel in 2 Kgs 18:17—19:37. It is described in *Prophet against Prophet*, 69–71. Its date is about a hundred years later than that of

Narrative A, i.e., *ca.* 700 B.C., the reign of Hezekiah. A story of this subgenre
has to do with a contest between rival claimants to revelation, and its purpose
is to demonstrate that Yahweh has power to counteract conflicting prophecy
for the fulfillment of his historical purposes. Neither Narrative A nor Narrative
B utilizes a strictly stereotyped pattern of language, but each does have a
peculiar structure designed to carry out its special function. Thus Narrative
A has the following closely integrated three-part structure: (1) the need for
supporting revelation; (2) the conflict between a favorable and an unfavorable
oracle; (3) the fulfillment of the unfavorable oracle. Narrative B also has
three episodes, but uses the first two to delineate a different kind of clash,
that between earth's court and heaven's court, with the third element bringing
a resolution between them: (1) the revelatory confrontation at Samaria; (2)
the revelatory confrontation in heaven; (3) the diatribe between two prophets,
Zedekiah and Micaiah. While both narratives feature Micaiah and have somewhat similar themes, each is actually concerned with a different issue. In
Narrative A the question is whether a king can prevent a superseding unfavorable oracle from coming to pass. In Narrative B the question is whether Yahweh
is actually in control of prophets who speak false oracles of good to the
king. In the first narrative the answer is no. In the second it is yes.

As generally happens, this pericope is burdened by a number of secondary
accretions. Isolated glosses occur in v 4bα and v 28b. Dtr is responsible for
the concluding Ahab summary in vv 39–40. The Jehuite redactor who created
the Omride-war cycle wrote the transition to Narrative A in vv 1–2a, the
reference to the king bleeding to death in v 35b, and the concluding statement
in v 38 that prophecy had been fulfilled. This leaves vv 12aβb, 13, the single
word וַיֹּאמֶר "and he said" at the beginning of v 19, and the words, "so
that he may go up and fall at Ramoth-Gilead," in v 20, all of which comes
from a later redactor (prior to Dtr) who did the interweaving of the two
narratives.

Comment

1–9 V 1 connects directly back to 20:43, with which it was originally
connected. The number three for the years of truce is offhand and conventional (cf. the gloss in 18:1), and should not be relied upon by biblical chronologists. In distinction from G^{BL}, which tendentiously insert Jehoshaphat's
introductory summary at 16:28$^+$ (see above on chronology), MT here allows
that king to appear prior to Dtr's original introductory summary in vv 41–
43. This is because by the time of Dtr the Micaiah story(ies) had come to
be applied to Ahab. Narrative A is told from the viewpoint of the North.
"Going down" to the king of Israel implies the customary biblical orientation,
with Jerusalem identified as the highest place; where the king of Israel himself
was is not stated, though the conclusion in v 37 makes it clear that it is
Samaria. What the king of Israel says to his retainers is in effect an accusatory
question, designed not for providing information but for arousing shame
and resentment. Ramoth-Gilead lay at the northeastern frontier of heavily
forested Gilead. The statement in 2 Kgs 8:28 that Joram was wounded at
this same place is to be interpreted not as indication of further warfare but

as the realistic, nonsymbolical source of the traditions behind the present account.

Apart from the gloss, "and Jehoshaphat said," v 4 depicts the king of Israel as requesting Jehoshaphat's assistance in a campaign against Ramoth-Gilead, explaining that he and his army can proceed only if Jehoshaphat and his army proceed (see *Notes*). Before Jehoshaphat will agree, he demands to hear a favoring oracle, and in response the king of Israel summons four hundred prophets (the same schematic number as in 1 Kgs 18:19), all of whom advise the king(s) to go up against Ramoth-Gilead, promising that Yahweh will allow its recapture. But their unanimity makes Jehoshaphat suspicious, and he demands one other oracle. The king of Israel reveals that there is still Micaiah son of Imlah (known from no other source), who has not been called because he always speaks evil concerning the king. He is summoned at Jehoshaphat's insistence.

10–14 V 10 is styled in characteristic exposition style, with noun-subjects foremost, followed by predicative participles. This is the introduction to Narrative B, not a resumptive parallel to vv 2–9. Though eventually this account will identify the king of Israel as Ahab (v 20), he is introduced here anonymously, alongside Jehoshaphat, who is identified as "king of Judah." The occasion is formal, for each king sits on his throne clad in the robes of his office. The locale is the "open place" גרן (not "threshing floor" since the gateway of Samaria lies too high), outside Samaria's gate. "All the prophets" have come, and probably there are so many of them that this quasi-sacral place (cf. 2 Sam 6:6, 24:16) is better suited to accommodate them than the king's audience chamber. The reader should take note here of a striking parallel in the Ugaritic literature, 2 Aqht V, 3–8, which speaks of the semidivine person, Danel, appearing for judgment at a *grn*, "open place" or "threshing floor" (*ANET* 151a; cf. J. Gray, 450). All the prophets are "prophesying before them"—simultaneously or successively—when one Zedekiah, son of Kenaanah, also not mentioned elsewhere, performs a symbolic act (cf. E. Haller, "Charisma und Ekstasis in 1 Kg 22," *ThEx* 82, Munich 1960; G. Fohrer, *Die symbolischen Handlungen der Propheten*, ATANT 54, 2nd ed. [Zürich: Zwingli Verlag, 1968], 22–23), to which all the prophets acquiesce. Zedekiah makes iron horns and interprets them oracularly to mean that the king would "push," i.e., smash or clash, Syria with them until it was destroyed. O. Keel has deduced from Egyptian and Canaanite iconography, showing the gods with horned helmets, that Zedekiah's horns were fixed to a helmet and were presented to the king to be worn by him (O. Keel, *Wirkmächtige Siegeszeichen im Alten Testament*, OBO 5; [Göttingen: 1974] 123–34, 142).

The redactor who combined Narrative A and Narrative B intrudes in v 12b by supplying words for "all the prophets," which are paraphrastic of Zedekiah's oracle. In v 13 he prepares for vv 15–18 by having a "messenger" advise Micaiah to agree with those prophets: "Let your words (i.e., oracles) be like the word (oracle) of one of them" shows that this redactor was quite well aware that in his redactional combination Micaiah would indeed speak more than one oracle, one in v 17 and another in vv 19–23. When Micaiah speaks in v 14, it is as someone who belongs in the prophet crowd at Samaria, but who has somehow been left out. Instead of agreeing with "all the prophets," he swears by Yahweh's life that he is even now receiving a vision from Yahweh, and will speak exactly as he sees and hears.

15–18 In Narrative A, which resumes at this place, Micaiah comes from wherever he has been. The king asks him the same question he asked the four hundred, and gets from Micaiah the same answer. But because it is a favorable answer, the king knows that it cannot be Micaiah's true word. He accordingly admonishes Micaiah with impressive sternness not to speak Yahweh's word to him except in truth. Though many interpreters suggest that Micaiah was deliberately lying, it is better to interpret his words as a preliminary message expressive of a patriotic strain in his ideology. But the king's adjuration makes him see clearly what Yahweh truly intends. In v 17 he reports a simple vision of Israel as scattered sheep, together with an auditory report of Yahweh's own enigmatic interpretation. Sheep returning home safely (בשלום) but without their masters signify the death of their masters. The oracle is unfavorable, and thus the king of Israel interprets it in his comment to Jehoshaphat.

19–25 Micaiah continues impassionedly from v 14. After a summons to hear, he reports a vision quite different than that of the other Micaiah in v 17. Over against the king of Israel and Jehoshaphat, he has seen Yahweh enthroned, with the "host of heaven" (the metaphorical court of heaven) on either side, asking for a volunteer to entice (פתה piel) Ahab. None of the heavenly retainers dare respond, but the Spirit (evidently the spirit of prophetic inspiration, personified) volunteers, and is commissioned. Modern students of the Bible hardly know how to comprehend this until they are reminded that both Jeremiah (20:7, 10) and Ezekiel (14:9) describe Yahweh as deceiving or enticing a prophet. This accords with Micaiah's explanation of his vision in v 23, to the effect that this heavenly Spirit has become a lying spirit in the mouth of the king's prophets. This ultimately means that Yahweh has spoken unfavorably against the king, because the encouraging oracles of his deceived prophets will deceive him into doing himself harm. This leads to the third episode in which the question of where the greater authority lies is brought to a head (vv 24–25). Zedekiah's rude blow and insulting reproach represent the court of Samaria. Following the preferred text, we interpret his question to mean that since he has prophetic inspiration, how can Micaiah presume to claim that same prophetic inspiration? Micaiah's vision-oracle already offered the answer to this dilemma: a particular prophet can be inspired by Yahweh, even if it is a lying spirit which entices the people to the judgment that Yahweh has prepared for them. Instead of repeating what he has already said, Micaiah makes a final rejoinder to the effect that Zedekiah would witness it on the day Yahweh has prepared for it (see YTT, 292–95), when he himself would be a victim of its fury.

26–28 This is the last part of episode 2 in Narrative A. Amon and Joash represent civil and regal authority, respectively. They are to be jointly responsible for keeping Micaiah under close arrest, with just enough food and water to keep him alive, until the king returns "in safety," בשלום. It is not so much that the king is punishing the prophet as guarding his spirit from reaching out and performing what he had said. Here is a strongly dynamistic notion, held by the king but surely not shared by the narrator, who goes on to tell that this attempt to stifle the power of Micaiah's prophecy could not, and did not, succeed. When Micaiah replies that if the king does indeed return בשלום, Yahweh has not spoken by him, he may be saying that in such an event some other supernatural being, a demon, has spoken.

29–38 Episode 3 begins with two sets of verbal instructions: that of the king of Israel to Jehoshaphat to dress as a king while he himself dresses as an ordinary soldier (v 30), and that of the king of Syria, telling his chariot commanders to attack the king of Israel (v 31). There is a suspense-producing interlude in which the Syrians correct their initial mistake in attacking Jehoshaphat (vv 32–33). The climax comes in v 34, where we are told that a chance shot gives the king of Israel a fatal wound. As the day is filled with increasing fighting, he keeps up the final subterfuge of standing in his chariot, propped up, facing the Syrians. At evening he dies, and the alarm to scatter homeward goes out, fulfilling the prophecy of the masterless sheep. "So the king died" in v 37 is resumptive. The narrator is finished, except with reporting the further fact that the king "came" to Samaria to be buried. This bitter, solemn conclusion is spoiled, however, by the Jehuite redactor's mocking words of v 38, which report how his blood came to be licked by dogs and used by harlots for washing.

39–40 This is Dtr's closing summary for Ahab. Among this king's notable deeds were the building of an "ivory house" or palace (see N. Avigad, *Eretz-Shomron* [Jerusalem: Israel Exploration Society, 1973], 75–85) and certain unnamed cities. The important thing in this summary is the statement that "Ahab slept with his fathers," which has to mean that he died in peace and honor, and therefore cannot apply to the king of v 37. As has been argued above, this confirms that both Micaiah narratives are imaginative reflexes of Joram's death reported in 2 Kgs 8–9. The real Ahab died peacefully in Samaria, probably in ripe old age. (See *Prophet against Prophet*, 97–99.)

Explanation

Evidently there was an historical prophet named Micaiah ben Imlah. He was not sufficiently well known to attract to himself a whole cycle of stories, like Elijah or Elisha, but he was remembered because he foretold the death of a king of Israel in a forthcoming battle with the Syrians at Ramoth-Gilead. That king was not Ahab, as Narrative B names him, nor was his Judahite ally the real Jehoshaphat. By the time Narrative B was written, *ca.* 700 B.C., the monarch of most atrocious reputation from within the northern-Israelite succession was Ahab, so quite understandably he was named as the wicked king of this story, though, as we have stated, the real historical Ahab is recorded as having died in peace and honor. It had to be Ahab's son, Joram, then, with whom the prophet Micaiah had actually dealt, and his Judahite ally had to have been Jehoshaphat's son, Ahaziah. 2 Kgs 9 tells us with a high level of historicity how the battle at Ramoth-Gilead actually went, and how both Joram and Ahaziah met their death by Jehu's arrows. The Micaiah story as we have it in Narrative A is an imaginative retelling of this event, itself carrying on a subtle Jehuite polemic against the house of Ahab. In any event, its purpose is not propaganda but didactic edification. Composed *ca.* 800 B.C., i.e., during the reigns of the early Jehuite kings, it soon found a wider focus as it was taken up into a four-story prophetic cycle, 1 Kgs 20:1-43, 22:1-38, brought together with numerous glosses and expansions by a redactor intent on underscoring the failure of the Omride kings. No more than the author of Narrative A, does this redactor specify the name of "the king of Israel." Historically, it can be only Joram; symbolically it is "Ahab" and his entire house. In this form, Narrative A was later taken up into a collection of prophet stories extending to 2 Kgs 13, and eventually the variant Micaiah story, Narrative B, was joined redactionally to Narrative A.

Seldom has a simple prophet story undergone so complex a process of editing and redaction, and seldom has a passage raised so wide a range of theological problems. Narrative A is about one hundred years earlier than Narrative B, yet it is already surprisingly sophisticated in its reflections about the ways of God. At the time of Jehu's revolt, 841 B.C., and in the following decades of Hazael's rule in Syria, the Northern Kingdom continued in puzzlement and chagrin over the fact that Yahweh was allowing a foreign nation to grind it under its heel. The viewpoint of Narrative A is that Israel's kings act like heroes when they march out to resist such aggression, but not if this endangers Yahweh's covenant people. It had always been the role of Hebrew prophetism to support the holy war in defense of Israel. The paradox that Micaiah faces is that he desires the deliverance of Israel but deplores the greed, ambition, and materialism of Israel's rulers. For a prophet like Micaiah to resist a king's "patriotic" program might make him look like a coward and a traitor; that is why, ostensibly, the Israelite king has him thrown in jail, though his real reason in this instance is to prevent anything of the prophet's influence from putting a hex on his campaign. But this is a forecast of things to come: Isaiah, Jeremiah, and Ezekiel will each brave the mark of cowardice and treason because they too will dare distinguish between a king's wild ambition and the nation's true good. The central lesson of Narrative A is, of course, that Yahweh's ultimate purpose supersedes his proximate, traditional purpose. The king was counting on the proximate goal: deliverance for Israel, fame and fortune for himself. But nothing could prevent the ultimate purpose of Yahweh from reaching fulfillment. Nothing—putting Micaiah in jail, dressing for battle as a common soldier, standing propped up in his chariot—could bring the king back home in peace. Four hundred popular prophets had advised him wrongly, but Yahweh had spoken truth through the one that resisted.

The Jehuite redactor who placed Narrative A in his Omride War collection shared much of the same viewpoint but gave it wider range and sharper focus. For him, too, the king of Israel was anonymous; yet it was clear that he had to be one of the House of Ahab rather than Jehu or his line. This redactor has two "historical-demonstration" narratives (1 Kgs 20:1-21; 26-30) featuring aggressions by Syria's Ben-Hadad against an anonymous king of Israel, first at Samaria and then at Aphek. In both stories things seem desperate until a prophet or "man of God" appears on the scene to promise that Yahweh will give Israel victory; this turns out in both instances to be true prophecy as Israel wins over the Syrians gloriously. Our redactor composes a bit of transitional narrative (20:22–25) to join these two stories, but he has another prophet story, that of 20:30b–43, which he intends to use as the climax of the entire new story he is creating. For this he first needs a transition at 20:30a, and then he offers the regal self-judgment narrative in which an anonymous king of Israel first lets Ben-Hadad go cheaply by calling him "my brother," and next provokes a prophet in disguise into predicting, "Because you have let go out of your hand the man whom I had devoted to destruction, therefore your life shall go for his life, and your people for his people" (v 42, RSV). In the redactor's time (later than Narrative A, *ca.* 700 B.C.) the Israelite people were feeling deeply the pain of this prophecy as the Syrians marched back and forth through their defenseless countryside. These former subjects of the Omride kings were indeed suffering for the short-sighted, self-seeking policies of Ahab and Joram and the rest.

So now Narrative A, originally placed in immediate juxtaposition to 20:43, took on an even more sharply anti-Omride aspect. In this story the king—this time resisted by a prophet—goes out again to do battle against the Syrians. He pretends that this is another defensive "holy war," and accordingly calls on patriots, allies, and prophets to support him. But unlike the battles of chap. 20, this is no battle of defense, but an ostentatious show of power. There are prophets aplenty—four hundred, to be exact, with only one true prophet to oppose him. The king has an ally too, mighty king Jehoshaphat of Judah. In the end Jehoshaphat escapes death, serving in the story to show how the king of Israel might have returned home in peace, had he given heed to the warning voice of Micaiah. Narrative A tells how the king of Israel was shot, and how be bled slowly to death, but it is the Jehuite redactor who writes 22:35b—about the blood flowing into the bottom of the chariot—as a preparation for v 38. Narrative A is at an end when it tells in v 37 that the king of Israel returned dead to Samaria, but the redactor's v 38 revels in the king's ignominious death. They wash the king's chariot; the dogs lick the blood; the harlots wash themselves in the water that has washed out the blood. This is the only kind of death gruesome enough to fulfill the alarming prophecy of 20:42: "Your life for his life!" It was that prophecy that was now fulfilled. All the wretched things that had happened to this Omride king had been "according to the word of Yahweh" that had come three years before (22:1).

The memory of Micaiah passed down in tradition. Though it was now part of a prophetic collection with only Narrative A, it was sometimes told in other forms; and after the Northern Kingdom had ceased to exist, as all the northern traditions were being gradually collected under the auspices of King Hezekiah and the Jerusalem temple, a variant story, dubbed by us "Narrative B," was written down, and then edited to be incorporated into Narrative A. It now looked as if the two were really one—and so it has seemed to every generation but our own. But it was really two stories blended together. They had in common the prophet Micaiah, the opposing prophets, the two kings, the Samaria locale, the contradicting oracles. But, because the spiritual problems of the time were now different, the two original narratives were different in spite of their similarities. In Narrative A, Micaiah is introduced as someone unknown, but in Narrative B he is without patronym, a well-

known typological figure like Elijah. In Narrative A Micaiah tells two prophecies which are at variance with each other, the first being superseded by
the second; but in Narrative B it is prophet against prophet—not one prophet
with two oracles, but two kinds of prophet. We can call them the "well-sayers"
and the "doom-sayers." They become decisive in the last years of Judah's
existence, and because the later kings preferred to listen to the well-sayers
rather than to the doom-sayers, the entire nationalistic structure of the Israelite
kingdom went into ruin. In Narrative B we have the court of Samaria and
the court of heaven. Micaiah tells only what he hears, and it is that a lying
spirit from Yahweh performs Yahweh's purpose to deceive (פתה piel) Ahab
by entering the mouths of his prophets. What an alarming thought! Does
Yahweh willingly deceive anybody, deluding one into sin? To answer this
we must contemplate profoundly biblical principles, to the effect that since
only one supernatural Being exists in the universe, even evil must somehow
be under his will. In this story, Yahweh does intend "Ahab's" ruin. The
quickest way to accomplish this is through his prophets, who will mislead
him by telling him what he wants to hear, and they want him to hear, something
pleasant that will put them in his favor.

It is well that the Micaiah account has also come down to us in this new
form. Especially those who aspire to a "prophetic" ministry may ponder its
message. We cannot work outside God's purposes, whatever we may intend.
Even when we speak good when he intends evil, our good-saying may become
the instrument by which his "evil" is performed.

The Reign of Jehoshaphat (22:41–51 [Eng. 22:41–50])

Bibliography

Stade, B. Miscellen.—9. 1 Kön. 22,48f." *ZAW* 5 (1885) 178. Yeivin, S. "King Yehoshaphat." *EI* 7 (1964) 6–17. *L. A. Mayer Memorial Volume.* Jerusalem: Israel Exploration Society.

Translation

[41ab]*Now Jehoshaphat son of Asa reigned over Judah* [bc] *in the fourth* [d] *year of Ahab* [e]*king of Israel.* [ce] [42] *And Jehoshaphat was thirty-five years old when he became king,* [a] *and for twenty-five years he reigned in Jerusalem. Now the name of his mother was Azubah, daughter of Shilhi.* [b] [43] *And he walked in all* [a] *the way of Asa his father, not departing from it, performing what is right in Yahweh's eyes.* [44] *However, the country shrines* [b]*he did not remove;* [b] *the people were still* [c]*sacrificing and making burnt-offerings at the country shrines.* [c] [45(44)]*And Jehoshaphat made peace with the king of Israel.* [a] [46(45)]*Now the remainder of the acts of Jehoshaphat,* [a] [b]*and all his acts of greatness which he did,* [c]*and how he fought,* [bc] *are they not written* [d]*in the Book of* [e]*the Chronicles of the kings of Judah?* [de] [47(46)]*And the remainder of the male prostitutes who were left in the days of Asa his father he exterminated from the land.* [48(47)] *And there was no king in Edom;* [a] *a deputy reigned.* [b]

[49(48)] *Jehoshaphat* [a] *made* [b]*Tarshish-style ships* [b] *to journey to Ophir for gold, but they did not make the voyage;* [c]*the ships were* [c] *wrecked at Ezion-Geber.* [50(49)] *Then* [a]*Ahaziah son of Ahab* [a] *said to Jehoshaphat, "*[b]*Let my servants journey with your servants* [b] *in ships," but Jehoshaphat would not agree.* [51(50)] *And Jehoshaphat* [a] *slept with his fathers and was buried with his fathers in the city of David his father. And his son Jehoram reigned in his place.*

Notes

41.a. G[L] omits vv 41–51. Cf. LXX 16:28[a-h], verse numbers follow the English text.

41.b-b. MT, G. Chr "and Jehoshaphat reigned over Judah."

41.c-c. MT, G. Chr omits.

41.d. MT, G. LXX 16:28[a] "eleventh."

41.e-e. MT. G[B] "reigned" (repeated from preceding context).

42.a. MT, G[B]. LXX 16:28[a] adds "he reigned thirty-five years in his kingdom" (influenced by chronological ideology).

42.b. MT. G[B] Σεμεεί is a corruption, substituting "m" for "l."

43.a. MT, G[B]. Chr omits.

44(43).b-b. G[B]; cf. G[L] in 16:28[b]. MT, C, and G[B] in 16:28[h] pl. Par "were still there" (paraphrase). Note variation in Hebrew verse division.

44.c-c. MT, G[B]. Chr "had confirmed their hearts for (Par Yahweh) the God of their fathers."

45(44).a-a. MT, G[B]. Chr (Par), LXX 16:28[+] omit.

46(45).a-a. MT, G[B]. G[L] 16:28[c] "and what Jehoshaphat added with (the) king of Israel."

45.b-b. MT. G[B] omits "how they fought." Chr (Par) "the first and the last."

45.c-c. MT. G[B] omits.

45.d-d. Chr *aliter.*
45.e-e. MT, G 16:28ᶜ. Gᴮ "Jehoshaphat."
47(46).a. Gᴮ omits vv 47–50, Chr 46–49; cf. LXX 16:28ᵈ⁻ᵉ.
48(47).a. LXX 16:28ᵉ "in Syria (Aram)"; cf. *HOTTP*, 330.
48.b. 2 MSS and LXX 16:28 נצי֯ב. "A deputy" for MT נצב niph ptcp "was being appointed."
49(48).a. LXX 16:28ᶠ omits.
49.b-b. LXX 16:28ᶠ "a ship in Tarshish."
49.c-c. Q, K, LXX 16:28ᶠ sing.
50(49).a-a. LXX 16:28ᵍ "the king of Israel."
50.b-b. LXX 16:28ᵍ "let me send out your (ᴸ my) servants and my (ᴸ your) servants."
51(50).a. MT. Gᴮ omits. LXXᴮᴸ 16:28ʰ *hab.*

Form/Structure/Setting

[Dtr: The reign of Jehoshaphat
  1. Introductory summary, vv 41–42
  2. Theological assessment, vv 43–44(43)
  3. Extract from the Book of the Chronicles of the Judahite Kings, v 45(44)
  4. Concluding summary (1), v 46(45)
  5. Further extracts from the Book of the Chronicles of the Judahite Kings, vv 47–48(46–47)]
Notice of prospective maritime ventures, vv 49–50(48–49)
[Dtr: Concluding summary for Jehoshaphat (2), v 51(50)]

Comment

Jehoshaphat receives high marks from Dtr, though one should note that it is Asa with whom he is compared, not David (cf. 15:11), evidently because there is still some blame to give Jehoshaphat with respect to his tolerance of the country shrines. Although it is noted that Jehoshaphat made peace with the king of Israel, Dtr observes in his summary that he was involved in warfare (v 46). Dtr also notes that with respect to the "male prostitutes" (females may also be included in the common gender of this masc pl), Jehoshaphat made amends for his father Asa's shortcoming (cf. 15:12). Dtr's note that there was no king in Edom, but that a deputy (not "Nasib," a proper name, with LXX 16:28⁺ and many scholars) was in charge, creates a serious problem with respect to the historicity of 2 Kgs 3:1–25 because 2 Kgs 8:20–22 confirms that Edom first got a king during the reign of Jehoshaphat's son Jehoram (see the discussion in De Vries, *Prophet against Prophet*, 134–45). Respecting the Tarshish-style ships of v 48, cf. 10:22. The cause of the wreck of these ships is not stated; on Ezion-Geber as port for the Red Sea trade, cf. 9:26. "Then" (אז) may be Dtr's connective, since v 49 and v 50 probably refer to separate ventures. That Jehoshaphat would not agree with Ahaziah's proposal may reveal commercial conservatism rather than personal or ideological hostility.

The Reign of Ahaziah, Son of Ahab (22:52-54 [Eng. 22:51-53])

Translation

⁵²⁽⁵¹⁾ *Ahaziah son of Ahab reigned over Israel in Samaria in the seventeenth* ^a *year of Jehoshaphat king of Judah. And he ruled over Israel for two years.* ⁵³⁽⁵²⁾ *And he* ^a *performed what was evil in the eyes of Yahweh. And he walked in the way of* ^b*his father* ^{bc} *and* ^d*in the way of* ^{de} *his mother; also in the way* ^f *of* ^g *Jeroboam son of Nebat, who made Israel to sin.* ⁵⁴⁽⁵³⁾ *And he worshiped Baal* ^a *and did obeisance to him,* ^b *enraging Yahweh the God of Israel according to all* ^c*that his father had done.* ^{cd}

Notes

52(51).a. MT, G^B (*Kaige*). G^L "twenty-seventh."
53(52).a. MT, G^B. G^L has explicative "Ahaziah."
53.b-b. MT, G^B. G^L omits.
53.c. MT. G^B adds explicative "Ahab."
53.d-d. MT, G^B. G^L omits.
53.e. MT, G^L. G^B inserts explicative "Jezebel."
53.f. MT. G^{BL} "sins."
53.g. MT, G^L. G^B inserts explicative "the house of."
54(53).a,b. MT. G^{BL} pl.
54.c-c. MT. G^{BL} add "that had been done before him" (interpretive).
54.d. G^{BL} have additional words belonging with the Heb. text at the beginning of 2 Kgs.

Form/Structure/Setting

[Dtr: The reign of Ahaziah
1. Introductory summary, v 52(51)
2. Theological assessment, vv 53–54(52–53)]

Comment

Ahaziah's reign was only somewhat longer than one year. Since Jezebel was so notorious a sinner, Ahaziah's mother's evil way is mentioned alongside his father's, yet all are subsumed under the "original" sin, that of Jeroboam son of Nebat. The Book of 1 Kgs ends with the note that Ahaziah enraged Yahweh by the devout worship of Baal.

Index of Authors Cited

Index of Principal Subjects

Index of Biblical Texts